D0826649

Collins *Gem*

English
Thesaurus

((Collins *Gem*

English
Thesaurus

Collins Gem

An Imprint of HarperCollinsPublishers

fourth edition 2004

© William Collins Sons & Co. Ltd. 1987
© HarperCollins Publishers 1994, 1999, 2004

HarperCollins Publishers
Westerhill Road, Bishopbriggs, Glasgow G64 2QT
Great Britain

www.collinsdictionaries.com

Collins Gem® and Bank of English® are registered
trademarks of HarperCollins Publishers Limited

ISBN 0-00-712639-5

Acknowledgements

We would like to thank those authors and publishers who
kindly gave permission for copyright material to be used
in the Bank of English. We would also like to thank
Times Newspapers Ltd for providing valuable data.

Note

Entered words that we have reason to believe constitute
trademarks have been designated as such. However, neither
the presence nor absence of such designation should be
regarded as affecting the legal status of any trademark.

A catalogue record for this book
is available from the British Library

Computing support by Thomas Callan and Mark Taylor

Typeset by Wordcraft, Glasgow

Printed in Italy by Legoprint, S.P.A.

Editorial Staff

Editor
Lorna Gilmour

Publishing Manager
Elaine Higgleton

Series Editor
Lorna Sinclair Knight

Editorial Assistance
Jennifer Baird   Kay Cullen

BANK of ENGLISH

This thesaurus has been compiled with constant reference to the Bank of English, a unique database containing over 524 million words of written and spoken English, enabling Collins lexicographers to analyse how the language is actually used and how it is changing. The Bank of English was set up to be a resource for language research and lexicography. It contains a very wide range of material from books, newspapers, radio, TV, magazines, letters and talks, thereby reflecting the whole spectrum of English today. Its size and range make it an unequalled resource, and the purpose-built software for its analysis is unique to Collins dictionaries.

This ensures that Collins dictionaries accurately reflect English as it is used today in a way that is most helpful to the dictionary or thesaurus user.

Contents

Introduction

When this thesaurus was first published in 1987, it proved to be an immensely popular language resource. This new edition has been completely revised to give you even more ways of expressing yourself, with a clear and attractive layout which highlights its many extra features.

The headword list has been selected on the basis of frequency as verified by the *Collins Bank of English®*, which means that the entry words given are those most likely to be looked up by the user. The key synonym for each sense is shown first, which not only offers you the most helpful alternative but also lets you identify the sense in question at a glance. Other synonyms are arranged in order of their frequency of occurrence.

The thesaurus offers extensive coverage of English as a world language, with words and phrases from all over the English-speaking world making this a truly international language resource.

As well as generous synonym lists, key antonyms are included for many entry words. But this new edition gives you much more than just synonyms and antonyms.

The *Related Words* feature enables you to find information such as adjectives and collective nouns connected with many main entry words.

Informative subject word lists provide a wealth of material connected with many entry words. In addition, the new *Word Power* supplement lists famous people such as actors, novelists, and politicians, all arranged by their occupations. It also lists geographical information such as countries, capitals, and currencies, arranged by subject. It is therefore a source of invaluable information for solving general-knowledge clues in crosswords and puzzles, and for boosting home study.

Helpful *Word Power* notes are also included at key entries. These give advice on good English and help you to avoid some of the more common language mistakes.

All these features mean that this new thesaurus is a treasury of useful and practical words and information, arranged in the most helpful way possible.

Features of the Thesaurus

Entry words

speed NOUN 1 = <u>rate</u>, pace
2 = <u>swiftness</u>, rush, hurry, haste, rapidity, quickness ≠ slowness

● VERB 1 = <u>race</u>, rush, hurry, zoom, career, tear, barrel (along) (*informal, chiefly U.S. & Canad.*), gallop ≠ crawl 2 = <u>help</u>, advance, aid, boost, assist, facilitate, expedite ≠ hinder

Synonyms offer a wide range of alternatives

Regional labels

Word Power notes give advice on good English

Word Power

speed – The past tense of *speed up* is *speeded up* (not *sped up*), for example *I speeded up to overtake the lorry*. The past participle is also *speeded up*, for example *I had already speeded up when I spotted the police car*.

Cross references

Related words expand your vocabulary

spider ▸ spiders and other arachnids
(Related Words)
fear of: arachnophobia

Subject word lists add an extra dimension to your vocabulary

Spiders and other arachnids

black widow
chigger, chigoe, *or* (*U.S. & Canad.*) redbug
chigoe, chigger, jigger, *or* sand
flea
harvestman *or* (*U.S. & Canad.*)
daddy-longlegs
katipo
mite

red-back (spider)
spider
spider mite
tarantula
tick
trap-door spider
whip scorpion
wolf spider *or* hunting spider

Sense numbers

spin VERB 1 = <u>revolve</u>, turn, rotate, reel, whirl, twirl, gyrate, pirouette
2 = <u>reel</u>, swim, whirl

● NOUN 1 (*Informal*) = <u>drive</u>, ride, joy ride (*informal*) = <u>revolution</u>, roll, whirl, gyration

● PHRASES **spin something out** = prolong, extend, lengthen, draw out, drag out, delay, amplify

Idioms and phrases add colour to your language

x

Features of the Thesaurus

International English from all regions of the world where English is spoken

Key synonyms given first

Part of speech labels

Fixed phrases

spirit NOUN 1 = <u>soul</u>, life 2 = <u>life force</u>, vital spark, mauri (N.Z.) 3 = <u>ghost</u>, phantom, spectre, apparition, atua (N.Z.), kehua (N.Z.) 4 = <u>courage</u>, guts (informal), grit, backbone, spunk (informal), gameness 5 = <u>liveliness</u>, energy, vigour, life, force, fire, enthusiasm, animation 6 = <u>attitude</u>, character, temper, outlook, temperament, disposition 7 = <u>heart</u>, sense, nature, soul, core, substance, essence, quintessence 8 = <u>intention</u>, meaning, purpose, purport, gist 9 = <u>feeling</u>, atmosphere, character, tone, mood, tenor, ambience
● PLURAL NOUN = <u>mood</u>, feelings, morale, temper, disposition, state of mind, frame of mind

spite NOUN = <u>malice</u>, malevolence, ill will, hatred, animosity, venom, spleen, spitefulness ≠ kindness
● VERB = <u>annoy</u>, hurt, injure, harm, vex ≠ benefit
● PHRASES **in spite of** = <u>despite</u>, regardless of, notwithstanding, (even) though

Labels identify areas of usage

Opposites given for many key words

xi

Lists in the Thesaurus

Lists in the Thesaurus

A

abandon VERB 1 = <u>leave</u>, strand, ditch, forsake, run out on, desert, dump 2 = <u>stop</u>, give up, halt, pack in (*Brit. informal*), discontinue, leave off ≠ continue 3 = <u>give up</u>, yield, surrender, relinquish ≠ keep
● NOUN = <u>recklessness</u>, wildness ≠ restraint

abandonment = <u>desertion</u>, leaving, forsaking

abbey = <u>monastery</u>, convent, priory, nunnery, friary

abduct = <u>kidnap</u>, seize, carry off, snatch (*slang*)

abide VERB = <u>tolerate</u>, suffer, accept, bear, endure, put up with, take, stand
● PHRASES **abide by something** = <u>obey</u>, follow, agree to, carry out, observe, fulfil, act on, comply with

abiding = <u>enduring</u>, lasting, continuing, permanent, persistent, everlasting ≠ brief

ability 1 = <u>capability</u>, potential, competence, proficiency ≠ inability 2 = <u>skill</u>, talent, expertise, competence, aptitude, proficiency, cleverness

able = <u>capable</u>, qualified, efficient, accomplished, competent, skilful, proficient ≠ incapable

abnormal = <u>unusual</u>, different, odd, strange, extraordinary, remarkable, exceptional, peculiar ≠ normal

abnormality 1 = <u>strangeness</u>, peculiarity, irregularity, singularity 2 = <u>anomaly</u>, oddity, exception, peculiarity, deformity, irregularity

abolish = <u>do away with</u>, end, destroy, eliminate, cancel, get rid of, ditch (*slang*), throw out ≠ establish

abolition = <u>eradication</u>, ending, end, destruction, wiping out, elimination, cancellation, termination

abort 1 = <u>terminate</u> (*a pregnancy*), miscarry 2 = <u>stop</u>, end, finish, check, arrest, halt, cease, axe (*informal*)

abortion = <u>termination</u>, miscarriage, deliberate miscarriage

abound = <u>be plentiful</u>, thrive, flourish, be numerous, proliferate, be abundant, be thick on the ground

about PREPOSITION 1 = <u>regarding</u>, on, concerning, dealing with, referring to, relating to, as regards 2 = <u>near</u>, around, close to, nearby, beside, adjacent to, in the neighbourhood of
● ADVERB = <u>approximately</u>, around, almost, nearly, approaching, close to, roughly, just about

above 1 = <u>over</u>, upon, beyond, on top of, exceeding, higher than

≠ under 2 = senior to, over, ahead of, in charge of, higher than, superior to, more powerful than

abroad = overseas, out of the country, in foreign lands

abrupt 1 = sudden, unexpected, rapid, surprising, quick, rash, precipitate ≠ slow 2 = curt, brief, short, rude, impatient, terse, gruff, succinct ≠ polite

absence 1 = time off, leave, break, vacation, recess, truancy, absenteeism, nonattendance 2 = lack, deficiency, omission, scarcity, want, need, shortage, dearth

absent ADJECTIVE 1 = away, missing, gone, elsewhere, unavailable, nonexistent ≠ present 2 = absent-minded, blank, vague, distracted, vacant, preoccupied, oblivious, inattentive ≠ alert
● PHRASES **absent yourself** = stay away, withdraw, keep away, play truant

absolute 1 = complete, total, perfect, pure, sheer, utter, outright, thorough 2 = supreme, sovereign, unlimited, ultimate, full, unconditional, unrestricted, pre-eminent 3 = autocratic, supreme, all-powerful, imperious, domineering, tyrannical

absolutely = completely, totally, perfectly, fully, entirely, altogether, wholly, utterly

≠ somewhat

absorb 1 = soak up, suck up, receive, digest, imbibe 2 = engross, involve, engage, fascinate, rivet, captivate

absorbed = engrossed, lost, involved, gripped, fascinated, caught up, wrapped up, preoccupied

absorbing = fascinating, interesting, engaging, gripping, compelling, intriguing, enticing, riveting ≠ boring

absorption 1 = soaking up, consumption, digestion, sucking up 2 = immersion, involvement, concentration, fascination, preoccupation, intentness

abstract ADJECTIVE = theoretical, general, academic, speculative, indefinite, hypothetical, notional, abstruse ≠ actual
● NOUN = summary, résumé, outline, digest, epitome, rundown, synopsis, précis ≠ expansion
● VERB = extract, draw, pull, remove, separate, withdraw, isolate, pull out ≠ add

absurd = ridiculous, crazy (informal), silly, foolish, ludicrous, unreasonable, irrational, senseless ≠ sensible

abundance = plenty, bounty, exuberance, profusion, plethora, affluence, fullness, fruitfulness ≠ shortage

abundant = plentiful, full, rich, liberal, generous, ample, exuberant, teeming ≠ scarce

abuse NOUN 1 = maltreatment, damage, injury, hurt, harm, exploitation, manhandling, ill-treatment 2 = insults, blame, slights, put-downs, censure, reproach, scolding, defamation 3 = misuse, misapplication
● VERB 1 = ill-treat, damage, hurt, injure, harm, molest, maltreat, knock around or around ≠ care for 2 = insult, offend, curse, put down, malign, scold, disparage, castigate ≠ praise

abusive 1 = violent, rough, cruel, savage, brutal, vicious, destructive, harmful ≠ kind 2 = insulting, offensive, rude, degrading, scathing, contemptuous, disparaging, scurrilous ≠ complimentary

academic ADJECTIVE
1 = scholastic, educational 2 = scholarly, learned, intellectual, literary, erudite, highbrow, studious 3 = theoretical, abstract, speculative, hypothetical, impractical, notional, conjectural
● NOUN = scholar, intellectual, don, master, professor, fellow, lecturer, tutor, acca (Austral. slang)

accelerate 1 = increase, grow, advance, extend, expand, raise, swell, enlarge ≠ fall 2 = expedite,

further, speed up, hasten ≠ delay 3 = speed up, advance, quicken, gather momentum ≠ slow down

acceleration = hastening, hurrying, stepping up (informal), speeding up, quickening

accent NOUN = pronunciation, tone, articulation, inflection, brogue, intonation, diction, modulation
● VERB = emphasize, stress, highlight, underline, underscore, accentuate

accept 1 = receive, take, gain, pick up, secure, collect, get, obtain 2 = acknowledge, believe, allow, admit, approve, recognize, yield, concede

acceptable = satisfactory, fair, all right, suitable, sufficient, good enough, adequate, tolerable ≠ unsatisfactory

acceptance 1 = accepting, taking, receiving, obtaining, acquiring, reception, receipt 2 = acknowledgement, agreement, approval, recognition, admission, consent, adoption, assent

accepted = agreed, common, established, traditional, approved, acknowledged, recognized, customary ≠ unconventional

access 1 = admission, entry, passage 2 = entrance, road, approach, entry, path, gate, opening, passage

accessible = handy, near,

nearby, at hand, within reach, at your fingertips, reachable, achievable ≠ inaccessible

accessory 1 = extra, addition, supplement, attachment, adjunct, appendage 2 = accomplice, partner, ally, associate (*in crime*), assistant, helper, colleague, collaborator

accident 1 = crash, smash, wreck, collision 2 = misfortune, disaster, tragedy, setback, calamity, mishap, misadventure 3 = chance, fortune, luck, fate, hazard, coincidence, fluke, fortuity

accidental 1 = unintentional, unexpected, incidental, unforeseen, unplanned ≠ deliberate 2 = chance, random, casual, unplanned, fortuitous, inadvertent

accidentally = unintentionally, incidentally, by accident, by chance, inadvertently, unwittingly, randomly, haphazardly ≠ deliberately

acclaim VERB = praise, celebrate, honour, cheer, admire, hail, applaud, compliment
● NOUN = praise, honour, celebration, approval, tribute, applause, kudos, commendation ≠ criticism

accommodate 1 = house, put up, take in, lodge, shelter, entertain, cater for 2 = help,

support, aid, assist, cooperate with, abet, lend a hand to
3 = adapt, fit, settle, alter, adjust, modify, comply, reconcile

accommodating = obliging, willing, kind, friendly, helpful, polite, cooperative, agreeable ≠ unhelpful

accommodation = housing, homes, houses, board, quarters, digs (*Brit. informal*), shelter, lodging(s)

accompaniment 1 = backing music, backing, support, obbligato 2 = supplement, extra, addition, companion, accessory, complement, decoration, adjunct

accompany 1 = go with, lead, partner, guide, attend, conduct, escort, shepherd 2 = occur with, belong to, come with, supplement, go together with, follow

accompanying = additional, extra, related, associated, attached, attendant, complementary, supplementary

accomplish = realize, produce, effect, finish, complete, manage, achieve, perform ≠ fail

accomplished = skilled, able, professional, expert, masterly, talented, gifted, polished ≠ unskilled

accomplishment
1 = achievement, feat, act, stroke, triumph, coup, exploit, deed
2 = accomplishing, finishing,

carrying out, conclusion, bringing about, execution, completion, fulfilment

accord NOUN 1 = <u>treaty</u>, contract, agreement, arrangement, settlement, pact, deal (*informal*) 2 = <u>sympathy</u>, agreement, harmony, unison, rapport, conformity ≠ conflict
● PHRASES **accord with something** = <u>agree with</u>, match, coincide with, fit with, correspond with, conform with, tally with, harmonize with

accordingly 1 = <u>consequently</u>, so, thus, therefore, hence, subsequently, in consequence, ergo 2 = <u>appropriately</u>, correspondingly, properly, suitably, fitly

account NOUN 1 = <u>description</u>, report, story, statement, version, tale, explanation, narrative 2 = <u>importance</u>, standing, concern, value, note, worth, weight, honour
● PLURAL NOUN (*Commerce*) = <u>ledgers</u>, books, charges, bills, statements, balances, tallies, invoices
● VERB = <u>consider</u>, rate, value, judge, estimate, think, count, reckon

accountability = <u>responsibility</u>, liability, culpability, answerability, chargeability

accountable = <u>answerable</u>,

subject, responsible, obliged, liable, amenable, obligated, chargeable

accountant = <u>auditor</u>, book-keeper, bean counter (*informal*)

accumulate = <u>build up</u>, increase, be stored, collect, gather, pile up, amass, hoard ≠ disperse

accumulation 1 = <u>collection</u>, increase, stock, store, mass, build-up, pile, stack 2 = <u>growth</u>, collection, gathering, build-up

accuracy = <u>exactness</u>, precision, fidelity, authenticity, correctness, closeness, veracity, truthfulness ≠ inaccuracy

accurate 1 = <u>precise</u>, close, correct, careful, strict, exact, faithful, explicit ≠ inaccurate 2 = <u>correct</u>, true, exact, spot-on (*Brit. informal*)

accurately 1 = <u>precisely</u>, correctly, closely, truly, strictly, exactly, faithfully, to the letter 2 = <u>exactly</u>, closely, correctly, precisely, strictly, faithfully, explicitly, scrupulously

accusation = <u>charge</u>, complaint, allegation, indictment, recrimination, denunciation, incrimination

accuse 1 = <u>point a or the finger at</u>, blame for, denounce, hold responsible for, impute blame to ≠ exonerate 2 = <u>charge with</u>, indict for, impeach for, censure

accustom = <u>familiarize</u>, train, discipline, adapt, instruct, school, acquaint, acclimatize

accustomed 1 = <u>used</u>, trained, familiar, given to, adapted, acquainted, in the habit of, familiarized ≠ unaccustomed **2** = <u>usual</u>, established, expected, common, standard, traditional, normal, regular ≠ unusual

ace NOUN **1** (*Cards, dice*) = <u>one</u>, single point **2** (*Informal*) = <u>expert</u>, star, champion, authority, professional, master, specialist, guru
• ADJECTIVE (*Informal*) = <u>great</u>, brilliant, fine, wonderful, excellent, outstanding, superb, fantastic (*informal*), booshit (*Austral. slang*), sik (*Austral. slang*), ka pai (*N.Z.*)

ache VERB = <u>hurt</u>, suffer, burn, pain, smart, sting, pound, throb
• NOUN = <u>pain</u>, discomfort, suffering, hurt, throbbing, irritation, tenderness, pounding

achieve = <u>accomplish</u>, fulfil, complete, gain, perform, do, get, carry out

achievement
= <u>accomplishment</u>, effort, feat, deed, stroke, triumph, coup, exploit

acid 1 = <u>sour</u>, tart, pungent, acerbic, acrid, vinegary ≠ sweet **2** = <u>sharp</u>, cutting, biting, bitter,

harsh, barbed, caustic, vitriolic ≠ kindly

acknowledge 1 = <u>admit</u>, own up, allow, accept, reveal, grant, declare, recognize ≠ deny **2** = <u>greet</u>, address, notice, recognize, salute, accost ≠ snub **3** = <u>reply to</u>, answer, notice, recognize, respond to, react to, retort to ≠ ignore

acquaintance 1 = <u>associate</u>, contact, ally, colleague, comrade ≠ intimate **2** = <u>relationship</u>, connection, fellowship, familiarity ≠ unfamiliarity

acquire = <u>get</u>, win, buy, receive, gain, earn, secure, collect ≠ lose

acquisition 1 = <u>acquiring</u>, gaining, procurement, attainment **2** = <u>purchase</u>, buy, investment, property, gain, prize, asset, possession

acquit VERB = <u>clear</u>, free, release, excuse, discharge, liberate, vindicate ≠ find guilty
• PHRASES **acquit yourself** = <u>behave</u>, bear yourself, conduct yourself, comport yourself

act VERB **1** = <u>do something</u>, perform, function **2** = <u>perform</u>, mimic
• NOUN **1** = <u>deed</u>, action, performance, achievement, undertaking, exploit, feat, accomplishment **2** = <u>pretence</u>, show, front, performance, display, attitude, pose, posture **3** = <u>law</u>,

bill, measure, resolution, decree, statute, ordinance, enactment **4** = <u>performance</u>, show, turn, production, routine, presentation, gig (informal), sketch

acting NOUN = <u>performance</u>, playing, performing, theatre, portrayal, impersonation, characterization, stagecraft
• ADJECTIVE = <u>temporary</u>, substitute, interim, provisional, surrogate, stopgap, pro tem

action 1 = <u>deed</u>, act, performance, achievement, exploit, feat, accomplishment **2** = <u>measure</u>, act, manoeuvre **3** = <u>lawsuit</u>, case, trial, suit, proceeding, dispute, prosecution, litigation **4** = <u>energy</u>, activity, spirit, force, vitality, vigour, liveliness, vim **5** = <u>effect</u>, working, process, operation, activity, movement, functioning, motion **6** = <u>battle</u>, fight, conflict, clash, contest, encounter, combat, engagement

activate = <u>start</u>, move, initiate, rouse, mobilize, set in motion, galvanize ≠ stop

active 1 = <u>busy</u>, involved, occupied, lively, energetic, bustling, on the move, strenuous ≠ sluggish **2** = <u>energetic</u>, quick, alert, dynamic, lively, vigorous, animated, forceful ≠ inactive **3** = <u>in operation</u>, working, acting, at work, in action, operative, in

force, effectual

activist = <u>militant</u>, partisan

activity 1 = <u>action</u>, labour, movement, energy, exercise, spirit, motion, bustle ≠ inaction **2** = <u>pursuit</u>, project, scheme, pleasure, interest, hobby, pastime

actor or **actress** = <u>performer</u>, player, Thespian, luvvie (informal)
➤ WORD POWER SUPPLEMENT **actors**

Word Power

actor/actress – The use of *actress* is now very much on the decline, and women who work in the profession invariably prefer to be referred to as *actors*.

actual = <u>real</u>, substantial, concrete, definite, tangible

Word Power

actual – The words *actual* and *actually* are often used when speaking, but should only be used in writing where they add something to the meaning of a sentence. For example, in the sentence *he actually rather enjoyed the film*, the word *actually* is only needed if there was originally some doubt as to whether he would enjoy it.

actually = <u>really</u>, in fact, indeed, truly, literally, genuinely, in reality, in truth

acute 1 = <u>serious</u>, important, dangerous, critical, crucial, severe, grave, urgent 2 = <u>sharp</u>, shooting, powerful, violent, severe, intense, fierce, piercing 3 = <u>perceptive</u>, sharp, keen, smart, sensitive, clever, astute, insightful ≠ slow

adamant = <u>determined</u>, firm, fixed, stubborn, uncompromising, resolute, unbending, obdurate ≠ flexible

adapt 1 = <u>adjust</u>, change, alter, modify, accommodate, conform, acclimatize 2 = <u>convert</u>, change, transform, alter, modify, tailor, remodel

adaptation 1 = <u>acclimatization</u>, naturalization, familiarization 2 = <u>conversion</u>, change, variation, adjustment, transformation, modification, alteration

add 1 = <u>count up</u>, total, reckon, compute, add up, tot up ≠ take away 2 = <u>include</u>, attach, supplement, adjoin, augment, affix, append

addict 1 = <u>junkie</u> (informal), freak (informal), fiend (informal) 2 = <u>fan</u>, lover, nut (slang), follower, enthusiast, admirer, buff (informal), junkie (informal)

addicted
• PHRASES **addicted to** = <u>hooked on</u>, dependent on, accustomed to (slang), habituated to

addiction = <u>dependence</u>, habit, obsession, craving, enslavement with **to** = <u>love of</u>, passion for, attachment to

addition NOUN 1 = <u>extra</u>, supplement, increase, gain, bonus, extension, accessory, additive 2 = <u>inclusion</u>, adding, increasing, extension, attachment, insertion, incorporation, augmentation ≠ removal 3 = <u>counting up</u>, totalling, adding up, computation, totting up ≠ subtraction
• PHRASES **in addition to** = <u>as well as</u>, along with, on top of, besides, to boot, additionally, over and above, to say nothing of

additional = <u>extra</u>, new, other, added, further, fresh, spare, supplementary

address NOUN 1 = <u>location</u>, home, place, house, point, position, situation, site 2 = <u>speech</u>, talk, lecture, discourse, sermon, dissertation, homily, oration
• VERB = <u>speak to</u>, talk to, greet, hail, approach, converse with, korero (N.Z.)

adept ADJECTIVE = <u>skilful</u>, able, skilled, expert, practised, accomplished, versed, proficient ≠ unskilled
• NOUN = <u>expert</u>, master, genius, hotshot (informal), dab hand (Brit. informal)

adequate 1 = <u>passable</u>, acceptable, average, fair, satisfactory, competent, mediocre, so-so (*informal*) ≠ <u>sufficient</u>, enough ≠ insufficient

adhere to = <u>stick to</u>, attach to, cling to, glue to, fix to, fasten to, hold fast to, paste to

adjacent ADJECTIVE = <u>adjoining</u>, neighbouring, nearby ≠ far away ● PREPOSITION *with* **to** = <u>next to</u>, touching, close to, neighbouring, beside, near to, adjoining, bordering on

adjoin = <u>connect with</u> *or* <u>to</u>, join, link with, touch on, border on

adjoining = <u>connecting</u>, touching, bordering, neighbouring, next door, adjacent, abutting

adjourn = <u>postpone</u>, delay, suspend, interrupt, put off, defer, discontinue ≠ continue

adjust 1 = <u>adapt</u>, change, alter, accustom, conform 2 = <u>change</u>, reform, alter, adapt, revise, modify, amend, make conform 3 = <u>modify</u>, alter, adapt

adjustable = <u>alterable</u>, flexible, adaptable, malleable, movable, modifiable

adjustment 1 = <u>alteration</u>, change, tuning, repair, conversion, modifying, adaptation, modification 2 = <u>acclimatization</u>, orientation, change, regulation, amendment, adaptation, revision, modification

administer 1 = <u>manage</u>, run, control, direct, handle, conduct, command, govern 2 = <u>dispense</u>, give, share, provide, apply, assign, allocate, allot 3 = <u>execute</u>, give, provide, apply, perform, carry out, impose, implement

administration
1 = <u>management</u>, government, running, control, handling, direction, conduct, application 2 = <u>directors</u>, board, executive(s), employers 3 = <u>government</u>, leadership, regime

administrative = <u>managerial</u>, executive, directing, regulatory, governmental, organizational, supervisory, directorial

administrator = <u>manager</u>, head, official, director, executive, boss (*informal*), governor, supervisor, baas (*S. African*)

admirable = <u>praiseworthy</u>, good, great, fine, wonderful, excellent, brilliant, outstanding, booshit (*Austral. slang*), exo (*Austral. slang*), sik (*Austral. slang*), ka pai (*N.Z.*) ≠ deplorable

admiration = <u>regard</u>, wonder, respect, praise, approval, recognition, esteem, appreciation

admire 1 = <u>respect</u>, value, prize, honour, praise, appreciate, esteem, approve of ≠ despise 2 = <u>adore</u>, like, love, take to, fancy

(*Brit. informal*), treasure, cherish, glorify **3** = <u>marvel at</u>, look at, appreciate, delight in, wonder at, be amazed by, take pleasure in, gape at

admirer 1 = <u>fan</u>, supporter, follower, enthusiast, partisan, disciple, devotee **2** = <u>suitor</u>, lover, boyfriend, sweetheart, beau, wooer

admission 1 = <u>admittance</u>, access, entry, introduction, entrance, acceptance, initiation, entrée **2** = <u>confession</u>, declaration, revelation, allowance, disclosure, acknowledgement, unburdening, divulgence

admit 1 = <u>confess</u>, confide, own up, come clean (*informal*) **2** = <u>allow</u>, agree, accept, reveal, grant, declare, acknowledge, recognize ≠ deny **3** = <u>let in</u>, allow, receive, accept, introduce, take in, initiate, give access to ≠ keep out

adolescence = <u>teens</u>, youth, minority, boyhood, girlhood

adolescent ADJECTIVE
1 = <u>young</u>, junior, teenage, juvenile, youthful, childish, immature, boyish **2** = <u>teenage</u>, young, teen (*informal*)
● NOUN = <u>teenager</u>, girl, boy, kid (*informal*), youth, lad, minor, young man

adopt 1 = <u>take on</u>, follow, choose, maintain, assume, take up, engage in, become involved

in **2** = <u>take in</u>, raise, nurse, mother, rear, foster, bring up, take care of ≠ abandon

adoption 1 = <u>fostering</u>, adopting, taking in **2** = <u>embracing</u>, choice, taking up, selection, assumption, endorsement, appropriation, espousal

adore = <u>love</u>, honour, admire, worship, esteem, cherish, revere, dote on ≠ hate

adoring = <u>admiring</u>, loving, devoted, fond, affectionate, doting ≠ hating

adorn = <u>decorate</u>, array, embellish, festoon

adrift ADJECTIVE **1** = <u>drifting</u>, afloat, unmoored, unanchored **2** = <u>aimless</u>, goalless, directionless, purposeless
● ADVERB = <u>wrong</u>, astray, off course, amiss, off target, wide of the mark

adult NOUN = <u>grown-up</u>, mature person, person of mature age, grown or grown-up person, man or woman
● ADJECTIVE **1** = <u>fully grown</u>, mature, grown-up, of age, ripe, fully fledged, fully developed, full grown **2** = <u>pornographic</u>, blue, dirty, obscene, filthy, indecent, lewd, salacious

advance VERB **1** = <u>progress</u>, proceed, come forward, make inroads, make headway ≠ retreat

2 = <u>accelerate</u>, speed, promote, hasten, bring forward
3 = <u>improve</u>, rise, develop, pick up, progress, upgrade, prosper, make strides **4** = <u>suggest</u>, offer, present, propose, advocate, submit, prescribe, put forward ≠ withhold **5** = <u>lend</u>, loan, supply on credit ≠ withhold payment
• **NOUN 1** = <u>down payment</u>, credit, loan, fee, deposit, retainer, prepayment **2** = <u>attack</u>, charge, strike, assault, raid, invasion, offensive, onslaught
3 = <u>improvement</u>, development, gain, growth, breakthrough, step, headway, inroads
• **ADJECTIVE** = <u>prior</u>, early, beforehand
• **PHRASES in advance** = <u>beforehand</u>, earlier, ahead, previously
advanced = <u>sophisticated</u>, foremost, modern, revolutionary, up-to-date, higher, leading, recent ≠ backward
advancement = <u>promotion</u>, rise, gain, progress, improvement, betterment, preferment
advantage 1 = <u>benefit</u>, help, profit, favour ≠ disadvantage
2 = <u>lead</u>, sway, dominance, precedence **3** = <u>superiority</u>, good
adventure 1 = <u>venture</u>, experience, incident, enterprise, undertaking, exploit, occurrence, caper **2** = <u>excitement</u>, action,

passion, thrill, animation, commotion
adventurous = <u>daring</u>, enterprising, bold, reckless, intrepid, daredevil ≠ cautious
adversary = <u>opponent</u>, rival, enemy, competitor, foe, contestant, antagonist ≠ ally
adverse 1 = <u>harmful</u>, damaging, negative, destructive, detrimental, hurtful, injurious, inopportune ≠ beneficial
2 = <u>unfavourable</u>, hostile, unlucky **3** = <u>negative</u>, opposing, hostile, contrary, dissenting, unsympathetic, ill-disposed
advert (*Brit. informal*) = <u>advertisement</u>, notice, commercial, ad (*informal*), announcement, poster, plug (*informal*), blurb
advertise = <u>publicize</u>, promote, plug (*informal*), announce, inform, hype, notify, tout
advertisement = <u>advert</u> (*Brit. informal*), notice, commercial, ad (*informal*), announcement, poster, plug (*informal*), blurb
advice = <u>guidance</u>, help, opinion, direction, suggestion, instruction, counsel, counselling
advise 1 = <u>recommend</u>, suggest, urge, counsel, advocate, caution, prescribe, commend **2** = <u>notify</u>, tell, report, announce, warn, declare, inform, acquaint
adviser = <u>counsellor</u>, guide,

consultant, aide, guru, mentor, helper, confidant

advisory = advising, helping, recommending, counselling, consultative

advocate VERB = recommend, support, champion, encourage, propose, promote, advise, endorse ≠ oppose

● NOUN 1 = supporter, spokesman, champion, defender, campaigner, promoter, counsellor, proponent

2 (*Law*) = lawyer, attorney, solicitor, counsel, barrister

affair 1 = matter, business, happening, event, activity, incident, episode, topic

2 = relationship, romance, intrigue, fling, liaison, flirtation, amour, dalliance

affect[1] 1 = influence, concern, alter, change, manipulate, act on, bear upon, impinge upon

2 = emotionally move, touch, upset, overcome, stir, disturb, perturb

affect[2] = put on, assume, adopt, pretend, imitate, simulate, contrive, aspire to

affected = pretended, artificial, contrived, put-on, mannered, unnatural, feigned, insincere ≠ genuine

affection = fondness, liking, feeling, love, care, warmth, attachment, goodwill, aroha (*N.Z.*)

affectionate = fond, loving,

kind, caring, friendly, attached, devoted, tender ≠ cool

affiliate = associate, unite, join, link, ally, combine, incorporate, amalgamate

affinity 1 = attraction, liking, leaning, sympathy, inclination, rapport, fondness, partiality, aroha (*N.Z.*) ≠ hostility

2 = similarity, relationship, connection, correspondence, analogy, resemblance, closeness, likeness ≠ difference

affirm 1 = declare, state, maintain, swear, assert, testify, pronounce, certify ≠ deny

2 = confirm, prove, endorse, ratify, verify, validate, bear out, substantiate ≠ refute

affirmative = agreeing, confirming, positive, approving, consenting, favourable, concurring, assenting ≠ negative

afflict = torment, trouble, pain, hurt, distress, plague, grieve, harass

affluent = wealthy, rich, prosperous, loaded (*slang*), well-off, opulent, well-heeled (*informal*), well-to-do ≠ poor

afford 1 = have the money for, manage, bear, pay for, spare, stand, stretch to 2 = bear, stand, sustain, allow yourself 3 = give, offer, provide, produce, supply, yield, render

affordable = inexpensive,

cheap, reasonable, moderate, modest, low-cost, economical ≠ expensive

afraid 1 = scared, frightened, nervous, terrified, shaken, startled, fearful, cowardly ≠ unafraid 2 = reluctant, frightened, scared, unwilling, hesitant, loath, disinclined, unenthusiastic 3 = sorry, apologetic, regretful, sad, distressed, unhappy ≠ pleased

after PREPOSITION = at the end of, following, subsequent to ≠ before
● ADVERB = following, later, next, succeeding, afterwards, subsequently, thereafter

Related Words
prefix: post-

aftermath = effects, results, wake, consequences, outcome, sequel, end result, upshot

again 1 = once more, another time, anew, afresh 2 = also, in addition, moreover, besides, furthermore

against 1 = beside, on, up against, in contact with, abutting 2 = opposed to, anti (*informal*), hostile to, in opposition to, averse to, opposite to 3 = in opposition to, resisting, versus, counter to, in the opposite direction of 4 = in preparation for, in case of, in anticipation of, in expectation of, in provision for

Related Words
prefixes: anti-, counter-

age NOUN 1 = years, days, generation, lifetime, length of existence 2 = old age, experience, maturity, seniority, majority, senility, decline (*of life*), advancing years ≠ youth 3 = time, day(s), period, generation, era, epoch
● VERB 1 = grow old, decline, weather, fade, deteriorate, wither 2 = mature, season, condition, soften, mellow, ripen

aged = old, getting on, grey, ancient, antique, elderly, antiquated ≠ young

agency 1 = business, company, office, firm, department, organization, enterprise, establishment 2 (*Old-fashioned*) = medium, means, activity, vehicle, instrument, mechanism

agenda = programme, list, plan, schedule, diary, calendar, timetable

agent 1 = representative, rep (*informal*), negotiator, envoy, surrogate, go-between 2 = author, worker, vehicle, instrument, operator, performer, catalyst, doer 3 = force, means, power, cause, instrument

aggravate 1 = make worse, exaggerate, intensify, worsen, exacerbate, magnify, inflame, increase ≠ improve 2 (*Informal*)

= <u>annoy</u>, bother, provoke, irritate, nettle, get on your nerves (*informal*) ≠ please

aggregate NOUN = <u>total</u>, body, whole, amount, collection, mass, sum, combination

● **ADJECTIVE** = <u>collective</u>, mixed, combined, collected, accumulated, composite, cumulative

● **VERB** = <u>combine</u>, mix, collect, assemble, heap, accumulate, pile, amass

aggression 1 = <u>hostility</u>, malice, antagonism, antipathy, ill will, belligerence, destructiveness, pugnacity **2** = <u>attack</u>, campaign, injury, assault, raid, invasion, offensive, onslaught

aggressive 1 = <u>hostile</u>, offensive, destructive, belligerent, unfriendly, contrary, antagonistic, pugnacious, aggers (*Austral. slang*), biffo (*Austral. slang*) ≠ friendly **2** = <u>forceful</u>, powerful, convincing, effective, enterprising, dynamic, bold, militant ≠ submissive

agitate 1 = <u>stir</u>, beat, shake, disturb, toss, rouse **2** = <u>upset</u>, worry, trouble, excite, distract, unnerve, disconcert, fluster ≠ calm

agony = <u>suffering</u>, pain, distress, misery, torture, discomfort, torment, hardship

agree 1 = <u>concur</u>, be as one,

sympathize, assent, see eye to eye, be of the same opinion ≠ disagree **2** = <u>correspond</u>, match, coincide, tally, conform **3** = <u>suit</u>, get on, befit

agreement 1 = <u>treaty</u>, contract, arrangement, alliance, deal (*informal*), understanding, settlement, bargain **2** = <u>concurrence</u>, harmony, compliance, union, agreeing, consent, unison, assent ≠ disagreement **3** = <u>correspondence</u>, similarity, consistency, correlation, conformity, compatibility, congruity ≠ difference

agricultural = <u>farming</u>, country, rural, rustic, agrarian

agriculture = <u>farming</u>, culture, cultivation, husbandry, tillage

ahead 1 = <u>in front</u>, in advance, towards the front, forwards **2** = <u>at an advantage</u>, in advance, in the lead **3** = <u>in the lead</u>, winning, leading, at the head, to the fore, at an advantage **4** = <u>in front</u>, before, in advance, in the lead

aid NOUN = <u>help</u>, backing, support, benefit, favour, relief, promotion, assistance ≠ hindrance

● **VERB 1** = <u>help</u>, support, serve, sustain, assist, avail, subsidize, be of service to ≠ hinder **2** = <u>promote</u>, help, further, forward, encourage, favour, facilitate, pave the way for

aide = <u>assistant</u>, supporter, attendant, helper, right-hand man, second

ailing 1 = <u>weak</u>, failing, poor, flawed, unstable, unsatisfactory, deficient 2 = <u>ill</u>, poorly, sick, weak, crook (*Austral. & N.Z. informal*), unwell, infirm, under the weather (*informal*), indisposed

ailment = <u>illness</u>, disease, complaint, disorder, sickness, affliction, malady, infirmity

aim VERB 1 = <u>try for</u>, seek, work for, plan for, strive, set your sights on 2 = <u>point</u>
● NOUN = <u>intention</u>, point, plan, goal, design, target, purpose, desire

air NOUN 1 = <u>wind</u>, breeze, draught, gust, zephyr 2 = <u>atmosphere</u>, sky, heavens, aerosphere 3 = <u>tune</u>, song, theme, melody, strain, lay, aria 4 = <u>manner</u>, appearance, look, aspect, atmosphere, mood, impression, aura
● PLURAL NOUN = <u>affectation</u>, arrogance, pretensions, pomposity, swank (*informal*), hauteur, haughtiness, superciliousness
● VERB 1 = <u>publicize</u>, reveal, exhibit, voice, express, display, circulate, make public 2 = <u>ventilate</u>, expose, freshen, aerate
(*Related Words*)
adjective: aerial

airborne 1 = <u>flying</u>, floating, in the air, hovering, gliding, in flight, on the wing

airing 1 = <u>ventilation</u>, drying, freshening, aeration 2 = <u>exposure</u>, display, expression, publicity, vent, utterance, dissemination

airplane (*U.S. & Canad.*) = <u>plane</u>, aircraft, jet, aeroplane, airliner

aisle = <u>passageway</u>, path, lane, passage, corridor, alley, gangway

alarm NOUN 1 = <u>fear</u>, panic, anxiety, fright, apprehension, nervousness, consternation, trepidation ≠ calmness 2 = <u>danger signal</u>, warning, bell, alert, siren, alarm bell, hooter, distress signal
● VERB = <u>frighten</u>, scare, panic, distress, startle, dismay, daunt, unnerve ≠ calm

alarming = <u>frightening</u>, shocking, scaring, disturbing, distressing, startling, horrifying, menacing

alcoholic NOUN = <u>drunkard</u>, drinker, drunk, toper, lush (*slang*), tippler, wino (*informal*), inebriate, alko or alco (*Austral. slang*)
● ADJECTIVE = <u>intoxicating</u>, hard, strong, stiff, brewed, fermented, distilled

alert ADJECTIVE 1 = <u>attentive</u>,

awake, vigilant, watchful, on the lookout, circumspect, observant, on guard ≠ careless 2 = **quick-witted**, bright, sharp
- NOUN = **warning**, signal, alarm, siren ≠ all clear
- VERB = **warn**, signal, inform, alarm, notify, tip off, forewarn ≠ lull

alien ADJECTIVE 1 = **foreign**, strange, imported, unknown, exotic, unfamiliar 2 = **strange**, new, foreign, novel, unknown, exotic, unfamiliar, untried ≠ similar
- NOUN = **foreigner**, incomer, immigrant, stranger, outsider, newcomer, asylum seeker ≠ citizen

alienate = **antagonize**, anger, annoy, offend, irritate, hassle (*informal*), estrange

alienation = **estrangement**, setting against, separation, turning away, disaffection, remoteness

alight[1] 1 = **get off**, descend, get down, disembark, dismount 2 = **land**, light, settle, come down, descend, perch, touch down, come to rest ≠ take off

alight[2] = **lit up**, bright, brilliant, shining, illuminated, fiery

align 1 = **ally**, side, join, associate, affiliate, cooperate, sympathize 2 = **line up**, order, range, regulate, straighten, even up

alike ADJECTIVE = **similar**, close, the same, parallel, resembling, identical, corresponding, akin ≠ different
- ADVERB = **similarly**, identically, equally, uniformly, correspondingly, analogously ≠ differently

alive 1 = **living**, breathing, animate, subsisting, existing, functioning, in the land of the living (*informal*) ≠ dead 2 = **in existence**, existing, functioning, active, in force, on-going, prevalent ≠ inoperative 3 = **lively**, active, vital, alert, energetic, animated, agile, perky ≠ dull

all PRONOUN 1 = **the whole amount**, everything, the total, the aggregate, the totality, the sum total, the entirety, the entire amount 2 = **every**, each, every single, every one of, each and every
- ADJECTIVE = **complete**, greatest, full, total, perfect, entire, utter
- ADVERB = **completely**, totally, fully, entirely, absolutely, altogether, wholly, utterly

allegation = **claim**, charge, statement, declaration, accusation, assertion, affirmation

allege = **claim**, charge, challenge, state, maintain, declare, assert, uphold ≠ deny

alleged = **claimed**, supposed, declared, assumed, so-called, apparent, stated, described

allegiance = **loyalty**, devotion, fidelity, obedience, constancy, faithfulness ≠ disloyalty

allergic = <u>sensitive</u>, affected by, susceptible, hypersensitive

allergy = <u>sensitivity</u>, reaction, susceptibility, antipathy, hypersensitivity, sensitiveness

alleviate = <u>ease</u>, reduce, relieve, moderate, soothe, lessen, lighten, allay

alley = <u>passage</u>, walk, lane, pathway, alleyway, passageway, backstreet

alliance = <u>union</u>, league, association, agreement, marriage, connection, combination, coalition ≠ division

allied 1 = <u>united</u>, linked, related, combined, integrated, affiliated, cooperating, in league
2 = <u>connected</u>, linked, associated

allocate = <u>assign</u>, grant, distribute, designate, set aside, earmark, give out, consign

allocation 1 = <u>allowance</u>, share, portion, quota, lot, ration
2 = <u>assignment</u>, allowance, allotment

allow VERB 1 = <u>permit</u>, approve, enable, sanction, endure, license, tolerate, authorize ≠ prohibit
2 = <u>let</u>, permit, sanction, authorize, license, tolerate, consent to, assent to ≠ forbid
3 = <u>give</u>, provide, grant, spare, devote, assign, allocate, set aside
4 = <u>acknowledge</u>, accept, admit, grant, recognize, yield, concede, confess

● PHRASES **allow for something** = <u>take something into account</u>, consider, plan for, accommodate, provide for, make provision for, make allowances for, make concessions for

allowance 1 = <u>portion</u>, lot, share, amount, grant, quota, allocation, stint
2 = <u>pocket money</u>, grant, fee, payment, ration, handout, remittance
3 = <u>concession</u>, discount, reduction, repayment, deduction, rebate

all right 1 = <u>satisfactory</u>, O.K. or okay (*informal*), average, fair, sufficient, standard, acceptable, good enough ≠ unsatisfactory
2 = <u>well</u>, O.K. or okay (*informal*), whole, sound, fit, safe, healthy, unharmed ≠ ill

ally NOUN = <u>partner</u>, friend, colleague, associate, mate, comrade, helper, collaborator, cobber (*Austral. & N.Z. old-fashioned informal*), E hoa (*N.Z.*) ≠ opponent

● PHRASES **ally yourself with something** or **someone** = <u>unite with</u>, associate with, unify, collaborate with, join forces with, band together with

almost = <u>nearly</u>, about, close to, virtually, practically, roughly, just about, not quite

alone ADJECTIVE 1 = <u>solitary</u>, isolated, separate, apart, by yourself, unaccompanied, on your tod (*slang*) ≠ accompanied **2** = **lonely**, abandoned, isolated, solitary, desolate, forsaken, forlorn, destitute

● ADVERB **1** = **solely**, only, individually, singly, exclusively, uniquely **2** = **by yourself**, independently, unaccompanied, without help, on your own, without assistance ≠ with help

aloud = **out loud**, clearly, plainly, distinctly, audibly, intelligibly

already = **before now**, before, previously, at present, by now, by then, even now, just now

also = **and**, too, further, in addition, as well, moreover, besides, furthermore

alter 1 = **modify**, change, reform, vary, transform, adjust, adapt, revise **2** = **change**, turn, vary, transform, adjust, adapt

alternate VERB **1** = **interchange**, change, fluctuate, take turns, oscillate, chop and change **2** = **intersperse**, interchange, exchange, swap, stagger, rotate

● ADJECTIVE = **alternating**, interchanging, every other, rotating, every second, sequential

alternative NOUN = **substitute**, choice, other (*of two*), option, preference, recourse

● ADJECTIVE = **different**, other, substitute, alternate

alternatively = **or**, instead, otherwise, on the other hand, if not, then again, as an alternative, as another option

although = **though**, while, even if, even though, whilst, albeit, despite the fact that, notwithstanding

altogether 1 = **absolutely**, quite, completely, totally, perfectly, fully, thoroughly, wholly **2** = **completely**, fully, entirely, thoroughly, wholly, in every respect ≠ partially **3** = **on the whole**, generally, mostly, in general, collectively, all things considered, on average, for the most part **4** = **in total**, in all, all told, taken together, in sum, everything included

---

Word Power

altogether – The single-word form *altogether* should not be used as an alternative to *all together* because the meanings are very distinct. *Altogether* is an adverb meaning 'absolutely' or, in a different sense, 'in total'. *All together*, however, means 'all at the same time' or 'all in the same place'. The distinction can be seen in the following example: *altogether there were six or seven families sharing the flat's facilities* means 'in total', while *there were six or seven families all together in one flat*, means 'all crowded in together'.

always 1 = habitually, regularly, every time, consistently, invariably, perpetually, without exception, customarily ≠ seldom 2 = forever, for keeps, eternally, for all time, evermore, till the cows come home (*informal*), till Doomsday 3 = continually, constantly, all the time, forever, repeatedly, persistently, perpetually, incessantly

amass = collect, gather, assemble, compile, accumulate, pile up, hoard

amateur = nonprofessional, outsider, layman, dilettante, layperson, non-specialist, dabbler

amaze = astonish, surprise, shock, stun, alarm, stagger, startle, bewilder

amazement = astonishment, surprise, wonder, shock, confusion, admiration, awe, bewilderment

amazing = astonishing, surprising, brilliant, stunning, overwhelming, staggering, sensational (*informal*), bewildering

ambassador = representative, minister, agent, deputy, diplomat, envoy, consul, attaché

ambiguity = vagueness, doubt, uncertainty, obscurity, equivocation, dubiousness

ambiguous = unclear, obscure, vague, dubious, enigmatic, indefinite, inconclusive, indeterminate ≠ clear

ambition 1 = goal, hope, dream, target, aim, wish, purpose, desire 2 = enterprise, longing, drive, spirit, desire, passion, enthusiasm, striving

ambitious 1 = enterprising, spirited, daring, eager, intent, enthusiastic, hopeful, striving ≠ unambitious

ambush VERB = trap, attack, surprise, deceive, dupe, ensnare, waylay, bushwhack (*U.S.*)
● NOUN = trap, snare, lure, waylaying

amend VERB = change, improve, reform, fix, correct, repair, edit, alter
● PLURAL NOUN (usually in *make amends*) = compensation, redress, reparation, restitution, atonement, recompense

amendment 1 = addition, change, adjustment, attachment, adaptation, revision, modification, alteration 2 = change, improvement, repair, edit, remedy, correction, revision, modification

amenity = facility, service, advantage, comfort, convenience

amid *or* **amidst** 1 = during, among, at a time of, in an atmosphere of 2 = in the middle of, among, surrounded by, amongst, in the midst of, in the thick of

ammunition = <u>munitions</u>, rounds, shot, shells, powder, explosives, armaments

amnesty = <u>general pardon</u>, mercy, pardoning, immunity, forgiveness, reprieve, remission (of penalty), clemency

among or **amongst** 1 = <u>in the midst of</u>, with, together with, in the middle of, amid, surrounded by, amidst, in the thick of 2 = <u>in the group of</u>, one of, part of, included in, in the company of, in the class of, in the number of 3 = <u>between</u>, to

amount NOUN = <u>quantity</u>, measure, size, supply, mass, volume, capacity, extent

● PHRASES **amount to something** 1 = <u>add up to</u>, mean, total, equal, constitute, comprise, be equivalent to 2 = <u>come to</u>, become, develop into, advance to, progress to, mature into

> ### Word Power
>
> **amount** – Although it is common to use a plural noun after *amount of*, for example in *the amount of people* and *the amount of goods*, this should be avoided. Preferred alternatives would be to use *quantity*, as in *the quantity of people*, or *number*, as in *the number of goods*.

amphibian ▸ **amphibians**

ample 1 = <u>plenty of</u>, generous, lavish, abundant, plentiful, expansive, copious, profuse ≠ insufficient 2 = <u>large</u>, full, extensive, generous, abundant, bountiful

amply = <u>fully</u>, completely, richly, generously, abundantly, profusely, copiously ≠ insufficiently

amuse 1 = <u>entertain</u>, please, delight, charm, cheer, tickle

> ### Amphibians
>
> | | |
> |---|---|
> | axolotl | midwife toad |
> | brown-striped frog (*Austral.*) | natterjack |
> | bullfrog | newt or (*dialect or archaic*) eft |
> | caecilian | olm |
> | cane toad (*Austral.*) | Queensland cane toad |
> | congo eel or snake | salamander |
> | frog or (*Caribbean*) crapaud | siren |
> | Goliath frog | toad or (*Caribbean*) crapaud |
> | hairy frog | tree frog |
> | hyla | |

≠ bore **2** = <u>occupy</u>, interest, involve, engage, entertain, absorb, engross

amusement 1 = <u>enjoyment</u>, entertainment, cheer, mirth, merriment ≠ boredom **2** = <u>diversion</u>, fun, pleasure, entertainment **3** = <u>pastime</u>, game, sport, joke, entertainment, hobby, recreation, diversion

amusing = <u>funny</u>, humorous, comical, droll, interesting, entertaining, comic, enjoyable ≠ boring

anaesthetic NOUN = <u>painkiller</u>, narcotic, sedative, opiate, anodyne, analgesic, soporific
● ADJECTIVE = <u>pain-killing</u>, dulling, numbing, sedative, deadening, anodyne, analgesic, soporific

analogy 1 = <u>similarity</u>, relation, comparison, parallel, correspondence, resemblance, correlation, likeness

analyse 1 = <u>examine</u>, test, study, research, survey, investigate, evaluate, inspect **2** = <u>break down</u>, separate, divide, resolve, dissect, think through

analysis 1 = <u>examination</u>, test, inquiry, investigation, interpretation, breakdown, scanning, evaluation

analytical or **analytic** = <u>rational</u>, organized, exact, precise, logical, systematic, inquiring, investigative

anarchy = <u>lawlessness</u>, revolution, riot, disorder, confusion, chaos, disorganization ≠ order

anatomy 1 = <u>structure</u>, build, make-up, frame, framework, composition **2** = <u>examination</u>, study, division, inquiry, investigation, analysis, dissection

ancestor 1 = <u>forefather</u>, predecessor, precursor, forerunner, forebear, antecedent, tupuna or tipuna (N.Z.) ≠ descendant

ancient 1 = <u>classical</u>, old, former, past, bygone, primordial, primeval, olden **2** = <u>very old</u>, aged, antique, archaic, timeworn **3** = <u>old-fashioned</u>, dated, outdated, obsolete, out of date, unfashionable, outmoded, passé ≠ up-to-date

and 1 = <u>also</u>, including, along with, together with, in addition to, as well as **2** = <u>moreover</u>, plus, furthermore

---

> ### Word Power
>
> **and** – The forms *try and do something* and *wait and do something* should only be used in informal or spoken English. In more formal writing, use *try to* and *wait to*, for example: *we must try to prevent this happening* (not *try and prevent this*).

---

anecdote = <u>story</u>, tale, sketch,

short story, yarn, reminiscence, urban myth, urban legend

angel 1 = <u>divine messenger</u>, cherub, archangel, seraph **2** (*Informal*) = <u>dear</u>, beauty, saint, treasure, darling, jewel, gem, paragon

anger NOUN = <u>rage</u>, outrage, temper, fury, resentment, wrath, annoyance, ire ≠ calmness

• VERB = <u>enrage</u>, outrage, annoy, infuriate, incense, gall, madden, exasperate ≠ soothe

angle 1 = <u>gradient</u>, bank, slope, incline, inclination **2** = <u>intersection</u>, point, edge, corner, bend, elbow, crook, nook **3** = <u>point of view</u>, position, approach, direction, aspect, perspective, outlook, viewpoint

angry = <u>furious</u>, cross, mad (*informal*), outraged, annoyed, infuriated, incensed, enraged, tooshie (*Austral. slang*), off the air (*Austral. slang*) ≠ calm

> ### Word Power
>
> **angry** – Some people feel it is more correct to talk about being *angry with* someone than being *angry at* them. In British English, *angry with* is still more common than *angry at*, but *angry at* is used more commonly in American English.

angst = <u>anxiety</u>, worry, unease, apprehension ≠ peace of mind

anguish = <u>suffering</u>, pain, distress, grief, misery, agony, torment, sorrow

animal NOUN **1** = <u>creature</u>, beast, brute **2** = <u>brute</u>, devil, monster, savage, beast, bastard (*informal, offensive*), villain, barbarian

• ADJECTIVE = <u>physical</u>, gross, bodily, sensual, carnal, brutish, bestial

> amphibians > animals
> birds > dinosaurs > fish
> insects > invertebrates
> mammals > reptiles

animate ADJECTIVE = <u>living</u>, live, moving, alive, breathing, alive and kicking

• VERB = <u>enliven</u>, excite, inspire, move, fire, stimulate, energize, kindle ≠ inhibit

animated = <u>lively</u>, spirited, excited, enthusiastic, passionate, energetic, ebullient, vivacious ≠ listless

animation = <u>liveliness</u>, energy, spirit, passion, enthusiasm, excitement, verve, zest

announce = <u>make known</u>, tell, report, reveal, declare, advertise, broadcast, disclose ≠ keep secret

announcement 1 = <u>statement</u>, communication, broadcast, declaration, advertisement, bulletin, communiqué, proclamation **2** = <u>declaration</u>, report, reporting, revelation, proclamation

Animals

Collective animals

antelopes	herd	geese	gaggle *or* skein
apes	shrewdness	giraffes	herd
asses	pace *or* herd	gnats	swarm *or* cloud
badgers	cete	goats	herd *or* tribe
bears	sloth	goldfinches	charm
bees	swarm *or* grist	grouse	brood, covey, *or* pack
birds	flock, congregation, flight, *or* volery	gulls	colony
		hares	down *or* husk
bitterns	sedge *or* siege	hawks	cast
boars	sounder	hens	brood
bucks	brace *or* lease	herons	sedge *or* siege
buffaloes	herd	herrings	shoal *or* glean
capercailzies	tok	hounds	pack, mute, *or* cry
cats	clowder	insects	swarm
cattle	drove *or* herd	kangaroos	troop
choughs	chattering	kittens	kindle
colts	rag	lapwings	desert
coots	covert	larks	exaltation
cranes	herd, sedge, *or* siege	leopards	leap
		lions	pride *or* troop
crows	murder	mallards	sord *or* sute
cubs	litter	mares	stud
curlews	herd	martens	richesse
curs	cowardice	moles	labour
deer	herd	monkeys	troop
dolphins	school	mules	barren
doves	flight *or* dule	nightingales	watch
ducks	paddling *or* team	owls	parliament
dunlins	flight	oxen	yoke, drove, team, *or* herd
elk	gang		
fish	shoal, draught, haul, run, *or* catch	partridges	covey
		peacocks	muster
		pheasants	nye *or* nide
flies	swarm *or* grist	pigeons	flock *or* flight
foxes	skulk		

Animals (continued)

Collective animals

pigs	litter	sparrows	host
plovers	stand *or* wing	starlings	murmuration
pochards	flight, rush, bunch, *or* knob	swallows	flight
		swans	herd *or* bevy
ponies	herd	swifts	flock
porpoises	school *or* gam	swine	herd, sounder, *or* dryft
poultry	run		
pups	litter	teal	bunch, knob, *or* spring
quails	bevy		
rabbits	nest	whales	school, gam, *or* run
racehorses	field *or* string		
ravens	unkindness	whelps	litter
roes	bevy	whiting	pod
rooks	building *or* clamour	wigeon	bunch, company, knob, *or* flight
ruffs	hill	wildfowl	plump, sord, *or* sute
seals	herd *or* pod		
sheep	flock	wolves	pack, rout, *or* herd
sheldrakes	dopping		
snipe	walk *or* wisp	woodcocks	fall

annoy = <u>irritate</u>, trouble, anger, bother, disturb, plague, hassle (*informal*), madden ≠ soothe

annoying = <u>irritating</u>, disturbing, troublesome, maddening, exasperating ≠ delightful

annual 1 = <u>once a year</u>, yearly 2 = <u>yearlong</u>, yearly

annually 1 = <u>once a year</u>, yearly, every year, per year, by the year, every twelve months, per annum 2 = <u>per year</u>, yearly, every year, by the year, per annum

anomaly = <u>irregularity</u>, exception, abnormality, inconsistency, eccentricity, oddity, peculiarity, incongruity

anonymous 1 = <u>unnamed</u>, unknown, unidentified, nameless, unacknowledged, incognito ≠ identified 2 = <u>unsigned</u>, uncredited, unattributed ≠ signed

answer VERB = <u>reply</u>, explain, respond, resolve, react, return, retort ≠ ask
• NOUN 1 = <u>reply</u>, response,

reaction, explanation, comeback, retort, return, defence ≠ **question**

2 = **solution**, resolution, explanation **3** = **remedy**, solution

ant ➤ **ants, bees, and wasps**

anthem = **song of praise**, carol, chant, hymn, psalm, paean, chorale, canticle

anthology = **collection**, selection, treasury, compilation, compendium, miscellany

anticipate 1 = **expect**, predict, prepare for, hope for, envisage, foresee, bank on, foretell

2 = **await**, look forward to, count the hours until

anticipation = **expectancy**, expectation, foresight, premonition, prescience, forethought

antics = **clowning**, tricks, mischief, pranks, escapades, playfulness, horseplay, tomfoolery

antique NOUN = **period piece**, relic, bygone, heirloom, collector's item, museum piece

● ADJECTIVE = **vintage**, classic,

Ants, bees, and wasps

Amazon ant	kootchar (*Austral.*)
ant *or* (*archaic or dialect*) emmet	leafcutter ant
army ant *or* legionary ant	leafcutter bee
bee	mason bee
blue ant (*Austral.*)	mason wasp
bulldog ant, bull ant, *or* (*Austral.*)	minga (*Austral.*)
bull Joe	mining bee
bumblebee *or* humblebee	mud dauber
carpenter bee	native bee *or* sugarbag fly
cicada hunter (*Austral.*)	(*Austral.*)
cuckoo bee	Pharaoh ant
digger wasp	policeman fly (*Austral.*)
driver ant	ruby-tail wasp
flower wasp (*Austral.*)	sand wasp
gall wasp	Sirex wasp (*Austral.*)
honeypot ant *or* honey ant	slave ant
(*Austral.*)	spider-hunting wasp
honeybee *or* hive bee	termite *or* white ant
horntail *or* wood wasp	velvet ant
ichneumon fly *or* ichneumon	wasp
wasp	wood ant
killer bee	yellow jacket (*U.S. & Canad.*)

antiquarian, olden

anxiety = <u>uneasiness</u>, concern, worry, doubt, tension, angst, apprehension, misgiving ≠ confidence

anxious 1 = <u>eager</u>, keen, intent, yearning, impatient, itching, desirous ≠ reluctant 2 = <u>uneasy</u>, concerned, worried, troubled, nervous, uncomfortable, tense, fearful ≠ confident

apart 1 = <u>to pieces</u>, to bits, asunder 2 = <u>away from each other</u>, distant from each other 3 = <u>aside</u>, away, alone, isolated, to one side, by yourself 4 *with from* = <u>except for</u>, excepting, other than, excluding, besides, not including, aside from, but

apartment 1 (*U.S.*) = <u>flat</u>, room, suite, penthouse, crib 2 = <u>rooms</u>, quarters, accommodation, living quarters

apathy = <u>lack of interest</u>, indifference, inertia, coolness, passivity, nonchalance, torpor, unconcern ≠ interest

apiece = <u>each</u>, individually, separately, for each, to each, respectively, from each ≠ all together

apologize = <u>say sorry</u>, express regret, ask forgiveness, make an apology, beg pardon

apology NOUN = <u>regret</u>, explanation, excuse, confession
● PHRASES **apology for**

something *or* someone = <u>mockery of</u>, excuse for, imitation of, caricature of, travesty of, poor substitute for

appal = <u>horrify</u>, shock, alarm, frighten, outrage, disgust, dishearten, revolt

appalling 1 = <u>horrifying</u>, shocking, alarming, awful, terrifying, horrible, dreadful, fearful ≠ reassuring 2 = <u>awful</u>, dreadful, horrendous

apparatus 1 = <u>organization</u>, system, network, structure, bureaucracy, hierarchy, setup (*informal*), chain of command 2 = <u>equipment</u>, tackle, gear, device, tools, mechanism, machinery, appliance

apparent 1 = <u>seeming</u>, outward, superficial, ostensible ≠ actual 2 = <u>obvious</u>, marked, visible, evident, distinct, manifest, noticeable, unmistakable ≠ unclear

apparently = <u>seemingly</u>, outwardly, ostensibly

appeal VERB = <u>plead</u>, ask, request, pray, beg, entreat ≠ refuse
● NOUN 1 = <u>plea</u>, call, application, request, prayer, petition, overture, entreaty ≠ refusal 2 = <u>attraction</u>, charm, fascination, beauty, allure ≠ repulsiveness
● PHRASES **appeal to someone** = <u>attract</u>, interest, draw, please,

charm, fascinate, tempt, lure

appealing = <u>attractive</u>, engaging, charming, desirable, alluring, winsome ≠ repellent

appear 1 = <u>look (like or as if)</u>, seem, occur, look to be, come across as, strike you as 2 = <u>come into view</u>, emerge, occur, surface, come out, turn up, be present, show up (*informal*) ≠ disappear

appearance 1 = <u>look</u>, form, figure, looks, manner, expression, demeanour, mien (*literary*) 2 = <u>arrival</u>, presence, introduction, emergence 3 = <u>impression</u>, air, front, image, illusion, guise, façade, pretence

appease 1 = <u>pacify</u>, satisfy, soothe, quiet, placate, mollify, conciliate ≠ anger 2 = <u>ease</u>, calm, relieve, soothe, alleviate, allay

appendix = <u>supplement</u>, postscript, adjunct, appendage, addendum, addition

appetite 1 = <u>hunger</u> 2 = <u>desire</u>, liking, longing, demand, taste, passion, stomach, hunger ≠ distaste

applaud 1 = <u>clap</u>, encourage, praise, cheer, acclaim ≠ boo 2 = <u>praise</u>, celebrate, approve, acclaim, compliment, salute, commend, extol ≠ criticize

applause = <u>ovation</u>, praise, cheers, approval, clapping, accolade, big hand

appliance = <u>device</u>, machine, tool, instrument, implement, mechanism, apparatus, gadget

applicable = <u>appropriate</u>, fitting, useful, suitable, relevant, apt, pertinent ≠ inappropriate

applicant = <u>candidate</u>, claimant, inquirer

application 1 = <u>request</u>, claim, appeal, inquiry, petition, requisition 2 = <u>effort</u>, work, industry, trouble, struggle, pains, commitment, hard work

apply VERB 1 = <u>request</u>, appeal, put in, petition, inquire, claim, requisition 2 = <u>be relevant</u>, relate, refer, be fitting, be appropriate, fit, pertain, be applicable 3 = <u>use</u>, exercise, carry out, employ, implement, practise, exert, enact 4 = <u>put on</u>, work in, cover with, lay on, paint on, spread on, rub in, smear on

● PHRASES **apply yourself to something** = <u>work hard at</u>, concentrate on, try at, commit yourself to, buckle down to (*informal*), devote yourself to, be diligent in, dedicate yourself to

appoint 1 = <u>assign</u>, name, choose, commission, select, elect, delegate, nominate ≠ fire 2 = <u>decide</u>, set, choose, establish, fix, arrange, assign, designate ≠ cancel

appointed 1 = <u>decided</u>, set, chosen, established, fixed, arranged, assigned, designated

2 = <u>assigned</u>, named, chosen, selected, elected, delegated, nominated **3** = <u>equipped</u>, provided, supplied, furnished, fitted out

appointment 1 = <u>selection</u>, naming, election, choice, nomination, assignment **2** = <u>job</u>, office, position, post, situation, place, employment, assignment **3** = <u>meeting</u>, interview, date, arrangement, engagement, fixture, rendezvous, assignation

appraisal 1 = <u>assessment</u>, opinion, estimate, judgment, evaluation, estimation

appreciate 1 = <u>enjoy</u>, like, value, respect, prize, admire, treasure, rate highly ≠ scorn **2** = <u>be aware of</u>, understand, realize, recognize, perceive, take account of, be sensitive to, sympathize with ≠ be unaware of **3** = <u>be grateful</u>, be obliged, be thankful, give thanks, be indebted, be in debt, be appreciative ≠ be ungrateful for **4** = <u>increase</u>, rise, grow, gain, improve, enhance, soar ≠ fall

appreciation 1 = <u>admiration</u>, enjoyment **2** = <u>gratitude</u>, thanks, recognition, obligation, acknowledgment, indebtedness, thankfulness, gratefulness ≠ ingratitude **3** = <u>awareness</u>, understanding, recognition, perception, sympathy, consciousness, sensitivity, realization ≠ ignorance **4** = <u>increase</u>, rise, gain, growth, improvement, escalation, enhancement ≠ fall

apprehension 1 = <u>anxiety</u>, concern, fear, worry, alarm, suspicion, dread, trepidation ≠ confidence **2** = <u>arrest</u>, catching, capture, taking, seizure ≠ release **3** = <u>awareness</u>, understanding, perception, grasp, comprehension ≠ incomprehension

apprentice = <u>trainee</u>, student, pupil, novice, beginner, learner, probationer ≠ master

approach VERB **1** = <u>move towards</u>, reach, near, come close, come near, draw near **2** = <u>make a proposal to</u>, speak to, apply to, appeal to, proposition, solicit, sound out, make overtures to **3** = <u>set about</u>, tackle, undertake, embark on, get down to, launch into, begin work on, commence on

● NOUN **1** = <u>advance</u>, coming, nearing, appearance, arrival, drawing near **2** = <u>access</u>, way, drive, road, passage, entrance, avenue, passageway **3** *often plural* = <u>proposal</u>, offer, appeal, advance, application, invitation, proposition, overture **4** = <u>way</u>, means, style, method, technique, manner

appropriate ADJECTIVE

= **suitable**, fitting, relevant, to the point, apt, pertinent, befitting, well-suited ≠ unsuitable

● VERB 1 = **seize**, claim, acquire, confiscate, usurp, impound, commandeer, take possession of ≠ relinquish 2 = **allocate**, allow, budget, devote, assign, designate, set aside, earmark ≠ withhold 3 = **steal**, take, nick (*slang, chiefly Brit.*), pocket, pinch (*informal*), lift (*informal*), embezzle, pilfer

approval 1 = **consent**, agreement, sanction, blessing, permission, recommendation, endorsement, assent 2 = **favour**, respect, praise, esteem, acclaim, appreciation, admiration, applause ≠ disapproval

approve VERB = **agree to**, allow, pass, recommend, permit, sanction, endorse, authorize ≠ veto

● PHRASES **approve of something** *or* **someone** = **favour**, like, respect, praise, admire, commend, have a good opinion of, regard highly

apt 1 = **appropriate**, fitting, suitable, relevant, to the point, pertinent ≠ inappropriate 2 = **inclined**, likely, ready, disposed, prone, liable, given, predisposed 3 = **gifted**, skilled, quick, talented, sharp, capable, smart, clever ≠ slow

arbitrary 1 = **random**, chance, subjective, inconsistent, erratic, personal, whimsical, capricious ≠ logical

arbitration = **decision**, settlement, judgment, determination, adjudication

arc = **curve**, bend, bow, arch, crescent, half-moon

arcade = **gallery**, cloister, portico, colonnade

arch¹ NOUN **1** = **archway**, curve, dome, span, vault 2 = **curve**, bend, bow, crook, arc, hunch, sweep, hump

● VERB = **curve**, bridge, bend, bow, span, arc

arch² = **playful**, sly, mischievous, saucy, pert, roguish, frolicsome, waggish

archetypal = **typical**, standard, model, original, classic, ideal, prototypic *or* prototypical

architect = **designer**, planner, draughtsman, master builder

architecture 1 = **design**, planning, building, construction 2 = **construction**, design, style 3 = **structure**, design, shape, make-up, construction, framework, layout, anatomy

archive NOUN = **record office**, museum, registry, repository

● PLURAL NOUN = **records**, papers, accounts, rolls, documents, files, deeds, chronicles

arctic (*Informal*) = **freezing**, cold, frozen, icy, chilly, glacial, frigid

Arctic = polar, far-northern, hyperborean

ardent 1 = enthusiastic, keen, eager, avid, zealous ≠ indifferent 2 = passionate, intense, impassioned, lusty, amorous, hot-blooded ≠ cold

area 1 = region, quarter, district, zone, neighbourhood, locality 2 = part, section, sector, portion 3 = realm, part, department, field, province, sphere, domain

arena 1 = ring, ground, field, theatre, bowl, pitch, stadium, enclosure 2 = scene, world, area, stage, field, sector, territory, province

argue 1 = quarrel, fight, row, clash, dispute, disagree, squabble, bicker 2 = discuss, debate, dispute 3 = claim, reason, challenge, insist, maintain, allege, assert, uphold

argument 1 = reason, case, reasoning, ground(s), defence, logic, polemic, dialectic 2 = debate, questioning, claim, discussion, dispute, controversy, plea, assertion 3 = quarrel, fight, row, clash, dispute, controversy, disagreement, feud ≠ agreement

arise 1 = happen, start, begin, follow, result, develop, emerge, occur 2 (Old-fashioned) = get to your feet, get up, rise, stand up, spring up, leap up 3 = get up, wake up, awaken, get out of bed

aristocrat = noble, lord, lady, peer, patrician, grandee, aristo (informal), peeress

aristocratic = upper-class, lordly, titled, elite, gentlemanly, noble, patrician, blue-blooded ≠ common

arm[1] = upper limb, limb, appendage

arm[2] VERB = equip, provide, supply, array, furnish, issue with, deck out, accoutre

● PLURAL NOUN = weapons, guns, firearms, weaponry, armaments, ordnance, munitions, instruments of war

armed = carrying weapons, protected, equipped, primed, fitted out

armour = protection, covering, shield, sheathing, armour plate, chain mail, protective covering

armoured = protected, mailed, reinforced, toughened, bulletproof, armour-plated, steel-plated, ironclad

army 1 = soldiers, military, troops, armed force, legions, infantry, military force, land force 2 = vast number, host, gang, mob, flock, array, legion, swarm

aroma = scent, smell, perfume, fragrance, bouquet, savour, odour, redolence

around PREPOSITION 1 = surrounding, about, enclosing, encompassing, framing, encircling, on all sides of, on every side of

2 = approximately, about, nearly, close to, roughly, just about, in the region of, circa (used with dates)

● ADVERB **1** = everywhere, about, throughout, all over, here and there, on all sides, in all directions, to and fro **2** = near, close, nearby, at hand, close at hand

arouse 1 = stimulate, encourage, inspire, prompt, spur, provoke, rouse, stir up ≠ quell **2** = inflame, move, excite, spur, provoke, stir up, agitate **3** = awaken, wake up, rouse, waken

arrange 1 = plan, agree, prepare, determine, organize, construct, devise, contrive, jack up (N.Z. informal) **2** = put in order, group, order, sort, position, line up, organize, classify, jack up (N.Z. informal) ≠ disorganize **3** = adapt, score, orchestrate, harmonize, instrument

arrangement 1 often plural = plan, planning, provision, preparation **2** = agreement, contract, settlement, appointment, compromise, deal (informal), pact, compact **3** = display, system, structure, organization, exhibition, presentation, classification, alignment **4** = adaptation, score,

version, interpretation, instrumentation, orchestration, harmonization

array NOUN 1 = arrangement, show, supply, display, collection, exhibition, line-up, mixture **2** (Poetic) = clothing, dress, clothes, garments, apparel, attire, finery, regalia

● VERB **1** = arrange, show, group, present, range, display, parade, exhibit **2** = dress, clothe, deck, decorate, adorn, festoon, attire

arrest VERB 1 = capture, catch, nick (slang, chiefly Brit.), seize, detain, apprehend, take prisoner ≠ release **2** = stop, end, limit, block, slow, delay, interrupt, suppress ≠ speed up **3** = fascinate, hold, occupy, engage, grip, absorb, entrance, intrigue

● NOUN **1** = capture, bust (informal), detention, seizure ≠ release **2** = stoppage, suppression, obstruction, blockage, hindrance ≠ acceleration

arresting = striking, surprising, engaging, stunning, impressive, outstanding, remarkable, noticeable ≠ unremarkable

arrival 1 = appearance, coming, arriving, entrance, advent, materialization **2** = coming, happening, taking place, emergence, occurrence, materialization 3 = <u>newcomer</u>, incomer, visitor, caller, entrant

arrive 1 = <u>come</u>, appear, turn up, show up (*informal*), draw near ≠ depart **2** = <u>occur</u>, happen, take place **3** (*Informal*) = <u>succeed</u>, make it (*informal*), triumph, do well, thrive, flourish, be successful, make good

arrogance = <u>conceit</u>, pride, swagger, insolence, high-handedness, haughtiness, superciliousness, disdainfulness ≠ modesty

arrogant = <u>conceited</u>, proud, cocky, overbearing, haughty, scornful, egotistical, disdainful ≠ modest

arrow 1 = <u>dart</u>, flight, bolt, shaft (*archaic*), quarrel **2** = <u>pointer</u>, indicator, marker

arsenal = <u>armoury</u>, supply, store, stockpile, storehouse, ammunition dump, arms depot, ordnance depot

art 1 = <u>artwork</u>, style of art, fine art, creativity **2** = <u>skill</u>, craft, expertise, competence, mastery, ingenuity, virtuosity, cleverness

article 1 = <u>feature</u>, story, paper, piece, item, creation, essay, composition **2** = <u>thing</u>, piece, unit, item, object, device, tool, implement **3** = <u>clause</u>, point, part, section, item, passage, portion, paragraph

articulate ADJECTIVE = <u>expressive</u>, clear, coherent, fluent, eloquent, lucid ≠ incoherent
● VERB **1** = <u>express</u>, say, state, word, declare, phrase, communicate, utter
2 = <u>pronounce</u>, say, talk, speak, voice, utter, enunciate

artificial 1 = <u>synthetic</u>, manufactured, plastic, man-made, non-natural **2** = <u>insincere</u>, forced, affected, phoney or phony (*informal*), false, contrived, unnatural, feigned ≠ genuine
3 = <u>fake</u>, mock, imitation, bogus, simulated, sham, counterfeit ≠ authentic

artillery = <u>big guns</u>, battery, cannon, ordnance, gunnery

artist ▶ WORD POWER SUPPLEMENT artists

artistic 1 = <u>creative</u>, cultured, original, sophisticated, refined, aesthetic, discerning, eloquent ≠ untalented **2** = <u>beautiful</u>, creative, elegant, stylish, aesthetic, tasteful ≠ unattractive

as CONJUNCTION = <u>when</u>, while, just as, at the time that
● PREPOSITION **1** = <u>in the role of</u>, being, under the name of, in the character of **2** = <u>in the way that</u>, like, in the manner that **3** = <u>since</u>, because, seeing that, considering that, on account of the fact that

ashamed 1 = <u>embarrassed</u>, sorry, guilty, distressed, humiliated, self-conscious, red-faced, mortified ≠ proud

2 = reluctant, embarrassed

ashore = on land, on the beach, on the shore, aground, to the shore, on dry land, shorewards, landwards

aside ADVERB = to one side, separately, apart, beside, out of the way, on one side, to the side

• NOUN = interpolation, parenthesis

ask **1** = inquire, question, quiz, query, interrogate ≠ answer **2** = request, appeal to, plead with, demand, beg **3** = invite, bid, summon

asleep = sleeping, napping, dormant, dozing, slumbering, snoozing (*informal*), fast asleep, sound asleep

aspect **1** = feature, side, factor, angle, characteristic, facet **2** = position, view, situation, scene, prospect, point of view, outlook **3** = appearance, look, air, condition, quality, bearing, attitude, cast

aspiration = aim, plan, hope, goal, dream, wish, desire, objective

aspire to = aim for, desire, hope for, long for, seek out, wish for, dream about, set your heart on

ass **1** = donkey, moke (*slang*) **2** = fool, idiot, twit (*informal*, *chiefly Brit.*), oaf, jackass,

blockhead, halfwit, numbskull or numskull, dorba or dorb (*Austral. slang*), bogan (*Austral. slang*)

assassin = murderer, killer, slayer, liquidator, executioner, hit man (*slang*), hatchet man (*slang*)

assassinate = murder, kill, eliminate (*slang*), take out (*slang*), terminate, hit (*slang*), slay, liquidate

assault NOUN = attack, raid, invasion, charge, offensive, onslaught, foray ≠ defence

• VERB = strike, attack, beat, knock, bang, slap, smack, thump

assemble **1** = gather, meet, collect, rally, come together, muster, congregate ≠ scatter **2** = bring together, collect, gather, rally, come together, muster, amass, congregate **3** = put together, join, set up, build up, connect, construct, piece together, fabricate ≠ take apart

assembly **1** = gathering, group, meeting, council, conference, crowd, congress, collection, hui (*N.Z.*), runanga (*N.Z.*) **2** = putting together, setting up, construction, building up, connecting, piecing together

assert VERB **1** = state, argue, maintain, declare, swear, pronounce, affirm, profess ≠ deny **2** = insist upon, stress, defend, uphold, put forward, press, stand up for ≠ retract

● PHRASES **assert yourself** = <u>be forceful</u>, put your foot down (*informal*), put yourself forward, make your presence felt, exert your influence

assertion 1 = <u>statement</u>, claim, declaration, pronouncement 2 = <u>insistence</u>, stressing, maintenance

assertive = <u>confident</u>, positive, aggressive, forceful, emphatic, insistent, feisty (*informal, chiefly U.S. & Canad.*), pushy (*informal*) ≠ meek

assess 1 = <u>judge</u>, estimate, analyse, evaluate, rate, value, check out, weigh up 2 = <u>evaluate</u>, rate, tax, value, estimate, fix, impose, levy

assessment 1 = <u>judgment</u>, analysis, evaluation, valuation, appraisal, rating, opinion, estimate 2 = <u>evaluation</u>, rating, charge, fee, toll, levy, valuation

asset NOUN = <u>benefit</u>, help, service, aid, advantage, strength, resource, attraction ≠ disadvantage

● PLURAL NOUN = <u>property</u>, goods, money, funds, effects, capital, riches, finance

assign 1 = <u>give</u>, set, grant, allocate, give out, consign, allot, apportion 2 = <u>select for</u>, post, commission, elect, appoint, delegate, nominate, name

3 = <u>attribute</u>, credit, put down, set down, ascribe, accredit

assignment = <u>task</u>, job, position, post, commission, exercise, responsibility, duty

assist 1 = <u>help</u>, support, aid, cooperate with, abet, lend a helping hand to 2 = <u>facilitate</u>, help, further, serve, aid, forward, promote, speed up ≠ hinder

assistance = <u>help</u>, backing, support, aid, cooperation, helping hand ≠ hindrance

assistant = <u>helper</u>, ally, colleague, supporter, aide, second, attendant, accomplice

associate VERB 1 = <u>connect</u>, link, ally, identify, join, combine, attach, fasten ≠ separate 2 = <u>socialize</u>, mix, accompany, mingle, consort, hobnob ≠ avoid

● NOUN = <u>partner</u>, friend, ally, colleague, mate (*informal*), companion, comrade, affiliate, cobber (*Austral. & N.Z. old-fashioned informal*), E hoa (*N.Z.*)

association 1 = <u>group</u>, club, society, league, band, set, pack, collection 2 = <u>connection</u>, union, joining, pairing, combination, mixture, blend, juxtaposition

assorted = <u>various</u>, different, mixed, varied, diverse, miscellaneous, sundry, motley ≠ similar

assume 1 = <u>presume</u>, think, believe, expect, suppose, imagine, fancy, take for granted ≠ know 2 = take on, accept, shoulder, take over, put on, enter upon 3 = simulate, affect, adopt, put on, imitate, mimic, feign, impersonate 4 = take over, take, appropriate, seize, commandeer ≠ give up

assumed = false, made-up, fake, bogus, counterfeit, fictitious, make-believe ≠ real

assumption 1 = presumption, belief, guess, hypothesis, inference, conjecture, surmise, supposition 2 = taking on, managing, handling, shouldering, putting on, taking up, takeover, acquisition 3 = seizure, taking, takeover, acquisition, appropriation, wresting, confiscation, commandeering

assurance 1 = promise, statement, guarantee, commitment, pledge, vow, declaration, assertion ≠ lie 2 = confidence, conviction, certainty, self-confidence, poise, faith, nerve, aplomb ≠ self-doubt

assure 1 = convince, encourage, persuade, satisfy, comfort, reassure, hearten, embolden 2 = make certain, ensure, confirm, guarantee, secure, make sure, complete, seal 3 = promise to, pledge to, vow to, guarantee to, swear to, confirm to, certify to, give your word to

assured 1 = confident, certain, positive, poised, fearless, self-confident, self-assured, dauntless ≠ self-conscious 2 = certain, sure, ensured, confirmed, settled, guaranteed, fixed, secure ≠ doubtful

astonish = amaze, surprise, stun, stagger, bewilder, astound, daze, confound

astounding = amazing, surprising, brilliant, impressive, astonishing, staggering, sensational (informal), bewildering

astute = intelligent, sharp, clever, subtle, shrewd, cunning, canny, perceptive ≠ stupid

asylum 1 (Old-fashioned) = mental hospital, hospital, institution, psychiatric hospital, madhouse (informal) 2 = refuge, haven, safety, protection, preserve, shelter, retreat, harbour

athlete = sportsperson, player, runner, competitor, sportsman, contestant, gymnast, sportswoman

athletic ADJECTIVE = fit, strong, powerful, healthy, active, trim, strapping, energetic ≠ feeble
● PLURAL NOUN = sports, games, races, exercises, contests, sporting events, gymnastics, track and field events

atmosphere 1 = air, sky, heavens, aerosphere 2 = feeling, character, environment, spirit, surroundings, tone, mood, climate

atom = <u>particle</u>, bit, spot, trace, molecule, dot, speck

atrocity 1 = <u>act of cruelty</u>, crime, horror, evil, outrage, abomination 2 = <u>cruelty</u>, horror, brutality, savagery, wickedness, barbarity, viciousness, fiendishness

attach 1 = <u>affix</u>, stick, secure, add, join, couple, link, tie ≠ detach 2 = <u>ascribe</u>, connect, attribute, assign, associate

attached ADJECTIVE = <u>spoken for</u>, married, partnered, engaged, accompanied

● PHRASES **attached to** = <u>fond of</u>, devoted to, affectionate towards, full of regard for

attachment 1 = <u>fondness</u>, liking, feeling, relationship, regard, attraction, affection, affinity, aroha (*N.Z.*) ≠ aversion 2 = <u>accessory</u>, fitting, extra, component, extension, supplement, fixture, accoutrement

attack VERB 1 = <u>assault</u>, strike (at), mug, ambush, tear into, set upon, lay into (*informal*) ≠ defend 2 = <u>invade</u>, occupy, raid, infringe, storm, encroach 3 = <u>criticize</u>, blame, abuse, condemn, knock (*informal*), put down, slate (*informal*), have a go (at) (*informal*)

● NOUN 1 = <u>assault</u>, charge, campaign, strike, raid, invasion, offensive, blitz ≠ defence 2 = <u>criticism</u>, censure, disapproval, abuse, bad press, vilification, denigration, disparagement 3 = <u>bout</u>, fit, stroke, seizure, spasm, convulsion, paroxysm

attacker = <u>assailant</u>, assaulter, raider, intruder, invader, aggressor, mugger

attain 1 = <u>obtain</u>, get, reach, complete, gain, achieve, acquire, fulfil 2 = <u>reach</u>, achieve, acquire, accomplish

attempt VERB = <u>try</u>, seek, aim, struggle, venture, undertake, strive, endeavour

● NOUN 1 = <u>try</u>, go (*informal*), shot (*informal*), effort, trial, bid, crack (*informal*), stab (*informal*) 2 = <u>attack</u>

attend VERB 1 = <u>be present</u>, go to, visit, frequent, haunt, appear at, turn up at, patronize ≠ be absent 2 = <u>pay attention</u>, listen, hear, mark, note, observe, heed, pay heed ≠ ignore

● PHRASES **attend to something** = <u>apply yourself to</u>, concentrate on, look after, take care of, see to, get to work on, devote yourself to, occupy yourself with

attendance 1 = <u>presence</u>, being there, attending,

appearance 2 = <u>turnout</u>, audience, gate, congregation, house, crowd, throng, number present

attendant NOUN = <u>assistant</u>, guard, servant, companion, aide, escort, follower, helper
● ADJECTIVE = <u>accompanying</u>, related, associated, accessory, consequent, resultant, concomitant

attention 1 = <u>thinking</u>, thought, mind, consideration, scrutiny, heed, deliberation, intentness 2 = <u>care</u>, support, concern, treatment, looking after, succour, ministration 3 = <u>awareness</u>, regard, notice, recognition, consideration, observation, consciousness ≠ inattention

attic = <u>loft</u>, garret, roof space

attitude 1 = <u>opinion</u>, view, position, approach, mood, perspective, point of view, stance 2 = <u>position</u>, bearing, pose, stance, carriage, posture

attract 1 = <u>allure</u>, draw, persuade, charm, appeal to, win over, tempt, lure (*informal*) ≠ repel 2 = <u>pull</u>, draw, magnetize

attraction 1 = <u>appeal</u>, pull (*informal*), charm, lure, temptation, fascination, allure, magnetism 2 = <u>pull</u>, magnetism

attractive = <u>seductive</u>, charming, tempting, pretty, fair, inviting, lovely, pleasant ≠ unattractive 2 = <u>appealing</u>, pleasing, inviting, tempting, irresistable ≠ unappealing

attribute VERB = <u>ascribe</u>, credit, refer, trace, assign, charge, allocate, put down
● NOUN = <u>quality</u>, feature, property, character, element, aspect, characteristic, distinction

audience 1 = <u>spectators</u>, company, crowd, gathering, gallery, assembly, viewers, listeners 2 = <u>interview</u>, meeting, hearing, exchange, reception, consultation

aura = <u>air</u>, feeling, quality, atmosphere, tone, mood, ambience

austerity 1 = <u>plainness</u>, simplicity, starkness 2 = <u>asceticism</u>, self-discipline, sobriety, puritanism, self-denial

authentic 1 = <u>real</u>, pure, genuine, valid, undisputed, lawful, bona fide, dinkum (*Austral. & N.Z. informal*), true-to-life ≠ fake 2 = <u>accurate</u>, legitimate, authoritative

authenticity 1 = <u>genuineness</u>, purity 2 = <u>accuracy</u>, certainty, validity, legitimacy, faithfulness, truthfulness

author 1 = <u>writer</u>, composer, novelist, hack, creator, scribbler, scribe, wordsmith 2 = <u>creator</u>, father, producer, designer, founder, architect, inventor, originator

authoritarian ADJECTIVE = strict, severe, autocratic, dictatorial, dogmatic, tyrannical, doctrinaire ≠ lenient

● NOUN = disciplinarian, dictator, tyrant, despot, autocrat, absolutist

authoritative

1 = commanding, masterly, imposing, assertive, imperious, self-assured ≠ timid 2 = reliable, accurate, valid, authentic, definitive, dependable, trustworthy ≠ unreliable

authority 1 usually plural = powers that be, government, police, officials, the state, management, administration, the system 2 = prerogative, influence, power, control, weight, direction, command, licence, mana (N.Z.) 3 = expert, specialist, professional, master, guru, virtuoso, connoisseur, fundi (S. African) 4 = command, power, control, rule, management, direction, mastery

authorize 1 = empower, commission, enable, entitle, mandate, accredit, give authority to 2 = permit, allow, grant, approve, sanction, license, warrant, consent to ≠ forbid

automatic 1 = mechanical, automated, mechanized, push-button, self-propelling ≠ done by

hand 2 = involuntary, natural, unconscious, mechanical, spontaneous, reflex, instinctive, unwilled ≠ conscious

autonomous = self-ruling, free, independent, sovereign, self-sufficient, self-governing, self-determining

autonomy = independence, freedom, sovereignty, self-determination, self-government, self-rule, self-sufficiency, home rule, rangatiratanga (N.Z.) ≠ dependency

availability = accessibility, readiness, handiness, attainability

available = accessible, ready, to hand, handy, at hand, free, to be had, achievable ≠ in use

avalanche 1 = snow-slide, landslide, landslip 2 = large amount, barrage, torrent, deluge, inundation

avant-garde = progressive, pioneering, experimental, innovative, unconventional, ground-breaking ≠ conservative

avenue = street, way, course, drive, road, approach, route, path

average NOUN = standard, normal, usual, par, mode, mean, medium, norm

● ADJECTIVE 1 = usual, standard, general, normal, regular, ordinary, typical, commonplace ≠ unusual 2 = mean, middle, medium, intermediate, median

≠ minimum

● VERB = make on average, be on average, even out to so on average, balance out to

● PHRASES on average = usually, generally, normally, typically, for the most part, as a rule

avert 1 = ward off, avoid, prevent, frustrate, fend off, preclude, stave off, forestall 2 = turn away, turn aside

avoid 1 = prevent, stop, frustrate, hamper, foil, inhibit, avert, thwart 2 = refrain from, bypass, dodge, eschew, escape, duck (out of) (informal), fight shy of, shirk from 3 = keep away from, dodge, shun, evade, steer clear of, bypass

await 1 = wait for, expect, look for, look forward to, anticipate, stay for 2 = be in store for, wait for, be ready for, lie in wait for, be in readiness for

awake ADJECTIVE = not sleeping, sleepless, wide-awake, aware, conscious, aroused, awakened, restless ≠ asleep

● VERB = wake up, come to, wake, stir, awaken, rouse 2 = alert, stimulate, provoke, revive, arouse, stir up, kindle

awaken 1 = stimulate, provoke, alert, stir up, kindle 2 = awake, wake, revive, arouse, rouse

award NOUN = prize, gift, trophy, decoration, grant, bonsela (S. African), koha (N.Z.)

● VERB 1 = present with, give, grant, hand out, confer, endow, bestow 2 = grant, give, confer

aware = informed, enlightened, knowledgeable, learned, expert, versed, up to date, in the picture ≠ ignorant

awareness

● PHRASES awareness of = knowledge of, understanding of, recognition of, perception of, consciousness of, realization of, familiarity with

away ADJECTIVE = absent, out, gone, elsewhere, abroad, not here, not present, on vacation

● ADVERB 1 = off, elsewhere, abroad, hence, from here 2 = aside, out of the way, to one side 3 = at a distance, far, apart, remote, isolated 4 = continuously, repeatedly, relentlessly, incessantly, interminably, unremittingly, uninterruptedly

awe NOUN = wonder, fear, respect, reverence, horror, terror, dread, admiration ≠ contempt

● VERB = impress, amaze, stun, frighten, terrify, astonish, horrify, intimidate

awesome = awe-inspiring, amazing, stunning, impressive, astonishing, formidable, intimidating, breathtaking

awful 1 = disgusting, offensive, gross, foul, dreadful, revolting, sickening, frightful, festy (*Austral. slang*), yucko (*Austral. slang*) **2** = **bad**, poor, terrible, appalling, foul, rubbish (*slang*), dreadful, horrendous ≠ **wonderful**, ka pai (*N.Z.*) **3** = **shocking**, dreadful **4** = **unwell**, poorly (*informal*), ill, terrible, sick, crook (*Austral. & N.Z. informal*), unhealthy, off-colour, under the weather (*informal*)

awfully 1 (*Informal*) = **very**, extremely, terribly, exceptionally, greatly, immensely, exceedingly, dreadfully **2** = **badly**, woefully, dreadfully, disgracefully, wretchedly, unforgivably, reprehensibly

awkward 1 = **embarrassing**, difficult, sensitive, delicate, uncomfortable, humiliating, disconcerting, inconvenient, barro (*Austral. slang*) ≠ **comfortable 2** = **inconvenient**, difficult, troublesome, cumbersome, unwieldy, unmanageable, clunky (*informal*) ≠ **convenient 3** = **clumsy**, lumbering, bumbling, unwieldy, ponderous, ungainly, gauche, gawky, unco (*Austral. slang*) ≠ **graceful**

axe NOUN = **hatchet**, chopper, tomahawk, cleaver, adze
● **VERB 1** (*Informal*) = **abandon**, end, eliminate, cancel, scrap, cut back, terminate, dispense with

2 (*Informal*) = **dismiss**, fire (*informal*), sack (*informal*), remove, get rid of
● **PHRASES the axe** (*Informal*) = **the sack** (*informal*), dismissal, the boot (*slang*), termination, the chop (*slang*)

axis = **pivot**, shaft, axle, spindle, centre line

B

baas (*S. African*) = **master**, bo (*informal*), chief, ruler, commander, head, overlord, overseer

baby NOUN = **child**, infant, babe, bairn (*Scot.*), newborn child, babe in arms, ankle-biter (*Austral. slang*), tacker (*Austral. slang*)
● **ADJECTIVE** = **small**, little, minute, tiny, mini, wee, miniature, petite

back NOUN 1 = **spine**, backbone, vertebrae, spinal column, vertebral column **2** = **rear** ≠ **front 3** = **reverse**, rear, other side, wrong side, underside, flip side
● **ADJECTIVE 1** = **rear** ≠ **front 2** = **rearmost**, hind, hindmost **3** = **previous**, earlier, former, past, elapsed ≠ **future 4** = **tail**, end, rear, posterior
● **VERB 1** = **support**, help, aid, champion, defend, promote, assist, advocate ≠ **oppose 2** = **subsidize**, help, support, sponsor, assist

backbone 1 = <u>spinal column</u>, spine, vertebrae, vertebral column **2** = <u>strength of character</u>, character, resolution, nerve, daring, courage, determination, pluck

backer 1 = <u>supporter</u>, second, angel (*informal*), patron, promoter, subscriber, helper, benefactor **2** = <u>advocate</u>, supporter, patron, sponsor, promoter

backfire = <u>fail</u>, founder, flop (*informal*), rebound, boomerang, miscarry, misfire

background 1 = <u>upbringing</u>, history, culture, environment, tradition, circumstances **2** = <u>experience</u>, grounding, education **3** = <u>circumstances</u>, history, conditions, situation, atmosphere, environment, framework, ambience

backing 1 = <u>support</u>, encouragement, endorsement, moral support **2** = <u>assistance</u>, support, help, aid, sponsorship, patronage

backlash = <u>reaction</u>, response, resistance, retaliation, repercussion, counterblast, counteraction

backward 1 = <u>underdeveloped</u>, undeveloped **2** = <u>slow</u>, behind, retarded, underdeveloped, subnormal, half-witted, slow-witted

backwards *or* **backward** = <u>towards the rear</u>, behind you, in reverse, rearwards

bacteria = <u>microorganisms</u>, viruses, bugs (*slang*), germs, microbes, pathogens, bacilli

---

Word Power

bacteria – *Bacteria* is a plural noun. It is therefore incorrect to talk about a *bacteria*, even though this is quite commonly heard, especially in the media. The correct singular is a *bacterium*.

---

bad 1 = <u>harmful</u>, damaging, dangerous, destructive, unhealthy, detrimental, hurtful, ruinous ≠ beneficial **2** = <u>poor</u> **3** = <u>unfavourable</u>, distressing, unfortunate, grim, unpleasant, gloomy, adverse **4** = <u>inferior</u>, poor, inadequate, faulty, unsatisfactory, defective, imperfect, substandard, bush-league (*Austral. & N.Z. informal*), half-pie (*N.Z. informal*), bodger or bodgie (*Austral. slang*) ≠ satisfactory **5** = <u>incompetent</u>, poor, useless, incapable, unfit, inexpert **6** = <u>grim</u>, severe, hard, tough **7** = <u>wicked</u>, criminal, evil, corrupt, immoral, sinful, depraved ≠ virtuous **8** = <u>naughty</u>, defiant, wayward, mischievous, wicked, unruly, impish, undisciplined ≠ well-behaved **9** = <u>rotten</u>, off, rank, sour, rancid, mouldy, putrid, festy (*Austral. slang*)

badge 1 = <u>image</u>, brand, stamp, identification, crest, emblem, insignia **2** = <u>mark</u>, sign, token

badger = <u>pester</u>, harry, harass, bug (*informal*), bully, plague, hound, harass

badly 1 = <u>poorly</u>, incorrectly, carelessly, inadequately, imperfectly, ineptly ≠ well **2** = <u>severely</u>, greatly, deeply, seriously, desperately, intensely, exceedingly **3** = <u>unfavourably</u>, unsuccessfully

baffle = <u>puzzle</u>, confuse, stump, bewilder, confound, perplex, mystify, flummox ≠ explain

bag NOUN = <u>sack</u>, container, sac, receptacle
● **VERB 1** = <u>get</u>, land, score (*slang*), capture, acquire, procure **2** = <u>catch</u>, kill, shoot, capture, acquire, trap

baggage = <u>luggage</u>, things, cases, bags, equipment, gear, suitcases, belongings

baggy = <u>loose</u>, slack, bulging, sagging, sloppy, floppy, roomy, ill-fitting ≠ tight

bail NOUN (*Law*) = <u>security</u>, bond, guarantee, pledge, warranty, surety
● **PHRASES bail out** = <u>escape</u>, withdraw, get away, retreat, make your getaway, break free *or* out
◆ **bail something** *or* **someone out** (*Informal*) = <u>save</u>, help, release, aid, deliver, recover,

rescue, get out

bait NOUN = <u>lure</u>, attraction, incentive, carrot (*informal*), temptation, snare, inducement, decoy
● **VERB** = <u>tease</u>, annoy, irritate, bother, mock, wind up (*Brit. slang*), hound, torment

baked = <u>dry</u>, desert, seared, scorched, barren, sterile, arid, torrid

bakkie (*S. African*) = <u>truck</u>, pick-up, van, lorry, pick-up truck

balance VERB 1 = <u>stabilize</u>, level, steady ≠ overbalance **2** = <u>weigh</u>, consider, compare, estimate, contrast, assess, evaluate, set against **3** (*Accounting*) = <u>calculate</u>, total, determine, estimate, settle, count, square, reckon
● **NOUN 1** = <u>equilibrium</u>, stability, steadiness, evenness ≠ instability **2** = <u>stability</u>, equanimity, steadiness **3** = <u>parity</u>, equity, fairness, impartiality, equality, correspondence, equivalence **4** = <u>remainder</u>, rest, difference, surplus, residue **5** = <u>composure</u>, stability, restraint, self-control, poise, self-discipline, equanimity, self-restraint

balcony 1 = <u>terrace</u>, veranda **2** = <u>upper circle</u>, gods, gallery

bald 1 = <u>hairless</u>, depilated, baldheaded **2** = <u>plain</u>, direct, frank, straightforward, blunt, rude, forthright, unadorned

ball = sphere, drop, globe, pellet, orb, globule, spheroid

balloon = expand, rise, increase, swell, blow up, inflate, bulge, billow

ballot = vote, election, voting, poll, polling, referendum, show of hands

ban VERB 1 = prohibit, bar, block, veto, forbid, boycott, outlaw, banish ≠ permit 2 = bar, prohibit, exclude, forbid, disqualify, preclude, debar, declare ineligible
• NOUN = prohibition, restriction, veto, boycott, embargo, injunction, taboo, disqualification, rahui (N.Z.) ≠ permission

band[1] 1 = ensemble, group, orchestra, combo 2 = gang, company, group, party, team, body, crowd, pack

band[2] = headband, strip, ribbon

bandage NOUN = dressing, plaster, compress, gauze
• VERB = dress, cover, bind, swathe

bandit = robber, outlaw, raider, plunderer, mugger (informal), looter, highwayman, desperado

bang NOUN 1 = explosion, pop, clash, crack, blast, slam, discharge, thump 2 = blow, knock, stroke, punch, bump, sock (slang), smack, thump
• VERB 1 = resound, boom, explode, thunder, thump, clang

2 = bump, knock, elbow, jostle 3 often with **on** = hit, strike, knock, belt (informal), slam, thump, clatter
• ADVERB = exactly, straight, square, squarely, precisely, slap, smack, plumb (informal)

banish 1 = exclude, ban, dismiss, expel, throw out, eject, evict 2 = expel, exile, outlaw, deport ≠ admit 3 = get rid of, remove

bank[1] NOUN 1 = financial institution, repository, depository 2 = store, fund, stock, source, supply, reserve, pool, reservoir
• VERB = deposit, keep, save

bank[2] NOUN 1 = side, edge, margin, shore, brink 2 = mound, banking, rise, hill, mass, pile, heap, ridge, kopje or koppie (S. African) 3 = mass
• VERB = tilt, tip, pitch, heel, slope, incline, slant, cant

bank[3] = row, group, line, range, series, file, rank, sequence

bankrupt = insolvent, broke (informal), ruined, wiped out (informal), impoverished, in the red, destitute, gone bust (informal) ≠ solvent

bankruptcy = insolvency, failure, disaster, ruin, liquidation

banner = flag, standard, colours, placard, pennant, ensign, streamer

banquet = feast, spread (informal), dinner, meal, revel, repast, hakari (*N.Z.*)

bar NOUN 1 = <u>public house</u>, pub (*informal, chiefly Brit.*), counter, inn, saloon, tavern, canteen, watering hole (*facetious slang*) 2 = <u>rod</u>, staff, stick, stake, rail, pole, paling, shaft 3 = <u>obstacle</u>, block, barrier, hurdle, hitch, barricade, snag, deterrent ≠ aid

● VERB 1 = <u>lock</u>, block, secure, attach, bolt, blockade, barricade, fortify 2 = <u>block</u>, restrict, restrain, hamper, thwart, hinder, obstruct, impede 3 = <u>exclude</u>, ban, forbid, prohibit, keep out of, disallow, shut out of, blackball ≠ admit

barbarian 1 = <u>savage</u>, monster, beast, brute, yahoo, swine, sadist 2 = <u>lout</u>, yahoo, bigot, philistine, hoon (*Austral. & N.Z.*), cougan (*Austral. slang*), scozza (*Austral. slang*), bogan (*Austral. slang*), boor, vulgarian

bare 1 = <u>naked</u>, nude, stripped, uncovered, undressed, unclothed, unclad, without a stitch on (*informal*) ≠ dressed 2 = <u>simple</u>, spare, stark, austere, spartan, unadorned, unembellished, unornamented ≠ adorned 3 = <u>plain</u>, simple, basic, obvious, sheer, patent, evident, stark

barely = <u>only just</u>, just, hardly, scarcely, at a push ≠ completely

bargain NOUN 1 = <u>good buy</u>, discount purchase, good deal, steal (*informal*), snip (*informal*),

giveaway, cheap purchase 2 = <u>agreement</u>, deal (*informal*), promise, contract, arrangement, settlement, pledge, pact

● VERB = <u>negotiate</u>, deal, contract, mediate, covenant, stipulate, transact, cut a deal

barge = <u>canal boat</u>, lighter, narrow boat, flatboat

bark¹ VERB = <u>yap</u>, bay, howl, snarl, growl, yelp, woof ● NOUN = <u>yap</u>, bay, howl, snarl, growl, yelp, woof

bark² = <u>covering</u>, casing, cover, skin, layer, crust, cortex (*Anatomy, botany*), rind

barracks = <u>camp</u>, quarters, garrison, encampment, billet

barrage 1 = <u>bombardment</u>, attack, bombing, assault, shelling, battery, volley, blitz 2 = <u>torrent</u>, mass, burst, stream, hail, spate, onslaught, deluge

barren 1 = <u>desolate</u>, empty, desert, waste ≠ fertile 2 (*Old-fashioned*) = <u>infertile</u>, sterile, childless, unproductive

barricade NOUN = <u>barrier</u>, wall, fence, blockade, obstruction, rampart, bulwark, palisade ● VERB = <u>bar</u>, block, defend, secure, lock, bolt, blockade, fortify

barrier = <u>barricade</u>, wall, bar, fence, boundary, obstacle, blockade, obstruction

base¹ NOUN 1 = <u>bottom</u>, floor, lowest part ≠ top 2 = <u>support</u>, stand, foot, rest, bed, bottom, foundation, pedestal **3** = <u>foundation</u>, institution, organization, establishment **4** = <u>centre</u>, post, station, camp, settlement, headquarters, starting point **5** = <u>home</u>, house, pad (slang), residence **6** = <u>essence</u>, source, basis, root, core

● VERB **1** = <u>ground</u>, found, build, establish, depend, construct, derive, hinge **2** = <u>place</u>, set, post, station, establish, locate, install

base² = <u>dishonourable</u>, evil, disgraceful, shameful, immoral, wicked, sordid, despicable, scungy (Austral. & N.Z.) ≠ honourable

bash NOUN (Informal) = <u>attempt</u>, go (informal), try, shot (informal), bid, crack (informal), stab (informal)

● VERB (Informal) = <u>hit</u>, beat, strike, knock, smash, belt (informal), slap, sock (slang)

basic ADJECTIVE **1** = <u>fundamental</u>, main, essential, primary, vital, principal, cardinal, elementary **2** = <u>vital</u>, needed, important, key, necessary, essential, primary, crucial **3** = <u>essential</u>, key, vital, fundamental ≠ secondary **4** = <u>main</u>, key, essential, primary **5** = <u>plain</u>, simple, classic, unfussy, unembellished

● PLURAL NOUN = <u>essentials</u>,

principles, fundamentals, nuts and bolts (informal), nitty-gritty (informal), rudiments, brass tacks (informal)

basically = <u>essentially</u>, mainly, mostly, principally, fundamentally, primarily, at heart, inherently

basis 1 = <u>arrangement</u>, way, system, footing, agreement **2** = <u>foundation</u>, support, base, ground, footing, bottom, groundwork

bask = <u>lie</u>, relax, lounge, sprawl, loaf, lie about, swim in, sunbathe, outspan (S. African)

bass = <u>deep</u>, low, resonant, sonorous, low-pitched, deep-toned

bat

Bats	
flying fox	noctule
fruit bat	pipistrelle
hammerhead	serotine
horseshoe bat	vampire bat
kalong	

batch = <u>group</u>, set, lot, crowd, pack, collection, quantity, bunch

bath NOUN = <u>wash</u>, cleaning, shower, soak, cleansing, scrub, scrubbing, douche

● VERB = <u>clean</u>, wash, shower, soak, cleanse, scrub, bathe, rinse

bathe 1 = <u>swim</u> **2** = <u>wash</u>, clean, bath, shower, soak, cleanse, scrub, rinse 3 = <u>cleanse</u>, clean, wash, soak, rinse 4 = <u>cover</u>, flood, steep, engulf, immerse, overrun, suffuse, wash over

baton = <u>stick</u>, club, staff, pole, rod, crook, cane, mace, mere (*N.Z.*), patu (*N.Z.*)

batter = <u>beat</u>, hit, strike, knock, bang, thrash, pound, buffet

battery = <u>artillery</u>, ordnance, gunnery, gun emplacement, cannonry

battle NOUN 1 = <u>fight</u>, attack, action, struggle, conflict, clash, encounter, combat, biffo (*Austral. slang*) ≠ peace 2 = <u>conflict</u>, campaign, struggle, dispute, contest, crusade 3 = <u>campaign</u>, drive, movement, push, struggle
● VERB 1 = <u>wrestle</u>, war, fight, argue, dispute, grapple, clamour, lock horns 2 = <u>struggle</u>, work, labour, strain, toil, go all out (*informal*), give it your best shot (*informal*)
➤ **famous battles**

battlefield = <u>battleground</u>, front, field, combat zone, field of battle

batty = <u>crazy</u>, odd, mad, eccentric, peculiar, daft (*informal*), touched, potty (*Brit. informal*), off the air (*Austral. slang*), porangi (*N.Z.*)

bay¹ = <u>inlet</u>, sound, gulf, creek, cove, fjord, bight, natural harbour

bay² = <u>recess</u>, opening, corner, niche, compartment, nook, alcove

bay³ VERB = <u>howl</u>, cry, roar (*used of hounds*), bark, wail, growl, bellow, clamour
● NOUN = <u>cry</u>, roar (*used of hounds*), bark, howl, wail, growl, bellow, clamour

bazaar 1 = <u>market</u>, exchange, fair, marketplace 2 = <u>fair</u>, fête, gala, bring-and-buy

be = <u>be alive</u>, live, exist, survive, breathe, be present, endure

beach = <u>shore</u>, coast, sands, seaside, water's edge, seashore

beached = <u>stranded</u>, grounded, abandoned, deserted, wrecked, ashore, marooned, aground

beacon = <u>signal</u>, sign, beam, flare, lighthouse, bonfire, watchtower

bead = <u>drop</u>, tear, bubble, pearl, dot, drip, blob, droplet

beam VERB 1 = <u>smile</u>, grin 2 = <u>transmit</u>, show, air, broadcast, cable, send out, relay, televise 3 = <u>radiate</u>, flash, shine, glow, glitter, glare, gleam
● NOUN 1 = <u>ray</u>, flash, stream, glow, streak, shaft, gleam, glint 2 = <u>rafter</u>, support, timber, spar, plank, girder, joist 3 = <u>smile</u>, grin

bear VERB 1 = <u>carry</u>, take, move, bring, transfer, conduct, transport, haul ≠ put down 2 = <u>support</u>, shoulder, sustain, endure, uphold, withstand ≠ give up 3 = <u>display</u>, have, show, hold, carry, possess

Famous battles

Aboukir Bay *or* Aboukir Bay	1798
Actium	31 B.C.
Agincourt	1415
Alamo	1836
Arnhem	1944
Austerlitz	1805
Balaklava *or* Balaclava	1854
Bannockburn	1314
Barnet	1471
Bautzen	1813
Belleau Wood	1918
Blenheim	1704
Borodino	1812
Bosworth Field	1485
Boyne	1690
Cannae	216 B.C.
Crécy	1346
Culloden	1746
Dien Bien Phu	1954
Edgehill	1642
El Alamein	1942
Falkirk	1298; 1746
Flodden	1513
Gettysburg	1863
Guadalcanal	1942–3
Hastings	1066
Imphal	1944
Inkerman	1854
Issus	333 B.C.
Jemappes	1792
Jena	1806
Killiecrankie	1689
Kursk	1943
Ladysmith	1899–1900
Leipzig	1813
Lepanto	1571
Leyte Gulf	1944
Little Bighorn	1876
Lützen	1632

Manassas	1861; 1862
Marathon	490 B.C.
Marengo	1800
Marston Moor	1644
Missionary Ridge	1863
Naseby	1645
Navarino	425 B.C.
Omdurman	1898
Passchendaele	1917
Philippi	42 B.C.
Plains of Abraham	1759
Plassey	1757
Plataea	479 B.C.
Poltava	1709
Prestonpans	1745
Pydna	168 B.C.
Quatre Bras	1815
Ramillies	1706
Roncesvalles	778
Sadowa *or* Sadová	1866
Saint-Mihiel	1918
Salamis	480 B.C.
Sedgemoor	1685
Sempach	1386
Shipka Pass	1877–78
Somme	1916; 1918
Stamford Bridge	1066
Tannenberg	1410; 1914
Tewkesbury	1471
Thermopylae	480 B.C.
Tobruk	1941; 1942
Trafalgar	1805
Trenton	1776
Verdun	1916
Vitoria	1813
Wagram	1809
Waterloo	1815
Ypres	1914;1915; 1917;1918
Zama	202 B.C.

4 = <u>suffer</u>, experience, go through, sustain, stomach, endure, brook, abide **5** = <u>bring yourself to</u>, allow, accept, permit, endure, tolerate **6** = <u>produce</u>, generate, yield, bring forth **7** = <u>give birth to</u>, produce, deliver, breed, bring forth, beget **8** = <u>exhibit</u>, hold, maintain **9** = <u>conduct</u>, carry, move, deport

● **PHRASES bear something out** = <u>support</u>, prove, confirm, justify, endorse, uphold, substantiate, corroborate

bearer 1 = <u>agent</u>, carrier, courier, herald, envoy, messenger, conveyor, emissary **2** = <u>carrier</u>, runner, servant, porter

bearing NOUN 1 *usually with on or upon* = <u>relevance</u>, relation, application, connection, import, reference, significance, pertinence ≠ irrelevance **2** = <u>manner</u>, attitude, conduct, aspect, behaviour, posture, demeanour, deportment

● **PLURAL NOUN** = <u>way</u>, course, position, situation, track, aim, direction, location

beast 1 = <u>animal</u>, creature, brute **2** = <u>brute</u>, monster, savage, barbarian, fiend, swine, ogre, sadist

beastly = <u>unpleasant</u>, mean, awful, nasty, rotten, horrid, disagreeable ≠ pleasant

beat VERB 1 = <u>batter</u>, hit, strike, knock, pound, smack, thrash, thump **2** = <u>pound</u>, strike, hammer, batter, thrash **3** = <u>throb</u>, thump, pound, quake, vibrate, pulsate, palpitate **4** = <u>hit</u>, strike, bang **5** = <u>flap</u>, thrash, flutter, wag **6** = <u>defeat</u>, outdo, trounce, overcome, crush, overwhelm, conquer, surpass

● **NOUN 1** = <u>throb</u>, pounding, pulse, thumping, vibration, pulsating, palpitation, pulsation **2** = <u>route</u>, way, course, rounds, path, circuit

● **PHRASES beat someone up** (*Informal*) = <u>assault</u>, attack, batter, thrash, set about, set upon, lay into (*informal*), beat the living daylights out of (*informal*)

beaten 1 = <u>stirred</u>, mixed, whipped, blended, whisked, frothy, foamy **2** = <u>defeated</u>, overcome, overwhelmed, cowed, thwarted, vanquished

beautiful = <u>attractive</u>, pretty, lovely, charming, tempting, pleasant, handsome, fetching ≠ ugly

beauty = <u>attractiveness</u>, charm, grace, glamour, elegance, loveliness, handsomeness, comeliness ≠ ugliness **2** = <u>good-looker</u>, lovely (*slang*), belle, stunner (*informal*)

because CONJUNCTION = <u>since</u>, as, in that

● **PHRASES because of** = <u>as a</u>

result of, on account of, by reason of, thanks to, owing to

> ### Word Power
>
> **because** – The phrase *on account of* can provide a useful alternative to *because* in writing. It occurs relatively infrequently in spoken language, where it is sometimes followed by a clause, as in *on account of I don't do drugs*. However, this use is considered nonstandard.

beckon = gesture, sign, wave, indicate, signal, nod, motion, summon

become 1 = come to be, develop into, be transformed into, grow into, change into, alter to, mature into, ripen into **2** = suit, fit, enhance, flatter, embellish, set off

becoming 1 = flattering, pretty, attractive, enhancing, neat, graceful, tasteful, well-chosen ≠ unflattering **2** = appropriate, seemly, fitting, suitable, proper, worthy, in keeping, compatible ≠ inappropriate

bed 1 = bedstead, couch, berth, cot, bunk, divan **2** = plot, area, row, strip, patch, ground, land, garden **3** = bottom, ground, floor **4** = base, footing, basis, bottom, foundation, underpinning, groundwork, bedrock

bee > ants, bees, and wasps
beetle > beetles
before PREPOSITION **1** = earlier than, ahead of, prior to, in advance of ≠ after **2** = in front of, ahead of, in advance of **3** = in the presence of, in front of **4** = ahead of, in front of, in advance of
● ADVERB **1** = previously, earlier, sooner, in advance, formerly ≠ after **2** = in the past, earlier, once, previously, formerly, hitherto, beforehand

Related Words
prefixes: ante-, fore-, pre-

beforehand = in advance, before, earlier, already, sooner, ahead, previously, in anticipation

beg 1 = implore, plead with, beseech, request, petition, solicit, entreat **2** = scrounge, bum (*informal*), touch (someone) for (*slang*), cadge, sponge on (someone) for, freeload (*slang*), seek charity, solicit charity ≠ give

beggar = tramp, bum (*informal*), derelict, drifter, down-and-out, pauper, vagrant, bag lady (*chiefly U.S.*), derro (*Austral. slang*)

begin 1 = start, commence, proceed ≠ stop **2** = commence, start, initiate, embark on, set about, instigate, institute, make a beginning **3** = start talking, start, initiate, commence **3** = come into existence, start, appear, emerge, arise, originate, come into being

Beetles

ambrosia beetle	dung beetle or chafer
Asiatic beetle	firefly
bacon beetle	flea beetle
bark beetle	furniture beetle
bee beetle	glow-worm
black beetle or (N.Z.) kekerengu or Māori bug	gold beetle or goldbug
	goldsmith beetle
blister beetle	ground beetle
bloody-nosed beetle	Japanese beetle
boll weevil	June bug, June beetle, May bug, or May beetle
bombardier beetle	
burying beetle or sexton	ladybird or (U.S. & Canad.) ladybug
cabinet beetle	
cardinal beetle	leaf beetle
carpet beetle or (U.S.) carpet bug chafer	leather beetle
	May beetle, cockchafer, or June bug
Christmas beetle or king beetle	
click beetle, snapping beetle, or skipjack	scarab
	scavenger beetle
cockchafer, May beetle, or May bug	snapping beetle
	water beetle
Colorado beetle or potato beetle	weevil or snout beetle
deathwatch beetle	weevil, pea weevil, or bean weevil
diving beetle	

5 = <u>emerge</u>, start, spring, stem, derive, originate ≠ end

beginner = <u>novice</u>, pupil, amateur, newcomer, starter, trainee, apprentice, learner ≠ expert

beginning 1 = <u>start</u>, opening, birth, origin, outset, onset, initiation, inauguration ≠ end **2** = <u>outset</u>, start, opening, birth, onset, commencement **3** = <u>origins</u>

behave 1 = <u>act</u> **2** often reflexive = <u>be well-behaved</u>, mind your manners, keep your nose clean, act correctly, conduct yourself properly ≠ misbehave

behaviour 1 = <u>conduct</u>, ways, actions, bearing, attitude, manner, manners, demeanour **2** = <u>action</u>, performance, operation, functioning

behind PREPOSITION **1** = <u>at the</u>

rear of, at the back of, at the heels of 2 = <u>after</u>, following 3 = <u>supporting</u>, for, backing, on the side of, in agreement with 4 = <u>causing</u>, responsible for, initiating, at the bottom of, instigating 5 = <u>later than</u>, after

• ADVERB 1 = <u>after</u>, next, following, afterwards, subsequently, in the wake (of) ≠ in advance of 2 = <u>behind schedule</u>, delayed, running late, behind time ≠ ahead 3 = <u>overdue</u>, in debt, in arrears, behindhand

• NOUN (*Informal*) = <u>bottom</u>, butt (*U.S. & Canad. informal*), buttocks, posterior

being 1 = <u>individual</u>, creature, human being, living thing 2 = <u>life</u>, reality ≠ nonexistence 3 = <u>soul</u>, spirit, substance, creature, essence, organism, entity

beleaguered 1 = <u>harassed</u>, troubled, plagued, hassled (*informal*), badgered, persecuted, pestered, vexed 2 = <u>besieged</u>, surrounded, blockaded, beset, encircled, assailed, hemmed in

belief 1 = <u>trust</u>, confidence, conviction ≠ disbelief 2 = <u>faith</u>, principles, doctrine, ideology, creed, dogma, tenet, credo 3 = <u>opinion</u>, feeling, idea, impression, assessment, notion, judgment, point of view

believe 1 = <u>think</u>, judge, suppose, estimate, imagine, assume, gather, reckon 2 = <u>accept</u>, trust, credit, depend on, rely on, have faith in, swear by, be certain of ≠ disbelieve

believer = <u>follower</u>, supporter, convert, disciple, devotee, apostle, adherent, zealot ≠ sceptic

bellow VERB = <u>shout</u>, cry (out), scream, roar, yell, howl, shriek, bawl

• NOUN = <u>shout</u>, cry, scream, roar, yell, howl, shriek, bawl

belly = <u>stomach</u>, insides (*informal*), gut, abdomen, tummy, paunch, potbelly, corporation (*informal*), puku (*N.Z.*)

belong = <u>go with</u>, fit into, be part of, relate to, be connected with, pertain to

belonging = <u>fellowship</u>, relationship, association, loyalty, acceptance, attachment, inclusion, affinity

belongings = <u>possessions</u>, goods, things, effects, property, stuff, gear, paraphernalia

beloved = <u>dear</u>, loved, valued, prized, admired, treasured, precious, darling

below PREPOSITION 1 = <u>under</u>, underneath, lower than 2 = <u>less than</u>, lower than 3 = <u>subordinate to</u>, subject to, inferior to, lesser than

• ADVERB 1 = <u>lower</u>, down, under, beneath, underneath

2 = <u>beneath</u>, following, at the end, underneath, at the bottom, further on

belt 1 = <u>waistband</u>, band, sash, girdle, girth, cummerbund **2** = <u>conveyor belt</u>, band, loop, fan belt, drive belt **3** (*Geography*) = <u>zone</u>, area, region, section, district, stretch, strip, layer

bemused = <u>puzzled</u>, confused, baffled, at sea, bewildered, muddled, perplexed, mystified

bench NOUN **1** = <u>seat</u>, stall, pew **2** = <u>worktable</u>, stand, table, counter, trestle table, workbench
• PHRASES **the bench** = <u>court</u>, judges, magistrates, tribunal, judiciary, courtroom

benchmark = <u>reference point</u>, gauge, yardstick, measure, level, standard, model, par

bend VERB **1** = <u>twist</u>, turn, wind, lean, hook, bow, curve, arch
• NOUN = <u>curve</u>, turn, corner, twist, angle, bow, loop, arc

beneath PREPOSITION **1** = <u>under</u>, below, underneath, lower than ≠ over **2** = <u>inferior to</u>, below **3** = <u>unworthy of</u>, unfitting for, unsuitable for, inappropriate for, unbefitting
• ADVERB = <u>underneath</u>, below, in a lower place
Related Words
prefix: sub-

beneficial = <u>favourable</u>, useful, valuable, helpful, profitable,

benign, wholesome, advantageous ≠ harmful

beneficiary 1 = <u>recipient</u>, receiver, payee **2** = <u>heir</u>, inheritor

benefit NOUN **1** = <u>good</u>, help, profit, favour, advantage ≠ harm **2** = <u>advantage</u>, aid, favour, assistance
• VERB **1** = <u>profit from</u>, make the most of, gain from, do well out of, reap benefits from, turn to your advantage **2** = <u>help</u>, aid, profit, improve, enhance, assist, avail ≠ harm

benign 1 = <u>benevolent</u>, kind, kindly, warm, friendly, obliging, sympathetic, compassionate ≠ unkind **2** (*Medical*) = <u>harmless</u>, innocent, innocuous, curable, inoffensive, remediable ≠ malignant

bent ADJECTIVE **1** = <u>misshapen</u>, twisted, angled, bowed, curved, arched, crooked, distorted ≠ straight **2** = <u>stooped</u>, bowed, arched, hunched
• NOUN = <u>inclination</u>, ability, leaning, tendency, preference, penchant, propensity, aptitude
• PHRASES **bent on** = <u>intent on</u>, set on, fixed on, predisposed to, resolved on, insistent on

bequeath 1 = <u>leave</u>, will, give, grant, hand down, endow, bestow, entrust **2** = <u>give</u>, accord, grant, afford, yield, lend, pass on, confer

berth NOUN 1 = <u>bunk</u>, bed, hammock, billet 2 (*Nautical*) = <u>anchorage</u>, haven, port, harbour, dock, pier, wharf, quay
● VERB (*Nautical*) = <u>anchor</u>, land, dock, moor, tie up, drop anchor

beside PREPOSITION = <u>next to</u>, near, close to, neighbouring, alongside, adjacent to, at the side of, abreast of
● PHRASES **beside yourself** = <u>distraught</u>, desperate, distressed, frantic, frenzied, demented, unhinged, overwrought

> ### Word Power
>
> **beside** – People occasionally confuse *beside* and *besides*. *Besides* is used for mentioning something that adds to what you have already said, for example: *I didn't feel like going and besides, I had nothing to wear*. *Beside* usually means *next to* or *at the side of something or someone*, for example: *he was standing beside me* (not *besides me*).

besides PREPOSITION = <u>apart from</u>, barring, excepting, other than, excluding, as well (as), in addition to, over and above
● ADVERB = <u>also</u>, too, further, otherwise, in addition, as well, moreover, furthermore

besiege 1 = <u>harass</u>, harry, plague, hound, hassle (*informal*), badger, pester 2 = <u>surround</u>, enclose, blockade, encircle, hem in, shut in, lay siege to

best ADJECTIVE = <u>finest</u>, leading, supreme, principal, foremost, pre-eminent, unsurpassed, most accomplished
● NOUN = <u>finest</u>, top, prime, pick, flower, cream, elite, crème de la crème (*French*)
● ADVERB = <u>most highly</u>, most fully, most deeply

bestow = <u>present</u>, give, award, grant, commit, hand out, lavish, impart ≠ obtain

bet VERB = <u>gamble</u>, chance, stake, venture, hazard, speculate, wager, risk money
● NOUN = <u>gamble</u>, risk, stake, venture, speculation, flutter (*informal*), punt, wager

betray 1 = <u>be disloyal to</u>, dob in (*Austral. slang*), double-cross (*informal*), stab in the back, be unfaithful to, inform on or against 2 = <u>give away</u>, reveal, expose, disclose, uncover, divulge, unmask, let slip

betrayal = <u>disloyalty</u>, sell-out (*informal*), deception, treason, treachery, trickery, double-cross (*informal*), breach of trust ≠ loyalty

better ADVERB 1 = <u>to a greater degree</u>, more completely, more thoroughly 2 = <u>in a more excellent manner</u>, more effectively, more attractively, more advantageously, more competently, in a superior way ≠ worse

● ADJECTIVE 1 = <u>well</u>, stronger, recovering, cured, fully recovered, on the mend (*informal*) ≠ worse 2 = <u>superior</u>, finer, higher-quality, surpassing, preferable, more desirable ≠ inferior

between = <u>amidst</u>, among, mid, in the middle of, betwixt

(Related Words)

prefix: inter-

Word Power

between – After *distribute* and words with a similar meaning, *among* should be used rather than *between*: share out the sweets among the children (not between the children, unless there are only two children).

---

beverage = <u>drink</u>, liquid, liquor, refreshment

beware 1 = <u>be careful</u>, look out, watch out, be wary, be cautious, take heed, guard against something 2 = <u>avoid</u>, mind

bewilder = <u>confound</u>, confuse, puzzle, baffle, perplex, mystify, flummox, bemuse

bewildered = <u>confused</u>, puzzled, baffled, at sea, muddled, perplexed, at a loss, mystified

beyond 1 = <u>on the other side of</u> 2 = <u>after</u>, over, past, above

3 = <u>past</u> 4 = <u>except for</u>, but, save, apart from, other than, excluding, besides, aside from 5 = <u>exceeding</u>, surpassing, superior to, out of reach of 6 = <u>outside</u>, over, above

bias NOUN = <u>prejudice</u>, leaning, tendency, inclination, favouritism, partiality ≠ impartiality

● VERB = <u>influence</u>, colour, weight, prejudice, distort, sway, warp, slant

biased = <u>prejudiced</u>, weighted, one-sided, partial, distorted, slanted

bid NOUN 1 = <u>attempt</u>, try, effort, go (*informal*), shot (*informal*), stab (*informal*), crack (*informal*) 2 = <u>offer</u>, price, amount, advance, proposal, sum, tender

● VERB 1 = <u>make an offer</u>, offer, propose, submit, tender, proffer 2 = <u>wish</u>, say, call, tell, greet 3 = <u>tell</u>, ask, order, require, direct, command, instruct

bidding = <u>order</u>, request, command, instruction, summons, beck and call

big 1 = <u>large</u>, great, huge, massive, vast, enormous, substantial, extensive ≠ small 2 = <u>important</u>, significant, urgent, far-reaching ≠ unimportant 3 = <u>powerful</u>, important, prominent, dominant, influential, eminent 4 = <u>grown-up</u>, adult, grown, mature, elder, full-grown

≠ young **5** = <u>generous</u>, good, noble, gracious, benevolent, altruistic, unselfish, magnanimous

bill¹ NOUN **1** = <u>charges</u>, rate, costs, score, account, statement, reckoning, expense **2** = <u>act of parliament</u>, measure, proposal, piece of legislation, projected law **3** = <u>list</u>, listing, programme, card, schedule, agenda, catalogue, inventory **4** = <u>advertisement</u>, notice, poster, leaflet, bulletin, circular, handout, placard

● VERB **1** = <u>charge</u>, debit, invoice, send a statement to, send an invoice to **2** = <u>advertise</u>, post, announce, promote, plug (*informal*), tout, publicize, give advance notice of

bill² = <u>beak</u>, nib, neb (*archaic, dialect*), mandible

bind VERB **1** = <u>oblige</u>, make, force, require, engage, compel, constrain, necessitate **2** = <u>tie</u>, join, stick, secure, wrap, knot, strap, lash ≠ untie

● NOUN (*Informal*) = <u>nuisance</u>, inconvenience, hassle (*informal*), drag (*informal*), spot (*informal*), difficulty, bore, dilemma, uphill (*S. African*)

binding = <u>compulsory</u>, necessary, mandatory, obligatory, irrevocable, unalterable, indissoluble ≠ optional

binge (*Informal*) = <u>bout</u>, spell, fling, feast, stint, spree, orgy, bender (*informal*)

biography = <u>life story</u>, life, record, account, profile, memoir, CV, curriculum vitae

bird = <u>feathered friend</u>, fowl, songbird

Related Words
adjective: avian
male: cock
female: hen
young: chick, fledg(e)ling, nestling
collective nouns: flock, flight
habitation: nest
▸ **birds** ▸ birds of prey
▸ **seabirds** ▸ types of fowl

bird of prey ▸ birds of prey

birth 1 = <u>childbirth</u>, delivery, nativity, parturition ≠ death **2** = <u>ancestry</u>, stock, blood, background, breeding, pedigree, lineage, parentage

Related Words
adjective: natal

bit¹ 1 = <u>slice</u>, fragment, crumb, morsel **2** = <u>piece</u>, scrap **3** = <u>jot</u>, iota **4** = <u>part</u>

bit² = <u>curb</u>, check, brake, restraint, snaffle

bite VERB = <u>nip</u>, cut, tear, wound, snap, pierce, pinch, chew

● NOUN **1** = <u>snack</u>, food, piece, taste, refreshment, mouthful, morsel, titbit **2** = <u>wound</u>, sting, pinch, nip, prick

biting 1 = <u>piercing</u>, cutting, sharp, frozen, harsh, penetrating,

Birds

accentor
amokura (*N.Z.*)
apostle bird *or* happy family bird (*Austral.*)
avocet
axebird (*Austral.*)
banded dotterel (*N.Z.*)
banded rail (*N.Z.*)
bee-eater
bellbird *or* (*N.Z.*) koromako *or* makomako
bittern
blackbird
blackcap
black-fronted tern *or* tara (*N.Z.*)
black robin (*N.Z.*)
blue duck, mountain duck, whio *or* whistling duck (*N.Z.*)
boobook (*Austral.*)
brain-fever bird *or* (*Austral.*) pallid cuckoo
brambling
brolga, Australian crane, *or* (*Austral.*) native companion
brown creeper *or* pipipi (*N.Z.*)
brown duck (*N.Z.*)
brown kiwi (*N.Z.*)
budgerigar *or* (*Austral.*) zebra parrot
bunting
bush wren (*N.Z.*)
bustard *or* (*Austral.*) plain turkey, plains turkey, *or* wild turkey
button quail *or* (*Austral.*) bustard quail
Californian quail (*N.Z.*)
canary

capercaillie *or* capercailzie
chaffinch
chicken *or* (*Austral. informal*) chook
chiffchaff
chough
chukar
crane
crossbill
crow *or* (*Scot.*) corbie
cuckoo
curlew
dipper *or* water ouzel
diver
dove *or* (*archaic or poetic*) culver
dunlin *or* red-backed sandpiper
egret
fernbird (*N.Z.*)
fieldfare
finch
firecrest
flamingo
flycatcher
galah *or* (*Austral.*) galar *or* gillar
godwit
goldcrest
grebe
greenshank
grey-crowned babbler, happy family bird, Happy Jack, *or* parson bird (*Austral.*)
grey warbler *or* riroriro (*N.Z.*)
grouse
hen harrier *or* (*U.S. & Canad.*) marsh harrier
heron
hoopoe

Birds (continued)

jabiru or (Austral.) policeman bird
jackdaw
jaeger (U.S. & Canad.)
jay
kaka (N.Z.)
kakapo (N.Z.)
kakariki (N.Z.)
karoro or blackbacked gull (N.Z.)
kea (N.Z.)
kingfisher or (N.Z.) kotare
kiwi or apteryx
knot
koel or (Austral.) black cuckoo or cooee bird
kokako or blue-wattled crow (N.Z.)
kookaburra, laughing jackass, or (Austral.) bushman's clock, settler's clock, goburra, or great brown kingfisher
kotuku or white heron (N.Z.)
lapwing or green plover
lark
linnet
lorikeet
lyrebird or (Austral.) buln-buln
magpie or (Austral.) piping shrike or piping crow-shrike
magpie lark or (Austral.)
mudlark, Murray magpie, mulga, or peewit
Major Mitchell or Leadbeater's cockatoo
makomako (Austral.)
martin
metallic starling or shining starling (Austral.)

miromiro (N.Z.)
mistletoe bird (Austral.)
mohua or bush canary (N.Z.)
New Zealand pigeon or kereru (N.Z.)
nightingale
nightjar, (U.S. & Canad.) goatsucker, or (Austral.) nighthawk
noisy miner or (Austral.) micky or soldier bird
nutcracker
nuthatch
ouzel or ousel
paradise duck or putangitangi (N.Z.)
pardalote (Austral.)
partridge
pheasant
pigeon
pipit or (N.Z.) pihoihoi
pipiwharauroa or bronze-winged cuckoo (N.Z.)
pitta (Austral.)
plover
ptarmigan
puffin
quail
rainbow lorikeet
raven
redpoll
redshank
redstart
redwing
ringneck parrot, Port Lincoln parrot, or buln-buln (Austral.)
robin or robin redbreast
roller

Birds (continued)

rook
ruff
saddlebill *or* jabiru
sanderling
sandpiper
serin
shrike *or* butcherbird
silver-eye (*Austral.*)
siskin *or* (*formerly*) aberdevine
skylark
snipe
sparrow
spoonbill
spotted crake *or* (*Austral.*) water crake
starling
stint
stonechat
stork
sulphur-crested cockatoo *or* white cockatoo
superb blue wren (*Austral.*)
superb lyrebird (*Austral.*)
swallow
swift

thrush *or* (*poetic*) throstle
tit
topknot pigeon (*Austral.*)
tree creeper
tui *or* parson bird (*N.Z.*)
twite
wagtail
warbler
waxwing
weka, weka rail, Maori hen, *or* wood hen (*N.Z.*)
whinchat
white-eye *or* (*N.Z.*) blighty, silvereye, tauhou *or* waxeye
white-fronted tern *or* kahawai bird (*N.Z.*)
whitethroat
woodcock
woodlark
woodpecker
wren
yellowhammer
yellowtail *or* yellowtail kingfisher (*Austral.*)

---

arctic, icy **2** = <u>sarcastic</u>, cutting, stinging, scathing, acrimonious, incisive, virulent, caustic

bitter 1 = <u>resentful</u>, angry, offended, sour, sore, acrimonious, sullen, miffed (*informal*) ≠ happy **2** = <u>freezing</u>, biting, severe, intense, raw, fierce, chill, stinging ≠ mild **3** = <u>sour</u>, sharp, acid, harsh, tart, astringent, acrid, unsweetened ≠ sweet

bitterness 1 = <u>resentment</u>, hostility, indignation, animosity, acrimony, rancour, ill feeling, bad blood **2** = <u>sourness</u>, acidity, sharpness, tartness, acerbity

bizarre = <u>strange</u>, unusual, extraordinary, fantastic, weird, peculiar, eccentric, ludicrous ≠ normal

black 1 = <u>dark</u>, raven, ebony, sable, jet, dusky, pitch-black,

Shades from black to white			
ash	gunmetal	pitch-black	slate
black	iron	platinum	steel grey
charcoal	ivory	putty	white
cream	jet	raven	
ebony	off-white	sable	
grey	pearl	silver	

swarthy ≠ light **2** = gloomy, sad, depressing, grim, bleak, hopeless, dismal, ominous ≠ happy **3** = terrible, bad, devastating, tragic, fatal, catastrophic, ruinous, calamitous **4** = wicked, bad, evil, corrupt, vicious, immoral, depraved, villainous ≠ good **5** = angry, cross, furious, hostile, sour, menacing, moody, resentful ≠ happy
➤ shades from black to white

Word Power

black – When referring to people with dark skin, the adjective *black* or *Black* is used. For people of the US whose origins lie in Africa, the preferred term is *African American*.

blackmail NOUN = threat, intimidation, ransom, extortion, hush money (*slang*)

● VERB = threaten, squeeze, compel, intimidate, coerce, dragoon, extort, hold to ransom

blame VERB **1** = hold responsible, accuse, denounce, indict, impeach, incriminate, impute ≠ absolve **2** = attribute to, credit to, assign to, put down to, impute to **3** (used in negative constructions) = criticize, condemn, censure, reproach, chide, find fault with ≠ praise

● NOUN = responsibility, liability, accountability, onus, culpability, answerability ≠ praise

bland 1 = dull, boring, plain, flat, dreary, run-of-the-mill, uninspiring, humdrum ≠ exciting **2** = tasteless, insipid, flavourless, thin

blank ADJECTIVE **1** = unmarked, white, clear, clean, empty, plain, bare, void ≠ marked **2** = expressionless, empty, vague, vacant, deadpan, impassive, poker-faced (*informal*) ≠ expressive

● NOUN **1** = empty space, space, gap **2** = void, vacuum, vacancy, emptiness, nothingness

blanket NOUN **1** = cover, rug, coverlet **2** = covering, sheet, coat, layer, carpet, cloak, mantle,

thickness
● VERB = coat, cover, hide, mask, conceal, obscure, cloak

blast NOUN 1 = explosion, crash, burst, discharge, eruption, detonation 2 = gust, rush, storm, breeze, puff, gale, tempest, squall 3 = blare, blow, scream, trumpet, wail, resound, clamour, toot
● VERB = blow up, bomb, destroy, burst, ruin, break up, explode, shatter

blatant = obvious, clear, plain, evident, glaring, manifest, noticeable, conspicuous ≠ subtle

blaze VERB 1 = burn, glow, flare, be on fire, go up in flames, be ablaze, fire, flame 2 = shine, flash, beam, glow, flare, glare, gleam, radiate
● NOUN 1 = inferno, fire, flames, bonfire, combustion, conflagration 2 = flash, glow, glitter, flare, glare, gleam, brilliance, radiance

bleach = lighten, wash out, blanch, whiten

bleak 1 = dismal, dark, depressing, grim, discouraging, gloomy, hopeless, dreary ≠ cheerful 2 = exposed, empty, bare, barren, desolate, windswept, weather-beaten, unsheltered ≠ sheltered 3 = stormy, severe, rough, harsh, tempestuous, intemperate

bleed 1 = lose blood, flow, gush,

spurt, shed blood 2 = blend, run, meet, unite, mix, combine, flow, fuse 3 (*Informal*) = extort, milk, squeeze, drain, exhaust, fleece

blend VERB 1 = mix, join, combine, compound, merge, unite, mingle, amalgamate 2 = go well, match, fit, suit, go with, correspond, complement, coordinate 3 = combine, mix, link, integrate, merge, unite, amalgamate
● NOUN = mixture, mix, combination, compound, brew, union, synthesis, alloy

bless 1 = sanctify, dedicate, ordain, exalt, anoint, consecrate, hallow ≠ curse 2 = endow, give to, provide for, grant for, favour, grace, bestow to ≠ afflict

blessed = holy, sacred, divine, adored, revered, hallowed, sanctified, beatified

blessing 1 = benefit, help, service, favour, gift, windfall, kindness, good fortune ≠ disadvantage 2 = approval, backing, support, agreement, favour, sanction, permission, leave ≠ disapproval 3 = benediction, grace, dedication, thanksgiving, invocation, commendation, consecration, benison ≠ curse

blight NOUN 1 = curse, suffering, evil, corruption, pollution, plague, hardship, woe ≠ blessing

blind → bloom

2 = <u>disease</u>, pest, fungus, mildew, infestation, pestilence, canker

• VERB = <u>frustrate</u>, destroy, ruin, crush, mar, dash, wreck, spoil, crool *or* cruel (*Austral. slang*)

blind 1 = <u>sightless</u>, unsighted, unseeing, eyeless, visionless ≠ sighted **2** *often with* **to** = <u>unaware of</u>, unconscious of, ignorant of, indifferent to, insensitive to, oblivious of, unconcerned about, inconsiderate of ≠ aware **3** = <u>unquestioning</u>, prejudiced, wholesale, indiscriminate, uncritical, unreasoning, undiscriminating

blindly 1 = <u>thoughtlessly</u>, carelessly, recklessly, indiscriminately, senselessly, heedlessly **2** = <u>wildly</u>, aimlessly

blink VERB **1** = <u>flutter</u>, wink, bat **2** = <u>flash</u>, flicker, wink, shimmer, twinkle, glimmer

• PHRASES **on the blink** (*Slang*) = <u>not working (properly)</u>, faulty, defective, playing up, out of action, malfunctioning, out of order

bliss 1 = <u>joy</u>, ecstasy, euphoria, rapture, nirvana, felicity, gladness, blissfulness ≠ misery **2** = <u>beatitude</u>, blessedness

blister = <u>sore</u>, boil, swelling, cyst, pimple, carbuncle, pustule

blitz = <u>attack</u>, strike, assault, raid, offensive, onslaught, bombardment, bombing campaign

bloc = <u>group</u>, union, league, alliance, coalition, axis

block NOUN **1** = <u>piece</u>, bar, mass, brick, lump, chunk, hunk, ingot **2** = <u>obstruction</u>, bar, barrier, obstacle, impediment, hindrance

• VERB **1** = <u>obstruct</u>, close, stop, plug, choke, clog, stop up, bung up (*informal*) ≠ clear **2** = <u>obscure</u>, bar, obstruct **3** = <u>shut off</u>, stop, bar, hamper, obstruct

blockade = <u>stoppage</u>, block, barrier, restriction, obstacle, barricade, obstruction, impediment

bloke (*Informal*) = <u>man</u>, person, individual, character (*informal*), guy (*informal*), fellow, chap

blonde *or* **blond 1** = <u>fair</u>, light, flaxen **2** = <u>fair-haired</u>, golden-haired, tow-headed

blood 1 = <u>lifeblood</u>, gore, vital fluid **2** = <u>family</u>, relations, birth, descent, extraction, ancestry, lineage, kinship

bloodshed = <u>killing</u>, murder, massacre, slaughter, slaying, carnage, butchery, blood-letting

bloody 1 = <u>cruel</u>, fierce, savage, brutal, vicious, ferocious, cut-throat, warlike **2** = <u>bloodstained</u>, raw, bleeding, blood-soaked, blood-spattered

bloom NOUN **1** = <u>flower</u>, bud, blossom **2** = <u>prime</u>, flower, beauty, height, peak, flourishing, heyday, zenith **3** = <u>glow</u>, freshness, lustre, radiance ≠ pallor

● VERB **1** = <u>flower</u>, blossom, open, bud ≠ wither **2** = <u>grow</u>, develop, wax **3** = <u>succeed</u>, flourish, thrive, prosper, fare well ≠ fail

blossom NOUN = <u>flower</u>, bloom, bud, efflorescence, floret

● VERB **1** = <u>bloom</u>, grow, develop, mature **2** = <u>succeed</u>, progress, thrive, flourish, prosper **3** = <u>flower</u>, bloom, bud

blow¹ VERB **1** = <u>move</u>, carry, drive, sweep, fling, buffet, waft **2** = <u>be carried</u>, flutter **3** = <u>exhale</u>, breathe, pant, puff **4** = <u>play</u>, sound, pipe, trumpet, blare, toot

● PHRASES **blow something up 1** = <u>explode</u>, bomb, blast, detonate, blow sky-high **2** = <u>inflate</u>, pump up, fill, expand, swell, enlarge, puff up, distend **3** = <u>magnify</u>, increase, extend, expand, widen, broaden, amplify

♦ **blow up 1** = <u>explode</u>, burst, shatter, erupt, detonate **2** (*Informal*) = <u>lose your temper</u>, rage, erupt, see red (*informal*), become angry, hit the roof

(*informal*), fly off the handle (*informal*), go crook (*Austral. & N.Z. slang*), blow your top

blow² **1** = <u>knock</u>, stroke, punch, bang, sock (*slang*), smack, thump, clout (*informal*) **2** = <u>setback</u>, shock, disaster, reverse, disappointment, catastrophe, misfortune, bombshell

bludge (*Austral. & N.Z. informal*) = <u>slack</u>, skive (*Brit. informal*), idle, shirk

blue ADJECTIVE **1** = <u>depressed</u>, low, sad, unhappy, melancholy, dejected, despondent, downcast ≠ happy **2** = <u>smutty</u>, obscene, indecent, lewd, risqué, X-rated (*informal*) ≠ respectable

● PLURAL NOUN = <u>depression</u>, gloom, melancholy, unhappiness, low spirits, the dumps (*informal*), doldrums

➤ **shades of blue**

blueprint **1** = <u>scheme</u>, plan, design, system, programme, proposal, strategy, pattern **2** = <u>plan</u>, scheme, pattern, draft, outline, sketch

bluff¹ NOUN = <u>deception</u>, fraud,

Shades of blue

aqua	cobalt blue	perse	steel blue
aquamarine	indigo	royal blue	teal
azure	navy blue	sapphire	turquoise
Cambridge blue	Oxford blue	saxe blue	ultramarine
clear blue	peacock blue	sky blue	

sham, pretence, deceit, bravado, bluster, humbug

● VERB = <u>deceive</u>, trick, fool, pretend, cheat, con, fake, mislead

bluff² NOUN = <u>precipice</u>, bank, peak, cliff, ridge, crag, escarpment, promontory

● ADJECTIVE = <u>hearty</u>, open, blunt, outspoken, genial, ebullient, jovial, plain-spoken ≠ tactful

blunder NOUN = <u>mistake</u>, slip, fault, error, oversight, gaffe, slip-up (*informal*), indiscretion ≠ correctness

● VERB 1 = <u>make a mistake</u>, blow it (*slang*), err, slip up (*informal*), foul up, put your foot in it (*informal*) ≠ be correct 2 = <u>stumble</u>, fall, reel, stagger, lurch

blunt ADJECTIVE 1 = <u>frank</u>, forthright, straightforward, rude, outspoken, bluff, brusque, plain-spoken ≠ tactful 2 = <u>dull</u>, rounded, dulled, edgeless, unsharpened ≠ sharp

● VERB = <u>dull</u>, weaken, soften, numb, dampen, water down, deaden, take the edge off ≠ stimulate

blur NOUN = <u>haze</u>, confusion, fog, obscurity, indistinctness

● VERB 1 = <u>become indistinct</u>, become vague, become hazy, become fuzzy 2 = <u>obscure</u>, make indistinct, mask, obfuscate, make vague, make hazy

blush VERB = <u>turn red</u>, colour,

glow, flush, redden, go red (as a beetroot), turn scarlet ≠ turn pale

● NOUN = <u>reddening</u>, colour, glow, flush, pink tinge, rosiness, ruddiness, rosy tint

board NOUN 1 = <u>plank</u>, panel, timber, slat, piece of timber 2 = <u>council</u>, directors, committee, congress, advisers, panel, assembly, trustees 3 = <u>meals</u>, provisions, victuals, daily meals

● VERB = <u>get on</u>, enter, mount, embark ≠ get off

boast VERB 1 = <u>brag</u>, crow, vaunt, talk big (*slang*), blow your own trumpet, show off, congratulate yourself on, skite (*Austral. & N.Z. informal*) ≠ cover up 2 = <u>possess</u>, exhibit

● NOUN = <u>bragging</u> ≠ disclaimer

bob = <u>bounce</u>, duck, hop, oscillate

bodily = <u>physical</u>, material, actual, substantial, tangible, corporal, carnal, corporeal

body 1 = <u>physique</u>, build, form, figure, shape, frame, constitution 2 = <u>torso</u>, trunk 3 = <u>corpse</u>, dead body, remains, stiff (*slang*), carcass, cadaver 4 = <u>organization</u>, company, group, society, association, band, congress, institution 5 = <u>main part</u>, matter, material, mass, substance, bulk, essence 6 = <u>expanse</u>, mass, sweep

Related Words

adjectives: corporal, physical

bog = <u>marsh</u>, swamp, slough,

wetlands, fen, mire, quagmire, morass, pakihi (*N.Z.*)

bogey = <u>bugbear</u>, bête noire, horror, nightmare, bugaboo

bogus = <u>fake</u>, false, artificial, forged, imitation, sham, fraudulent, counterfeit ≠ genuine

Bohemian ADJECTIVE *often not cap.* = <u>unconventional</u>, alternative, artistic, unorthodox, arty (*informal*), offbeat, left bank, nonconformist ≠ conventional

● NOUN *often not cap.* = <u>nonconformist</u>, rebel, radical, eccentric, maverick, hippy, dropout, individualist

boil¹ = <u>simmer</u>, bubble, foam, seethe, fizz, froth, effervesce

boil² = <u>pustule</u>, gathering, swelling, blister, carbuncle

bold 1 = <u>fearless</u>, enterprising, brave, daring, heroic, adventurous, courageous, audacious ≠ timid 2 = <u>impudent</u>, forward, confident, rude, cheeky, brazen, shameless, insolent ≠ shy

bolster = <u>support</u>, help, boost, strengthen, reinforce, shore up, augment

bolt NOUN 1 = <u>pin</u>, rod, peg, rivet 2 = <u>bar</u>, catch, lock, latch, fastener, sliding bar

● VERB 1 = <u>lock</u>, close, bar, secure, fasten, latch 2 = <u>dash</u>, fly 3 = <u>gobble</u>, stuff, wolf, cram, gorge, devour, gulp, guzzle

bomb NOUN = <u>explosive</u>, mine,

shell, missile, device, rocket, grenade, torpedo

● VERB = <u>blow up</u>, attack, destroy, assault, shell, blitz, bombard, torpedo

bombard 1 = <u>attack</u>, assault, besiege, beset, assail 2 = <u>bomb</u>, shell, blitz, open fire, strafe, fire upon

bombardment = <u>bombing</u>, attack, assault, shelling, blitz, barrage, fusillade

bond NOUN 1 = <u>tie</u>, union, coupling, link, association, relation, connection, alliance 2 = <u>fastening</u>, tie, chain, cord, shackle, fetter, manacle 3 = <u>agreement</u>, word, promise, contract, guarantee, pledge, obligation, covenant

● VERB 1 = <u>form friendships</u>, connect 2 = <u>fix</u>, hold, bind, connect, glue, stick, paste, fasten

bonus 1 = <u>extra</u>, prize, gift, reward, premium, dividend 2 = <u>advantage</u>, benefit, gain, extra, plus, asset, icing on the cake

book NOUN 1 = <u>work</u>, title, volume, publication, tract, tome 2 = <u>notebook</u>, album, journal, diary, pad, notepad, exercise book, jotter

● VERB = <u>reserve</u>, schedule, engage, organize, charter, arrange for, make reservations

●PHRASES **book in** = <u>register</u>,

enter

booklet = brochure, leaflet, hand-out, pamphlet, folder, mailshot, handbill

boom NOUN 1 = expansion, increase, development, growth, jump, boost, improvement, upsurge ≠ decline 2 = bang, crash, clash, blast, burst, explosion, roar, thunder

● VERB 1 = increase, flourish, grow, develop, expand, strengthen, swell, thrive ≠ fall 2 = bang, roll, crash, blast, explode, roar, thunder, rumble

boon 1 = benefit, blessing, godsend, gift 2 = gift, favour

boost VERB = increase, develop, raise, expand, add to, heighten, enlarge, amplify ≠ decrease

● NOUN 1 = rise, increase, jump, addition, improvement, expansion, upsurge, upturn ≠ fall 2 = encouragement, help

boot = kick, punt, put the boot in(to) (slang), drop-kick

border NOUN 1 = frontier, line, limit, bounds, boundary, perimeter, borderline 2 = edge, margin, verge, rim

● VERB = edge, bound, decorate, trim, fringe, rim, hem

bore¹ = drill, mine, sink, tunnel, pierce, penetrate, burrow, puncture

bore² VERB = tire, fatigue, weary, wear out, jade, be tedious, pall

on, send to sleep ≠ excite

● NOUN = nuisance, pain (informal), yawn (informal), anorak (informal)

bored = fed up, tired, wearied, uninterested, sick and tired (informal), listless, brassed off (Brit. slang), hoha (N.Z.)

boredom = tedium, apathy, weariness, monotony, sameness, ennui, flatness, world-weariness ≠ excitement

boring = uninteresting, dull, tedious, tiresome, monotonous, flat, humdrum, mind-numbing

borrow 1 = take on loan, touch (someone) for (slang), scrounge (informal), cadge, use temporarily ≠ lend 2 = steal, take, copy, adopt, pinch (informal)

boss NOUN = manager, head, leader, director, chief, master, employer, supervisor, baas (S. African)

●PHRASES **boss someone around** (Informal) = order around, dominate, bully, oppress, push around (slang)

bother VERB 1 = trouble, concern, worry, alarm, disturb, disconcert, perturb 2 = pester, plague, harass, hassle (informal), inconvenience ≠ help

● NOUN = trouble, problem, worry, difficulty, fuss, irritation, hassle (informal), nuisance, uphill (S. African) ≠ help

bottle shop (*Austral. & N.Z.*) = off-licence (*Brit.*), liquor store (*U.S. & Canad.*), bottle store (*S. African*), package store (*U.S. & Canad.*), offie *or* offy (*Brit. informal*)

bottle store (*S. African*) = off-licence (*Brit.*), liquor store (*U.S. & Canad.*), bottle shop (*Austral. & N.Z.*), package store (*U.S. & Canad.*), offie *or* offy (*Brit. informal*)

bottom NOUN 1 = lowest part, base, foot, bed, floor, foundation, depths ≠ top 2 = underside, sole, underneath, lower side 3 = buttocks, behind (*informal*), rear, backside, rump, seat, posterior
• ADJECTIVE = lowest, last ≠ higher

bounce VERB 1 = rebound, recoil, ricochet 2 = bound, spring, jump, leap, skip, gambol
• NOUN 1 = springiness, give, spring, resilience, elasticity, recoil 2 (*Informal*) = life, go (*informal*), energy, zip (*informal*), vigour, exuberance, dynamism, vivacity

bound¹ 1 = compelled, obliged, forced, committed, pledged, constrained, beholden, duty-bound 2 = tied, fixed, secured, attached, tied up, fastened, pinioned 3 = certain, sure, fated, doomed, destined

bound² 1 = surround, confine, enclose, encircle, hem in, demarcate 2 = limit, restrict, confine, restrain, circumscribe

bound³ VERB = leap, bob, spring, jump, bounce, skip, vault
• NOUN = leap, bob, spring, jump, bounce, hurdle, skip, vault

boundary 1 = frontier, edge, border, barrier, margin, brink 2 = edges, limits, fringes, extremities 3 = dividing line, borderline

bounds = boundary, limit, edge, border, confine, verge, rim, perimeter

bouquet 1 = bunch of flowers, spray, garland, wreath, posy, buttonhole, corsage, nosegay 2 = aroma, smell, scent, perfume, fragrance, savour, odour, redolence

bourgeois = middle-class, traditional, conventional, materialistic, hidebound

bout 1 = period, term, fit, spell, turn, interval 2 = round, series, session, cycle, sequence, stint 3 = fight, match, competition, struggle, contest, set-to, encounter, engagement

bow¹ VERB = bend, bob, nod, stoop, droop, genuflect
• NOUN = bending, bob, nod, obeisance, kowtow, genuflection

bow² (*Nautical*) = prow, head, stem, fore, beak

bowels 1 = guts, insides (*informal*), intestines, innards

(*informal*), entrails, viscera, vitals
2 = <u>depths</u>, hold, inside, deep,
interior, core, belly

bowl¹ = <u>basin</u>, plate, dish, vessel

bowl² = <u>throw</u>, hurl, launch, cast,
pitch, toss, fling, chuck (*informal*)

box¹ NOUN = <u>container</u>, case,
chest, trunk, pack, package,
carton, casket

● VERB = <u>pack</u>, package, wrap,
encase, bundle up

box² = <u>fight</u>, spar, exchange
blows

boxer = <u>fighter</u>, pugilist,
prizefighter

boy = <u>lad</u>, kid (*informal*), youth,
fellow, youngster, schoolboy,
junior, stripling

boycott = <u>embargo</u>, reject, snub,
black ≠ support

boyfriend = <u>sweetheart</u>, man,
lover, beloved, admirer, suitor,
beau, date

brace VERB 1 = <u>steady</u>, support,
secure, stabilize 2 = <u>support</u>,
strengthen, steady, reinforce,
bolster, fortify, buttress

● NOUN = <u>support</u>, stay, prop,
bolster, bracket, reinforcement,
strut, truss

bracing = <u>refreshing</u>, fresh,
stimulating, crisp, brisk,
exhilarating, invigorating ≠ tiring

brain = <u>intelligence</u>,
understanding, sense, intellect

brake NOUN = <u>control</u>, check,
curb, restraint, constraint, rein

● VERB = <u>slow</u>, decelerate, reduce
speed

branch 1 = <u>bough</u>, shoot, arm,
spray, limb, sprig, offshoot
2 = <u>office</u>, department, unit, wing,
chapter, bureau 3 = <u>division</u>, part,
section, subdivision,
4 = <u>discipline</u>, section,
subdivision

brand NOUN 1 = <u>trademark</u>
2 = <u>label</u>, mark, sign, stamp,
symbol, logo, trademark, marker

● VERB 1 = <u>stigmatize</u>, mark,
expose, denounce, disgrace,
discredit, censure 2 = <u>mark</u>, burn,
label, stamp, scar

brash = <u>bold</u>, rude, cocky, pushy
(*informal*), brazen, impertinent,
insolent, impudent ≠ timid

brave ADJECTIVE = <u>courageous</u>,
daring, bold, heroic, adventurous,
fearless, resolute, audacious
≠ timid

● VERB = <u>confront</u>, face, suffer,
tackle, endure, defy, withstand,
stand up to ≠ give in to

bravery = <u>courage</u>, nerve,
daring, pluck, spirit, fortitude,
heroism, mettle ≠ cowardice

brawl NOUN = <u>fight</u>, clash, fray,
skirmish, scuffle, punch-up (*Brit.
informal*), fracas, altercation, biffo
(*Austral. slang*)

● VERB = <u>fight</u>, scrap (*informal*),
wrestle, tussle, scuffle

breach 1 = <u>nonobservance</u>,
abuse, violation, infringement,

trespass, transgression, contravention, infraction ≠ **compliance 2** = <u>opening</u>, crack, split, gap, rift, rupture, cleft, fissure

bread 1 = <u>food</u>, fare, kai (*N.Z. informal*) nourishment, sustenance **2** (*Slang*) = <u>money</u>, cash, dough (*slang*)

breadth 1 = <u>width</u>, spread, span, latitude, broadness, wideness **2** = <u>extent</u>, range, scale, scope, compass, expanse

break VERB **1** = <u>shatter</u>, separate, destroy, crack, snap, smash, crush, fragment ≠ repair **2** = <u>fracture</u>, crack, smash **3** = <u>burst</u>, tear, split **4** = <u>disobey</u>, breach, defy, violate, disregard, flout, infringe, contravene ≠ obey **5** = <u>stop</u>, cut, suspend, interrupt, cut short, discontinue **6** = <u>disturb</u>, interrupt **7** = <u>end</u>, stop, cut, drop, give up, abandon, suspend, interrupt **8** = <u>weaken</u>, undermine, tame, subdue, demoralize, dispirit **9** = <u>be revealed</u>, be published, be announced, be made public, be proclaimed, be let out **10** = <u>reveal</u>, tell, announce, declare, disclose, proclaim, make known **11** = <u>beat</u>, top, better, exceed, go beyond, excel, surpass, outstrip

● NOUN **1** = <u>fracture</u>, opening, tear, hole, split, crack, gap, fissure **2** = <u>interval</u>, pause, interlude,

intermission **3** = <u>holiday</u>, leave, vacation, time off, recess, awayday **4** (*Informal*) = <u>stroke of luck</u>, chance, opportunity, advantage, fortune, opening

● PHRASES **break off** = <u>stop talking</u>, pause ◆ **break out** = <u>begin</u>, start, happen, occur, arise, set in, commence, spring up ◆ **break something off** = <u>detach</u>, separate, divide, cut off, pull off, sever, part, remove ◆ **break something up** = <u>stop</u>, end, suspend, dismantle, terminate, disband, diffuse ◆ **break up 1** = <u>finish</u>, be suspended, adjourn **2** = <u>split up</u>, separate, part, divorce

breakdown = <u>collapse</u>

break-in = <u>burglary</u>, robbery, breaking and entering

breakthrough = <u>development</u>, advance, progress, discovery, find, invention, step forward, leap forwards

breast = <u>bosom(s)</u>, front, chest, bust

breath = <u>inhalation</u>, breathing, pant, gasp, gulp, wheeze, exhalation, respiration

breathe 1 = <u>inhale and exhale</u>, pant, gasp, puff, gulp, wheeze, respire, draw in breath **2** = <u>whisper</u>, sigh, murmur

breathless 1 = <u>out of breath</u>, panting, gasping, gulping, wheezing, short-winded

2 = excited, curious, eager, enthusiastic, impatient, on tenterhooks, in suspense

breathtaking = amazing, exciting, stunning (*informal*), impressive, thrilling, magnificent, astonishing, sensational

breed NOUN **1** = variety, race, stock, type, species, strain, pedigree **2** = kind, sort, type, variety, brand, stamp

● VERB **1** = rear, tend, keep, raise, maintain, farm, look after, care for **2** = reproduce, multiply, propagate, procreate, produce offspring, bear young, bring forth young **3** = produce, cause, create, generate, bring about, arouse, give rise to, stir up

breeding = refinement, culture, taste, manners, polish, courtesy, sophistication, cultivation

breeze NOUN = light wind, air, draught, gust, waft, zephyr, breath of wind, current of air

● VERB = sweep, move briskly, pass, sail, hurry, glide, flit

brew VERB **1** = boil, make, soak, steep, stew, infuse (*tea*) **2** = make, ferment **3** = start, develop, gather, foment **4** = develop, form, gather, foment

● NOUN = drink, preparation, mixture, blend, liquor, beverage, infusion, concoction

bribe NOUN = inducement, pay-off (*informal*), sweetener (*slang*),

kickback (*U.S.*), backhander (*slang*), enticement, allurement

● VERB = buy off, reward, pay off (*informal*), corrupt, suborn, grease the palm *or* hand of (*slang*)

bribery = corruption, inducement, buying off, payola (*informal*), palm-greasing (*slang*)

bridge NOUN **1** = arch, span, viaduct, flyover, overpass

● VERB **1** = span, cross **2** = reconcile, resolve

brief ADJECTIVE = short, quick, fleeting, swift, short-lived, momentary, ephemeral, transitory ≠ long

● VERB = inform, prime, prepare, advise, fill in (*informal*), instruct, put in the picture (*informal*), keep (someone) posted

● NOUN = summary, résumé, outline, sketch, abstract, digest, epitome, rundown

briefing 1 = conference, priming **2** = instructions, information, priming, directions, preparation, guidance, rundown

briefly 1 = quickly, shortly, hastily, momentarily, hurriedly **2** = in outline, in brief, in a nutshell, concisely

brigade 1 = corps, company, force, unit, division, troop, squad, team **2** = group, band, squad, organization

bright 1 = vivid, rich, brilliant,

glowing, colourful **2** = <u>shining</u>, glowing, dazzling, gleaming, shimmering, radiant, luminous, lustrous **3** = <u>intelligent</u>, smart, clever, aware, sharp, enlightened, astute, wide-awake ≠ stupid **4** = <u>clever</u>, smart, ingenious **5** = <u>sunny</u>, clear, fair, pleasant, lucid, cloudless, unclouded ≠ cloudy

brighten 1 = <u>light up</u>, shine, glow, gleam, lighten ≠ dim **2** = <u>enliven</u>, animate, make brighter, vitalize **3** = <u>become brighter</u>, light up, glow, gleam

brilliance or **brilliancy 1** = <u>cleverness</u>, talent, wisdom, distinction, genius, excellence, greatness, inventiveness ≠ stupidity **2** = <u>brightness</u>, intensity, sparkle, dazzle, lustre, radiance, luminosity, vividness ≠ darkness **3** = <u>splendour</u>, glamour, grandeur, magnificence, éclat, illustriousness

brilliant 1 = <u>intelligent</u>, sharp, intellectual, clever, profound, penetrating, inventive, perspicacious ≠ stupid **2** = <u>expert</u>, masterly, talented, gifted, accomplished ≠ untalented **3** = <u>splendid</u>, famous, celebrated, outstanding, superb, magnificent, glorious, notable **4** = <u>bright</u>, shining, intense, sparkling, glittering, dazzling, vivid, radiant ≠ dark

brim NOUN = <u>rim</u>, edge, border, lip, margin, verge, brink
● VERB **1** = <u>be full</u>, spill, well over, run over **2** = <u>fill</u>, well over, fill up, overflow

bring VERB **1** = <u>fetch</u>, take, carry, bear, transfer, deliver, transport, convey **2** = <u>take</u>, guide, conduct, escort **3** = <u>cause</u>, produce, create, effect, occasion, result in, contribute to, inflict
● PHRASES **bring someone up** = <u>rear</u>, raise, support, train, develop, teach, breed, foster
♦ **bring something about** = <u>cause</u>, produce, create, effect, achieve, generate, accomplish, give rise to ♦ **bring something off** = <u>accomplish</u>, achieve, perform, succeed, execute, pull off, carry off ♦ **bring something up** = <u>mention</u>, raise, introduce, point out, refer to, allude to, broach

brink = <u>edge</u>, limit, border, lip, margin, boundary, skirt, frontier

brisk 1 = <u>quick</u>, lively, energetic, active, vigorous, bustling, sprightly, spry ≠ slow **2** = <u>short</u>, brief, blunt, abrupt, terse, gruff, brusque, monosyllabic

briskly = <u>quickly</u>, smartly, promptly, rapidly, readily, actively, efficiently, energetically

bristle NOUN = <u>hair</u>, spine, thorn, whisker, barb, stubble, prickle
● VERB **1** = <u>stand up</u>, rise, stand on

end 2 = **be angry**, rage, seethe, flare up, bridle, see red

brittle = **fragile**, delicate, crisp, crumbling, frail, crumbly, breakable, friable ≠ tough

broad 1 = **wide**, large, ample, generous, expansive **2** = **large**, huge, vast, extensive, ample, spacious, expansive, roomy ≠ narrow **3** = **full**, general, comprehensive, complete, wide, sweeping, wide-ranging, thorough **4** = **universal**, general, common, wide, sweeping, worldwide, widespread, wide-ranging **5** = **general**, loose, vague, approximate, indefinite, ill-defined, inexact, unspecific

broadcast NOUN = **transmission**, show, programme, telecast
● VERB **1** = **transmit**, show, air, radio, cable, beam, send out, relay **2** = **make public**, report, announce, publish, spread, advertise, proclaim, circulate

broaden = **expand**, increase, develop, spread, extend, stretch, swell, supplement ≠ restrict

brochure = **booklet**, advertisement, leaflet, hand-out, circular, pamphlet, folder, mailshot

broekies (S. African informal) = **underpants**, pants, briefs, drawers, knickers, panties, boxer shorts, Y-fronts®, underdaks (Austral. slang)

broke (Informal) = **penniless**, short, ruined, bust (informal), bankrupt, impoverished, in the red, insolvent ≠ rich

broken 1 = **interrupted**, incomplete, erratic, intermittent, fragmentary, spasmodic, discontinuous **2** = **imperfect**, halting, hesitating, stammering, disjointed **3** = **smashed**, burst, shattered, fragmented, fractured, severed, ruptured, separated **4** = **defective**, not working, imperfect, out of order, on the blink (slang), kaput (informal)

broker = **dealer**, agent, trader, supplier, merchant, negotiator, mediator, intermediary

bronze = **reddish-brown**, copper, tan, rust, chestnut, brownish
➤ **shades of brown**

brood NOUN 1 = **offspring**, issue, clutch, litter, progeny **2** = **children**, family, nearest and dearest, flesh and blood, ainga (N.Z.)
● VERB = **think**, obsess, muse, ponder, agonize, mull over, mope, ruminate

brook = **stream**, burn (Scot. & Northern English), rivulet, beck, watercourse, rill

brother 1 = **male sibling 2** = **monk**, cleric, friar, religious
(Related Words)
adjective: fraternal

Shades of brown

amber	café au lait	ginger	rust
auburn	camel	hazel	sable
bay	chestnut	henna	sepia
beige	chocolate	khaki	sienna
biscuit	cinnamon	liver	tan
bisque	cocoa	mahogany	taupe
bronze	coffee	mocha	tawny
buff	copper	nutbrown	terracotta
burnt sienna	dun	oxblood	tortoiseshell
burnt umber	fawn	russet	walnut

brotherly = <u>fraternal</u>, friendly, neighbourly, sympathetic, affectionate, benevolent, kind, amicable

brown ADJECTIVE 1 = <u>brunette</u>, bay, coffee, chocolate, chestnut, hazel, dun, auburn 2 = <u>tanned</u>, bronze, tan, sunburnt

● VERB = <u>fry</u>, cook, grill, sear, sauté

➤ **shades of brown**

browse 1 = <u>skim</u>, scan, glance at, survey, look through, look round, dip into, leaf through 2 = <u>graze</u>, eat, feed, nibble

bruise NOUN = <u>discoloration</u>, mark, injury, blemish, contusion

● VERB 1 = <u>hurt</u>, injure, mark 2 = <u>damage</u>, mark, mar, discolour

brush¹ NOUN 1 = <u>broom</u>, sweeper, besom 2 = <u>conflict</u>, clash, confrontation, skirmish, tussle 3 = <u>encounter</u>, meeting, confrontation, rendezvous

● VERB 1 = <u>clean</u>, wash, polish, buff 2 = <u>touch</u>, sweep, kiss, stroke,

glance, flick, scrape, graze

● PHRASES **brush someone off** (*Slang*) = <u>ignore</u>, reject, dismiss, snub, disregard, scorn, disdain, spurn ◆ **brush something up** or **brush up on something** = <u>revise</u>, study, go over, cram, polish up, read up on, relearn, bone up on (*informal*)

brush² = <u>shrubs</u>, bushes, scrub, undergrowth, thicket, copse, brushwood

brutal 1 = <u>cruel</u>, savage, vicious, ruthless, callous, sadistic, heartless, inhuman ≠ kind 2 = <u>harsh</u>, tough, severe, rough, rude, impolite, insensitive, callous ≠ sensitive

brutality = <u>cruelty</u>, atrocity, ferocity, savagery, ruthlessness, barbarism, inhumanity, viciousness

bubble NOUN = <u>air ball</u>, drop, bead, blister, blob, droplet, globule

• VERB 1 = <u>boil</u>, seethe 2 = <u>foam</u>, fizz, froth, percolate, effervesce
3 = <u>gurgle</u>, splash, murmur, trickle, ripple, babble, burble, lap

bubbly 1 = <u>lively</u>, happy, excited, animated, merry, bouncy, elated, sparky 2 = <u>frothy</u>, sparkling, fizzy, effervescent, carbonated, foamy

buckle NOUN = <u>fastener</u>, catch, clip, clasp, hasp

• VERB 1 = <u>fasten</u>, close, secure, hook, clasp 2 = <u>distort</u>, bend, warp, crumple, contort
3 = <u>collapse</u>, bend, twist, fold, give way, subside, cave in, crumple

bud NOUN = <u>shoot</u>, branch, sprout, sprig, offshoot

• VERB = <u>develop</u>, grow, shoot, sprout, burgeon, burst forth

budding = <u>developing</u>, beginning, growing, promising, potential, burgeoning, fledgling, embryonic

budge 1 = <u>move</u>, stir
2 = <u>dislodge</u>, move, push, transfer, shift, stir

budget NOUN = <u>allowance</u>, means, funds, income, finances, resources, allocation

• VERB = <u>plan</u>, estimate, allocate, cost, ration, apportion

buff¹ ADJECTIVE = <u>fawn</u>, tan, beige, yellowish, straw-coloured, sand-coloured, yellowish-brown

• VERB = <u>polish</u>, smooth, brush, shine, rub, wax, brighten, burnish

➤ **shades of brown** ➤ **shades**

of yellow

buff² (*Informal*) = <u>expert</u>, fan, addict, enthusiast, admirer, devotee, connoisseur, aficionado, fundi (*S. African*)

buffer = <u>safeguard</u>, screen, shield, cushion, intermediary, bulwark

buffet 1 = <u>smorgasbord</u>
2 = <u>snack bar</u>, café, cafeteria, brasserie, refreshment counter

bug NOUN 1 (*Informal*) = <u>illness</u>, disease, virus, infection, disorder, sickness, ailment, affliction
2 = <u>fault</u>, error, defect, flaw, glitch, gremlin

• VERB 1 = <u>tap</u>, eavesdrop, listen in on 2 (*Informal*) = <u>annoy</u>, bother, disturb, irritate, hassle (*informal*), pester, vex, get on your nerves (*informal*)

build VERB = <u>construct</u>, make, raise, put up, assemble, erect, fabricate, form ≠ demolish

• NOUN = <u>physique</u>, form, body, figure, shape, structure, frame

building = <u>structure</u>, house, construction, dwelling, erection, edifice, domicile

build-up = <u>increase</u>, development, growth, expansion, accumulation, enlargement, escalation

bulge VERB 1 = <u>swell out</u>, project, expand, stick out, protrude, puff out, distend 2 = <u>stick out</u>, stand out, protrude

● NOUN **1** = <u>lump</u>, swelling, bump, projection, hump, protuberance, protrusion ≠ hollow **2** = <u>increase</u>, rise, boost, surge, intensification

bulk 1 = <u>size</u>, volume, dimensions, magnitude, substance, immensity, largeness **2** = <u>weight</u>, size, mass, heaviness, poundage **3** = <u>majority</u>, mass, most, body, best part, lion's share, better part, preponderance

> ## Word Power
>
> **bulk** – The use of a plural noun after *bulk*, as in sense 3, although common, is considered by some to be incorrect and should be avoided. This usage is most commonly encountered, according to the Bank of English, when referring to *funds* and *profits*: *the bulk of our profits stem from the sale of beer*. The synonyms *majority* and *most* would work better in this context.

bullet = <u>projectile</u>, ball, shot, missile, slug, pellet
bulletin = <u>report</u>, account, statement, message, communication, announcement, dispatch, communiqué
bully NOUN = <u>persecutor</u>, tough, oppressor, tormentor, bully boy, browbeater, coercer, ruffian
● VERB **1** = <u>persecute</u>, intimidate, torment, oppress, pick on,

victimize, terrorize, push around (*slang*) **2** = <u>force</u>, coerce, browbeat, hector, domineer
bump VERB **1** = <u>knock</u>, hit, strike, crash, smash, slam, bang **2** = <u>jerk</u>, shake, bounce, rattle, jog, lurch, jolt
● NOUN **1** = <u>knock</u>, blow, impact, collision, thump **2** = <u>thud</u>, crash, knock, bang, smack, thump **3** = <u>lump</u>, swelling, bulge, hump, nodule, protuberance, contusion
bumper = <u>exceptional</u>, excellent, exo (*Austral. slang*), massive, jumbo (*informal*), abundant, whopping (*informal*), bountiful
bunch NOUN **1** = <u>group</u>, band, crowd, party, team, gathering, gang, flock **2** = <u>bouquet</u>, sheaf **3** = <u>cluster</u>, clump
●PHRASES **bunch together** or **up** = <u>group</u>, mass, collect, assemble, cluster, huddle
bundle NOUN = <u>bunch</u>, group, collection, mass, pile, stack, heap, batch
● VERB = <u>push</u>, thrust, shove, throw, rush, hurry, jostle, hustle
●PHRASES **bundle someone up** = <u>wrap up</u>, swathe
bungle = <u>mess up</u>, blow (*slang*), ruin, spoil, blunder, botch, make a mess of, muff, crool *or* cruel (*Austral. slang*) ≠ accomplish
bungling = <u>incompetent</u>, blundering, clumsy, inept, cack-handed (*informal*), maladroit,

ham-fisted (*informal*), unco (*Austral. slang*)

bunk or **bunkum** (*informal*) = nonsense, rubbish, garbage (*informal*), hot air (*informal*), twaddle, moonshine, baloney (*informal*), hogwash, bizzo (*Austral. slang*), bull's wool (*Austral. & N.Z. slang*), kak (*S. African taboo slang*)

buoy = float, guide, signal, marker, beacon

buoyant ADJECTIVE 1 = cheerful, happy, upbeat (*informal*), carefree, jaunty, chirpy (*informal*), light-hearted ≠ gloomy
● ADJECTIVE 2 = floating, light

burden NOUN 1 = trouble, worry, weight, responsibility, strain, affliction, onus, millstone 2 = load, weight, cargo, freight, consignment, encumbrance
● VERB = weigh down, worry, load, tax, bother, handicap, oppress, inconvenience

bureau 1 = agency 2 = office, department, section, branch, station, unit, division, subdivision 3 = desk, writing desk

bureaucracy 1 = government, officials, authorities, administration, the system, civil service, corridors of power 2 = red tape, regulations, officialdom

bureaucrat = official, officer, administrator, civil servant, public

servant, functionary, mandarin

burglar = housebreaker, thief, robber, pilferer, filcher, cat burglar, sneak thief

burglary = breaking and entering, housebreaking, break-in

burial = funeral, interment, obsequies, entombment, exequies

burn 1 = be on fire, blaze, be ablaze, smoke, flame, glow, flare, go up in flames 2 = set on fire, light, ignite, kindle, incinerate 3 = scorch, toast, sear, char, singe 4 = be passionate, be aroused, be inflamed 5 = seethe, fume, be angry, simmer, smoulder

burning 1 = intense, passionate, eager, ardent, fervent, impassioned, vehement ≠ mild 2 = blazing, fiery, smouldering, glowing 3 = flashing, blazing, flaming, gleaming, fiery 4 = crucial, important, pressing, significant, essential, vital, critical, acute

burrow NOUN = hole, shelter, tunnel, den, lair, retreat
● VERB 1 = dig, tunnel, excavate 2 = delve, search, probe, ferret, rummage, forage, fossick (*Austral. & N.Z.*)

burst VERB 1 = explode, blow up, break, split, crack, shatter, puncture, rupture 2 = rush, run, break, break out, erupt, spout, gush forth 3 = barge, charge, rush, shove

● NOUN 1 = <u>rush</u>, surge, outbreak, outburst, spate, gush, torrent, spurt 2 = <u>explosion</u>, crack, blast, bang, discharge

● ADJECTIVE = <u>ruptured</u>, flat, punctured, split, rent

bury 1 = <u>inter</u>, lay to rest, entomb, consign to the grave, inhume ≠ dig up 2 = <u>hide</u>, cover, conceal, stash (informal), secrete, stow away ≠ uncover 3 = <u>sink</u>, embed, immerse, enfold 4 = <u>forget</u>

bush NOUN = <u>shrub</u>, plant, hedge, thicket, shrubbery

● PHRASES the bush = <u>the wilds</u>, brush, scrub, woodland, backwoods, scrubland

business 1 = <u>trade</u>, selling, industry, manufacturing, commerce, dealings 2 = <u>establishment</u>, company, firm, concern, organization, corporation, venture, enterprise 3 = <u>profession</u>, work, job, line, trade, career, function, employment 4 = <u>matter</u>, issue, subject, point, problem, responsibility, task, duty 5 = <u>concern</u>, affair

businessman = <u>executive</u>, director, manager, merchant, capitalist, administrator, entrepreneur, tycoon

bust[1] = <u>bosom</u>, breasts, chest, front

bust[2] (Informal) VERB 1 = <u>break</u>, smash, split, burst, shatter, fracture, rupture 2 = <u>arrest</u>, catch, raid

● PHRASES go bust = <u>go bankrupt</u>, fail, be ruined, become insolvent

bustle VERB = <u>hurry</u>, rush, fuss, hasten, scuttle, scurry, scamper ≠ idle

● NOUN = <u>activity</u>, to-do, stir, excitement, fuss, flurry, commotion, ado ≠ inactivity

bustling = <u>busy</u>, full, crowded, active, lively, buzzing, humming, swarming

busy ADJECTIVE 1 = <u>active</u>, industrious, rushed off your feet ≠ idle 2 = <u>occupied with</u>, working, engaged in, on duty, employed in, hard at work ≠ unoccupied 3 = <u>hectic</u>, full, exacting, energetic

● PHRASES busy yourself = <u>occupy yourself</u>, be engrossed, immerse yourself, involve yourself, absorb yourself, employ yourself, engage yourself

but CONJUNCTION = <u>however</u>, still, yet, nevertheless

● PREPOSITION = <u>except (for)</u>, save, bar, barring, excepting, excluding, with the exception of

● ADVERB = <u>only</u>, just, simply, merely

butcher NOUN = <u>murderer</u>, killer, slaughterer, slayer, destroyer,

Butterflies and moths

argus	house moth	skipper
bag moth (N.Z.)	lackey moth	small white
brown-tail moth	large white or	snout
cabbage white	cabbage white	speckled wood
cactoblastis	leopard moth	swallowtail
cardinal	magpie moth	swift
carpet moth	marbled white	tapestry moth
clearwing or	monarch	tiger (moth)
clearwing moth	orange-tip	umber (moth)
death's-head moth	painted lady	wax moth,
ermine moth or	peacock butterfly	honeycomb moth, or
ermine	peppered moth	bee moth
ghost moth	privet hawk	white
gipsy moth	processionary moth	white admiral
grayling	purple emperor	winter moth
hairstreak	puss moth	yellow underwing
herald moth	red admiral	
hawk moth, sphinx	red underwing	
moth, or	ringlet	
hummingbird moth	silver-Y	

executioner, cut-throat, exterminator

● VERB 1 = <u>slaughter</u>, prepare, carve, cut up, dress, cut, clean, joint 2 = <u>kill</u>, slaughter, massacre, destroy, cut down, assassinate, slay, liquidate

butt¹ 1 = <u>end</u>, handle, shaft, stock, shank, hilt, haft 2 = <u>stub</u>, tip, leftover, fag end (*informal*)

butt² = <u>target</u>, victim, dupe, laughing stock, Aunt Sally

butt³ VERB = <u>knock</u>, push, bump, thrust, ram, shove, poke, prod

● PHRASES **butt in** 1 = <u>interfere</u>, meddle, intrude, heckle, barge in

(*informal*), stick your nose in, put your oar in 2 = <u>interrupt</u>, cut in, break in, chip in (*informal*)

butt⁴ = <u>cask</u>, barrel

butterfly
Related Words
young: caterpillar, chrysalis or chrysalid
enthusiast: lepidopterist

> butterflies and moths

buy VERB = <u>purchase</u>, get, pay for, obtain, acquire, invest in, shop for, procure ≠ sell

● NOUN = <u>purchase</u>, deal, bargain, acquisition, steal (*informal*), snip (*informal*), giveaway

by PREPOSITION **1** = <u>through</u>,
through the agency of **2** = <u>via</u>,
over, by way of **3** = <u>near</u>, past,
along, close to, closest to,
neighbouring, next to, beside
• ADVERB = <u>nearby</u>, close, handy,
at hand, within reach

bypass 1 = <u>get round</u>, avoid
2 = <u>go round</u>, circumvent, depart
from, deviate from, pass round,
detour round ≠ cross

C

cab = <u>taxi</u>, minicab, taxicab,
hackney carriage

cabin 1 = <u>room</u>, berth, quarters,
compartment **2** = <u>hut</u>, shed,
cottage, lodge, shack, chalet,
shanty, whare (*N.Z.*)

cabinet 1 = <u>cupboard</u>, case,
locker, dresser, closet, press,
chiffonier **2** *often cap.* = <u>council</u>,
committee, administration,
ministry, assembly, board

cad (*Old-fashioned, informal*)
= <u>scoundrel</u> (*slang*), rat (*informal*),
bounder (*Brit. old-fashioned
slang*), rotter (*slang, chiefly Brit.*),
heel

café = <u>snack bar</u>, restaurant,
cafeteria, coffee shop, brasserie,
coffee bar, tearoom, lunchroom

cage = <u>enclosure</u>, pen, coop,
hutch, pound

cake = <u>block</u>, bar, slab, lump,

cube, loaf, mass

calculated = <u>deliberate</u>,
planned, considered, intended,
intentional, designed, aimed,
purposeful ≠ unplanned

calculating = <u>scheming</u>, sharp,
shrewd, cunning, sly, devious,
manipulative, crafty ≠ direct

calculation 1 = <u>computation</u>,
working out, reckoning, estimate,
forecast, judgment, result, answer
2 = <u>planning</u>, intention,
deliberation, foresight,
contrivance, forethought,
premeditation

calibre *or* (*U.S.*) **caliber**
1 = <u>worth</u>, quality, ability, talent,
capacity, merit, distinction,
stature **2** = <u>standard</u>, level,
quality, grade **3** = <u>diameter</u>, bore,
gauge, measure

call VERB **1** = <u>name</u>, entitle, dub,
designate, term, style, label,
describe as **2** = <u>cry</u>, shout, scream,
yell, whoop ≠ whisper **3** = <u>phone</u>,
telephone, ring (up) (*informal,
chiefly Brit.*) **4** = <u>hail</u>, summon
5 = <u>summon</u>, gather, rally,
assemble, muster, convene
≠ dismiss **6** = <u>waken</u>, arouse,
rouse
• NOUN **1** = <u>visit</u> **2** = <u>request</u>, order,
demand, appeal, notice,
command, invitation, plea
3 (*usually used in a negative
construction*) = <u>need</u>, cause,
reason, grounds, occasion,

excuse, justification
4 = attraction, pull (*informal*), appeal, lure, allure, magnetism
5 = cry, shout, scream, yell, whoop ≠ whisper

● **PHRASES call for someone** = fetch, pick up, collect ◆ **call for something 1** = demand, order, request, insist on, cry out for **2** = require, need, involve, demand, occasion, entail, necessitate

calling = profession, trade, career, mission, vocation, life's work

calm ADJECTIVE **1** = cool, relaxed, composed, sedate, collected, dispassionate, unemotional, self-possessed ≠ excited **2** = still, quiet, smooth, mild, serene, tranquil, balmy, windless ≠ rough

● NOUN **1** = peacefulness, peace, serenity **2** = stillness, peace, quiet, hush, serenity, tranquillity, repose, peacefulness **3** = peace, calmness ≠ disturbance

● VERB **1** = soothe, quiet, relax, appease, still, allay, assuage, quieten ≠ excite **2** = placate, hush, pacify, mollify ≠ aggravate

camouflage NOUN
1 = protective colouring
2 = disguise, cover, screen, blind, mask, cloak, masquerade, subterfuge

● VERB = disguise, cover, screen, hide, mask, conceal, obscure, veil

≠ reveal

camp[1] = camp site, tents, encampment, bivouac, camping ground

camp[2] (*Informal*) = affected, mannered, artificial, posturing, ostentatious, effeminate

campaign 1 = drive, appeal, movement, push (*informal*), offensive, crusade **2** = operation, drive, attack, movement, push, offensive, expedition, crusade

canal = waterway, channel, passage, conduit, duct, watercourse

cancel VERB **1** = call off, drop, forget about **2** = annul, abolish, repeal, abort, do away with, revoke, eliminate

● **PHRASES cancel something out** = counterbalance, offset, make up for, compensate for, neutralize, nullify, balance out

cancellation 1 = abandonment
2 = annulment, abolition, repeal, elimination, revocation

cancer 1 = growth, tumour, malignancy **2** = evil, corruption, sickness, pestilence

candidate = contender, competitor, applicant, nominee, entrant, claimant, contestant, runner

cannabis = marijuana, pot (*slang*), dope (*slang*), grass (*slang*), hemp, dagga (*S. African*)

cannon = gun, big gun, field

gun, mortar

canon 1 = <u>rule</u>, standard, principle, regulation, formula, criterion, dictate, statute 2 = <u>list</u>, index, catalogue, roll

canopy = <u>awning</u>, covering, shade, sunshade

cap 1 (*Informal*) = <u>beat</u>, top, better, exceed, eclipse, surpass, transcend, outstrip 2 = <u>top</u>, crown 3 = <u>complete</u>, crown

capability = <u>ability</u>, means, power, potential, capacity, qualification(s), competence, proficiency ≠ inability

capable 1 = <u>able</u> ≠ incapable 2 = <u>accomplished</u>, qualified, talented, gifted, efficient, competent, proficient ≠ incompetent

capacity 1 = <u>ability</u>, facility, gift, genius, capability, aptitude, aptness, competence *or* competency 2 = <u>size</u>, room, range, space, volume, extent, dimensions, scope 3 = <u>function</u>, position, role, post, office

cape = <u>headland</u>, point, head, peninsula, promontory

capital NOUN = <u>money</u>, funds, investment(s), cash, finances, resources, assets, wealth
• ADJECTIVE (*Old-fashioned*) = <u>first-rate</u>, fine, excellent, superb
➤ WORD POWER SUPPLEMENT **capital cities**

capitalism = <u>private enterprise</u>, free enterprise, private ownership, laissez faire *or* laisser faire

capsule 1 = <u>pill</u>, tablet, lozenge 2 (*Botany*) = <u>pod</u>, case, shell, vessel, sheath, receptacle, seed case

captain 1 = <u>leader</u>, boss, master, skipper, head, chief 2 = <u>commander</u>, skipper

captivate = <u>charm</u>, attract, fascinate, entrance, enchant, enthral, beguile, allure ≠ repel

captive ADJECTIVE = <u>confined</u>, caged, imprisoned, locked up, enslaved, incarcerated, ensnared, subjugated
• NOUN = <u>prisoner</u>, hostage, convict, prisoner of war, detainee, internee

captivity = <u>confinement</u>, custody, detention, imprisonment, incarceration, internment

capture VERB = <u>catch</u>, arrest, take, bag, secure, seize, collar (*informal*), apprehend ≠ release
• NOUN = <u>arrest</u>, catching, trapping, imprisonment, seizure, apprehension, taking, taking captive

car 1 = <u>vehicle</u>, motor, wheels (*informal*), auto (*U.S.*), automobile, jalopy (*informal*), motorcar, machine 2 (*U.S. & Canad.*) = <u>(railway) carriage</u>, coach, cable car, dining car, sleeping car, buffet car, van

cardinal = <u>principal</u>, first, leading, chief, main, central, key, essential ≠ secondary

care VERB = <u>be concerned</u>, mind, bother, be interested, be bothered, give a damn, concern yourself

● NOUN 1 = <u>custody</u>, keeping, control, charge, management, protection, supervision, guardianship 2 = <u>caution</u>, attention, pains, consideration, heed, prudence, vigilance, forethought ≠ carelessness

3 = <u>worry</u>, concern, pressure, trouble, responsibility, stress, anxiety, disquiet ≠ pleasure

● PHRASES **care for someone** 1 = <u>look after</u>, mind, tend, attend, nurse, minister to, watch over 2 = <u>love</u>, desire, be fond of, want, prize ◆ **care for something or someone** = <u>like</u>, enjoy, take to, relish, be fond of, be keen on, be partial to ◆ **take care of** 1 = <u>look after</u>, mind, watch, protect, tend, nurse, care for, provide for 2 = <u>deal with</u>, manage, cope with, see to, handle

career NOUN = <u>occupation</u>, calling, employment, pursuit, vocation, livelihood, life's work

● VERB = <u>rush</u>, race, speed, tear, dash, barrel (along) (informal, (chiefly U.S. & Canad.), bolt, hurtle

careful 1 = <u>cautious</u>, scrupulous, circumspect, chary, thoughtful, discreet ≠ careless 2 = <u>thorough</u>, full, particular, precise, intensive, in-depth, meticulous, conscientious ≠ casual

3 = <u>prudent</u>, sparing, economical, canny, provident, frugal, thrifty

careless 1 = <u>slapdash</u>, irresponsible, sloppy (informal), cavalier, offhand, neglectful, slipshod, lackadaisical ≠ careful

2 = <u>negligent</u>, hasty, thoughtless, unthinking, forgetful, absent-minded, remiss ≠ careful

3 = <u>nonchalant</u>, casual, offhand, artless, unstudied ≠ careful

caretaker = <u>warden</u>, keeper, porter, superintendent, curator, custodian, watchman, janitor

cargo = <u>load</u>, goods, contents, shipment, freight, merchandise, baggage, consignment

caricature NOUN = <u>parody</u>, cartoon, distortion, satire, send-up (Brit. informal), travesty, takeoff (informal), lampoon

● VERB = <u>parody</u>, take off (informal), mock, distort, ridicule, mimic, send up (Brit. informal), lampoon

carnage = <u>slaughter</u>, murder, massacre, holocaust, havoc, bloodshed, shambles, mass murder

carnival = <u>festival</u>, fair, fête, celebration, gala, jubilee, jamboree, revelry

carnivore > **carnivores**

carol = song, hymn, Christmas song

carp = find fault, complain,

criticize, reproach, quibble, cavil, pick holes ≠ praise

carpenter = joiner, cabinet-maker, woodworker

carriage 1 = vehicle, coach, trap,

Carnivores

aardwolf	grizzly bear or grizzly	polar bear or (N.
arctic fox	hyena or hyaena	Canad.) nanook
badger	ichneumon	polecat
bear	jackal	prairie dog
binturong	jaguar	puma or cougar
black bear	jaguarondi,	raccoon, racoon, or
bobcat	jaguarundi, or	coon
brown bear	(Austral.) eyra	raccoon dog
caracal or desert lynx	kinkajou, honey bear,	ratel
cat	or potto	red fox
catamount,	Kodiak bear	sable
catamountain, or	laughing hyena or	sea otter
cat-o'-mountain	spotted hyena	serval
cheetah or chetah	leopard or panther	silver fox
cinnamon bear	linsang	skunk
civet	lion	sloth bear
coyote or prairie wolf	lynx	snow leopard or
dhole	margay	ounce
dingo or (Austral.)	marten	stoat
native dog or	meerkat	strandwolf
warrigal	mink	sun bear
dog	mongoose	swift fox or kit fox
ermine	mountain lion	tayra
fennec	ocelot	teledu
ferret	otter	tiger
fox	otter shrew	tiger cat
genet or genette	palm civet	timber wolf
giant panda	panda	weasel
grey fox (U.S.)	panther	wolf
grey wolf or timber	pine marten or sweet	wolverine, glutton, or
wolf	marten	carcajou

gig, cab, wagon, hackney, conveyance 2 = **bearing**, posture, gait, deportment, air

carry VERB 1 = **convey**, take, move, bring, bear, transfer, conduct, transport 2 = **transport**, take, transfer 3 = **transmit**, transfer, spread, pass on 4 = **win**, gain, secure, capture, accomplish

● PHRASES **carry on** 1 = **continue**, last, endure, persist, keep going, persevere 2 (*Informal*) = **make a fuss**, misbehave, create (*slang*), raise Cain ◆ **carry something on** = **engage in**, conduct, carry out, undertake, embark on, enter into ◆ **carry something out** = **perform**, effect, achieve, realize, implement, fulfil, accomplish, execute

carry-on (*Informal, chiefly Brit.*) = **fuss**, disturbance, racket, commotion

carton = **box**, case, pack, package, container

cartoon 1 = **drawing**, parody, satire, caricature, comic strip, takeoff (*informal*), lampoon, sketch 2 = **animation**, animated film, animated cartoon

carve 1 = **sculpt**, cut, chip, whittle, chisel, hew, fashion 2 = **etch**, engrave

cascade NOUN = **waterfall**, falls, torrent, flood, shower, fountain, avalanche, deluge

● VERB = **flow**, fall, flood, pour, plunge, surge, spill, tumble

case¹ 1 = **situation**, event, circumstance(s), state, position, condition, context, contingency 2 = **instance**, example, occasion, specimen, occurrence 3 (*Law*) = **lawsuit**, trial, suit, proceedings, dispute, action

case² 1 = **cabinet**, box, chest, holder 2 = **container**, carton, canister, casket, receptacle 3 = **suitcase**, bag, grip, holdall, portmanteau, valise 4 = **crate**, box 5 = **covering**, casing, shell, jacket, envelope, capsule, sheath, wrapper

cash = **money**, funds, notes, currency, silver, brass (*Northern English dialect*), dough (*slang*), coinage

cast NOUN 1 = **actors**, company, players, characters, troupe, dramatis personae 2 = **type**, sort, kind, style, stamp

● VERB 1 = **choose**, select, appoint, assign, allot 2 = **bestow**, give, level, direct 3 = **give out**, spread, deposit, shed, distribute, scatter, emit, radiate 4 = **throw**, launch, pitch, toss, thrust, hurl, fling, sling 5 = **mould**, set, found, form, model, shape

caste = **class**, order, rank, status, stratum, social order

castle = **fortress**, keep, palace,

tower, chateau, stronghold, citadel

casual 1 = careless, relaxed, unconcerned, blasé, offhand, nonchalant, lackadaisical ≠ serious 2 = chance, unexpected, random, accidental, incidental ≠ planned 3 = informal, leisure, sporty, non-dressy ≠ formal

casualty 1 = fatality, death, loss, wounded 2 = victim, sufferer

cat = feline, pussy (informal), moggy (slang), puss (informal), ballarat (Austral. informal), tabby

(Related Words)
adjective: feline
male: tom
female: tabby
young: kitten

catalogue or (U.S.) **catalog** NOUN = list, record, schedule, index, register, directory, inventory, gazetteer
● VERB = list, file, index, register, classify, inventory, tabulate, alphabetize

catastrophe = disaster, tragedy, calamity, cataclysm, trouble, adversity, fiasco

catch VERB 1 = capture, arrest, trap, seize, snare, apprehend, ensnare, entrap ≠ free 2 = trap, capture, snare, ensnare, entrap 3 = seize, get, grab, snatch 4 = grab, take, grip, seize, grasp, clutch, lay hold of ≠ release

5 = discover, surprise, find out, expose, detect, catch in the act, take unawares 6 = contract, get, develop, suffer from, incur, succumb to, go down with ≠ escape
● NOUN 1 = fastener, clip, bolt, latch, clasp 2 (Informal) = drawback, trick, trap, disadvantage, hitch, snag, stumbling block, fly in the ointment ≠ advantage
● PHRASES **catch on** 1 (Informal) = understand, see, find out, grasp, see through, comprehend, twig (Brit. informal), get the picture 2 = become popular, take off, become trendy, come into fashion

catching = infectious, contagious, transferable, communicable, transmittable ≠ non-infectious

category = class, grouping, heading, sort, department, type, division, section

cater
● PHRASES **cater for something** or **someone** 1 = provide for, supply, purvey 2 = take into account, consider, bear in mind, make allowance for, have regard for

cattle = cows, stock, beasts, livestock, bovines

(Related Words)
adjective: bovine

collective nouns: drove, herd

cause NOUN 1 = <u>origin</u>, source, spring, agent, maker, producer, root, beginning ≠ result 2 = <u>reason</u>, call, need, grounds, basis, incentive, motive, motivation 3 = <u>aim</u>, movement, principle, ideal, enterprise
● VERB = <u>produce</u>, create, lead to, result in, generate, induce, bring about, give rise to ≠ prevent

caution NOUN 1 = <u>care</u>, discretion, heed, prudence, vigilance, alertness, forethought, circumspection ≠ carelessness 2 = <u>reprimand</u>, warning, injunction, admonition
● VERB 1 = <u>warn</u>, urge, advise, alert, tip off, forewarn 2 = <u>reprimand</u>, warn, admonish, give an injunction to

cautious = <u>careful</u>, guarded, wary, tentative, prudent, judicious, circumspect, cagey (*informal*) ≠ careless

cavalry = <u>horsemen</u>, horse, mounted troops ≠ infantrymen

cave = <u>hollow</u>, cavern, grotto, den, cavity

cavity = <u>hollow</u>, hole, gap, pit, dent, crater

cease 1 = <u>stop</u>, end, finish, come to an end ≠ start 2 = <u>discontinue</u>, end, stop, finish, conclude, halt, terminate, break off ≠ begin

celebrate 1 = <u>rejoice</u>, party, enjoy yourself, carouse, live it up (*informal*), make merry, put the flags out, kill the fatted calf 2 = <u>commemorate</u>, honour, observe, toast, drink to, keep 3 = <u>perform</u>, observe, preside over, officiate at, solemnize

celebrated = <u>renowned</u>, popular, famous, distinguished, well-known, prominent, acclaimed, notable ≠ unknown

celebration 1 = <u>party</u>, festival, gala, jubilee, festivity, revelry, red-letter day, merrymaking 2 = <u>commemoration</u>, honouring, remembrance 3 = <u>performance</u>, observance, solemnization

celebrity 1 = <u>personality</u>, star, superstar, big name, dignitary, luminary, big shot (*informal*), V.I.P. ≠ nobody 2 = <u>fame</u>, reputation, distinction, prestige, prominence, stardom, renown, repute ≠ obscurity

cell 1 = <u>room</u>, chamber, lock-up, compartment, cavity, cubicle, dungeon, stall 2 = <u>unit</u>, group, section, core, nucleus, caucus, coterie

cement NOUN 1 = <u>mortar</u>, plaster, paste 2 = <u>sealant</u>, glue, gum, adhesive
● VERB = <u>stick</u>, join, bond, attach, seal, glue, plaster, weld

cemetery = <u>graveyard</u>,

churchyard, burial ground, necropolis, God's acre

censor = expurgate, cut, blue-pencil, bowdlerize

censure VERB = criticize, blame, condemn, denounce, rebuke, reprimand, reproach, scold ≠ applaud

• NOUN = disapproval, criticism, blame, condemnation, rebuke, reprimand, reproach, stick (slang) ≠ approval

central 1 = inner, middle, mid, interior ≠ outer 2 = main, chief, key, essential, primary, principal, fundamental, focal ≠ minor

centre NOUN = middle, heart, focus, core, nucleus, hub, pivot, kernel ≠ edge

• VERB = focus, concentrate, cluster, revolve, converge

ceremonial ADJECTIVE = formal, public, official, ritual, stately, solemn, liturgical, courtly ≠ informal

• NOUN = ritual, ceremony, rite, formality, solemnity

ceremony 1 = ritual, service, rite, observance, commemoration, solemnities 2 = formality, ceremonial, propriety, decorum

certain 1 = sure, convinced, positive, confident, satisfied, assured ≠ unsure 2 = bound, sure, fated, destined ≠ unlikely 3 = inevitable, unavoidable,

inescapable 4 = known, true, positive, conclusive, unequivocal, undeniable, irrefutable, unquestionable ≠ doubtful 5 = fixed, decided, established, settled, definite ≠ indefinite

certainly 1 = definitely, surely, truly, undoubtedly, without doubt, undeniably, indisputably, assuredly

certainty 1 = confidence, trust, faith, conviction, assurance, sureness, positiveness ≠ doubt 2 = inevitability ≠ uncertainty 3 = fact, truth, reality, sure thing (informal), banker

certificate = document, licence, warrant, voucher, diploma, testimonial, authorization, credential(s)

certify = confirm, declare, guarantee, assure, testify, verify, validate, attest

chain NOUN 1 = tether, coupling, link, bond, shackle, fetter, manacle 2 = series, set, train, string, sequence, succession, progression

• VERB = bind, confine, restrain, handcuff, shackle, tether, fetter, manacle

chairman or **chairwoman** 1 = director, president, chief, executive, chairperson 2 = master of ceremonies, spokesman, chair, speaker, MC, chairperson

> ### Word Power
>
> **chairman/chairwoman** –
> The general trend of nonsexist
> language is to find a term which
> can apply to both sexes equally,
> as in the use of *actor* to refer to
> both men and women.
> *Chairman* can seem
> inappropriate when applied to a
> woman, while *chairwoman*
> specifies gender, and so, as the
> entry above illustrates, the terms
> *chair* and *chairperson* are often
> preferred as alternatives.

challenge NOUN 1 = <u>dare</u>,
provocation, wero (*N.Z.*) 2 = <u>test</u>,
trial, opposition, confrontation,
ultimatum

• VERB 1 = <u>dispute</u>, question,
tackle, confront, defy, object to,
disagree with, take issue with
2 = <u>dare</u>, invite, defy, throw down
the gauntlet 3 = <u>test</u>
4 = <u>question</u>, interrogate

chamber 1 = <u>hall</u>, room
2 = <u>council</u>, assembly, legislature,
legislative body 3 = <u>room</u>,
bedroom, apartment, enclosure,
cubicle 4 = <u>compartment</u>

champion NOUN 1 = <u>winner</u>,
hero, victor, conqueror, title
holder 2 = <u>defender</u>, guardian,
patron, backer, protector,
upholder

• VERB = <u>support</u>, back, defend,
promote, advocate, fight for,

uphold, espouse

chance NOUN 1 = <u>probability</u>,
odds, possibility, prospect,
likelihood ≠ certainty
2 = <u>opportunity</u>, opening,
occasion, time 3 = <u>accident</u>,
fortune, luck, fate, destiny,
coincidence, providence ≠ design
4 = <u>risk</u>, speculation, gamble,
hazard

• VERB = <u>risk</u>, try, stake, venture,
gamble, hazard, wager

change NOUN 1 = <u>alteration</u>,
innovation, transformation,
modification, mutation,
metamorphosis, difference,
revolution 2 = <u>variety</u>, break
(*informal*), departure, variation,
novelty, diversion ≠ monotony
3 = <u>exchange</u>, trade, conversion,
swap, substitution, interchange

• VERB 1 = <u>alter</u>, reform, transform,
adjust, revise, modify, reorganize,
restyle ≠ keep 2 = <u>shift</u>, vary,
transform, alter, modify, mutate
≠ stay 3 = <u>exchange</u>, trade,
replace, substitute, swap,
interchange

channel NOUN 1 = <u>means</u>, way,
course, approach, medium, route,
path, avenue 2 = <u>strait</u>, sound,
route, passage, canal, waterway
3 = <u>duct</u>, artery, groove, gutter,
furrow, conduit

• VERB = <u>direct</u>, guide, conduct,
transmit, convey

chant NOUN = <u>song</u>, carol, chorus,

melody, psalm
● VERB = sing, chorus, recite, intone, carol

chaos = disorder, confusion, mayhem, anarchy, lawlessness, pandemonium, bedlam, tumult ≠ orderliness

chaotic = disordered, confused, uncontrolled, anarchic, tumultuous, lawless, riotous, topsy-turvy

chap (Informal) = fellow, man, person, individual, character, guy (informal), bloke (Brit. informal)

chapter 1 = section, part, stage, division, episode, topic, segment, instalment 2 = period, time, stage, phase

character 1 = personality, nature, attributes, temperament, complexion, disposition 2 = nature, kind, quality, calibre 3 = reputation, honour, integrity, good name, rectitude 4 = role, part, persona 5 = eccentric, card (informal), original, oddball (informal) 6 = symbol, mark, sign, letter, figure, device, rune, hieroglyph

characteristic NOUN = feature, mark, quality, property, attribute, faculty, trait, quirk
● ADJECTIVE = typical, special, individual, representative, distinguishing, distinctive, peculiar, singular ≠ rare

characterize = distinguish, mark, identify, brand, stamp, typify

charge VERB 1 = accuse, indict, impeach, incriminate, arraign ≠ acquit 2 = attack, assault, assail ≠ retreat 3 = rush, storm, stampede 4 = fill, load
● NOUN 1 = price, rate, cost, amount, payment, expense, toll, expenditure 2 = accusation, allegation, indictment, imputation ≠ acquittal 3 = care, trust, responsibility, custody, safekeeping 4 = duty, office, responsibility, remit 5 = ward, pupil, protégé, dependant 6 = attack, rush, assault, onset, onslaught, stampede, sortie ≠ retreat

charisma = charm, appeal, personality, attraction, lure, allure, magnetism, force of personality

charismatic = charming, appealing, attractive, influential, magnetic, enticing, alluring

charitable 1 = benevolent, liberal, generous, lavish, philanthropic, bountiful, beneficent ≠ mean 2 = kind, understanding, forgiving, sympathetic, favourable, tolerant, indulgent, lenient ≠ unkind

charity 1 = charitable organization, fund, movement, trust, endowment 2 = donations, help, relief, gift, contributions, assistance, hand-out,

philanthropy, koha (N.Z.)
≠ meanness 3 = <u>kindness</u>,
humanity, goodwill, compassion,
generosity, indulgence, altruism,
benevolence, aroha (N.Z.) ≠ ill will

charm NOUN 1 = <u>attraction</u>,
appeal, fascination, allure,
magnetism ≠ repulsiveness
2 = <u>talisman</u>, trinket, amulet,
fetish 3 = <u>spell</u>, magic,
enchantment, sorcery, makutu
(N.Z.)

● VERB 1 = <u>attract</u>, delight,
fascinate, entrance, win over,
enchant, captivate, beguile
≠ repel 2 = <u>persuade</u>, seduce,
coax, beguile, sweet-talk
(informal)

charming = <u>attractive</u>, pleasing,
appealing, fetching, delightful,
cute, seductive, captivating
≠ unpleasant

chart NOUN = <u>table</u>, diagram,
blueprint, graph, plan, map

● VERB 1 = <u>plot</u>, map out,
delineate, sketch, draft, tabulate
2 = <u>monitor</u>, follow, record, note,
document, register, trace, outline

charter NOUN 1 = <u>document</u>,
contract, permit, licence, deed,
prerogative 2 = <u>constitution</u>,
laws, rules, code

● VERB 1 = <u>hire</u>, commission,
employ, rent, lease 2 = <u>authorize</u>,
permit, sanction, entitle, license,
empower, give authority

chase VERB 1 = <u>pursue</u>, follow,

track, hunt, run after, course
2 = <u>drive away</u>, drive, expel,
hound, send away, send packing,
put to flight 3 = <u>rush</u>, run, race,
shoot, fly, speed, dash, bolt

● NOUN = <u>pursuit</u>, race, hunt,
hunting

chat VERB = <u>talk</u>, gossip, jaw
(slang), natter, blather, blether
(Scot.)

● NOUN = <u>talk</u>, tête-à-tête,
conversation, gossip, heart-to-
heart, natter, blather, blether
(Scot.), korero (N.Z.)

chatter VERB = <u>prattle</u>, chat,
rabbit on (Brit. informal), babble,
gab (informal), natter, blather,
schmooze (slang)

● NOUN = <u>prattle</u>, chat, gossip,
babble, gab (informal), natter,
blather, blether (Scot.)

cheap 1 = <u>inexpensive</u>, reduced,
keen, reasonable, bargain, low-
priced, low-cost, cut-price
≠ expensive 2 = <u>inferior</u>, poor,
worthless, second-rate, shoddy,
tawdry, tatty, trashy, bodger or
bodgie (Austral. slang) ≠ good
3 (Informal) = <u>despicable</u>, mean,
contemptible, scungy (Austral. &
N.Z.) ≠ decent

cheat VERB = <u>deceive</u>, trick, fool,
con (informal), mislead, rip off
(slang), fleece, defraud

● NOUN = <u>deceiver</u>, sharper, shark,
charlatan, trickster, con man
(informal), double-crosser

(*informal*), swindler, rorter (*Austral. slang*)

check VERB 1 *often with out* = <u>examine</u>, test, study, look at, research, investigate, monitor, vet ≠ overlook 2 = <u>stop</u>, limit, delay, halt, restrain, inhibit, hinder, obstruct ≠ further

● NOUN 1 = <u>examination</u>, test, research, investigation, inspection, scrutiny, once-over (*informal*) 2 = <u>control</u>, limitation, restraint, constraint, obstacle, curb, obstruction, stoppage

cheek (*Informal*) = <u>impudence</u>, nerve, disrespect, audacity, lip (*slang*), temerity, chutzpah (*U.S. & Canad. informal*), insolence

cheeky = <u>impudent</u>, rude, forward, insulting, saucy, audacious, pert, disrespectful ≠ respectful

cheer VERB 1 = <u>applaud</u>, hail, acclaim, clap ≠ boo 2 = <u>hearten</u>, encourage, comfort, uplift, brighten, cheer up, buoy up, gladden ≠ dishearten

● NOUN = <u>applause</u>, ovation, plaudits, acclamation

● PHRASES **cheer someone up** = <u>comfort</u>, encourage, hearten, enliven, gladden, gee up, jolly along (*informal*) ◆ **cheer up** = <u>take heart</u>, rally, perk up, buck up (*informal*)

cheerful 1 = <u>happy</u>, optimistic, enthusiastic, jolly, merry, upbeat

(*informal*), buoyant, cheery ≠ sad 2 = <u>pleasant</u> ≠ gloomy

chemical = <u>compound</u>, drug, substance, synthetic substance, potion

chemist = <u>pharmacist</u>, apothecary (*obsolete*), dispenser

cherish 1 = <u>cling to</u>, prize, treasure, hold dear, cleave to ≠ despise 2 = <u>care for</u>, love, support, comfort, look after, shelter, nurture, hold dear ≠ neglect 3 = <u>harbour</u>, nurse, sustain, foster, entertain

chest 1 = <u>breast</u>, front 2 = <u>box</u>, case, trunk, crate, coffer, casket, strongbox

(Related Words)
adjective: pectoral

chew = <u>munch</u>, bite, grind, champ, crunch, gnaw, chomp, masticate

chic = <u>stylish</u>, smart, elegant, fashionable, trendy (*Brit. informal*) ≠ unfashionable

chief NOUN = <u>head</u>, leader, director, manager, boss (*informal*), captain, master, governor, baas (*S. African*), ariki (*N.Z.*) ≠ subordinate

● ADJECTIVE = <u>primary</u>, highest, leading, main, prime, key, premier, supreme ≠ minor

chiefly 1 = <u>especially</u>, essentially, principally, primarily, above all 2 = <u>mainly</u>, largely, usually, mostly, in general, on the whole,

child → chorus

predominantly, in the main

child 1 = <u>youngster</u>, baby, kid (*informal*), infant, babe, juvenile, toddler, tot, littlie (*Austral. informal*), ankle-biter (*Austral. slang*), tacker (*Austral. slang*) 2 = <u>offspring</u>

Related Words

adjective: filial

prefix: paedo-

childbirth = <u>child-bearing</u>, labour, delivery, lying-in, confinement, parturition

childhood = <u>youth</u>, minority, infancy, schooldays, immaturity, boyhood *or* girlhood

childish 1 = <u>youthful</u>, young, boyish *or* girlish 2 = <u>immature</u>, juvenile, foolish, infantile, puerile ≠ mature

chill VERB 1 = <u>cool</u>, refrigerate, freeze 2 = <u>dishearten</u>, depress, discourage, dismay, dampen, deject

● NOUN 1 = <u>coldness</u>, bite, nip, sharpness, coolness, rawness, crispness, frigidity 2 = <u>shiver</u>, frisson

● ADJECTIVE = <u>chilly</u>, biting, sharp, freezing, raw, bleak, chilly, wintry

chilly 1 = <u>cool</u>, fresh, sharp, crisp, penetrating, brisk, draughty, nippy ≠ warm 2 = <u>unfriendly</u>, hostile, unsympathetic, frigid, unresponsive, unwelcoming ≠ friendly

china[1] = <u>pottery</u>, ceramics, ware, porcelain, crockery, tableware, service

china[2] (*Brit. & S. African informal*) = <u>friend</u>, pal, mate (*informal*), buddy (*informal*), companion, best friend, intimate, comrade, cobber (*Austral. & N.Z. old-fashioned informal*), E hoa (*N.Z.*)

chip NOUN 1 = <u>fragment</u>, shaving, wafer, sliver, shard 2 = <u>scratch</u>, nick, notch 3 = <u>counter</u>, disc, token

● VERB 1 = <u>nick</u>, damage, gash 2 = <u>chisel</u>, whittle

choice NOUN 1 = <u>range</u>, variety, selection, assortment

2 = <u>selection</u>, preference, pick

3 = <u>option</u>, say, alternative

● ADJECTIVE = <u>best</u>, prime, select, excellent, exclusive, elite, booshit (*Austral. slang*), exo (*Austral. slang*), sik (*Austral. slang*)

choke 1 = <u>suffocate</u>, stifle, smother, overpower, asphyxiate 2 = <u>strangle</u>, throttle, asphyxiate 3 = <u>block</u>, clog, obstruct, bung, constrict, congest, stop, bar

choose 1 = <u>pick</u>, prefer, select, elect, adopt, opt for, designate, settle upon ≠ reject 2 = <u>wish</u>, want

chop = <u>cut</u>, fell, hack, sever, cleave, hew, lop

chore = <u>task</u>, job, duty, burden, hassle (*informal*), errand

chorus NOUN 1 = <u>refrain</u>, response, strain, burden 2 = <u>choir</u>, singers, ensemble, vocalists, choristers

• PHRASES **in chorus** = in unison, as one, all together, in concert, in harmony, in accord, with one voice

christen 1 = <u>baptize</u>, name 2 = <u>name</u>, call, term, style, title, dub, designate

Christmas = <u>festive season</u>, Noël, Xmas, Yule (*archaic*), Yuletide (*archaic*)

chronicle VERB = <u>record</u>, tell, report, enter, relate, register, recount, set down

• NOUN = <u>record</u>, story, history, account, register, journal, diary, narrative

chuck (*Informal*) 1 = <u>throw</u>, cast, pitch, toss, hurl, fling, sling, heave 2 *often with* **away** *or* **out** = <u>throw out</u>, dump (*informal*), scrap, get rid of, ditch (*slang*), dispose of, dispense with, jettison 3 = <u>give up</u> *or* **over**, leave, abandon, cease, resign from, pack in 4 (*Austral. & N.Z. informal*) = <u>vomit</u>, throw up (*informal*), spew, heave (*slang*), puke (*slang*), barf (*U.S. slang*), chunder (*slang, chiefly Austral.*)

chuckle = <u>laugh</u>, giggle, snigger, chortle, titter

chum (*Informal*) = <u>friend</u>, mate (*informal*), pal (*informal*), companion, comrade, crony, cobber (*Austral. & N.Z. old-fashioned informal*), E hoa (*N.Z.*)

chunk = <u>piece</u>, block, mass, portion, lump, slab, hunk, nugget

churn 1 = <u>stir up</u>, beat, disturb, swirl, agitate 2 = <u>swirl</u>, toss

cinema 1 = <u>pictures</u>, movies, picture-house, flicks (*slang*) 2 = <u>films</u>, pictures, movies, big screen (*informal*), motion pictures, silver screen

circle NOUN 1 = <u>ring</u>, disc, hoop, halo 2 = <u>group</u>, company, set, club, society, clique, coterie

• VERB 1 = <u>go round</u>, ring, surround, enclose, envelop, encircle, circumscribe, circumnavigate 2 = <u>wheel</u>, spiral

circuit 1 = <u>course</u>, tour, track, route, journey 2 = <u>racetrack</u>, course, track, racecourse 3 = <u>lap</u>, tour, revolution, orbit

circular ADJECTIVE 1 = <u>round</u>, ring-shaped 2 = <u>circuitous</u>, cyclical, orbital

• NOUN = <u>advertisement</u>, notice, ad (*informal*), announcement, advert (*Brit. informal*), press release

circulate 1 = <u>spread</u>, issue, publish, broadcast, distribute, publicize, disseminate, promulgate 2 = <u>flow</u>, revolve, rotate, radiate

circulation 1 = <u>distribution</u>, currency, readership 2 = <u>bloodstream</u>, blood flow 3 = <u>flow</u>, circling, motion, rotation 4 = <u>spread</u>, distribution, transmission, dissemination

circumstance 1 *usually plural* = <u>situation</u>, condition, contingency, state of affairs, lie of the land 2 *usually plural* = <u>detail</u>, event, particular, respect 3 *usually plural* = <u>situation</u>, state, means, position, station, status 4 = <u>chance</u>, the times, accident, fortune, luck, fate, destiny, providence

cite = <u>quote</u>, name, advance, mention, extract, specify, allude to, enumerate

citizen = <u>inhabitant</u>, resident, dweller, denizen, subject, townsman

Related Words
adjective: civil

city = <u>town</u>, metropolis, municipality, conurbation

Related Words
adjective: civic

civic = <u>public</u>, municipal, communal, local

civil 1 = <u>civic</u>, political, domestic, municipal ≠ state 2 = <u>polite</u>, obliging, courteous, considerate, affable, well-mannered ≠ rude

civilization 1 = <u>society</u>, people, community, nation, polity 2 = <u>culture</u>, development, education, progress, enlightenment, sophistication, advancement, cultivation

civilize = <u>cultivate</u>, educate, refine, tame, enlighten,

sophisticate

civilized 1 = <u>cultured</u>, educated, sophisticated, enlightened, humane ≠ primitive 2 = <u>polite</u>, mannerly, tolerant, gracious, courteous, well-behaved, well-mannered

claim VERB 1 = <u>assert</u>, insist, maintain, allege, uphold, profess 2 = <u>demand</u>, call for, ask for, insist on

● NOUN 1 = <u>assertion</u>, statement, allegation, declaration, pretension, affirmation, protestation 2 = <u>demand</u>, application, request, petition, call 3 = <u>right</u>, title, entitlement

clamour = <u>noise</u>, shouting, racket, outcry, din, uproar, commotion, hubbub

clamp NOUN = <u>vice</u>, press, grip, bracket, fastener

● VERB = <u>fasten</u>, fix, secure, brace, make fast

clan 1 = <u>family</u>, group, society, tribe, fraternity, brotherhood, ainga (*N.Z.*), ngai (*N.Z.*) 2 = <u>group</u>, set, circle, gang, faction, coterie, cabal

clap = <u>applaud</u>, cheer, acclaim ≠ boo

clarify = <u>explain</u>, interpret, illuminate, clear up, simplify, make plain, elucidate, throw or shed light on

clarity 1 = <u>clearness</u>, precision, simplicity, transparency, lucidity,

straightforwardness ≠ obscurity
2 = <u>transparency</u>, clearness ≠ cloudiness

clash VERB **1** = <u>conflict</u>, grapple, wrangle, lock horns, cross swords, war, feud, quarrel **2** = <u>disagree</u>, conflict, vary, counter, differ, contradict, diverge, run counter to **3** = <u>not go</u>, jar, not match **4** = <u>crash</u>, bang, rattle, jar, clatter, jangle, clang, clank

• NOUN **1** = <u>conflict</u>, fight, brush, confrontation, collision, showdown (informal)

2 = <u>disagreement</u>, difference, argument, dispute, dissent, difference of opinion

clasp VERB = <u>grasp</u>, hold, press, grip, seize, squeeze, embrace, clutch

• NOUN **1** = <u>grasp</u>, hold, grip, embrace, hug **2** = <u>fastening</u>, catch, grip, hook, pin, clip, buckle, brooch

class NOUN **1** = <u>group</u>, set, division, rank **2** = <u>type</u>, set, sort, kind, category, genre

• VERB = <u>classify</u>, group, rate, rank, brand, label, grade, designate

classic ADJECTIVE **1** = <u>typical</u>, standard, model, regular, usual, ideal, characteristic, definitive, dinki-di (Austral. informal) **2** = <u>masterly</u>, best, finest, world-class, consummate, first-rate ≠ second-rate **3** = <u>lasting</u>, enduring, abiding, immortal,

undying, ageless, deathless

• NOUN = <u>standard</u>, masterpiece, prototype, paradigm, exemplar, model

classification
= <u>categorization</u>, grading, taxonomy, sorting, analysis, arrangement

classify = <u>categorize</u>, sort, rank, arrange, grade, catalogue, pigeonhole, tabulate

classy (Informal) = <u>high-class</u>, exclusive, superior, elegant, stylish, posh (informal, chiefly Brit.), up-market, top-drawer

clause = <u>section</u>, condition, article, chapter, passage, part, paragraph

claw NOUN **1** = <u>nail</u>, talon **2** = <u>pincer</u>

• VERB = <u>scratch</u>, tear, dig, rip, scrape, maul, mangulate (Austral. slang), lacerate

clean ADJECTIVE **1** = <u>hygienic</u>, fresh, sterile, pure, purified, antiseptic, sterilized, uncontaminated ≠ contaminated **2** = <u>spotless</u>, fresh, immaculate, impeccable, flawless, unblemished, unsullied ≠ dirty **3** = <u>moral</u>, good, pure, decent, innocent, respectable, upright, honourable ≠ immoral **4** = <u>complete</u>, final, whole, total, perfect, entire, decisive, thorough

• VERB = <u>cleanse</u>, wash, scrub, rinse, launder, scour, purify, disinfect ≠ dirty

cleanse = <u>purify</u>, clear, purge
1 = <u>absolve</u>, clear, purge, purify
2 = <u>clean</u>, wash, scrub, rinse, scour

clear ADJECTIVE
1 = <u>comprehensible</u>, explicit, understandable ≠ confused
2 = <u>distinct</u> ≠ indistinct
3 = <u>obvious</u>, plain, apparent, evident, distinct, pronounced, manifest, blatant ≠ ambiguous
4 = <u>certain</u>, sure, convinced, positive, satisfied, resolved, definite, decided ≠ confused
5 = <u>transparent</u>, see-through, translucent, crystalline, glassy, limpid, pellucid ≠ opaque
6 = <u>unobstructed</u>, open, free, empty, unhindered, unimpeded ≠ blocked 7 = <u>bright</u>, fine, fair, shining, sunny, luminous, cloudless, light ≠ cloudy
8 = <u>untroubled</u>, clean, pure, innocent, immaculate, unblemished, untarnished
● VERB 1 = <u>unblock</u>, free, loosen, extricate, open, disentangle
2 = <u>remove</u>, clean, wipe, cleanse, tidy (up), sweep away
3 = <u>brighten</u>, break up, lighten
4 = <u>pass over</u>, jump, leap, vault, miss 5 = <u>absolve</u>, acquit, vindicate, exonerate ≠ blame

clear-cut = <u>straightforward</u>, specific, plain, precise, black-and-white, explicit, definite, unequivocal

clearly 1 = <u>obviously</u>, undoubtedly, evidently, distinctly, markedly, overtly, undeniably, beyond doubt 2 = <u>legibly</u>, distinctly 3 = <u>audibly</u>, distinctly, intelligibly, comprehensibly

clergy = <u>priesthood</u>, ministry, clerics, clergymen, churchmen, the cloth, holy orders

clever 1 = <u>intelligent</u>, bright, talented, gifted, smart, knowledgeable, quick-witted ≠ stupid 2 = <u>shrewd</u>, bright, ingenious, resourceful, canny ≠ unimaginative 3 = <u>skilful</u>, talented, gifted ≠ inept

cliché = <u>platitude</u>, stereotype, commonplace, banality, truism, hackneyed phrase

client = <u>customer</u>, consumer, buyer, patron, shopper, patient

cliff = <u>rock face</u>, overhang, crag, precipice, escarpment, scar, bluff

climate = <u>weather</u>, temperature

climax = <u>culmination</u>, top, summit, height, highlight, peak, high point, zenith

climb VERB 1 = <u>ascend</u>, scale, mount, go up, clamber, shin up
2 = <u>clamber</u>, descend, scramble, dismount 3 = <u>rise</u>, go up, soar, ascend, fly up
● PHRASES **climb down** = <u>back down</u>, withdraw, yield, concede, retreat, surrender, give in, cave in (informal)

clinch 1 = <u>secure</u>, close, confirm,

conclude, seal, sew up (*informal*), set the seal on 2 = <u>settle</u>, decide, determine

cling 1 = <u>clutch</u>, grip, embrace, grasp, hug, hold on to, clasp 2 = <u>stick to</u>, adhere to

clinical = <u>unemotional</u>, cold, scientific, objective, detached, analytic, impersonal, dispassionate

clip¹ VERB 1 = <u>trim</u>, cut, crop, prune, shorten, shear, snip, pare 2 (*Informal*) = <u>smack</u>, strike, knock, punch, thump, clout (*informal*), cuff, whack

● NOUN (*Informal*) = <u>smack</u>, strike, knock, punch, thump, clout (*informal*), cuff, whack

clip² = <u>attach</u>, fix, secure, connect, pin, staple, fasten, hold

cloak NOUN 1 = <u>cape</u>, coat, wrap, mantle 2 = <u>covering</u>, layer, blanket, shroud

● VERB 1 = <u>cover</u>, coat, wrap, blanket, shroud, envelop 2 = <u>hide</u>, cover, screen, mask, disguise, conceal, obscure, veil

clog = <u>obstruct</u>, block, jam, hinder, impede, congest

close¹ VERB 1 = <u>shut</u>, lock, fasten, secure ≠ open 2 = <u>shut down</u>, finish, cease 3 = <u>wind up</u>, shut down, terminate 4 = <u>block up</u>, bar, seal ≠ open 5 = <u>end</u>, finish, complete, conclude, wind up, terminate ≠ begin 6 = <u>clinch</u>, confirm, secure, conclude, seal,

sew up (*informal*), set the seal on 7 = <u>come together</u>, join, connect ≠ separate

● NOUN = <u>end</u>, ending, finish, conclusion, finale, culmination, denouement

close² 1 = <u>near</u>, neighbouring, nearby, handy, adjacent, adjoining, cheek by jowl ≠ far 2 = <u>intimate</u>, loving, familiar, thick (*informal*), attached, devoted, confidential, inseparable ≠ distant 3 = <u>noticeable</u>, marked, strong, distinct, pronounced 4 = <u>careful</u>, detailed, intense, minute, thorough, rigorous, painstaking 5 = <u>even</u>, level, neck and neck, fifty-fifty (*informal*), evenly matched 6 = <u>imminent</u>, near, impending, at hand, nigh ≠ far away 7 = <u>stifling</u>, oppressive, suffocating, stuffy, humid, sweltering, airless, muggy ≠ airy

closed 1 = <u>shut</u>, locked, sealed, fastened ≠ open 2 = <u>shut down</u>, out of service 3 = <u>exclusive</u>, select, restricted 4 = <u>finished</u>, over, ended, decided, settled, concluded, resolved, terminated

cloth = <u>fabric</u>, material, textiles

clothe = <u>dress</u>, array, robe, drape, swathe, attire, fit out, garb ≠ undress

clothes = <u>clothing</u>, wear, dress, gear (*informal*), outfit, costume, wardrobe, garments

clothing = <u>clothes</u>, wear, dress,

gear (*informal*), outfit, costume, wardrobe, garments

cloud NOUN = <u>mist</u>, haze, vapour, murk, gloom

● VERB 1 = <u>confuse</u>, distort, impair, muddle, disorient 2 = <u>darken</u>, dim, be overshadowed

clout (*Informal*) VERB = <u>hit</u>, strike, punch, slap, sock (*slang*), smack, thump, clobber (*slang*)

● NOUN 1 = <u>thump</u>, blow, punch, slap, sock (*slang*), wallop (*informal*) 2 = <u>influence</u>, power, authority, pull, weight, prestige, mana (*N.Z.*)

clown NOUN 1 = <u>comedian</u>, fool, comic, harlequin, joker, jester, prankster, buffoon 2 = <u>fool</u>, idiot, twit (*informal, chiefly Brit.*), imbecile (*informal*), ignoramus, dolt, blockhead, dorba or dorb (*Austral. slang*), bogan (*Austral. slang*)

● VERB *usually with* **around** = <u>play the fool</u>, mess about, jest, act the fool

club NOUN 1 = <u>association</u>, company, group, union, society, lodge, guild, fraternity 2 = <u>stick</u>, bat, bludgeon, truncheon, cosh (*Brit.*), cudgel

● VERB = <u>beat</u>, strike, hammer, batter, bash, bludgeon, pummel, cosh (*Brit.*)

clue NOUN = <u>indication</u>, lead, sign, evidence, suggestion, trace, hint, suspicion

clump NOUN = <u>cluster</u>, group, bunch, bundle

● VERB = <u>stomp</u>, thump, lumber, tramp, thud

clumsy = <u>awkward</u>, lumbering, bumbling, ponderous, ungainly, gauche, gawky, uncoordinated, unco (*Austral. slang*) ≠ skilful

cluster NOUN = <u>gathering</u>, group, collection, bunch, knot, clump, assemblage

● VERB = <u>gather</u>, group, collect, bunch, assemble, flock, huddle

clutch VERB 1 = <u>hold</u>, grip, embrace, grasp, cling to, clasp 2 = <u>seize</u>, catch, grab, grasp, snatch

● PLURAL NOUN = <u>power</u>, hands, control, grip, possession, grasp, custody, sway

clutter NOUN = <u>untidiness</u>, mess, disorder, confusion, litter, muddle, disarray, jumble ≠ order

● VERB = <u>litter</u>, scatter, strew, mess up ≠ tidy

coach NOUN 1 = <u>instructor</u>, teacher, trainer, tutor, handler 2 = <u>bus</u>, charabanc

● VERB = <u>instruct</u>, train, prepare, exercise, drill, tutor

coalition = <u>alliance</u>, union, association, combination, merger, conjunction, bloc, confederation

coarse 1 = <u>rough</u>, crude, unfinished, homespun, impure, unrefined, unprocessed, unpolished ≠ smooth 2 = <u>vulgar</u>, rude, indecent, improper, earthy, smutty, ribald, indelicate

coast NOUN = <u>shore</u>, border, beach, seaside, coastline, seaboard

• VERB = <u>cruise</u>, sail, drift, taxi, glide, freewheel

coat NOUN 1 = <u>fur</u>, hair, skin, hide, wool, fleece, pelt 2 = <u>layer</u>, covering, coating, overlay

• VERB = <u>cover</u>, spread, plaster, smear

coax = <u>persuade</u>, cajole, talk into, wheedle, sweet-talk (*informal*), prevail upon, entice, allure ≠ bully

cobber (*Austral. & N.Z. old-fashioned informal*) = <u>friend</u>, pal, mate (*informal*), buddy (*informal*), china (*Brit. & S. African informal*), best friend, intimate, comrade, E hoa (*N.Z.*)

cocktail = <u>mixture</u>, combination, compound, blend, mix

cocky or **cockie** (*Austral. & N.Z. informal*) = <u>farmer</u>, smallholder, crofter (*Scot.*), grazier, agriculturalist, rancher

code 1 = <u>principles</u>, rules, manners, custom, convention, ethics, maxim, etiquette, kawa (*N.Z.*), tikanga (*N.Z.*) 2 = <u>cipher</u>, cryptograph

coherent 1 = <u>consistent</u>, reasoned, organized, rational, logical, meaningful, systematic, orderly ≠ inconsistent

2 = <u>articulate</u>, lucid, comprehensible, intelligible ≠ unintelligible

coil 1 = <u>wind</u>, twist, curl, loop, spiral, twine 2 = <u>curl</u>, wind, twist, snake, loop, twine, wreathe

coin NOUN = <u>money</u>, change, cash, silver, copper, specie

• VERB = <u>invent</u>, create, make up, forge, originate, fabricate

coincide 1 = <u>occur simultaneously</u>, coexist, synchronize, be concurrent 2 = <u>agree</u>, match, accord, square, correspond, tally, concur, harmonize ≠ disagree

coincidence = <u>chance</u>, accident, luck, fluke, stroke of luck, happy accident

cold ADJECTIVE 1 = <u>chilly</u>, freezing, bleak, arctic, icy, frosty, wintry, frigid ≠ hot 2 = <u>distant</u>, reserved, indifferent, aloof, frigid, undemonstrative, standoffish ≠ emotional 3 = <u>unfriendly</u>, indifferent, frigid ≠ friendly

• NOUN = <u>coldness</u>, chill, frigidity, frostiness, iciness

collaborate 1 = <u>work together</u>, team up, join forces, cooperate, play ball (*informal*), participate 2 = <u>conspire</u>, cooperate, collude, fraternize

collaboration 1 = <u>teamwork</u>, partnership, cooperation, association, alliance 2 = <u>conspiring</u>, cooperation, collusion, fraternization

collaborator 1 = <u>co-worker</u>, partner, colleague, associate, team-mate, confederate 2 = <u>traitor</u>, turncoat, quisling, fraternizer

collapse VERB 1 = <u>fall down</u>, fall, give way, subside, cave in, crumple, fall apart at the seams 2 = <u>fail</u>, fold, founder, break down, fall through, come to nothing, go belly-up (*informal*)
● NOUN 1 = <u>falling down</u>, ruin, falling apart, cave-in, disintegration, subsidence 2 = <u>failure</u>, slump, breakdown, flop, downfall 3 = <u>faint</u>, breakdown, blackout, prostration

collar (*Informal*) = <u>seize</u>, catch, arrest, grab, capture, nail (*informal*), nab (*informal*), apprehend

colleague = <u>fellow worker</u>, partner, ally, associate, assistant, team-mate, comrade, helper

collect 1 = <u>gather</u>, save, assemble, heap, accumulate, amass, stockpile, hoard ≠ scatter 2 = <u>assemble</u>, meet, rally, cluster, come together, convene, converge, congregate ≠ disperse

collected = <u>calm</u>, cool, composed, poised, serene, unperturbed, unruffled, self-possessed ≠ nervous

collection 1 = <u>accumulation</u>,

set, store, mass, pile, heap, stockpile, hoard 2 = <u>compilation</u>, accumulation, anthology 3 = <u>group</u>, company, crowd, assembly, cluster, assortment 4 = <u>gathering</u> 5 = <u>contribution</u>, donation, alms 6 = <u>offering</u>, offertory

collective 1 = <u>joint</u>, united, shared, combined, corporate, unified ≠ individual 2 = <u>combined</u>, aggregate, composite, cumulative ≠ separate

collide 1 = <u>crash</u>, clash, meet head-on, come into collision 2 = <u>conflict</u>, clash, be incompatible, be at variance

collision 1 = <u>crash</u>, impact, accident, smash, bump, pile-up (*informal*), prang (*informal*) 2 = <u>conflict</u>, opposition, clash, encounter, disagreement, incompatibility

colony = <u>settlement</u>, territory, province, possession, dependency, outpost, dominion, satellite state

colour or (*U.S.*) **color** NOUN 1 = <u>hue</u>, tone, shade, tint, colourway 2 = <u>paint</u>, stain, dye, tint, pigment, colorant
● VERB = <u>blush</u>, flush, redden
▸ **shades from black to white** ▸ **shades of blue** ▸ **shades of brown** ▸ **shades of green** ▸ **shades of**

orange ▸ shades of purple ▸ shades of red ▸ shades of yellow

colourful 1 = <u>bright</u>, brilliant, psychedelic, variegated, multicoloured ≠ drab **2** = <u>interesting</u>, rich, graphic, lively, distinctive, vivid, picturesque ≠ boring

column 1 = <u>pillar</u>, support, post, shaft, upright, obelisk **2** = <u>line</u>, row, file, rank, procession, cavalcade

coma = <u>unconsciousness</u>, trance, oblivion, stupor

comb 1 = <u>untangle</u>, arrange, groom, dress **2** = <u>search</u>, hunt through, rake, sift, scour, rummage, ransack, forage, fossick (Austral. & N.Z.)

combat NOUN = <u>fight</u>, war, action, battle, conflict, engagement, warfare, skirmish ≠ peace

● **VERB** = <u>fight</u>, oppose, resist, defy, withstand, do battle with ≠ support

combination 1 = <u>mixture</u>, mix, blend, composite, amalgamation, coalescence **2** = <u>association</u>, union, alliance, coalition, federation, consortium, syndicate, confederation

combine 1 = <u>amalgamate</u>, mix, blend, integrate, merge ≠ separate **2** = <u>join together</u>, link, connect, integrate, merge,

amalgamate **3** = <u>unite</u>, associate, team up, get together, collaborate, join forces, join together, pool resources ≠ split up

come VERB 1 = <u>approach</u>, near, advance, move towards, draw near **2** = <u>arrive</u>, turn up (informal), show up (informal) **3** = <u>reach</u>, extend, come up to, come as far as **4** = <u>happen</u>, fall, occur, take place, come about, come to pass **5** = <u>be available</u>, be made, be offered, be produced, be on offer

● **PHRASES come across something** or **someone** = <u>seem</u>, look, seem to be, appear to be, give the impression of being ◆ **come across someone** = <u>meet</u>, encounter, run into, bump into (informal) ◆ **come across something** = <u>find</u>, discover, notice, unearth, stumble upon, chance upon = <u>be obtained</u>, be from, issue, emerge, flow, arise, originate, emanate

comeback 1 (Informal) = <u>return</u>, revival, rebound, resurgence, rally, recovery, triumph **2** = <u>response</u>, reply, retort, retaliation, riposte, rejoinder

comedian = <u>comic</u>, wit, clown, funny man, humorist, wag, joker, jester, dag (N.Z. informal)

comedy 1 = <u>light entertainment</u>

≠ tragedy, soapie (*Austral.* slang)
2 = <u>humour</u>, fun, joking, farce, jesting, hilarity ≠ seriousness

comfort NOUN 1 = <u>ease</u>, luxury, wellbeing, opulence
2 = <u>consolation</u>, succour, help, support, relief, compensation ≠ annoyance
● VERB = <u>console</u>, reassure, soothe, hearten, commiserate with ≠ distress

comfortable 1 = <u>pleasant</u>, homely, relaxing, cosy, agreeable, restful ≠ unpleasant 2 = <u>at ease</u>, happy, at home, contented, relaxed, serene ≠ uncomfortable
3 (*Informal*) = <u>well-off</u>, prosperous, affluent, well-to-do, comfortably-off, in clover (*informal*)

comforting = <u>consoling</u>, encouraging, cheering, reassuring, soothing, heart-warming ≠ upsetting

comic ADJECTIVE = <u>funny</u>, amusing, witty, humorous, farcical, comical, droll, jocular ≠ sad
● NOUN = <u>comedian</u>, funny man, humorist, wit, clown, wag, jester, dag (*N.Z. informal*), buffoon

coming ADJECTIVE
= <u>approaching</u>, near, forthcoming, imminent, in store, impending, at hand, nigh
● NOUN = <u>arrival</u>, approach, advent

command VERB 1 = <u>order</u>, tell, charge, demand, require, direct, bid, compel ≠ beg 2 = <u>have authority over</u>, lead, head, control, rule, manage, handle, dominate ≠ be subordinate to
● NOUN = <u>order</u>, demand, instruction, requirement, decree, directive, ultimatum, commandment 2 = <u>domination</u>, control, rule, mastery, power, government 3 = <u>management</u>, power, control, charge, authority, supervision

commander = <u>leader</u>, chief, officer, boss, head, captain, bass (*S. African*), ruler

commanding = <u>dominant</u>, controlling, dominating, superior, decisive, advantageous

commemorate = <u>celebrate</u>, remember, honour, recognize, salute, pay tribute to, immortalize ≠ ignore

commence 1 = <u>embark on</u>, start, open, begin, initiate, originate, instigate, enter upon ≠ stop 2 = <u>start</u>, open, begin, go ahead ≠ end

commend 1 = <u>praise</u>, acclaim, applaud, compliment, extol, approve, speak highly of ≠ criticize 2 = <u>recommend</u>, suggest, approve, advocate, endorse

comment VERB 1 = <u>remark</u>, say, note, mention, point out, observe,

utter 2 *usually with* **on** = <u>remark on</u>, explain, talk about, discuss, speak about, say something about, allude to, elucidate
● NOUN 1 = <u>remark</u>, statement, observation 2 = <u>note</u>, explanation, illustration, commentary, exposition, annotation, elucidation

commentary 1 = <u>narration</u>, report, review, explanation, description, voice-over 2 = <u>analysis</u>, notes, review, critique, treatise

commentator 1 = <u>reporter</u>, special correspondent, sportscaster 2 = <u>critic</u>, interpreter, annotator

commercial 1 = <u>mercantile</u>, trading 2 = <u>materialistic</u>, mercenary, profit-making

commission VERB = <u>appoint</u>, order, contract, select, engage, delegate, nominate, authorize
● NOUN 1 = <u>duty</u>, task, mission, mandate, errand 2 = <u>fee</u>, cut, percentage, royalties, rake-off (*slang*) 3 = <u>committee</u>, board, representatives, commissioners, delegation, deputation

commit 1 = <u>do</u>, perform, carry out, execute, enact, perpetrate 2 = <u>put in custody</u>, confine, imprison ≠ release

commitment 1 = <u>dedication</u>, loyalty, devotion ≠ indecisiveness

2 = <u>responsibility</u>, tie, duty, obligation, liability, engagement

common 1 = <u>usual</u>, standard, regular, ordinary, familiar, conventional, routine, frequent ≠ rare 2 = <u>popular</u>, general, accepted, standard, routine, widespread, universal, prevailing 3 = <u>shared</u>, collective 4 = <u>ordinary</u>, average, typical, dinki-di (*Austral. informal*) ≠ important 5 = <u>vulgar</u>, inferior, coarse, plebeian ≠ refined 6 = <u>collective</u>, public, community, social, communal ≠ personal

commonplace ADJECTIVE = <u>everyday</u>, common, ordinary, widespread, mundane, banal, run-of-the-mill, humdrum ≠ rare
● NOUN = <u>cliché</u>, platitude, banality, truism

common sense = <u>good sense</u>, sound judgment, level-headedness, prudence, gumption (*Brit. informal*), horse sense, native intelligence, wit

communal = <u>public</u>, shared, general, joint, collective ≠ private

commune = <u>community</u>, collective, cooperative, kibbutz

communicate 1 = <u>contact</u>, talk, speak, make contact, get in contact 2 = <u>make known</u>, declare, disclose, pass on, proclaim, transmit, convey, impart ≠ keep secret 3 = <u>pass on</u>, transfer, spread, transmit

communication 1 = <u>contact</u>, conversation, correspondence, link, relations 2 = <u>passing on</u>, circulation, transmission, disclosure, imparting, dissemination, conveyance 3 = <u>message</u>, news, report, word, information, statement, announcement, disclosure

communism *usually cap.* = <u>socialism</u>, Marxism, collectivism, Bolshevism, state socialism

communist *often cap.* = <u>socialist</u>, Red (*informal*), Marxist, Bolshevik, collectivist

community = <u>society</u>, people, public, residents, commonwealth, general public, populace, state

commuter = <u>daily traveller</u>, passenger, suburbanite

compact[1] ADJECTIVE 1 = <u>closely packed</u>, solid, thick, dense, compressed, condensed, pressed together ≠ loose 2 = <u>concise</u>, brief, to the point, succinct, terse ≠ lengthy

● VERB = <u>pack closely</u>, stuff, cram, compress, condense, tamp ≠ loosen

compact[2] = <u>agreement</u>, deal, understanding, contract, bond, arrangement, treaty, bargain

companion 1 = <u>friend</u>, partner, ally, colleague, associate, mate (*informal*), comrade, accomplice, cobber (*Austral. & N.Z. old-fashioned informal*) 2 = <u>assistant</u>, aide, escort, attendant

company 1 = <u>business</u>, firm, association, corporation, partnership, establishment, syndicate, house 2 = <u>group</u>, set, community, band, crowd, collection, gathering, assembly 3 = <u>troop</u>, unit, squad, team 4 = <u>companionship</u>, society, presence, fellowship 5 = <u>guests</u>, party, visitors, callers

comparable 1 = <u>equal</u>, equivalent, on a par, tantamount, a match for, proportionate, commensurate, as good as ≠ unequal 2 = <u>similar</u>, related, alike, corresponding, akin, analogous, of a piece, cognate

comparative = <u>relative</u>, qualified, by comparison

compare VERB = <u>contrast</u>, balance, weigh, set against, juxtapose

● PHRASES **compare to something** = <u>liken to</u>, parallel, identify with, equate to, correlate to, mention in the same breath as ◆ **compare with something** = <u>be as good as</u>, match, approach, equal, compete with, be on a par with, be the equal of, hold a candle to

comparison 1 = <u>contrast</u>, distinction, differentiation, juxtaposition 2 = <u>similarity</u>, analogy, resemblance, correlation, likeness, comparability

compartment 1 = <u>section</u>, carriage, berth 2 = <u>bay</u>, booth, locker, niche, cubicle, alcove, pigeonhole, cubbyhole

compass = <u>range</u>, field, area, reach, scope, limit, extent, boundary

compassion = <u>sympathy</u>, understanding, pity, humanity, mercy, sorrow, kindness, tenderness, aroha (*N.Z.*) ≠ indifference

compassionate = <u>sympathetic</u>, understanding, pitying, humanitarian, charitable, humane, benevolent, merciful ≠ uncaring

compatible 1 = <u>consistent</u>, in keeping, congruous ≠ inappropriate 2 = <u>like-minded</u>, harmonious, in harmony ≠ incompatible

compel = <u>force</u>, make, railroad (*informal*), oblige, constrain, coerce, impel, dragoon

compelling 1 = <u>convincing</u>, telling, powerful, forceful, conclusive, weighty, cogent, irrefutable 2 = <u>pressing</u>, binding, urgent, overriding, imperative,

unavoidable, coercive, peremptory 3 = <u>fascinating</u>, gripping, irresistible, enchanting, enthralling, hypnotic, spellbinding, mesmeric ≠ boring

compensate 1 = <u>recompense</u>, repay, refund, reimburse, remunerate, make good 2 = <u>make amends</u>, make up for, atone, make it up to someone, pay for, do penance, cancel out, make reparation 3 = <u>balance</u>, cancel (out), offset, make up for, redress, counteract, counterbalance

compensation 1 = <u>reparation</u>, damages, recompense, remuneration, restitution, reimbursement 2 = <u>recompense</u>, amends, reparation, restitution, atonement

compete 1 = <u>contend</u>, fight, vie, challenge, struggle, contest, strive 2 = <u>take part</u>, participate, be in the running, be a competitor, be a contestant, be a play

competence 1 = <u>ability</u>, skill, talent, capacity, expertise, proficiency, capability ≠ incompetence 2 = <u>fitness</u>, suitability, adequacy, appropriateness ≠ inadequacy

competent 1 = <u>able</u>, skilled, capable, proficient ≠ incompetent 2 = <u>fit</u>, qualified, suitable, adequate

≠ unqualified

competition 1 = rivalry, opposition, struggle, strife 2 = opposition, field, rivals, challengers 3 = contest, event, championship, tournament, head-to-head

competitive 1 = cut-throat, aggressive, fierce, ruthless, relentless, antagonistic, dog-eat-dog 2 = ambitious, pushing, opposing, aggressive, vying, contentious, combative

competitor 1 = rival, adversary, antagonist 2 = contestant, participant, contender, challenger, entrant, player, opponent

compilation = collection, treasury, accumulation, anthology, assortment, assemblage

compile = put together, collect, gather, organize, accumulate, marshal, garner, amass

complacency = smugness, satisfaction, contentment, self-congratulation, self-satisfaction

complacent = smug, self-satisfied, pleased with yourself, resting on your laurels, contented, satisfied, serene, unconcerned ≠ insecure

complain = find fault, moan, grumble, whinge (*informal*), carp, groan, lament, whine

complaint 1 = protest, objection, grievance, charge 2 = grumble, criticism, moan, lament, grievance, grouse, gripe (*informal*) 3 = disorder, problem, disease, upset, illness, sickness, ailment, affliction

complement VERB = enhance, complete, improve, boost, crown, add to, set off, heighten
● NOUN 1 = accompaniment, companion, accessory, completion, finishing touch, rounding-off, adjunct, supplement 2 = total, capacity, quota, aggregate, contingent, entirety

> ### Word Power
>
> **complement** – This is sometimes confused with *compliment* but the two words have very different meanings. As the synonyms show, the verb form of *complement* means 'to enhance' and 'to complete' something. In contrast, common synonyms of *compliment* as a verb are *praise*, *commend*, and *flatter*.

complementary = matching, companion, corresponding, compatible, reciprocal, interrelating, interdependent, harmonizing, ≠ incompatible

complete ADJECTIVE 1 = total,

perfect, absolute, utter, outright, thorough, consummate, out-and-out **2** = <u>whole</u>, full, entire ≠ partial **3** = <u>entire</u>, full, whole, intact, unbroken, faultless ≠ incomplete **4** = <u>unabridged</u>, full, entire **5** = <u>finished</u>, done, ended, achieved, concluded, fulfilled, accomplished ≠ unfinished **6** = <u>perfect</u>, finish off, round off, crown ≠ spoil

● **VERB 1** = <u>finish</u>, conclude, end, close, settle, wrap up (*informal*), finalize ≠ start **2** = <u>fill in</u>, fill out

completely = <u>totally</u>, entirely, wholly, utterly, perfectly, fully, absolutely, altogether

completion = <u>finishing</u>, end, close, conclusion, fulfilment, culmination, fruition

complex ADJECTIVE
1 = <u>compound</u>, multiple, composite, manifold, heterogeneous, multifarious
2 = <u>complicated</u>, difficult, involved, elaborate, tangled, intricate, tortuous, convoluted ≠ simple

● **NOUN 1** = <u>structure</u>, system, scheme, network, organization, aggregate, composite
2 (*Informal*) = <u>obsession</u>, preoccupation, phobia, fixation, fixed idea, idée fixe (*French*)

> ### Word Power
>
> **complex** – Although *complex* and *complicated* are close in meaning, care should be taken when using one as a synonym of the other. *Complex* should be used to say that something consists of several parts rather than that it is difficult to understand, analyse, or deal with, which is what *complicated* inherently means. In the following real example a clear distinction is made between the two words: *the British benefits system is phenomenally complex and is administered by a complicated range of agencies*.

complexion 1 = <u>skin</u>, colour, colouring, hue, skin tone, pigmentation **2** = <u>nature</u>, character, make-up
3 = <u>perspective</u>, look, light, appearance, aspect, angle, slant

complexity = <u>complication</u>, involvement, intricacy, entanglement

complicate = <u>make difficult</u>, confuse, muddle, entangle, involve ≠ simplify

complicated 1 = <u>involved</u>, difficult, puzzling, troublesome, problematic, perplexing ≠ simple
2 = <u>complex</u>, involved, elaborate, intricate, convoluted, labyrinthine ≠ understandable

complication 1 = problem, difficulty, obstacle, drawback, snag, uphill (*S. African*) 2 = complexity, web, confusion, intricacy, entanglement

compliment NOUN = praise, honour, tribute, bouquet, flattery, eulogy ≠ criticism

● PLURAL NOUN 1 = greetings, regards, respects, good wishes, salutation ≠ insult

2 = congratulations, praise, commendation

● VERB = praise, flatter, salute, congratulate, pay tribute to, commend, extol, wax lyrical about ≠ criticize

> ### Word Power
>
> **compliment** – *Compliment* is sometimes confused with complement.

complimentary 1 = flattering, approving, appreciative, congratulatory, commendatory ≠ critical 2 = free, donated, courtesy, honorary, on the house, gratuitous, gratis

comply = obey, follow, observe, submit to, conform to, adhere to, abide by, acquiesce with ≠ defy

component NOUN = part, piece, unit, item, element, ingredient, constituent

● ADJECTIVE = constituent, inherent, intrinsic

compose VERB 1 = put together, make up, constitute, comprise, make, build, form, fashion ≠ destroy 2 = create, write, produce, invent, devise, contrive 3 = arrange, make up, construct, put together, order, organize

● PHRASES **compose yourself** = calm, control, collect, quiet, soothe, pull yourself together

composed = calm, cool, collected, relaxed, poised, at ease, serene, sedate ≠ agitated

composition 1 = design, structure, make-up, organization, arrangement, formation, layout, configuration 2 = creation, work, piece, production, opus, masterpiece 3 = essay, exercise, treatise, literary work 4 = production, creation, making, fashioning, formation, putting together, compilation, formulation

compound NOUN = combination, mixture, blend, composite, fusion, synthesis, alloy, medley ≠ element

● ADJECTIVE = complex, multiple, composite, intricate ≠ simple

● VERB 1 = intensify, add to, complicate, worsen, heighten, exacerbate, aggravate, magnify ≠ lessen 2 = combine, unite, mix, blend, synthesize, amalgamate, intermingle ≠ divide

comprehend = understand,

see, take in, perceive, grasp,
conceive, make out, fathom
≠ misunderstand

comprehension
= understanding, grasp,
conception, realization,
intelligence, perception,
discernment ≠ incomprehension

comprehensive = broad, full,
complete, blanket, thorough,
inclusive, exhaustive, all-inclusive
≠ limited

compress 1 = squeeze, crush,
squash, press 2 = condense,
contract, concentrate, shorten,
abbreviate

comprise 1 = be composed of,
include, contain, consist of, take
in, embrace, encompass 2 = make
up, form, constitute, compose

Word Power

comprise – The use of *of* after
comprise should be avoided: *the
library comprises* (not *comprises
of*) *6,500,000 books and
manuscripts. Consist,* however,
should be followed by *of* when
used in this way: *Her crew
consisted of children from Devon
and Cornwall.*

---

compromise NOUN = give-and-
take, agreement, settlement,
accommodation, concession,
adjustment, trade-off
≠ disagreement

● VERB 1 = meet halfway, concede,

make concessions, give and take,
strike a balance, strike a happy
medium, go fifty-fifty (*informal*)
≠ disagree 2 = undermine,
expose, embarrass, weaken,
prejudice, discredit, jeopardize,
dishonour ≠ support

compulsive 1 = obsessive,
confirmed, chronic, persistent,
addictive, uncontrollable,
incurable, inveterate
2 = fascinating, gripping,
absorbing, compelling,
captivating, enthralling, hypnotic,
engrossing 3 = irresistible,
overwhelming, compelling,
urgent, neurotic, uncontrollable,
driving

compulsory = obligatory,
forced, required, binding,
mandatory, imperative, requisite,
de rigueur (*French*) ≠ voluntary

compute = calculate, total,
count, reckon, figure out, add up,
tally, enumerate

comrade = companion, friend,
partner, ally, colleague, associate,
fellow, co-worker, cobber (*Austral.
& N.Z. old-fashioned informal*)

con (*Informal*) VERB = swindle,
trick, cheat, rip off (*slang*),
deceive, defraud, dupe, hoodwink
● NOUN = swindle, trick, fraud,
deception, scam (*slang*), sting
(*informal*)

conceal 1 = hide, bury, cover,
screen, disguise, obscure,

camouflage ≠ reveal 2 = keep secret, hide, disguise, mask, suppress, veil ≠ show

concede 1 = admit, allow, accept, acknowledge, own, grant, confess ≠ deny 2 = give up, yield, hand over, surrender, relinquish, cede ≠ conquer

conceive 1 = imagine, envisage, comprehend, visualize, think, believe, suppose, fancy 2 = think up, create, design, devise, formulate, contrive 3 = become pregnant, get pregnant, become impregnated

concentrate 1 = focus your attention on, focus on, pay attention to, be engrossed in, put your mind to, keep your mind on, apply yourself to, give your mind to ≠ pay no attention to 2 = focus, centre, converge, bring to bear 3 = gather, collect, cluster, accumulate, congregate ≠ scatter

concentrated 1 = condensed, rich, undiluted, reduced, evaporated, thickened, boiled down 2 = intense, hard, deep, intensive, all-out (*informal*)

concentration 1 = attention, application, absorption, single-mindedness, intentness ≠ inattention 2 = focusing, centring, consolidation, convergence, bringing to bear, intensification, centralization 3 = convergence, collection,

mass, cluster, accumulation, aggregation ≠ scattering

concept = idea, view, image, theory, notion, conception, hypothesis, abstraction

conception 1 = idea, plan, design, image, concept, notion 2 = impregnation, insemination, fertilization, germination

concern NOUN 1 = anxiety, fear, worry, distress, unease, apprehension, misgiving, disquiet 2 = worry, care, anxiety 3 = affair, issue, matter, consideration 4 = care, interest, attentiveness 5 = business, job, affair, responsibility, task 6 = company, business, firm, organization, corporation, enterprise, establishment 7 = importance, interest, bearing, relevance

● VERB 1 = worry, trouble, bother, disturb, distress, disquiet, perturb, make anxious 2 = be about, cover, deal with, go into, relate to, have to do with 3 = be relevant to, involve, affect, regard, apply to, bear on, have something to do with, pertain to

concerned 1 = worried, troubled, upset, bothered, disturbed, anxious, distressed, uneasy ≠ indifferent 2 = involved, interested, active, mixed up, implicated, privy to

concerning = regarding, about, re, touching, respecting, relating

to, on the subject of, with
reference to

concession 1 = <u>compromise</u>,
agreement, settlement,
accommodation, adjustment,
trade-off, give-and-take
2 = <u>privilege</u>, right, permit,
licence, entitlement, indulgence,
prerogative **3** = <u>reduction</u>, saving,
grant, discount, allowance
4 = <u>surrender</u>, yielding,
conceding, renunciation,
relinquishment

conclude 1 = <u>decide</u>, judge,
assume, gather, work out, infer,
deduce, surmise **2** = <u>come to an
end</u>, end, close, finish, wind up
≠ begin **3** = <u>bring to an end</u>, end,
close, finish, complete, wind up,
terminate, round off ≠ begin
4 = <u>accomplish</u>, effect, bring
about, carry out, pull off

conclusion 1 = <u>decision</u>,
opinion, conviction, verdict,
judgment, deduction, inference
2 = <u>end</u>, ending, close, finish,
completion, finale, termination,
bitter end **3** = <u>outcome</u>, result,
upshot, consequence,
culmination, end result

concrete 1 = <u>specific</u>, precise,
explicit, definite, clear-cut,
unequivocal ≠ vague **2** = <u>real</u>,
material, actual, substantial,
sensible, tangible, factual
≠ abstract

condemn 1 = <u>denounce</u>, damn,

criticize, disapprove, censure,
reprove, upbraid, blame
≠ approve **2** = <u>sentence</u>, convict,
damn, doom, pass sentence on
≠ acquit

condemnation
= <u>denunciation</u>, blame, censure,
disapproval, reproach, stricture,
reproof

condition NOUN **1** = <u>state</u>, order,
shape, nick (*Brit. informal*), trim
2 = <u>situation</u>, state, position,
status, circumstances
3 = <u>requirement</u>, terms, rider,
restriction, qualification,
limitation, prerequisite, proviso
4 = <u>health</u>, shape, fitness, trim,
form, kilter, state of health, fettle
5 = <u>ailment</u>, problem, complaint,
weakness, malady, infirmity
● PLURAL NOUN = <u>circumstances</u>,
situation, environment,
surroundings, way of life, milieu
● VERB = <u>train</u>, teach, adapt,
accustom

conditional = <u>dependent</u>,
limited, qualified, subject to,
contingent, provisional, with
reservations ≠ unconditional

condone = <u>overlook</u>, excuse,
forgive, pardon, turn a blind eye
to, look the other way, make
allowance for, let pass
≠ condemn

conduct VERB **1** = <u>carry out</u>, run,
control, manage, direct, handle,
organize, administer

2 = <u>accompany</u>, lead, escort, guide, steer, convey, usher

● NOUN 1 = <u>management</u>, running, control, handling, administration, direction, organization, guidance 2 = <u>behaviour</u>, ways, bearing, attitude, manners, demeanour, deportment

● PHRASES **conduct yourself** = <u>behave yourself</u>, act, carry yourself, acquit yourself, deport yourself, comport yourself

confer 1 = <u>discuss</u>, talk, consult, deliberate, discourse, converse 2 = <u>grant</u>, give, present, accord, award, hand out, bestow

conference = <u>meeting</u>, congress, discussion, convention, forum, consultation, seminar, symposium, hui (*N.Z.*)

confess 1 = <u>admit</u>, acknowledge, disclose, confide, own up, come clean (*informal*), divulge ≠ cover up 2 = <u>declare</u>, allow, reveal, confirm, concede, assert, affirm, profess

confession = <u>admission</u>, revelation, disclosure, acknowledgment, exposure, unbosoming

confidant *or* **confidante** = <u>close friend</u>, familiar, intimate, crony, alter ego, bosom friend

confide = <u>tell</u>, admit, reveal, confess, whisper, disclose, impart, divulge

confidence NOUN 1 = <u>trust</u>, belief, faith, dependence, reliance, credence ≠ <u>distrust</u> 2 = <u>self-assurance</u>, courage, assurance, aplomb, boldness, self-possession, nerve ≠ shyness 3 = <u>secret</u>

● PHRASES **in confidence** = <u>in secrecy</u>, privately, confidentially, between you and me (and the gatepost), (just) between ourselves

confident 1 = <u>certain</u>, sure, convinced, positive, secure, satisfied, counting on ≠ unsure 2 = <u>self-assured</u>, positive, assured, bold, self-confident, self-reliant, sure of yourself ≠ insecure

confidential 1 = <u>secret</u>, private, intimate, classified, privy, off the record, hush-hush (*informal*) 2 = <u>secretive</u>, low, soft, hushed

confine VERB 1 = <u>imprison</u>, enclose, shut up, intern, incarcerate, hem in, keep, cage 2 = <u>restrict</u>, limit

● PLURAL NOUN = <u>limits</u>, bounds, boundaries, compass, precincts, circumference, edge

confirm 1 = <u>prove</u>, support, establish, back up, verify, validate, bear out, substantiate 2 = <u>ratify</u>, establish, sanction, endorse, authorize 3 = <u>strengthen</u>, establish, fix, secure, reinforce, fortify

confirmation 1 = <u>proof</u>,

evidence, testimony, verification, ratification, validation, corroboration, authentication ≠ repudiation 2 = <u>affirmation</u>, approval, acceptance, endorsement, ratification, assent, agreement ≠ disapproval

confirmed = <u>long-established</u>, seasoned, chronic, hardened, habitual, ingrained, inveterate, dyed-in-the-wool

confiscate = <u>seize</u>, appropriate, impound, commandeer, sequester ≠ give back

conflict NOUN 1 = <u>dispute</u>, difference, opposition, hostility, disagreement, friction, strife, fighting ≠ agreement

2 = <u>struggle</u>, battle, clash, strife

3 = <u>battle</u>, war, fight, clash, contest, encounter, combat, strife ≠ peace

● VERB = be incompatible, clash, differ, disagree, collide, be at variance ≠ agree

conflicting = <u>incompatible</u>, opposing, clashing, contrary, contradictory, inconsistent, paradoxical, discordant ≠ agreeing

conform 1 = <u>fit in</u>, follow, adjust, adapt, comply, obey, fall in with, toe the line 2 = <u>fulfil</u>, meet, match, suit, satisfy, agree with, obey, abide by

confound = <u>bewilder</u>, baffle, confuse, astound, perplex,

mystify, flummox, dumbfound

confront 1 = <u>tackle</u>, deal with, cope with, meet head-on

2 = <u>trouble</u>, face, perturb, bedevil

3 = <u>challenge</u>, face, oppose, tackle, encounter, defy, stand up to, accost ≠ evade

confrontation = <u>conflict</u>, fight, contest, set-to (*informal*), encounter, showdown (*informal*), head-to-head

confuse 1 = <u>mix up with</u>, take for, muddle with 2 = <u>bewilder</u>, puzzle, baffle, perplex, mystify, fluster, faze, flummox

3 = <u>obscure</u>, cloud, make more difficult

confused 1 = <u>bewildered</u>, puzzled, baffled, at sea, muddled, perplexed, taken aback, disorientated ≠ enlightened

2 = <u>disorderly</u>, disordered, chaotic, mixed up, jumbled, untidy, in disarray, topsy-turvy ≠ tidy

confusing = <u>bewildering</u>, puzzling, misleading, unclear, baffling, contradictory, perplexing ≠ clear

confusion 1 = <u>bewilderment</u>, doubt, uncertainty ≠ enlightenment 2 = <u>disorder</u>, chaos, turmoil, upheaval, muddle, shambles, commotion ≠ order

congestion = <u>overcrowding</u>, crowding, jam, clogging, bottleneck

congratulate = compliment, pat on the back, wish joy to

congratulations PLURAL NOUN = <u>good wishes</u>, greetings, compliments, best wishes, felicitations

• INTERJECTION = <u>good wishes</u>, greetings, compliments, best wishes, felicitations

congregation = <u>parishioners</u>, brethren, crowd, assembly, flock, fellowship, multitude, throng

congress 1 = <u>meeting</u>, council, conference, assembly, convention, conclave, hui (*N.Z.*), runanga (*N.Z.*) **2** = <u>legislature</u>, council, parliament, House of Representatives (*N.Z.*)

conjure VERB = <u>produce</u>, generate, bring about, give rise to, make, create, effect, produce as if by magic

• PHRASES **conjure something up** = <u>bring to mind</u>, recall, evoke, recreate, recollect, produce as if by magic

connect 1 = <u>link</u>, join, couple, attach, fasten, affix, unite ≠ separate **2** = <u>associate</u>, join, link, identify, lump together

connected = <u>linked</u>, united, joined, coupled, related, allied, associated, combined

connection 1 = <u>association</u>, relationship, link, bond, relevance, tie-in **2** = <u>communication</u>, alliance, attachment, liaison, affinity, union **3** = <u>link</u>, coupling, junction, fastening, tie **4** = <u>contact</u>, friend, ally, associate, acquaintance

conquer 1 = <u>seize</u>, obtain, acquire, occupy, overrun, annex, win **2** = <u>defeat</u>, overcome, overthrow, beat, master, crush, overpower, quell ≠ lose to **3** = <u>overcome</u>, beat, defeat, master, overpower

conquest 1 = <u>takeover</u>, coup, invasion, occupation, annexation, subjugation **2** = <u>defeat</u>, victory, triumph, overthrow, rout, mastery

conscience 1 = <u>principles</u>, scruples, moral sense, sense of right and wrong, still small voice **2** = <u>guilt</u>, shame, regret, remorse, contrition, self-reproach

conscious 1 often with **of** = <u>aware of</u>, alert to, responsive to, sensible of ≠ unaware **2** = <u>deliberate</u>, knowing, studied, calculated, self-conscious, intentional, wilful, premeditated ≠ unintentional **3** = <u>awake</u>, wide-awake, sentient, alive ≠ asleep

consciousness = <u>awareness</u>, understanding, knowledge, recognition, sensibility, realization, apprehension

consecutive = <u>successive</u>, running, succeeding, in turn, uninterrupted, sequential, in sequence

consensus = <u>agreement</u>,

general agreement, unanimity, common consent, unity, harmony, assent, concord, kotahitanga (*N.Z.*)

> ### Word Power
>
> **consensus** – The original meaning of the word *consensus* is *a collective opinion*. Because the concept of 'opinion' is contained within this word, a few people argue that the phrase *a consensus of opinion* is incorrect and should be avoided. However, this common use of the word is unlikely to jar with the majority of speakers.

consent NOUN = <u>agreement</u>, sanction, approval, go-ahead (*informal*), permission, compliance, assent, acquiescence ≠ refusal

● VERB = <u>agree</u>, approve, permit, concur, assent, acquiesce ≠ refuse

consequence 1 = <u>result</u>, effect, outcome, repercussion, issue, sequel, end result, upshot **2** = <u>importance</u>, concern, moment, value, account, weight, import, significance

consequently = <u>as a result</u>, thus, therefore, hence, subsequently, accordingly, for that reason, thence

conservation 1 = <u>preservation</u>, saving, protection, maintenance, safeguarding, upkeep, guardianship, safekeeping **2** = <u>economy</u>, saving, thrift, husbandry

conservative ADJECTIVE = <u>traditional</u>, conventional, cautious, sober, reactionary, die-hard, hidebound ≠ radical

● NOUN = <u>traditionalist</u>, reactionary, die-hard, stick-in-the-mud (*informal*) ≠ radical

Conservative ADJECTIVE = <u>Tory</u>, Republican (*U.S.*), right-wing

● NOUN = <u>Tory</u>, Republican (*U.S.*), right-winger

conserve 1 = <u>save</u>, husband, take care of, hoard, store up, use sparingly ≠ waste **2** = <u>protect</u>, keep, save, preserve

consider 1 = <u>think</u>, see, believe, rate, judge, deem, view as **2** = <u>think about</u>, reflect on, weigh, contemplate, deliberate, ponder, meditate, ruminate **3** = <u>bear in mind</u>, remember, respect, think about, take into account, reckon with, take into consideration, make allowance for

considerable = <u>large</u>, goodly, great, marked, substantial, noticeable, plentiful, appreciable ≠ small

considerably = <u>greatly</u>, very much, significantly, remarkably, substantially, markedly, noticeably, appreciably

consideration 1 = <u>thought</u>,

review, analysis, examination, reflection, scrutiny, deliberation **2** = thoughtfulness, concern, respect, kindness, tact, considerateness **3** = factor, point, issue, concern, element, aspect **4** = payment, fee, reward, remuneration, recompense, tip

considering = taking into account, in the light of, bearing in mind, in view of, keeping in mind, taking into consideration

consist VERB
● PHRASES **consist in something** = lie in, involve, reside in, be expressed by, subsist in, be found or contained in
◆ **consist of something** = be made up of, include, contain, incorporate, amount to, comprise, be composed of

consistency 1 = agreement, regularity, uniformity, constancy, steadiness, steadfastness, evenness **2** = texture, density, thickness, firmness, viscosity, compactness

consistent 1 = steady, even, regular, stable, constant, persistent, dependable, unchanging ≠ erratic **2** = compatible, agreeing, in keeping, harmonious, in harmony, consonant, in accord, congruous ≠ incompatible **3** = coherent, logical, compatible, harmonious, consonant ≠ contradictory

consolation = comfort, help, support, relief, cheer, encouragement, solace, succour

console = comfort, cheer, soothe, support, encourage, calm, succour, express sympathy for ≠ distress

consolidate 1 = strengthen, secure, reinforce, fortify, stabilize **2** = combine, unite, join, merge, unify, amalgamate, federate

conspicuous = obvious, clear, patent, evident, noticeable, blatant, salient ≠ inconspicuous

conspiracy = plot, scheme, intrigue, collusion, machination

conspire 1 = plot, scheme, intrigue, manoeuvre, contrive, machinate, plan **2** = work together, combine, contribute, cooperate, concur, tend

constant 1 = continuous, sustained, perpetual, interminable, unrelenting, incessant, ceaseless, nonstop ≠ occasional **2** = unchanging, even, fixed, permanent, stable, steady, uniform, invariable ≠ changing **3** = faithful, true, devoted, loyal, stalwart, staunch, trustworthy, trusty ≠ undependable

constantly = continuously, always, all the time, invariably, continually, endlessly, perpetually, incessantly

≠ occasionally

constituent NOUN 1 = <u>voter</u>, elector, member of the electorate 2 = <u>component</u>, element, ingredient, part, unit, factor
• ADJECTIVE = <u>component</u>, basic, essential, integral, elemental

constitute 1 = <u>represent</u>, be, consist of, embody, exemplify, be equivalent to 2 = <u>make up</u>, form, compose, comprise

constitution 1 = <u>state of health</u>, build, body, frame, physique, physical condition 2 = <u>structure</u>, form, nature, make-up, composition, character, disposition

constitutional = <u>legitimate</u>, official, legal, chartered, statutory, vested

constrain 1 = <u>restrict</u>, confine, curb, restrain, constrict, straiten, check 2 = <u>force</u>, bind, compel, oblige, necessitate, coerce, impel, pressurize

constraint 1 = <u>restriction</u>, limitation, curb, rein, deterrent, hindrance, check 2 = <u>force</u>, pressure, necessity, restraint, compulsion, coercion

construct 1 = <u>build</u>, make, form, create, fashion, shape, manufacture, assemble ≠ demolish 2 = <u>create</u>, make, form, compose, put together

construction 1 = <u>building</u>, creation, composition 2 (*Formal*)

= <u>interpretation</u>, reading, explanation, rendering, inference

constructive = <u>helpful</u>, positive, useful, practical, valuable, productive ≠ unproductive

consult 1 = <u>ask</u>, refer to, turn to, take counsel, pick (someone's) brains, question 2 = <u>confer</u>, talk, compare notes 3 = <u>refer to</u>, check in, look in

consultant = <u>specialist</u>, adviser, counsellor, authority

consultation 1 = <u>discussion</u>, talk, council, conference, dialogue 2 = <u>meeting</u>, interview, session, appointment, examination, deliberation, hearing

consume 1 = <u>eat</u>, swallow, devour, put away, gobble (up), eat up 2 = <u>use up</u>, spend, waste, absorb, exhaust, squander, dissipate, expend 3 = <u>destroy</u>, devastate, demolish, ravage, annihilate, lay waste 4 *often passive* = <u>obsess</u>, dominate, absorb, preoccupy, eat up, monopolize, engross

consumer = <u>buyer</u>, customer, user, shopper, purchaser

consumption 1 = <u>using up</u>, use, loss, waste, expenditure, exhaustion, depletion, dissipation 2 (*Old-fashioned*) = <u>tuberculosis</u>, T.B.

contact NOUN 1 = <u>communication</u>, link,

association, connection, correspondence 2 = <u>touch</u>, contiguity 3 = <u>connection</u>, colleague, associate, liaison, acquaintance, confederate
● **VERB** = <u>get</u> *or* be in touch with, call, reach, approach, write to, speak to, communicate with

contain 1 = <u>hold</u>, incorporate, accommodate, enclose, have capacity for 2 = <u>include</u>, consist of, embrace, comprise, embody, comprehend 3 = <u>restrain</u>, control, hold in, curb, suppress, hold back, stifle, repress

container = <u>holder</u>, vessel, repository, receptacle

contaminate = <u>pollute</u>, infect, stain, corrupt, taint, defile, adulterate, befoul ≠ purify

contamination = <u>pollution</u>, infection, corruption, poisoning, taint, impurity, contagion, defilement

contemplate 1 = <u>consider</u>, plan, think of, intend, envisage, foresee 2 = <u>think about</u>, consider, ponder, reflect upon, ruminate (upon), muse over, deliberate over 3 = <u>look at</u>, examine, inspect, gaze at, eye up, view, study, regard

contemporary ADJECTIVE
1 = <u>modern</u>, recent, current, up-to-date, present-day, à la mode, newfangled, present ≠ old-fashioned 2 = <u>coexisting</u>,

concurrent, contemporaneous
● **NOUN** = <u>peer</u>, fellow, equal

> ### Word Power
> **contemporary** – Since *contemporary* can mean either 'of the same period' or 'of the present period', it is best to avoid it where ambiguity might arise, as in *a production of Othello in contemporary dress.* A synonym such as *modern* or *present-day* would clarify if the first sense were being used, while a specific term, such as *Elizabethan,* would be appropriate for the second sense.

contempt = <u>scorn</u>, disdain, mockery, derision, disrespect, disregard ≠ respect

contend 1 = <u>argue</u>, hold, maintain, allege, assert, affirm 2 = <u>compete</u>, fight, struggle, clash, contest, strive, vie, jostle

content¹ NOUN 1 = <u>subject matter</u>, material, theme, substance, essence, gist 2 = <u>amount</u>, measure, size, load, volume, capacity
● **PLURAL NOUN** = <u>constituents</u>, elements, load, ingredients

content² ADJECTIVE = <u>satisfied</u>, happy, pleased, contented, comfortable, fulfilled, at ease, gratified
● **NOUN** = <u>satisfaction</u>, ease,

pleasure, comfort, peace of mind, gratification, contentment

● PHRASES **content yourself with something** = <u>satisfy yourself with</u>, be happy with, be satisfied with, be content with

contented = <u>satisfied</u>, happy, pleased, content, comfortable, glad, thankful, gratified ≠ discontented

contentious = <u>argumentative</u>, wrangling, bickering, quarrelsome, querulous, cavilling, disputatious, captious

contest NOUN 1 = <u>competition</u>, game, match, trial, tournament 2 = <u>struggle</u>, fight, battle, conflict, dispute, controversy, combat
● VERB 1 = <u>compete in</u>, take part in, fight in, go in for, contend for, vie in 2 = <u>oppose</u>, question, challenge, argue, debate, dispute, object to, call in or into question

contestant = <u>competitor</u>, candidate, participant, contender, entrant, player

context 1 = <u>circumstances</u>, conditions, situation, ambience 2 = <u>frame of reference</u>, background, framework, relation, connection

contingency = <u>possibility</u>, happening, chance, event, incident, accident, emergency, eventuality

continual 1 = <u>constant</u>, interminable, incessant,

unremitting ≠ erratic
2 = <u>frequent</u>, regular, repeated, recurrent ≠ occasional

continually 1 = <u>constantly</u>, always, all the time, forever, incessantly, nonstop, interminably 2 = <u>repeatedly</u>, often, frequently, many times, over and over, persistently

continuation 1 = <u>continuing</u>, lasting, carrying on, keeping up, endurance, perpetuation, prolongation 2 = <u>addition</u>, extension, supplement, sequel, resumption, postscript

continue 1 = <u>keep on</u>, go on, maintain, sustain, carry on, persist in, persevere, stick at ≠ stop
2 = <u>go on</u>, progress, proceed, carry on, keep going 3 = <u>resume</u>, return to, take up again, proceed, carry on, recommence, pick up where you left off ≠ stop
4 = <u>remain</u>, last, stay, survive, carry on, live on, endure, persist ≠ quit

continuing = <u>lasting</u>, sustained, enduring, ongoing, in progress

continuity = <u>cohesion</u>, flow, connection, sequence, succession, progression

continuous = <u>constant</u>, extended, prolonged, unbroken, uninterrupted, unceasing ≠ occasional

contract NOUN = <u>agreement</u>, commitment, arrangement,

settlement, bargain, pact, covenant
● VERB 1 = <u>agree</u>, negotiate, pledge, bargain, undertake, come to terms, covenant, make a deal ≠ refuse 2 = <u>constrict</u>, confine, tighten, shorten, compress, condense, shrivel 3 = <u>tighten</u>, narrow, shorten ≠ stretch 4 = <u>lessen</u>, reduce, shrink, diminish, decrease, dwindle ≠ increase 5 = <u>catch</u>, get, develop, acquire, incur, be infected with, go down with, be afflicted with ≠ avoid

contraction 1 = <u>tightening</u>, narrowing, shortening, constricting, shrinkage 2 = <u>abbreviation</u>, reduction, shortening, compression

contradict 1 = <u>dispute</u>, deny, challenge, belie, fly in the face of, be at variance with 2 = <u>negate</u>, deny, rebut, controvert ≠ confirm

contradiction 1 = <u>conflict</u>, inconsistency, contravention, incongruity 2 = <u>negation</u>, opposite, denial

contradictory = <u>inconsistent</u>, conflicting, opposed, opposite, contrary, incompatible, paradoxical

contrary ADJECTIVE 1 = <u>opposite</u>, different, opposed, clashing, counter, reverse, adverse, contradictory ≠ in agreement 2 = <u>perverse</u>, difficult, awkward,

intractable, obstinate, stroppy (*Brit. slang*), cantankerous, disobliging ≠ cooperative
● NOUN = <u>opposite</u>, reverse, converse, antithesis

contrast NOUN = <u>difference</u>, opposition, comparison, distinction, foil, disparity, divergence, dissimilarity
● VERB 1 = <u>differentiate</u>, compare, oppose, distinguish, set in opposition 2 = <u>differ</u>, be contrary, be at variance, be dissimilar

contribute VERB = <u>give</u>, provide, supply, donate, subscribe, chip in (*informal*), bestow
● PHRASES **contribute to something** = <u>be partly responsible for</u>, lead to, be instrumental in, be conducive to, help

contribution = <u>gift</u>, offering, grant, donation, input, subscription, koha (*N.Z.*)

contributor = <u>donor</u>, supporter, patron, subscriber, giver

contrive 1 = <u>devise</u>, plan, fabricate, create, design, scheme, manufacture, plot 2 = <u>manage</u>, succeed, arrange, manoeuvre

contrived = <u>forced</u>, planned, laboured, belie, artificial, elaborate, unnatural, overdone ≠ natural

control NOUN 1 = <u>power</u>, authority, management, command, guidance, supervision,

supremacy, charge **2** = <u>restraint</u>, check, regulation, brake, limitation, curb **3** = <u>self-discipline</u>, self-restraint, restraint, self-command **4** = <u>switch</u>, instrument, button, dial, lever, knob
● PLURAL NOUN = <u>instruments</u>, dash, dials, console, dashboard, control panel
● VERB **1** = <u>have power over</u>, manage, direct, handle, command, govern, administer, supervise **2** = <u>limit</u>, restrict, curb **3** = <u>restrain</u>, limit, check, contain, curb, hold back, subdue, repress

controversial 1 = <u>disputed</u>, contentious, at issue, debatable, under discussion, open to question, disputable

controversy 1 = <u>argument</u>, debate, row, dispute, quarrel, squabble, wrangling, altercation

convene 1 = <u>call</u>, gather, assemble, summon, bring together, convoke **2** = <u>meet</u>, gather, assemble, come together, congregate

convenience 1 = <u>benefit</u>, good, advantage **2** = <u>suitability</u>, fitness, appropriateness **3** = <u>usefulness</u>, utility ≠ uselessness **4** = <u>accessibility</u>, availability, nearness **5** = <u>appliance</u>, facility, comfort, amenity, labour-saving device, help

convenient 1 = <u>suitable</u>, fit, handy, satisfactory **2** = <u>useful</u>, practical, handy, serviceable, labour-saving, serviceable, labour-saving ≠ useless
3 = <u>nearby</u>, available, accessible, handy, at hand, within reach, close at hand, just round the corner ≠ inaccessible
4 = <u>appropriate</u>, timely, suitable, helpful

convention 1 = <u>custom</u>, practice, tradition, code, usage, protocol, etiquette, propriety, kawa (N.Z.), tikanga (N.Z.)
2 = <u>agreement</u>, contract, treaty, bargain, pact, protocol **3** = <u>assembly</u>, meeting, council, conference, congress, convocation, hui (N.Z.), runanga (N.Z.)

conventional 1 = <u>proper</u>, conservative, respectable, genteel, conformist **2** = <u>ordinary</u>, standard, normal, regular, usual **3** = <u>traditional</u>, accepted, orthodox, customary **4** = <u>unoriginal</u>, routine, stereotyped, banal, prosaic, run-of-the-mill, hackneyed ≠ unconventional

converge VERB = <u>come together</u>, meet, join, combine, gather, merge, coincide, intersect
● PHRASES **converge on something** = <u>close in on</u>, arrive at, move towards, home in on, come together at

conversation = <u>talk</u>, discussion, dialogue, tête-à-tête, conference, chat, gossip, discourse, korero (N.Z.)

Related Words

adjective: colloquial

conversion 1 = change, transformation, metamorphosis 2 = adaptation, reconstruction, modification, alteration, remodelling, reorganization

convert VERB 1 = change, turn, transform, alter, transpose 2 = adapt, modify, remodel, reorganize, customize, restyle 3 = reform, convince, proselytize
• NOUN = neophyte, disciple, proselyte

convey 1 = communicate, impart, reveal, relate, disclose, make known, tell 2 = carry, transport, move, bring, bear, conduct, fetch

convict VERB = find guilty, sentence, condemn, imprison, pronounce guilty
• NOUN = prisoner, criminal, lag (slang), felon, jailbird

conviction 1 = belief, view, opinion, principle, faith, persuasion, creed, tenet, kaupapa (N.Z.) 2 = certainty, confidence, assurance, firmness, certitude

convince 1 = assure, persuade, satisfy, reassure 2 = persuade, induce, coax, talk into, prevail upon, bring round to the idea of

---

> *Word Power*
>
> **convince** – The use of *convince* to talk about persuading someone to do something is considered by many British speakers to be wrong or unacceptable. It would be preferable to use an alternative such as *persuade* or *talk into*.

---

convincing = persuasive, credible, conclusive, telling, powerful, impressive, plausible, cogent ≠ unconvincing

cool ADJECTIVE 1 = cold, chilled, refreshing, chilly, nippy ≠ warm 2 = calm, collected, relaxed, composed, sedate, self-controlled, unruffled, unemotional ≠ agitated 3 = unfriendly, distant, indifferent, aloof, lukewarm, offhand, unenthusiastic, unwelcoming ≠ friendly 4 = unenthusiastic, indifferent, lukewarm, unwelcoming
• VERB 1 = lose heat, cool off ≠ warm (up) 2 = make cool, freeze, chill, refrigerate, cool off ≠ warm (up)
• NOUN 1 = coldness, chill, coolness 2 (Slang) = calmness, control, temper, composure, self-control, poise, self-discipline, self-possession

cooperate = work together, collaborate, coordinate, join forces, conspire, pull together, pool resources, combine your efforts ≠ conflict

cooperation = teamwork, unity, collaboration, give-and-take, combined effort, esprit de corps, kotahitanga (*N.Z.*) ≠ opposition

cooperative 1 = shared, joint, combined, collective, collaborative 2 = helpful, obliging, accommodating, supportive, responsive, onside (*informal*)

cope VERB = manage, get by (*informal*), struggle through, survive, carry on, make the grade, hold your own
● PHRASES **cope with something** = deal with, handle, struggle with, grapple with, wrestle with, contend with, weather

copy NOUN = reproduction, duplicate, replica, imitation, forgery, counterfeit, likeness, facsimile ≠ original
● VERB 1 = reproduce, replicate, duplicate, transcribe, counterfeit ≠ create 2 = imitate, act like, emulate, behave like, follow, repeat, mirror, ape

cord = rope, line, string, twine

cordon NOUN = chain, line, ring, barrier, picket line

● PHRASES **cordon something off** = surround, isolate, close off, fence off, separate, enclose, picket, encircle

core 1 = centre 2 = heart, essence, nucleus, kernel, crux, gist, nub, pith

corner NOUN 1 = angle, joint, crook 2 = bend, curve 3 = space, hideaway, nook, hide-out
● VERB 1 = trap, catch, run to earth 2 (usually with *market* as object) = monopolize, take over, dominate, control, hog (*slang*), engross

corporation 1 = business, company, concern, firm, society, association, organization, enterprise 2 = town council, council, municipal authorities, civic authorities

corps = team, unit, regiment, detachment, company, band, division, troop

corpse = body, remains, carcass, cadaver, stiff (*slang*)

correct ADJECTIVE 1 = accurate, right, true, exact, precise, flawless, faultless, O.K. *or* okay (*informal*) ≠ inaccurate 2 = right, standard, appropriate, acceptable, proper, precise 3 = proper, seemly, standard, fitting, kosher (*informal*) ≠ inappropriate
● VERB 1 = rectify, remedy, redress, right, reform, cure, adjust, amend ≠ spoil 2 = rebuke, discipline,

reprimand, chide, admonish, chastise, chasten, reprove ≠ praise

correction 1 = <u>rectification</u>, improvement, amendment, adjustment, modification, alteration, emendation **2** = <u>punishment</u>, discipline, reformation, admonition, chastisement, reproof, castigation

correctly = <u>rightly</u>, right, perfectly, properly, precisely, accurately

correctness 1 = <u>truth</u>, accuracy, precision, exactitude, exactness, faultlessness **2** = <u>decorum</u>, propriety, good manners, civility, good breeding

correspond 1 = <u>be consistent</u>, match, agree, accord, fit, square, tally, conform ≠ differ **2** = <u>communicate</u>, write, keep in touch, exchange letters

correspondence 1 = <u>communication</u>, writing, contact **2** = <u>letters</u>, post, mail **3** = <u>relation</u>, match, agreement, comparison, harmony, coincidence, similarity, correlation

correspondent 1 = <u>reporter</u>, journalist, contributor, hack **2** = <u>letter writer</u>, pen friend or pen pal

corresponding = <u>equivalent</u>, matching, similar, related, complementary, reciprocal, analogous

corridor = <u>passage</u>, alley, aisle, hallway, passageway

corrupt ADJECTIVE **1** = <u>dishonest</u>, bent (slang), crooked (informal), fraudulent, unscrupulous, venal, unprincipled ≠ honest **2** = <u>depraved</u>, vicious, degenerate, debased, profligate, dissolute **3** = <u>distorted</u>, doctored, altered, falsified

● VERB **1** = <u>bribe</u>, fix (informal), buy off, suborn, grease (someone's) palm (slang) **2** = <u>deprave</u>, pervert, subvert, debauch ≠ reform **3** = <u>distort</u>, doctor, tamper with

corruption 1 = <u>dishonesty</u>, fraud, bribery, extortion, venality, shady dealings (informal) **2** = <u>depravity</u>, vice, evil, perversion, decadence, wickedness, immorality **3** = <u>distortion</u>, doctoring, falsification

cosmetic = <u>superficial</u>, surface, nonessential

cosmic 1 = <u>extraterrestrial</u>, stellar **2** = <u>universal</u>, general, overarching

cosmopolitan = <u>sophisticated</u>, cultured, refined, cultivated, urbane, well-travelled, worldly-wise ≠ unsophisticated

cost NOUN **1** = <u>price</u>, worth, expense, charge, damage (informal), amount, payment, outlay **2** = <u>loss</u>, suffering, damage, injury, penalty, hurt, expense, harm

● PLURAL NOUN = expenses, spending, expenditure, overheads, outgoings, outlay, budget

● VERB 1 = sell at, come to, set (someone) back (*informal*), be priced at, command a price of 2 = lose, deprive of, cheat of

costly 1 = expensive, dear, stiff, steep (*informal*), highly-priced, exorbitant, extortionate ≠ inexpensive 2 = damaging, disastrous, harmful, catastrophic, loss-making, ruinous, deleterious

costume = outfit, dress, clothing, uniform, ensemble, livery, apparel, attire

cosy 1 = comfortable, homely, warm, intimate, snug, comfy (*informal*), sheltered 2 = snug, warm, comfortable, sheltered, comfy (*informal*), tucked up 3 = intimate, friendly, informal

cottage = cabin, lodge, hut, shack, chalet, whare (*N.Z.*)

cough VERB = clear your throat, bark, hack

● NOUN = frog or tickle in your throat, bark, hack

council 1 = committee, governing body, board 2 = governing body, parliament, congress, cabinet, panel, assembly, convention, conference, runanga (*N.Z.*)

counsel NOUN 1 = advice, information, warning, direction, suggestion, recommendation, guidance 2 = legal adviser, lawyer, attorney, solicitor, advocate, barrister

● VERB = advise, recommend, advocate, warn, urge, instruct, exhort

count VERB 1 = often with **up** = add (up), total, reckon (up), tot up, calculate, compute, tally, number 2 = matter, be important, carry weight, tell, rate, weigh, signify 3 = consider, judge, regard, deem, think of, rate, look upon 4 = include, number among, take into account or consideration

● NOUN = calculation, poll, reckoning, sum, tally, numbering, computation, enumeration

● PHRASES **count on** or **upon something** or **someone** = depend on, trust, rely on, bank on, take for granted, lean on, reckon on, take on trust

counter VERB 1 = oppose, meet, block, resist, parry, deflect, repel, rebuff 2 = retaliate, answer, reply, respond, retort, hit back, rejoin, strike back ≠ yield

● ADVERB = opposite to, against, versus, conversely, in defiance of, at variance with, contrariwise ≠ in accordance with

counterpart = opposite number, equal, twin, equivalent,

match, fellow, mate

countless = <u>innumerable</u>, legion, infinite, myriad, untold, limitless, incalculable, immeasurable ≠ limited

country 1 = <u>nation</u>, state, land, commonwealth, kingdom, realm, people 2 = <u>people</u>, community, nation, society, citizens, inhabitants, populace, public 3 = <u>countryside</u>, provinces, sticks (*informal*), farmland, outback (*Austral. & N.Z.*), green belt, backwoods, bush (*N.Z. & S. African*) ≠ town 4 = <u>territory</u>, land, region, terrain
➤ WORD POWER SUPPLEMENT
countries

countryside = <u>country</u>, rural areas, outback (*Austral. & N.Z.*), green belt, sticks (*informal*)

county = <u>province</u>, district, shire
➤ WORD POWER SUPPLEMENT
counties

coup = <u>masterstroke</u>, feat, stunt, action, exploit, manoeuvre, deed, accomplishment

couple NOUN = <u>pair</u>, two, brace, duo, twosome
● PHRASES **couple something to something** = <u>link to</u>, connect to, pair with, unite with, join to, hitch to, yoke to

coupon = <u>slip</u>, ticket, certificate, token, voucher, card

courage = <u>bravery</u>, nerve, resolution, daring, pluck, heroism, mettle, gallantry ≠ cowardice

courageous = <u>brave</u>, daring, bold, gritty, fearless, gallant, intrepid, valiant ≠ cowardly

courier 1 = <u>messenger</u>, runner, carrier, bearer, envoy 2 = <u>guide</u>, representative, escort, conductor

course NOUN 1 = <u>route</u>, way, line, road, track, direction, path, passage 2 = <u>procedure</u>, plan, policy, programme, method, conduct, behaviour, manner 3 = <u>progression</u>, order, unfolding, development, movement, progress, flow, sequence 4 = <u>classes</u>, programme, schedule, lectures, curriculum 5 = <u>racecourse</u>, circuit 6 = <u>period</u>, time, duration, term, passing
● VERB 1 = <u>run</u>, flow, stream, gush, race, speed, surge 2 = <u>hunt</u>, follow, chase, pursue
● PHRASES **of course** = <u>naturally</u>, certainly, obviously, definitely, undoubtedly, needless to say, without a doubt, indubitably

court NOUN 1 = <u>law court</u>, bar, bench, tribunal 2 = <u>palace</u>, hall, castle, manor 3 = <u>royal household</u>, train, suite, attendants, entourage, retinue, cortege
● VERB 1 = <u>cultivate</u>, seek, flatter, solicit, pander to, curry favour with, fawn upon 2 = <u>invite</u>, seek, attract, prompt, provoke, bring about, incite 3 = <u>woo</u>, go (out) with, date, take out, run after,

walk out with, set your cap at

courtesy 1 = <u>politeness</u>, good manners, civility, gallantry, graciousness, affability, urbanity 2 = <u>favour</u>, kindness, indulgence

courtyard = <u>yard</u>, square, piazza, quadrangle, plaza, enclosure, cloister, quad (*informal*)

cove = <u>bay</u>, sound, inlet, anchorage

covenant = <u>promise</u>, contract, agreement, commitment, arrangement, pledge, pact

cover VERB 1 = <u>conceal</u>, hide, mask, disguise, obscure, veil, cloak, shroud ≠ reveal 2 = <u>clothe</u>, dress, wrap, envelop ≠ uncover 3 = <u>overlay</u>, blanket 4 = <u>coat</u>, cake, plaster, smear, envelop, spread, encase, daub 5 = <u>submerge</u>, flood, engulf, overrun, wash over 6 = <u>travel over</u>, cross, traverse, pass through or over 7 = <u>protect</u>, guard, defend, shield 8 = <u>consider</u>, deal with, investigate, describe, tell of 9 = <u>report on</u>, write about, commentate on, relate, tell of, narrate, write up 10 = <u>pay for</u>, fund, provide for, offset, be enough for

● NOUN 1 = <u>protection</u>, shelter, shield, defence, guard, camouflage, concealment 2 = <u>insurance</u>, protection, compensation, indemnity, reimbursement 3 = <u>covering</u>, case, top, coating, envelope, lid, canopy, wrapper 4 = <u>bedclothes</u>, bedding, sheets, blankets, quilt, duvet, eiderdown 5 = <u>jacket</u>, case, wrapper 6 = <u>disguise</u>, front, screen, mask, veil, façade, pretext, smoke screen

covering NOUN = <u>cover</u>, coating, casing, wrapping, layer, blanket
● ADJECTIVE = <u>explanatory</u>, accompanying, introductory, descriptive

covet = <u>long for</u>, desire, envy, crave, aspire to, yearn for, lust after, set your heart on

coward = <u>wimp</u>, chicken (*slang*), scaredy-cat (*informal*), yellow-belly (*slang*)

cowardly = <u>faint-hearted</u>, scared, spineless, soft, yellow (*informal*), weak, chicken (*slang*), fearful, sookie (*N.Z.*) ≠ brave

cowboy = <u>cowhand</u>, drover, rancher, stockman, cattleman, herdsman, gaucho (*S. American*)

crack VERB 1 = <u>break</u>, split, burst, snap, fracture, splinter 2 = <u>snap</u>, ring, crash, burst, explode, pop, detonate 3 (*Informal*) = <u>hit</u>, clip (*informal*), slap, smack, clout (*informal*), cuff, whack 4 = <u>break</u>, cleave 5 = <u>solve</u>, work out, resolve, clear up, fathom, decipher, suss (out) (*slang*), get to the bottom of 6 = <u>break down</u>, collapse, yield, give in, give way, succumb, lose control, be overcome

● NOUN 1 = <u>break</u>, chink, gap, fracture, rift, cleft, crevice, fissure 2 = <u>split</u>, break, fracture 3 = <u>snap</u>, pop, crash, burst, explosion, clap, report 4 (*Informal*) = <u>blow</u>, slap, smack, clout (*informal*), cuff, whack, clip (*informal*) 5 (*Informal*) = <u>joke</u>, dig, gag (*informal*), quip, jibe, wisecrack, witticism, funny remark

● ADJECTIVE (*Slang*) = <u>first-class</u>, choice, excellent, ace, elite, superior, world-class, first-rate

crackdown = <u>clampdown</u>, crushing, repression, suppression

cracked = <u>broken</u>, damaged, split, chipped, flawed, faulty, defective, imperfect

cradle NOUN 1 = <u>crib</u>, cot, Moses basket, bassinet 2 = <u>birthplace</u>, beginning, source, spring, origin, fount, fountainhead, wellspring

● VERB 1 = <u>hold</u>, support, rock, nurse, nestle

craft 1 = <u>vessel</u>, boat, ship, plane, aircraft, spacecraft 2 = <u>occupation</u>, work, business, trade, employment, pursuit, vocation, handicraft 3 = <u>skill</u>, art, ability, technique, know-how (*informal*), expertise, aptitude, artistry

craftsman = <u>skilled worker</u>, artisan, master, maker, wright, technician, smith

cram 1 = <u>stuff</u>, force, jam, shove, compress 2 = <u>pack</u>, fill, stuff 3 = <u>squeeze</u>, press, pack in 4 = <u>study</u>, revise, swot, bone up (*informal*), mug up (*slang*)

cramp[1] = <u>spasm</u>, pain, ache, contraction, pang, stitch, convulsion, twinge

cramp[2] = <u>restrict</u>, hamper, inhibit, hinder, handicap, constrain, obstruct, impede

cramped = <u>restricted</u>, confined, overcrowded, crowded, packed, uncomfortable, closed in, congested ≠ spacious

crash NOUN 1 = <u>collision</u>, accident, smash, wreck, prang (*informal*), bump, pile-up (*informal*) 2 = <u>smash</u>, clash, boom, bang, thunder, racket, din, clatter 3 = <u>collapse</u>, failure, depression, ruin, downfall

● VERB 1 = <u>fall</u>, plunge, topple, lurch, hurtle, overbalance, fall headlong 2 = <u>plunge</u>, hurtle 3 = <u>collapse</u>, fail, go under, be ruined, go bust (*informal*), fold up, go to the wall, go belly up (*informal*)

● PHRASES **crash into** = <u>collide with</u>, hit, bump into, drive into, plough into

crate = <u>container</u>, case, box, packing case, tea chest

crater = <u>hollow</u>, hole, depression, dip, cavity

crave 1 = <u>long for</u>, yearn for,

hanker after, want, desire, hope for, lust after **2** (*Informal*) = **beg**, ask for, seek, petition, pray for, plead for, solicit, implore

craving = <u>longing</u>, hope, desire, yen (*informal*), hunger, appetite, yearning, thirst

crawl VERB = <u>creep</u>, slither, inch, wriggle, writhe, worm your way, advance slowly ≠ **run**
  ● PHRASES **crawl to someone** = <u>grovel</u>, creep, fawn, toady, humble yourself

craze = <u>fad</u>, fashion, trend, rage, enthusiasm, vogue, mania, infatuation

crazed = <u>mad</u>, crazy, raving, insane, lunatic, berko (*Austral. slang*), off the air (*Austral. slang*), porangi (*N.Z.*)

crazy 1 (*Informal*) = <u>ridiculous</u>, absurd, foolish, ludicrous, senseless, preposterous, idiotic, nonsensical, porangi (*N.Z.*) ≠ **sensible 2** = <u>insane</u>, mad, unbalanced, deranged, nuts (*slang*), crazed, demented, off the air (*Austral. slang*), out of your mind, porangi (*N.Z.*) ≠ **sane 3** = <u>fanatical</u>, wild (*informal*), mad, devoted, enthusiastic, passionate, infatuated ≠ **uninterested**

cream NOUN **1** = <u>lotion</u>, ointment, oil, essence, cosmetic, paste, emulsion, salve **2** = <u>best</u>, elite, prime, pick, flower, crème de la crème (*French*)

● NOUN *or* ADJECTIVE = <u>off-white</u>, ivory, yellowish-white
  ➤ **shades from black to white**

creamy 1 = <u>milky</u>, buttery **2** = <u>smooth</u>, soft, velvety, rich

crease NOUN **1** = <u>fold</u>, line, ridge, groove, corrugation **2** = <u>wrinkle</u>, line, crow's-foot
  ● VERB **1** = <u>crumple</u>, rumple, fold, double up, corrugate **2** = <u>wrinkle</u>, crumple, screw up

create 1 = <u>cause</u>, lead to, occasion, bring about **2** = <u>make</u>, produce, invent, compose, devise, originate, formulate, spawn ≠ **destroy 3** = <u>appoint</u>, make, establish, set up, invest, install, constitute

creation 1 = <u>universe</u>, world, nature, cosmos **2** = <u>invention</u>, production, achievement, brainchild (*informal*), concoction, handiwork, pièce de résistance (*French*), magnum opus **3** = <u>making</u>, generation, formation, conception, genesis **4** = <u>setting up</u>, development, production, institution, foundation, establishment, formation, inception

creative = <u>imaginative</u>, gifted, artistic, inventive, original, inspired, clever, ingenious

creativity = <u>imagination</u>, inspiration, ingenuity, originality, inventiveness, cleverness

creator 1 = maker, father, author, designer, architect, inventor, originator **2** *usually with cap.* = God, Maker

creature 1 = living thing, being, animal, beast, brute **2** = person, man, woman, individual, soul, human being, mortal

credentials 1 = qualifications, ability, skill, fitness, attribute, capability, eligibility, aptitude **2** = certification, document, reference(s), papers, licence, passport, testimonial, authorization

credibility = believability, reliability, plausibility, trustworthiness

credible 1 = believable, possible, likely, reasonable, probable, plausible, conceivable, imaginable ≠ unbelievable **2** = reliable, honest, dependable, trustworthy, sincere, trusty ≠ unreliable

credit NOUN **1** = praise, honour, recognition, approval, tribute, acclaim, acknowledgment, kudos **2** = source of satisfaction, asset, honour, feather in your cap **3** = prestige, reputation, standing, position, influence, regard, status, esteem **4** = belief, trust, confidence, faith, reliance, credence
● VERB = believe, rely on, have faith in, trust, accept

● PHRASES **credit someone with something** = attribute to, assign to, ascribe to, impute to

creed = belief, principles, doctrine, dogma, credo, catechism, articles of faith

creek 1 = inlet, bay, cove, bight, firth *or* frith (*Scot.*) **2** (*U.S., Canad., Austral., & N.Z.*) = stream, brook, tributary, bayou, rivulet, watercourse, runnel

creep VERB = sneak, steal, tiptoe, slink, skulk, approach unnoticed
● NOUN (*Slang*) = bootlicker (*informal*), sneak, sycophant, crawler (*slang*), toady
● PHRASES **give someone the creeps** (*Informal*) = disgust, frighten, scare, repel, repulse, make your hair stand on end, make you squirm

crescent = meniscus, sickle, new moon

crest 1 = top, summit, peak, ridge, highest point, pinnacle, apex, crown **2** = tuft, crown, comb, plume, mane **3** = emblem, badge, symbol, insignia, bearings, device

crew 1 = (ship's) company, hands, (ship's) complement **2** = team, squad, gang, corps, posse **3** (*Informal*) = crowd, set, bunch (*informal*), band, pack, gang, mob, horde

crime 1 = offence, violation, trespass, felony, misdemeanour, misdeed, transgression, unlawful act **2** = <u>lawbreaking</u>, corruption, illegality, vice, misconduct, wrongdoing

criminal NOUN = <u>lawbreaker</u>, convict, offender, crook (*informal*), villain, culprit, sinner, felon, rorter (*Austral. slang*), skelm (*S. African*)

● ADJECTIVE **1** = <u>unlawful</u>, illicit, lawless, wrong, illegal, corrupt, crooked (*informal*), immoral ≠ lawful **2** (*Informal*) = <u>disgraceful</u>, ridiculous, foolish, senseless, scandalous, preposterous, deplorable

cripple 1 = <u>disable</u>, paralyse, lame, maim, incapacitate, weaken, hamstring **2** = <u>damage</u>, destroy, ruin, spoil, impair, put paid to, put out of action ≠ help

crippled = <u>disabled</u>, handicapped, paralysed, lame, incapacitated

crisis 1 = <u>emergency</u>, plight, predicament, trouble, deep water, meltdown (*informal*), dire straits **2** = <u>critical point</u>, climax, height, crunch (*informal*), turning point, culmination, crux, moment of truth

crisp 1 = <u>firm</u>, crunchy, crispy, crumbly, fresh, brittle, unwilted ≠ soft **2** = <u>bracing</u>, fresh, refreshing, brisk, invigorating ≠ warm **3** = <u>clean</u>, smart, trim, neat, tidy, spruce, well-groomed, well-pressed

criterion = <u>standard</u>, test, rule, measure, principle, gauge, yardstick, touchstone

> ### Word Power
> **criterion**–The word *criteria* is the plural of *criterion* and it is incorrect to use it as an alternative singular form; *these criteria are not valid* is correct, and so is *this criterion is not valid*, but not *this criteria is not valid.*

critic 1 = <u>judge</u>, authority, expert, analyst, commentator, pundit, reviewer, connoisseur **2** = <u>fault-finder</u>, attacker, detractor, knocker (*informal*)

critical 1 = <u>crucial</u>, decisive, pressing, serious, vital, urgent, all-important, pivotal ≠ unimportant **2** = <u>grave</u>, serious, acute, precarious ≠ safe **3** = <u>disparaging</u>, disapproving, scathing, derogatory, nit-picking (*informal*), censorious, fault-finding, captious ≠ complimentary **4** = <u>analytical</u>, penetrating, discriminating, discerning, perceptive, judicious ≠ undiscriminating

criticism 1 = <u>fault-finding</u>, censure, disapproval, disparagement, stick (*slang*), flak (*informal*), bad press, character assassination 2 = <u>analysis</u>, assessment, judgment, commentary, evaluation, appreciation, appraisal, critique

criticize = <u>find fault with</u>, censure, disapprove of, knock (informal), condemn, carp, put down, slate (informal) ≠ praise

crook NOUN (Informal) = <u>criminal</u>, rogue, cheat, thief, shark, villain, robber, racketeer, skelm (S. African)

• ADJECTIVE (Austral. & N.Z. informal) = <u>ill</u>, sick, poorly (informal), unhealthy, seedy (informal), unwell, queasy, out of sorts (informal)

• PHRASES **go (off) crook** (Austral. & N.Z. informal) = <u>lose your temper</u>, be furious, rage, go mad, lose it (informal), crack up (informal), see red (informal), blow your top

crooked 1 = <u>bent</u>, twisted, curved, irregular, warped, out of shape, misshapen ≠ straight 2 = <u>deformed</u>, distorted 3 = <u>zigzag</u>, winding, twisting 4 = <u>at an angle</u>, uneven, slanting, squint, skew, lopsided, askew, off-centre 5 (Informal) = <u>dishonest</u>, criminal, illegal, corrupt, unlawful, shady (informal), fraudulent, bent (slang) ≠ honest

crop NOUN = <u>yield</u>, produce, gathering, fruits, harvest, vintage, reaping

• VERB 1 = <u>graze</u>, eat, browse, feed on, nibble 2 = <u>cut</u>, trim, clip, prune, shear, snip, pare, lop

• PHRASES **crop up** (Informal) = <u>happen</u>, appear, emerge, occur, arise, turn up, spring up

cross VERB 1 = <u>go across</u>, pass over, traverse, cut across, move across, travel across 2 = <u>span</u>, bridge, go across, extend over 3 = <u>intersect</u>, intertwine, crisscross 4 = <u>oppose</u>, interfere with, obstruct, block, resist, impede 5 = <u>interbreed</u>, mix, blend, cross-pollinate, crossbreed, hybridize, cross-fertilize, intercross

• NOUN 1 = <u>crucifix</u> 2 = <u>trouble</u>, worry, trial, load, burden, grief, woe, misfortune 3 = <u>mixture</u>, combination, blend, amalgam, amalgamation 4 = <u>crossroads</u>, crossing, junction, intersection

• ADJECTIVE = <u>angry</u>, annoyed, put out, grumpy, short, ill-tempered, irascible, tooshie (Austral. slang), in a bad mood, hoha (N.Z.) ≠ good-humoured

• PHRASES **cross something out** or **off** = <u>strike off</u> or <u>out</u>, eliminate, cancel, delete, blue-pencil, score off or out

crouch = <u>bend down</u>, kneel, squat, stoop, bow, duck, hunch

crow = <u>gloat</u>, triumph, boast, swagger, brag, exult, blow your own trumpet

crowd NOUN 1 = <u>multitude</u>, mass,

throng, army, host, pack, mob, swarm 2 = <u>group</u>, set, lot, circle, gang, bunch (*informal*), clique 3 = <u>audience</u>, spectators, house, gate, attendance
● VERB 1 = <u>flock</u>, mass, collect, gather, stream, surge, swarm, throng 2 = <u>squeeze</u>, pack, pile, bundle, cram 3 = <u>congest</u>, pack, cram

crowded = <u>packed</u>, full, busy, cramped, swarming, teeming, congested, jam-packed

crown NOUN 1 = <u>coronet</u>, tiara, diadem, circlet 2 = <u>laurel wreath</u>, trophy, prize, honour, garland, laurels, wreath 3 = <u>high point</u>, top, tip, summit, crest, pinnacle, apex
● VERB 1 = <u>install</u>, honour, dignify, ordain, inaugurate 2 = <u>top</u>, cap, be on top of, surmount 3 = <u>cap</u>, finish, complete, perfect, round off, put the finishing touch to, be the climax *or* culmination of 4 (*Slang*) = <u>strike</u>, belt (*informal*), bash, hit over the head, box, punch, cuff, biff (*slang*)
● PHRASES **the Crown** 1 = <u>monarch</u>, ruler, sovereign, emperor *or* empress, king *or* queen 2 = <u>monarchy</u>, sovereignty, royalty

crucial 1 (*Informal*) = <u>vital</u>, important, pressing, essential, urgent, momentous, high-priority 2 = <u>critical</u>, central, key,

psychological, decisive, pivotal

crude 1 = <u>rough</u>, basic, makeshift 2 = <u>simple</u>, rudimentary, basic, primitive, coarse, clumsy, rough-and-ready 3 = <u>vulgar</u>, dirty, rude, obscene, coarse, indecent, tasteless, smutty ≠ tasteful 4 = <u>unrefined</u>, natural, raw, unprocessed ≠ processed

crudely 1 = <u>roughly</u>, basically 2 = <u>simply</u>, roughly, basically, coarsely 3 = <u>vulgarly</u>, rudely, coarsely, crassly, obscenely, lewdly, impolitely, tastelessly

cruel 1 = <u>brutal</u>, ruthless, callous, sadistic, inhumane, vicious, monstrous, unkind ≠ kind 2 = <u>bitter</u>, ruthless, traumatic, grievous, unrelenting, merciless, pitiless

cruelly 1 = <u>brutally</u>, severely, mercilessly, in cold blood, callously, monstrously, sadistically, pitilessly 2 = <u>bitterly</u>, deeply, severely, ruthlessly, mercilessly, grievously, pitilessly, traumatically

cruelty = <u>brutality</u>, ruthlessness, depravity, inhumanity, barbarity, callousness, spitefulness, mercilessness

cruise NOUN = <u>sail</u>, voyage, boat trip, sea trip
● VERB 1 = <u>sail</u>, coast, voyage 2 = <u>travel along</u>, coast, drift, keep a steady pace

crumb 1 = <u>bit</u>, grain, fragment,

shred, morsel 2 = <u>morsel</u>, scrap, shred, snippet, soupçon (French)

crumble 1 = <u>disintegrate</u>, collapse, deteriorate, decay, fall apart, degenerate, tumble down, go to pieces 2 = <u>crush</u>, fragment, pulverize, pound, grind, powder, granulate 3 = <u>collapse</u>, deteriorate, decay, fall apart, degenerate, go to pieces, go to wrack and ruin

crumple 1 = <u>crush</u>, squash, screw up, scrumple 2 = <u>crease</u>, wrinkle, rumple, ruffle, pucker 3 = <u>collapse</u>, sink, go down, fall 4 = <u>break down</u>, fall, collapse, give way, cave in, go to pieces 5 = <u>screw up</u>

crunch VERB = <u>chomp</u>, champ, munch, chew noisily, grind
● NOUN (Informal) = <u>critical point</u>, test, crisis, emergency, crux, moment of truth

crusade NOUN 1 = <u>campaign</u>, drive, movement, cause, push 2 = <u>holy war</u>
● VERB = <u>campaign</u>, fight, push, struggle, lobby, agitate, work

crush VERB 1 = <u>squash</u>, break, squeeze, compress, press, pulverize 2 = <u>crease</u>, wrinkle, crumple 3 = <u>overcome</u>, overwhelm, put down, subdue, overpower, quash, quell, stamp out 4 = <u>demoralize</u>, depress, devastate, discourage, humble, put down (slang), humiliate, squash
● NOUN = <u>crowd</u>, mob, horde, throng, pack, mass, jam, huddle

crust = <u>layer</u>, covering, coating, skin, surface, shell

crustacean ▸ crustaceans

cry VERB 1 = <u>weep</u>, sob, shed tears, blubber, snivel ≠ laugh 2 = <u>shout</u>, scream, roar, yell, howl,

---

Crustaceans

barnacle	lobster
crab	oyster crab
crayfish, crawfish, (U.S.) or	prawn
(Austral. & N.Z. informal) craw	robber crab
freshwater shrimp	sand shrimp
hermit crab	scorpion
horseshoe crab or king crab	sea spider
king prawn	shrimp
koura (N.Z.)	soft-shell crab
krill	spider crab
land crab	spiny lobster, rock lobster,
langoustine	crawfish, or langouste

call out, exclaim, shriek ≠ whisper
- NOUN 1 = <u>weep</u>, sob, bawl, blubber 2 = <u>shout</u>, call, scream, roar, yell, howl, shriek, bellow 3 = <u>appeal</u>, plea
- PLURAL NOUN = <u>weeping</u>, sobbing, blubbering, snivelling
- PHRASES **cry off** (*Informal*) = <u>back out</u>, withdraw, quit, excuse yourself

cuddle VERB 1 = <u>hug</u>, embrace, fondle, cosset 2 = <u>pet</u>, hug, bill and coo
- PHRASES **cuddle up** = <u>snuggle</u>

cue = <u>signal</u>, sign, hint, prompt, reminder, suggestion

culminate = <u>end up</u>, close, finish, conclude, wind up, climax, come to a head, come to a climax

culprit = <u>offender</u>, criminal, felon, guilty party, wrongdoer, miscreant, evildoer, transgressor

cult 1 = <u>sect</u>, faction, school, religion, clique, hauhau (*N.Z.*) 2 = <u>craze</u>, fashion, trend, fad 3 = <u>obsession</u>, worship, devotion, idolization

cultivate 1 = <u>farm</u>, work, plant, tend, till, plough 2 = <u>develop</u>, establish, foster 3 = <u>court</u>, seek out, run after, dance attendance upon 4 = <u>improve</u>, refine

cultural 1 = <u>ethnic</u>, national, native, folk, racial 2 = <u>artistic</u>, educational, aesthetic, enriching, enlightening, civilizing, edifying

culture 1 = <u>the arts</u>

2 = <u>civilization</u>, society, customs, way of life 3 = <u>lifestyle</u>, habit, way of life, mores 4 = <u>refinement</u>, education, enlightenment, sophistication, good taste, urbanity

cultured = <u>refined</u>, intellectual, educated, sophisticated, enlightened, well-informed, urbane, highbrow ≠ uneducated

cunning ADJECTIVE 1 = <u>crafty</u>, sly, devious, artful, sharp, wily, Machiavellian, shifty ≠ frank 2 = <u>ingenious</u>, imaginative, sly, devious, artful, Machiavellian 3 = <u>skilful</u>, clever ≠ clumsy
- NOUN 1 = <u>craftiness</u>, guile, trickery, deviousness, artfulness, slyness ≠ candour 2 = <u>skill</u>, subtlety, ingenuity, artifice, cleverness ≠ clumsiness

cup 1 = <u>mug</u>, goblet, chalice, teacup, beaker, bowl 2 = <u>trophy</u>

cupboard = <u>cabinet</u>, press

curb VERB = <u>restrain</u>, control, check, restrict, suppress, inhibit, hinder, retard
- NOUN = <u>restraint</u>, control, check, brake, limitation, rein, deterrent, bridle

cure VERB 1 = <u>make better</u>, correct, heal, relieve, remedy, mend, ease 2 = <u>restore to health</u>, restore, heal 3 = <u>preserve</u>, smoke, dry, salt, pickle
- NOUN = <u>remedy</u>, treatment, antidote, panacea, nostrum

curiosity 1 = <u>inquisitiveness</u>, interest, prying, snooping (*informal*), nosiness (*informal*) **2** = <u>oddity</u>, wonder, sight, phenomenon, spectacle, freak, novelty, rarity

curious ADJECTIVE **1** = <u>inquisitive</u>, interested, questioning, searching, inquiring, meddling, prying, nosy (*informal*)
≠ uninterested **2** = <u>strange</u>, unusual, bizarre, odd, novel, rare, extraordinary, unexpected
● ADJECTIVE ≠ ordinary

curl NOUN **1** = <u>ringlet</u>, lock **2** = <u>twist</u>, spiral, coil, kink, whorl **3** = <u>crimp</u>, wave, perm
● VERB **1** = <u>twirl</u>, turn, bend, twist, curve, loop, spiral, coil **2** = <u>wind</u>

curly 1 = <u>wavy</u>, curled, curling, fuzzy, frizzy

currency 1 = <u>money</u>, coinage, legal tender, notes, coins **2** = <u>acceptance</u>, popularity, circulation, vogue, prevalence
➤ WORD POWER SUPPLEMENT currencies

current NOUN **1** = <u>flow</u>, course, undertow, jet, stream, tide, progression, river **2** = <u>draught</u>, flow, breeze, puff **3** = <u>mood</u>, feeling, spirit, atmosphere, trend, tendency, undercurrent
● ADJECTIVE **1** = <u>present</u>, fashionable, up-to-date, contemporary, trendy (*Brit. informal*), topical, present-day, in fashion ≠ out-of-date

2 = <u>prevalent</u>, common, accepted, popular, widespread, customary, in circulation

curse VERB **1** = <u>swear</u>, cuss (*informal*), blaspheme, take the Lord's name in vain **2** = <u>abuse</u>, damn, scold, vilify
● NOUN **1** = <u>oath</u>, obscenity, blasphemy, expletive, profanity, imprecation, swearword **2** = <u>malediction</u>, jinx, anathema, hoodoo (*informal*), excommunication **3** = <u>affliction</u>, plague, scourge, trouble, torment, hardship, bane

cursed = <u>under a curse</u>, damned, doomed, jinxed, bedevilled, accursed, ill-fated

curtail = <u>reduce</u>, diminish, decrease, dock, cut back, shorten, lessen, cut short

curtain = <u>hanging</u>, drape (*chiefly U.S.*), portière

curve NOUN = <u>bend</u>, turn, loop, arc, curvature
● VERB = <u>bend</u>, turn, wind, twist, arch, snake, arc, coil

curved = <u>bent</u>, rounded, twisted, bowed, arched, serpentine, sinuous

cushion NOUN = <u>pillow</u>, pad, bolster, headrest, beanbag, hassock
● VERB **1** = <u>protect</u> **2** = <u>soften</u>, dampen, muffle, mitigate, deaden, suppress, stifle

custody 1 = <u>care</u>, charge,

protection, supervision, safekeeping, keeping **2** = <u>imprisonment</u>, detention, confinement, incarceration

custom 1 = <u>tradition</u>, practice, convention, ritual, policy, rule, usage, kaupapa (*N.Z.*) **2** = <u>habit</u>, way, practice, procedure, routine, wont **3** = <u>customers</u>, business, trade, patronage

customary 1 = <u>usual</u>, common, accepted, established, traditional, normal, ordinary, conventional ≠ unusual **2** = <u>accustomed</u>, regular, usual

customer = <u>client</u>, consumer, regular (*informal*), buyer, patron, shopper, purchaser

customs = <u>import charges</u>, tax, duty, toll, tariff

cut VERB **1** = <u>slit</u>, score, slice, slash, pierce, penetrate **2** = <u>chop</u>, split, slice, dissect **3** = <u>carve</u>, slice **4** = <u>sever</u>, cut in two **5** = <u>shape</u>, carve, engrave, chisel, form, score, fashion, whittle **6** = <u>slash</u>, wound **7** = <u>clip</u>, mow, trim, prune, snip, pare, lop **8** = <u>trim</u>, shave, snip **9** = <u>reduce</u>, lower, slim (down), diminish, slash, decrease, cut back ≠ increase **10** = <u>abridge</u>, edit, shorten, curtail, condense, abbreviate ≠ extend **11** = <u>delete</u>, take out, expurgate **12** = <u>hurt</u>, wound, upset, sting, hurt someone's feelings **13** (*Informal*) = <u>ignore</u>, avoid, slight, blank

(*slang*), snub, spurn, cold-shoulder, turn your back on ≠ greet **14** = <u>cross</u>, bisect
● NOUN **1** = <u>incision</u>, nick, stroke, slash, slit **2** = <u>gash</u>, nick, wound, slash, laceration **3** = <u>reduction</u>, fall, lowering, slash, decrease, cutback **4** (*Informal*) = <u>share</u>, piece, slice, percentage, portion **5** = <u>style</u>, look, fashion, shape

cutback = <u>reduction</u>, cut, retrenchment, economy, decrease, lessening

cute = <u>appealing</u>, sweet, attractive, engaging, charming, delightful, lovable, winsome

cutting = <u>hurtful</u>, wounding, bitter, malicious, scathing, acrimonious, barbed, sarcastic ≠ kind

cycle = <u>series of events</u>, circle, revolution, rotation

cynic = <u>sceptic</u>, doubter, pessimist, misanthrope, misanthropist, scoffer

cynical 1 = <u>sceptical</u>, mocking, pessimistic, scoffing, contemptuous, scornful, distrustful, derisive ≠ trusting **2** = <u>unbelieving</u>, sceptical, disillusioned, pessimistic, disbelieving, mistrustful ≠ optimistic

cynicism 1 = <u>scepticism</u>, pessimism, misanthropy **2** = <u>disbelief</u>, doubt, scepticism, mistrust

D

dab VERB 1 = <u>pat</u>, touch, tap
2 = <u>apply</u>, daub, stipple
● NOUN 1 = <u>spot</u>, bit, drop, pat, smudge, speck 2 = <u>touch</u>, stroke, flick

daft (*Informal, chiefly Brit.*)
1 = <u>stupid</u>, crazy, silly, absurd, foolish, idiotic, witless, crackpot (*informal*), off the air (*Austral. slang*) 2 = <u>crazy</u>, mad, touched, nuts (*slang*), crackers (*Brit. slang*), insane, demented, deranged, off the air (*Austral. slang*), porangi (*N.Z.*)

dag NOUN (*N.Z. informal*) = <u>joker</u>, comic, wag, wit, comedian, clown, humorist, prankster
● PHRASES **rattle your dags**
(*N.Z. informal*) = <u>hurry up</u>, get a move on, step on it (*informal*), get your skates on (*informal*), make haste

dagga (*S. African*) = <u>cannabis</u>, marijuana, pot (*slang*), dope (*slang*), hash (*slang*), grass (*slang*), weed (*slang*), hemp

daily ADVERB = <u>every day</u>, day by day, once a day
● ADJECTIVE = <u>everyday</u>, diurnal, quotidian

dam NOUN = <u>barrier</u>, wall, barrage, obstruction, embankment
● VERB = <u>block up</u>, restrict, hold back, barricade, obstruct

damage VERB = <u>spoil</u>, hurt, injure, harm, ruin, crush, devastate, wreck ≠ fix
● NOUN 1 = <u>destruction</u>, harm, loss, injury, suffering, hurt, ruin, devastation ≠ improvement
2 (*Informal*) = <u>cost</u>, price, charge, bill, amount, payment, expense, outlay
● PLURAL NOUN (*Law*)
= <u>compensation</u>, fine, satisfaction, amends, reparation, restitution, reimbursement, atonement

damaging = <u>harmful</u>, detrimental, hurtful, ruinous, deleterious, injurious, disadvantageous ≠ helpful

dame = <u>lady</u>, baroness, dowager, grande dame (*French*), noblewoman, peeress

damn = <u>criticize</u>, condemn, blast, denounce, put down, censure ≠ praise

damned (*Slang*) = <u>infernal</u>, detestable, confounded, hateful, loathsome

damp ADJECTIVE = <u>moist</u>, wet, soggy, humid, dank, sopping, clammy, dewy ≠ dry
● NOUN = <u>moisture</u>, liquid, drizzle, dampness, wetness, dankness ≠ dryness
● VERB = <u>moisten</u>, wet, soak, dampen, moisturize
● PHRASES **damp something down** = <u>curb</u>, reduce, check,

diminish, inhibit, stifle, allay, pour cold water on

dampen 1 = <u>reduce</u>, check, moderate, dull, restrain, stifle, lessen 2 = <u>moisten</u>, wet, spray, make damp

dance VERB 1 = <u>prance</u>, trip, hop, skip, sway, whirl, caper, jig 2 = <u>caper</u>, trip, spring, jump, bound, skip, frolic, cavort
• NOUN = <u>ball</u>, social, hop (*informal*), disco, knees-up (*Brit. informal*), discotheque, B and S (*Austral. informal*)

dancer = <u>ballerina</u>, Terpsichorean

danger 1 = <u>jeopardy</u>, vulnerability 2 = <u>hazard</u>, risk, threat, menace, peril, pitfall

dangerous = <u>perilous</u>, risky, hazardous, vulnerable, insecure, unsafe, precarious, breakneck ≠ safe

dangerously = <u>perilously</u>, alarmingly, precariously, recklessly, riskily, hazardously, unsafely

dangle 1 = <u>hang</u>, swing, trail, sway, flap, hang down 2 = <u>wave</u> 3 = <u>offer</u>, flourish, brandish, flaunt

dare 1 = <u>risk doing</u>, venture, presume, make bold (*archaic*), hazard doing 2 = <u>challenge</u>, provoke, defy, taunt, goad, throw down the gauntlet

daring ADJECTIVE = <u>brave</u>, bold, adventurous, reckless, fearless, audacious, intrepid, daredevil ≠ timid
• NOUN = <u>bravery</u>, nerve (*informal*), courage, spirit, bottle (*Brit. slang*), pluck, audacity, boldness ≠ timidity

dark ADJECTIVE 1 = <u>dim</u>, murky, shady, shadowy, grey, dingy, unlit, poorly lit 2 = <u>black</u>, brunette, ebony, dark-skinned, sable, dusky, swarthy ≠ fair 3 = <u>evil</u>, foul, sinister, vile, wicked, infernal 4 = <u>secret</u>, hidden, mysterious, concealed 5 = <u>gloomy</u>, sad, grim, miserable, bleak, dismal, pessimistic, melancholy ≠ cheerful
• NOUN 1 = <u>darkness</u>, shadows, gloom, dusk, obscurity, murk, dimness, semi-darkness 2 = <u>night</u>, twilight, evening, evo (*Austral. slang*), dusk, night-time, nightfall

darken 1 = <u>cloud</u>, obscure, dim, overshadow, blacken ≠ brighten 2 = <u>make dark</u>, blacken

darkness = <u>dark</u>, shadows, shade, gloom, blackness, murk, duskiness

darling NOUN = <u>beloved</u>, love, dear, dearest, angel, treasure, precious, sweetheart
• ADJECTIVE = <u>beloved</u>, dear, treasured, precious, adored, cherished

dart = <u>dash</u>, run, race, shoot, fly, speed, spring, tear

dash VERB 1 = <u>rush</u>, run, race, shoot, fly, career, speed, tear ≠ dawdle 2 = <u>throw</u>, cast, pitch, slam, toss, hurl, fling, chuck (*informal*) 3 = <u>crash</u>, break, smash, shatter, splinter

• NOUN 1 = <u>rush</u>, run, race, sprint, dart, spurt, sortie 2 = <u>drop</u>, little, bit, shot (*informal*), touch, spot, trace, hint ≠ lot 3 (*Old-fashioned*) = <u>style</u>, spirit, flair, flourish, verve, panache, élan, brio

dashing 1 (*Old-fashioned*) = <u>stylish</u>, smart, elegant, flamboyant, sporty, jaunty, showy 2 = <u>bold</u>, spirited, gallant, swashbuckling, debonair ≠ dull

data = <u>information</u>, facts, figures, details, intelligence, statistics

date NOUN 1 = <u>time</u>, stage, period 2 = <u>appointment</u>, meeting, arrangement, commitment, engagement, rendezvous, tryst, assignation 3 = <u>partner</u>, escort, friend

• VERB 1 = <u>put a date on</u>, assign a date to, fix the period of 2 = <u>become dated</u>, become old-fashioned

• PHRASES **date from** or **date back to** (with a *time* or *date* as object) = <u>come from</u>, belong to, originate in, exist from, bear a date of

dated = <u>old-fashioned</u>, outdated, out of date, obsolete, unfashionable, outmoded, passé,

old hat ≠ modern

daunting = <u>intimidating</u>, alarming, frightening, discouraging, unnerving, disconcerting, demoralizing, off-putting (*Brit. informal*) ≠ reassuring

dawn NOUN 1 = <u>daybreak</u>, morning, sunrise, daylight, aurora (*poetic*), crack of dawn, sunup, cockcrow 2 (*Literary*) = <u>beginning</u>, start, birth, rise, origin, emergence, advent, genesis

• VERB 1 = <u>begin</u>, start, rise, develop, emerge, unfold, originate 2 = <u>grow light</u>, break, brighten, lighten

• PHRASES **dawn on** or **upon someone** = <u>hit</u>, strike, occur to, register (*informal*), become apparent, come to mind, come into your head

day 1 = <u>twenty-four hours</u> 2 = <u>daytime</u>, daylight 3 = <u>date</u> 4 = <u>time</u>, age, era, period, epoch

daylight = <u>sunlight</u>, sunshine, light of day

daze VERB = <u>stun</u>, shock, paralyse, numb, stupefy, benumb

• NOUN (usually used in the phrase *in a daze*) = <u>shock</u>, confusion, distraction, trance, bewilderment, stupor, trancelike state

dazzle VERB 1 = <u>impress</u>, amaze, overwhelm, astonish, overpower, bowl over (*informal*), take your breath away **2** = **blind**, confuse, daze, bedazzle

● NOUN = **splendour**, sparkle, glitter, brilliance, magnificence, razzmatazz (*slang*)

dazzling = **splendid**, brilliant, stunning, glorious, sparkling, glittering, sensational (*informal*), virtuoso ≠ ordinary

dead ADJECTIVE **1** = **deceased**, departed, late, perished, extinct, defunct, passed away ≠ alive **2** = **boring**, dull, dreary, flat, plain, humdrum, uninteresting **3** = **not working**, useless, inactive, inoperative ≠ working **4** = **numb**, frozen, paralysed, insensitive, inert, deadened, immobilized, unfeeling **5** (usually used of *centre, silence,* or *stop*) = **total**, complete, absolute, utter, outright, thorough, unqualified **6** (*Informal*) = **exhausted**, tired, worn out, spent, done in (*informal*), all in (*slang*), drained, knackered (*slang*)

● NOUN = **middle**, heart, depth, midst

● ADVERB (*Informal*) = **exactly**, completely, totally, directly, fully, entirely, absolutely, thoroughly

deadline 1 = **time limit**, cutoff point, target date or time, limit

deadlock 1 = **impasse**, stalemate, standstill, gridlock, standoff **2** = **tie**, draw, stalemate,

impasse, standstill, gridlock, standoff, dead heat

deadly 1 = **lethal**, fatal, deathly, dangerous, devastating, mortal, murderous, malignant **2** (*Informal*) = **boring**, dull, tedious, flat, monotonous, uninteresting, mind-numbing, wearisome

deaf 1 = **hard of hearing**, without hearing, stone deaf **2** = **oblivious**, indifferent, unmoved, unconcerned, unsympathetic, impervious, unhearing

➤ **disabled**

deal NOUN **1** (*Informal*) = **agreement**, understanding, contract, arrangement, bargain, transaction, pact **2** = **amount**, quantity, measure, degree, mass, volume, share, portion

● PHRASES **deal in something** = **sell**, trade in, stock, traffic in, buy and sell ◆ **deal something out** = **distribute**, give, share, assign, allocate, dispense, allot, mete out ◆ **deal with something** = **be concerned with**, involve, concern, touch, regard, apply to, bear on, pertain to ◆ **deal with something or someone** = **handle**, manage, treat, cope with, take care of, see to, attend to, get to grips with

dealer = **trader**, merchant, supplier, wholesaler, purveyor, tradesman

dear ADJECTIVE 1 = <u>beloved</u>, close, valued, favourite, prized, treasured, precious, intimate ≠ hated 2 (*Brit. informal*) = <u>expensive</u>, costly, high-priced, pricey (*informal*), at a premium, overpriced, exorbitant ≠ cheap

• NOUN = <u>darling</u>, love, dearest, angel, treasure, precious, beloved, loved one

dearly (*Formal*) 1 = <u>very much</u>, greatly, extremely, profoundly 2 = <u>at great cost</u>, at a high price

death 1 = <u>dying</u>, demise, end, passing, departure ≠ birth 2 = <u>destruction</u>, finish, ruin, undoing, extinction, downfall ≠ beginning

(Related Words)

adjectives: fatal, lethal, mortal

deathly = <u>deathlike</u>, white, pale, ghastly, wan, pallid, ashen

debacle or **débâcle** = <u>disaster</u>, catastrophe, fiasco

debate NOUN = <u>discussion</u>, talk, argument, dispute, analysis, conversation, controversy, dialogue

• VERB 1 = <u>discuss</u>, question, talk about, argue about, dispute, examine, deliberate 2 = <u>consider</u>, reflect, think about, weigh, contemplate, deliberate, ponder, ruminate

debris = <u>remains</u>, bits, waste, ruins, fragments, rubble, wreckage, detritus

debt NOUN = <u>debit</u>, commitment, obligation, liability

• PHRASES in debt = <u>owing</u>, liable, in the red (*informal*), in arrears

debtor = <u>borrower</u>, mortgagor

debut = <u>entrance</u>, beginning, launch, coming out, introduction, presentation, first appearance, initiation

decay VERB 1 = <u>rot</u>, spoil, crumble, deteriorate, perish, decompose, moulder, go bad 2 = <u>decline</u>, diminish, crumble, deteriorate, fall off, dwindle, lessen, wane ≠ grow

• NOUN 1 = <u>rot</u>, corruption, mould, blight, decomposition, gangrene, canker, caries 2 = <u>decline</u>, collapse, deterioration, failing, fading, degeneration ≠ growth

deceased = <u>dead</u>, late, departed, expired, defunct, lifeless

deceive = <u>take in</u>, trick, fool (*informal*), cheat, con (*informal*), mislead, dupe, swindle

decency 1 = <u>propriety</u>, correctness, decorum, respectability, etiquette 2 = <u>courtesy</u>, politeness, civility, graciousness, urbanity, courteousness

decent 1 = <u>satisfactory</u>, fair, all right, reasonable, sufficient, good enough, adequate, ample ≠ unsatisfactory 2 = <u>proper</u>, becoming, seemly, fitting, appropriate, suitable, respectable,

befitting ≠ improper 3 (*Informal*)
= good, kind, friendly,
neighbourly, generous, helpful,
obliging, accommodating
4 = respectable, pure, proper,
modest, chaste, decorous

deception 1 = trickery, fraud,
deceit, cunning, treachery, guile,
legerdemain ≠ honesty 2 = trick,
lie, bluff, hoax, decoy, ruse,
subterfuge

decide 1 = make a decision,
make up your mind, reach or
come to a decision, choose,
determine, conclude ≠ hesitate
2 = resolve, answer, determine,
conclude, clear up, ordain,
adjudicate, adjudge 3 = settle,
determine, resolve

decidedly = definitely, clearly,
positively, distinctly, downright,
unequivocally, unmistakably

decision 1 = judgment, finding,
ruling, sentence, resolution,
conclusion, verdict, decree
2 = decisiveness, purpose,
resolution, resolve,
determination, firmness,
forcefulness, strength of mind or
will

decisive 1 = crucial, significant,
critical, influential, momentous,
conclusive, fateful ≠ uncertain
2 = resolute, decided, firm,
determined, forceful, incisive,
trenchant, strong-minded
≠ indecisive

deck = decorate, dress, clothe,
array, adorn, embellish, festoon,
beautify

declaration
1 = announcement,
proclamation, decree, notice,
notification, edict,
pronouncement 2 = affirmation,
profession, assertion, revelation,
disclosure, acknowledgment,
protestation, avowal
3 = statement, testimony

declare 1 = state, claim,
announce, voice, express,
maintain, assert, proclaim
2 = testify, state, swear, assert,
affirm, bear witness, vouch
3 = make known, reveal, show,
broadcast, confess, communicate,
disclose

decline VERB 1 = fall, drop, lower,
sink, fade, shrink, diminish,
decrease ≠ rise 2 = deteriorate,
weaken, pine, decay, worsen,
languish, degenerate, droop
≠ improve 3 = refuse, reject, turn
down, avoid, spurn, abstain, say
'no' ≠ accept
● NOUN 1 = depression, recession,
slump, falling off, downturn,
dwindling, lessening ≠ rise
2 = deterioration, failing,
weakening, decay, worsening,
degeneration ≠ improvement

décor or **decor** = decoration,
colour scheme, ornamentation,
furnishing style

decorate 1 = <u>adorn</u>, trim, embroider, ornament, embellish, festoon, beautify, grace **2** = <u>do up</u>, paper, paint, wallpaper, renovate (*informal*), furbish **3** = <u>pin a medal on</u>, cite, confer an honour on *or* upon

decoration 1 = <u>adornment</u>, trimming, enhancement, elaboration, embellishment, ornamentation, beautification **2** = <u>ornament</u>, trimmings, garnish, frill, bauble **3** = <u>medal</u>, award, star, ribbon, badge

decorative = <u>ornamental</u>, fancy, pretty, attractive, for show, embellishing, showy, beautifying

decrease VERB **1** = <u>drop</u>, decline, lessen, lower, shrink, diminish, dwindle, subside **2** = <u>reduce</u>, cut, lower, moderate, weaken, diminish, cut down, shorten ≠ increase

• NOUN = <u>lessening</u>, decline, reduction, loss, falling off, dwindling, contraction, cutback ≠ growth

decree NOUN **1** = <u>law</u>, order, ruling, act, command, statute, proclamation, edict **2** = <u>judgment</u>, finding, ruling, decision, verdict, arbitration

• VERB = <u>order</u>, rule, command, demand, proclaim, prescribe, pronounce, ordain

dedicate 1 = <u>devote</u>, give, apply, commit, pledge, surrender, give

over to **2** = <u>offer</u>, address, inscribe

dedicated = <u>committed</u>, devoted, enthusiastic, single-minded, zealous, purposeful, wholehearted ≠ indifferent

dedication 1 = <u>commitment</u>, loyalty, devotion, allegiance, adherence, single-mindedness, faithfulness, wholeheartedness ≠ indifference **2** = <u>inscription</u>, message, address

deduct = <u>subtract</u>, remove, take off, take away, reduce by, knock off (*informal*), decrease by ≠ add

deduction 1 = <u>conclusion</u>, finding, verdict, judgment, assumption, inference **2** = <u>reasoning</u>, thinking, thought, analysis, logic **3** = <u>discount</u>, reduction, cut, concession, decrease, rebate, diminution **4** = <u>subtraction</u>, reduction, concession

deed 1 = <u>action</u>, act, performance, achievement, exploit, feat **2** (*Law*) = <u>document</u>, title, contract

deep ADJECTIVE **1** = <u>big</u>, wide, broad, profound, yawning, bottomless, unfathomable ≠ shallow **2** = <u>intense</u>, great, serious (*informal*), acute, extreme, grave, profound, heartfelt ≠ superficial **3** = <u>sound</u>, profound, unbroken, undisturbed, untroubled **4** = <u>absorbed</u>, lost, gripped, preoccupied, immersed, engrossed, rapt **5** = <u>dark</u>, strong, rich, intense, vivid ≠ light **6** = <u>low</u>, booming, bass, resonant, sonorous, low-pitched ≠ high **7** = <u>secret</u>, hidden, mysterious, obscure, abstract, esoteric, mystifying, arcane **8** = <u>far</u>, a long way, a good way, miles, a great distance

● NOUN **1** = <u>middle</u>, heart, midst, dead

● PHRASES **the deep** (*Poetic*) = <u>the ocean</u>, the sea, the waves, the main, the high seas, the briny (*informal*)

deepen 1 = <u>intensify</u>, increase, grow, strengthen, reinforce, escalate, magnify **2** = <u>dig out</u>, excavate, scoop out, hollow out

deeply = <u>thoroughly</u>, completely, seriously, sadly, severely, gravely, profoundly, intensely

de facto ADJECTIVE = <u>actual</u>, real, existing

● ADVERB = <u>in fact</u>, really, actually, in effect, in reality

default VERB = <u>fail to pay</u>, dodge, evade, neglect

● NOUN **1** (usually in phrase *by default* or *in default of*) = <u>failure</u>, neglect, deficiency, lapse, omission, dereliction **2** = <u>nonpayment</u>, evasion

defeat VERB **1** = <u>beat</u>, crush, overwhelm, conquer, master, rout, trounce, vanquish

≠ surrender **2** = <u>frustrate</u>, foil, thwart, ruin, baffle, confound, balk, get the better of

● NOUN **1** = <u>conquest</u>, beating, overthrow, rout ≠ victory **2** = <u>frustration</u>, failure, reverse, setback, thwarting

defect NOUN = <u>deficiency</u>, failing, fault, error, flaw, imperfection

● VERB = <u>desert</u>, rebel, quit, revolt, change sides

defence *or* (*U.S.*) **defense** NOUN **1** = <u>protection</u>, cover, security, guard, shelter, safeguard, immunity **2** = <u>armaments</u>, weapons **3** = <u>argument</u>, explanation, excuse, plea, justification, vindication, rationalization **4** = <u>plea</u> (*Law*), testimony, denial, alibi, rebuttal

● PLURAL NOUN = <u>shield</u>, barricade, fortification, buttress, rampart, bulwark, fortified pa (*N.Z.*)

defend 1 = <u>protect</u>, cover, guard, screen, preserve, look after, shelter, shield **2** = <u>support</u>, champion, justify, endorse, uphold, vindicate, stand up for, speak up for

defendant = <u>the accused</u>, respondent, prisoner at the bar

defender 1 = <u>supporter</u>, champion, advocate, sponsor, follower **2** = <u>protector</u>, guard, guardian, escort, bodyguard

defensive 1 = <u>protective</u>, watchful, on the defensive, on guard 2 = <u>oversensitive</u>, uptight (*informal*)

defer = <u>postpone</u>, delay, put off, suspend, shelve, hold over, procrastinate, put on ice (*informal*)

defiance = <u>resistance</u>, opposition, confrontation, contempt, disregard, disobedience, insolence, insubordination ≠ obedience

defiant = <u>resisting</u>, rebellious, daring, bold, provocative, audacious, antagonistic, insolent ≠ obedient

deficiency 1 = <u>lack</u>, want, deficit, absence, shortage, scarcity, dearth ≠ sufficiency 2 = <u>failing</u>, fault, weakness, defect, flaw, drawback, shortcoming, imperfection

deficit = <u>shortfall</u>, shortage, deficiency, loss, arrears

define 1 = <u>mark out</u>, outline, limit, bound, delineate, circumscribe, demarcate 2 = <u>describe</u>, interpret, characterize, explain, spell out, expound 3 = <u>establish</u>, specify, designate

definite 1 = <u>specific</u>, exact, precise, clear, particular, fixed, black-and-white, cut-and-dried (*informal*) ≠ vague 2 = <u>clear</u>, black-and-white, unequivocal, unambiguous, guaranteed, cut-and-dried (*informal*)

3 = <u>noticeable</u>, marked, clear, decided, striking, particular, distinct, conspicuous 4 = <u>certain</u>, decided, sure, settled, convinced, positive, confident, assured ≠ uncertain

definitely = <u>certainly</u>, clearly, surely, absolutely, positively, without doubt, unquestionably, undeniably

definition 1 = <u>description</u>, interpretation, explanation, clarification, exposition, elucidation, statement of meaning 2 = <u>sharpness</u>, focus, clarity, contrast, precision, distinctness

definitive 1 = <u>final</u>, convincing, absolute, clinching, decisive, definite, conclusive, irrefutable 2 = <u>authoritative</u>, greatest, ultimate, reliable, exhaustive, superlative

deflect = <u>turn aside</u>, bend

defy = <u>resist</u>, oppose, confront, brave, disregard, stand up to, spurn, flout

degenerate VERB = <u>decline</u>, slip, sink, decrease, deteriorate, worsen, decay, lapse

● ADJECTIVE = <u>depraved</u>, corrupt, low, perverted, immoral, decadent, debauched, dissolute

degrade = <u>demean</u>, disgrace, humiliate, shame, humble, discredit, debase, dishonour ≠ ennoble

degree = <u>amount</u>, stage, grade

delay VERB 1 = <u>put off</u>, suspend, postpone, shelve, defer, hold over 2 = <u>hold up</u>, detain, hold back, hinder, obstruct, impede, bog down, set back ≠ speed (up)
● NOUN = <u>hold-up</u>, wait, setback, interruption, stoppage, impediment, hindrance

delegate NOUN = <u>representative</u>, agent, deputy, ambassador, commissioner, envoy, proxy, legate
● VERB 1 = <u>entrust</u>, transfer, hand over, give, pass on, assign, consign, devolve 2 = <u>appoint</u>, commission, select, contract, engage, nominate, designate, mandate

delegation 1 = <u>deputation</u>, envoys, contingent, commission, embassy, legation
2 = <u>commissioning</u>, assignment, devolution, committal

delete = <u>remove</u>, cancel, erase, strike out, obliterate, efface, cross out, expunge

deliberate ADJECTIVE
1 = <u>intentional</u>, meant, planned, intended, conscious, calculated, wilful, purposeful ≠ accidental
2 = <u>careful</u>, measured, slow, cautious, thoughtful, circumspect, methodical, unhurried ≠ hurried
● VERB = <u>consider</u>, think, ponder, discuss, debate, reflect, consult, weigh

deliberately = <u>intentionally</u>, on purpose, consciously, knowingly, wilfully, by design, in cold blood, wittingly

deliberation 1 = <u>consideration</u>, thought, reflection, calculation, meditation, forethought, circumspection 2 = <u>discussion</u>, talk, conference, debate, analysis, conversation, dialogue, consultation

delicacy 1 = <u>fragility</u>, flimsiness 2 = <u>daintiness</u>, charm, grace, elegance, neatness, prettiness, slenderness, exquisiteness
3 = <u>difficulty</u> 4 = <u>sensitivity</u>, understanding, consideration, diplomacy, discretion, tact, thoughtfulness, sensitiveness
5 = <u>treat</u>, luxury, savoury, dainty, morsel, titbit 6 = <u>lightness</u>, accuracy, precision, elegance, sensibility, purity, subtlety, refinement

delicate 1 = <u>fine</u>, elegant, exquisite, graceful 2 = <u>subtle</u>, fine, delicious, faint, refined, understated, dainty ≠ bright
3 = <u>fragile</u>, weak, frail, brittle, tender, flimsy, dainty, breakable
4 = <u>skilled</u>, precise, deft
5 = <u>diplomatic</u>, sensitive, thoughtful, discreet, considerate, tactful ≠ insensitive

delicious = <u>delectable</u>, tasty, choice, savoury, dainty, mouthwatering, scrumptious (*informal*), appetizing, lekker (*S. African slang*), yummo (*Austral. slang*) ≠ unpleasant

delight NOUN = <u>pleasure</u>, joy, satisfaction, happiness, ecstasy, enjoyment, bliss, glee ≠ displeasure

● VERB = <u>please</u>, satisfy, thrill, charm, cheer, amuse, enchant, gratify ≠ displease

● PHRASES **delight in** or **take (a) delight in something** or **someone** = <u>like</u>, love, enjoy, appreciate, relish, savour, revel in, take pleasure in

delightful = <u>pleasant</u>, charming, thrilling, enjoyable, enchanting, agreeable, pleasurable, rapturous ≠ unpleasant

deliver 1 = <u>bring</u>, carry, bear, transport, distribute, convey, cart 2 *sometimes with up* = <u>hand over</u>, commit, give up, yield, surrender, turn over, relinquish, make over 3 = <u>give</u>, read, present, announce, declare, utter 4 = <u>strike</u>, give, deal, launch, direct, aim, administer, inflict 5 (*Dated*) = <u>release</u>, free, save, rescue, loose, liberate, ransom, emancipate

delivery 1 = <u>handing over</u>, transfer, distribution, transmission, dispatch, consignment, conveyance 2 = <u>consignment</u>, goods, shipment, batch 3 = <u>speech</u>, utterance, articulation, intonation, elocution, enunciation 4 = <u>childbirth</u>, labour, confinement, parturition

delusion = <u>misconception</u>, mistaken idea, misapprehension, fancy, illusion, hallucination, fallacy, false impression

demand VERB 1 = <u>request</u>, ask (for), order, expect, claim, seek, insist on, exact 2 = <u>challenge</u>, ask, question, inquire 3 = <u>require</u>, want, need, involve, call for, entail, necessitate, cry out for ≠ provide

● NOUN 1 = <u>request</u>, order 2 = <u>need</u>, want, call, market, claim, requirement

demanding = <u>difficult</u>, trying, hard, taxing, wearing, challenging, tough, exacting ≠ easy

demise 1 = <u>failure</u>, end, fall, defeat, collapse, ruin, breakdown, overthrow 2 (*Euphemistic*) = <u>death</u>, end, dying, passing, departure, decease

democracy = <u>self-government</u>, republic, commonwealth

Democrat ADJECTIVE = <u>left-wing</u>, Labour

● NOUN = <u>left-winger</u>

democratic = <u>self-governing</u>, popular, representative, autonomous, populist, egalitarian

demolish 1 = <u>knock down</u>, level, destroy, dismantle, flatten, tear down, bulldoze, raze ≠ build

2 = <u>destroy</u>, wreck, overturn, overthrow, undo

demolition = <u>knocking down</u>, levelling, destruction, explosion, wrecking, tearing down, bulldozing, razing

demon 1 = <u>evil spirit</u>, devil, fiend, goblin, ghoul, malignant spirit, atua (*N.Z.*), wairua (*N.Z.*) **2** = <u>wizard</u>, master, ace (*informal*), fiend

demonstrate 1 = <u>prove</u>, show, indicate, make clear, manifest, testify to **2** = <u>show</u>, express, display, indicate, exhibit, manifest **3** = <u>march</u>, protest, rally, object, parade, picket, remonstrate, express disapproval, hikoi (*N.Z.*) **4** = <u>describe</u>, show, explain, teach, illustrate

demonstration 1 = <u>march</u>, protest, rally, sit-in, parade, picket, mass lobby, hikoi (*N.Z.*) **2** = <u>display</u>, show, performance, explanation, description, presentation, exposition **3** = <u>indication</u>, proof, testimony, confirmation, substantiation **4** = <u>exhibition</u>, display, expression, illustration

den 1 = <u>lair</u>, hole, shelter, cave, haunt, cavern, hide-out **2** (*Chiefly U.S.*) = <u>study</u>, retreat, sanctuary, hideaway, sanctum, cubbyhole

denial 1 = <u>negation</u>, contradiction, dissent, retraction, repudiation ≠ admission

2 = <u>refusal</u>, veto, rejection, prohibition, rebuff, repulse **3** = <u>renunciation</u>, giving up, rejection, abdication, repudiation, forswearing, disavowal, relinquishment

denomination 1 = <u>religious group</u>, belief, sect, persuasion, creed, school, hauhau (*N.Z.*) **2** = <u>unit</u>, value, size, grade

denounce 1 = <u>condemn</u>, attack, censure, revile, vilify, stigmatize **2** = <u>report</u>, dob in (*Austral. slang*)

dense 1 = <u>thick</u>, heavy, solid, compact, condensed, impenetrable, close-knit ≠ thin **2** = <u>heavy</u>, thick, opaque, impenetrable **3** = <u>stupid</u> (*Informal*), thick, dull, dumb (*informal*), dozy (*Brit. informal*), stolid, dopey (*informal*), moronic ≠ bright

density 1 = <u>tightness</u>, thickness, compactness, impenetrability, denseness **2** = <u>mass</u>, bulk, consistency, solidity

dent VERB = <u>make a dent in</u>, press in, gouge, hollow, push in
● NOUN = <u>hollow</u>, chip, indentation, depression, impression, pit, dip, crater, ding (*Austral. & N.Z. dated informal*)

deny 1 = <u>contradict</u>, disagree with, rebuff, negate, rebut, refute ≠ admit **2** = <u>renounce</u>, reject, retract, repudiate, disown, recant, disclaim ≠ refuse, forbid, reject, rule out, turn down, prohibit, withhold, preclude ≠ permit

depart 1 = <u>leave</u>, go, withdraw, retire, disappear, quit, retreat, exit ≠ arrive 2 = <u>deviate</u>, vary, differ, stray, veer, swerve, diverge, digress

department = <u>section</u>, office, unit, station, division, branch, bureau, subdivision

departure 1 = <u>leaving</u>, going, retirement, withdrawal, exit, going away, removal, exodus ≠ arrival 2 = <u>retirement</u>, going, withdrawal, exit, going away, removal 3 = <u>shift</u>, change, difference, variation, innovation, novelty, deviation, divergence

depend 1 = <u>be determined by</u>, be based on, be subject to, hang on, rest on, revolve around, hinge on, be subordinate to 2 = <u>count on</u>, turn to, trust in, bank on, lean on, rely upon, reckon on

dependent or (U.S. sometimes) **dependant** ADJECTIVE = <u>reliant</u>, vulnerable, helpless, powerless, weak, defenceless ≠ independent
• PHRASES **dependent on** or **upon** 1 = <u>reliant on</u>, relying on 2 = <u>determined by</u>, depending on, subject to, influenced by, conditional on, contingent on

depict 1 = <u>illustrate</u>, portray, picture, paint, outline, draw, sketch, delineate 2 = <u>describe</u>, present, represent, outline, characterize

deplete = <u>use up</u>, reduce, drain, exhaust, consume, empty, lessen, impoverish ≠ increase

deplore = <u>disapprove of</u>, condemn, object to, denounce, censure, abhor, take a dim view of

deploy (used of troops or military resources) = <u>use</u>, station, position, arrange, set out, utilize

deployment (used of troops or military resources) = <u>use</u>, stationing, spread, organization, arrangement, positioning, utilization

deport = <u>expel</u>, exile, throw out, oust, banish, expatriate, extradite, evict

depose = <u>oust</u>, dismiss, displace, demote, dethrone, remove from office

deposit NOUN 1 = <u>down payment</u>, security, stake, pledge, instalment, retainer, part payment 2 = <u>accumulation</u>, mass, build-up, layer 3 = <u>sediment</u>, grounds, residue, lees, precipitate, silt, dregs
• VERB 1 = <u>put</u>, place, lay, drop 2 = <u>store</u>, keep, put, bank, lodge, entrust, consign

depot 1 = <u>arsenal</u>, warehouse, storehouse, repository, depository 2 (Chiefly U.S. & Canad.) = <u>bus station</u>, station, garage, terminus

depreciation = <u>devaluation</u>, fall, drop, depression, slump, deflation

depress 1 = <u>sadden</u>, upset, distress, discourage, grieve, oppress, weigh down, make sad ≠ cheer 2 = <u>lower</u>, cut, reduce, diminish, decrease, lessen ≠ raise 3 = <u>devalue</u>, depreciate, cheapen 4 = <u>press down</u>, push, squeeze, lower, flatten, compress, push down

depressed 1 = <u>sad</u>, blue, unhappy, discouraged, fed up, mournful, dejected, despondent 2 = <u>poverty-stricken</u>, poor, deprived, disadvantaged, run-down, impoverished, needy 3 = <u>lowered</u>, devalued, weakened, depreciated, cheapened 4 = <u>sunken</u>, hollow, recessed, indented, concave

depressing = <u>bleak</u>, sad, discouraging, gloomy, dismal, harrowing, saddening, dispiriting

depression 1 = <u>despair</u>, misery, sadness, dumps (*informal*), the blues, melancholy, unhappiness, despondency 2 = <u>recession</u>, slump, economic decline, stagnation, inactivity, hard *or* bad times 3 = <u>hollow</u>, pit, dip, bowl, valley, dent, cavity, indentation

deprivation 1 = <u>lack</u>, denial, withdrawal, removal, expropriation, dispossession 2 = <u>want</u>, need, hardship, suffering, distress, privation, destitution

deprive = <u>dispossess</u>, rob, strip, despoil, bereave

deprived = <u>poor</u>, disadvantaged, needy, in need, lacking, bereft, destitute, down at heel ≠ prosperous

depth 1 = <u>deepness</u>, drop, measure, extent 2 = <u>insight</u>, wisdom, penetration, profundity, discernment, sagacity, astuteness, profoundness ≠ superficiality 3 = <u>breadth</u>

deputy = <u>substitute</u>, representative, delegate, lieutenant, proxy, surrogate, second-in-command, legate

derelict ADJECTIVE = <u>abandoned</u>, deserted, ruined, neglected, discarded, forsaken, dilapidated • NOUN = <u>tramp</u>, outcast, drifter, down-and-out, vagrant, bag lady, derro (*Austral. slang*)

descend VERB 1 = <u>fall</u>, drop, sink, go down, plunge, dive, tumble, plummet ≠ rise 2 = <u>get off</u> 3 = <u>go down</u>, come down, walk down, move down, climb down 4 = <u>slope</u>, dip, incline, slant • PHRASES be descended from = <u>originate from</u>, derive from, spring from, proceed from, issue from

descent 1 = <u>fall</u>, drop, plunge, coming down, swoop 2 = <u>slope</u>, drop, dip, incline, slant, declivity

3 = <u>decline</u>, deterioration, degeneration 4 = <u>origin</u>, extraction, ancestry, lineage, family tree, parentage, genealogy, derivation

describe 1 = <u>relate</u>, tell, report, explain, express, recount, recite, narrate 2 = <u>portray</u>, depict 3 = <u>trace</u>, draw, outline, mark out, delineate

description 1 = <u>account</u>, report, explanation, representation, sketch, narrative, portrayal, depiction 2 = <u>calling</u>, naming, branding, labelling, dubbing, designation 3 = <u>kind</u>, sort, type, order, class, variety, brand, category

desert[1] = <u>wilderness</u>, waste, wilds, wasteland

desert[2] 1 = <u>abandon</u>, leave, quit (*informal*), forsake 2 = <u>leave</u>, abandon, strand, maroon, walk out on (*informal*), forsake, jilt, leave stranded ≠ take care of 3 = <u>abscond</u>

deserted 1 = <u>empty</u>, abandoned, desolate, neglected, vacant, derelict, unoccupied 2 = <u>abandoned</u>, neglected, forsaken

deserve = <u>merit</u>, warrant, be entitled to, have a right to, rate, earn, justify, be worthy of

deserved = <u>well-earned</u>, fitting, due, earned, justified, merited, proper, warranted

deserving = <u>worthy</u>, righteous, commendable, laudable, praiseworthy, meritorious, estimable ≠ undeserving

design VERB 1 = <u>plan</u>, draw, draft, trace, outline, devise, sketch, formulate 2 = <u>create</u>, plan, fashion, propose, invent, conceive, originate, fabricate 3 = <u>intend</u>, mean, plan, aim, purpose
• NOUN 1 = <u>pattern</u>, form, style, shape, organization, arrangement, construction 2 = <u>plan</u>, drawing, model, scheme, draft, outline, sketch, blueprint 3 = <u>intention</u>, end, aim, goal, target, purpose, object, objective

designate 1 = <u>name</u>, call, term, style, label, entitle, dub 2 = <u>choose</u>, reserve, select, label, flag, assign, allocate, set aside 3 = <u>appoint</u>, name, choose, commission, select, elect, delegate, nominate

designer 1 = <u>couturier</u> 2 = <u>producer</u>, architect, deviser, creator, planner, inventor, originator

desirable 1 = <u>advantageous</u>, useful, valuable, helpful, profitable, of service, convenient, worthwhile ≠ disadvantageous 2 = <u>popular</u> ≠ unpopular 3 = <u>attractive</u>, appealing, pretty, fair, inviting, lovely, charming, sexy (*informal*) ≠ unattractive

desire NOUN 1 = <u>wish</u>, want, longing, hope, urge, aspiration, craving, thirst 2 = <u>lust</u>, passion, libido, appetite, lasciviousness
● VERB = <u>want</u>, long for, crave, hope for, ache for, wish for, yearn for, thirst for

despair NOUN 1 = <u>despondency</u>, depression, misery, gloom, desperation, anguish, hopelessness, dejection
● VERB = <u>lose hope</u>, give up, lose heart

despatch ▸ dispatch

desperate 1 = <u>grave</u>, pressing, serious, severe, extreme, urgent, drastic 2 = <u>last-ditch</u>, daring, furious, risky, frantic, audacious

desperately = <u>gravely</u>, badly, seriously, severely, dangerously, perilously

desperation 1 = <u>misery</u>, worry, trouble, despair, agony, anguish, unhappiness, hopelessness 2 = <u>recklessness</u>, madness, frenzy, impetuosity, rashness, foolhardiness

despise = <u>look down on</u>, loathe, scorn, detest, revile, abhor ≠ admire

despite = <u>in spite of</u>, in the face of, regardless of, even with, notwithstanding, in the teeth of, undeterred by

destination = <u>stop</u>, station, haven, resting-place, terminus,

journey's end

destined = <u>fated</u>, meant, intended, certain, bound, doomed, predestined

destiny 1 = <u>fate</u>, fortune, lot, portion, doom, nemesis 2 *usually cap.* = <u>fortune</u>, chance, karma, providence, kismet, predestination, divine will

destroy 1 = <u>ruin</u>, crush, devastate, wreck, shatter, wipe out, demolish, eradicate 2 = <u>slaughter</u>, kill

destruction 1 = <u>ruin</u>, havoc, wreckage, demolition, devastation, annihilation 2 slaughter, extermination, eradication 3 = <u>slaughter</u>

destructive = <u>devastating</u>, fatal, deadly, lethal, harmful, damaging, catastrophic, ruinous

detach 1 = <u>separate</u>, remove, divide, cut off, sever, disconnect, tear off, disengage ≠ attach 2 = <u>free</u>, remove, separate, isolate, cut off, disengage

detached 1 = <u>objective</u>, neutral, impartial, reserved, impersonal, disinterested, unbiased, dispassionate ≠ subjective 2 = <u>separate</u>, disconnected, discrete, unconnected, undivided

detachment 1 = <u>indifference</u>, fairness, neutrality, objectivity, impartiality, coolness, remoteness, nonchalance 2 (*Military*) = <u>unit</u>, party, force, body, squad, patrol, task force

detail NOUN 1 = point, fact, feature, particular, respect, factor, element, aspect 2 = fine point, particular, nicety, triviality 3 (*Military*) = party, force, body, duty, squad, assignment, fatigue, detachment

● VERB = list, relate, catalogue, recount, rehearse, recite, enumerate, itemize

detailed = comprehensive, full, complete, minute, particular, thorough, exhaustive, all-embracing ≠ brief

detain 1 = hold, arrest, confine, restrain, imprison, intern, take prisoner, hold in custody 2 = delay, hold up, hamper, hinder, retard, impede, keep back, slow up *or* down

detect 1 = discover, find, uncover, track down, unmask 2 = notice, see, spot, note, identify, observe, recognize, perceive

detective = investigator, cop (*slang*), private eye, sleuth (*informal*), private investigator, gumshoe (*U.S. slang*)

detention = imprisonment, custody, quarantine, confinement, incarceration ≠ release

deter 1 = discourage, inhibit, put off, frighten, intimidate, dissuade, talk out of 2 = prevent, stop

deteriorate = decline, worsen, degenerate, slump, go downhill ≠ improve

determination = resolution, purpose, resolve, dedication, fortitude, persistence, tenacity, perseverance ≠ indecision

determine 1 = affect, decide, regulate, ordain 2 = settle, learn, establish, discover, find out, work out, detect, verify 3 = decide on, choose, elect, resolve 4 = decide, conclude, resolve, make up your mind

determined = resolute, firm, dogged, intent, persistent, persevering, single-minded, tenacious

deterrent = discouragement, obstacle, curb, restraint, impediment, check, hindrance, disincentive ≠ incentive

devastate = destroy, ruin, sack, wreck, demolish, level, ravage, raze

devastation = destruction, ruin, havoc, demolition, desolation

develop 1 = grow, advance, progress, mature, evolve, flourish, ripen 2 = establish, set up, promote, generate, undertake, initiate, embark on, cultivate 3 = form, establish, breed, generate, originate 4 = expand, extend, work out, elaborate, unfold, enlarge, broaden, amplify

development 1 = growth,

increase, advance, progress, spread, expansion, evolution, enlargement **2** = <u>establishment</u>, forming, generation, institution, invention, initiation, inauguration, instigation **3** = <u>event</u>, happening, result, incident, improvement, evolution, unfolding, occurrence

deviant ADJECTIVE = <u>perverted</u>, sick (informal), twisted, warped, kinky (slang) ≠ normal

• NOUN = <u>pervert</u>, freak, misfit

device 1 = <u>gadget</u>, machine, tool, instrument, implement, appliance, apparatus, contraption **2** = <u>ploy</u>, scheme, plan, trick, manoeuvre, gambit, stratagem, wile

devil NOUN **1** = <u>evil spirit</u>, demon, fiend, atua (N.Z.), wairua (N.Z.) **2** = <u>brute</u>, monster, beast, barbarian, fiend, terror, swine, ogre **3** = <u>person</u>, individual, soul, creature, thing, beggar **4** = <u>scamp</u>, rogue, rascal, scoundrel, scallywag (informal), nointer (Austral. slang)

• PHRASES **the Devil** = <u>Satan</u>, Lucifer, Prince of Darkness, Mephistopheles, Evil One, Beelzebub, Old Nick (informal)

devise = <u>work out</u>, design, construct, invent, conceive, formulate, contrive, dream up

devoid with **of** = <u>lacking in</u>, without, free from, wanting in,

bereft of, empty of, deficient in

devote = <u>dedicate</u>, give, commit, apply, reserve, pledge, surrender, assign

devoted = <u>dedicated</u>, committed, true, constant, loyal, faithful, ardent, staunch ≠ disloyal

devotee = <u>enthusiast</u>, fan, supporter, follower, admirer, buff (informal), fanatic, adherent

devotion NOUN **1** = <u>love</u>, passion, affection, attachment, fondness **2** = <u>dedication</u>, commitment, loyalty, allegiance, fidelity, adherence, constancy, faithfulness ≠ indifference **3** = <u>worship</u>, reverence, spirituality, holiness, piety, godliness, devoutness ≠ irreverence

• PLURAL NOUN = <u>prayers</u>, religious observance, church service, divine office

devour 1 = <u>eat</u>, consume, swallow, wolf, gulp, gobble, guzzle, polish off (informal) **2** = <u>enjoy</u>, take in, read compulsively or voraciously

devout = <u>religious</u>, godly, pious, pure, holy, orthodox, saintly, reverent ≠ irreverent

diagnose = <u>identify</u>, determine, recognize, distinguish, interpret, pronounce, pinpoint

diagnosis = <u>identification</u>, discovery, recognition, detection

diagram = <u>plan</u>, figure, drawing,

chart, representation, sketch, graph

dialogue 1 = <u>discussion</u>, conference, exchange, debate 2 = <u>conversation</u>, discussion, communication, discourse

diary 1 = <u>journal</u>, chronicle 2 = <u>engagement book</u>, Filofax®, appointment book

dictate VERB = <u>speak</u>, say, utter, read out

● NOUN 1 = <u>command</u>, order, decree, demand, direction, injunction, fiat, edict 2 = <u>principle</u>, law, rule, standard, code, criterion, maxim

● PHRASES **dictate to someone** = <u>order (about)</u>, direct, lay down the law, pronounce to

dictator = <u>absolute ruler</u>, tyrant, despot, oppressor, autocrat, absolutist, martinet

dictatorship = <u>absolute rule</u>, tyranny, totalitarianism, authoritarianism, despotism, autocracy, absolutism

dictionary = <u>wordbook</u>, vocabulary, glossary, lexicon

die VERB 1 = <u>pass away</u>, expire, perish, croak (slang), give up the ghost, snuff it (slang), peg out (informal), kick the bucket (slang), cark it (Austral. & N.Z. slang) ≠ live 2 = <u>stop</u>, fail, halt, break down, run down, stop working, peter out, fizzle out 3 = <u>dwindle</u>, decline, sink, fade,

diminish, decrease, decay, wither ≠ increase

● PHRASES **be dying for something** = <u>long for</u>, want, desire, crave, yearn for, hunger for, pine for, hanker after

diet¹ NOUN 1 = <u>food</u>, provisions, fare, rations, kai (N.Z. informal), nourishment, sustenance, victuals 2 = <u>fast</u>, regime, abstinence, regimen

● VERB = <u>slim</u>, fast, lose weight, abstain, eat sparingly ≠ overindulge

diet² often cap. = <u>council</u>, meeting, parliament, congress, chamber, convention, legislature

differ 1 = <u>be dissimilar</u>, contradict, contrast with, vary, belie, depart from, diverge, negate ≠ accord 2 = <u>disagree</u>, clash, dispute, dissent ≠ agree

difference 1 = <u>dissimilarity</u>, contrast, variation, change, variety, diversity, alteration, discrepancy ≠ similarity 2 = <u>remainder</u>, rest, balance, remains, excess 3 = <u>disagreement</u>, conflict, argument, clash, dispute, quarrel, contretemps ≠ agreement

different 1 = <u>dissimilar</u>, opposed, contrasting, changed, unlike, altered, inconsistent, disparate 2 = <u>various</u>, varied, diverse, assorted, miscellaneous, sundry 3 = <u>unusual</u>, special, strange, extraordinary, distinctive, peculiar, uncommon, singular

---

Word Power

different – On the whole, *different from* is preferable to *different to* and *different than*, both of which are considered unacceptable by some people. *Different to* is often heard in British English, but is thought by some people to be incorrect; and *different than*, though acceptable in American English, is often regarded as unacceptable in British English. This makes *different from* the safest option: *this result is only slightly different from that obtained in the US* – or you can rephrase the sentence: *this result differs only slightly from that obtained in the US*.

---

differentiate 1 = <u>distinguish</u>, separate, discriminate, contrast, mark off, make a distinction, tell apart, set off *or* apart 2 = <u>make different</u>, separate, distinguish, characterize, single out, segregate, individualize, mark off 3 = <u>become different</u>, change, convert, transform, alter, adapt, modify

difficult 1 = <u>hard</u>, tough, taxing, demanding, challenging, exacting, formidable, uphill ≠ easy 2 = <u>problematical</u>,

involved, complex, complicated, obscure, baffling, intricate, knotty ≠ simple 3 = <u>troublesome</u>, demanding, perverse, fussy, fastidious, hard to please, refractory, unaccommodating ≠ cooperative

difficulty 1 = <u>problem</u>, trouble, obstacle, hurdle, dilemma, complication, snag, uphill (*S. African*) 2 = <u>hardship</u>, strain, awkwardness, strenuousness, arduousness, laboriousness

dig VERB 1 = <u>hollow out</u>, mine, quarry, excavate, scoop out 2 = <u>delve</u>, tunnel, burrow 3 = <u>turn over</u> 4 = <u>search</u>, hunt, root, delve, forage, dig down, fossick (*Austral. & N.Z.*) 5 = <u>poke</u>, drive, push, stick, punch, stab, thrust, shove
● NOUN 1 = <u>cutting remark</u>, crack (*slang*), insult, taunt, sneer, jeer, barb, wisecrack (*informal*)
2 = <u>poke</u>, thrust, nudge, prod, jab, punch

digest VERB 1 = <u>ingest</u>, absorb, incorporate, dissolve, assimilate 2 = <u>take in</u>, absorb, grasp, soak up
● NOUN = <u>summary</u>, résumé, abstract, epitome, synopsis, précis, abridgment

dignity 1 = <u>decorum</u>, gravity, majesty, grandeur, respectability, nobility, solemnity, courtliness 2 = <u>self-importance</u>, pride, self-esteem, self-respect

dilemma = <u>predicament</u>,

problem, difficulty, spot (*informal*), mess, puzzle, plight, quandary

> ### Word Power
>
> **dilemma** – The use of *dilemma* to refer to a problem that seems incapable of solution is considered by some people to be incorrect. To avoid this misuse of the word, an appropriate alternative such as *predicament* could be used.

dilute 1 = <u>water down</u>, thin (out), weaken, adulterate, make thinner, cut (*informal*) ≠ condense **2** = <u>reduce</u>, weaken, diminish, temper, decrease, lessen, diffuse, mitigate ≠ intensify

dim ADJECTIVE 1 = <u>poorly lit</u>, dark, gloomy, murky, shady, shadowy, dusky, tenebrous **2** = <u>cloudy</u>, grey, gloomy, dismal, overcast, leaden ≠ bright **3** = <u>unclear</u>, obscured, faint, blurred, fuzzy, shadowy, hazy, bleary ≠ distinct **4** = <u>stupid</u> (*Informal*), thick, dull, dense, dumb (*informal*), daft (*informal*), dozy (*Brit. informal*), obtuse ≠ bright
● **VERB 1** = <u>turn down</u>, fade, dull **2** = <u>grow or become faint</u>, fade, dull, grow or become dim **3** = <u>darken</u>, dull, cloud over

dimension 1 = <u>aspect</u>, side, feature, angle, facet **2** = <u>extent</u>, size

diminish 1 = <u>decrease</u>, decline, lessen, shrink, dwindle, wane, recede, subside ≠ grow **2** = <u>reduce</u>, cut, decrease, lower, curtail ≠ increase

din = <u>noise</u>, row, racket, crash, clamour, clatter, uproar, commotion ≠ silence

dine = <u>eat</u>, lunch, feast, sup

dinkum (*Austral. & N.Z. informal*) = <u>genuine</u>, honest, natural, frank, sincere, candid, upfront (*informal*), artless

dinner 1 = <u>meal</u>, main meal, spread (*informal*), repast **2** = <u>banquet</u>, feast, repast, hakari (*N.Z.*)

dinosaur ▸ dinosaurs

dip VERB 1 = <u>plunge</u>, immerse, bathe, duck, douse, dunk **2** = <u>drop (down)</u>, fall, lower, sink, descend, subside **3** = <u>slope</u>, drop (down), descend, fall, decline, sink, incline, drop away
● **NOUN 1** = <u>plunge</u>, ducking, soaking, drenching, immersion, douche **2** = <u>nod</u>, drop, lowering, slump, sag **3** = <u>hollow</u>, hole, depression, pit, basin, trough, concavity
● **PHRASES dip into something** = <u>sample</u>, skim, glance at, browse, peruse

diplomacy 1 = <u>statesmanship</u>, statecraft, international negotiation **2** = <u>tact</u>, skill,

---

Dinosaurs

allosaur(us)	elasmosaur(us)	protoceratops
ankylosaur(us)	hadrosaur(us)	stegodon *or*
apatosaur(us)	ichthyosaur(us)	stegodont
atlantosaur(us)	iguanodon *or*	stegosaur(us)
brachiosaur(us)	iguanodont	theropod
brontosaur(us)	megalosaur(us)	titanosaur(us)
ceratosaur(us)	mosasaur(us)	trachodon
compsognathus	oviraptor	triceratops
dimetrodon	plesiosaur(us)	tyrannosaur(us)
diplodocus	pteranodon	velociraptor
dolichosaur(us)	pterodactyl *or*	
dromiosaur(us)	pterosaur	

---

sensitivity, craft, discretion, subtlety, delicacy, finesse ≠ tactlessness

diplomat = <u>official</u>, ambassador, envoy, statesman, consul, attaché, emissary, chargé d'affaires

diplomatic 1 = <u>consular</u>, official, foreign-office, ambassadorial, foreign-politic **2** = <u>tactful</u>, politic, sensitive, subtle, delicate, polite, discreet, prudent ≠ tactless

dire = <u>desperate</u>, pressing, critical, terrible, crucial, extreme, awful, urgent

direct ADJECTIVE = <u>quickest</u>, shortest

● ADVERB **1** = <u>straight</u>, through ≠ circuitous **2** = <u>first-hand</u>, personal, immediate ≠ indirect **3** = <u>clear</u>, specific, plain, absolute, definite, explicit, downright, point-blank ≠ ambiguous **4** = <u>straightforward</u>, open,

straight, frank, blunt, honest, candid, forthright ≠ indirect **5** = <u>verbatim</u>, exact, word-for-word, strict, accurate, faithful, letter-for-letter **6** = <u>non-stop</u>, straight

● VERB **1** = <u>aim</u>, point, level, train, focus **2** = <u>guide</u>, show, lead, point the way, point in the direction of **3** = <u>control</u>, run, manage, lead, guide, handle, conduct, oversee **4** = <u>order</u>, command, instruct, charge, demand, require, bid **5** = <u>address</u>, send, mail, route, label

direction NOUN **1** = <u>way</u>, course, line, road, track, bearing, route, path **2** = <u>management</u>, control, charge, administration, leadership, command, guidance, supervision

● PLURAL NOUN = <u>instructions</u>, rules, information, plan, briefing, regulations, recommendations, guidelines

directive = <u>order</u>, ruling, regulation, command, instruction, decree, mandate, injunction

directly 1 = <u>straight</u>, unswervingly, without deviation, by the shortest route, in a beeline 2 = <u>immediately</u>, promptly, right away, straightaway 3 (*Old-fashioned*) = <u>at once</u>, as soon as possible, straightaway, forthwith 4 = <u>honestly</u>, openly, frankly, plainly, point-blank, unequivocally, truthfully, unreservedly

director = <u>controller</u>, head, leader, manager, chief, executive, governor, administrator, baas (*S. African*)

dirt 1 = <u>filth</u>, muck, grime, dust, mud, impurity, kak (*S. African taboo slang*) 2 = <u>soil</u>, ground, earth, clay, turf, loam

dirty ADJECTIVE 1 = <u>filthy</u>, soiled, grubby, foul, muddy, polluted, messy, grimy, festy (*Austral. slang*) ≠ clean 2 = <u>dishonest</u>, illegal, unfair, cheating, crooked, fraudulent, treacherous, unscrupulous ≠ honest 3 = <u>obscene</u>, indecent, blue, offensive, filthy, pornographic, sleazy, lewd ≠ decent
● VERB = <u>soil</u>, foul, stain, spoil, muddy, pollute, blacken, defile ≠ clean

disability = <u>handicap</u>, affliction, disorder, defect, impairment, infirmity

disable = <u>handicap</u>, cripple, damage, paralyse, impair, incapacitate, immobilize, enfeeble

disabled = <u>differently abled</u>, physically challenged, handicapped, weakened, crippled, paralysed, lame, incapacitated ≠ able-bodied

---

Word Power

disabled – Referring to people with disabilities as *the disabled* can cause offence and should be avoided. Instead, refer to them as people *with disabilities* or *who are physically challenged*, or, possibly, *disabled people* or *differently abled people*. In general, the terms used for disabilities or medical conditions should be avoided as collective nouns for people who have them – so, for example, instead of *the blind*, it is preferable to refer to *sightless people*, *vision-impaired people*, or *partially-sighted people*, depending on the degree of their condition.

---

disadvantage 1 = <u>drawback</u>, trouble, handicap, nuisance, snag, inconvenience, downside

≠ advantage 2 = <u>harm</u>, loss, damage, injury, hurt, prejudice, detriment, disservice ≠ benefit

disagree 1 = <u>differ (in opinion)</u>, argue, clash, dispute, dissent, quarrel, take issue with, cross swords ≠ agree 2 = <u>make ill</u>, upset, sicken, trouble, hurt, bother, distress, discomfort

disagreement 1 = <u>argument</u>, row, conflict, clash, dispute, dissent, quarrel, squabble ≠ agreement

disappear 1 = <u>vanish</u>, recede, evanesce ≠ appear 2 = <u>pass</u>, fade away 3 = <u>cease</u>, dissolve, evaporate, perish, die out, pass away, melt away, leave no trace

disappearance 1 = <u>vanishing</u>, going, passing, melting, eclipse, evaporation, evanescence 2 = <u>flight</u>, departure 3 = <u>loss</u>, losing, mislaying

disappoint = <u>let down</u>, dismay, fail, disillusion, dishearten, disenchant, dissatisfy, disgruntle

disappointment 1 = <u>regret</u>, discontent, dissatisfaction, disillusionment, chagrin, disenchantment, dejection, despondency 2 = <u>letdown</u>, blow, setback, misfortune, calamity, choker (informal) 3 = <u>frustration</u>

disapproval = <u>displeasure</u>, criticism, objection, condemnation, dissatisfaction, censure, reproach, denunciation

disapprove = <u>condemn</u>, object to, dislike, deplore, frown on, take exception to, take a dim view of, find unacceptable ≠ approve

disarm 1 = <u>demilitarize</u>, disband, demobilize, deactivate 2 = <u>win over</u>, persuade

disarmament = <u>arms reduction</u>, demobilization, arms limitation, demilitarization, de-escalation

disarming = <u>charming</u>, winning, irresistible, persuasive, likable or likeable

disarray 1 = <u>confusion</u>, disorder, indiscipline, disunity, disorganization, unruliness ≠ order 2 = <u>untidiness</u>, mess, chaos, muddle, clutter, shambles, jumble, hotchpotch ≠ tidiness

disaster 1 = <u>catastrophe</u>, trouble, tragedy, ruin, misfortune, adversity, calamity, cataclysm 2 = <u>failure</u>, mess, flop (informal), catastrophe, debacle, cock-up (Brit. slang), washout (informal)

disastrous 1 = <u>terrible</u>, devastating, tragic, fatal, catastrophic, ruinous, calamitous, cataclysmic 2 = <u>unsuccessful</u>

disbelief = <u>scepticism</u>, doubt, distrust, mistrust, incredulity, unbelief, dubiety ≠ belief

discard = <u>get rid of</u>, drop, throw away or out, reject, abandon, dump (informal), dispose of, dispense with ≠ keep

discharge VERB 1 = <u>release</u>, free, clear, liberate, pardon, allow to go, set free 2 = <u>dismiss</u>, sack (*informal*), fire (*informal*), remove, expel, discard, oust, cashier 3 = <u>carry out</u>, perform, fulfil, accomplish, do, effect, realize, observe 4 = <u>pay</u>, meet, clear, settle, square (up), honour, satisfy, relieve 5 = <u>pour forth</u>, release, leak, emit, dispense, ooze, exude, give off 6 = <u>fire</u>, shoot, set off, explode, let off, detonate, let loose (*informal*)
● NOUN 1 = <u>release</u>, liberation, clearance, pardon, acquittal 2 = <u>dismissal</u>, notice, removal, the boot (*slang*), expulsion, the push (*slang*), marching orders (*informal*), ejection 3 = <u>emission</u>, ooze, secretion, excretion, pus, seepage, suppuration 4 = <u>firing</u>, report, shot, blast, burst, explosion, volley, salvo

disciple 1 = <u>apostle</u> 2 = <u>follower</u>, student, supporter, pupil, devotee, apostle, adherent ≠ teacher

discipline NOUN 1 = <u>control</u>, authority, regulation, supervision, orderliness, strictness 2 = <u>punishment</u>, penalty, correction, chastening, chastisement, castigation 3 = <u>self-control</u>, control, restraint, self-discipline, willpower, self-restraint, orderliness 4 = <u>training</u>,

practice, exercise, method, regulation, drill, regimen 5 = <u>field of study</u>, area, subject, theme, topic, course, curriculum, speciality
● VERB 1 = <u>punish</u>, correct, reprimand, castigate, chastise, chasten, penalize, bring to book 2 = <u>train</u>, educate

disclose 1 = <u>make known</u>, reveal, publish, relate, broadcast, confess, communicate, divulge ≠ keep secret 2 = <u>show</u>, reveal, expose, unveil, uncover, lay bare, bring to light ≠ hide

disclosure 1 = <u>revelation</u>, announcement, publication, leak, admission, declaration, confession, acknowledgment 2 = <u>uncovering</u>, publication, revelation, divulgence

discomfort 1 = <u>pain</u>, hurt, ache, throbbing, irritation, tenderness, pang, malaise ≠ comfort 2 = <u>uneasiness</u>, worry, anxiety, doubt, distress, misgiving, qualms, trepidation ≠ reassurance 3 = <u>inconvenience</u>, trouble, difficulty, bother, hardship, irritation, nuisance, uphill (*S. African*)

discontent = <u>dissatisfaction</u>, unhappiness, displeasure, regret, envy, restlessness, uneasiness

discontented = <u>dissatisfied</u>, unhappy, fed up, disgruntled, disaffected, vexed, displeased

≠ satisfied

discount NOUN = <u>deduction</u>, cut, reduction, concession, rebate
• VERB 1 = <u>mark down</u>, reduce, lower 2 = <u>disregard</u>, reject, ignore, overlook, discard, set aside, dispel, pass over

discourage 1 = <u>dishearten</u>, depress, intimidate, overawe, demoralize, put a damper on, dispirit, deject ≠ hearten 2 = <u>put off</u>, deter, prevent, dissuade, talk out of ≠ encourage

discourse 1 = <u>conversation</u>, talk, discussion, speech, communication, chat, dialogue 2 = <u>speech</u>, essay, lecture, sermon, treatise, dissertation, homily, oration, whaikorero (N.Z.)

discover 1 = <u>find out</u>, learn, notice, realize, recognize, perceive, detect, uncover 2 = <u>find</u>, come across, uncover, unearth, turn up, dig up, come upon

discovery 1 = <u>finding out</u>, news, revelation, disclosure, realization 2 = <u>invention</u>, launch, institution, pioneering, innovation, inauguration 3 = <u>breakthrough</u>, find, development, advance, leap, invention, step forward, quantum leap 4 = <u>finding</u>, revelation, uncovering, disclosure, detection

discredit VERB 1 = <u>disgrace</u>, shame, smear, humiliate, taint, disparage, vilify, slander ≠ honour 2 = <u>dispute</u>, question, challenge,

deny, reject, discount, distrust, mistrust
• NOUN = <u>disgrace</u>, scandal, shame, disrepute, stigma, ignominy, dishonour, ill-repute ≠ honour

discreet = <u>tactful</u>, diplomatic, guarded, careful, cautious, wary, prudent, considerate ≠ tactless

discrepancy = <u>disagreement</u>, difference, variation, conflict, contradiction, inconsistency, disparity, divergence

discretion 1 = <u>tact</u>, consideration, caution, diplomacy, prudence, wariness, carefulness, judiciousness ≠ tactlessness 2 = <u>choice</u>, will, pleasure, preference, inclination, volition

discriminate VERB = <u>differentiate</u>, distinguish, separate, tell the difference, draw a distinction
• PHRASES **discriminate against someone** = <u>treat differently</u>, single out, victimize, treat as inferior, show bias against, show prejudice against

discriminating = <u>discerning</u>, particular, refined, cultivated, selective, tasteful, fastidious ≠ undiscriminating

discrimination 1 = <u>prejudice</u>, bias, injustice, intolerance, bigotry, favouritism, unfairness 2 = <u>discernment</u>, taste, judgment, perception, subtlety, refinement

discuss = <u>talk about</u>, consider, debate, examine, argue about, deliberate about, converse about, confer about

discussion 1 = <u>talk</u>, debate, argument, conference, conversation, dialogue, consultation, discourse, korero (N.Z.) 2 = <u>examination</u>, investigation, analysis, scrutiny, dissection

disdain NOUN = <u>contempt</u>, scorn, arrogance, derision, haughtiness, superciliousness

● VERB = <u>scorn</u>, reject, slight, disregard, spurn, deride, look down on, sneer at

disease = <u>illness</u>, condition, complaint, infection, disorder, sickness, ailment, affliction

diseased = <u>unhealthy</u>, sick, infected, rotten, ailing, sickly, unwell, crook (Austral. & N.Z. informal)

disgrace NOUN 1 = <u>shame</u>, degradation, disrepute, ignominy, dishonour, infamy, opprobrium, odium ≠ honour 2 = <u>scandal</u>, stain, stigma, blot, blemish

● VERB = <u>shame</u>, humiliate, discredit, degrade, taint, sully, dishonour, bring shame upon ≠ honour

disgraceful = <u>shameful</u>, shocking, scandalous, unworthy, ignominious, disreputable,

contemptible, dishonourable

disgruntled = <u>discontented</u>, dissatisfied, annoyed, irritated, put out, grumpy, vexed, displeased, hoha (N.Z.)

disguise NOUN = <u>costume</u>, mask, camouflage

● VERB = <u>hide</u>, cover, conceal, screen, mask, suppress, withhold, veil

disguised 1 = <u>in disguise</u>, masked, camouflaged, undercover, incognito 2 = <u>false</u>, artificial, forged, fake, mock, imitation, sham, counterfeit

disgust NOUN 1 = <u>loathing</u>, revulsion, hatred, dislike, nausea, distaste, aversion, repulsion ≠ liking 2 = <u>outrage</u>, shock, anger, hurt, fury, resentment, wrath, indignation

● VERB = <u>sicken</u>, offend, revolt, put off, repel, nauseate ≠ delight

disgusting 1 = <u>sickening</u>, foul, revolting, gross, repellent, nauseating, repugnant, loathsome, festy (Austral. slang), yucko (Austral. slang) 2 = <u>appalling</u>, shocking, awful, offensive, dreadful, horrifying

dish 1 = <u>bowl</u>, plate, platter, salver 2 = <u>food</u>, fare, recipe

dishonest = <u>deceitful</u>, corrupt, crooked (informal), lying, bent (slang), false, cheating, treacherous ≠ honest

disintegrate = <u>break up</u>,

crumble, fall apart, separate, shatter, splinter, break apart, go to pieces

dislike VERB = <u>hate</u>, object to, loathe, despise, disapprove of, detest, recoil from, take a dim view of ≠ like

• NOUN = <u>hatred</u>, hostility, disapproval, distaste, animosity, aversion, displeasure, antipathy ≠ liking

dismal 1 = <u>bad</u>, awful, dreadful, rotten (*informal*), terrible, poor, dire, abysmal 2 = <u>sad</u>, gloomy, dark, depressing, discouraging, bleak, dreary, sombre ≠ happy 3 = <u>gloomy</u>, depressing, dull, dreary ≠ cheerful

dismantle = <u>take apart</u>, strip, demolish, disassemble, take to pieces *or* bits

dismay NOUN 1 = <u>alarm</u>, fear, horror, anxiety, dread, apprehension, nervousness, consternation 2 = <u>disappointment</u>, frustration, dissatisfaction, disillusionment, chagrin, disenchantment, discouragement

• VERB 1 = <u>alarm</u>, frighten, scare, panic, distress, terrify, appal, startle 2 = <u>disappoint</u>, upset, discourage, daunt, disillusion, let down, dishearten, dispirit

dismiss 1 = <u>reject</u>, disregard 2 = <u>banish</u>, dispel, discard, set aside, cast out, lay aside, put out of your mind 3 = <u>sack</u>, fire (*informal*), remove (*informal*), axe (*informal*), discharge, lay off, cashier, give notice to 4 = <u>let go</u>, free, release, discharge, dissolve, liberate, disperse, send away

dismissal = <u>the sack</u>, removal, the boot (*slang*), expulsion (*informal*), the push (*slang*), marching orders (*informal*)

disobey 1 = <u>defy</u>, ignore, rebel, disregard, refuse to obey 2 = <u>infringe</u>, defy, refuse to obey, flout, violate, contravene, overstep, transgress

disorder 1 = <u>illness</u>, disease, complaint, condition, sickness, ailment, affliction, malady 2 = <u>untidiness</u>, mess, confusion, chaos, muddle, clutter, shambles, disarray 3 = <u>disturbance</u>, riot, turmoil, unrest, uproar, commotion, unruliness, biffo (*Austral. slang*)

disorderly 1 = <u>untidy</u>, confused, chaotic, messy, jumbled, shambolic (*informal*), disorganized, higgledy-piggledy (*informal*) ≠ tidy 2 = <u>unruly</u>, disruptive, rowdy, turbulent, tumultuous, lawless, riotous, ungovernable

dispatch *or* **despatch** VERB 1 = <u>send</u>, consign 2 = <u>kill</u>, murder, destroy, execute, slaughter, assassinate, slay, liquidate 3 = <u>carry out</u>, perform, fulfil, effect, finish, achieve, settle, dismiss

● NOUN = <u>message</u>, news, report, story, account, communication, bulletin, communiqué

dispel = <u>drive away</u>, dismiss, eliminate, expel, disperse, banish, chase away

dispense VERB 1 = <u>distribute</u>, assign, allocate, allot, dole out, share out, apportion, deal out 2 = <u>prepare</u>, measure, supply, mix 3 = <u>administer</u>, operate, carry out, implement, enforce, execute, apply, discharge

● PHRASES **dispense with something** or **someone** 1 = <u>do away with</u>, give up, cancel, abolish, brush aside, forgo 2 = <u>do without</u>, get rid of, dispose of, relinquish

disperse 1 = <u>scatter</u>, spread, distribute, strew, diffuse, disseminate, throw about 2 = <u>break up</u>, separate, scatter, dissolve, disband ≠ gather 3 = <u>dissolve</u>, break up

displace 1 = <u>replace</u>, succeed, supersede, oust, usurp, supplant, take the place of 2 = <u>move</u>, shift, disturb, budge, misplace

display VERB 1 = <u>show</u>, present, exhibit, put on view ≠ conceal 2 = <u>expose</u>, show, reveal, exhibit, uncover 3 = <u>demonstrate</u>, show, reveal, register, expose, disclose, manifest 4 = <u>show off</u>, parade,

exhibit, sport (informal), flash (informal), flourish, brandish, flaunt

● NOUN 1 = <u>proof</u>, exhibition, demonstration, evidence, expression, illustration, revelation, testimony 2 = <u>exhibition</u>, show, demonstration, presentation, array 3 = <u>ostentation</u>, show, flourish, fanfare, pomp 4 = <u>show</u>, exhibition, parade, spectacle, pageant

disposable 1 = <u>throwaway</u>, nonreturnable 2 = <u>available</u>, expendable, consumable

disposal NOUN = <u>throwing away</u>, dumping (informal), scrapping, removal, discarding, jettisoning, ejection, riddance

● PHRASES **at your disposal** = <u>available</u>, ready, to hand, accessible, handy, at hand, on tap, expendable

dispose VERB = <u>arrange</u>, put, place, group, order, distribute, array

● PHRASES **dispose of someone** = <u>kill</u>, murder, destroy, execute, slaughter, assassinate, slay, liquidate ◆ **dispose of something** 1 = <u>get rid of</u>, destroy, dump (informal), scrap, discard, unload, jettison, throw out or away 2 = <u>deal with</u>, manage, treat, handle, settle, cope with, take care of, see to

disposition 1 = <u>character</u>, nature, spirit, make-up, constitution, temper, temperament 2 = <u>tendency</u>, inclination, propensity, habit, leaning, bent, bias, proclivity 3 = <u>arrangement</u>, grouping, ordering, organization, distribution, placement

dispute NOUN 1 = <u>disagreement</u>, conflict, argument, dissent, altercation 2 = <u>argument</u>, row, clash, controversy, contention, feud, quarrel, squabble
● VERB 1 = <u>contest</u>, question, challenge, deny, doubt, oppose, object to, contradict 2 = <u>argue</u>, fight, clash, disagree, fall out (*informal*), quarrel, squabble, bicker

disqualify = <u>ban</u>, rule out, prohibit, preclude, debar, declare ineligible

disregard VERB = <u>ignore</u>, discount, overlook, neglect, pass over, turn a blind eye to, make light of, pay no heed to ≠ pay attention to
● NOUN = <u>ignoring</u>, neglect, contempt, indifference, negligence, disdain, disrespect

disrupt 1 = <u>interrupt</u>, stop, upset, hold up, interfere with, unsettle, obstruct, cut short 2 = <u>disturb</u>, upset, confuse, disorder, spoil, disorganize, disarrange

disruption = <u>disturbance</u>, interference, interruption, stoppage

disruptive = <u>disturbing</u>, upsetting, disorderly, unsettling, troublesome, unruly ≠ well-behaved

dissatisfaction = <u>discontent</u>, frustration, resentment, disappointment, irritation, unhappiness, annoyance, displeasure

dissatisfied = <u>discontented</u>, frustrated, unhappy, disappointed, fed up, disgruntled, displeased, unsatisfied ≠ satisfied

dissent = <u>disagreement</u>, opposition, protest, resistance, refusal, objection, discord, demur ≠ assent

dissident NOUN = <u>protester</u>, rebel, dissenter, demonstrator, agitator
● ADJECTIVE = <u>dissenting</u>, disagreeing, nonconformist, heterodox

dissolve 1 = <u>melt</u>, soften, thaw, liquefy, deliquesce 2 = <u>end</u>, suspend, break up, wind up, terminate, discontinue, dismantle, disband

distance 1 = <u>space</u>, length, extent, range, stretch, gap, interval, span 2 = <u>aloofness</u>, reserve, detachment, restraint, stiffness, coolness, coldness, standoffishness

distant 1 = <u>far-off</u>, far, remote, abroad, out-of-the-way, far-flung, faraway, outlying ≠ close **2** = <u>remote</u> **3** = <u>reserved</u>, withdrawn, cool, remote, detached, aloof, unfriendly, reticent ≠ friendly **4** = <u>faraway</u>, blank, vague, distracted, vacant, preoccupied, oblivious, absent-minded

distinct 1 = <u>different</u>, individual, separate, discrete, unconnected ≠ similar **2** = <u>striking</u>, dramatic, outstanding, noticeable, well-defined **3** = <u>definite</u>, marked, clear, decided, obvious, evident, noticeable, conspicuous ≠ vague

distinction 1 = <u>difference</u>, contrast, variation, differential, discrepancy, disparity, dissimilarity **2** = <u>excellence</u>, importance, fame, merit, prominence, greatness, eminence, repute **3** = <u>feature</u>, quality, characteristic, mark, individuality, peculiarity, distinctiveness, particularity **4** = <u>merit</u>, honour, integrity, excellence, rectitude

distinctive = <u>characteristic</u>, special, individual, unique, typical, peculiar, singular, idiosyncratic ≠ ordinary

distinctly 1 = <u>definitely</u>, clearly, obviously, plainly, patently, decidedly, markedly, noticeably **2** = <u>clearly</u>, plainly

distinguish 1 = <u>differentiate</u>, determine, separate, discriminate, decide, judge, ascertain, tell the difference **2** = <u>characterize</u>, mark, separate, single out, set apart **3** = <u>make out</u>, recognize, perceive, know, see, tell, pick out, discern

distinguished = <u>eminent</u>, noted, famous, celebrated, well-known, prominent, esteemed, acclaimed ≠ unknown

distort 1 = <u>misrepresent</u>, twist, bias, disguise, pervert, slant, colour, misinterpret **2** = <u>deform</u>, bend, twist, warp, buckle, mangle, mangulate (*Austral. slang*), disfigure, contort

distortion 1 = <u>misrepresentation</u>, bias, slant, perversion, falsification **2** = <u>deformity</u>, bend, twist, warp, buckle, contortion, malformation, crookedness

distract 1 = <u>divert</u>, sidetrack, draw away, turn aside, lead astray, draw *or* lead away from **2** = <u>amuse</u>, occupy, entertain, beguile, engross

distracted = <u>agitated</u>, troubled, puzzled, at sea, perplexed, flustered, in a flap (*informal*)

distraction 1 = <u>disturbance</u>, interference, diversion, interruption **2** = <u>entertainment</u>, recreation, amusement, diversion, pastime

distraught = <u>frantic</u>, desperate,

distressed, distracted, worked-up, agitated, overwrought, out of your mind

distress NOUN **1** = suffering, pain, worry, grief, misery, torment, sorrow, heartache **2** = need, trouble, difficulties, poverty, hard times, hardship, misfortune, adversity

● VERB = upset, worry, trouble, disturb, grieve, torment, harass, agitate

distressed 1 = upset, worried, troubled, distracted, tormented, distraught, agitated, wretched **2** = poverty-stricken, poor, impoverished, needy, destitute, indigent, down at heel, straitened

distressing = upsetting, worrying, disturbing, painful, sad, harrowing, heart-breaking

distribute 1 = hand out, pass round **2** = circulate, deliver, convey **3** = share, deal, allocate, dispense, allot, dole out, apportion

distribution 1 = delivery, mailing, transportation, handling **2** = sharing, division, assignment, rationing, allocation, allotment, apportionment **3** = spread, organization, arrangement, placement

district = area, region, sector, quarter, parish, neighbourhood, vicinity, locality

distrust VERB = suspect, doubt, be wary of, mistrust, disbelieve, be suspicious of ≠ trust

● NOUN = suspicion, question, doubt, disbelief, scepticism, mistrust, misgiving, wariness ≠ trust

disturb 1 = interrupt, trouble, bother, plague, disrupt, interfere with, hassle, inconvenience **2** = upset, concern, worry, trouble, alarm, distress, unsettle, unnerve ≠ calm **3** = muddle, disorder, mix up, mess up, jumble up, disarrange

disturbance 1 = disorder, fray, brawl, fracas, commotion, rumpus **2** = upset, bother, distraction, intrusion, interruption, annoyance

disturbed 1 (Psychiatry) = unbalanced, troubled, disordered, unstable, neurotic, upset, deranged, maladjusted ≠ balanced **2** = worried, concerned, troubled, upset, bothered, nervous, anxious, uneasy ≠ calm

disturbing = worrying, upsetting, alarming, frightening, distressing, startling, unsettling, harrowing

ditch NOUN = channel, drain, trench, dyke, furrow, gully, moat, watercourse

● VERB **1** (Slang) = get rid of, dump (informal), scrap, discard, dispose of, dispense with, jettison, throw

out *or* overboard 2 (*Slang*)
= <u>leave</u>, drop, abandon, dump
(*informal*), get rid of, forsake

dive VERB 1 = <u>plunge</u>, drop, duck,
dip, descend, plummet 2 = <u>go
underwater</u> 3 = <u>nose-dive</u>,
plunge, crash, swoop, plummet
● NOUN = <u>plunge</u>, spring, jump,
leap, lunge, nose dive

diverse 1 = <u>various</u>, mixed,
varied, assorted, miscellaneous,
several, sundry, motley
2 = <u>different</u>, unlike, varying,
separate, distinct, disparate,
discrete, dissimilar

diversify = <u>vary</u>, change,
expand, spread out, branch out

diversion 1 = <u>distraction</u>,
deviation, digression 2 = <u>pastime</u>,
game, sport, entertainment,
hobby, relaxation, recreation,
distraction 3 (*Chiefly Brit.*)
= <u>detour</u>, roundabout way,
indirect course 4 (*Chiefly Brit.*)
= <u>deviation</u>, departure, straying,
divergence, digression

diversity 1 = <u>difference</u>,
multiplicity, heterogeneity,
diverseness 2 = <u>range</u>, variety,
scope, sphere

divert 1 = <u>redirect</u>, switch, avert,
deflect, deviate, turn aside
2 = <u>distract</u>, sidetrack, lead astray,
draw *or* lead away from
3 = <u>entertain</u>, delight, amuse,
please, charm, gratify, beguile,
regale

divide 1 = <u>separate</u>, split,
segregate, bisect ≠ join
2 *sometimes with* **up** = <u>share</u>,
distribute, allocate, dispense,
allot, mete, deal out 3 = <u>split</u>,
break up, come between,
estrange, cause to disagree

dividend = <u>bonus</u>, share, cut
(*informal*), gain, extra, plus,
portion, divvy (*informal*)

divine ADJECTIVE 1 = <u>heavenly</u>,
spiritual, holy, immortal,
supernatural, celestial, angelic,
superhuman 2 = <u>sacred</u>, religious,
holy, spiritual, blessed, revered,
hallowed, consecrated
3 (*Informal*) = <u>wonderful</u>, perfect,
beautiful, excellent, lovely,
glorious, marvellous, splendid
● VERB = <u>guess</u>, suppose, perceive,
discern, infer, deduce, apprehend,
surmise

division 1 = <u>separation</u>, dividing,
splitting up, partition, cutting up
2 = <u>sharing</u>, sharing, distribution,
assignment, rationing, allocation,
allotment, apportionment
3 = <u>disagreement</u>, split, rift,
rupture, abyss, chasm, variance,
discord ≠ unity 4 = <u>department</u>,
group, branch 5 = <u>part</u>, bit, piece,
section, class, category, fraction

divorce NOUN = <u>separation</u>, split,
break-up, parting, split-up, rift,
dissolution, annulment
● VERB = <u>separate</u>, split up, part
company, dissolve your marriage

dizzy 1 = <u>giddy</u>, faint, light-headed, swimming, reeling, shaky, wobbly, off balance 2 = <u>confused</u>, dazzled, at sea, bewildered, muddled, bemused, dazed, disorientated

do VERB 1 = <u>perform</u>, achieve, carry out, complete, accomplish, execute, pull off 2 = <u>make</u>, prepare, fix, arrange, look after, see to, get ready 3 = <u>solve</u>, work out, resolve, figure out, decode, decipher, puzzle out 4 = <u>be adequate</u>, be sufficient, satisfy, suffice, pass muster, cut the mustard, meet requirements 5 = <u>produce</u>, make, create, develop, manufacture, construct, invent, fabricate
● NOUN (*Informal, chiefly Brit. & N.Z.*) = <u>party</u>, gathering, function, event, affair, occasion, celebration, reception
● PHRASES **do away with something** = <u>get rid of</u>, remove, eliminate, abolish, discard, put an end to, dispense with, discontinue ◆ **do without something** *or* **someone** = <u>manage without</u>, give up, dispense with, forgo, kick (*informal*), abstain from, get along without

dock[1] NOUN 1 = <u>port</u>, haven, harbour, pier, wharf, quay, waterfront, anchorage
● VERB 1 = <u>moor</u>, land, anchor, put in, tie up, berth, drop anchor 2 (*of spacecraft*) = <u>link up</u>, unite, join, couple, rendezvous, hook up

dock[2] 1 = <u>cut</u>, reduce, decrease, diminish, lessen ≠ increase 2 = <u>deduct</u>, subtract 3 = <u>cut off</u>, crop, clip, shorten, curtail, cut short

doctor NOUN = <u>physician</u>, medic (*informal*), general practitioner, medical practitioner, G.P.
● VERB 1 = <u>change</u>, alter, interfere with, disguise, pervert, tamper with, tinker with, misrepresent 2 = <u>add to</u>, spike, cut, mix something with something, dilute, water down, adulterate

doctrine = <u>teaching</u>, principle, belief, opinion, conviction, creed, dogma, tenet, kaupapa (*N.Z.*)

document NOUN = <u>paper</u>, form, certificate, report, record, testimonial, authorization
● VERB = <u>support</u>, certify, verify, detail, validate, substantiate, corroborate, authenticate

dodge VERB 1 = <u>duck</u>, dart, swerve, sidestep, shoot, turn aside 2 = <u>evade</u>, avoid, escape, get away from, elude 3 = <u>avoid</u>, evade, shirk
● NOUN = <u>trick</u>, scheme, ploy, trap, device, fraud, manoeuvre, deception

dodgy 1 (*Brit., Austral., & N.Z*) = <u>nasty</u>, offensive, unpleasant, revolting, distasteful, repellent, obnoxious, repulsive **2** (*Brit., Austral., & N.Z.*) = <u>risky</u>, difficult, tricky, dangerous, delicate, uncertain, dicey (*informal, chiefly Brit.*), chancy (*informal*) **3** = <u>second rate</u>, poor, inferior, mediocre, shoddy, bush-league (*Austral. & N.Z. informal*), half-pie (*N.Z. informal*), bodger or bodgie (*Austral. slang*)

dog NOUN **1** = <u>hound</u>, canine, pooch (*slang*), cur, man's best friend, kuri or goorie (*N.Z.*), brak (*S. African*)
● VERB **1** = <u>plague</u>, follow, trouble, haunt, hound, torment **2** = <u>pursue</u>, follow, track, chase, trail, hound, stalk
● PHRASES **go to the dogs** (*Informal*) = <u>deteriorate</u>, degenerate, be in decline, go downhill (*informal*), go down the drain, go to pot, go to ruin

Related Words
adjective: canine
female: bitch
young: pup, puppy

dogged **1** = <u>determined</u>, persistent, stubborn, resolute, tenacious, steadfast, obstinate, indefatigable ≠ irresolute

dole NOUN = <u>share</u>, grant, gift, allowance, handout, koha (*N.Z.*)
● PHRASES **dole something out** = <u>give out</u>, distribute, assign, allocate, hand out, dispense, allot, apportion

dolphin

Related Words
collective noun: school
➤ whales and dolphins

domestic ADJECTIVE **1** = <u>home</u>, internal, native, indigenous **2** = <u>household</u>, home, family, private **3** = <u>home-loving</u>, homely, housewifely, stay-at-home, domesticated **4** = <u>domesticated</u>, trained, tame, pet, house-trained
● NOUN = <u>servant</u>, help, maid, daily, char (*informal*), charwoman

dominant **1** = <u>main</u>, chief, primary, principal, prominent, predominant, pre-eminent ≠ minor **2** = <u>controlling</u>, ruling, commanding, supreme, governing, superior, authoritative

dominate **1** = <u>control</u>, rule, direct, govern, monopolize, tyrannize, have the whip hand over **2** = <u>tower above</u>, overlook, survey, stand over, loom over, stand head and shoulders above

domination = <u>control</u>, power, rule, authority, influence, command, supremacy, ascendancy

don = <u>put on</u>, get into, dress in, pull on, change into, get dressed in, clothe yourself in, slip on or into

donate = <u>give</u>, present, contribute, grant, subscribe, endow, entrust, impart

donation = <u>contribution</u>, gift, subscription, offering, present, grant, hand-out, koha (N.Z.)

donor = giver, contributor, benefactor, philanthropist, donator ≠ recipient

doom NOUN 1 = destruction, ruin, catastrophe, downfall 2 = fate, fortune
• VERB = condemn, sentence, consign, destine

doomed = hopeless, condemned, ill-fated, fated, unhappy, unfortunate, cursed, unlucky

door = opening, entry, entrance, exit, doorway

dope NOUN 1 (Slang) = drugs, narcotics, opiates, dadah (Austral. slang) 2 (Informal) = idiot, fool, twit (informal, chiefly Brit.), dunce, simpleton, dimwit (informal), nitwit (informal), dumb-ass (slang), dorba or dorb (Austral. slang), bogan (Austral. slang)
• VERB = drug, knock out, sedate, stupefy, anaesthetize, narcotize

dorp (S. African) = town, village, settlement, municipality, kainga or kaika (N.Z.)

dose 1 = measure, amount, allowance, portion, prescription, ration, draught, dosage 2 = quantity, measure, supply, portion

dot NOUN = spot, point, mark, fleck, jot, speck, speckle
• VERB = spot, stud, fleck, speckle
• PHRASES on the dot = on time,

promptly, precisely, exactly (informal), to the minute, on the button (informal), punctually

double ADJECTIVE 1 = matching, coupled, paired, twin, duplicate, in pairs 2 = dual, enigmatic, twofold
• VERB 1 = multiply by two, duplicate, increase twofold, enlarge, magnify 2 = fold up or over
• NOUN = twin, lookalike, spitting image, clone, replica, dead ringer (slang), Doppelgänger, duplicate
• PHRASES at or on the double = at once, now, immediately, directly, quickly, promptly, straight away, right away
◆ double as something or someone = function as, serve as

doubt NOUN 1 = uncertainty, confusion, hesitation, suspense, indecision, hesitancy, lack of conviction, irresolution ≠ certainty 2 = suspicion, scepticism, distrust, apprehension, mistrust, misgivings, qualms ≠ belief
• VERB 1 = be uncertain, be sceptical, be dubious 2 = waver, hesitate, vacillate, fluctuate 3 = disbelieve, question, suspect, query, distrust, mistrust, lack confidence in ≠ believe

doubtful 1 = unlikely, unclear, dubious, questionable, improbable, debatable, equivocal

≠ certain 2 = <u>unsure</u>, uncertain, hesitant, suspicious, hesitating, sceptical, tentative, wavering ≠ certain

doubtless = <u>probably</u>, presumably, most likely

down ADJECTIVE = <u>depressed</u>, low, sad, unhappy, discouraged, miserable, fed up, dejected

• VERB (Informal) = <u>swallow</u>, drink (down), drain, gulp (down), put away (informal), toss off

downfall = <u>ruin</u>, fall, destruction, collapse, disgrace, overthrow, undoing, comeuppance (slang)

downgrade = <u>demote</u>, degrade, take down a peg (informal), lower or reduce in rank ≠ promote

downright = <u>complete</u>, absolute, utter, total, plain, outright, unqualified, out-and-out

down-to-earth = <u>sensible</u>, practical, realistic, matter-of-fact, sane, no-nonsense, unsentimental, plain-spoken

downward = <u>descending</u>, declining, heading down, earthward

draft NOUN 1 = <u>outline</u>, plan, sketch, version, rough, abstract 2 = <u>money order</u>, bill (of exchange), cheque, postal order

• VERB = <u>outline</u>, write, plan, produce, create, design, draw, compose

drag VERB = <u>pull</u>, draw, haul, trail, tow, tug, jerk, lug

• NOUN (Slang) = <u>nuisance</u>, bore, bother, pest, hassle (informal), inconvenience, annoyance

drain VERB 1 = <u>remove</u>, draw, empty, withdraw, tap, pump, bleed 2 = <u>empty</u> 3 = <u>flow out</u>, leak, trickle, ooze, seep, exude, well out, effuse 4 = <u>drink up</u>, swallow, finish, put away (informal), quaff, gulp down 5 = <u>exhaust</u>, wear out, strain, weaken, fatigue, debilitate, tire out, enfeeble 6 = <u>consume</u>, exhaust, empty, use up, sap, dissipate

• NOUN 1 = <u>sewer</u>, channel, pipe, sink, ditch, trench, conduit, duct 2 = <u>reduction</u>, strain, drag, exhaustion, sapping, depletion

drama 1 = <u>play</u>, show, stage show, dramatization 2 = <u>theatre</u>, acting, stagecraft, dramaturgy 3 = <u>excitement</u>, crisis, spectacle, turmoil, histrionics

dramatic 1 = <u>exciting</u>, thrilling, tense, sensational, breathtaking, electrifying, melodramatic, climactic 2 = <u>theatrical</u>, Thespian, dramaturgical 3 = <u>expressive</u> 4 = <u>powerful</u>, striking, impressive, vivid, jaw-dropping ≠ ordinary

dramatist > WORD POWER SUPPLEMENT dramatists

drape = <u>cover</u>, wrap, fold, swathe

drastic = <u>extreme</u>, strong, radical, desperate, severe, harsh

draught 1 = <u>breeze</u>, current, movement, flow, puff, gust, current of air **2** = <u>drink</u>

draw VERB **1** = <u>sketch</u>, design, outline, trace, portray, paint, depict, mark out **2** = <u>pull</u>, drag, haul, tow, tug **3** = <u>extract</u>, take, remove **4** = <u>deduce</u>, make, take, derive, infer **5** = <u>attract</u> **6** = <u>entice</u>
● NOUN **1** = <u>tie</u>, deadlock, stalemate, impasse, dead heat **2** (*Informal*) = <u>appeal</u>, pull (*informal*), charm, attraction, lure, temptation, fascination, allure
● PHRASES **draw on** or **upon something** = <u>make use of</u>, use, employ, rely on, exploit, extract, take from, fall back on

drawback = <u>disadvantage</u>, difficulty, handicap, deficiency, flaw, hitch, snag, downside ≠ advantage

drawing = <u>picture</u>, illustration, representation, cartoon, sketch, portrayal, depiction, study

drawn = <u>tense</u>, worn, stressed, tired, pinched, haggard

dread VERB = <u>fear</u>, shrink from, cringe at the thought of, quail from, shudder to think about, have cold feet about (*informal*), tremble to think about
● NOUN = <u>fear</u>, alarm, horror, terror, dismay, fright, apprehension, trepidation

dreadful 1 = <u>terrible</u>, shocking, awful, appalling, horrible, fearful, hideous, atrocious **2** = <u>serious</u>, terrible, awful, horrendous,

monstrous, abysmal **3** = <u>awful</u>, terrible, horrendous, frightful

dream NOUN **1** = <u>vision</u>, illusion, delusion, hallucination **2** = <u>ambition</u>, wish, fantasy, desire, pipe dream **3** = <u>daydream</u> **4** = <u>delight</u>, pleasure, joy, beauty, treasure, gem, marvel, pearler (*Austral. slang*)
● VERB **1** = <u>have dreams</u>, hallucinate **2** = <u>daydream</u>, stargaze, build castles in the air or in Spain
● PHRASES **dream of something** or **someone** = <u>daydream about</u>, fantasize about

dreamer = <u>idealist</u>, visionary, daydreamer, utopian, escapist, Walter Mitty, fantasist

dreary = <u>dull</u>, boring, tedious, drab, tiresome, monotonous, humdrum, uneventful ≠ exciting

drench = <u>soak</u>, flood, wet, drown, steep, swamp, saturate, inundate

dress NOUN **1** = <u>frock</u>, gown, robe **2** = <u>clothing</u>, clothes, costume, garments, apparel, attire, garb, togs
● VERB **1** = <u>put on clothes</u>, don clothes, slip on or into something ≠ undress **2** = <u>clothe</u> **3** = <u>bandage</u>, treat, plaster, bind up **4** = <u>arrange</u>, prepare, get ready

dribble 1 = <u>run</u>, drip, trickle,

drop, leak, ooze, seep, fall in drops **2** = <u>drool</u>, drivel, slaver, slobber

drift VERB **1** = <u>float</u>, go (aimlessly), bob, coast, slip, sail, slide, glide **2** = <u>wander</u>, stroll, stray, roam, meander, rove, range **3** = <u>stray</u>, wander, digress, get off the point **4** = <u>pile up</u>, gather, accumulate, amass, bank up
● NOUN **1** = <u>pile</u>, bank, mass, heap, mound, accumulation **2** = <u>meaning</u>, point, gist, direction, import, intention, tendency, significance

drill NOUN **1** = <u>bit</u>, borer, gimlet, boring tool **2** = <u>training</u>, exercise, discipline, instruction, preparation, repetition **3** = <u>practice</u>
● VERB **1** = <u>bore</u>, pierce, penetrate, sink in, puncture, perforate **2** = <u>train</u>, coach, teach, exercise, discipline, practise, instruct, rehearse

drink VERB **1** = <u>swallow</u>, sip, suck, gulp, sup, guzzle, imbibe, quaff **2** = <u>booze</u> (informal), tipple, tope, hit the bottle (informal)
● NOUN **1** = <u>glass</u>, cup, draught **2** = <u>beverage</u>, refreshment, potion, liquid **3** = <u>alcohol</u>, booze (informal), liquor, spirits, the bottle (informal), hooch or hootch (informal, chiefly U.S. & Canad.)

drip VERB **1** = <u>drop</u>, splash, sprinkle, trickle, dribble, exude, plop
● NOUN **1** = <u>drop</u>, bead, trickle,

dribble, droplet, globule, pearl **2** (Informal) = <u>weakling</u>, wet (Brit. informal), weed (informal), softie (informal), mummy's boy (informal), namby-pamby

drive VERB **1** = <u>go (by car)</u>, ride (by car), motor, travel by car **2** = <u>operate</u>, manage, direct, guide, handle, steer **3** = <u>push</u>, propel **4** = <u>thrust</u>, push, hammer, ram **5** = <u>herd</u>, urge, impel **6** = <u>force</u>, press, prompt, spur, prod, constrain, coerce, goad
● NOUN **1** = <u>run</u>, ride, trip, journey, spin (informal), outing, excursion, jaunt **2** = <u>initiative</u>, energy, enterprise, ambition, motivation, zip (informal), vigour, get-up-and-go (informal) **3** = <u>campaign</u>, push (informal), crusade, action, effort, appeal

drop VERB **1** = <u>fall</u>, decline, diminish **2** often with **away** = <u>decline</u>, fall, sink **3** = <u>plunge</u>, fall, tumble, descend, plummet **4** = <u>drip</u>, trickle, dribble, fall in drops **5** = <u>sink</u>, fall, descend **6** = <u>quit</u>, give up, axe (informal), kick (informal), relinquish, discontinue
● NOUN **1** = <u>decrease</u>, fall, cut, lowering, decline, reduction, slump, fall-off **2** = <u>droplet</u>, bead, globule, bubble, pearl, drip **3** = <u>dash</u>, shot (informal), spot, trace, sip, tot, trickle, mouthful **4** = <u>fall</u>, plunge, descent

• PHRASES **drop off 1** = <u>fall asleep</u>, nod (off), doze (off), snooze (*informal*), have forty winks (*informal*) **2** = <u>decrease</u>, lower, decline, shrink, diminish, dwindle, lessen, subside ♦ **drop out** = <u>leave</u>, stop, give up, withdraw, quit, pull out, fall by the wayside ♦ **drop out of something** = <u>discontinue</u>, give up, quit

drought = <u>water shortage</u>, dryness, dry spell, aridity ≠ flood

drove often plural = <u>herd</u>, company, crowds, collection, mob, flocks, swarm, horde

drown 1 = <u>go down</u>, go under **2** = <u>drench</u>, flood, soak, steep, swamp, saturate, engulf, submerge **3** = <u>overwhelm</u>, overcome, wipe out, overpower, obliterate, swallow up

drug NOUN 1 = <u>medication</u>, medicine, remedy, physic, medicament **2** = <u>dope</u> (*slang*), narcotic (*slang*), stimulant, opiate, dadah (*Austral. slang*)

• VERB = <u>knock out</u>, dope (*slang*), numb, deaden, stupefy, anaesthetize

drum VERB = <u>pound</u>, beat, tap, rap, thrash, tattoo, throb, pulsate

• PHRASES **drum something into someone** = <u>drive into</u>, hammer into, instil into, din into, harp on about to

drunk ADJECTIVE = <u>intoxicated</u>,

plastered (*slang*), drunken, merry (*Brit. informal*), under the influence (*informal*), tipsy, legless (*informal*), inebriated, out to it (*Austral. & N.Z. slang*), babalas (*S. African*)

• NOUN = <u>drunkard</u>, alcoholic, lush (*slang*), boozer (*informal*), wino (*informal*), inebriate, alko or alco (*Austral. slang*)

dry ADJECTIVE 1 = <u>dehydrated</u>, dried-up, arid, parched, desiccated ≠ wet **2** = <u>thirsty</u>, parched **3** = <u>sarcastic</u>, cynical, low-key, sly, sardonic, deadpan, droll, ironical **4** = <u>dull</u>, boring, tedious, dreary, tiresome, monotonous, run-of-the-mill, humdrum ≠ interesting **5** = <u>plain</u>, simple, bare, basic, stark, unembellished

• VERB 1 = <u>drain</u>, make dry **2** often with out = <u>dehydrate</u>, make dry, desiccate, sear, parch, dehumidify ≠ wet

• PHRASES **dry up** or **out** = <u>become dry</u>, harden, wither, shrivel up, wizen

dual = <u>twofold</u>, double, twin, matched, paired, duplicate, binary, duplex

dubious 1 = <u>suspect</u>, suspicious, crooked, dodgy (*Brit., Austral., & N.Z. informal*), questionable, unreliable, fishy (*informal*), disreputable ≠ trustworthy **2** = <u>unsure</u>, uncertain, suspicious, hesitating, doubtful, sceptical, tentative, wavering ≠ sure

duck 1 = bob, drop, lower, bend, bow, dodge, crouch, stoop 2 (*Informal*) = dodge, avoid, escape, evade, elude, sidestep, shirk 3 = dunk, wet, plunge, dip, submerge, immerse, douse, souse

due ADJECTIVE 1 = expected, scheduled 2 = fitting, deserved, appropriate, justified, suitable, merited, proper, rightful 3 = payable, outstanding, owed, owing, unpaid, in arrears

● ADVERB = directly, dead, straight, exactly, undeviatingly

● NOUN = right(s), privilege, deserts, merits, comeuppance (*informal*)

● PLURAL NOUN = membership fee, charges, fee, contribution, levy

duel NOUN 1 = single combat, affair of honour 2 = contest, fight, competition, clash, encounter, engagement, rivalry

● VERB = fight, struggle, clash, compete, contest, contend, vie with, lock horns

duff (*Brit., Austral., & N.Z. informal*) = bad, poor, useless, inferior, unsatisfactory, defective, imperfect, substandard, bodger or bodgie (*Austral. slang*)

dull ADJECTIVE 1 = boring, tedious, dreary, flat, plain, monotonous, run-of-the-mill, humdrum ≠ exciting 2 = lifeless, indifferent,

apathetic, listless, unresponsive, passionless ≠ lively 3 = cloudy, dim, gloomy, dismal, overcast, leaden ≠ bright 4 = blunt, blunted, unsharpened ≠ sharp

● VERB = relieve, blunt, lessen, moderate, soften, alleviate, allay, take the edge off

duly 1 = properly, fittingly, correctly, appropriately, accordingly, suitably, deservedly, rightfully 2 = on time, promptly, punctually, at the proper time

dumb 1 = unable to speak, mute ≠ articulate 2 = silent, mute, speechless, tongue-tied, wordless, voiceless, soundless, mum 3 (*Informal*) = stupid, thick, dull, foolish, dense, unintelligent, asinine, dim-witted (*informal*) ≠ clever

dummy NOUN 1 = model, figure, mannequin, form, manikin 2 = imitation, copy, duplicate, sham, counterfeit, replica 3 (*Slang*) = fool, idiot, dunce, oaf, simpleton, nitwit (*informal*), blockhead, dumb-ass (*slang*), dorba or dorb (*Austral. slang*), bogan (*Austral. slang*)

● ADJECTIVE = imitation, false, fake, artificial, mock, bogus, simulated, sham

dump VERB 1 = drop, deposit, throw down, let fall, fling down 2 = get rid of, tip, dispose of, unload, jettison, empty out, throw away *or* out **3** = scrap, get rid of, abolish, put an end to, discontinue, jettison, put paid to

● NOUN **1** = rubbish tip, tip, junkyard, rubbish heap, refuse heap **2** (*Informal*) = pigsty, hole (*informal*), slum, hovel

dunny (*Austral. & N.Z. old-fashioned informal*) = toilet, lavatory, bathroom, loo (*Brit. informal*), W.C., bog (*slang*), Gents *or* Ladies, can (*U.S. & Canad. slang*), bogger (*Austral. slang*), brasco (*Austral. slang*)

duplicate VERB **1** = repeat, reproduce, copy, clone, replicate **2** = copy

● ADJECTIVE = identical, matched, matching, twin, corresponding, twofold

● NOUN **1** = copy, facsimile **2** = photocopy, copy, reproduction, replica, carbon copy

durable 1 = hard-wearing, strong, tough, reliable, resistant, sturdy, long-lasting ≠ fragile **2** = enduring, continuing, dependable, unwavering, unfaltering

duration = length, time, period, term, stretch, extent, spell, span

dusk = twilight, evening, evo (*Austral. slang*), nightfall, sunset, dark, sundown, eventide, gloaming (*Scot. poetic*) ≠ dawn

dust NOUN **1** = grime, grit, powder **2** = particles

● VERB = sprinkle, cover, powder, spread, spray, scatter, sift, dredge

dusty = dirty, grubby, unclean, unswept

duty NOUN **1** = responsibility, job, task, work, role, function, obligation, assignment **2** = tax, toll, levy, tariff, excise

● PHRASES **on duty** = at work, busy, engaged, on active service

dwarf VERB **1** = tower above *or* over, dominate, overlook, stand over, loom over, stand head and shoulders above **2** = eclipse, tower above *or* over, put in the shade, diminish

● ADJECTIVE = miniature, small, baby, tiny, diminutive, bonsai, undersized

● NOUN = gnome, midget, Lilliputian, Tom Thumb, pygmy *or* pigmy

dwell (*Formal or literary*) = live, reside, lodge, abide

dwelling (*Formal or literary*) = home, house, residence, abode, quarters, lodging, habitation, domicile, whare (*N.Z.*)

dwindle = lessen, decline, fade, shrink, diminish, decrease, wane, subside ≠ increase

dye VERB = colour, stain, tint, tinge, pigment

● NOUN = colouring, colour, pigment, stain, tint, tinge, colorant

dying 1 = near death, moribund, in extremis (*Latin*), at death's

door, not long for this world
2 = <u>final</u>, last, parting, departing
3 = <u>failing</u>, declining, foundering, diminishing, decreasing, dwindling, subsiding

dynamic = <u>energetic</u>, powerful, vital, go-ahead, lively, animated, high-powered, forceful ≠ apathetic

dynasty = <u>empire</u>, house, rule, regime, sovereignty

E

each DETERMINER = <u>every</u>, every single

● PRONOUN = <u>every one</u>, all, each one, each and every one, one and all

● ADVERB = <u>apiece</u>, individually, for each, to each, respectively, per person, per head, per capita

> ### Word Power
>
> **each** – *Each* is a singular pronoun and should be used with a singular verb – for example, *each of the candidates was interviewed separately* (not *were interviewed separately*).

eager 1 = <u>anxious</u>, keen, hungry, impatient, itching, thirsty ≠ unenthusiastic **2** = <u>keen</u>, interested, intense, enthusiastic, passionate, avid (*informal*), fervent ≠ uninterested

ear = <u>sensitivity</u>, taste, discrimination, appreciation
(Related Words)
adjective: aural

early ADVERB **1** = <u>in good time</u>, beforehand, ahead of schedule, in advance, with time to spare ≠ late **2** = <u>too soon</u>, before the usual time, prematurely, ahead of time ≠ late

● ADJECTIVE **1** = <u>first</u>, opening, initial, introductory

2 = <u>premature</u>, forward, advanced, untimely, unseasonable ≠ belated

3 = <u>primitive</u>, first, earliest, young, original, undeveloped, primordial, primeval ≠ developed

earmark 1 = <u>set aside</u>, reserve, label, flag, allocate, designate, mark out **2** = <u>mark out</u>, identify, designate

earn 1 = <u>be paid</u>, make, get, receive, gain, net, collect, bring in **2** = <u>deserve</u>, win, gain, attain, justify, merit, warrant, be entitled to

earnest 1 = <u>serious</u>, grave, intense, dedicated, sincere, thoughtful, solemn, ardent ≠ frivolous

2 = <u>determined</u>, dogged, intent, persistent, persevering, resolute, wholehearted ≠ half-hearted

earnings = <u>income</u>, pay, wages, revenue, proceeds, salary, receipts, remuneration

earth 1 = <u>world</u>, planet, globe, sphere, orb, earthly sphere **2** = <u>ground</u>, land, dry land, terra firma 3 = soil, ground, land, dust, clay, dirt, turf, silt

earthly 1 = worldly, material, secular, mortal, temporal, human ≠ spiritual 2 = sensual, worldly, physical, fleshly, bodily, carnal 3 (*Informal*) = possible, likely, practical, feasible, conceivable, imaginable

ease NOUN 1 = straightforwardness, simplicity, readiness 2 = comfort, luxury, leisure, relaxation, prosperity, affluence, rest, repose ≠ hardship 3 = peace of mind, peace, content, quiet, comfort, happiness, serenity, tranquillity ≠ agitation

● VERB 1 = relieve, calm, soothe, lessen, alleviate, lighten, lower, relax ≠ aggravate 2 = reduce, diminish, lessen, slacken 3 = move carefully, edge, slip, inch, slide, creep, manoeuvre

easily = without difficulty, smoothly, readily, comfortably, effortlessly, with ease, straightforwardly

easy 1 = simple, straightforward, no trouble, not difficult, effortless, painless, uncomplicated, child's play (*informal*) ≠ hard 2 = untroubled, relaxed, peaceful, serene, tranquil, quiet 3 = carefree, comfortable, leisurely, trouble-free, untroubled, cushy (*informal*) ≠ difficult 4 = tolerant, soft, mild, laid-back

(*informal*), indulgent, easy-going, lenient, permissive ≠ strict

eat 1 = consume, swallow, chew, scoff (*slang*), devour, munch, tuck into (*informal*), put away 2 = have a meal, lunch, breakfast, dine, snack, feed, graze (*informal*), have lunch

ebb VERB 1 = flow back, go out, withdraw, retreat, wane, recede 2 = decline, flag, diminish, decrease, dwindle, lessen, subside, fall away

● NOUN = flowing back, going out, withdrawal, retreat, wane, low water, low tide, outgoing tide

eccentric ADJECTIVE = odd, strange, peculiar, irregular, quirky, unconventional, idiosyncratic, outlandish ≠ normal

● NOUN = crank (*informal*), character (*informal*), oddball (*informal*), nonconformist, weirdo or weirdie (*informal*)

echo NOUN 1 = reverberation, ringing, repetition, answer, resonance, resounding 2 = copy, reflection, clone, reproduction, imitation, duplicate, double, reiteration

● VERB 1 = reverberate, repeat, resound, ring, resonate 2 = recall, reflect, copy, mirror, resemble, imitate, ape

eclipse NOUN = obscuring, covering, blocking, shading, dimming, extinction, darkening, blotting out

● VERB = <u>surpass</u>, exceed, overshadow, excel, transcend, outdo, outclass, outshine

economic 1 = <u>financial</u>, industrial, commercial 2 = <u>profitable</u>, successful, commercial, rewarding, productive, lucrative, worthwhile, viable 3 (*Informal*) = <u>economical</u>, cheap, reasonable, modest, low-priced, inexpensive

economical 1 = <u>thrifty</u>, sparing, careful, prudent, provident, frugal, parsimonious, scrimping ≠ extravagant 2 = <u>efficient</u>, sparing, cost-effective, money-saving, time-saving ≠ wasteful

economy 1 = <u>financial system</u>, financial state 2 = <u>thrift</u>, restraint, prudence, husbandry, frugality, parsimony

ecstasy = <u>rapture</u>, delight, joy, bliss, euphoria, fervour, elation ≠ agony

ecstatic = <u>rapturous</u>, entranced, joyous, elated, overjoyed, blissful, euphoric, enraptured

edge NOUN 1 = <u>border</u>, side, limit, outline, boundary, fringe, verge, brink 2 = <u>verge</u>, point, brink, threshold 3 = <u>advantage</u>, lead, dominance, superiority, upper hand, head start, ascendancy, whip hand 4 = <u>power</u>, force, bite, effectiveness, incisiveness, powerful quality 5 = <u>sharpness</u>, point, bitterness, keenness

● VERB 1 = <u>inch</u>, ease, creep, slink, steal, sidle, move slowly 2 = <u>border</u>, fringe, hem, pipe

● PHRASES on edge = <u>tense</u>, nervous, impatient, irritable, apprehensive, edgy, ill at ease, on tenterhooks

edit = <u>revise</u>, improve, correct, polish, adapt, rewrite, condense, redraft

edition = <u>version</u>, copy, issue, programme (*TV, Radio*), printing, volume, impression, publication

educate = <u>teach</u>, school, train, develop, improve, inform, discipline, tutor

educated 1 = <u>cultured</u>, intellectual, learned, sophisticated, refined, cultivated, enlightened, knowledgeable ≠ uncultured 2 = <u>taught</u>, schooled, coached, informed, tutored, instructed, nurtured, well-informed ≠ uneducated

education 1 = <u>teaching</u>, schooling, training, development, discipline, instruction, nurture, tuition 2 = <u>learning</u>, schooling, cultivation, refinement

educational 1 = <u>academic</u>, school, learning, teaching, scholastic, pedagogical, pedagogic 2 = <u>instructive</u>, useful, cultural, illuminating, enlightening, informative, instructional, edifying

eerie = uncanny, strange, frightening, ghostly, weird, mysterious, scary (*informal*), sinister

effect NOUN 1 = result, consequence, conclusion, outcome, event, end result, upshot 2 = impression, feeling, impact, influence 3 = purpose, impression, sense, intent, essence, thread, tenor
● PLURAL NOUN = belongings, goods, things, property, stuff, gear, possessions, paraphernalia
● VERB = bring about, produce, complete, achieve, perform, fulfil, accomplish, execute

> ### Word Power
>
> **effect** – It is quite common for the verb *effect* to be mistakenly used where *affect* is intended. *Effect* is relatively uncommon and rather formal, and is a synonym of 'bring about'. Conversely, the noun *effect* is quite often mistakenly written with an initial *a*. The following are correct: *the group is still recovering from the effects of the recession; they really are powerless to effect any change.* The next two examples are incorrect: *the full affects of the shutdown won't be felt for several more days; men whose lack of hair doesn't effect their self-esteem.*

effective 1 = efficient, successful, useful, active, capable, valuable, helpful, adequate ≠ ineffective 2 = powerful, strong, convincing, persuasive, telling, impressive, compelling, forceful ≠ weak 3 = virtual, essential, practical, implied, implicit, tacit, unacknowledged 4 = in operation, official, current, legal, active, in effect, valid, operative ≠ inoperative

efficiency 1 = effectiveness, power, economy, productivity, organization, cost-effectiveness, orderliness 2 = competence, expertise, capability, professionalism, proficiency, adeptness

efficient 1 = effective, successful, structured, productive, systematic, streamlined, cost-effective, methodical ≠ inefficient 2 = competent, professional, capable, organized, productive, proficient, businesslike, well-organized ≠ incompetent

effort 1 = attempt, try, endeavour, bid, essay, go (*informal*), stab (*informal*) 2 = exertion, work, trouble, energy, struggle, application, graft, toil

egg NOUN = ovum, gamete, germ cell
● PHRASES **egg someone on** = incite, push, encourage, urge,

prompt, spur, provoke, prod

eject 1 = <u>throw out</u>, remove, turn out, expel (*slang*), oust, banish, drive out, evict 2 = <u>bail out</u>, escape, get out

elaborate ADJECTIVE
1 = <u>complicated</u>, detailed, studied, complex, precise, thorough, intricate, painstaking 2 = <u>ornate</u>, involved, complex, fancy, complicated, intricate, baroque, ornamented ≠ plain

● VERB 1 = <u>develop</u>, flesh out 2 = <u>expand (upon)</u>, extend, enlarge (on), amplify, embellish, flesh out, add detail (to) ≠ simplify

elastic 1 = <u>flexible</u>, supple, rubbery, pliable, plastic, springy, pliant, tensile ≠ rigid 2 = <u>adaptable</u>, yielding, variable, flexible, accommodating, tolerant, adjustable, supple ≠ inflexible

elbow = <u>joint</u>, angle, curve

elder ADJECTIVE = <u>older</u>, first, senior, first-born

● NOUN = <u>older person</u>, senior

elect 1 = <u>vote for</u>, choose, pick, determine, select, appoint, opt for, settle on 2 = <u>choose</u>, decide, prefer, select, opt

election 1 = <u>vote</u>, poll, ballot, referendum, franchise, plebiscite, show of hands 2 = <u>appointment</u>, picking, choice, selection

electric 1 = <u>electric-powered</u>, powered, cordless, battery-operated, electrically-charged, mains-operated 2 = <u>charged</u>, exciting, stirring, thrilling, stimulating, dynamic, tense, rousing

elegance = <u>style</u>, taste, grace, dignity, sophistication, grandeur, refinement, gracefulness

elegant = <u>stylish</u>, fine, sophisticated, delicate, handsome, refined, chic, exquisite ≠ inelegant

element NOUN 1 = <u>component</u>, part, unit, section, factor, principle, aspect, foundation 2 = <u>group</u>, faction, clique, set, party, circle 3 = <u>trace</u>, suggestion, hint, dash, suspicion, tinge, smattering, soupçon

● PLURAL NOUN = <u>weather conditions</u>, climate, the weather, wind and rain, atmospheric conditions, powers of nature

● PHRASES **be in your element** = be in a situation you enjoy, be in your natural environment, be in familiar surroundings

elementary = <u>simple</u>, clear, easy, plain, straightforward, rudimentary, uncomplicated, undemanding ≠ complicated

elevate 1 = <u>promote</u>, raise, advance, upgrade, exalt, kick upstairs (*informal*), aggrandize, give advancement to 2 = <u>increase</u>, lift, raise, step up, intensify, move up, hoist, raise high **3** = <u>raise</u>, lift, heighten, uplift, hoist, lift up, raise up, hike up

elevated 1 = <u>exalted</u>, important, august, grand, superior, noble, dignified, high-ranking **2** = <u>high-minded</u>, fine, grand, noble, inflated, dignified, sublime, lofty ≠ humble **3** = <u>raised</u>, high, lifted up, upraised

elicit 1 = <u>bring about</u>, cause, derive, bring out, evoke, give rise to, draw out, bring forth **2** = <u>obtain</u>, extract, exact, evoke, wrest, draw out, extort

eligible 1 = <u>entitled</u>, fit, qualified, suitable ≠ ineligible **2** = <u>available</u>, free, single, unmarried, unattached

eliminate = <u>remove</u>, end, stop, withdraw, get rid of, abolish, cut out, dispose of

elite = <u>aristocracy</u>, best, pick, cream, upper class, nobility, crème de la crème (*French*), flower ≠ rabble

eloquent 1 = <u>silver-tongued</u>, moving, powerful, effective, stirring, articulate, persuasive, forceful ≠ inarticulate **2** = <u>expressive</u>, telling, pointed, significant, vivid, meaningful, indicative, suggestive

elsewhere = <u>in</u> *or* <u>to another place</u>, away, abroad, hence (*archaic*), somewhere else, not here, in other places, in *or* to a different place

elude 1 = <u>evade</u>, escape, lose, avoid, flee, duck (*informal*), dodge, get away from **2** = <u>escape</u>, baffle, frustrate, puzzle, stump, foil, be beyond (someone), thwart

> ### Word Power
> **elude** – Elude is sometimes wrongly used where *allude* is meant: *he was alluding* (not *eluding*) *to his previous visit to the city.*

elusive 1 = <u>difficult to catch</u>, tricky, slippery, difficult to find, evasive, shifty **2** = <u>indefinable</u>, fleeting, subtle, indefinite, transient, intangible, indescribable, transitory

> ### Word Power
> **elusive** – The spelling of *elusive*, as in *a shy, elusive character*, should be noted. This adjective derives from the verb *elude*, and should not be confused with the rare word *illusive* meaning 'not real' or 'based on illusion'.

emanate = <u>flow</u>, emerge, spring, proceed, arise, stem, derive, originate

embargo NOUN = <u>ban</u>, bar, restriction, boycott, restraint,

prohibition, moratorium, stoppage, rahui (*N.Z.*)
● VERB = block, stop, bar, ban, restrict, boycott, prohibit, blacklist

embark VERB = go aboard, climb aboard, board ship, step aboard, go on board, take ship ≠ get off
● PHRASES **embark on something** = begin, start, launch, enter, take up, set out, set about, plunge into

embarrass = shame, distress, show up (*informal*), humiliate, disconcert, fluster, mortify, discomfit

embarrassed = ashamed, shamed, uncomfortable, awkward, abashed, humiliated, uneasy, unsettled

embarrassing = humiliating, upsetting, compromising, delicate, uncomfortable, awkward, sensitive, troublesome, barro (*Austral. slang*)

embarrassment 1 = shame, distress, showing up (*informal*), humiliation, discomfort, unease, self-consciousness, awkwardness 2 = problem, difficulty, nuisance, source of trouble, thorn in your flesh 3 = predicament, problem, difficulty (*informal*), mess, jam (*informal*), plight, scrape (*informal*), pickle (*informal*)

embody 1 = personify, represent, stand for, manifest, exemplify, symbolize, typify,

actualize 2 = incorporate, include, contain, combine, collect, take in, encompass

embrace VERB 1 = hug, hold, cuddle, seize, squeeze, clasp, envelop, canoodle (*slang*) 2 = accept, support, welcome, adopt, take up, seize, espouse, take on board 3 = include, involve, cover, contain, take in, incorporate, comprise, encompass
● NOUN = hug, hold, cuddle, squeeze, clinch (*slang*), clasp

embroil = involve, mix up, implicate, entangle, mire, ensnare, enmesh

embryo 1 = foetus, unborn child, fertilized egg 2 = germ, beginning, source, root, seed, nucleus, rudiment

emerge 1 = come out, appear, surface, rise, arise, turn up, spring up, emanate ≠ withdraw 2 = become apparent, come out, become known, come to light, crop up, transpire, become evident, come out in the wash

emergence 1 = coming, development, arrival, surfacing, rise, appearance, arising, turning up 2 = disclosure, publishing, broadcasting, broadcast, publication, declaration, revelation, becoming known

emergency NOUN = crisis, danger, difficulty, accident,

disaster, necessity, plight, scrape (*informal*)

• ADJECTIVE 1 = <u>urgent</u>, crisis, immediate 2 = <u>alternative</u>, extra, additional, substitute, replacement, temporary, makeshift, stopgap

emigrate = <u>move abroad</u>, move, relocate, migrate, resettle, leave your country

eminent = <u>prominent</u>, noted, respected, famous, celebrated, distinguished, well-known, esteemed ≠ unknown

emission = <u>giving off</u> or out, release, shedding, leak, radiation, discharge, transmission, ejaculation

emit 1 = <u>give off</u>, release, leak, transmit, discharge, send out, radiate, eject ≠ absorb 2 = <u>utter</u>, produce, voice, give out, let out

emotion 1 = <u>feeling</u>, spirit, soul, passion, excitement, sensation, sentiment, fervour 2 = <u>instinct</u>, sentiment, sensibility, intuition, tenderness, gut feeling, soft-heartedness

emotional 1 = <u>psychological</u>, private, personal, hidden, spiritual, inner 2 = <u>moving</u>, touching, affecting, stirring, sentimental, poignant, emotive, heart-rending 3 = <u>passionate</u>, sentimental, temperamental, excitable, demonstrative, hot-blooded 4 = <u>emotive</u>, sensitive,

controversial, delicate, contentious, heated, inflammatory, touchy

emphasis 1 = <u>importance</u>, attention, weight, significance, stress, priority, prominence 2 = <u>stress</u>, accent, force, weight

emphasize 1 = <u>highlight</u>, stress, underline, draw attention to, dwell on, play up, make a point of, give priority to ≠ minimize 2 = <u>stress</u>, accentuate, lay stress on

emphatic 1 = <u>forceful</u>, positive, definite, vigorous, unmistakable, insistent, unequivocal, vehement ≠ hesitant 2 = <u>significant</u>, pronounced, decisive, resounding, conclusive

empire 1 = <u>kingdom</u>, territory, province, federation, commonwealth, realm, domain 2 = <u>organization</u>, company, business, firm, concern, corporation, consortium, syndicate

(Related Words)
adjective: imperial

empirical or **empiric** = <u>first-hand</u>, direct, observed, practical, actual, experimental, pragmatic, factual ≠ hypothetical

employ 1 = <u>hire</u>, commission, appoint, take on, retain, engage, recruit, sign up 2 = <u>use</u>, apply, exercise, exert, make use of, utilize, ply, bring to bear 3 = <u>spend</u>, fill, occupy, involve, engage, take up, make use of, use up

employed 1 = <u>working</u>, in work, having a job, in employment, in a job, earning your living ≠ out of work 2 = <u>busy</u>, active, occupied, engaged, hard at work, in harness, rushed off your feet ≠ idle

employee = <u>worker</u>, labourer, workman, staff member, member of staff, hand, wage-earner, white-collar worker

employer 1 = <u>boss</u> (*informal*), manager, head, leader, director, chief, owner, master, baas (*S. African*) 2 = <u>company</u>, business, firm, organization, establishment, outfit (*informal*)

employment 1 = <u>job</u>, work, position, trade, post, situation, profession, occupation 2 = <u>taking on</u>, commissioning, appointing, hire, hiring, retaining, engaging, appointment 3 = <u>use</u>, application, exertion, exercise, utilization

empower 1 = <u>authorize</u>, allow, commission, qualify, permit, sanction, entitle, delegate 2 = <u>enable</u>, equip, emancipate, give means to, enfranchise

empty ADJECTIVE 1 = <u>bare</u>, clear, abandoned, deserted, vacant, free, void, desolate ≠ full 2 = <u>meaningless</u>, cheap, hollow, vain, idle, futile, insincere 3 = <u>worthless</u>, meaningless, hollow, pointless, futile, senseless,

fruitless, inane ≠ meaningful

● VERB 1 = <u>clear</u>, drain, void, unload, pour out, unpack, remove the contents of ≠ fill 2 = <u>exhaust</u>, consume the contents of, void, deplete, use up ≠ replenish 3 = <u>evacuate</u>, clear, vacate

emulate = <u>imitate</u>, follow, copy, mirror, echo, mimic, model yourself on

enable 1 = <u>allow</u>, permit, empower, give someone the opportunity, give someone the means ≠ prevent 2 = <u>authorize</u>, allow, permit, qualify, sanction, entitle, license, warrant ≠ stop

enact 1 = <u>establish</u>, order, command, approve, sanction, proclaim, decree, authorize 2 = <u>perform</u>, play, present, stage, represent, put on, portray, depict

enchant = <u>fascinate</u>, delight, charm, entrance, dazzle, captivate, enthral, beguile

enclose *or* **inclose** 1 = <u>surround</u>, circle, bound, fence, confine, close in, wall in, encircle 2 = <u>send with</u>, include, put in, insert

encompass 1 = <u>include</u>, hold, cover, admit, deal with, contain, take in, embrace 2 = <u>surround</u>, circle, enclose, close in, envelop, encircle, fence in, ring

encounter VERB 1 = <u>experience</u>, meet, face, suffer, have, go through, sustain, endure

2 = <u>meet</u>, confront, come across, bump into (*informal*), run across, come upon, chance upon, meet by chance

● NOUN 1 = <u>meeting</u>, brush, confrontation, rendezvous, chance meeting 2 = <u>battle</u>, conflict, clash, contest, run-in (*informal*), confrontation, head-to-head

encourage 1 = <u>inspire</u>, comfort, cheer, reassure, console, hearten, cheer up, embolden ≠ discourage 2 = <u>urge</u>, persuade, prompt, spur, coax, egg on ≠ dissuade 3 = <u>promote</u>, back, support, increase, foster, advocate, stimulate, endorse ≠ prevent

encouragement
1 = <u>inspiration</u>, support, comfort, comforting, cheer, cheering, reassurance, morale boosting 2 = <u>urging</u>, prompting, stimulus, persuasion, coaxing, egging on, incitement 3 = <u>promotion</u>, backing, support, endorsement, stimulation, furtherance

end NOUN 1 = <u>close</u>, ending, finish, expiry, expiration ≠ beginning 2 = <u>conclusion</u>, ending, climax, completion, finale, culmination, denouement, consummation ≠ start 3 = <u>finish</u>, close, stop, resolution, conclusion, closure, completion, termination 4 = <u>extremity</u>, limit, edge, border, extent, extreme, margin,

boundary 5 = <u>tip</u>, point, head, peak, extremity 6 = <u>purpose</u>, point, reason, goal, target, aim, object, mission 7 = <u>outcome</u>, resolution, conclusion 8 = <u>death</u>, dying, ruin, destruction, passing on, doom, demise, extinction 9 = <u>remnant</u>, butt, stub, scrap, fragment, stump, remainder, leftover

● VERB 1 = <u>stop</u>, finish, halt, cease, wind up, terminate, call off, discontinue ≠ start 2 = <u>finish</u>, close, conclude, wind up, culminate, terminate, come to an end, draw to a close ≠ begin

(*Related Words*)
adjectives: final, terminal, ultimate

endanger = <u>put at risk</u>, risk, threaten, compromise, jeopardize, imperil, put in danger, expose to danger ≠ save

endearing = <u>attractive</u>, winning, pleasing, appealing, sweet, engaging, charming, pleasant

endeavour (*Formal*) VERB = <u>try</u>, labour, attempt, aim, struggle, venture, strive, aspire

● NOUN = <u>attempt</u>, try, effort, trial, bid, venture, enterprise, undertaking

ending = <u>finish</u>, end, close, conclusion, summing up, completion, finale, culmination ≠ start

endless = <u>eternal</u>, infinite, continual, unlimited, interminable, incessant,

boundless, everlasting
≠ temporary

endorse 1 = <u>approve</u>, back, support, champion, promote, recommend, advocate, uphold **2** = <u>sign</u>, initial, countersign, sign on the back of

endorsement = <u>approval</u>, backing, support, favour, recommendation, acceptance, agreement, upholding

endow 1 = <u>provide</u>, favour, grace, bless, supply, furnish, endue **2** = <u>finance</u>, fund, pay for, award, confer, bestow, bequeath, donate money to **3** = <u>imbue</u>

endowment = <u>provision</u>, funding, award, grant, gift, contribution, subsidy, donation, koha (*N.Z.*)

endurance 1 = <u>staying power</u>, strength, resolution, determination, patience, stamina, fortitude, persistence **2** = <u>permanence</u>, stability, continuity, duration, longevity, durability, continuance

endure 1 = <u>experience</u>, suffer, bear, meet, encounter, cope with, sustain, undergo **2** = <u>last</u>, continue, remain, stay, stand, go on, survive, live on

enemy = <u>foe</u>, rival, opponent, the opposition, competitor, the other side, adversary, antagonist ≠ friend

energetic 1 = <u>forceful</u>, determined, active, aggressive, dynamic, vigorous, hard-hitting, strenuous **2** = <u>lively</u>, active, dynamic, vigorous, animated, tireless, bouncy, indefatigable ≠ lethargic **3** = <u>strenuous</u>, hard, taxing, demanding, tough, exhausting, vigorous, arduous

energy 1 = <u>strength</u>, might, stamina, forcefulness **2** = <u>liveliness</u>, drive, determination, pep, vitality, vigour, verve, resilience **3** = <u>power</u>

enforce 1 = <u>carry out</u>, apply, implement, fulfil, execute, administer, put into effect, put into action **2** = <u>impose</u>, force, insist on

engage 1 *with* **in** = <u>participate in</u>, join in, take part in, undertake, embark on, enter into, become involved in, set about **2** = <u>captivate</u>, catch, arrest, fix, capture **3** = <u>occupy</u>, involve, draw, grip, absorb, preoccupy, immerse, engross **4** = <u>employ</u>, appoint, take on, hire, retain, recruit, enlist, enrol ≠ dismiss **5** = <u>set going</u>, apply, trigger, activate, switch on, energize, bring into operation **6** (*Military*) = <u>begin battle with</u>, attack, take on, encounter, fall on, battle with, meet, assail

engaged 1 = <u>occupied</u>, working, employed, busy, tied up **2** = <u>betrothed</u>, promised, pledged, affianced, promised in marriage ≠ unattached **3** = <u>in use</u>, busy, tied up, unavailable ≠ free

engagement 1 = <u>appointment</u>, meeting, interview, date, commitment, arrangement, rendezvous **2** = <u>betrothal</u>, marriage contract, troth (*archaic*), agreement to marry **3** = <u>battle</u>, fight, conflict, action, struggle, clash, encounter, combat **4** = <u>participation</u>, joining, taking part, involvement

engaging = <u>charming</u>, interesting, pleasing, attractive, lovely, entertaining, winning, fetching (*informal*) ≠ unpleasant

engine = <u>machine</u>, motor, mechanism, generator, dynamo

engineer NOUN **1** = <u>designer</u>, producer, architect, developer, deviser, creator, planner, inventor **2** = <u>worker</u>, specialist, operator, practitioner, operative, driver, conductor, technician
● VERB **1** = <u>design</u>, plan, create, construct, devise **2** = <u>bring about</u>, plan, effect, set up (*informal*), scheme, arrange, plot, mastermind

engraving = <u>print</u>, carving, etching, inscription, plate, woodcut, dry point

engulf 1 = <u>immerse</u>, swamp, submerge, overrun, inundate, envelop, swallow up

2 = <u>overwhelm</u>, overcome, crush, swamp

enhance = <u>improve</u>, better, increase, lift, boost, add to, strengthen, reinforce ≠ reduce

enjoy 1 = <u>take pleasure in</u> *or* <u>from</u>, like, love, appreciate, relish, delight in, be pleased with, be fond of ≠ hate **2** = <u>have</u>, use, own, experience, possess, have the benefit of, reap the benefits of, be blessed *or* favoured with

enjoyable = <u>pleasurable</u>, good, great, fine, nice, satisfying, lovely, entertaining ≠ unpleasant

enjoyment 1 = <u>pleasure</u>, liking, fun, delight, entertainment, joy, happiness, relish **2** = <u>benefit</u>, use, advantage, favour, possession, blessing

enlarge VERB **1** = <u>expand</u>, increase, extend, add to, build up, widen, intensify, broaden ≠ reduce **2** = <u>grow</u>, increase, extend, expand, swell, become bigger, puff up, grow larger
● PHRASES **enlarge on something** = <u>expand on</u>, develop, add to, fill out, elaborate on, flesh out, expatiate on, give further details about

enlighten = <u>inform</u>, tell, teach, advise, counsel, educate, instruct, illuminate

enlightened = <u>informed</u>, aware, reasonable, educated, sophisticated, cultivated, open-

minded, knowledgeable
≠ ignorant

enlightenment
= understanding, learning,
education, knowledge,
instruction, awareness, wisdom,
insight

enlist 1 = join up, join, enter
(into), register, volunteer, sign up,
enrol 2 = recruit, take on, hire,
sign up, call up, muster, mobilize,
conscript 3 = obtain, get, gain,
secure, engage, procure

enormous = huge, massive,
vast, extensive, tremendous,
gross, immense, gigantic ≠ tiny

enough DETERMINER = sufficient,
adequate, ample, abundant, as
much as you need, as much as is
necessary

● PRONOUN = sufficiency, plenty,
sufficient, abundance, adequacy,
right amount, ample supply

● ADVERB = sufficiently, amply,
reasonably, adequately,
satisfactorily, abundantly,
tolerably

enquire ➤ inquire

enquiry ➤ inquiry

enrage = anger, infuriate,
incense, madden, inflame,
exasperate, antagonize, make you
angry ≠ calm

enrich 1 = enhance, develop,
improve, boost, supplement,
refine, heighten, augment
2 = make rich, make wealthy,

make affluent, make prosperous,
make well-off

enrol 1 = enlist, register, be
accepted, be admitted, join up,
put your name down for, sign up
or on 2 = recruit, take on, enlist

en route = on or along the way,
travelling, on the road, in transit,
on the journey

ensemble 1 = group, company,
band, troupe, cast, orchestra,
chorus 2 = collection, set, body,
whole, total, sum, combination,
entity 3 = outfit, suit, get-up
(informal), costume

ensue = follow, result, develop,
proceed, arise, stem, derive, issue
≠ come first

ensure 1 = make certain,
guarantee, secure, make sure,
confirm, warrant, certify
2 = protect, defend, secure,
safeguard, guard, make safe

entail = involve, require,
produce, demand, call for,
occasion, need, bring about

enter 1 = come or go in or into,
arrive, set foot in somewhere,
cross the threshold of
somewhere, make an entrance
≠ exit 2 = penetrate, get in,
pierce, pass into, perforate
3 = join, start work at, begin work
at, enrol, enlist in ≠ leave
4 = participate in, join (in), be
involved in, get involved in, play a
part in, partake in, associate

yourself with, start to be in
5 = <u>begin</u>, start, take up, move
into, commence, set out on,
embark upon **6** = <u>compete in</u>,
contest, join in, fight, sign up for,
go in for **7** = <u>record</u>, note, register,
log, list, write down, take down,
inscribe

enterprise 1 = <u>firm</u>, company,
business, concern, operation,
organization, establishment,
commercial undertaking
2 = <u>venture</u>, operation, project,
adventure, undertaking,
programme, pursuit, endeavour
3 = <u>initiative</u>, energy, daring,
enthusiasm, imagination, drive,
ingenuity, originality

enterprising = <u>resourceful</u>,
original, spirited, daring, bold,
enthusiastic, imaginative,
energetic

entertain 1 = <u>amuse</u>, interest,
please, delight, charm, enthral,
cheer, regale **2** = <u>show hospitality
to</u>, receive, accommodate, treat,
put up, lodge, be host to, have
company of **3** = <u>consider</u>,
imagine, think about,
contemplate, conceive of, bear in
mind, keep in mind, give thought
to

entertainment 1 = <u>enjoyable</u>,
fun, pleasure, leisure, relaxation,
recreation, enjoyment,
amusement **2** = <u>pastime</u>, show,
sport, performance, treat,

presentation, leisure activity

enthusiasm = <u>keenness</u>,
interest, passion, motivation,
relish, zeal, zest, fervour

enthusiast = <u>fan</u>, supporter,
lover, follower, addict, buff
(*informal*), fanatic, devotee

enthusiastic = <u>keen</u>,
committed, eager, passionate,
vigorous, avid, fervent, zealous
≠ apathetic

entice = <u>lure</u>, attract, invite,
persuade, tempt, induce, seduce,
lead on

entire = <u>whole</u>, full, complete,
total, gross

entirely = <u>completely</u>, totally,
absolutely, fully, altogether,
thoroughly, wholly, utterly
≠ partly

entitle 1 = <u>give the right to</u>,
allow, enable, permit, sanction,
license, authorize, empower
2 = <u>call</u>, name, title, term, label,
dub, christen, give the title of

entity = <u>thing</u>, being, individual,
object, substance, creature,
organism

entrance¹ 1 = <u>way in</u>, opening,
door, approach, access, entry,
gate, passage ≠ exit
2 = <u>appearance</u>, coming in, entry,
arrival, introduction ≠ exit
3 = <u>admission</u>, access, entry,
entrée, admittance, permission to
enter, right of entry

entrance² 1 = <u>enchant</u>, delight,

charm, fascinate, dazzle, captivate, enthral, beguile ≠ bore **2** = <u>mesmerize</u>, bewitch, hypnotize, put a spell on, cast a spell on, put in a trance

entrant = <u>competitor</u>, player, candidate, entry, participant, applicant, contender, contestant

entrenched or **intrenched** = <u>fixed</u>, set, rooted, well-established, ingrained, deep-seated, deep-rooted, unshakeable or unshakable

entrepreneur = <u>businessman</u> or <u>businesswoman</u>, tycoon, executive, industrialist, speculator, magnate, impresario, business executive

entrust or **intrust 1** = <u>give custody of</u>, deliver, commit, delegate, hand over, turn over, confide **2** = <u>assign</u>

entry 1 = <u>admission</u>, access, entrance, admittance, entrée, permission to enter, right of entry **2** = <u>coming in</u>, entering, appearance, arrival, entrance ≠ exit **3** = <u>introduction</u>, presentation, initiation, inauguration, induction, debut, investiture **4** = <u>record</u>, listing, account, note, statement, item **5** = <u>way in</u>, opening, door, approach, access, gate, passage, entrance

envelope = <u>wrapping</u>, casing, case, covering, cover, jacket,

sleeve, wrapper

environment 1 = <u>surroundings</u>, setting, conditions, situation, medium, circumstances, background, atmosphere **2** = <u>habitat</u>, home, surroundings, territory, terrain, locality, natural home

environmental = <u>ecological</u>, green

environmentalist = <u>conservationist</u>, ecologist, green

envisage 1 = <u>imagine</u>, contemplate, conceive (of), visualize, picture, fancy, think up, conceptualize **2** = <u>foresee</u>, see, expect, predict, anticipate, envision

envoy 1 = <u>ambassador</u>, diplomat, emissary **2** = <u>messenger</u>, agent, representative, delegate, courier, intermediary, emissary

envy NOUN = <u>covetousness</u>, resentment, jealousy, bitterness, resentfulness, enviousness (*informal*)

● VERB **1** = <u>be jealous (of)</u>, resent, begrudge, be envious (of) **2** = <u>covet</u>, desire, crave, aspire to, yearn for, hanker after

epidemic 1 = <u>outbreak</u>, plague, growth, spread, scourge, contagion **2** = <u>spate</u>, plague, outbreak, wave, rash, eruption, upsurge

episode 1 = <u>event</u>, experience,

happening, matter, affair, incident, adventure, occurrence **2** = instalment, part, act, scene, section, chapter, passage **3** = period, attack, spell, phase, bout

equal ADJECTIVE **1** = identical, the same, matching, equivalent, uniform, alike, corresponding ≠ unequal **2** = fair, just, impartial, egalitarian, unbiased, even-handed ≠ unfair **3** = even, balanced, fifty-fifty (*informal*), evenly matched ≠ uneven

● NOUN = match, equivalent, twin, counterpart

● VERB **1** = amount to, make, come to, total, level, parallel, tie with, equate ≠ be unequal to **2** = be equal to, match, reach **3** = be as good as, match, compare with, equate with, measure up to, be as great as

equality 1 = fairness, equal opportunity, equal treatment, egalitarianism, fair treatment, justness ≠ inequality **2** = sameness, balance, identity, similarity, correspondence, parity, likeness, uniformity ≠ disparity

equate 1 = identify, associate, connect, compare, relate, mention in the same breath, think of in connection with **2** = make equal, match, even up **3** = be equal to, parallel, compare with, liken, be commensurate with, correspond with *or* to

equation = equating, comparison, parallel, correspondence

equilibrium = stability, balance, symmetry, steadiness, evenness, equipoise

equip 1 = supply, provide for, stock, arm, array, furnish, fit out, kit out **2** = prepare, qualify, educate, get ready

equipment = apparatus, stock, supplies, stuff, tackle, gear, tools, provisions

equitable = even-handed, just, fair, reasonable, proper, honest, impartial, unbiased

equivalent NOUN = equal, counterpart, twin, parallel, match, opposite number

● ADJECTIVE = equal, same, comparable, parallel, identical, alike, corresponding, tantamount ≠ different

era = age, time, period, date, generation, epoch, day *or* days

eradicate = wipe out, eliminate, remove, destroy, get rid of, erase, extinguish, obliterate

erase 1 = delete, cancel out, wipe out, remove, eradicate, obliterate, blot out, expunge **2** = rub out, remove, wipe out, delete

erect VERB **1** = build, raise, set up, construct, put up, assemble, put together ≠ demolish **2** = found,

establish, form, create, set up, institute, organize, put up
● ADJECTIVE = **upright**, straight, stiff, vertical, elevated, perpendicular, pricked-up ≠ bent

erode 1 = **disintegrate**, crumble, deteriorate, corrode, break up, grind down, waste away, wear down or away **2** = **destroy**, consume, crumble, eat away, corrode, break up, grind down, abrade **3** = **weaken**, undermine, diminish, impair, lessen, wear away

erosion 1 = **disintegration**, deterioration, wearing down or away, grinding down **2** = **deterioration**, undermining, destruction, weakening, attrition, eating away, abrasion, grinding down

erotic = **sexual**, sexy (informal), crude, explicit, sensual, seductive, vulgar, voluptuous

erratic = **unpredictable**, variable, unstable, irregular, inconsistent, uneven, unreliable, wayward ≠ regular

error = **mistake**, slip, blunder, oversight, howler (informal), bloomer (Brit. informal), miscalculation, solecism

erupt 1 = **explode**, blow up, emit lava **2** = **discharge**, expel, emit, eject, spout, throw off, pour forth, spew forth or out **3** = **gush**, burst out, pour forth, belch forth, spew forth or out **4** = **start**, break out, began, explode, flare up, burst out, boil over **5** (Medical) = **break out**, appear, flare up

escalate 1 = **grow**, increase, extend, intensify, expand, surge, mount, heighten ≠ decrease **2** = **increase**, develop, extend, intensify, expand, build up, heighten ≠ lessen

escape VERB **1** = **get away**, flee, take off, fly, bolt, slip away, abscond, make a break for it **2** = **avoid**, miss, evade, dodge, shun, elude, duck, steer clear of **3** = **leak out**, flow out, gush out, emanate, seep out, exude, spill out, pour forth
● NOUN **1** = **getaway**, break, flight, break-out **2** = **avoidance**, evasion, circumvention **3** = **relaxation**, recreation, distraction, diversion, pastime **4** = **leak**, emission, outpouring, seepage, issue, emanation

escort NOUN **1** = **guard**, bodyguard, train, convoy, entourage, retinue, cortege **2** = **companion**, partner, attendant, guide, beau, chaperon
● VERB = **accompany**, lead, partner, conduct, guide, shepherd, usher, chaperon

especially 1 = **notably**, mostly, strikingly, conspicuously, outstandingly **2** = **very**, specially, extremely, remarkably, unusually, exceptionally, markedly, uncommonly

espionage = spying, intelligence, surveillance, counter-intelligence, undercover work

essay NOUN = composition, study, paper, article, piece, assignment, discourse, tract
● VERB (Formal) = attempt, try, undertake, endeavour

essence 1 = fundamental nature, nature, being, heart, spirit, soul, core, substance
2 = concentrate, spirits, extract, tincture, distillate

essential ADJECTIVE 1 = vital, important, needed, necessary, critical, crucial, key, indispensable
≠ unimportant 2 = fundamental, main, basic, principal, cardinal, elementary, innate, intrinsic
≠ secondary
● NOUN = prerequisite, fundamental, necessity, must, basic, sine qua non (Latin), rudiment

establish 1 = set up, found, create, institute, constitute, inaugurate 2 = prove, confirm, demonstrate, certify, verify, substantiate, corroborate, authenticate 3 = secure, form, ground, settle

establishment NOUN
1 = creation, founding, setting up, foundation, institution,

organization, formation, installation 2 = organization, company, business, firm, concern, operation, institution, corporation
● PHRASES the Establishment = the authorities, the system, the powers that be, the ruling class

estate 1 = lands, property, area, grounds, domain, manor, holdings 2 = area, centre, park, development, site, zone, plot
3 (Law) = property, capital, assets, fortune, goods, effects, wealth, possessions

esteem NOUN = respect, regard, honour, admiration, reverence, estimation, veneration
● VERB = respect, admire, think highly of, love, value, prize, treasure, revere

estimate VERB 1 = calculate roughly, value, guess, judge, reckon, assess, evaluate, gauge
2 = think, believe, consider, rate, judge, hold, rank, reckon
● NOUN 1 = approximate calculation, guess, assessment, judgment, valuation, guesstimate (informal), rough calculation, ballpark figure (informal)
2 = assessment, opinion, belief, appraisal, evaluation, judgment, estimation

estuary = inlet, mouth, creek, firth, fjord

etch 1 = engrave, cut, impress,

stamp, carve, imprint, inscribe
2 = <u>corrode</u>, eat into, burn into

etching = <u>print</u>, impression, carving, engraving, imprint, inscription

eternal 1 = <u>everlasting</u>, lasting, permanent, enduring, endless, perpetual, timeless, unending ≠ transitory 2 = <u>interminable</u>, endless, infinite, continual, immortal, never-ending, everlasting ≠ occasional

eternity 1 (*Theology*) = <u>the afterlife</u>, heaven, paradise, the next world, the hereafter
2 = <u>perpetuity</u>, immortality, infinity, timelessness, endlessness
3 = <u>ages</u>

ethical 1 = <u>moral</u>, behavioural
2 = <u>right</u>, morally acceptable, good, just, fair, responsible, principled ≠ unethical

ethics = <u>moral code</u>, standards, principles, morals, conscience, morality, moral values, moral principles, tikanga (*N.Z.*)

ethnic *or* **ethnical** = <u>cultural</u>, national, traditional, native, folk, racial, genetic, indigenous

euphoria = <u>elation</u>, joy, ecstasy, rapture, exhilaration, jubilation ≠ despondency

Europe ► **WORD POWER SUPPLEMENT European Union**

evacuate 1 = <u>remove</u>, clear, withdraw, expel, move out, send to a safe place 2 = <u>abandon</u>, leave, clear, desert, quit, withdraw from, pull out of, move out of

evade 1 = <u>avoid</u>, escape, dodge, get away from, elude, steer clear of, sidestep, duck ≠ face 2 = <u>avoid</u> answering, parry, fend off, fudge, hedge, equivocate

evaluate = <u>assess</u>, rate, judge, estimate, reckon, weigh, calculate, gauge

evaporate 1 = <u>disappear</u>, vaporize, dematerialize, vanish, dissolve, dry up, fade away, melt away 2 = <u>dry up</u>, dry, dehydrate, vaporize, desiccate 3 = <u>fade away</u>, disappear, vanish, dissolve, melt away

eve 1 = <u>night before</u>, day before, vigil 2 = <u>brink</u>, point, edge, verge, threshold

even 1 = <u>regular</u>, stable, constant, steady, smooth, uniform, unbroken, uninterrupted ≠ variable
2 = <u>level</u>, straight, flat, smooth, true, steady, uniform, parallel ≠ uneven 3 = <u>equal</u>, like, matching, similar, identical, comparable ≠ unequal
4 = <u>equally matched</u>, level, tied, on a par, neck and neck, fifty-fifty (*informal*), all square ≠ ill-matched 5 = <u>square</u>, quits, on the same level, on an equal footing
6 = <u>calm</u>, composed, cool, well-balanced, placid, unruffled, imperturbable, even-tempered

≠ **excitable**

evening = <u>dusk</u> (*archaic*), night, sunset, twilight, sundown, gloaming (*Scot. poetic*), close of day, evo (*Austral. slang*)

event 1 = <u>incident</u>, happening, experience, affair, occasion, proceeding, business, circumstance **2** = <u>competition</u>, game, tournament, contest, bout

eventual = <u>final</u>, overall, concluding, ultimate

eventually = <u>in the end</u>, finally, one day, after all, some time, ultimately, at the end of the day, when all is said and done

ever 1 = <u>at any time</u>, at all, in any case, at any point, by any chance, on any occasion, at any period **2** = <u>always</u>, for ever, at all times, evermore **3** = <u>constantly</u>, continually, perpetually

every = <u>each</u>, each and every, every single

everybody = <u>everyone</u>, each one, the whole world, each person, every person, all and sundry, one and all
> **everyone**

everyday = <u>ordinary</u>, common, usual, routine, stock, customary, mundane, run-of-the-mill
≠ **unusual**

everyone = <u>everybody</u>, each one, the whole world, each person, every person, all and sundry, one and all

> ### Word Power
>
> **everyone** – *Everyone* and *everybody* are interchangeable, and can be used as synonyms of each other in any context. Care should be taken, however, to distinguish between *everyone* as a single word and *every one* as two words, the latter form correctly being used to refer to each individual person or thing in a particular group: *every one of them is wrong*.

everything = <u>all</u>, the lot, the whole lot, each thing

everywhere 1 = <u>all over</u>, all around, the world over, high and low, in every nook and cranny, far and wide *or* near, to *or* in every place **2** = <u>all around</u>, all over, in every nook and cranny, ubiquitously, far and wide *or* near, to *or* in every place

evidence NOUN **1** = <u>proof</u>, grounds, demonstration, confirmation, verification, corroboration, authentication, substantiation **2** = <u>sign(s)</u>, suggestion, trace, indication **3** = <u>testimony</u>, statement, submission, avowal
● VERB = <u>show</u>, prove, reveal, display, indicate, witness, demonstrate, exhibit

evident = <u>obvious</u>, clear, plain,

apparent, visible, manifest, noticeable, unmistakable ≠ hidden

evidently 1 = <u>obviously</u>, clearly, plainly, undoubtedly, manifestly, without question, unmistakably 2 = <u>apparently</u>, seemingly, outwardly, ostensibly, so it seems, to all appearances

evil NOUN 1 = <u>wickedness</u>, bad, vice, sin, wrongdoing, depravity, badness, villainy 2 = <u>harm</u>, suffering, hurt, woe 3 = <u>act of cruelty</u>, crime, ill, horror, outrage, misfortune, mischief, affliction
● ADJECTIVE 1 = <u>wicked</u>, bad, malicious, immoral, sinful, malevolent, depraved, villainous 2 = <u>harmful</u>, disastrous, destructive, ruinous, catastrophic, pernicious, ruinous 3 = <u>demonic</u>, satanic, diabolical, hellish, devilish, infernal, fiendish 4 = <u>offensive</u>, nasty, foul, unpleasant, vile, noxious, disagreeable, pestilential 5 = <u>unfortunate</u>, unfavourable, ruinous, calamitous

evoke = <u>arouse</u>, cause, induce, awaken, give rise to, stir up, rekindle, summon up ≠ suppress

evolution 1 = <u>rise</u>, development, adaptation, natural selection, Darwinism, survival of the fittest 2 = <u>development</u>, growth, advance, progress, working out, expansion, extension, unfolding

evolve 1 = <u>develop</u>, metamorphose, adapt yourself 2 = <u>grow</u>, develop, advance, progress, mature 3 = <u>work out</u>, develop, progress, expand, unfold

exact ADJECTIVE = <u>accurate</u>, correct, true, right, specific, precise, definite, faultless ≠ approximate
● VERB 1 = <u>demand</u>, claim, force, command, extract, compel, extort 2 = <u>inflict</u>, apply, administer, mete out, deal out

exacting 1 = <u>demanding</u>, hard, taxing, difficult, tough ≠ easy 2 = <u>strict</u>, severe, harsh, rigorous, stringent

exactly 1 = <u>accurately</u>, correctly, precisely, faithfully, explicitly, scrupulously, truthfully, unerringly 2 = <u>precisely</u>, specifically, bang on (informal), to the letter

exaggerate = <u>overstate</u>, enlarge, embroider, amplify, embellish, overestimate, overemphasize, pile it on about (informal)

examination 1 = <u>checkup</u>, analysis, going-over (informal), exploration, health check, check 2 = <u>exam</u>, test, research, paper, investigation, practical, assessment, quiz

examine 1 = <u>inspect</u>, study, survey, investigate, explore, analyse, scrutinize, peruse

2 = <u>check</u>, analyse, check over
3 = <u>test</u>, question, assess, quiz, evaluate, appraise **4** = <u>question</u>, quiz, interrogate, cross-examine, grill (*informal*), give the third degree to (*informal*)

example 1 = <u>instance</u>, specimen, case, sample, illustration, particular case, particular instance, typical case **2** = <u>illustration</u>, model, ideal, standard, prototype, paradigm, archetype, paragon **3** = <u>warning</u>, lesson, caution, deterrent

exceed 1 = <u>surpass</u>, better, pass, eclipse, beat, cap (*informal*), be over **2** = <u>go over the limit of</u>, go beyond, overstep

excel VERB = <u>be superior</u>, eclipse, beat, surpass, transcend, outdo, outshine

● PHRASES **excel in** or **at something** = <u>be good at</u>, shine at, be proficient in, show talent in, be skilful at, be talented at

excellence = <u>high quality</u>, merit, distinction, goodness, superiority, greatness, supremacy, eminence

excellent = <u>outstanding</u>, good, great, fine, cool (*informal*), brilliant, very good, superb, booshit (*Austral. slang*), exo (*Austral. slang*), sik (*Austral. slang*) ≠ terrible

except or **except for**
PREPOSITION = <u>apart from</u>, but for, saving, barring, excepting, other than, excluding, omitting
● VERB = <u>exclude</u>, leave out, omit, disregard, pass over

exception = <u>special case</u>, freak, anomaly, inconsistency, deviation, oddity, peculiarity, irregularity

exceptional 1 = <u>remarkable</u>, special, excellent, extraordinary, outstanding, superior, first-class, marvellous ≠ average **2** = <u>unusual</u>, special, odd, strange, extraordinary, unprecedented, peculiar, abnormal ≠ ordinary

excerpt = <u>extract</u>, part, piece, section, selection, passage, fragment, quotation

excess 1 = <u>surfeit</u>, surplus, overload, glut, superabundance, superfluity ≠ shortage **2** = <u>overindulgence</u>, extravagance, profligacy, debauchery, dissipation, intemperance, indulgence, prodigality ≠ moderation

excessive 1 = <u>immoderate</u>, too much, extreme, exaggerated, unreasonable, disproportionate, undue, uncontrolled **2** = <u>inordinate</u>, unfair, unreasonable, disproportionate, undue, unwarranted, exorbitant, extortionate

exchange VERB = <u>interchange</u>, change, trade, switch, swap, barter, give to each other, give to one another

● NOUN 1 = <u>conversation</u>, talk, word, discussion, chat, dialogue, natter, powwow 2 = <u>interchange</u>, trade, switch, swap, trafficking, swapping, substitution, barter

excite 1 = <u>thrill</u>, inspire, stir, provoke, animate, rouse, exhilarate, inflame 2 = <u>arouse</u>, provoke, rouse, stir up 3 = <u>titillate</u>, thrill, stimulate, turn on (slang), arouse, get going (informal), electrify

excitement = <u>exhilaration</u>, action, activity, passion, thrill, animation, furore, agitation

exciting 1 = <u>stimulating</u>, dramatic, gripping, stirring, thrilling, sensational, rousing, exhilarating ≠ boring 2 = <u>titillating</u>, stimulating, arousing, erotic

exclaim = <u>cry out</u>, declare, shout, proclaim, yell, utter, call out

exclude 1 = <u>keep out</u>, bar, ban, refuse, forbid, boycott, prohibit, disallow ≠ let in 2 = <u>omit</u>, reject, eliminate, rule out, miss out, leave out ≠ include 3 = <u>eliminate</u>, reject, ignore, rule out, leave out, set aside, omit, pass over

exclusion 1 = <u>ban</u>, bar, veto, boycott, embargo, prohibition, disqualification 2 = <u>elimination</u>, missing out, rejection, leaving out, omission

exclusive 1 = <u>select</u>,

fashionable, stylish, restricted, posh (informal, chiefly Brit.), chic, high-class, up-market ≠ unrestricted 2 = <u>sole</u>, full, whole, complete, total, entire, absolute, undivided ≠ shared 3 = <u>entire</u>, full, whole, complete, total, absolute, undivided 4 = <u>limited</u>, unique, restricted, confined, peculiar

excursion = <u>trip</u>, tour, journey, outing, expedition, ramble, day trip, jaunt

excuse NOUN = <u>justification</u>, reason, explanation, defence, grounds, plea, apology, vindication ≠ accusation

● VERB 1 = <u>justify</u>, explain, defend, vindicate, mitigate, apologize for, make excuses for ≠ blame 2 = <u>forgive</u>, pardon, overlook, tolerate, acquit, turn a blind eye to, exonerate, make allowances for 3 = <u>free</u>, relieve, exempt, release, spare, discharge, let off, absolve ≠ convict

execute 1 = <u>put to death</u>, kill, shoot, hang, behead, decapitate, guillotine, electrocute 2 = <u>carry out</u>, effect, implement, accomplish, discharge, administer, prosecute, enact 3 = <u>perform</u>, carry out, accomplish

execution 1 = <u>killing</u>, hanging, the death penalty, the rope, capital punishment, beheading,

the electric chair, the guillotine
2 = <u>carrying out</u>, performance, operation, administration, prosecution, enforcement, implementation, accomplishment

executive NOUN
1 = <u>administrator</u>, official, director, manager, chairman, managing director, controller, chief executive officer
2 = <u>administration</u>, government, directors, management, leadership, hierarchy, directorate
• ADJECTIVE = <u>administrative</u>, controlling, directing, governing, regulating, decision-making, managerial

exemplify = <u>show</u>, represent, display, demonstrate, illustrate, exhibit, embody, serve as an example of

exempt ADJECTIVE = <u>immune</u>, free, excepted, excused, released, spared, not liable to ≠ liable
• VERB = <u>grant immunity</u>, free, excuse, release, spare, relieve, discharge, let off

exemption = <u>immunity</u>, freedom, relief, exception, discharge, release, dispensation, absolution

exercise VERB **1** = <u>put to use</u>, use, apply, employ, exert, utilize, bring to bear, avail yourself of
2 = <u>train</u>, work out, practise, keep fit, do exercises

• NOUN **1** = <u>use</u>, practice, application, operation, discharge, implementation, fulfilment, utilization **2** = <u>exertion</u>, training, activity, work, labour, effort, movement, toil **3** = <u>manoeuvre</u>, campaign, operation, movement, deployment **4** = <u>task</u>, problem, lesson, assignment, practice

exert VERB = <u>apply</u>, use, exercise, employ, wield, make use of, utilize, bring to bear
• PHRASES **exert yourself** = <u>make an effort</u>, work, labour, struggle, strain, strive, endeavour, toil

exhaust 1 = <u>tire out</u>, fatigue, drain, weaken, weary, sap, wear out, debilitate **2** = <u>use up</u>, spend, consume, waste, go through, run through, deplete, squander

exhausted 1 = <u>worn out</u>, tired out, drained, spent, bushed (informal), done in (informal), all in (slang), fatigued ≠ invigorated
2 = <u>used up</u>, consumed, spent, finished, depleted, dissipated, expended ≠ replenished

exhaustion 1 = <u>tiredness</u>, fatigue, weariness, debilitation
2 = <u>depletion</u>, emptying, consumption, using up

exhibit 1 = <u>show</u>, reveal, display, demonstrate, express, indicate, manifest **2** = <u>display</u>, show, set out, parade, unveil, put on view

exhibition 1 = <u>show</u>, display,

representation, presentation, spectacle, showcase, exposition **2** = <u>display</u>, show, performance, demonstration, revelation

exile NOUN **1** = <u>banishment</u>, expulsion, deportation, eviction, expatriation **2** = <u>expatriate</u>, refugee, outcast, émigré, deportee

● VERB = <u>banish</u>, expel, throw out, deport, drive out, eject, expatriate, cast out

exist 1 = <u>live</u>, be present, survive, endure, be in existence, be, have breath **2** = <u>occur</u>, be present **3** = <u>survive</u>, stay alive, make ends meet, subsist, eke out a living, scrape by, scrimp and save, support yourself

existence 1 = <u>reality</u>, being, life, subsistence, actuality **2** = <u>life</u>, situation, way of life, life style

existent = <u>in existence</u>, living, existing, surviving, standing, present, alive, extant

exit NOUN **1** = <u>way out</u>, door, gate, outlet, doorway, gateway, escape route ≠ entry **2** = <u>departure</u>, withdrawal, retreat, farewell, going, goodbye, exodus, decamping

● VERB = <u>depart</u>, leave, go out, withdraw, retire, quit, retreat, go away ≠ enter

exodus = <u>departure</u>, withdrawal, retreat, leaving, flight, exit, migration, evacuation

exotic 1 = <u>unusual</u>, striking, strange, fascinating, mysterious, colourful, glamorous, unfamiliar ≠ ordinary **2** = <u>foreign</u>, alien, tropical, external, naturalized

expand VERB **1** = <u>get bigger</u>, increase, grow, extend, swell, widen, enlarge, become bigger ≠ contract **2** = <u>make bigger</u>, increase, develop, extend, widen, enlarge, broaden, magnify ≠ reduce **3** = <u>spread (out)</u>, stretch (out), unfold, unravel, diffuse, unfurl, unroll

● PHRASES **expand on something** = <u>go into detail about</u>, embellish, elaborate on, develop, flesh out, expound on, enlarge on, expatiate on

expansion 1 = <u>increase</u>, development, growth, spread, magnification, amplification **2** = <u>enlargement</u>, increase, growth, opening out

expatriate NOUN = <u>exile</u>, refugee, emigrant, émigré

● ADJECTIVE = <u>exiled</u>, refugee, banished, emigrant, émigré, expat

expect 1 = <u>think</u>, believe, suppose, assume, trust, imagine, reckon, presume **2** = <u>anticipate</u>, look forward to, predict, envisage, await, hope for, contemplate **3** = <u>require</u>, demand, want, call for, ask for, hope for, insist on

expectation 1 = <u>projection</u>,

supposition, assumption, belief, forecast, likelihood, probability, presumption **2** = <u>anticipation</u>, hope, promise, excitement, expectancy, apprehension, suspense

expedition = <u>journey</u>, mission, voyage, tour, quest, trek

expel 1 = <u>throw out</u>, exclude, ban, dismiss, kick out (*informal*), ask to leave, turf out (*informal*), debar ≠ let in **2** = <u>banish</u>, exile, deport, evict, force to leave ≠ take in **3** = <u>drive out</u>, discharge, force out, let out, eject, issue, spew, belch

expenditure 1 = <u>spending</u>, payment, expense, outgoings, cost, outlay **2** = <u>consumption</u>, using, output

expense = <u>cost</u>, charge, expenditure, payment, spending, outlay

expensive = <u>costly</u>, high-priced, lavish, extravagant, dear, stiff, steep (*informal*), pricey ≠ cheap

experience NOUN
1 = <u>knowledge</u>, practice, skill, contact, expertise, involvement, exposure, participation **2** = <u>event</u>, affair, incident, happening, encounter, episode, adventure, occurrence

● VERB = <u>undergo</u>, feel, face, taste, go through, sample, encounter, endure

experienced = <u>knowledgeable</u>, skilled, tried, tested, seasoned, expert, veteran, practised ≠ inexperienced

experiment NOUN **1** = <u>test</u>, trial, investigation, examination, procedure, demonstration, observation, try-out **2** = <u>research</u>, investigation, analysis, observation, research and development, experimentation

● VERB = <u>test</u>, investigate, trial, research, try, examine, pilot, sample

experimental 1 = <u>test</u>, trial, pilot, preliminary, provisional, tentative, speculative, exploratory **2** = <u>innovative</u>, new, original, radical, creative, ingenious, avant-garde, inventive

expert NOUN = <u>specialist</u>, authority, professional, master, genius, guru, pundit, maestro, fundi (*S. African*) ≠ amateur

● ADJECTIVE = <u>skilful</u>, experienced, professional, masterly, qualified, talented, outstanding, practised ≠ unskilled

expertise = <u>skill</u>, knowledge, know-how (*informal*), facility, judgment, mastery, proficiency, adroitness

expire 1 = <u>become invalid</u>, end, finish, conclude, close, stop, run out, cease **2** = <u>die</u>, depart, perish, kick the bucket (*informal*), depart this life, meet your maker, cark it (*Austral. & N.Z. slang*), pass away or on

explain 1 = <u>make clear</u> or plain, describe, teach, define, resolve, clarify, clear up, simplify
2 = <u>account for</u>, excuse, justify, give a reason for

explanation 1 = <u>reason</u>, answer, account, excuse, motive, justification, vindication
2 = <u>description</u>, report, definition, teaching, interpretation, illustration, clarification, simplification

explicit 1 = <u>clear</u>, obvious, specific, direct, precise, straightforward, definite, overt ≠ vague 2 = <u>frank</u>, specific, graphic, unambiguous, unrestricted, unrestrained, uncensored ≠ indirect

explode 1 = <u>blow up</u>, erupt, burst, go off, shatter
2 = <u>detonate</u>, set off, discharge, let off 3 = <u>lose your temper</u>, rage, erupt, become angry, hit the roof (informal), go crook (Austral. & N.Z. slang) 4 = <u>increase</u>, grow, develop, extend, advance, shoot up, soar, boost 5 = <u>disprove</u>, discredit, refute, demolish, repudiate, put paid to, invalidate, debunk

exploit VERB 1 = <u>take advantage of</u>, abuse, use, manipulate, milk, misuse, ill-treat, play on or upon 2 = <u>make the best use of</u>, use, make use of, utilize, cash in on (informal), capitalize on, use to good advantage, profit by or from
● NOUN = <u>feat</u>, act, achievement,

enterprise, adventure, stunt, deed, accomplishment

exploitation = <u>misuse</u>, abuse, manipulation, using, ill-treatment

exploration 1 = <u>expedition</u>, tour, trip, survey, travel, journey, reconnaissance 2 = <u>investigation</u>, research, survey, search, inquiry, analysis, examination, inspection

explore 1 = <u>travel around</u>, tour, survey, scout, reconnoitre 2 = <u>investigate</u>, consider, research, survey, search, examine, probe, look into

explosion 1 = <u>blast</u>, crack, burst, bang, discharge, report, blowing up, clap 2 = <u>increase</u>, rise, development, growth, boost, expansion, enlargement, escalation 3 = <u>outburst</u>, fit, storm, attack, surge, flare-up, eruption 4 = <u>outbreak</u>, flare-up, eruption, upsurge

explosive NOUN = <u>bomb</u>, mine, shell, missile, rocket, grenade, charge, torpedo
● ADJECTIVE 1 = <u>unstable</u>, dangerous, volatile, hazardous, unsafe, perilous, combustible, inflammable 2 = <u>sudden</u>, rapid, marked, unexpected, startling, swift, abrupt 3 = <u>fiery</u>, violent, volatile, stormy, touchy, vehement

expose 1 = <u>uncover</u>, show, reveal, display, exhibit, present, unveil, lay bare ≠ hide 2 = <u>make vulnerable</u>, subject, endanger, leave open, jeopardize, put at risk, imperil, lay open

exposure 1 = hypothermia, frostbite, extreme cold, intense cold **2** = uncovering, showing, display, exhibition, revelation, presentation, unveiling

express VERB **1** = state, communicate, convey, articulate, say, word, voice, declare **2** = show, indicate, exhibit, demonstrate, reveal, intimate, convey, signify
● ADJECTIVE **1** = explicit, clear, plain, distinct, definite, unambiguous, categorical **2** = specific, exclusive, particular, sole, special, singular, clear-cut, especial **3** = fast, direct, rapid, priority, prompt, swift, high-speed, speedy

expression 1 = statement, declaration, announcement, communication, utterance, articulation **2** = indication, demonstration, exhibition, display, showing, show, sign, symbol **3** = look, countenance, face, air, appearance, aspect **4** = phrase, saying, word, term, remark, maxim, idiom, adage

expressive = vivid, striking, telling, moving, poignant, eloquent ≠ impassive

expulsion 1 = ejection, exclusion, dismissal, removal, eviction, banishment **2** = discharge, emission, spewing,

secretion, excretion, ejection, seepage, suppuration

exquisite 1 = beautiful, elegant, graceful, pleasing, attractive, lovely, charming, comely ≠ unattractive **2** = fine, beautiful, lovely, elegant, precious, delicate, dainty **3** = intense, acute, severe, sharp, keen, extreme

extend 1 = spread out, reach, stretch **2** = stretch, stretch out, spread out, straighten out **3** = last, continue, go on, stretch, carry on **4** = protrude, project, stand out, bulge, stick out, hang, overhang, jut out **5** = widen, increase, expand, add to, enhance, supplement, enlarge, broaden ≠ reduce **6** = make longer, prolong, lengthen, draw out, spin out, drag out ≠ shorten **7** = offer, present, confer, stick out, impart, proffer ≠ withdraw

extension 1 = annexe, addition, supplement, appendix, appendage **2** = lengthening, extra time, continuation, additional period of time **3** = development, expansion, widening, increase, broadening, enlargement, diversification

extensive ADJECTIVE = large, considerable, substantial, spacious, wide, broad, expansive
● ADJECTIVE ≠ confined **2** = comprehensive, complete, wide, pervasive ≠ restricted

3 = **great**, vast, widespread, large-scale, far-reaching, far-flung, voluminous ≠ limited

extent 1 = **magnitude**, amount, scale, level, stretch, expanse 2 = **size**, area, length, width, breadth

exterior NOUN = **outside**, face, surface, covering, skin, shell, coating, façade
● ADJECTIVE = **outer**, outside, external, surface, outward, outermost ≠ inner

external 1 = **outer**, outside, surface, outward, exterior, outermost ≠ internal 2 = **foreign**, international, alien, extrinsic ≠ domestic 3 = **outside**, visiting ≠ inside

extinct = **dead**, lost, gone, vanished, defunct ≠ living

extinction = **dying out**, destruction, abolition, oblivion, extermination, annihilation, eradication, obliteration

extra ADJECTIVE 1 = **additional**, more, added, further, supplementary, auxiliary, ancillary ≠ vital 2 = **surplus**, excess, spare, redundant, unused, leftover, superfluous
● NOUN = **addition**, bonus, supplement, accessory ≠ necessity
● ADVERB 1 = **in addition**, additionally, over and above 2 = **exceptionally**, very, specially, especially, particularly, extremely, remarkably, unusually

extract VERB 1 = **take out**, draw, pull, remove, withdraw, pull out, bring out 2 = **pull out**, remove, take out, draw, uproot, pluck out 3 = **elicit**, obtain, force, draw, derive, glean, coerce
● NOUN 1 = **passage**, selection, excerpt, cutting, clipping, quotation, citation 2 = **essence**, solution, concentrate, juice, distillation

> ### Word Power
>
> **extract** – People sometimes use *extract* where *extricate* would be better. Although both words can refer to a physical act of removal from a place, *extract* has a more general sense than *extricate*. *Extricate* has additional overtones of 'difficulty', and is most commonly used with reference to getting a person – particularly *yourself* – out of a situation. So, for example, you might say *he will find it difficult to extricate himself* (not *extract himself*) from this situation.

extraordinary 1 = **remarkable**, outstanding, amazing, fantastic, astonishing, exceptional, phenomenal, extremely good ≠ unremarkable 2 = **unusual**, strange, remarkable, uncommon ≠ ordinary

extravagant 1 = **wasteful**, lavish, prodigal, profligate,

spendthrift ≠ economical
2 = <u>excessive</u>, outrageous, over the top (*slang*), unreasonable, preposterous ≠ moderate

extreme ADJECTIVE **1** = <u>great</u>, highest, supreme, acute, severe, maximum, intense, ultimate ≠ mild **2** = <u>severe</u>, radical, strict, harsh, rigid, drastic, uncompromising **3** = <u>radical</u>, excessive, fanatical, immoderate ≠ moderate **4** = <u>farthest</u>, furthest, far, remotest, far-off, outermost, most distant ≠ nearest
● NOUN = <u>limit</u>, end, edge, opposite, pole, boundary, antithesis, extremity

extremely ADVERB = <u>very</u>, particularly, severely, terribly, unusually, exceptionally, extraordinarily, tremendously

extremist NOUN = <u>radical</u>, activist, militant, fanatic, die-hard, bigot, zealot
● ADJECTIVE = <u>extreme</u>, wild, passionate, frenzied, obsessive, fanatical, fervent, zealous

eye NOUN **1** = <u>eyeball</u>, optic (*informal*), organ of vision, organ of sight **2** *often plural* = <u>eyesight</u>, sight, vision, perception, ability to see, power of seeing **3** = <u>appreciation</u>, taste, recognition, judgment, discrimination, perception, discernment **4** = <u>observance</u>, observation, surveillance, vigil, watch, lookout **5** = <u>centre</u>, heart,

middle, mid, core, nucleus
● VERB = <u>look at</u>, view, study, watch, survey, observe, contemplate, check out (*informal*)
Related Words
adjectives: ocular, ophthalmic, optic

F

fable 1 = <u>legend</u>, myth, parable, allegory, story, tale **2** = <u>fiction</u>, fantasy, myth, invention, yarn (*informal*), fabrication, urban myth, tall story (*informal*) ≠ fact

fabric 1 = <u>cloth</u>, material, stuff, textile, web **2** = <u>framework</u>, structure, make-up, organization, frame, foundations, construction, constitution **3** = <u>structure</u>, foundations, construction, framework

fabulous 1 (*Informal*) = <u>wonderful</u>, excellent, brilliant, superb, spectacular, fantastic (*informal*), marvellous, sensational (*informal*) ≠ ordinary **2** = <u>astounding</u>, amazing, extraordinary, remarkable, incredible, astonishing, unbelievable, breathtaking **3** = <u>legendary</u>, imaginary, mythical, fictitious, made-up, fantastic, invented, unreal

façade 1 = <u>front</u>, face, exterior **2** = <u>show</u>, front, appearance, mask, exterior, guise, pretence, semblance

face NOUN 1 = <u>countenance</u>, features, profile, mug (*slang*), visage 2 = <u>expression</u>, look, air, appearance, aspect, countenance 3 = <u>side</u>, front, outside, surface, exterior, elevation, vertical surface • VERB 1 = <u>look onto</u>, overlook, be opposite, look out on, front onto 2 = <u>confront</u>, meet, encounter, deal with, oppose, tackle, experience, brave 3 *often with* **up to** = <u>accept</u>, deal with, tackle, acknowledge, cope with, confront, come to terms with, meet head-on

facilitate = <u>further</u>, help, forward, promote, speed up, pave the way for, make easy, expedite ≠ hinder

facility 1 *often plural* = <u>amenity</u>, means, aid, opportunity, advantage, resource, equipment, provision 2 = <u>opportunity</u>, possibility, convenience 3 = <u>ability</u>, skill, efficiency, fluency, proficiency, dexterity, adroitness 4 = <u>ease</u>, fluency, effortlessness ≠ difficulty

fact 1 = <u>truth</u>, reality, certainty, verity ≠ fiction 2 = <u>event</u>, happening, act, performance, incident, deed, occurrence, fait accompli (*French*)

faction 1 = <u>group</u>, set, party, gang, bloc, contingent, clique, coterie 2 = <u>dissension</u>, division, conflict, rebellion, disagreement, variance, discord, infighting ≠ agreement

factor = <u>element</u>, part, cause, influence, item, aspect, characteristic, consideration

> ### *Word Power*
>
> **factor** – In strict usage, *factor* should only be used to refer to something which contributes to a result. It should not be used to refer to a part of something, such as a plan or arrangement; more appropriate alternatives to *factor* in this sense are words such as *component* or *element*.

factory = <u>works</u>, plant, mill, workshop, assembly line, shop floor

factual = <u>true</u>, authentic, real, correct, genuine, exact, precise, dinkum (*Austral. & N.Z. informal*), true-to-life ≠ fictitious

faculty NOUN 1 = <u>ability</u>, power, skill, facility, capacity, propensity, aptitude ≠ failing 2 = <u>department</u>, school 3 = <u>teaching staff</u>, staff, teachers, professors, lecturers (*chiefly U.S.*) • PLURAL NOUN = <u>powers</u>, reason, senses, intelligence, wits, capabilities, mental abilities, physical abilities

fad = <u>craze</u>, fashion, trend, rage, vogue, whim, mania

fade 1 = <u>become pale</u>, bleach, wash out, discolour, lose colour, decolour 2 = <u>make pale</u>, dim, bleach, wash out, blanch, discolour, decolour 3 = <u>grow dim</u>, fade away, become less loud 4 = <u>dwindle</u>, disappear, vanish, melt away, decline, dissolve, wane, die away

fail VERB 1 = <u>be unsuccessful</u>, founder, fall, break down, flop (*informal*), fizzle out (*informal*), come unstuck, miscarry ≠ succeed 2 = <u>disappoint</u>, abandon, desert, neglect, omit, let down, forsake, be disloyal to 3 = <u>stop working</u>, stop, die, break down, stall, cut out, malfunction, conk out (*informal*) 4 = <u>wither</u>, perish, sag, waste away, shrivel up 5 = <u>go bankrupt</u>, collapse, fold (*informal*), close down, go under, go bust (*informal*), go out of business, be wound up 6 = <u>decline</u>, deteriorate, degenerate 7 = <u>give out</u>, dim, peter out, die away, grow dim
● PHRASES **without fail** = <u>without exception</u>, regularly, constantly, invariably, religiously, unfailingly, conscientiously, like clockwork

failing NOUN = <u>shortcoming</u>, fault, weakness, defect, deficiency, flaw, drawback, blemish ≠ strength
● PREPOSITION = <u>in the absence of</u>, lacking, in default of

failure 1 = <u>lack of success</u>, defeat, collapse, breakdown, overthrow, miscarriage, fiasco, downfall ≠ success 2 = <u>loser</u>, disappointment, flop (*informal*), write-off, no-hoper (*chiefly Austral.*), dud (*informal*), black sheep, washout (*informal*), dead duck (*slang*) 3 = <u>bankruptcy</u>, crash, collapse, ruin, closure, winding up, downfall, going under ≠ prosperity

faint ADJECTIVE 1 = <u>dim</u>, low, soft, faded, distant, vague, unclear, muted ≠ clear 2 = <u>slight</u>, weak, feeble, unenthusiastic, remote, slim, vague, slender 3 = <u>dizzy</u>, giddy, light-headed, weak, exhausted, wobbly, muzzy, woozy (*informal*) ≠ energetic
● VERB = <u>pass out</u>, black out, lose consciousness, keel over (*informal*), go out, collapse, swoon (*literary*), flake out (*informal*)
● NOUN = <u>blackout</u>, collapse, coma, swoon (*literary*), unconsciousness

faintly 1 = <u>slightly</u>, rather, a little, somewhat, dimly 2 = <u>softly</u>, weakly, feebly, in a whisper, indistinctly, unclearly

fair¹ 1 = <u>unbiased</u>, impartial, even-handed, unprejudiced, just, reasonable, proper, legitimate ≠ unfair 2 = <u>respectable</u>, average, reasonable, decent, acceptable, moderate, adequate, satisfactory 3 = <u>light</u>, golden, blonde, blond, yellowish, fair-haired, light-coloured, flaxen-haired 4 = <u>fine</u>, clear, dry, bright, pleasant, sunny,

cloudless, unclouded
5 = <u>beautiful</u>, pretty, attractive, lovely, handsome, good-looking, bonny, comely ≠ ugly

fair² = <u>carnival</u>, show, fête, festival, exhibition, mart, bazaar, gala

fairly 1 = <u>equitably</u>, objectively, legitimately, honestly, justly, lawfully, without prejudice, dispassionately **2** = <u>moderately</u>, rather, quite, somewhat, reasonably, adequately, pretty well, tolerably **3** = <u>positively</u>, really, simply, absolutely **4** = <u>deservedly</u>, objectively, honestly, justifiably, justly, impartially, equitably, without fear or favour

fairness = <u>impartiality</u>, justice, equity, legitimacy, decency, disinterestedness, rightfulness, equitableness

fairy = <u>sprite</u>, elf, brownie, pixie, puck, imp, leprechaun, peri

fairy tale *or* **fairy story**
1 = <u>folk tale</u>, romance, traditional story **2** = <u>lie</u>, fiction, invention, fabrication, untruth, urban myth, tall story, urban legend

faith 1 = <u>confidence</u>, trust, credit, conviction, assurance, dependence, reliance, credence ≠ distrust **2** = <u>religion</u>, church, belief, persuasion, creed, communion, denomination, dogma ≠ agnosticism

faithful 1 = <u>loyal</u>, true,

committed, constant, devoted, dedicated, reliable, staunch ≠ disloyal **2** = <u>accurate</u>, close, true, strict, exact, precise

fake ADJECTIVE = <u>artificial</u>, false, forged, counterfeit, put-on, pretend (*informal*), mock, imitation ≠ genuine
● **NOUN 1** = <u>forgery</u>, copy, fraud, reproduction, dummy, imitation, hoax, counterfeit **2** = <u>charlatan</u>, deceiver, sham, quack
● **VERB 1** = <u>forge</u>, copy, reproduce, fabricate, counterfeit, falsify
2 = <u>sham</u>, put on, pretend, simulate, feign, go through the motions of

fall VERB 1 = <u>drop</u>, plunge, tumble, plummet, collapse, sink, go down, come down ≠ rise **2** = <u>decrease</u>, drop, decline, go down, slump, diminish, dwindle, lessen ≠ increase **3** = <u>be overthrown</u>, surrender, succumb, submit, capitulate, be conquered, pass into enemy hands ≠ triumph **4** = <u>be killed</u>, die, perish, meet your end ≠ survive **5** = <u>occur</u>, happen, come about, chance, take place, befall, come to pass
● **NOUN 1** = <u>drop</u>, slip, plunge, dive, tumble, descent, plummet, nose dive **2** = <u>decrease</u>, drop, lowering, decline, reduction, slump, dip, lessening **3** = <u>collapse</u>, defeat, downfall, ruin, destruction, overthrow, submission,

capitulation

false 1 = <u>incorrect</u>, wrong,
mistaken, misleading, faulty,
inaccurate, invalid, erroneous
≠ correct **2** = <u>untrue</u>, fraudulent,
trumped up, fallacious, untruthful
≠ true **3** = <u>artificial</u>, forged, fake,
reproduction, replica, imitation,
bogus, simulated ≠ real

falter 1 = <u>hesitate</u>, delay, waver,
vacillate ≠ persevere **2** = <u>tumble</u>,
totter **3** = <u>stutter</u>, pause, stumble,
hesitate, stammer

fame = <u>prominence</u>, glory,
celebrity, stardom, reputation,
honour, prestige, stature
≠ obscurity

familiar 1 = <u>well-known</u>,
recognized, common, ordinary,
routine, frequent, accustomed,
customary ≠ unfamiliar
2 = <u>friendly</u>, close, dear, intimate,
amicable ≠ formal **3** = <u>relaxed</u>,
easy, friendly, comfortable,
intimate, casual, amicable
4 = <u>disrespectful</u>, forward, bold,
intrusive, presumptuous,
impudent, overfamiliar

familiarity 1 = <u>acquaintance</u>,
experience, understanding,
knowledge, awareness, grasp
≠ unfamiliarity **2** = <u>friendliness</u>,
intimacy, ease, openness,
informality, sociability ≠ formality
3 = <u>disrespect</u>, forwardness,
overfamiliarity, cheek,
presumption, boldness ≠ respect

family 1 = <u>relations</u>, relatives,
household, folk (*informal*), kin,
nuclear family, next of kin, kith
and kin (*N.Z.*) **2** = <u>children</u>,
kids (*informal*), offspring, little
ones, littlies (*Austral. informal*)
3 = <u>ancestors</u>, house, race, tribe,
clan, dynasty, line of descent
4 = <u>species</u>, group, class, system,
order, network, genre, subdivision

Word Power

family – Some careful writers
insist that a singular verb
should always be used with
collective nouns such as
*government, team, family,
committee,* and *class,* for
example: *the class is doing a
project on Vikings; the company
is mounting a big sales
campaign.* In British usage,
however, a plural verb is often
used with a collective noun,
especially where the emphasis is
on a collection of individual
objects or people rather than a
group regarded as a unit: *the
family are all on holiday.* The
most important thing to
remember is never to treat the
same collective noun as both
singular and plural in the same
sentence: *the family is well and
sends its best wishes* or *the family
are well and send their best
wishes,* but not *the family is well
and send their best wishes.*

famine = hunger, want, starvation, deprivation, scarcity, dearth

famous = well-known, celebrated, acclaimed, noted, distinguished, prominent, legendary, renowned ≠ unknown

fan¹ NOUN = blower, ventilator, air conditioner

● VERB = blow, cool, refresh, air-condition, ventilate

fan² = supporter, lover, follower, enthusiast, admirer, buff (*informal*), devotee, aficionado

fanatic = extremist, activist, militant, bigot, zealot

fancy ADJECTIVE = elaborate, decorative, extravagant, intricate, baroque, ornamental, ornate, embellished ≠ plain

● NOUN 1 = whim, thought, idea, desire, urge, notion, humour, impulse 2 = delusion, dream, vision, fantasy, daydream, chimera

● VERB 1 = wish for, want, desire, hope for, long for, crave, yearn for, thirst for 2 (*Informal*) = be attracted to, find attractive, lust after, like, take to, be captivated by, have a thing about (*informal*), have eyes for 3 = suppose, think, believe, imagine, reckon, conjecture, think likely

fantastic 1 (*Informal*) = wonderful, great, excellent, very good, smashing (*informal*), superb, tremendous (*informal*), magnificent, booshit (*Austral. slang*), exo (*Austral. slang*), sik (*Austral. slang*) ≠ ordinary 2 = strange, bizarre, grotesque, fanciful, outlandish 3 = implausible, unlikely, incredible, absurd, preposterous, cock-and-bull (*informal*)

fantasy or (*Archaic*) **phantasy** 1 = daydream, dream, wish, reverie, flight of fancy, pipe dream 2 = imagination, fancy, invention, creativity, originality

far ADVERB 1 = a long way, miles, deep, a good way, afar, a great distance 2 = much, greatly, very much, extremely, significantly, considerably, decidedly, markedly

● ADJECTIVE often with *off* = remote, distant, far-flung, faraway, out-of-the-way, far-off, outlying, off the beaten track ≠ near

farce 1 = comedy, satire, slapstick, burlesque, buffoonery 2 = mockery, joke, nonsense, parody, shambles, sham, travesty

fare NOUN 1 = charge, price, ticket price, ticket money 2 = food, provisions, board, rations, kai (*N.Z. informal*), nourishment, sustenance, victuals, nutriment

● VERB = get on, do, manage, make out, prosper, get along

farewell INTERJECTION = goodbye, bye (*informal*), so

long, see you, take care, good
morning, bye-bye (informal),
good day, haere ra (N.Z.)
● NOUN = goodbye, parting,
departure, leave-taking, adieu,
valediction, sendoff (informal)

farm NOUN = smallholding, ranch
(chiefly U.S. & Canad.), farmstead,
station (Austral. & N.Z.), vineyard,
plantation, croft (Scot.), grange,
homestead
● VERB = cultivate, work, plant,
grow crops on, keep animals on

fascinate = entrance, absorb,
intrigue, rivet, captivate, enthral,
beguile, transfix ≠ bore

fascinating = captivating,
engaging, gripping, compelling,
intriguing, very interesting,
irresistible, enticing ≠ boring

fascination = attraction, pull,
magic, charm, lure, allure,
magnetism, enchantment

fashion NOUN 1 = style, look,
trend, rage, custom, mode, vogue,
craze 2 = method, way, style,
manner, mode
● VERB = make, shape, cast,
construct, form, create,
manufacture, forge

fashionable = popular, in
fashion, trendy (Brit. informal), in
(informal), modern, with it
(informal), stylish, chic
≠ unfashionable

fast[1] ADJECTIVE 1 = quick, flying,
rapid, fleet, swift, speedy, brisk,

hasty ≠ slow 2 = fixed, firm,
sound, stuck, secure, tight,
jammed, fastened ≠ unstable
3 = dissipated, wild, exciting,
loose, extravagant, reckless, self-
indulgent, wanton 4 = close, firm,
devoted, faithful, steadfast
● ADVERB 1 = quickly, rapidly,
swiftly, hastily, hurriedly, speedily,
in haste, at full speed ≠ slowly
2 = securely, firmly, tightly, fixedly
3 = fixedly, firmly, soundly, deeply,
securely, tightly

fast[2] VERB = go hungry, abstain,
go without food, deny yourself
● NOUN = fasting, diet, abstinence

fasten 1 = secure, close, do up
2 = tie, bind, tie up 3 = fix, join,
link, connect, attach, affix

fat ADJECTIVE 1 = overweight,
large, heavy, plump, stout, obese,
tubby, portly ≠ thin 2 = fatty,
greasy, adipose, oleaginous, oily
≠ lean
● NOUN = fatness, flesh, bulk,
obesity, flab, blubber, paunch,
fatty tissue

fatal 1 = disastrous, devastating,
crippling, catastrophic, ruinous,
calamitous, baleful, baneful
≠ minor 2 = lethal, deadly, mortal,
causing death, final, killing,
terminal, malignant ≠ harmless

fate 1 = destiny, chance, fortune,
luck, the stars, providence, nemesis,
kismet 2 = fortune, destiny, lot,
portion, cup, horoscope

fated = <u>destined</u>, doomed, predestined, preordained, foreordained

father NOUN 1 = <u>daddy</u> (*informal*), dad (*informal*), male parent, pop (*U.S. informal*), old man (*Brit. informal*), pa (*informal*), papa (*old-fashioned informal*), pater (*informal*) 2 = <u>founder</u>, author, maker, architect, creator, inventor, originator, prime mover 3 *usually cap.* = <u>priest</u>, minister, vicar, parson, pastor, cleric, churchman, padre (*informal*) 4 *usually plural* = <u>forefather</u>, predecessor, ancestor, forebear, progenitor, tupuna or tipuna (*N.Z.*)
● **VERB** = <u>sire</u>, parent, conceive, bring to life, beget, procreate, bring into being, give life to

(*Related Words*)

adjective: paternal

fatherly = <u>paternal</u>, kindly, protective, supportive, benign, affectionate, patriarchal, benevolent

fatigue NOUN = <u>tiredness</u>, lethargy, weariness, heaviness, languor, listlessness ≠ freshness
● **VERB** = <u>tire</u>, exhaust, weaken, weary, drain, wear out, take it out of (*informal*), tire out ≠ refresh

fatty = <u>greasy</u>, fat, creamy, oily, adipose, oleaginous, suety, rich

fault NOUN 1 = <u>responsibility</u>, liability, guilt, accountability, culpability 2 = <u>mistake</u>, slip, error, blunder, lapse, oversight,

indiscretion, howler (*informal*) 3 = <u>failing</u>, weakness, defect, deficiency, flaw, shortcoming, blemish, imperfection ≠ strength
● **VERB** = <u>criticize</u>, blame, complain, condemn, moan about, censure, hold (someone) responsible, find fault with
● **PHRASES find fault with something** *or* **someone** = <u>criticize</u>, complain about, whinge about (*informal*), whine about (*informal*), quibble, carp at, take to task, pick holes in ◆ **to a fault** = <u>excessively</u>, unduly, in the extreme, overmuch, immoderately

faulty 1 = <u>defective</u>, damaged, malfunctioning, broken, flawed, impaired, imperfect, out of order 2 = <u>incorrect</u>, flawed, unsound

favour NOUN 1 = <u>approval</u>, goodwill, commendation, approbation ≠ disapproval 2 = <u>favouritism</u>, preferential treatment 3 = <u>support</u>, backing, aid, assistance, patronage, good opinion 4 = <u>good turn</u>, service, benefit, courtesy, kindness, indulgence, boon, good deed ≠ wrong
● **VERB** 1 = <u>prefer</u>, opt for, like better, incline towards, choose, pick, desire, go for ≠ object to 2 = <u>indulge</u>, reward, side with, smile upon 3 = <u>support</u>, champion, encourage, approve,

advocate, subscribe to, commend, stand up for ≠ oppose 4 = **help**, benefit

favourable 1 = positive, encouraging, approving, praising, reassuring, enthusiastic, sympathetic, commending ≠ disapproving 2 = affirmative, agreeing, confirming, positive, assenting, corroborative 3 = advantageous, promising, encouraging, suitable, helpful, beneficial, auspicious, opportune ≠ disadvantageous

favourite ADJECTIVE = preferred, favoured, best-loved, most-liked, special, choice, dearest, pet
• NOUN = darling, pet, blue-eyed boy (*informal*), beloved, idol, fave (*informal*), teacher's pet, the apple of your eye

fear NOUN 1 = dread, horror, panic, terror, fright, alarm, trepidation, fearfulness 2 = bugbear, bête noire, horror, nightmare, anxiety, terror, dread, spectre
• VERB 1 = be afraid of, dread, shudder at, be fearful of, tremble at, be terrified by, take fright at, shake in your shoes about 2 = regret, feel, suspect, have a feeling, have a hunch, have a sneaking suspicion, have a funny feeling
• PHRASES **fear for something** *or* **someone** = worry about, be

anxious about, feel concern for

fearful 1 = scared, afraid, alarmed, frightened, nervous, terrified, petrified ≠ unafraid 2 = timid, afraid, frightened, scared, alarmed, nervous, uneasy, jumpy ≠ brave 3 = frightful, terrible, awful, dreadful, horrific, dire, horrendous, gruesome

feasible = practicable, possible, reasonable, viable, workable, achievable, attainable, likely ≠ impracticable

feast NOUN 1 = banquet, repast, spread (*informal*), dinner, treat, hakari (*N.Z.*) 2 = festival, holiday, fête, celebration, holy day, red-letter day, religious festival, saint's day
• VERB = eat your fill, wine and dine, overindulge, consume, indulge, gorge, devour, pig out (*slang*)

feat = accomplishment, act, performance, achievement, enterprise, undertaking, exploit, deed

feather NOUN = plume
• PLURAL NOUN = plumage, plumes, down

feature NOUN 1 = aspect, quality, characteristic, property, factor, trait, hallmark, facet 2 = article, report, story, piece, item, column 3 = highlight, attraction, speciality, main item
• PLURAL NOUN = face,

countenance, physiognomy, lineaments

● VERB 1 = spotlight, present, emphasize, play up, foreground, give prominence to 2 = star, appear, participate, play a part

federation = union, league, association, alliance, combination, coalition, partnership, consortium

fed up = cheesed off, depressed, bored, tired, discontented, dissatisfied, glum, sick and tired (informal), hoha (N.Z.)

fee = charge, price, cost, bill, payment, wage, salary, toll

feeble 1 = weak, frail, debilitated, sickly, puny, weedy (informal), infirm, effete ≠ strong

2 = inadequate, pathetic, insufficient, lame

3 = unconvincing, poor, thin, tame, pathetic, lame, flimsy, paltry ≠ effective

feed VERB 1 = cater for, provide for, nourish, provide with food, supply, sustain, cook for, wine and dine 2 = graze, eat, browse, pasture 3 = eat, drink milk

● NOUN 1 = food, fodder, provender, pasturage 2 (Informal) = meal, spread (informal), dinner, lunch, tea, breakfast, feast, supper

feel VERB 1 = experience, bear 2 = touch, handle, manipulate, finger, stroke, paw, caress, fondle 3 = be aware of 4 = perceive,

detect, discern, experience, notice, observe 5 = sense, be aware, be convinced, have a feeling, intuit 6 = believe, consider, judge, deem, think, hold

● NOUN 1 = texture, finish, touch, surface, surface quality

2 = impression, feeling, air, sense, quality, atmosphere, mood, aura

feeling 1 = emotion, sentiment

2 = opinion, view, attitude, belief, point of view, instinct, inclination

3 = passion, emotion, intensity, warmth 4 = ardour, love, care, warmth, tenderness, fervour

5 = sympathy, understanding, concern, pity, sensitivity, compassion, sorrow, sensibility

6 = sensation, sense, impression, awareness 7 = sense of touch, perception, sensation

8 = impression, idea, sense, notion, suspicion, hunch, inkling, presentiment 9 = atmosphere, mood, aura, ambience, feel, air, quality

fell 1 = cut down, cut, level, demolish, knock down, hew

2 = knock down

fellow 1 (Old-fashioned) = man, person, individual, character, guy (informal), bloke (Brit. informal), chap (informal) 2 = associate, colleague, peer, partner, companion, comrade, crony

fellowship 1 = society, club, league, association, organization,

guild, fraternity, brotherhood
2 = <u>camaraderie</u>; brotherhood, companionship, sociability

feminine = <u>womanly</u>, pretty, soft, gentle, tender, delicate, ladylike ≠ masculine

fence NOUN = <u>barrier</u>, wall, defence, railings, hedge, barricade, hedgerow, rampart
• VERB *often with in* or *off* = <u>enclose</u>, surround, bound, protect, pen, confine, encircle

ferocious 1 = <u>fierce</u>, violent, savage, ravening, predatory, rapacious, wild ≠ gentle **2** = <u>cruel</u>, bitter, brutal, vicious, ruthless, bloodthirsty

ferry NOUN = <u>ferry boat</u>, boat, ship, passenger boat, packet boat, packet
• VERB = <u>transport</u>, bring, carry, ship, take, run, shuttle, convey

fertile 1 = <u>productive</u>, rich, lush, prolific, abundant, plentiful, fruitful, teeming ≠ barren

fertility = <u>fruitfulness</u>, abundance, richness, fecundity, luxuriance, productiveness

fertilizer = <u>compost</u>, muck, manure, dung, bone meal, dressing

festival 1 = <u>celebration</u>, fair, carnival, gala, fête, entertainment, jubilee, fiesta **2** = <u>holy day</u>, holiday, feast, commemoration, feast day, red-letter day, saint's day, fiesta

festive = <u>celebratory</u>, happy, merry, jubilant, cheery, joyous, joyful, jovial ≠ mournful

fetch 1 = <u>bring</u>, pick up, collect, go and get, get, carry, deliver, transport **2** = <u>sell for</u>, make, raise, earn, realize, go for, yield, bring in

fetching = <u>attractive</u>, charming, cute, enticing, captivating, alluring, winsome

feud NOUN = <u>hostility</u>, row, conflict, argument, disagreement, rivalry, quarrel, vendetta
• VERB = <u>quarrel</u>, row, clash, dispute, fall out, contend, war, squabble

fever = <u>excitement</u>, frenzy, ferment, agitation, fervour, restlessness, delirium

few = <u>not many</u>, one or two, scarcely any, rare, meagre, negligible, sporadic, sparse

fiasco = <u>flop</u>, failure, disaster, mess (*informal*), catastrophe, debacle, cock-up (*Brit. slang*), washout (*informal*)

fibre = <u>thread</u>, strand, filament, tendril, pile, texture, wisp

fiction 1 = <u>tale</u>, story, novel, legend, myth, romance, narration, creative writing **2** = <u>lie</u>, invention, fabrication, falsehood, untruth, urban myth, tall story, urban legend

fictional = <u>imaginary</u>, made-up, invented, legendary, unreal, nonexistent

fiddle VERB 1 *usually with with* = fidget, play, finger, tamper, mess about *or* around *or* around 2 *usually with with* = tinker, adjust, interfere, mess about *or* around 3 (*informal*) = cheat, cook (*informal*), fix, diddle (*informal*), wangle (*informal*)
● NOUN 1 (*Brit. informal*) = fraud, racket, scam (*slang*), fix, swindle 2 = violin

fiddling = trivial, small, petty, trifling, insignificant, unimportant, pettifogging, futile

fidelity 1 = loyalty, devotion, allegiance, constancy, faithfulness, dependability, trustworthiness, staunchness ≠ disloyalty 2 = accuracy, precision, correspondence, closeness, faithfulness, exactness, scrupulousness ≠ inaccuracy

field NOUN 1 = meadow, land, green, lea (*poetic*), pasture 2 = speciality, line, area, department, territory, discipline, province, sphere 3 = line, reach, sweep 4 = competitors, competition, candidates, runners, applicants, entrants, contestants
● VERB 1 (*Informal*) = deal with, answer, handle, respond to, reply to, deflect, turn aside 2 (*Sport*) = retrieve, return, stop, catch, pick up

fierce 1 = ferocious, wild, dangerous, cruel, savage, brutal, aggressive, menacing, aggers (*Austral. slang*), biffo (*Austral. slang*) ≠ gentle 2 = intense, strong, keen, relentless, cut-throat 3 = stormy, strong, powerful, violent, intense, raging, furious, howling ≠ tranquil

fiercely = ferociously, savagely, passionately, furiously, viciously, tooth and nail, tigerishly, with no holds barred

fiery 1 = burning, flaming, blazing, on fire, ablaze, aflame, afire 2 = excitable, fierce, passionate, irritable, impetuous, irascible, hot-headed

fight VERB 1 = oppose, campaign against, dispute, contest, resist, defy, contend, withstand 2 = battle, combat, do battle 3 = engage in, conduct, wage, pursue, carry on
● NOUN 1 = battle, campaign, movement, struggle 2 = conflict, clash, contest, encounter 3 = brawl, scrap (*informal*), confrontation, rumble (*U.S. & N.Z. slang*), duel, skirmish, tussle, biffo (*Austral. slang*) 4 = row, argument, dispute, quarrel, squabble 5 = resistance, spirit, pluck, militancy, belligerence, pluckiness

fighter 1 = boxer, wrestler, pugilist, prize fighter 2 = soldier, warrior, fighting man, man-at-arms

figure NOUN 1 = <u>digit</u>, character, symbol, number, numeral 2 = <u>shape</u>, build, body, frame, proportions, physique 3 = <u>personage</u>, person, individual, character, personality, celebrity, big name, dignitary 4 = <u>diagram</u>, drawing, picture, illustration, representation, sketch 5 = <u>design</u>, shape, pattern 6 = <u>price</u>, cost, value, amount, total, sum

● VERB 1 *usually with* **in** = <u>feature</u>, act, appear, contribute to, play a part, be featured 2 = <u>calculate</u>, work out, compute, tot up, total, count, reckon, tally

● PHRASES **figure something** *or* **someone out** = <u>understand</u>, make out, fathom, see, solve, comprehend, make sense of, decipher

figurehead = <u>nominal head</u>, titular head, front man, puppet, mouthpiece

file¹ NOUN 1 = <u>folder</u>, case, portfolio, binder 2 = <u>dossier</u>, record, information, data, documents, case history, report, case 3 = <u>line</u>, row, chain, column, queue, procession

● VERB 1 = <u>arrange</u>, order, classify, put in place, categorize, pigeonhole, put in order 2 = <u>register</u>, record, enter, log, put on record 3 = <u>march</u>, troop, parade, walk in line, walk behind one another

file² = <u>smooth</u>, shape, polish, rub, scrape, rasp, abrade

fill 1 = <u>top up</u>, fill up, make full, become full, brim over 2 = <u>swell</u>, expand, become bloated, extend, balloon, fatten 3 = <u>pack</u>, crowd, squeeze, cram, throng 4 = <u>stock</u>, supply, pack, load 5 = <u>plug</u>, close, stop, seal, cork, bung, block up, stop up 6 = <u>saturate</u>, charge, pervade, permeate, imbue, impregnate, suffuse 7 = <u>fulfil</u>, hold, perform, carry out, occupy, execute, discharge 8 *often with* **up** = <u>satisfy</u>, stuff, glut

filling NOUN = <u>stuffing</u>, padding, filler, wadding, inside, insides, contents

● ADJECTIVE = <u>satisfying</u>, heavy, square, substantial, ample

film NOUN 1 = <u>movie</u>, picture, flick (*slang*), motion picture 2 = <u>cinema</u>, the movies 3 = <u>layer</u>, covering, cover, skin, coating, dusting, tissue, membrane

● VERB 1 = <u>photograph</u>, record, shoot, video, videotape, take 2 = <u>adapt for the screen</u>, make into a film

filter VERB 1 = <u>purify</u>, treat, strain, refine, riddle, sift, sieve, winnow 2 = <u>trickle</u>, seep, percolate, escape, leak, penetrate, ooze, dribble

● NOUN = <u>sieve</u>, mesh, gauze, strainer, membrane, riddle, sifter

filthy 1 = <u>dirty</u>, foul, polluted,

squalid, slimy, unclean, putrid, festy (*Austral. slang*) **2** = <u>grimy</u>, muddy, blackened, grubby, begrimed, festy (*Austral. slang*) **3** = <u>obscene</u>, corrupt, indecent, pornographic, lewd, depraved, impure, smutty

final 1 = <u>last</u>, latest, closing, finishing, concluding, ultimate, terminal ≠ first **2** = <u>irrevocable</u>, absolute, definitive, decided, settled, definite, conclusive, irrefutable

finale = <u>climax</u>, ending, close, conclusion, culmination, denouement, last part, epilogue ≠ opening

finally 1 = <u>eventually</u>, at last, in the end, ultimately, at length, at long last, after a long time **2** = <u>lastly</u>, in the end, ultimately **3** = <u>in conclusion</u>, lastly, in closing, to conclude, to sum up, in summary

finance VERB = <u>fund</u>, back, support, pay for, guarantee, invest in, underwrite, endow
● NOUN = <u>economics</u>, business, money, banking, accounts, investment, commerce
● PLURAL NOUN = <u>resources</u>, money, funds, capital, cash, affairs, budgeting, assets

financial = <u>economic</u>, business, commercial, monetary, fiscal, pecuniary

find VERB **1** = <u>discover</u>, uncover,

spot, locate, detect, come across, hit upon, put your finger on ≠ lose **2** = <u>encounter</u>, meet, recognize **3** = <u>observe</u>, learn, note, discover, notice, realize, come up with, perceive
● NOUN = <u>discovery</u>, catch, asset, bargain, acquisition, good buy
● PHRASES **find something out** = <u>learn</u>, discover, realize, observe, perceive, detect, become aware, come to know

fine¹ 1 = <u>excellent</u>, good, striking, masterly, very good, impressive, outstanding, magnificent ≠ poor **2** = <u>satisfactory</u>, good, all right, suitable, acceptable, convenient, fair, O.K. or okay (*informal*) **3** = <u>thin</u>, light, narrow, wispy **4** = <u>delicate</u>, light, thin, sheer, flimsy, wispy, gossamer, diaphanous ≠ coarse **5** = <u>stylish</u>, expensive, elegant, refined, tasteful, quality **6** = <u>exquisite</u>, delicate, fragile, dainty **7** = <u>minute</u>, exact, precise, nice **8** = <u>keen</u>, minute, nice, sharp, acute, subtle, precise, hairsplitting **9** = <u>brilliant</u>, quick, keen, alert, clever, penetrating, astute **10** = <u>sunny</u>, clear, fair, dry, bright, pleasant, clement, balmy ≠ cloudy

fine² NOUN = <u>penalty</u>, damages, punishment, forfeit, financial penalty
● VERB = <u>penalize</u>, charge, punish

finger = <u>touch</u>, feel, handle, play with, manipulate, paw (*informal*), maul, toy with

finish VERB 1 = <u>stop</u>, close, complete, conclude, cease, wrap up (*informal*), terminate, round off ≠ start 2 = <u>get done</u>, complete, conclude 3 = <u>end</u>, stop, conclude, wind up, terminate 4 = <u>consume</u>, dispose of, devour, polish off, eat, get through 5 = <u>use up</u>, empty, exhaust 6 = <u>coat</u>, polish, stain, texture, wax, varnish, gild, veneer 7 *usually with* **off** = <u>destroy</u>, defeat, overcome, bring down, ruin, dispose of, rout, put an end to 8 *usually with* **off** = <u>kill</u>, murder, destroy, massacre, butcher, slaughter, slay, exterminate
● NOUN 1 = <u>end</u>, close, conclusion, run-in, completion, finale, culmination, cessation ≠ beginning 2 = <u>surface</u>, polish, shine, gloss, glaze, veneer, lacquer, lustre

finished 1 = <u>over</u>, done, through, ended, closed, complete, executed, finalized ≠ begun 2 = <u>ruined</u>, done for (*informal*), doomed, through, lost, defeated, wiped out, undone

fire NOUN 1 = <u>flames</u>, blaze, combustion, inferno, conflagration, holocaust 2 = <u>passion</u>, energy, spirit, enthusiasm, excitement, intensity, sparkle, vitality 3 = <u>bombardment</u>, shooting, firing, shelling, hail, volley, barrage, gunfire
● VERB 1 = <u>let off</u>, shoot, shell, set off, discharge, detonate 2 = <u>shoot</u>, explode, discharge, detonate, pull the trigger 3 (*Informal*) = <u>dismiss</u>, sack (*informal*), get rid of, discharge, lay off, make redundant, cashier, give notice 4 *sometimes with* **up** = <u>inspire</u>, excite, stir, stimulate, motivate, awaken, animate, rouse

fireworks 1 = <u>pyrotechnics</u>, illuminations, feux d'artifice 2 (*Informal*) = <u>trouble</u>, row, storm, rage, uproar, hysterics

firm[1] 1 = <u>hard</u>, solid, dense, set, stiff, compacted, rigid, inflexible ≠ soft 2 = <u>secure</u>, fixed, rooted, stable, steady, fast, embedded, immovable ≠ unstable 3 = <u>strong</u>, close, tight, steady 4 = <u>strict</u>, unshakeable, resolute, inflexible, unyielding, unbending 5 = <u>determined</u>, resolved, definite, set on, adamant, resolute, inflexible, unyielding ≠ wavering 6 = <u>definite</u>, hard, clear, confirmed, settled, fixed, hard-and-fast, cut-and-dried (*informal*)

firm[2] = <u>company</u>, business, concern, association, organization, corporation, venture, enterprise

firmly 1 = <u>securely</u>, safely, tightly
2 = <u>immovably</u>, securely, steadily, like a rock, unflinchingly, unshakeably **3** = <u>steadily</u>, securely, tightly, unflinchingly
4 = <u>resolutely</u>, staunchly, steadfastly, definitely, unwaveringly, unchangeably

first ADJECTIVE 1 = <u>earliest</u>, original, primordial **2** = <u>initial</u>, opening, earliest, maiden, introductory **3** = <u>top</u>, best, winning, premier **4** = <u>elementary</u>, key, basic, primary, fundamental, cardinal, rudimentary, elemental **5** = <u>foremost</u>, highest, greatest, leading, head, ruling, chief, prime
● **ADVERB** = <u>to begin with</u>, firstly, initially, at the beginning, in the first place, beforehand, to start with, at the outset
● **NOUN** = <u>novelty</u>, innovation, originality, new experience
● **PHRASES from the first** = <u>from the start</u>, from the beginning, from the outset, from the very beginning, from the introduction, from the starting point, from the inception, from the commencement

fish = <u>angle</u>, net, cast, trawl
➤ **types of fish** ➤ **sharks**

fit¹ VERB 1 = <u>adapt</u>, shape, arrange, alter, adjust, modify, tweak (*informal*), customize **2** = <u>place</u>, insert **3** = <u>suit</u>, meet, match, belong to, conform to,

correspond to, accord with, be appropriate to **4** = <u>equip</u>, provide, arm, prepare, fit out, kit out
● **ADJECTIVE 1** = <u>appropriate</u>, suitable, right, becoming, seemly, fitting, skilled, correct
≠ inappropriate **2** = <u>healthy</u>, strong, robust, sturdy, well, trim, strapping, hale ≠ unfit

fit² 1 = <u>seizure</u>, attack, bout, spasm, convulsion, paroxysm
2 = <u>bout</u>, burst, outbreak, outburst, spell

fitness 1 = <u>appropriateness</u>, competence, readiness, eligibility, suitability, propriety, aptness
2 = <u>health</u>, strength, good health, vigour, good condition, wellness, robustness

fitting NOUN = <u>accessory</u>, part, piece, unit, component, attachment
● **ADJECTIVE** = <u>appropriate</u>, suitable, proper, apt, right, becoming, seemly, correct
≠ unsuitable

fix VERB 1 = <u>place</u>, join, stick, attach, set, position, plant, link
2 = <u>decide</u>, set, choose, establish, determine, settle, arrange, arrive at **3** = <u>arrange</u>, organize, sort out, see to, fix up, make arrangements for **4** = <u>repair</u>, mend, service, correct, restore, see to, overhaul, patch up **5** = <u>focus</u>, direct at, fasten on **6** (*Informal*) = <u>rig</u>, set up (*informal*), influence,

Types of fish

ahuru (*N.Z.*)
alewife
albacore
alfonsino
amberjack
anabas
anchovy
angelfish
archerfish
argentine
aua (*N.Z.*)
Australian salmon, native salmon, salmon trout, bay trout *or* kahawai (*N.Z. & Austral.*)
barbel
barracouta *or* (*Austral.*) hake
barracuda
barramundi *or* (*Austral.*) barra *or* giant perch
bass
beluga
bib, pout, *or* whiting pout
black cod *or* Māori chief (*N.Z.*)
blackfish *or* (*Austral.*) nigger
bleak
blenny
blowfish *or* (*Austral.*) toado
blue cod, rock cod, *or* (*N.Z.*) rawaru, pakirikiri, *or* patutuki
bluefin tuna
bluefish *or* snapper
blue nose (*N.Z.*)
bonito *or* (*Austral.*) horse mackerel
bony bream (*Austral.*)
bowfin *or* dogfish
bream *or* (*Austral.*) brim

brill
brook trout *or* speckled trout
brown trout
bullhead
bully *or* (*N.Z.*) pakoko, titarakura, *or* toitoi
burbot, eelpout, *or* ling
butterfish, greenbone, *or* (*N.Z.*) koaea *or* marari
capelin *or* caplin
carp
catfish
Chinook salmon, quinnat salmon, *or* king salmon
chub
cisco *or* lake herring
clingfish
coalfish *or* (*Brit.*) saithe *or* coley
cockabully
cod *or* codfish
coelacanth
coho *or* silver salmon
coley
conger
coral trout
dab
dace
dart (*Austral.*)
darter
dory
dragonet
eel *or* (*N.Z.*) tuna
eelpout
electric eel
fighting fish *or* betta
filefish
flatfish *or* (*N.Z.*) flattie

Types of fish (continued)

flathead
flounder *or* (N.Z.) patiki
flying fish
flying gurnard
garpike, garfish, gar, *or* (Austral.)
 ballahoo
geelbek
gemfish *or* (Austral.) hake
goby
golden perch, freshwater bream,
 Murray perch, *or* yellow-belly
 (Austral.)
goldfish
gourami
grayling *or* (Austral.) yarra
 herring
grenadier *or* rat-tail
groper *or* grouper
grunion
grunt
gudgeon
gunnel
guppy
gurnard *or* gurnet
haddock
hagfish, hag *or* blind eel
hake
halfbeak
halibut
hapuku (Austral. & N.Z.)
herring
hogfish
hoki (N.Z.)
horse mackerel
jewelfish
jewfish *or* (Austral. informal)
 jewie

John Dory
kelpfish *or* (Austral. informal)
 kelpie
killifish
kingfish
kingklip (S. Afr.)
kokanee
kokopu (N.Z.)
lamprey *or* lamper eel
leatherjacket
lemon sole
ling *or* (Austral.) beardie
loach
luderick *or* (N.Z.) parore
lumpfish *or* lumpsucker
lungfish
mackerel *or* (*colloquial*) shiner
mangrove Jack (Austral.)
manta, manta ray, devilfish, *or*
 devil ray
maomao (N.Z.)
marlin *or* spearfish
menhaden
miller's thumb
minnow *or* (Scot.) baggie minnow
mirror carp
moki *or* blue moki (N.Z.)
molly
monkfish *or* (U.S.) goosefish
moray
morwong, black perch, *or* (N.Z.)
 porae
mudfish
mudskipper
opah, moonfish, *or* kingfish
orange roughy (Austral.)
orfe

Types of fish *(continued)*

ouananiche
ox-eye herring *(Austral.)*
parore, blackfish, black
 rockfish *or* mangrove fish
 (N.Z.)
parrotfish
pearl perch *(Austral.)*
perch *or (Austral.)* redfin
pickerel
pike, luce, *or* jackfish
pikeperch
pilchard *or (Austral. informal)*
 pillie
pilot fish
pipefish *or* needlefish
piranha *or* piraña
plaice
pollack *or* pollock
pollan
pompano
porae *(N.Z.)*
porcupine fish *or* globefish
porgy *or* pogy
pout
powan *or* lake herring
puffer *or* globefish
rainbow trout
ray
redfin
redfish
red mullet *or (U.S.)* goatfish
red salmon
red snapper
remora
ribbonfish
roach
rock bass

rockfish *or (formerly)* rock
 salmon
rockling
rudd
ruffe, ruff, *or* pope
salmon
sand eel, sand lance, *or* launce
sardine
sauger
saury *or* skipper
sawfish
scad
scaldfish
scorpion fish
scup *or* northern porgy
sea bass
sea bream
sea horse
sea scorpion
sea snail *or* snailfish
sea trout
Sergeant Baker
shad
shanny
shiner
Siamese fighting fish
sild
silver belly *(N.Z.)*
silverfish
silverside *or* silversides
skate
skipjack *or* skipjack tuna
smelt
smooth hound
snapper, red bream, *or (Austral.)*
 wollomai *or* wollamai
snipefish *or* bellows fish

Types of fish (continued)

snoek	trevalla (*Austral.*)
snook	trevally, araara *or* samson fish
sockeye *or* red salmon	(*Austral.* & *N.Z.*)
sole	triggerfish
Spanish mackerel *or* Queensland	trout
kingfish	trunkfish, boxfish, *or* cowfish
sprat	tuna *or* tunny
steelhead	turbot
stickleback	vendace
stingray	wahoo
stonefish	walleye, walleyed pike, *or* dory
sturgeon	warehou (*N.Z.*)
sucker	weever
sunfish	whitebait
surgeonfish	whitefish
swordfish	whiting
swordtail	witch
tailor	wobbegong, wobbygong, *or*
tarakihi *or* terakihi (*N.Z.*)	wobegong
tarpon	wolffish *or* catfish
tarwhine	wrasse
tautog *or* blackfish	yellowfin (*N.Z.*)
tench	yellow jack
toadfish	
tommy rough *or* tommy ruff	
(*Austral.*)	

manipulate, fiddle (*informal*)
● NOUN (*Informal*) = mess, corner, difficulty, dilemma, embarrassment, plight, pickle (*informal*)
● PHRASES **fix someone up** = provide, supply, bring about, lay on, arrange for ◆ **fix something up** = arrange, plan, settle, fix, organize, sort out, agree on, make arrangements for

fixed 1 = inflexible, set, steady, resolute, unwavering ≠ wavering 2 = immovable, set, established, secure, rooted, permanent, rigid ≠ mobile 3 = agreed, set, planned, decided, established, settled, arranged, resolved

fizz 1 = bubble, froth, fizzle,

effervesce, produce bubbles
2 = <u>sputter</u>, buzz, sparkle, hiss, crackle

flag¹ NOUN = <u>banner</u>, standard, colours, pennant, ensign, streamer, pennon

● VERB = <u>mark</u>, identify, indicate, label, pick out, note

● PHRASES **flag something or someone down** = <u>hail</u>, stop, signal, wave down

flag² = <u>weaken</u>, fade, weary, falter, wilt, wane, sag, languish

flagging = <u>weakening</u>, declining, waning, fading, deteriorating, wearying, faltering, wilting

flair 1 = <u>ability</u>, feel, talent, gift, genius, faculty, mastery, knack
2 = <u>style</u>, taste, dash, chic, elegance, panache, discernment, stylishness

flake NOUN = <u>chip</u>, scale, layer, peeling, shaving, wafer, sliver
● VERB = <u>chip</u>, peel (off), blister

flamboyant 1 = <u>camp</u> (informal), dashing, theatrical, swashbuckling **2** = <u>showy</u>, elaborate, extravagant, ornate, ostentatious **3** = <u>colourful</u>, striking, brilliant, glamorous, stylish, dazzling, glitzy (slang), showy

flame NOUN **1** = <u>fire</u>, light, spark, glow, blaze, brightness, inferno
2 (Informal) = <u>sweetheart</u>, partner, lover, girlfriend,

boyfriend, heart-throb (Brit.), beau
● VERB = <u>burn</u>, flash, shine, glow, blaze, flare, glare

flank 1 = <u>side</u>, hip, thigh, loin
2 = <u>wing</u>, side, sector, aspect

flap VERB **1** = <u>flutter</u>, wave, flail
2 = <u>beat</u>, wave, thrash, flutter, wag, vibrate, shake
● NOUN **1** = <u>flutter</u>, beating, waving, shaking, swinging, swish
2 (Informal) = <u>panic</u>, state (informal), agitation, commotion, sweat (informal), dither (chiefly Brit.), fluster, tizzy (informal)

flare NOUN = <u>flame</u>, burst, flash, blaze, glare, flicker
● VERB **1** = <u>blaze</u>, flame, glare, flicker, burn up **2** = <u>widen</u>, spread, broaden, spread out, dilate, splay

flash NOUN = <u>blaze</u>, burst, spark, beam, streak, flare, dazzle, glare
● VERB **1** = <u>blaze</u>, shine, beam, sparkle, flare, glare, gleam, light up **2** = <u>speed</u>, race, shoot, fly, tear, dash, whistle, streak **3** (Informal) = <u>show quickly</u>, display, expose, exhibit, flourish, show off, flaunt
● ADJECTIVE (Informal) = <u>ostentatious</u>, smart, trendy, showy

flat¹ ADJECTIVE **1** = <u>even</u>, level, levelled, smooth, horizontal ≠ uneven **2** = <u>punctured</u>, collapsed, burst, blown out, deflated, empty **3** = <u>used up</u>, finished, empty, drained, expired

4 = absolute, firm, positive, explicit, definite, outright, downright, unequivocal **5** = dull, dead, empty, boring, depressing, tedious, lacklustre, tiresome ≠ exciting **6** = without energy, empty, weak, tired, depressed, drained, weary, worn out **7** = monotonous, boring, dull, tedious, tiresome, unchanging

● ADVERB = completely, directly, absolutely, categorically, precisely, exactly, utterly, outright

● PHRASES **flat out** (*Informal*) = at full speed, all out, to the full, hell for leather (*informal*), as hard as possible, at full tilt, for all you are worth

flat² = apartment, rooms, quarters, digs, suite, penthouse, living quarters

flatly = absolutely, completely, positively, categorically, unequivocally, unhesitatingly

flatten 1 = level, squash, compress, trample, iron out, even out, smooth off **2** = destroy, level, ruin, demolish, knock down, pull down, raze

flatter 1 = praise, compliment, pander to, sweet-talk (*informal*), wheedle, soft-soap (*informal*), butter up **2** = suit, become, enhance, set off, embellish, do something for, show to advantage

flattering 1 = becoming, kind,

effective, enhancing, well-chosen ≠ unflattering **2** = ingratiating, complimentary, fawning, fulsome, laudatory, adulatory ≠ uncomplimentary

flavour NOUN **1** = taste, seasoning, flavouring, savour, relish, smack, aroma, zest ≠ blandness **2** = quality, feeling, feel, style, character, tone, essence, tinge

● VERB = season, spice, add flavour to, enrich, infuse, imbue, pep up, leaven

flaw = weakness, failing, defect, weak spot, fault, blemish, imperfection, chink in your armour

flawed 1 = damaged, defective, imperfect, blemished, faulty **2** = erroneous, incorrect, invalid, wrong, mistaken, false, faulty, unsound

flee = run away, escape, bolt, fly, take off (*informal*), depart, run off, take flight

fleet = navy, task force, flotilla, armada

fleeting = momentary, passing, brief, temporary, short-lived, transient, ephemeral, transitory ≠ lasting

flesh NOUN **1** = fat, muscle, tissue, brawn **2** = fatness, fat, adipose tissue, corpulence, weight **3** = meat **4** = physical nature, carnality, human nature, flesh and blood, sinful nature

● PHRASES **your own flesh and blood** = <u>family</u>, blood, relations, relatives, kin, kith and kin, blood relations, kinsfolk, ainga (N.Z.)

flexibility 1 = <u>elasticity</u>, pliability, springiness, pliancy, give (informal) 2 = <u>adaptability</u>, openness, versatility, adjustability 3 = <u>complaisance</u>, accommodation, give and take, amenability

flexible 1 = <u>pliable</u>, plastic, elastic, supple, lithe, springy, pliant, stretchy ≠ rigid 2 = <u>adaptable</u>, open, variable, adjustable, discretionary ≠ inflexible

flick VERB 1 = <u>jerk</u>, pull, tug, lurch, jolt 2 = <u>strike</u>, tap, remove quickly, hit, touch, stroke, flip, whisk

● PHRASES **flick through something** = <u>browse</u>, glance at, skim, leaf through, flip through, thumb through, skip through

flicker VERB 1 = <u>twinkle</u>, flash, sparkle, flare, shimmer, gutter, glimmer 2 = <u>flutter</u>, waver, quiver, vibrate

● NOUN 1 = <u>glimmer</u>, flash, spark, flare, gleam 2 = <u>trace</u>, breath, spark, glimmer, iota

flight[1] 1 = <u>journey</u>, trip, voyage 2 = <u>aviation</u>, flying, aeronautics 3 = <u>flock</u>, group, unit, cloud, formation, squadron, swarm,

flying group

flight[2] = <u>escape</u>, fleeing, departure, retreat, exit, running away, exodus, getaway

fling VERB = <u>throw</u>, toss, hurl, launch, cast, propel, sling, catapult

● NOUN = <u>binge</u>, good time, bash, party, spree, night on the town, rave-up (Brit. slang)

flip VERB 1 = <u>flick</u>, switch, snap, slick 2 = <u>spin</u>, turn, overturn, turn over, roll over 3 = <u>toss</u>, throw, flick, fling, sling

● NOUN = <u>toss</u>, throw, spin, snap, flick

flirt VERB 1 = <u>chat up</u>, lead on (informal), make advances at, make eyes at, philander, make sheep's eyes at 2 usually with **with** = <u>toy with</u>, consider, entertain, play with, dabble in, trifle with, give a thought to, expose yourself to

● NOUN = <u>tease</u>, philanderer, coquette, heart-breaker

float 1 = <u>glide</u>, sail, drift, move gently, bob, coast, slide, be carried 2 = <u>be buoyant</u>, hang, hover ≠ sink 3 = <u>launch</u>, offer, sell, set up, promote, get going ≠ dissolve

floating 1 = <u>uncommitted</u>, wavering, undecided, indecisive, vacillating, sitting on the fence (informal), unaffiliated, independent 2 = <u>free</u>, wandering, variable, fluctuating, unattached, movable

flock NOUN 1 = <u>herd</u>, group, flight, drove, colony, gaggle, skein 2 = <u>crowd</u>, company, group, host, collection, mass, gathering, herd
● VERB 1 = <u>stream</u>, crowd, mass, swarm, throng 2 = <u>gather</u>, crowd, mass, collect, assemble, herd, huddle, converge

flog = <u>beat</u>, whip, lash, thrash, whack, scourge, hit hard, trounce

flood NOUN 1 = <u>deluge</u>, downpour, inundation, tide, overflow, torrent, spate 2 = <u>torrent</u>, flow, rush, stream, tide, abundance, glut, profusion 3 = <u>series</u>, stream, avalanche, barrage, spate, torrent 4 = <u>outpouring</u>, rush, stream, surge, torrent
● VERB 1 = <u>immerse</u>, swamp, submerge, inundate, drown, cover with water 2 = <u>pour over</u>, swamp, run over, overflow, inundate 3 = <u>engulf</u>, sweep into, overwhelm, surge into, swarm into, pour into 4 = <u>saturate</u>, fill, choke, swamp, glut, oversupply, overfill 5 = <u>stream</u>, flow, rush, pour, surge

floor NOUN 1 = <u>ground</u> 2 = <u>storey</u>, level, stage, tier
● VERB 1 (Informal) = <u>disconcert</u>, stump, baffle, confound, throw (informal), defeat, puzzle, bewilder 2 = <u>knock down</u>, fell,

knock over, prostrate, deck (slang)

flop VERB 1 = <u>slump</u>, fall, drop, collapse, sink 2 = <u>hang down</u>, hang, dangle, sag, droop 3 (Informal) = <u>fail</u>, fold (informal), founder, fall flat, come unstuck, misfire, go belly-up (slang) ≠ succeed
● NOUN (Informal) = <u>failure</u>, disaster, fiasco, debacle, washout (informal), nonstarter ≠ success

floppy = <u>droopy</u>, soft, loose, limp, sagging, baggy, flaccid, pendulous

floral = <u>flowery</u>, flower-patterned

flounder 1 = <u>falter</u>, struggle, stall, slow down, run into trouble, come unstuck (informal), be in difficulties, hit a bad patch 2 = <u>dither</u>, struggle, blunder, be confused, falter, be in the dark, be out of your depth 3 = <u>struggle</u>, struggle, toss, thrash, stumble, fumble, grope

> ### Word Power
>
> **flounder** – *Flounder* is sometimes wrongly used where *founder* is meant: *the project foundered* (not *floundered*) *because of lack of funds.*

flourish VERB 1 = <u>thrive</u>, increase, advance, progress, boom, bloom, blossom, prosper ≠ fail

2 = <u>succeed</u>, move ahead, go places (*informal*) **3** = <u>grow</u>, thrive, flower, succeed, bloom, blossom, prosper **4** = <u>wave</u>, brandish, display, shake, wield, flaunt

• NOUN **1** = <u>wave</u>, sweep, brandish, swish, swing, twirl **2** = <u>show</u>, display, parade, fanfare **3** = <u>curlicue</u>, sweep, decoration, swirl, plume, embellishment, ornamentation

flourishing = <u>thriving</u>, successful, blooming, prospering, rampant, going places, in the pink

flow VERB **1** = <u>run</u>, course, rush, sweep, move, pass, roll, flood **2** = <u>pour</u>, move, sweep, flood, stream **3** = <u>issue</u>, follow, result, emerge, spring, proceed, arise, derive

• NOUN = <u>stream</u>, current, movement, motion, course, flood, drift, tide

flower NOUN **1** = <u>bloom</u>, blossom, efflorescence **2** = <u>elite</u>, best, prime, finest, pick, choice, cream, crème de la crème (*French*) **3** = <u>height</u>, prime, peak

• VERB **1** = <u>bloom</u>, open, mature, flourish, unfold, blossom **2** = <u>blossom</u>, grow, develop, progress, mature, thrive, flourish, bloom

Related Words
adjective: floral

fluctuate 1 = <u>change</u>, swing,

vary, alternate, waver, veer, seesaw **2** = <u>shift</u>, oscillate

fluent = <u>effortless</u>, natural, articulate, well-expressed, voluble

fluid NOUN = <u>liquid</u>, solution, juice, liquor, sap

• ADJECTIVE = <u>liquid</u>, flowing, watery, molten, melted, runny, liquefied ≠ solid

flurry 1 = <u>commotion</u>, stir, bustle, flutter, excitement, fuss, disturbance, ado **2** = <u>gust</u>, shower, gale, swirl, squall, storm

flush[1] VERB **1** = <u>blush</u>, colour, glow, redden, turn red, go red **2** *often with* **out** = <u>cleanse</u>, wash out, rinse out, flood, swill, hose down **3** = <u>expel</u>, drive, dislodge

• NOUN = <u>blush</u>, colour, glow, reddening, redness, rosiness

flush[2] **1** = <u>level</u>, even, true, flat, square **2** (*Informal*) = <u>wealthy</u>, rich, well-off, in the money (*informal*), well-heeled (*informal*), replete, moneyed

flutter VERB **1** = <u>beat</u>, flap, tremble, ripple, waver, quiver, vibrate, palpitate **2** = <u>flit</u>

• NOUN **1** = <u>tremor</u>, tremble, shiver, shudder, palpitation **2** = <u>vibration</u>, twitching, quiver **3** = <u>agitation</u>, state (*informal*), confusion, excitement, flap (*informal*), dither (*chiefly Brit.*), commotion, fluster

fly[1] **1** = <u>take wing</u>, soar, glide,

Types of fly

aphid *or* plant louse	gallfly
aphis	gnat
blackfly *or* bean aphid	green blowfly *or* (*Austral. informal*) blue-arsed fly
blowfly, bluebottle, *or* (*Austral. informal*) blowie	greenfly
botfly	horsefly *or* cleg
bushfly	housefly
crane fly *or* (*Brit.*) daddy-longlegs	hover fly
damselfly	lacewing
dragonfly *or* (*colloquial*) devil's darning-needle	mayfly *or* dayfly
	sandfly
drosophila, fruit fly, *or* vinegar fly	stonefly
fly	tsetse fly *or* tzetze fly
fruit fly	warble fly
gadfly	whitefly

wing, sail, hover, flutter, flit
2 = <u>pilot</u>, control, operate, steer,
manoeuvre, navigate **3** = <u>airlift</u>,
send by plane, take by plane, take
in an aircraft **4** = <u>flutter</u>, wave,
float, flap **5** = <u>display</u>, show,
flourish, brandish **6** = <u>rush</u>, race,
shoot, career, speed, tear, dash,
hurry **7** = <u>pass swiftly</u>, pass, glide,
slip away, roll on, flit, elapse, run
its course **8** = <u>leave</u>, get away,
escape, flee, run for it,
skedaddle (*informal*), take to
your heels

fly² ▸ types of fly

flying = <u>hurried</u>, brief, rushed,
fleeting, short-lived, hasty,
transitory

foam NOUN = <u>froth</u>, spray,
bubbles, lather, suds, spume,
head
● VERB = <u>bubble</u>, boil, fizz, froth,
lather, effervesce

focus VERB **1** = <u>concentrate</u>,
centre, spotlight, direct, aim,
pinpoint, zoom in **2** = <u>fix</u>, train,
direct, aim
● NOUN **1** = <u>centre</u>, focal point,
central point **2** = <u>focal point</u>,
heart, target, hub

foe = <u>enemy</u>, rival, opponent,
adversary, antagonist ≠ friend

fog = <u>mist</u>, gloom, haze, smog,
murk, miasma, peasouper
(*informal*)

foil¹ = <u>thwart</u>, stop, defeat,
disappoint, counter, frustrate,
hamper, balk

foil² = <u>complement</u>, relief,
contrast, antithesis

fold VERB 1 = <u>bend</u>, crease, double over 2 (*Informal*) = <u>go bankrupt</u>, fail, crash, collapse, founder, shut down, go under, go bust (*informal*)

• NOUN = <u>crease</u>, gather, bend, overlap, wrinkle, pleat, ruffle, furrow

folk 1 = <u>people</u>, persons, individuals, men and women, humanity, inhabitants, mankind, mortals 2 *usually plural* = <u>family</u>, parents, relations, relatives, tribe, clan, kin, kindred, ainga (*N.Z.*)

follow 1 = <u>accompany</u>, attend, escort, go behind, tag along behind, come behind 2 = <u>pursue</u>, track, dog, hunt, chase, shadow, trail, hound ≠ avoid 3 = <u>come after</u>, go after, come next ≠ precede 4 = <u>result</u>, issue, develop, spring, flow, proceed, arise, ensue 5 = <u>obey</u>, observe, adhere to, stick to, heed, conform to, keep to, pay attention to ≠ ignore 6 = <u>succeed</u>, replace, come after, take over from, come next, supersede, supplant, take the place of 7 = <u>understand</u>, realize, appreciate, take in, grasp, catch on (*informal*), comprehend, fathom 8 = <u>keep up with</u>, support, be interested in, cultivate, be a fan of, keep abreast of

follower = <u>supporter</u>, fan, disciple, devotee, apostle, pupil, adherent, groupie (*slang*) ≠ leader

following ADJECTIVE 1 = <u>next</u>, subsequent, successive, ensuing, later, succeeding, consequent 2 = <u>coming</u>, about to be mentioned

• NOUN = <u>supporters</u>, backing, train, fans, suite, clientele, entourage, coterie

folly = <u>foolishness</u>, nonsense, madness, stupidity, indiscretion, lunacy, imprudence, rashness ≠ wisdom

fond ADJECTIVE 1 = <u>loving</u>, caring, warm, devoted, tender, adoring, affectionate, indulgent ≠ indifferent 2 = <u>unrealistic</u>, empty, naive, vain, foolish, deluded, overoptimistic, delusive ≠ sensible

• PHRASES **fond of** 1 = <u>attached to</u>, in love with, keen on, attracted to, having a soft spot for, enamoured of 2 = <u>keen on</u>, into (*informal*), hooked on, partial to, having a soft spot for, addicted to

fondly 1 = <u>lovingly</u>, tenderly, affectionately, amorously, dearly, possessively, with affection, indulgently 2 = <u>unrealistically</u>, stupidly, vainly, foolishly, naively, credulously

food = <u>nourishment</u>, fare, diet, tucker (*Austral. & N.Z. informal*), rations, nutrition, cuisine, refreshment, nibbles, kai (*N.Z. informal*)

fool NOUN 1 = simpleton, idiot, mug (*Brit. slang*), dummy (*slang*), git (*Brit. slang*), twit (*informal, chiefly Brit.*), dunce, imbecile (*informal*), dorba or dorb (*Austral. slang*), bogan (*Austral. slang*) ≠ genius 2 = dupe, mug (*Brit. slang*), sucker (*slang*), stooge (*slang*), laughing stock, pushover (*informal*), fall guy (*informal*) 3 = jester, clown, harlequin, buffoon, court jester
● VERB = deceive, mislead, delude, trick, take in, con (*informal*), dupe, beguile

foolish = unwise, silly, absurd, rash, senseless, foolhardy, ill-judged, imprudent ≠ sensible

footing 1 = basis, foundation, base position, groundwork 2 = relationship, position, basis, standing, rank, status, grade

footpath (*Austral. & N.Z.*) = pavement, sidewalk (*U.S. & Canad.*)

footstep = step, tread, footfall

foray = raid, sally, incursion, inroad, attack, assault, invasion, swoop

forbid = prohibit, ban, disallow, exclude, rule out, veto, outlaw, preclude ≠ permit

---

Word Power

forbid – Traditionally, it has been considered more correct to talk about *forbidding someone to do something*, rather than *forbidding someone from doing something*. Recently, however, the *from* option has become generally more acceptable, so that *he was forbidden to come in* and *he was forbidden from coming in* may both now be considered correct.

---

forbidden = prohibited, banned, vetoed, outlawed, taboo, out of bounds, proscribed

forbidding = threatening, severe, frightening, hostile, menacing, sinister, daunting, ominous ≠ inviting

force VERB 1 = compel, make, drive, press, oblige, constrain, coerce, impel 2 = push, thrust, propel 3 = break open, blast, wrench, prise, wrest
● NOUN 1 = compulsion, pressure, violence, constraint, oppression, coercion, duress, arm-twisting (*informal*) 2 = power, might, pressure, energy, strength, momentum, impulse, vigour ≠ weakness 3 = intensity, vigour, vehemence, fierceness, emphasis 4 = army, unit, company, host, troop, squad, patrol, regiment
● PHRASES **in force** 1 = valid

working, current, effective, binding, operative, operational, in operation **2** = **in great numbers**, all together, in full strength

forced 1 = **compulsory**, enforced, mandatory, obligatory, involuntary, conscripted ≠ voluntary **2** = **false**, affected, strained, wooden, stiff, artificial, contrived, unnatural ≠ natural

forceful 1 = **dynamic**, powerful, assertive ≠ weak **2** = **powerful**, strong, convincing, effective, compelling, persuasive, cogent

forecast NOUN = **prediction**, prognosis, guess, prophecy, conjecture, forewarning
● VERB = **predict**, anticipate, foresee, foretell, divine, prophesy, augur, forewarn

forefront = **lead**, centre, front, fore, spearhead, prominence, vanguard, foreground

foreign = **alien**, exotic, unknown, strange, imported, remote, external, unfamiliar ≠ native

foreigner = **alien**, incomer, immigrant, non-native, stranger, settler

foremost = **leading**, best, highest, chief, prime, primary, supreme, most important

foresee = **predict**, forecast, anticipate, envisage, prophesy, foretell

forever 1 = **evermore**, always, ever, for good, for keeps, for all time, in perpetuity, till the cows come home (*informal*)
2 = **constantly**, always, all the time, continually, endlessly, persistently, eternally, perpetually

> ### *Word Power*
> **forever** – *Forever* and *for ever* can both be used to say that something is without end. For all other meanings, *forever* is the preferred form.

forfeit VERB = **relinquish**, lose, give up, surrender, renounce, be deprived of, say goodbye to, be stripped of
● NOUN = **penalty**, fine, damages, forfeiture, loss, mulct

forge 1 = **form**, build, create, establish, set up, fashion, shape, frame **2** = **fake**, copy, reproduce, imitate, counterfeit, feign, falsify **3** = **create**, make, work, found, form, model, fashion, shape

forget 1 = **neglect**, overlook, omit, not remember, be remiss, fail to remember **2** = **leave behind**, lose, lose sight of, mislay

forgive = **excuse**, pardon, not hold something against, understand, acquit, condone, let off (*informal*), turn a blind eye to ≠ blame

forgiveness = **pardon**, mercy, absolution, exoneration, amnesty, acquittal, remission

forgotten = <u>unremembered</u>, lost, past, left behind, omitted, bygone, past recall

fork = <u>branch</u>, part, separate, split, divide, diverge, subdivide, bifurcate

forked = <u>branching</u>, split, branched, divided, angled, pronged, zigzag, Y-shaped

form NOUN 1 = <u>type</u>, sort, kind, variety, class, style 2 = <u>shape</u>, formation, configuration, structure, pattern, appearance 3 = <u>condition</u>, health, shape, nick (*informal*), fitness, trim, fettle 4 = <u>document</u>, paper, sheet, questionnaire, application 5 = <u>procedure</u>, etiquette, use, custom, convention, usage, protocol, wont, kawa (*N.Z.*), tikanga (*N.Z.*) 6 = <u>class</u>, year, set, rank, grade, stream
• VERB 1 = <u>arrange</u>, combine, line up, assemble, draw up 2 = <u>make</u>, produce, fashion, build, create, shape, construct, forge 3 = <u>constitute</u>, make up, compose, comprise 4 = <u>establish</u>, start, launch 5 = <u>take shape</u>, grow, develop, materialize, rise, appear, come into being, crystallize 6 = <u>draw up</u>, devise, formulate, organize 7 = <u>develop</u>, pick up, acquire, cultivate, contract

formal 1 = <u>serious</u>, stiff, detached, official, correct, conventional, remote, precise ≠ informal 2 = <u>official</u>, authorized, endorsed, certified, solemn 3 = <u>ceremonial</u>, traditional, solemn, ritualistic, dressy 4 = <u>conventional</u>, established, traditional

formality 1 = <u>correctness</u>, seriousness, decorum, protocol, etiquette 2 = <u>convention</u>, procedure, custom, ritual, rite

format = <u>arrangement</u>, form, style, make-up, look, plan, design, type

formation 1 = <u>establishment</u>, founding, forming, setting up, starting, production, generation, manufacture 2 = <u>development</u>, shaping, constitution, moulding, genesis 3 = <u>arrangement</u>, grouping, design, structure, pattern, organization, array, configuration

former = <u>previous</u>, one-time, erstwhile, earlier, prior, sometime, foregoing ≠ current

formerly = <u>previously</u>, earlier, in the past, at one time, before, lately, once

formidable 1 = <u>impressive</u>, great, powerful, tremendous, mighty, terrific, awesome, invincible 2 = <u>intimidating</u>, threatening, terrifying, menacing, dismaying, fearful, daunting, frightful ≠ encouraging

formula = <u>method</u>, plan, policy,

rule, principle, procedure, recipe, blueprint

formulate 1 = <u>devise</u>, plan, develop, prepare, work out, invent, forge, draw up **2** = <u>express</u>, detail, frame, define, specify, articulate, set down, put into words

fort NOUN = <u>fortress</u>, keep, camp, tower, castle, garrison, stronghold, citadel, fortified pa (*N.Z.*)

● PHRASES **hold the fort** (*Informal*) = <u>take responsibility</u>, cover, stand in, carry on, take over the reins, deputize, keep things on an even keel

forte = <u>speciality</u>, strength, talent, strong point, métier, long suit (*informal*), gift ≠ weak point

forth 1 (*Formal or old-fashioned*) = <u>forward</u>, out, away, ahead, onward, outward **2** = <u>out</u>

forthcoming 1 = <u>approaching</u>, coming, expected, future, imminent, prospective, impending, upcoming **2** = <u>available</u>, ready, accessible, at hand, in evidence, obtainable, on tap (*informal*) **3** = <u>communicative</u>, open, free, informative, expansive, sociable, chatty, talkative

fortify 1 = <u>protect</u>, defend, strengthen, reinforce, support, shore up, augment, buttress **2** = <u>strengthen</u>, add alcohol to

≠ dishearten

fortitude = <u>courage</u>, strength, resolution, grit, bravery, backbone, perseverance, valour

fortress = <u>castle</u>, fort, stronghold, citadel, redoubt, fastness, fortified pa (*N.Z.*)

fortunate 1 = <u>lucky</u>, favoured, jammy (*Brit. slang*), in luck ≠ unfortunate **2** = <u>well-off</u>, rich, successful, wealthy, prosperous, affluent, opulent, well-heeled (*informal*) **3** = <u>providential</u>, fortuitous, felicitous, timely, helpful, convenient, favourable, advantageous

fortunately = <u>luckily</u>, happily, as luck would have it, providentially, by good luck, by a happy chance

fortune NOUN **1** = <u>wealth</u>, means, property, riches, resources, assets, possessions, treasure ≠ poverty **2** = <u>luck</u>, fluke (*informal*), stroke of luck, serendipity, twist of fate, run of luck **3** = <u>chance</u>, fate, destiny, providence, the stars, Lady Luck, kismet

● PLURAL NOUN = <u>destiny</u>, lot, experiences, history, condition, success, means, adventures

forward ADVERB **1** = <u>forth</u>, on, ahead, onwards ≠ backward(s) **2** = <u>on</u>, onward, onwards

● ADJECTIVE **1** = <u>leading</u>, first, head, front, advance, foremost **2** = <u>future</u>, advanced, premature, prospective **3** = <u>presumptuous</u>, familiar, bold, cheeky, brash, pushy (*informal*), brazen, shameless ≠ shy

● VERB 1 = <u>further</u>, advance, promote, assist, hurry, hasten, expedite 2 = <u>send on</u>, send, post, pass on, dispatch, redirect

fossick (*Austral. & N.Z.*) = <u>search</u>, hunt, explore, ferret, check, forage, rummage

foster 1 = <u>bring up</u>, mother, raise, nurse, look after, rear, care for, take care of 2 = <u>develop</u>, support, further, encourage, feed, promote, stimulate, uphold ≠ suppress

foul ADJECTIVE 1 = <u>dirty</u>, unpleasant, stinking, filthy, grubby, repellent, squalid, repulsive, festy (*Austral. slang*), yucko (*Austral. slang*) ≠ clean 2 = <u>obscene</u>, crude, indecent, blue, abusive, coarse, vulgar, lewd 3 = <u>unfair</u>, illegal, crooked, shady (*informal*), fraudulent, dishonest, unscrupulous, underhand 4 = <u>offensive</u>, bad, wrong, evil, corrupt, disgraceful, shameful, immoral ≠ admirable

● VERB = <u>dirty</u>, stain, contaminate, pollute, taint, sully, defile, besmirch ≠ clean

found = <u>establish</u>, start, set up, begin, create, institute, organize, constitute

foundation 1 = <u>basis</u> 2 often plural = <u>substructure</u>,

underpinning, groundwork, bedrock, base, footing, bottom 3 = <u>setting up</u>, institution, instituting, organization, settlement, establishment, initiating, originating

founder[1] = <u>initiator</u>, father, author, architect, creator, beginner, inventor, originator

founder[2] 1 = <u>fail</u>, collapse, break down, fall through, be unsuccessful, come unstuck, miscarry, misfire 2 = <u>sink</u>, go down, be lost, submerge, capsize, go to the bottom

---

Word Power

founder – *Founder* is sometimes wrongly used where *flounder* is meant: *this unexpected turn of events left him floundering* (not *foundering*).

---

fountain 1 = <u>font</u>, spring, reservoir, spout, fount, water feature, well 2 = <u>jet</u>, stream, spray, gush 3 = <u>source</u>, fount, wellspring, cause, origin, derivation, fountainhead

fowl = <u>poultry</u>
➤ types of fowl

foyer = <u>entrance hall</u>, lobby, reception area, vestibule, anteroom, antechamber

fraction = <u>percentage</u>, share, section, slice, portion

fracture NOUN 1 = <u>break</u>, split,

Types of fowl

barnacle goose	Muscovy duck *or* musk duck
brush turkey *or* scrub turkey	mute swan
bufflehead	paradise duck
Canada goose	pintail
canvasback	pochard
chicken *or* (*Austral. slang*) chook	redhead
cock *or* cockerel	Rhode Island Red chicken
duck	scaup *or* scaup duck
eider *or* eider duck	screamer
gadwall	shelduck
goldeneye	shoveler
goosander	smew
goose	snow goose
greylag *or* greylag goose	sultan
hen	swan
mallard	teal
mallee fowl *or* (*Austral.*) gnow	trumpeter swan
mandarin duck	turkey
megapode	whooper *or* whooper swan
merganser *or* sawbill	wigeon *or* widgeon
moorhen	

crack 2 = <u>cleft</u>, opening, split, crack, rift, rupture, crevice, fissure

● VERB 1 = <u>break</u>, crack 2 = <u>split</u>, separate, divide, rend, fragment, splinter, rupture

fragile 1 = <u>unstable</u>, weak, vulnerable, delicate, uncertain, insecure, precarious, flimsy 2 = <u>fine</u>, weak, delicate, frail, brittle, flimsy, dainty, easily broken ≠ durable 3 = <u>delicate</u>, fine, charming, elegant, neat, exquisite, graceful, petite 4 = <u>unwell</u>, poorly, weak, delicate,

crook (*Austral. & N.Z. informal*), shaky, frail, feeble, sickly

fragment NOUN = <u>piece</u>, bit, scrap, particle, portion, shred, speck, sliver

● VERB 1 = <u>break</u>, shatter, crumble, disintegrate, splinter, come apart, break into pieces, come to pieces ≠ fuse 2 = <u>break up</u>, split up

fragrance 1 = <u>scent</u>, smell, perfume, bouquet, aroma, sweet smell, sweet odour, redolence ≠ stink 2 = <u>perfume</u>, scent, cologne, eau de toilette, eau de

Cologne, toilet water, Cologne water

fragrant = <u>aromatic</u>, perfumed, balmy, redolent, sweet-smelling, sweet-scented, odorous ≠ stinking

frail 1 = <u>feeble</u>, weak, puny, infirm ≠ strong **2** = <u>flimsy</u>, weak, vulnerable, delicate, fragile, insubstantial

frame NOUN **1** = <u>casing</u>, framework, structure, shell, construction, skeleton, chassis **2** = <u>physique</u>, build, form, body, figure, anatomy, carcass
● VERB **1** = <u>mount</u>, case, enclose **2** = <u>surround</u>, ring, enclose, encompass, envelop, encircle, hem in **3** = <u>devise</u>, draft, compose, sketch, put together, draw up, formulate, map out
● PHRASES **frame of mind** = <u>mood</u>, state, attitude, humour, temper, outlook, disposition, mind-set

framework 1 = <u>system</u>, plan, order, scheme, arrangement, the bare bones **2** = <u>structure</u>, body, frame, foundation, shell, skeleton

frank = <u>candid</u>, open, direct, straightforward, blunt, sincere, outspoken, honest ≠ secretive

frankly 1 = <u>honestly</u>, sincerely, in truth, candidly, to tell you the truth, to be frank, to be frank with someone, to be honest **2** = <u>openly</u>, freely, directly, plainly,

bluntly, candidly, without reserve

frantic 1 = <u>frenzied</u>, wild, furious, distracted, distraught, berserk, at the end of your tether, beside yourself, berko (Austral. slang) ≠ calm **2** = <u>hectic</u>, desperate, frenzied, fraught (informal), frenetic

fraternity 1 = <u>companionship</u>, fellowship, brotherhood, kinship, camaraderie **2** = <u>circle</u>, company, guild **3** = <u>brotherhood</u>, club, union, society, league, association

fraud 1 = <u>deception</u>, deceit, treachery, swindling, trickery, duplicity, double-dealing, chicanery ≠ honesty **2** = <u>scam</u>, deception (slang) **3** = <u>hoax</u>, trick, con (informal), deception, sham, spoof (informal), prank, swindle **4** (Informal) = <u>impostor</u>, fake, hoaxer, pretender, charlatan, fraudster, swindler, phoney or phony (informal)

fraudulent = <u>deceitful</u>, crooked (informal), untrue, sham, treacherous, dishonest, swindling, double-dealing ≠ genuine

fray = <u>wear thin</u>, wear, rub, wear out, chafe

freak ADJECTIVE = <u>abnormal</u>, chance, unusual, exceptional, unparalleled
● NOUN **1** (Informal) = <u>enthusiast</u>, fan, nut (slang), addict, buff (informal), fanatic, devotee, fiend (informal) **2** = <u>aberration</u>,

eccentric, anomaly, oddity, monstrosity, malformation

3 = <u>weirdo</u> *or* **weirdie** (*informal*), eccentric, character (*informal*), oddball (*informal*), nonconformist

free ADJECTIVE

1 = <u>complimentary</u>, for free (*informal*), for nothing, unpaid, for love, free of charge, on the house, without charge **2** = <u>allowed</u>, permitted, unrestricted, unimpeded, clear, able **3** = <u>at liberty</u>, loose, liberated, at large, on the loose ≠ confined **4** = <u>independent</u>, unfettered, footloose **5** = <u>available</u>, empty, spare, vacant, unused, unoccupied, untaken **6** = <u>generous</u>, liberal, lavish, unstinting, unsparing ≠ mean

● VERB **1** = <u>clear</u>, disengage, cut loose, release, rescue, extricate **2** = <u>release</u>, liberate, let out, set free, deliver, loose, untie, unchain ≠ confine **3** = <u>disentangle</u>, extricate, disengage, loose, unravel, disconnect, untangle

freedom 1 = <u>independence</u>, democracy, sovereignty, self-determination, emancipation, autarchy, rangatiratanga (*N.Z.*) **2** = <u>liberty</u>, release, discharge, emancipation, deliverance ≠ captivity **3** = <u>licence</u>, latitude, free rein, opportunity, discretion,

carte blanche, blank cheque ≠ restriction

freely 1 = <u>abundantly</u>, liberally, lavishly, extravagantly, copiously, unstintingly, amply **2** = <u>openly</u>, frankly, plainly, candidly, unreservedly, straightforwardly, without reserve **3** = <u>willingly</u>, readily, voluntarily, spontaneously, without prompting, of your own free will, of your own accord

freeway (*U.S. & Austral.*) = <u>motorway</u> (*Brit.*), autobahn (*German*), autoroute (*French*), autostrada (*Italian*)

freeze 1 = <u>ice over</u> *or* **up**, harden, stiffen, solidify, become solid **2** = <u>chill</u> **3** = <u>fix</u>, hold, limit, hold up **4** = <u>suspend</u>, stop, shelve, curb, cut short, discontinue

freezing 1 = <u>icy</u>, biting, bitter, raw, chill, arctic, frosty, glacial **2** = <u>frozen</u>, very cold

freight 1 = <u>transportation</u>, traffic, delivery, carriage, shipment, haulage, conveyance, transport **2** = <u>cargo</u>, goods, load, delivery, burden, shipment, merchandise, consignment

French = <u>Gallic</u>

frenzied = <u>uncontrolled</u>, wild, crazy, furious, frantic, frenetic, feverish, rabid

frenzy = <u>fury</u>, passion, rage, seizure, hysteria, paroxysm, derangement ≠ calm

frequent ADJECTIVE = <u>common</u>, repeated, usual, familiar, everyday, persistent, customary, recurrent ≠ infrequent

● VERB = <u>visit</u>, attend, haunt, be found at, patronize, hang out at (*informal*), visit often, go to regularly ≠ keep away

frequently = <u>often</u>, commonly, repeatedly, many times, habitually, not infrequently, much ≠ infrequently

fresh 1 = <u>additional</u>, more, new, other, added, further, extra, supplementary 2 = <u>natural</u>, unprocessed, unpreserved ≠ preserved 3 = <u>new</u>, original, novel, different, recent, modern, up-to-date, unorthodox ≠ old 4 = <u>invigorating</u>, clean, pure, crisp, bracing, refreshing, brisk, unpolluted ≠ stale 5 = <u>cool</u>, cold, refreshing, brisk, chilly, nippy 6 = <u>lively</u>, keen, alert, refreshed, vigorous, energetic, sprightly, spry ≠ weary 7 = <u>cheeky</u> (*Informal*), impertinent, forward, familiar, audacious, disrespectful, presumptuous, insolent ≠ well-mannered

fret = <u>worry</u>, brood, agonize, obsess, lose sleep, upset yourself, distress yourself

friction 1 = <u>conflict</u>, hostility, resentment, disagreement, animosity, discord, bad blood, dissension 2 = <u>resistance</u>, rubbing, scraping, grating, rasping, chafing, abrasion 3 = <u>rubbing</u>, scraping, grating, rasping, chafing, abrasion

friend 1 = <u>companion</u>, pal, mate (*informal*), buddy (*informal*), best friend, close friend, comrade, chum (*informal*), cobber (*Austral. & N.Z.*), E hoa (*N.Z. old-fashioned informal*) ≠ foe 2 = <u>supporter</u>, ally, associate, sponsor, patron, well-wisher

friendly = <u>amiable</u>, welcoming, warm, neighbourly, pally (*informal*), helpful, sympathetic, affectionate = <u>amicable</u>, warm, familiar, pleasant, intimate, informal, cordial, congenial ≠ unfriendly

friendship 1 = <u>attachment</u>, relationship, bond, link, association, tie 2 = <u>friendliness</u>, affection, harmony, goodwill, intimacy, familiarity, rapport, companionship ≠ unfriendliness

fright 1 = <u>fear</u>, shock, alarm, horror, panic, dread, consternation, trepidation ≠ courage 2 = <u>scare</u>, start, turn, surprise, shock, jolt, the creeps (*informal*), the willies (*slang*)

frighten = <u>scare</u>, shock, alarm, terrify, startle, intimidate, unnerve, petrify ≠ reassure

frightened = <u>afraid</u>, alarmed, scared, terrified, shocked, startled, petrified, flustered

frightening = terrifying, shocking, alarming, startling, horrifying, menacing, scary (*Informal*), fearful

fringe NOUN 1 = border, edging, edge, trimming, hem, frill, flounce 2 = edge, limits, border, margin, outskirts, perimeter, periphery, borderline

● ADJECTIVE = unofficial, alternative, radical, innovative, avant-garde, unconventional, unorthodox

frog ➤ **amphibians**

front NOUN 1 = head, start, lead, forefront 2 = exterior, face, façade, frontage 3 = foreground, fore, forefront, nearest part 4 = front line, trenches, vanguard, firing line 5 (*Informal*) = disguise, cover, blind, mask, cover-up, cloak, façade, pretext

● ADJECTIVE = foremost, at the front ≠ back 2 = leading, first, lead, head, foremost, topmost

● VERB = face onto, overlook, look out on, have a view of, look over or onto

frontier = border, limit, edge, boundary, verge, perimeter, borderline, dividing line

frost = hoarfrost, freeze, rime

frown VERB = glare, scowl, glower, make a face, look daggers, knit your brows, lour or lower

● NOUN = scowl, glare, glower, dirty look

frozen 1 = icy, hard, solid, frosted, arctic, ice-covered, icebound 2 = chilled, cold, iced, refrigerated, ice-cold 3 = ice-cold, freezing, numb, very cold, frigid, frozen stiff

fruit 1 = produce, crop, yield, harvest 2 *often plural* = result, reward, outcome, end result, return, effect, benefit, profit

frustrate = thwart, stop, check, block, defeat, disappoint, counter, spoil, crool or cruel (*Austral. slang*) ≠ further

frustrated = disappointed, discouraged, infuriated, exasperated, resentful, embittered, disheartened

frustration 1 = annoyance, disappointment, resentment, irritation, grievance, dissatisfaction, exasperation, vexation 2 = obstruction, blocking, foiling, spoiling, thwarting, circumvention

fudge = misrepresent, hedge, stall, flannel (*Brit. informal*), equivocate

fuel = incitement, ammunition, provocation, incentive

fugitive = runaway, refugee, deserter, escapee

fulfil 1 = carry out, perform, complete, achieve, accomplish ≠ neglect 2 = achieve, realize, satisfy, attain, consummate, bring to fruition 3 = satisfy, please, content, cheer, refresh, gratify, make happy **4** = **comply with**, meet, fill, satisfy, observe, obey, conform to, answer

fulfilment = **achievement**, implementation, completion, accomplishment, realization, attainment, consummation

full 1 = **filled**, stocked, brimming, replete, complete, loaded, saturated ≠ empty **2** = **satiated**, having had enough, replete **3** = **extensive**, complete, generous, adequate, ample, abundant, plentiful ≠ incomplete **4** = **comprehensive**, complete, exhaustive, all-embracing **5** = **rounded**, strong, rich, powerful, intense, pungent **6** = **plump**, rounded, voluptuous, shapely, well-rounded, buxom, curvaceous **7** = **voluminous**, large, loose, baggy, billowing, puffy, capacious, loose-fitting ≠ tight **8** = **rich**, strong, deep, loud, distinct, resonant, sonorous, clear ≠ thin

full-scale = **major**, wide-ranging, all-out, sweeping, comprehensive, thorough, in-depth, exhaustive

fully 1 = **completely**, totally, perfectly, entirely, altogether, thoroughly, wholly, utterly **2** = **in all respects**, completely, totally, entirely, altogether, thoroughly, wholly

fumble = **grope**, flounder, scrabble, feel around

fume VERB = **rage**, seethe, see red (*informal*), storm, rant, smoulder, get hot under the collar (*informal*)
● PLURAL NOUN = **smoke**, gas, exhaust, pollution, vapour, smog

fun NOUN **1** = **amusement**, sport, pleasure, entertainment, recreation, enjoyment, merriment, jollity **2** = **enjoyment**, pleasure, mirth ≠ gloom
● ADJECTIVE = **enjoyable**, entertaining, pleasant, amusing, lively, diverting, witty, convivial
● PHRASES **make fun of something** *or* **someone** = **mock**, tease, ridicule, poke fun at, laugh at, mimic, parody, send up (*Brit. informal*)

function NOUN **1** = **purpose**, business, job, use, role, responsibility, task, duty **2** = **reception**, party, affair, gathering, bash (*informal*), social occasion, soiree, do (*informal*)
● VERB **1** = **work**, run, operate, perform, go **2** = **act**, operate, perform, behave, do duty, have the role of

functional 1 = **practical**, utilitarian, serviceable, hard-wearing, useful **2** = **working**, operative, operational, going, prepared, ready, viable, up and running

fund NOUN = <u>reserve</u>, stock, supply, store, collection, pool

● PLURAL NOUN = <u>money</u>, capital, cash, finance, means, savings, resources, assets

● VERB = <u>finance</u>, back, support, pay for, subsidize, provide money for, put up the money for

fundamental 1 = <u>central</u>, key, basic, essential, primary, principal, cardinal ≠ incidental 2 = <u>basic</u>, essential, underlying, profound, elementary, rudimentary

fundamentally 1 = <u>basically</u>, at heart, at bottom 2 = <u>essentially</u>, radically, basically, primarily, profoundly, intrinsically

fundi (S. African) = <u>expert</u>

funeral = <u>burial</u>, committal, laying to rest, cremation, interment, obsequies, entombment

funny 1 = <u>humorous</u>, amusing, comical, entertaining, comic, witty, hilarious, riotous ≠ unfunny 2 = <u>comic</u>, comical 3 = <u>peculiar</u>, odd, strange, unusual, bizarre, curious, weird, mysterious 4 = <u>ill</u>, poorly (informal), sick, odd, crook (Austral. & N.Z. informal), ailing, unhealthy, unwell, off-colour (informal)

furious 1 = <u>angry</u>, raging, fuming, infuriated, incensed, enraged, inflamed, very angry, tooshie (Austral. slang) ≠ pleased 2 = <u>violent</u>, intense, fierce, savage, turbulent, vehement, unrestrained

furnish 1 = <u>decorate</u>, fit out, stock, equip 2 = <u>supply</u>, give, offer, provide, present, grant, hand out

furniture = <u>household goods</u>, furnishings, fittings, house fittings, goods, things (informal), possessions, appliances

furore = <u>commotion</u>, to-do, stir, disturbance, outcry, uproar, hullabaloo

further or **farther** ADVERB = <u>in addition</u>, moreover, besides, furthermore, also, to boot, additionally, into the bargain

● ADJECTIVE = <u>additional</u>, more, new, other, extra, fresh, supplementary

● VERB = <u>promote</u>, help, develop, forward, encourage, advance, work for, assist ≠ hinder

furthermore = <u>moreover</u>, further, in addition, besides, too, as well to boot, additionally

furthest or **farthest** = <u>most distant</u>, extreme, ultimate, remotest, furthermost, outmost

fury 1 = <u>anger</u>, passion, rage, madness, frenzy, wrath, impetuosity ≠ calmness 2 = <u>violence</u>, force, intensity, severity, ferocity, savagery, vehemence, fierceness ≠ peace

fuss NOUN 1 = <u>commotion</u>, to-do, bother, stir, excitement, ado, hue and cry, palaver 2 = <u>bother</u>, trouble, struggle, hassle (*informal*), nuisance, inconvenience, hindrance 3 = <u>complaint</u>, row, protest, objection, trouble, argument, squabble, furore

● VERB = <u>worry</u>, flap (*informal*), fret, fidget, take pains, be agitated, get worked up

futile = <u>useless</u>, vain, unsuccessful, pointless, worthless, fruitless, ineffectual, unprofitable ≠ useful

future NOUN 1 = <u>time to come</u>, hereafter, what lies ahead 2 = <u>prospect</u>, expectation, outlook

● ADJECTIVE = <u>forthcoming</u>, coming, later, approaching, to come, succeeding, fated, subsequent ≠ past

fuzzy 1 = <u>frizzy</u>, fluffy, woolly, downy 2 = <u>indistinct</u>, blurred, vague, distorted, unclear, bleary, out of focus, ill-defined ≠ distinct

G

gadget = <u>device</u>, thing, appliance, machine, tool, implement, invention, instrument

gag¹ NOUN = <u>muzzle</u>, tie, restraint

● VERB 1 = <u>suppress</u>, silence, muffle, curb, stifle, muzzle, quieten 2 = <u>retch</u>, heave

gag² (*Informal*) = <u>joke</u>, crack

(*slang*), funny (*informal*), quip, pun, jest, wisecrack (*informal*), witticism

gain VERB 1 = <u>acquire</u>, get, receive, pick up, secure, collect, gather, obtain 2 = <u>profit</u>, get, land, secure, collect, gather, capture, acquire ≠ lose 3 = <u>put on</u>, increase, gather, build up 4 = <u>attain</u>, get, reach, get to, secure, obtain, acquire, arrive at

● NOUN 1 = <u>rise</u>, increase, growth, advance, improvement, upsurge, upturn, upswing 2 = <u>profit</u>, return, benefit, advantage, yield, dividend ≠ loss

● PLURAL NOUN = <u>profits</u>, earnings, revenue, proceeds, winnings, takings

● PHRASES **gain on something** *or* **someone** = <u>get nearer to</u>, close in on, approach, catch up with, narrow the gap on

gala = <u>festival</u>, fête, celebration, carnival, festivity, pageant, jamboree

gale 1 = <u>storm</u>, hurricane, tornado, cyclone, blast, typhoon, tempest, squall 2 (*Informal*) = <u>outburst</u>, scream, roar, fit, storm, shout, burst, explosion

gall = <u>annoy</u>, provoke, irritate, trouble, disturb, madden, exasperate, vex

gallop 1 = <u>run</u>, race, career, speed, bolt 2 = <u>dash</u>, run, race, career, speed, rush, sprint

gamble NOUN 1 = <u>risk</u>, chance,

venture, lottery, speculation, uncertainty, leap in the dark ≠ certainty 2 = **bet**, flutter (*informal*) 2 = **risk**, chance, hazard, wager 3 = **bet**, play, game, speculate, punt, wager, have a flutter (*informal*)

● VERB 1 = **take a chance**, speculate, stick your neck out (*informal*) 2 = **risk**, chance, hazard, wager 3 = **bet**, play, game, speculate, punt, wager, have a flutter (*informal*)

game NOUN 1 = **pastime**, sport, activity, entertainment, recreation, distraction, amusement, diversion ≠ job 2 = **match**, meeting, event, competition, tournament, clash, contest, head-to-head 3 = **amusement**, joke, entertainment, diversion 4 = **wild animals** *or* **birds**, prey, quarry 5 = **scheme**, plan, design, trick, plot, tactic, manoeuvre, ploy

● ADJECTIVE 1 = **willing**, prepared, ready, keen, eager, interested, desirous 2 = **brave**, courageous, spirited, daring, persistent, gritty, intrepid, plucky ≠ cowardly

gang = **group**, crowd, pack, company, band, bunch, mob

gangster = **hoodlum** (*chiefly U.S.*), crook (*informal*), bandit, hood (*U.S. slang*), robber, mobster (*U.S. slang*), racketeer, ruffian, tsotsi (*S. African*)

gap 1 = **opening**, space, hole, break, crack, slot, aperture, cleft 2 = **interval**, pause, interruption,

respite, lull, interlude, breathing space, hiatus 3 = **difference**, gulf, contrast, disagreement, discrepancy, inconsistency, disparity, divergence

gape 1 = **stare**, wonder, goggle, gawp (*Brit. slang*), gawk 2 = **open**, split, crack, yawn

gaping = **wide**, great, open, broad, vast, yawning, wide open, cavernous

garland NOUN = **wreath**, band, bays, crown, honours, laurels, festoon, chaplet

● VERB = **adorn**, crown, deck, festoon, wreathe

garment *often plural* = **clothes**, dress, clothing, gear (*slang*), uniform, outfit, costume, apparel

garnish NOUN = **decoration**, embellishment, adornment, ornamentation, trimming

● VERB = **decorate**, adorn, ornament, embellish, trim ≠ strip

garrison NOUN 1 = **troops**, group, unit, section, command, armed force, detachment 2 = **fort**, fortress, camp, base, post, station, stronghold, fortification, fortified pa (*N.Z.*)

● VERB = **station**, position, post, install, assign, put on duty

gas 1 = **fumes**, vapour 2 (*U.S., Canad., & N.Z.*) = **petrol**, gasoline

gasp VERB = **pant**, blow, puff, choke, gulp, catch your breath

● NOUN = **pant**, puff, gulp, sharp

intake of breath

gate = <u>barrier</u>, opening, door, entrance, exit, gateway, portal

gather 1 = <u>congregate</u>, assemble, collect, meet, mass, come together, muster, converge ≠ scatter 2 = <u>assemble</u>, collect, bring together, muster, call together ≠ disperse 3 = <u>collect</u>, assemble, accumulate, mass, muster, garner, amass, stockpile 4 = <u>pick</u>, harvest, pluck, reap, garner, glean 5 = <u>build up</u>, rise, increase, grow, expand, swell, intensify, heighten 6 = <u>understand</u>, believe, hear, learn, assume, conclude, presume, infer 7 = <u>fold</u>, tuck, pleat

gathering 1 = <u>assembly</u>, group, crowd, meeting, conference, company, congress, mass, hui (N.Z.), runanga (N.Z.) 2 = <u>collecting</u>, obtaining, attainment

gauge VERB 1 = <u>measure</u>, calculate, evaluate, value, determine, count, weigh, compute 2 = <u>judge</u>, estimate, guess, assess, evaluate, rate, appraise, reckon ● NOUN = <u>meter</u>, dial, measuring instrument

gay ADJECTIVE 1 = <u>homosexual</u>, lesbian, queer (informal or derogatory), moffie (S. African slang) 2 = <u>cheerful</u>, lively, sparkling, merry, upbeat (informal), buoyant, cheery, carefree ≠ sad 3 = <u>colourful</u>, rich,

bright, brilliant, vivid, flamboyant, flashy, showy ≠ drab ● NOUN = <u>homosexual</u>, lesbian, auntie or aunty (Austral. slang), lily (Austral. slang) ≠ heterosexual

> ### Word Power
>
> **gay** – By far the most common and up-to-date use of the word *gay* is in reference to being homosexual. Other senses of the word have become uncommon and dated.

gaze VERB = <u>stare</u>, look, view, watch, regard, gape ● NOUN = <u>stare</u>, look, fixed look

gazette = <u>newspaper</u>, paper, journal, periodical, news-sheet

gear NOUN 1 = <u>mechanism</u>, works, machinery, cogs, cogwheels, gearwheels 2 = <u>equipment</u>, supplies, tackle, tools, instruments, apparatus, paraphernalia, accoutrements 3 = <u>clothing</u>, wear, dress, clothes, outfit, costume, garments, togs ● VERB with **to** or **towards** = <u>equip</u>, fit, adjust, adapt

gem 1 = <u>precious stone</u>, jewel, stone 2 = <u>treasure</u>, prize, jewel, pearl, masterpiece, humdinger (slang), taonga (N.Z.)

general 1 = <u>widespread</u>, accepted, popular, public, common, broad, extensive, universal ≠ individual 2 = <u>overall</u>, complete, total, global, comprehensive, blanket, inclusive, all-embracing ≠ restricted 3 = <u>universal</u>, overall, widespread, collective, across-the-board ≠ exceptional 4 = <u>vague</u>, loose, blanket, sweeping, unclear, approximate, woolly, indefinite ≠ specific

generally 1 = <u>usually</u>, commonly, typically, normally, on the whole, by and large, ordinarily, as a rule ≠ occasionally 2 = <u>commonly</u>, widely, publicly, universally, extensively, popularly, conventionally, customarily ≠ individually

generate = <u>produce</u>, create, make, cause, give rise to, engender ≠ end

generation 1 = <u>age group</u>, peer group 2 = <u>age</u>, period, era, time, lifetime, span, epoch

generic = <u>collective</u>, general, common, wide, comprehensive, universal, blanket, inclusive ≠ specific

generosity 1 = <u>liberality</u>, charity, bounty, munificence, beneficence, largesse or largess 2 = <u>magnanimity</u>, goodness, kindness, selflessness, charity, unselfishness, high-mindedness, nobleness

generous 1 = <u>liberal</u>, lavish, charitable, hospitable, bountiful, open-handed, unstinting, beneficent ≠ mean

2 = <u>magnanimous</u>, kind, noble, good, high-minded, unselfish, big-hearted 3 = <u>plentiful</u>, lavish, ample, abundant, full, rich, liberal, copious ≠ meagre

genesis = <u>beginning</u>, origin, start, birth, creation, formation, inception ≠ end

genius 1 = <u>brilliance</u>, ability, talent, capacity, gift, bent, excellence, flair 2 = <u>master</u>, expert, mastermind, maestro, virtuoso, whiz (*informal*), hotshot (*informal*), brainbox, fundi (*S. African*) ≠ dunce

genre = <u>type</u>, group, order, sort, kind, class, style, species

gentle 1 = <u>kind</u>, kindly, tender, mild, humane, compassionate, meek, placid ≠ unkind 2 = <u>slow</u>, easy, slight, moderate, gradual, imperceptible 3 = <u>moderate</u>, light, soft, slight, mild, soothing ≠ violent

gentlemanly = <u>chivalrous</u>, refined, polite, civil, courteous, gallant, genteel, well-mannered

genuine 1 = <u>authentic</u>, real, actual, true, valid, legitimate, veritable, bona fide, dinkum (*Austral. & N.Z. informal*) ≠ counterfeit 2 = <u>heartfelt</u>, sincere, honest, earnest, real, true, frank, unaffected ≠ affected 3 = <u>sincere</u>, honest, frank, candid, dinkum (*Austral. & N.Z. informal*), guileless ≠ hypocritical

germ 1 = <u>microbe</u>, virus, bug (*informal*), bacterium, bacillus, microorganism **2** = <u>beginning</u>, root, seed, origin, spark, embryo, rudiment

gesture NOUN = <u>sign</u>, action, signal, motion, indication, gesticulation

◆ VERB = <u>signal</u>, sign, wave, indicate, motion, beckon, gesticulate

get VERB **1** = <u>become</u>, grow, turn, come to be **2** = <u>persuade</u>, convince, induce, influence, entice, incite, impel, prevail upon **3** (*Informal*) = <u>annoy</u>, anger, disturb, trouble, bug (*informal*), irritate, gall **4** = <u>obtain</u>, receive, gain, acquire, win, land, net, pick up **5** = <u>fetch</u>, bring, collect **6** = <u>understand</u>, follow, catch, see, realize, take in, perceive, grasp **7** = <u>catch</u>, develop, contract, succumb to, fall victim to, go down with, come down with **8** = <u>arrest</u>, catch, grab, capture, seize, take, nab (*informal*), apprehend

◆ PHRASES **get at someone** = <u>criticize</u>, attack, blame, put down, knock (*informal*), nag, pick on, disparage ◆ **get at something 1** = <u>reach</u>, touch, grasp, get (a) hold of, stretch to **2** = <u>find out</u>, learn, reach, reveal, discover, acquire, detect, uncover **3** = <u>imply</u>, mean, suggest, hint,

intimate, lead up to, insinuate ◆ **get by** = <u>manage</u>, survive, cope, fare, exist, get along, make do, muddle through ◆ **get something across** = <u>communicate</u>, pass on, transmit, convey, impart, bring home, make known, put over

ghastly = <u>horrible</u>, shocking, terrible, awful, dreadful, horrendous, hideous, frightful ≠ lovely

ghost 1 = <u>spirit</u>, soul, phantom, spectre, spook (*informal*), apparition, wraith, atua (*N.Z.*), kehua (*N.Z.*), wairua (*N.Z.*) **2** = <u>trace</u>, shadow, suggestion, hint, suspicion, glimmer, semblance

(Related Words)

adjective: spectral

ghostly = <u>unearthly</u>, phantom, eerie, supernatural, spooky (*informal*), spectral

giant ADJECTIVE = <u>huge</u>, vast, enormous, tremendous, immense, titanic, gigantic, monumental ≠ tiny

◆ NOUN = <u>ogre</u>, monster, titan, colossus

gidday or **g'day** (*Austral. & N.Z.*) = <u>hello</u>, hi (*informal*), greetings, how do you do?, good morning, good evening, good afternoon, welcome, kia ora (*N.Z.*)

gift 1 = <u>donation</u>, offering, present, contribution, grant, legacy, hand-out, endowment, bonsela (*S. African*), koha (*N.Z.*) **2** = <u>talent</u>, ability, capacity, genius, power, capability, flair, knack

gifted = <u>talented</u>, able, skilled, expert, masterly, brilliant, capable, clever ≠ talentless

gigantic = <u>huge</u>, large, giant, massive, enormous, tremendous, immense, titanic ≠ tiny

giggle VERB = <u>laugh</u>, chuckle, snigger, chortle, titter, twitter
• NOUN = <u>laugh</u>, chuckle, snigger, chortle, titter, twitter

girl = <u>female child</u>, lass, lassie (*informal*), miss, maiden (*archaic*), maid (*archaic*)

give VERB **1** = <u>perform</u>, do, carry out, execute **2** = <u>communicate</u>, announce, transmit, pronounce, utter, issue **3** = <u>produce</u>, make, cause, occasion, engender **4** = <u>present</u>, contribute, donate, provide, supply, award, grant, deliver ≠ take **5** = <u>concede</u>, allow, grant **6** = <u>surrender</u>, yield, devote, hand over, relinquish, part with
• PHRASES **give in** = <u>admit defeat</u>, yield, concede, collapse, quit, submit, surrender, succumb
♦ **give something away** = <u>reveal</u>, expose, leak, disclose, betray, uncover, let out, divulge
♦ **give something off** or **out** = <u>emit</u>, produce, release, discharge, send out, throw out, exude ♦ **give something up**

= <u>abandon</u>, stop, quit, cease, renounce, leave off, desist

glad 1 = <u>happy</u>, pleased, delighted, contented, gratified, joyful, overjoyed ≠ unhappy **2** (*Archaic*) = <u>pleasing</u>, happy, cheering, pleasant, cheerful, gratifying

gladly 1 = <u>happily</u>, cheerfully, gleefully **2** = <u>willingly</u>, freely, happily, readily, cheerfully, with pleasure ≠ reluctantly

glamorous 1 = <u>attractive</u>, elegant, dazzling ≠ unglamorous **2** = <u>exciting</u>, glittering, prestigious, glossy ≠ unglamorous

glamour 1 = <u>charm</u>, appeal, beauty, attraction, fascination, allure, enchantment **2** = <u>excitement</u>, magic, thrill, romance, prestige, glitz (*slang*)

glance VERB = <u>peek</u>, look, view, glimpse, peep ≠ scrutinize
• NOUN = <u>peek</u>, look, glimpse, peep, dekko (*slang*) ≠ good look

---

Word Power

glance – Care should be taken not to confuse *glance* and *glimpse*: he caught a *glimpse* (not *glance*) of her making her way through the crowd; he gave a quick *glance* (not *glimpse*) at his watch. A *glance* is a deliberate action, while a *glimpse* seems opportunistic.

glare VERB 1 = <u>scowl</u>, frown, glower, look daggers, lour or lower 2 = <u>dazzle</u>, blaze, flare, flame

• NOUN 1 = <u>scowl</u>, frown, glower, dirty look, black look, lour or lower 2 = <u>dazzle</u>, glow, blaze, flame, brilliance

glaring 1 = <u>obvious</u>, gross, outrageous, manifest, blatant, conspicuous, flagrant, unconcealed ≠ inconspicuous 2 = <u>dazzling</u>, strong, bright, glowing, blazing ≠ subdued

glaze NOUN = <u>coat</u>, finish, polish, shine, gloss, varnish, enamel, lacquer

• VERB = <u>coat</u>, polish, gloss, varnish, enamel, lacquer

gleam VERB = <u>shine</u>, flash, glow, sparkle, glitter, shimmer, glint, glimmer

• NOUN 1 = <u>glimmer</u>, flash, beam, glow, sparkle 2 = <u>trace</u>, suggestion, hint, flicker, glimmer, inkling

glide = <u>slip</u>, sail, slide

glimpse NOUN = <u>look</u>, sighting, sight, glance, peep, peek

• VERB = <u>catch sight of</u>, spot, sight, view, spy, espy

glitter VERB = <u>shine</u>, flash, sparkle, glare, gleam, shimmer, twinkle, glint

• NOUN 1 = <u>glamour</u>, show, display, splendour, tinsel, pageantry, gaudiness, showiness

2 = <u>sparkle</u>, flash, shine, glare, gleam, sheen, shimmer, brightness

global 1 = <u>worldwide</u>, world, international, universal 2 = <u>comprehensive</u>, general, total, unlimited, exhaustive, all-inclusive ≠ limited

globe = <u>planet</u>, world, earth, sphere, orb

gloom 1 = <u>darkness</u>, dark, shadow, shade, twilight, dusk, obscurity, blackness ≠ light 2 = <u>depression</u>, sorrow, woe, melancholy, unhappiness, despondency, dejection, low spirits ≠ happiness

gloomy 1 = <u>dark</u>, dull, dim, dismal, black, grey, murky, dreary ≠ light 2 = <u>miserable</u>, sad, pessimistic, melancholy, glum, dejected, dispirited, downcast ≠ happy 3 = <u>depressing</u>, bad, dreary, sombre, dispiriting, disheartening, cheerless

glorious 1 = <u>splendid</u>, beautiful, brilliant, shining, superb, gorgeous, dazzling ≠ dull 2 = <u>delightful</u>, fine, wonderful, excellent, marvellous, gorgeous 3 = <u>illustrious</u>, famous, celebrated, distinguished, honoured, magnificent, renowned, eminent ≠ ordinary

glory NOUN 1 = <u>honour</u>, praise, fame, distinction, acclaim, prestige, eminence, renown

≠ shame 2 = <u>splendour</u>, majesty, greatness, grandeur, nobility, pomp, magnificence, pageantry ● VERB = <u>triumph</u>, boast, relish, revel, exult, take delight, pride yourself

gloss[1] = <u>shine</u>, gleam, sheen, polish, brightness, veneer, lustre, patina

gloss[2] NOUN = <u>interpretation</u>, comment, note, explanation, commentary, translation, footnote, elucidation ● VERB = <u>interpret</u>, explain, comment, translate, annotate, elucidate

glossy = <u>shiny</u>, polished, shining, glazed, bright, silky, glassy, lustrous ≠ dull

glow NOUN = <u>light</u>, gleam, splendour, glimmer, brilliance, brightness, radiance, luminosity ≠ dullness ● VERB 1 = <u>shine</u>, burn, gleam, brighten, glimmer, smoulder 2 = be pink

glowing 1 = <u>complimentary</u>, enthusiastic, rave (informal), ecstatic, rhapsodic, laudatory, adulatory ≠ scathing 2 = aglow, bright, radiant ≠ pale

glue NOUN = <u>adhesive</u>, cement, gum, paste ● VERB = <u>stick</u>, fix, seal, cement, gum, paste, affix

go VERB 1 = <u>move</u>, travel, advance, journey, proceed, pass, set off

≠ stay 2 = <u>leave</u>, withdraw, depart, move out, slope off, make tracks 3 = <u>elapse</u>, pass, flow, fly by, expire, lapse, slip away 4 = <u>be given</u>, be spent, be awarded, be allotted 5 = <u>function</u>, work, run, move, operate, perform ≠ fail 6 = <u>match</u>, blend, correspond, fit, suit, chime, harmonize 7 = <u>serve</u>, help, tend ● NOUN 1 = <u>attempt</u>, try, effort, bid, shot (informal), crack (informal) 2 = <u>turn</u>, shot (informal), stint 3 (informal) = <u>energy</u>, life, drive, spirit, vitality, vigour, verve, force ● PHRASES **go off** 1 = <u>depart</u>, leave, quit, go away, move out, decamp, slope off 2 = <u>explode</u>, fire, blow up, detonate, come about 3 (informal) = <u>go bad</u>, turn, spoil, rot, go stale ◆ **go out** 1 = <u>see someone</u>, court, date (informal, chiefly U.S.), woo, go steady (informal), be romantically involved with 2 = <u>be extinguished</u>, die out, fade out ◆ **go through something** 1 = <u>suffer</u>, experience, bear, endure, brave, undergo, tolerate, withstand 2 = <u>search</u>, look through, rummage through, rifle through, hunt through, fossick through (Austral. & N.Z.), ferret about in 3 = <u>examine</u>, check, search, explore, look through

goal = <u>aim</u>, end, target, purpose, object, intention, objective, ambition

god = <u>deity</u>, immortal, divinity, divine being, supreme being, atua (*N.Z.*)

> **gods and goddesses**

godly = <u>devout</u>, religious, holy, righteous, pious, good, saintly, god-fearing

gogga (*S. African*) = <u>insect</u>, bug, creepy-crawly (*Brit. informal*)

golden 1 = <u>yellow</u>, blonde, blond, flaxen ≠ dark
2 = <u>successful</u>, glorious, prosperous, rich, flourishing, halcyon ≠ worst **3** = <u>promising</u>, excellent, favourable, opportune ≠ unfavourable

> **shades of orange**
> **shades of yellow**

gone 1 = <u>missing</u>, lost, away, vanished, absent, astray **2** = <u>past</u>, over, ended, finished, elapsed

good ADJECTIVE **1** = <u>excellent</u>, great, fine, pleasing, acceptable, first-class, splendid, satisfactory, booshit (*Austral. slang*), sik (*Austral. slang*) ≠ bad **2** = <u>proficient</u>, able, skilled, expert, talented, clever, accomplished, first-class ≠ bad **3** = <u>beneficial</u>, useful, helpful, favourable, wholesome, advantageous ≠ harmful **4** = <u>honourable</u>, moral, worthy, ethical, upright, admirable, honest, righteous ≠ bad **5** = <u>well-behaved</u>, polite, orderly,

obedient, dutiful, well-mannered ≠ naughty **6** = <u>kind</u>, kindly, friendly, obliging, charitable, humane, benevolent, merciful ≠ unkind **7** = <u>true</u>, real, genuine, proper, dinkum (*Austral. & N.Z. informal*) **8** = <u>full</u>, complete, extensive ≠ scant **9** = <u>considerable</u>, large, substantial, sufficient, adequate, ample **10** = <u>valid</u>, convincing, compelling, legitimate, authentic, persuasive, bona fide ≠ invalid **11** = <u>convenient</u>, timely, fitting, appropriate, suitable ≠ inconvenient

● NOUN **1** = <u>benefit</u>, interest, gain, advantage, use, profit, welfare, usefulness ≠ disadvantage **2** = <u>virtue</u>, goodness, righteousness, worth, merit, excellence, morality, rectitude ≠ evil

● PHRASES **for good** = <u>permanently</u>, finally, for ever, once and for all, irrevocably

goodbye NOUN = <u>farewell</u>, parting, leave-taking ● INTERJECTION = <u>farewell</u>, see you, see you later, ciao (*Italian*), cheerio, adieu, ta-ta, au revoir (*French*), haere ra (*N.Z.*)

goodness 1 = <u>virtue</u>, honour, merit, integrity, morality, honesty, righteousness, probity ≠ badness **2** = <u>excellence</u>, value, quality, worth, merit, superiority

Gods and goddesses

Greek

Aeolus	winds	Hephaestus	fire and metalworking
Aphrodite	love and beauty	Hera	queen of the gods
Apollo	light, youth, and music	Hermes	messenger of the gods
Ares	war	Horae *or the Hours*	seasons
Artemis	hunting and the moon	Hymen	marriage
Asclepius	healing	Hyperion	sun
Athene *or Pallas Athene*	wisdom	Hypnos	sleep
Bacchus	wine	Iris	rainbow
Boreas	north wind	Momus	blame and mockery
Cronos	fertility of the earth	Morpheus	sleep and dreams
Demeter	agriculture	Nemesis	vengeance
Dionysus	wine	Nike	victory
Eos	dawn	Pan	woods and shepherds
Eros	love		
Fates	destiny	Poseidon	sea and earthquakes
Gaea *or Gaia*	the earth		
Graces	charm and beauty	Rhea	fertility
		Selene	moon
Hades	underworld	Uranus	sky
Hebe	youth and spring	Zephyrus	west wind
Hecate	underworld	Zeus	king of the gods
Helios	sun		

Roman

Aesculapius	medicine	Cupid	love
Apollo	light, youth, and music	Cybele	nature
		Diana	hunting and the moon
Aurora	dawn		
Bacchus	wine	Faunus	forests
Bellona	war	Flora	flowers
Bona Dea	fertility	Janus	doors and beginnings
Ceres	agriculture		

Roman *(continued)*			
Juno	queen of the gods	Pluto	underworld
Jupiter *or* Jove	king of the gods	Quirinus	war
Lares	household	Saturn	agriculture and
Luna	moon		vegetation
Mars	war	Sol	sun
Mercury	messenger of the gods	Somnus	sleep
		Trivia	crossroads
Minerva	wisdom	Venus	love
Neptune	sea	Victoria	victory
Penates	storeroom	Vulcan	fire and
Phoebus	sun		metalworking

3 = <u>nutrition</u>, benefit, advantage, wholesomeness, salubriousness
4 = <u>kindness</u>, charity, humanity, goodwill, mercy, compassion, generosity, friendliness
goods 1 = <u>merchandise</u>, stock, products, stuff, commodities, wares **2** = <u>property</u>, things, effects, gear, possessions, belongings, trappings, paraphernalia
goodwill = <u>friendliness</u>, friendship, benevolence, amity, kindliness
gore[1] = <u>blood</u>, slaughter, bloodshed, carnage, butchery
gore[2] = <u>pierce</u>, wound, transfix, impale
gorge NOUN = <u>ravine</u>, canyon, pass, chasm, cleft, fissure, defile, gulch
 ● VERB **1** = <u>overeat</u>, devour, gobble, wolf, gulp, guzzle

2 *usually reflexive* = <u>stuff</u>, feed, cram, glut
gorgeous 1 = <u>magnificent</u>, beautiful, superb, spectacular, splendid, dazzling, sumptuous ≠ shabby **2** = <u>delightful</u>, good, great, wonderful, excellent, lovely, fantastic, pleasant ≠ awful **3** (*Informal*) = <u>beautiful</u>, lovely, stunning (*informal*), elegant, handsome, exquisite, ravishing ≠ ugly
gospel 1 = <u>doctrine</u>, news, teachings, message, revelation, creed, credo, tidings **2** = <u>truth</u>, fact, certainty, the last word
gossip NOUN **1** = <u>idle talk</u>, scandal, hearsay, tittle-tattle, small talk, chitchat, blether, chinwag (*Brit. informal*) **2** = <u>busybody</u>, chatterbox (*informal*), chatterer, scandalmonger, gossipmonger
 ● VERB = <u>chat</u>, chatter, jaw (*slang*),

blether

gourmet = <u>connoisseur</u>, foodie (*informal*), bon vivant (*French*), epicure, gastronome

govern 1 = <u>rule</u>, lead, control, command, manage, direct, guide, handle **2** = <u>restrain</u>, control, check, master, discipline, regulate, curb, tame

government 1 = <u>administration</u>, executive, ministry, regime, powers-that-be **2** = <u>rule</u>, authority, administration, sovereignty, governance, statecraft

governor = <u>leader</u>, administrator, ruler, head, director, manager, chief, executive, baas (*S. African*)

gown = <u>dress</u>, costume, garment, robe, frock, garb, habit

grab = <u>snatch</u>, catch, seize, capture, grip, grasp, clutch, snap up

grace NOUN **1** = <u>elegance</u>, poise, ease, polish, refinement, fluency, suppleness, gracefulness ≠ ungainliness **2** = <u>manners</u>, decency, etiquette, consideration, propriety, tact, decorum ≠ bad manners **3** = <u>indulgence</u>, mercy, pardon, reprieve **4** = <u>benevolence</u>, favour, goodness, goodwill, generosity, kindness, kindliness ≠ ill will **5** = <u>prayer</u>, thanks, blessing, thanksgiving, benediction

6 = <u>favour</u>, regard, respect, approval, approbation, good opinion ≠ disfavour
● VERB **1** = <u>adorn</u>, enhance, decorate, enrich, set off, ornament, embellish **2** = <u>honour</u>, favour, dignify ≠ insult

graceful 1 = <u>elegant</u>, easy, pleasing, beautiful ≠ inelegant **2** = <u>polite</u>, mannerly, charming, gracious, civil, courteous, well-mannered

gracious = <u>courteous</u>, polite, civil, accommodating, kind, friendly, cordial, well-mannered ≠ ungracious

grade VERB = <u>classify</u>, rate, order, class, group, sort, range, rank
● NOUN **1** = <u>class</u> **2** degree **3** = <u>level</u>, rank, group, class, stage, category, echelon

gradual = <u>steady</u>, slow, regular, gentle, progressive, piecemeal, unhurried ≠ sudden

gradually = <u>steadily</u>, slowly, progressively, gently, step by step, little by little, by degrees, unhurriedly

graduate 1 = <u>mark off</u>, grade, proportion, regulate, gauge, calibrate, measure out **2** = <u>classify</u>, rank, grade, group, order, sort, arrange

graft NOUN **1** = <u>shoot</u>, bud, implant, sprout, splice, scion **2** (*Informal*) = <u>labour</u>, work, effort, struggle, sweat, toil, slog, exertion

● VERB 1 = <u>join</u>, insert, transplant, implant, splice, affix 2 = <u>work</u>, labour, struggle, sweat (informal), slave, strive, toil

grain 1 = <u>seed</u>, kernel, grist 2 = <u>cereal</u>, corn 3 = <u>bit</u>, piece, trace, scrap, particle, fragment, speck, morsel 4 = <u>texture</u>, pattern, surface, fibre, weave, nap

grand 1 = <u>impressive</u>, great, large, magnificent, imposing, splendid, regal, stately ≠ unimposing 2 = <u>ambitious</u>, great, grandiose 3 = <u>superior</u>, great, dignified, stately 4 = <u>excellent</u>, great (informal), fine, wonderful, outstanding, smashing (informal), first-class, splendid ≠ bad

grandeur = <u>splendour</u>, glory, majesty, nobility, pomp, magnificence, sumptuousness, sublimity

grant NOUN = <u>award</u>, allowance, donation, endowment, gift, subsidy, hand-out
● VERB 1 = <u>give</u>, allow, present, award, permit, assign, allocate, hand out 2 = <u>accept</u>, allow, admit, acknowledge, concede

graphic 1 = <u>vivid</u>, clear, detailed, striking, explicit, expressive ≠ vague 2 = <u>pictorial</u>, visual, diagrammatic ≠ impressionistic

grapple 1 = <u>deal</u>, tackle, struggle, take on, confront, get to grips with, address yourself to

2 = <u>struggle</u>, fight, combat, wrestle, battle, clash, tussle, scuffle

grasp VERB 1 = <u>grip</u>, hold, catch, grab, seize, snatch, clutch, clinch 2 = <u>understand</u>, realize, take in, get, see, catch on, comprehend, catch or get the drift of
● NOUN 1 = <u>grip</u>, hold, possession, embrace, clutches, clasp 2 = <u>understanding</u>, knowledge, grip, awareness, mastery, comprehension 3 = <u>reach</u>, power, control, scope

grasping = <u>greedy</u>, acquisitive, rapacious, avaricious, covetous, snoep (S. African informal) ≠ generous

grate 1 = <u>shred</u>, mince, pulverize 2 = <u>scrape</u>, grind, rub, scratch, creak, rasp

grateful = <u>thankful</u>, obliged, in (someone's) debt, indebted, appreciative, beholden

grating[1] = <u>grille</u>, grid, grate, lattice, trellis, gridiron

grating[2] = <u>irritating</u>, harsh, annoying, jarring, unpleasant, raucous, strident, discordant ≠ pleasing

gratitude = <u>thankfulness</u>, thanks, recognition, obligation, appreciation, indebtedness, gratefulness ≠ ingratitude

grave[1] = <u>tomb</u>, vault, crypt, mausoleum, sepulchre, pit, burying place

grave² 1 = <u>serious</u>, important, critical, pressing, threatening, dangerous, acute, severe ≠ trifling 2 = <u>solemn</u>, sober, sombre, dour, unsmiling ≠ carefree

graveyard = <u>cemetery</u>, churchyard, burial ground, charnel house, necropolis

gravity 1 = <u>seriousness</u>, importance, significance, urgency, severity, acuteness, weightiness, momentousness ≠ triviality 2 = <u>solemnity</u>, seriousness, gravitas ≠ frivolity

graze¹ = <u>feed</u>, crop, browse, pasture

graze² VERB 1 = <u>scratch</u>, skin, scrape, chafe, abrade 2 = <u>touch</u>, brush, rub, scrape, shave, skim, glance off
● NOUN = <u>scratch</u>, scrape, abrasion

greasy = <u>fatty</u>, slippery, oily, slimy, oleaginous

great 1 = <u>large</u>, big, huge, vast, enormous, immense, gigantic, prodigious ≠ small 2 = <u>important</u>, serious, significant, critical, crucial, momentous ≠ unimportant 3 = <u>famous</u>, outstanding, remarkable, prominent, renowned, eminent, illustrious, noteworthy 4 (Informal) = <u>excellent</u>, fine, wonderful, superb, fantastic (informal), tremendous (informal), marvellous (informal), terrific (informal), booshit

(Austral. slang), exo (Austral. slang), sik (Austral. slang) ≠ poor 5 = <u>very</u>, really, extremely, exceedingly

greatly = <u>very much</u>, hugely, vastly, considerably, remarkably, enormously, immensely, tremendously

greatness 1 = <u>grandeur</u>, glory, majesty, splendour, pomp, magnificence 2 = <u>fame</u>, glory, celebrity, distinction, eminence, note, renown, illustriousness

greed or **greediness** 1 = <u>gluttony</u>, voracity 2 = <u>avarice</u>, longing, desire, hunger, craving, selfishness, acquisitiveness, covetousness ≠ generosity

greedy 1 = <u>gluttonous</u>, insatiable, voracious, ravenous, piggish 2 = <u>avaricious</u>, grasping, selfish, insatiable, acquisitive, rapacious, materialistic, desirous ≠ generous

green ADJECTIVE 1 = <u>verdant</u>, leafy, grassy 2 = <u>ecological</u>, conservationist, environment-friendly, ozone-friendly, non-polluting 3 = <u>inexperienced</u>, new, raw, naive, immature, gullible, untrained, wet behind the ears (informal) 4 = <u>jealous</u>, grudging, resentful, envious, covetous
● NOUN = <u>lawn</u>, common, turf, sward
➤ **shades of green**

greet 1 = <u>salute</u>, hail, say hello to,

Shades of green			
apple green	emerald green	Lincoln green	pea green
aquamarine	jade	Nile green	pistachio
avocado	lime green	olive	sea green

address, accost **2** = <u>welcome</u>, meet, receive, karanga (*N.Z.*), mihi (*N.Z.*) **3** = <u>receive</u>, take, respond to, react to

greeting = <u>welcome</u>, reception, salute, address, salutation, hongi (*N.Z.*)

grey 1 = <u>dull</u>, dark, dim, gloomy, drab **2** = <u>boring</u>, dull, anonymous, faceless, colourless, nondescript, characterless **3** = <u>pale</u>, wan, pallid, ashen **4** = <u>ambiguous</u>, uncertain, neutral, unclear, debatable
➤ **shades from black to white**

grief = <u>sadness</u>, suffering, regret, distress, misery, sorrow, woe, anguish ≠ joy

grievance = <u>complaint</u>, gripe (*informal*), axe to grind

grieve 1 = <u>mourn</u>, suffer, weep, lament **2** = <u>sadden</u>, hurt, injure, distress, wound, pain, afflict, upset ≠ gladden

grim = <u>terrible</u>, severe, harsh, forbidding, formidable, sinister

grind VERB **1** = <u>crush</u>, mill, powder, grate, pulverize, pound, abrade, granulate **2** = <u>press</u>, push, crush, jam, mash, force down **3** = <u>grate</u>, scrape, gnash

4 = <u>sharpen</u>, polish, sand, smooth, whet
● NOUN = <u>hard work</u> (*Informal*), labour, sweat (*informal*), chore, toil, drudgery

grip VERB **1** = <u>grasp</u>, hold, catch, seize, clutch, clasp, take hold of **2** = <u>engross</u>, fascinate, absorb, entrance, hold, compel, rivet, enthral
● NOUN **1** = <u>clasp</u>, hold, grasp **2** = <u>control</u>, rule, influence, command, power, possession, domination, mastery **3** = <u>hold</u>, purchase, friction, traction **4** = <u>understanding</u>, sense, command, awareness, grasp, appreciation, mastery, comprehension

gripping = <u>fascinating</u>, exciting, thrilling, entrancing, compelling, riveting, enthralling, engrossing

grit NOUN **1** = <u>gravel</u>, sand, dust, pebbles **2** = <u>courage</u>, spirit, resolution, determination, guts (*informal*), backbone, fortitude, tenacity
● VERB = <u>clench</u>, grind, grate, gnash

gritty 1 = <u>rough</u>, sandy, dusty, rasping, gravelly, granular

2 = courageous, dogged, determined, spirited, brave, resolute, tenacious, plucky

groan VERB **1** = moan, cry, sigh **2** (Informal) = complain, object, moan, grumble, gripe (informal), carp, lament, whine

● NOUN **1** = moan, cry, sigh, whine **2** (Informal) = complaint, protest, objection, grumble, grouse, gripe (informal)

groom NOUN **1** = stableman, stableboy, hostler or ostler (archaic) **2** = newly-wed, husband, bridegroom, marriage partner

● VERB **1** = brush, clean, tend, rub down, curry **2** = smarten up, clean, tidy, preen, spruce up, primp **3** = train, prime, prepare, coach, ready, educate, drill, nurture

groove = indentation, cut, hollow, channel, trench, flute, trough, furrow

grope = feel, search, fumble, flounder, fish, scrabble, cast about, fossick (Austral. & N.Z.)

gross ADJECTIVE **1** = flagrant, blatant, rank, sheer, utter, grievous, heinous, unmitigated ≠ qualified **2** = vulgar, offensive, crude, obscene, coarse, indelicate ≠ decent **3** = fat, obese, overweight, hulking, corpulent ≠ slim **4** = total, whole, entire, aggregate, before tax, before

deductions ≠ net

● VERB = earn, make, take, bring in, rake in (informal)

grotesque 1 = unnatural, bizarre, strange, fantastic, distorted, deformed, outlandish, freakish ≠ natural **2** = absurd, preposterous ≠ natural

ground NOUN **1** = earth, land, dry land, terra firma **2** = arena, pitch, stadium, park (informal), field, enclosure

● PLURAL NOUN **1** = estate, land, fields, gardens, territory **2** = reason, cause, basis, occasion, foundation, excuse, motive, justification **3** = dregs, lees, deposit, sediment

● VERB **1** = base, found, establish, set, settle, fix **2** = instruct, train, teach, initiate, tutor, acquaint with, familiarize with

group NOUN **1** = crowd, party, band, pack, gang, bunch

● VERB = arrange, order, sort, class, classify, marshal, bracket

grove = wood, plantation, covert, thicket, copse, coppice, spinney

grow 1 = develop, get bigger ≠ shrink **2** = get bigger, spread, swell, stretch, expand, enlarge, multiply **3** = cultivate, produce, raise, farm, breed, nurture, propagate **4** = become, get, turn, come to be **5** = originate, spring, arise, stem, issue **6** = improve, advance, progress, succeed, thrive, flourish, prosper

grown-up NOUN = <u>adult</u>, man, woman

• ADJECTIVE = <u>mature</u>, adult, of age, fully-grown

growth 1 = <u>increase</u>, development, expansion, proliferation, enlargement, multiplication ≠ decline

2 = <u>progress</u>, success, improvement, expansion, advance, prosperity ≠ failure

3 (*Medical*) = <u>tumour</u>, cancer, swelling, lump, carcinoma (*Pathology*), sarcoma (*Medical*)

grudge NOUN = <u>resentment</u>, bitterness, grievance, dislike, animosity, antipathy, enmity, rancour ≠ goodwill

• VERB = <u>resent</u>, mind, envy, covet, begrudge ≠ welcome

gruelling = <u>exhausting</u>, demanding, tiring, taxing, severe, punishing, strenuous, arduous ≠ easy

gruesome = <u>horrific</u>, shocking, terrible, horrible, grim, ghastly, grisly, macabre ≠ pleasant

grumble VERB 1 = <u>complain</u>, moan, gripe (*informal*), whinge (*informal*), carp, whine, grouse, bleat 2 = <u>rumble</u>, growl, gurgle

• NOUN 1 = <u>complaint</u>, protest, objection, moan, grievance, grouse, gripe (*informal*), grouch (*informal*) 2 = <u>rumble</u>, growl, gurgle

guarantee VERB 1 = <u>ensure</u>, secure, assure, warrant, make certain 2 = <u>promise</u>, pledge, undertake

• NOUN 1 = <u>promise</u>, pledge, assurance, certainty, word of honour 2 = <u>warranty</u>, contract, bond

guard VERB = <u>protect</u>, defend, secure, mind, preserve, shield, safeguard, watch over

• NOUN 1 = <u>sentry</u>, warder, warden, custodian, watch, lookout, watchman, sentinel 2 = <u>shield</u>, security, defence, screen, protection, safeguard, buffer

guarded = <u>cautious</u>, reserved, careful, suspicious, wary, prudent, reticent, circumspect

guardian = <u>keeper</u>, champion, defender, guard, warden, curator, protector, custodian

guerrilla = <u>freedom fighter</u>, partisan, underground fighter

guess VERB 1 = <u>estimate</u>, predict, work out, speculate, conjecture, postulate, hypothesize ≠ know 2 = <u>suppose</u>, think, believe, suspect, judge, imagine, reckon, fancy

• NOUN 1 = <u>estimate</u>, speculation, judgment, hypothesis, conjecture, shot in the dark ≠ certainty 2 = <u>supposition</u>, idea, theory, hypothesis

guest = <u>visitor</u>, company, caller,

manu(w)hiri (*N.Z.*)

guidance = <u>advice</u>, direction, leadership, instruction, help, management, teaching, counselling

guide NOUN 1 = <u>handbook</u>, manual, guidebook, instructions, catalogue 2 = <u>directory</u>, street map 3 = <u>escort</u>, leader, usher 4 = <u>pointer</u>, sign, landmark, marker, beacon, signpost, guiding light, lodestar 5 = <u>model</u>, example, standard, ideal, inspiration, paradigm
● VERB 1 = <u>lead</u>, direct, escort, conduct, accompany, shepherd, usher, show the way 2 = <u>steer</u>, control, manage, direct, handle, command, manoeuvre 3 = <u>supervise</u>, train, teach, influence, advise, counsel, instruct, oversee

guild = <u>society</u>, union, league, association, company, club, order, organization

guilt 1 = <u>shame</u>, regret, remorse, contrition, guilty conscience, self-reproach ≠ pride 2 = <u>culpability</u>, blame, responsibility, misconduct, wickedness, sinfulness, guiltiness ≠ innocence

guilty 1 = <u>ashamed</u>, sorry, rueful, sheepish, contrite, remorseful, regretful, shamefaced ≠ proud 2 = <u>culpable</u>, responsible, to blame, offending, erring, at fault, reprehensible, blameworthy

≠ innocent

guise 1 = <u>form</u>, appearance, shape, aspect, mode, semblance 2 = <u>pretence</u>, disguise, aspect, semblance

gulf 1 = <u>bay</u>, bight, sea inlet 2 = <u>chasm</u>, opening, split, gap, separation, void, rift, abyss

gum NOUN = <u>glue</u>, adhesive, resin, cement, paste
● VERB = <u>stick</u>, glue, affix, cement, paste

gun = <u>firearm</u>, shooter (*slang*), piece (*slang*), handgun

gunman = <u>armed man</u>, gunslinger (*U.S. slang*)

guru 1 = <u>authority</u>, expert, leader, master, pundit, Svengali, fundi (*S. African*) 2 = <u>teacher</u>, mentor, sage, master, tutor

gush VERB 1 = <u>flow</u>, run, rush, flood, pour, stream, cascade, spurt 2 = <u>enthuse</u>, rave, spout, overstate, effuse
● NOUN = <u>stream</u>, flow, rush, flood, jet, cascade, torrent, spurt

gut NOUN = <u>paunch</u> (*Informal*), belly, spare tyre (*Brit. slang*), potbelly, puku (*N.Z.*)
● PLURAL NOUN 1 = <u>intestines</u>, insides (*informal*), stomach, belly, bowels, innards (*informal*), entrails 2 (*Informal*) = <u>courage</u>, spirit, nerve, daring, pluck, backbone, bottle (*slang*), audacity
● VERB 1 = <u>disembowel</u>, clean 2 = <u>ravage</u>, empty, clean out,

despoil

• **ADJECTIVE** = <u>instinctive</u>, natural, basic, spontaneous, intuitive, involuntary, heartfelt, unthinking

gutter = <u>drain</u>, channel, ditch, trench, trough, conduit, sluice

guy (*Informal*) = <u>man</u>, person, fellow, lad, bloke (*Brit. informal*), chap

Gypsy or **Gipsy** = <u>traveller</u>, roamer, wanderer, Bohemian, rover, rambler, nomad, Romany

H

habit 1 = <u>mannerism</u>, custom, way, practice, characteristic, tendency, quirk, propensity 2 = <u>addiction</u>, dependence, compulsion

hack¹ = <u>cut</u>, chop, slash, mutilate, mangle, mangulate (*Austral. slang*), hew, lacerate

hack² = <u>reporter</u>, writer, correspondent, journalist, scribbler, contributor, literary hack

hail¹ **VERB** 1 = <u>acclaim</u>, honour, acknowledge, cheer, applaud ≠ condemn 2 = <u>salute</u>, greet, address, welcome, say hello to, halloo ≠ snub 3 = <u>flag down</u>, summon, signal to, wave down

• **PHRASES hail from somewhere** = <u>come from</u>, be born in, originate in, be a native of, have your roots in

hail² **NOUN** 1 = <u>hailstones</u>, sleet, hailstorm, frozen rain 2 = <u>shower</u>, rain, storm, battery, volley, barrage, bombardment, downpour

• **VERB** 1 = <u>rain</u>, shower, pelt 2 = <u>batter</u>, rain, bombard, pelt, rain down on, beat down upon

hair = <u>locks</u>, mane, tresses, shock, mop, head of hair

hairdresser = <u>stylist</u>, barber, coiffeur or coiffeuse

hairy 1 = <u>shaggy</u>, woolly, furry, stubbly, bushy, unshaven, hirsute 2 (*Slang*) = <u>dangerous</u>, risky, unpredictable, hazardous, perilous

hale (*Old-fashioned*) = <u>healthy</u>, well, strong, sound, fit, flourishing, robust, vigorous

half NOUN = <u>fifty per cent</u>, equal part

• **ADJECTIVE** = <u>partial</u>, limited, moderate, halved

• **ADVERB** = <u>partially</u>, partly, in part

Related Words

prefixes: bi-, demi-, hemi-, semi-

halfway ADVERB = <u>midway</u>, to or in the middle

• **ADJECTIVE** = <u>midway</u>, middle, mid, central, intermediate, equidistant

hall 1 = <u>passage</u>, lobby, corridor, hallway, foyer, entry, passageway, entrance hall 2 = <u>meeting place</u>, chamber, auditorium, concert hall, assembly room

hallmark 1 = <u>trademark</u>, sure

sign, telltale sign 2 (*Brit.*) = <u>mark</u>, sign, device, stamp, seal, symbol

halt VERB 1 = <u>stop</u>, break off, stand still, wait, rest ≠ continue 2 = <u>come to an end</u>, stop, cease 3 = <u>hold back</u>, end, check, block, curb, terminate, cut short, bring to an end ≠ aid

● NOUN = <u>stop</u>, end, close, pause, standstill, stoppage ≠ continuation

halting = <u>faltering</u>, stumbling, awkward, hesitant, laboured, stammering, stuttering

halve 1 = <u>cut in half</u>, reduce by fifty per cent, decrease by fifty per cent, lessen by fifty per cent 2 = <u>split in two</u>, cut in half, bisect, divide in two, share equally, divide equally

hammer 1 = <u>hit</u>, drive, knock, beat, strike, tap, bang 2 (*Informal*) = <u>defeat</u>, beat, thrash, trounce, run rings around (*informal*), wipe the floor with (*informal*), drub

hamper = <u>hinder</u>, handicap, prevent, restrict, frustrate, hamstring, interfere with, obstruct ≠ help

hand NOUN 1 = <u>palm</u>, fist, paw (*informal*), mitt (*slang*) 2 = <u>worker</u>, employee, labourer, workman, operative, craftsman, artisan, hired man 3 = <u>round of applause</u>, clap, ovation, big hand 4 = <u>writing</u>, script, handwriting, calligraphy

● VERB = <u>give</u>, pass, hand over, present to, deliver

handbook = <u>guidebook</u>, guide, manual, instruction book

handcuff VERB = <u>shackle</u>, secure, restrain, fetter, manacle

● PLURAL NOUN = <u>shackles</u>, cuffs (*informal*), fetters, manacles

handful = <u>few</u>, sprinkling, small amount, smattering, small number ≠ a lot

handicap NOUN 1 = <u>disability</u>, defect, impairment, physical abnormality 2 = <u>disadvantage</u>, barrier, restriction, obstacle, limitation, drawback, stumbling block, impediment ≠ advantage 3 = <u>advantage</u>, head start

● VERB = <u>hinder</u>, limit, restrict, burden, hamstring, hamper, hold back, impede ≠ help

handle NOUN = <u>grip</u>, hilt, haft, stock

● VERB 1 = <u>manage</u>, deal with, tackle, cope with 2 = <u>deal with</u>, manage 3 = <u>control</u>, manage, direct, guide, manipulate, manoeuvre 4 = <u>hold</u>, feel, touch, pick up, finger, grasp

handsome 1 = <u>good-looking</u>, attractive, gorgeous, elegant, personable, dishy (*informal*, *chiefly Brit.*), comely ≠ ugly 2 = <u>generous</u>, large, princely, liberal, considerable, lavish, ample, abundant ≠ mean

handy 1 = <u>useful</u>, practical,

helpful, neat, convenient, easy to use, manageable, user-friendly ≠ useless 2 = <u>convenient</u>, close, available, nearby, accessible, on hand, at hand, within reach ≠ inconvenient 3 = <u>skilful</u>, skilled, expert, adept, deft, proficient, adroit, dexterous ≠ unskilled

hang VERB 1 = <u>dangle</u>, swing, suspend 2 = <u>lower</u>, suspend, dangle 3 = <u>lean</u> 4 = <u>execute</u>, lynch, string up (informal)

● PHRASES **get the hang of something** = <u>grasp</u>, understand, learn, master, comprehend, catch on to, acquire the technique of

♦ **hang back** = <u>be reluctant</u>, hesitate, hold back, recoil, demur

hangover = <u>aftereffects</u>, morning after (informal)

hang-up (Informal) = <u>preoccupation</u>, thing (informal), problem, block, difficulty, obsession, mania, inhibition

hank = <u>coil</u>, roll, length, bunch, piece, loop, clump, skein

happen 1 = <u>occur</u>, take place, come about, result, develop, transpire (informal), come to pass 2 = <u>chance</u>, turn out (informal)

happening = <u>event</u>, incident, experience, affair, proceeding, episode, occurrence

happily 1 = <u>luckily</u>, fortunately, providentially, opportunely 2 = <u>joyfully</u>, cheerfully, gleefully, blithely, merrily, gaily, joyously 3 = <u>willingly</u>, freely, gladly, with pleasure

happiness = <u>pleasure</u>, delight, joy, satisfaction, ecstasy, bliss, contentment, elation ≠ unhappiness

happy 1 = <u>pleased</u>, delighted, content, thrilled, glad, cheerful, merry, ecstatic 2 = <u>contented</u>, joyful, blissful ≠ sad 3 = <u>fortunate</u>, lucky, timely, favourable, auspicious, propitious, advantageous ≠ unfortunate

harass = <u>annoy</u>, trouble, bother, harry, plague, hound, hassle (informal), persecute

harassed = <u>hassled</u>, worried, troubled, strained, under pressure, tormented, distraught (informal), vexed

harassment = <u>hassle</u>, trouble, bother, irritation, persecution (informal), nuisance, annoyance, pestering

harbour NOUN = <u>port</u>, haven, dock, mooring, marina, pier, wharf, anchorage

● VERB 1 = <u>hold</u>, bear, maintain, nurse, retain, foster, entertain, nurture 2 = <u>shelter</u>, protect, hide, shield, provide refuge, give asylum to

hard ADJECTIVE 1 = <u>tough</u>, strong, firm, solid, stiff, rigid, resistant, compressed ≠ soft 2 = <u>difficult</u>, involved, complicated, puzzling,

intricate, perplexing, impenetrable, thorny ≠ easy
3 = exhausting, tough, exacting, rigorous, gruelling, strenuous, arduous, laborious ≠ easy
4 = harsh, cold, cruel, stern, callous, unkind, unsympathetic, pitiless ≠ kind **5** = grim, painful, distressing, harsh, unpleasant, intolerable, grievous, disagreeable

● ADVERB **1** = strenuously, steadily, persistently, doggedly, diligently, energetically, industriously, untiringly **2** = intently, closely, carefully, sharply, keenly
3 = forcefully, strongly, heavily, sharply, severely, fiercely, vigorously, intensely ≠ softly

harden 1 = solidify, set, freeze, cake, bake, clot, thicken, stiffen
2 = accustom, season, toughen, train, inure, habituate

hardened 1 = habitual, chronic, shameless, inveterate, incorrigible ≠ occasional **2** = seasoned, experienced, accustomed, toughened, inured, habituated ≠ naive

hardly 1 = barely, only just, scarcely, just, with difficulty, with effort ≠ completely **2** = only just, just, barely, scarcely

hardship = suffering, need, difficulty, misfortune, adversity, tribulation, privation ≠ ease

hardy = strong, tough, robust,

sound, rugged, sturdy, stout ≠ frail

hare

(Related Words)
adjective: leporine
male: buck
female: leveret
habitation: down, husk

harm VERB **1** = injure, hurt, wound, abuse, ill-treat, maltreat ≠ heal **2** = damage, hurt, ruin, spoil

● NOUN **1** = injury, suffering, damage, ill, hurt, distress
2 = damage, loss, ill, hurt, misfortune, mischief ≠ good

harmful = damaging, dangerous, negative, destructive, hazardous, unhealthy, detrimental, hurtful ≠ harmless

harmless 1 = safe, benign, wholesome, innocuous, nontoxic ≠ dangerous **2** = inoffensive, innocent, innocuous, gentle, tame, unobjectionable

harmony 1 = accord, peace, agreement, friendship, sympathy, cooperation, rapport, compatibility ≠ conflict **2** = tune, melody, unison, tunefulness, euphony ≠ discord

harness VERB = exploit, control, channel, employ, utilize, mobilize
● NOUN = equipment, tackle, gear, tack

harrowing = distressing, disturbing, painful, terrifying, traumatic, tormenting, agonizing, nerve-racking

harry = <u>pester</u>, bother, plague, harass, hassle (*informal*), badger, chivvy

harsh 1 = <u>severe</u>, hard, tough, stark, austere, inhospitable 2 = <u>bleak</u>, freezing, severe, icy 3 = <u>cruel</u>, savage, ruthless, barbarous, pitiless 4 = <u>hard</u>, severe, cruel, stern, pitiless ≠ kind 5 = <u>drastic</u>, punitive, Draconian 6 = <u>raucous</u>, rough, grating, strident, rasping, discordant, guttural, dissonant ≠ soft

harshly = <u>severely</u>, roughly, cruelly, strictly, sternly, brutally

harvest NOUN 1 = <u>harvesting</u>, picking, gathering, collecting, reaping, harvest-time 2 = <u>crop</u>, yield, year's growth, produce
● VERB = <u>gather</u>, pick, collect, bring in, pluck, reap

hassle (*Informal*) NOUN = <u>trouble</u>, problem, difficulty, bother, grief (*informal*), uphill (*S. African*), inconvenience
● VERB = <u>bother</u>, bug (*informal*), annoy, harass, badger, pester

hasten = <u>rush</u>, race, fly, speed, dash, hurry (up), scurry, make haste ≠ dawdle

hastily 1 = <u>quickly</u>, rapidly, promptly, speedily 2 = <u>hurriedly</u>, rashly, precipitately, impetuously

hatch 1 = <u>incubate</u>, breed, sit on,

brood, bring forth 2 = <u>devise</u>, design, invent, put together, conceive, brew, formulate, contrive

hate VERB 1 = <u>detest</u>, loathe, despise, dislike, abhor, recoil from, not be able to bear ≠ love 2 = <u>dislike</u>, detest, shrink from, recoil from, not be able to bear ≠ like 3 = <u>be unwilling</u>, regret, be reluctant, hesitate, be sorry, be loath, feel disinclined
● NOUN = <u>dislike</u>, hostility, hatred, loathing, animosity, aversion, antipathy, enmity ≠ love

hatred = <u>hate</u>, dislike, animosity, aversion, revulsion, antipathy, enmity, repugnance ≠ love

haul VERB = <u>drag</u>, draw, pull, heave
● NOUN = <u>yield</u>, gain, spoils, catch, harvest, loot, takings, booty

haunt VERB = <u>plague</u>, trouble, obsess, torment, possess, stay with, recur, prey on
● NOUN = <u>meeting place</u>, hangout (*informal*), rendezvous, stamping ground

haunted 1 = <u>possessed</u>, ghostly, cursed, eerie, spooky (*informal*), jinxed 2 = <u>preoccupied</u>, worried, troubled, plagued, obsessed, tormented

haunting = <u>evocative</u>, poignant, unforgettable

have VERB 1 = <u>own</u>, keep, possess, hold, retain, boast, be the owner of 2 = get, obtain, take, receive, accept, gain, secure, acquire 3 = suffer, experience, undergo, sustain, endure, be suffering from 4 = give birth to, bear, deliver, bring forth, beget 5 = experience, go through, undergo, meet with, come across, run into, be faced with

• **PHRASES have someone on** = tease, kid (informal), wind up (Brit. slang), trick, deceive, take the mickey, pull someone's leg

♦ **have something on** = wear, be wearing, be dressed in, be clothed in, be attired in ♦ **have to 1** = must, should, be forced, ought, be obliged, be bound, have got to, be compelled **2** = have got to, must

haven = sanctuary, shelter, retreat, asylum, refuge, oasis, sanctum

havoc 1 = devastation, damage, destruction, ruin **2** (Informal) = disorder, confusion, chaos, disruption, mayhem, shambles

hazard NOUN = danger, risk, threat, problem, menace, peril, jeopardy, pitfall

• **VERB** = jeopardize, risk, endanger, threaten, expose, imperil, put in jeopardy

• **PHRASES hazard a guess** = guess, conjecture, presume, take a guess

hazardous = dangerous, risky, difficult, insecure, unsafe,

precarious, perilous, dicey (informal, chiefly Brit.) ≠ safe

haze = mist, cloud, fog, obscurity, vapour

head NOUN **1** = skull, crown, pate, nut (slang), loaf (slang) **2** = mind, reasoning, understanding, thought, sense, brain, brains (informal), intelligence **3** = top, crown, summit, peak, crest, pinnacle **4** (Informal) = head teacher, principal **5** = leader, president, director, manager, chief, boss (informal), captain, master

• **ADJECTIVE** = chief, main, leading, first, prime, premier, supreme, principal

• **VERB 1** = lead, precede, be the leader of, be or go first, be or go at the front of, lead the way **2** = top, lead, crown, cap **3** = be in charge of, run, manage, lead, control, direct, guide, command

• **PHRASES go to your head 1** = intoxicate **2** = make someone conceited, puff someone up, make someone full of themselves

♦ **head over heels** = completely, thoroughly, utterly, intensely, wholeheartedly, uncontrollably

headache 1 = migraine, head (informal), neuralgia **2** = problem (Informal), worry, trouble, bother, nuisance, inconvenience, bane, vexation

heading = title, name, caption,

headline, rubric

heady 1 = <u>exciting</u>, thrilling, stimulating, exhilarating, intoxicating **2** = <u>intoxicating</u>, strong, potent, inebriating

heal ≠ *sometimes with* **up** = <u>mend</u>, get better, get well, cure, regenerate, show improvement **2** = <u>cure</u>, restore, mend, make better, remedy, make good, make well **≠** injure

health 1 = <u>condition</u>, state, shape, constitution, fettle **2** = <u>wellbeing</u>, strength, fitness, vigour, good condition, soundness, robustness, healthiness **≠** illness **3** = <u>state</u>, condition, shape

healthy 1 = <u>well</u>, fit, strong, active, robust, in good shape (*informal*), in the pink, in fine fettle **≠** ill **2** = <u>wholesome</u>, beneficial, nourishing, nutritious, salutary, hygienic, salubrious **≠** unwholesome **3** = <u>invigorating</u>, beneficial, salutary, salubrious

heap NOUN 1 = <u>pile</u>, lot, collection, mass, stack, mound, accumulation, hoard **2** *often plural* (*Informal*) = <u>a lot</u>, lots (*informal*), plenty, masses, load(s) (*informal*), great deal, tons, stack(s)
• VERB *sometimes with* **up** = <u>pile</u>, collect, gather, stack, accumulate, amass, hoard
• PHRASES **heap something on someone** = <u>load with</u>, confer on, assign to, bestow on, shower upon

hear 1 = <u>overhear</u>, catch, detect **2** = <u>listen to</u> **3** (*Law*) = <u>try</u>, judge, examine, investigate **4** = <u>learn</u>, discover, find out, pick up, gather, ascertain, get wind of (*informal*)

hearing = <u>inquiry</u>, trial, investigation, industrial tribunal

heart NOUN 1 = <u>emotions</u>, feelings, love, affection **2** = <u>nature</u>, character, soul, constitution, essence, temperament, disposition **3** = <u>root</u>, core, centre, nucleus, hub, gist, nitty-gritty (*informal*), nub **4** = <u>courage</u>, will, spirit, purpose, bottle (*Brit. informal*), resolution, resolve, stomach
• PHRASES **by heart** = <u>from</u> *or* by memory, verbatim, word for word, pat, word-perfect, by rote, off by heart, off pat
Related Words
adjective: cardiac

heat VERB *sometimes with* **up** = <u>warm (up)</u>, cook, boil, roast, reheat, make hot **≠** chill
• NOUN **1** = <u>warmth</u>, hotness, temperature **≠** cold **2** = <u>hot weather</u>, warmth, closeness, high temperature, heatwave, warm weather, hot climate, mugginess **3** = <u>passion</u>, excitement, intensity, fury, fervour, vehemence **≠** calmness
Related Words
adjective: thermal

heated 1 = <u>impassioned</u>, intense, spirited, excited, angry,

furious, fierce, lively ≠ calm
2 = wound up, worked up, keyed up, het up (informal)

heaven NOUN **1** = paradise, next world, hereafter, nirvana (Buddhism, Hinduism), bliss, Zion (Christianity), life everlasting, Elysium or Elysian fields (Greek myth) **2** (Informal) = happiness, paradise, ecstasy, bliss, utopia, rapture, seventh heaven
● PHRASES **the heavens** (Old-fashioned) = sky, ether, firmament

heavenly 1 = celestial, holy, divine, blessed, immortal, angelic ≠ earthly **2** (Informal) = wonderful, lovely, delightful, beautiful, divine (informal), exquisite, sublime, blissful ≠ awful

heavily 1 = excessively, to excess, very much, a great deal, considerably, copiously, without restraint, immoderately **2** = densely, closely, thickly, compactly **3** = hard, clumsily, awkwardly, weightily

heavy 1 = weighty, large, massive, hefty, bulky, ponderous ≠ light **2** = intensive, severe, serious, concentrated, fierce, excessive, relentless **3** = considerable, large, huge, substantial, abundant, copious, profuse ≠ slight

hectic = frantic, chaotic, heated, animated, turbulent, frenetic, feverish ≠ peaceful

hedge VERB = prevaricate, evade, sidestep, duck, dodge, flannel (Brit. informal), equivocate, temporize
● PHRASES **hedge against something** = protect against, insure against, guard against, safeguard against, shield against, cover against

heed (Formal) VERB = pay attention to, listen to, take notice of, follow, consider, note, observe, obey ≠ ignore
● NOUN = thought, care, mind, attention, regard, respect, notice ≠ disregard

heel (Slang) = swine, cad (Brit. informal), bounder (Brit. old-fashioned slang), rotter (slang, chiefly Brit.)

hefty (Informal) = big, strong, massive, strapping, robust, muscular, burly, hulking ≠ small

height 1 = tallness, stature, highness, loftiness ≠ shortness **2** = altitude, measurement, highness, elevation, tallness ≠ depth **3** = peak, top, crown, summit, crest, pinnacle, apex ≠ valley **4** = culmination, climax, zenith, limit, maximum, ultimate ≠ low point

heighten = intensify, increase, add to, improve, strengthen, enhance, sharpen, magnify

heir = successor, beneficiary, inheritor, heiress (fem.), next in line

hell 1 = the underworld, the abyss, Hades (*Greek myth*), hellfire, the inferno, fire and brimstone, the nether world, the bad fire (*informal*) 2 (*Informal*) = torment, suffering, agony, nightmare, misery, ordeal, anguish, wretchedness

hello = hi (*informal*), greetings, how do you do?, good morning, good evening, good afternoon, welcome, kia ora (*N.Z.*), gidday or g'day (*Austral. & N.Z.*)

helm (*Nautical*) = tiller, wheel, rudder

help VERB 1 *sometimes with out* = aid, support, assist, cooperate with, abet, lend a hand, succour ≠ hinder 2 = improve, ease, relieve, facilitate, alleviate, mitigate, ameliorate ≠ make worse 3 = assist, aid, support 4 = resist, refrain from, avoid, prevent, keep from
● NOUN = assistance, aid, support, advice, guidance, cooperation, helping hand ≠ hindrance

helper = assistant, ally, supporter, mate, second, aide, attendant, collaborator

helpful 1 = cooperative, accommodating, kind, friendly, neighbourly, sympathetic, supportive, considerate 2 = useful, practical, profitable, constructive 3 = beneficial, advantageous

helping = portion, serving, ration, piece, dollop (*informal*), plateful

helpless = powerless, weak, disabled, incapable, paralysed, impotent, infirm ≠ powerful

hem NOUN = edge, border, margin, trimming, fringe
● PHRASES **hem something** or **someone in** 1 = surround, confine, enclose, shut in 2 = restrict, confine, beset, circumscribe

hence = therefore, thus, consequently, for this reason, in consequence, ergo, on that account

herald VERB = indicate, promise, usher in, presage, portend, foretoken
● NOUN 1 (*Often literary*) = forerunner, sign, signal, indication, token, omen, precursor, harbinger 2 = messenger, courier, proclaimer, announcer, crier, town crier

herd = flock, crowd, collection, mass, drove, mob, swarm, horde

hereditary 1 = genetic, inborn, inbred, transmissible, inheritable 2 (*Law*) = inherited, passed down, traditional, ancestral

heritage = inheritance, legacy, birthright, tradition, endowment, bequest

hero 1 = protagonist, leading

man 2 = <u>star</u>, champion, victor, superstar, conqueror 3 = <u>idol</u>, favourite, pin-up (*slang*), fave (*informal*)

heroic = <u>courageous</u>, brave, daring, fearless, gallant, intrepid, valiant, lion-hearted ≠ cowardly

heroine 1 = <u>protagonist</u>, leading lady, diva, prima donna 2 = <u>idol</u>, favourite, pin-up (*slang*), fave (*informal*)

> ### Word Power
>
> **heroine** – Note that the word *heroine*, meaning 'a female hero', has an *e* at the end. The drug *heroin* is spelled without a final *e*.

hesitate 1 = <u>waver</u>, delay, pause, wait, doubt, falter, dither (*chiefly Brit.*), vacillate ≠ be decisive 2 = <u>be reluctant</u>, be unwilling, shrink from, think twice, scruple, demur, hang back, be disinclined ≠ be determined

hesitation = <u>reluctance</u>, reservation(s), misgiving(s), ambivalence, qualm(s), unwillingness, scruple(s), compunction

hidden 1 = <u>secret</u>, veiled, latent 2 = <u>concealed</u>, secret, covert, unseen, clandestine, secreted, under wraps

hide[1] = <u>conceal</u>, stash (*informal*), secrete, put out of

sight ≠ display 2 = <u>go into hiding</u>, take cover, keep out of sight, hole up, lie low, go underground, go to ground, go to earth 3 = <u>keep secret</u>, suppress, withhold, keep quiet about, hush up, draw a veil over, keep dark, keep under your hat ≠ disclose 4 = <u>obscure</u>, cover, mask, disguise, conceal, veil, cloak, shroud ≠ reveal

hide[2] = <u>skin</u>, leather, pelt

hideous = <u>ugly</u>, revolting, ghastly, monstrous, grotesque, gruesome, grisly, unsightly ≠ beautiful

hiding (*Informal*) = <u>beating</u>, whipping, thrashing, licking (*informal*), spanking, walloping (*informal*), drubbing

hierarchy = <u>grading</u>, ranking, social order, pecking order, class system, social stratum

high ADJECTIVE 1 = <u>tall</u>, towering, soaring, steep, elevated, lofty ≠ short 2 = <u>extreme</u>, great, acute, severe, extraordinary, excessive ≠ low 3 = <u>strong</u>, violent, blustery, squally, sharp 4 = <u>important</u>, chief, powerful, superior, eminent, exalted ≠ lowly 5 = <u>high-pitched</u>, piercing, shrill, penetrating, strident, sharp, acute, piping ≠ deep 6 (*Informal*) = <u>intoxicated</u>, stoned (*slang*), tripping (*informal*)

● ADVERB = <u>way up</u>, aloft, far up, to a great height

high-flown = <u>extravagant</u>,

elaborate, pretentious, exaggerated, inflated, lofty, grandiose, overblown ≠ straightforward

highlight VERB = <u>emphasize</u>, stress, accent, show up, underline, spotlight, accentuate, call attention to ≠ play down

● NOUN = <u>high point</u>, peak, climax, feature, focus, focal point, high spot ≠ low point

highly = <u>extremely</u>, very, greatly, vastly, exceptionally, immensely, tremendously

hijack = <u>seize</u>, take over, commandeer, expropriate

hike = <u>walk</u>, march, trek, ramble, tramp, traipse

● VERB = <u>walk</u>, march, trek, ramble, tramp, back-pack

hilarious 1 = <u>funny</u>, entertaining, amusing, hysterical, humorous, comical, side-splitting 2 = <u>merry</u>, uproarious, rollicking ≠ serious

hill = <u>mount</u>, fell, height, mound, hilltop, tor, knoll, hillock, kopje or koppie (S. African)

hinder = <u>obstruct</u>, stop, check, block, delay, frustrate, handicap, interrupt ≠ help

hint NOUN 1 = <u>clue</u>, suggestion, implication, indication, pointer, allusion, innuendo, intimation 2 often plural = <u>advice</u>, help, tip(s), suggestion(s), pointer(s) 3 = <u>trace</u>, touch, suggestion, dash,

suspicion, tinge, undertone

● VERB sometimes with **at** = <u>suggest</u>, indicate, imply, intimate, insinuate

hire VERB 1 = <u>employ</u>, commission, take on, engage, appoint, sign up, enlist 2 = <u>rent</u>, charter, lease, let, engage

● NOUN 1 = <u>rental</u>, hiring, rent, lease 2 = <u>charge</u>, rental, price, cost, fee

hiss VERB 1 = <u>whistle</u>, wheeze, whiz, whirr, sibilate 2 = <u>jeer</u>, mock, deride

● NOUN = <u>fizz</u>, buzz, hissing, fizzing, sibilation

historic = <u>significant</u>, notable, momentous, famous, extraordinary, outstanding, remarkable, groundbreaking ≠ unimportant

---

Word Power

historic – Although *historic* and *historical* are similarly spelt they are very different in meaning and should not be used interchangeably. A distinction is usually made between *historic*, which means 'important' or 'significant', and *historical*, which means 'pertaining to history': *a historic decision*; *a historical perspective*.

---

historical = <u>factual</u>, real, documented, actual, authentic, attested ≠ contemporary

➤ **historic**

history 1 = <u>the past</u>, antiquity,

yesterday, yesteryear, olden days
2 = <u>chronicle</u>, record, story,
account, narrative, recital, annals

hit VERB 1 = <u>strike</u>, beat, knock,
bang, slap, smack, thump, clout
(*informal*) 2 = <u>collide with</u>, run
into, bump into, clash with, smash
into, crash against, bang into
3 = <u>affect</u>, damage, harm, ruin,
devastate, overwhelm, touch,
impact on 4 = <u>reach</u>, gain,
achieve, arrive at, accomplish,
attain

● NOUN 1 = <u>shot</u>, blow 2 = <u>blow</u>,
knock, stroke, belt (*informal*), rap,
slap, smack, clout (*informal*)
3 = <u>success</u>, winner, triumph,
smash (*informal*), sensation

● PHRASES **hit it off** (*Informal*)
= <u>get on (well) with</u>, click (*slang*),
be on good terms, get on like a
house on fire (*informal*) ◆ **hit on**
or **upon something** = <u>think up</u>,
discover, arrive at, invent, stumble
on, light upon, strike upon

hitch NOUN = <u>problem</u>, catch,
difficulty, hold-up, obstacle,
drawback, snag, uphill (*S. African*),
impediment

● VERB 1 (*Informal*) = <u>hitchhike</u>,
thumb a lift 2 = <u>fasten</u>, join,
attach, couple, tie, connect,
harness, tether

● PHRASES **hitch something up**
= <u>pull up</u>, tug, jerk, yank

hitherto (*Formal*) = <u>previously</u>,
so far, until now, thus far,
heretofore

hobby = <u>pastime</u>, relaxation,
leisure pursuit, diversion,
avocation, (leisure) activity

hoist VERB = <u>raise</u>, lift, erect,
elevate, heave

● NOUN = <u>lift</u>, crane, elevator,
winch

hold VERB 1 = <u>embrace</u>, grasp,
clutch, hug, squeeze, cradle, clasp,
enfold 2 = <u>restrain</u> ≠ release
3 = <u>accommodate</u>, take, contain,
seat, have a capacity for
4 = <u>consider</u>, think, believe, judge,
regard, assume, reckon, deem
≠ deny 5 = <u>occupy</u>, have, fill,
maintain, retain, possess, hold
down (*informal*) 6 = <u>conduct</u>,
convene, call, run, preside over
≠ cancel 7 = <u>detain</u>, confine,
imprison, impound ≠ release

● NOUN 1 = <u>grip</u>, grasp, clasp
2 = <u>foothold</u>, footing 3 = <u>control</u>,
influence, mastery, mana (*N.Z.*)

holder 1 = <u>owner</u>, bearer,
possessor, keeper, proprietor
2 = <u>case</u>, cover, container

hold-up 1 = <u>robbery</u>, theft,
mugging (*informal*), stick-up
(*slang, chiefly U.S.*) 2 = <u>delay</u>, wait,
hitch, setback, snag, traffic jam,
stoppage, bottleneck

hole 1 = <u>cavity</u>, pit, hollow,
chamber, cave, cavern
2 = <u>opening</u>, crack, tear, gap,
breach, vent, puncture, aperture
3 = <u>burrow</u>, den, earth, shelter, lair

4 (*Informal*) = <u>hovel</u>, dump (*informal*), dive (*slang*), slum **5** (*Informal*) = <u>predicament</u>, spot (*informal*), fix (*informal*), mess, jam (*informal*), dilemma, scrape (*informal*), hot water (*informal*)

holiday 1 = <u>vacation</u>, leave, break, time off, recess **2** = <u>festival</u>, fête, celebration, feast, gala

hollow ADJECTIVE **1** = <u>empty</u>, vacant, void, unfilled ≠ solid **2** = <u>worthless</u>, useless, vain, meaningless, pointless, futile, fruitless ≠ meaningful **3** = <u>dull</u>, low, deep, muted, toneless, reverberant ≠ vibrant

● NOUN **1** = <u>cavity</u>, hole, bowl, depression, pit, basin, crater, trough ≠ mound **2** = <u>valley</u>, dale, glen, dell, dingle ≠ hill

● VERB *often followed by out* = <u>scoop out</u>, dig out, excavate, gouge out

holocaust 1 = <u>devastation</u>, destruction, genocide, annihilation, conflagration **2** = <u>genocide</u>, massacre, annihilation

holy 1 = <u>sacred</u>, blessed, hallowed, venerable, consecrated, sacrosanct, sanctified ≠ unsanctified **2** = <u>devout</u>, godly, religious, pure, righteous, pious, virtuous, saintly ≠ sinful

homage = <u>respect</u>, honour, worship, devotion, reverence, deference, adulation, adoration ≠ contempt

home NOUN **1** = <u>dwelling</u>, house, residence, abode, habitation, pad (*slang*), domicile **2** = <u>birthplace</u>, homeland, home town, native land

● ADJECTIVE **1** = <u>domestic</u>, local, internal, native

● PHRASES **at home 1** = <u>in</u>, present, available **2** = <u>at ease</u>, relaxed, comfortable, content, at peace ◆ **bring something home to someone** = <u>make clear</u>, emphasize, drive home, press home, impress upon

homeland = <u>native land</u>, birthplace, motherland, fatherland, country of origin, mother country

homeless = <u>destitute</u>, displaced, dispossessed, down-and-out

homely 1 = <u>comfortable</u>, welcoming, friendly, cosy, homespun **2** = <u>plain</u>, simple, ordinary, modest ≠ elaborate

homicide = <u>murder</u>, killing, manslaughter, slaying, bloodshed

hone 1 = <u>improve</u>, better, enhance, upgrade, refine, sharpen, help **2** = <u>sharpen</u>, point, grind, edge, file, polish, whet

---

Word Power

hone – *Hone* is sometimes wrongly used where *home* is meant: *this device makes it easier to home in on* (not *hone in on*) *the target.*

honest 1 = <u>trustworthy</u>, upright, ethical, honourable, reputable, truthful, virtuous, law-abiding ≠ dishonest 2 = <u>open</u>, direct, frank, plain, sincere, candid, forthright, upfront (informal) ≠ secretive

honestly 1 = <u>ethically</u>, legally, lawfully, honourably, by fair means 2 = <u>frankly</u>, plainly, candidly, straight (out), truthfully, to your face, in all sincerity

honesty 1 = <u>integrity</u>, honour, virtue, morality, probity, rectitude, truthfulness, trustworthiness 2 = <u>frankness</u>, openness, sincerity, candour, bluntness, outspokenness, straightforwardness

honorary = <u>nominal</u>, unofficial, titular, in name or title only

honour NOUN 1 = <u>integrity</u>, morality, honesty, goodness, fairness, decency, probity, rectitude ≠ dishonour 2 = <u>prestige</u>, credit, reputation, glory, fame, distinction, dignity, renown ≠ disgrace 3 = <u>reputation</u>, standing, prestige, image, status, stature, good name, cachet ≠ disgrace 4 = <u>acclaim</u>, praise, recognition, compliments, homage, accolades, commendation ≠ contempt 5 = <u>privilege</u>, credit, pleasure, compliment ● VERB 1 = <u>acclaim</u>, praise, decorate, commemorate, commend 2 = <u>respect</u>, value, esteem, prize, appreciate, adore ≠ scorn 3 = <u>fulfil</u>, keep, carry out, observe, discharge, live up to, be true to 4 = <u>pay</u>, take, accept, pass, acknowledge ≠ refuse

honourable 1 = <u>principled</u>, moral, ethical, fair, upright, honest, virtuous, trustworthy 2 = <u>proper</u>, respectable, virtuous, creditable

hook NOUN = <u>fastener</u>, catch, link, peg, clasp ● VERB 1 = <u>fasten</u>, fix, secure, clasp 2 = <u>catch</u>, land, trap, entrap

hooked 1 = <u>bent</u>, curved, aquiline, hook-shaped 2 (Informal) = <u>obsessed</u>, addicted, taken, devoted, turned on (slang), enamoured 3 (Informal) = <u>addicted</u>, dependent, using (informal), having a habit

hooligan = <u>delinquent</u>, vandal, hoon (Austral. & N.Z.), ruffian, lager lout, yob or yobbo (Brit. slang), cougan (Austral. slang), scozza (Austral. slang), bogan (Austral. slang)

hoop = <u>ring</u>, band, loop, wheel, round, girdle, circlet

hop VERB = <u>jump</u>, spring, bound, leap, skip, vault, caper ● NOUN = <u>jump</u>, step, spring, bound, leap, bounce, skip, vault

hope VERB = <u>believe</u>, look forward to, cross your fingers ● NOUN = <u>belief</u>, confidence, expectation, longing, dream, desire, ambition, assumption ≠ despair

hopeful 1 = <u>optimistic</u>, confident, looking forward to, buoyant, sanguine, expectant ≠ despairing
2 = <u>promising</u>, encouraging, bright, reassuring, rosy, heartening, auspicious ≠ unpromising

hopefully = <u>optimistically</u>, confidently, expectantly, with anticipation

> ### Word Power
> **hopefully** –Some people object to the use of *hopefully* as a synonym for the phrase 'it is hoped that' in a sentence such as *hopefully I'll be able to attend the meeting.* This use of the adverb first appeared in America in the 1960s, but it has rapidly established itself elsewhere. There are really no strong grounds for objecting to it, since we accept other sentence adverbials that fulfil a similar function, for example *unfortunately,* which means 'it is unfortunate that' in a sentence such as *unfortunately I won't be able to attend the meeting.*

hopeless = <u>impossible</u>, pointless, futile, useless, vain, no-win, unattainable

horde = <u>crowd</u>, mob, swarm, host, band, pack, drove, gang

horizon = <u>skyline</u>, view, vista

horizontal = <u>level</u>, flat, parallel

horrible 1 (*Informal*) = <u>dreadful</u>, terrible, awful, nasty, cruel, mean, unpleasant, horrid ≠ wonderful
2 = <u>terrible</u>, appalling, terrifying, shocking, grim, dreadful, revolting, ghastly

horrific = <u>horrifying</u>, shocking, appalling, awful, terrifying, dreadful, horrendous, ghastly

horrify 1 = <u>terrify</u>, alarm, frighten, scare, intimidate, petrify, make your hair stand on end ≠ comfort 2 = <u>shock</u>, appal, dismay, sicken, outrage ≠ delight

horror 1 = <u>terror</u>, fear, alarm, panic, dread, fright, consternation, trepidation
2 = <u>hatred</u>, disgust, loathing, aversion, revulsion, repugnance, odium, detestation ≠ love

horse = <u>nag</u>, mount, mare, colt, filly, stallion, steed (*archaic or literary*), moke (*Austral. slang*), yarraman *or* yarramin (*Austral.*), gee-gee (*slang*)

(I) **Related Words**
adjectives: equestrian, equine
male: stallion
female: mare
young: foal, colt, filly

hospitality = <u>welcome</u>, warmth, kindness, friendliness, sociability, conviviality, neighbourliness, cordiality

host[1] *or* **hostess** NOUN
1 = <u>master of ceremonies</u>, proprietor, innkeeper, landlord *or*

landlady 2 = <u>presenter</u>, compere
(*Brit.*), anchorman *or* anchorwoman
● VERB = <u>present</u>, introduce,
compere (*Brit.*), front (*informal*)

host² 1 = <u>multitude</u>, lot, load
(*informal*), wealth, array, myriad,
great quantity, large number
2 = <u>crowd</u>, army, pack, drove,
mob, herd, legion, swarm

hostage = <u>captive</u>, prisoner, pawn

hostile 1 = <u>antagonistic</u>,
opposed, contrary, ill-disposed
2 = <u>unfriendly</u>, belligerent,
antagonistic, rancorous, ill-
disposed ≠ friendly
3 = <u>inhospitable</u>, adverse,
uncongenial, unsympathetic,
unwelcoming ≠ hospitable

hostility NOUN
1 = <u>unfriendliness</u>, hatred,
animosity, spite, bitterness,
malice, venom, enmity
≠ friendliness 2 = <u>opposition</u>,
resentment, antipathy, aversion,
antagonism, ill feeling, ill-will,
animus ≠ approval
● PLURAL NOUN = <u>warfare</u>, war,
fighting, conflict, combat, armed
conflict ≠ peace

hot 1 = <u>heated</u>, boiling, steaming,
roasting, searing, scorching,
scalding 2 = <u>warm</u>, close, stifling,
humid, torrid, sultry, sweltering,
balmy ≠ cold 3 = <u>spicy</u>, pungent,
peppery, piquant, biting, sharp
≠ mild 4 = <u>intense</u>, passionate,
heated, spirited, fierce, lively,

animated, ardent 5 = <u>new</u>, latest,
fresh, recent, up to date, just out,
up to the minute, bang up to
date (*informal*) ≠ old 6 = <u>popular</u>,
hip, fashionable, cool, in demand,
sought-after, must-see, in vogue
≠ unpopular 7 = <u>fierce</u>, intense,
strong, keen, competitive, cut-
throat 8 = <u>fiery</u>, violent, raging,
passionate, stormy ≠ calm

hound = <u>harass</u>, harry, bother,
provoke, annoy, torment, hassle
(*informal*), badger
Related Words
collective noun: pack

house NOUN 1 = <u>home</u>, residence,
dwelling, pad (*slang*), homestead,
abode, habitation, domicile,
whare (*N.Z.*) 2 = <u>household</u>,
family 3 = <u>firm</u>, company,
business, organization, outfit
(*informal*) 4 = <u>assembly</u>,
parliament, Commons, legislative
body 5 = <u>dynasty</u>, tribe, clan
● VERB 1 = <u>accommodate</u>, quarter,
take in, put up, lodge, harbour,
billet 2 = <u>contain</u>, keep, hold,
cover, store, protect, shelter
3 = <u>take</u>, accommodate, sleep,
provide shelter for, give a bed to
● PHRASES on the house = <u>free</u>,
for free (*informal*), for nothing,
free of charge, gratis

household = <u>family</u>, home,
house, family circle, ainga (*N.Z.*)

housing 1 = <u>accommodation</u>,
homes, houses, dwellings,

domiciles 2 = <u>case</u>, casing, covering, cover, shell, jacket, holder, container

hover 1 = <u>float</u>, fly, hang, drift, flutter **2** = <u>linger</u>, loiter, hang about *or* around (*informal*) **3** = <u>waver</u>, fluctuate, dither (*chiefly Brit.*), oscillate, vacillate

however = <u>but</u>, nevertheless, still, though, yet, nonetheless, notwithstanding, anyhow

howl VERB **1** = <u>bay</u>, cry **2** = <u>cry</u>, scream, roar, weep, yell, wail, shriek, bellow
● NOUN **1** = <u>baying</u>, cry, bay, bark, barking, yelping **2** = <u>cry</u>, scream, roar, bay, wail, shriek, clamour, bawl

hub = <u>centre</u>, heart, focus, core, middle, focal point, nerve centre

huddle VERB **1** = <u>curl up</u>, crouch, hunch up **2** = <u>crowd</u>, press, gather, collect, squeeze, cluster, flock, herd
● NOUN (*informal*) = <u>discussion</u>, conference, meeting, hui (N.Z.), powwow, confab (*informal*), korero (N.Z.)

hue = <u>colour</u>, tone, shade, dye, tint, tinge

hug VERB = <u>embrace</u>, cuddle, squeeze, clasp, enfold, hold close, take in your arms
● NOUN = <u>embrace</u>, squeeze, bear hug, clinch (*slang*), clasp

huge = <u>enormous</u>, large, massive, vast, tremendous, immense, gigantic, monumental ≠ tiny

hui (N.Z.) = <u>meeting</u>, gathering, assembly, conference, congress, rally, convention, get-together (*informal*)

hull = <u>framework</u>, casing, body, covering, frame

hum 1 = <u>drone</u>, buzz, murmur, throb, vibrate, purr, thrum, whir **2** (*Informal*) = <u>be busy</u>, buzz, bustle, stir, pulse, pulsate

human ADJECTIVE = <u>mortal</u>, manlike ≠ nonhuman
● NOUN = <u>human being</u>, person, individual, creature, mortal, man *or* woman ≠ nonhuman

humane = <u>kind</u>, compassionate, understanding, forgiving, tender, sympathetic, benign, merciful ≠ cruel

humanitarian ADJECTIVE **1** = <u>compassionate</u>, charitable, humane, benevolent, altruistic **2** = <u>charitable</u>, philanthropic, public-spirited
● NOUN = <u>philanthropist</u>, benefactor, Good Samaritan, altruist

humanity 1 = <u>the human race</u>, man, mankind, people, mortals, humankind, Homo sapiens **2** = <u>human nature</u>, mortality **3** = <u>kindness</u>, charity, compassion, sympathy, mercy, philanthropy, fellow feeling, kind-heartedness

humble ADJECTIVE **1** = <u>modest</u>, meek, unassuming, self-effacing, unpretentious, self-effacing,

unostentatious ≠ proud
2 = **lowly**, poor, mean, simple, ordinary, modest, obscure, undistinguished ≠ distinguished
● VERB = **humiliate**, disgrace, crush, subdue, chasten, put (someone) in their place, take down a peg (*informal*) ≠ exalt

humidity = **damp**, moisture, dampness, wetness, moistness, dankness, clamminess, mugginess

humiliate = **embarrass**, shame, humble, crush, put down, degrade, chasten, mortify ≠ honour

humiliating = **embarrassing**, shaming, humbling, mortifying, crushing, degrading, ignominious, barro (*Austral. slang*)

humiliation = **embarrassment**, shame, disgrace, humbling, put-down, degradation, indignity, ignominy

humorous = **funny**, comic, amusing, entertaining, witty, comical, droll, jocular ≠ serious

humour NOUN 1 = **comedy**, funniness, fun, amusement, funny side, jocularity, facetiousness, ludicrousness ≠ seriousness
2 = **mood**, spirits, temper, disposition, frame of mind
3 = **joking**, comedy, wit, farce, jesting, wisecracks (*informal*), witticisms
● VERB = **indulge**, accommodate, go along with, flatter, gratify,

pander to, mollify ≠ oppose

hunch NOUN = **feeling**, idea, impression, suspicion, intuition, premonition, inkling, presentiment
● VERB = **crouch**, bend, curve, arch, draw in

hunger NOUN 1 = **appetite**, emptiness, hungriness, ravenousness 2 = **starvation**, famine, malnutrition, undernourishment 3 = **desire**, appetite, craving, ache, lust, yearning, itch, thirst
● PHRASES **hunger for** or **after something** = **want**, desire, crave, long for, wish for, yearn for, hanker after, ache for

hungry 1 = **starving**, ravenous, famished, starved, empty, voracious, peckish (*informal, chiefly Brit.*) 2 = **eager**, keen, craving, yearning, greedy, avid, desirous, covetous

hunk = **lump**, piece, chunk, block, mass, wedge, slab, nugget

hunt VERB = **stalk**, track, chase, pursue, trail, hound
● NOUN = **search**, hunting, investigation, chase, pursuit, quest
● PHRASES **hunt for something** or **someone** = **search for**, look for, seek for, forage for, scour for, fossick for (*Austral. & N.Z.*), ferret about for

hurdle 1 = **obstacle**, difficulty, barrier, handicap, hazard, uphill

(*S. African*), obstruction, stumbling block **2** = <u>fence</u>, barrier, barricade

hurl = <u>throw</u>, fling, launch, cast, pitch, toss, propel, sling

hurricane = <u>storm</u>, gale, tornado, cyclone, typhoon, tempest, twister (*U.S. informal*), willy-willy (*Austral.*)

hurried 1 = <u>hasty</u>, quick, brief, rushed, short, swift, speedy **2** = <u>rushed</u>, perfunctory, speedy, hasty, cursory

hurry VERB 1 = <u>rush</u>, fly, dash, scurry, scoot ≠ dawdle **2** = <u>make haste</u>, rush, get a move on (*informal*), step on it (*informal*)
● **NOUN** = <u>rush</u>, haste, speed, urgency, flurry, quickness ≠ slowness

hurt VERB 1 = <u>injure</u>, damage, wound, cut, disable, bruise, scrape, impair ≠ heal **2** = <u>ache</u>, be sore, be painful, burn, smart, sting, throb, be tender **3** = <u>harm</u>, injure, ill-treat, maltreat **4** = <u>upset</u>, distress, pain, wound, annoy, grieve, sadden
● **NOUN** = <u>distress</u>, suffering, pain, grief, misery, sorrow, heartache, wretchedness ≠ happiness
● **ADJECTIVE 1** = <u>injured</u>, wounded, damaged, harmed, cut, bruised, scarred ≠ healed **2** = <u>upset</u>, wounded, crushed, offended, aggrieved, tooshie (*Austral. slang*) ≠ calmed

hurtle = <u>rush</u>, charge, race, shoot, fly, speed, tear, crash

husband NOUN = <u>partner</u>, spouse, mate, better half (*humorous*)
● **VERB** = <u>conserve</u>, budget, save, store, hoard, economize on, use economically ≠ squander

hush VERB = <u>quieten</u>, silence, mute, muzzle, shush
● **NOUN** = <u>quiet</u>, silence, calm, peace, tranquillity, stillness

hut 1 = <u>cabin</u>, shack, shanty, hovel, whare (*N.Z.*) **2** = <u>shed</u>, outhouse, lean-to, lockup

hybrid 1 = <u>crossbreed</u>, cross, mixture, compound, composite, amalgam, mongrel, half-breed **2** = <u>mixture</u>, compound, composite, amalgam

hygiene = <u>cleanliness</u>, sanitation, disinfection, sterility

hymn 1 = <u>religious song</u>, song of praise, carol, chant, anthem, psalm, paean **2** = <u>song of praise</u>, anthem, paean

hype (*Slang*) = <u>publicity</u>, promotion, plugging (*informal*), razzmatazz (*slang*), brouhaha, ballyhoo (*informal*)

hypocrisy = <u>insincerity</u>, pretence, deception, cant, duplicity, deceitfulness ≠ sincerity

hypothesis = <u>theory</u>, premise, proposition, assumption, thesis, postulate, supposition

hysteria = <u>frenzy</u>, panic, madness, agitation, delirium, hysterics

hysterical 1 = <u>frenzied</u>, frantic, raving, distracted, distraught, crazed, overwrought, berko (*Austral. slang*) ≠ calm **2** (*Informal*) = <u>hilarious</u>, uproarious, side-splitting, comical ≠ serious

I

icy 1 = <u>cold</u>, freezing, bitter, biting, raw, chill, chilly, frosty ≠ hot **2** = <u>slippery</u>, glassy, slippy (*informal or dialect*), like a sheet of glass **3** = <u>unfriendly</u>, cold, distant, aloof, frosty, frigid, unwelcoming ≠ friendly

idea 1 = <u>notion</u>, thought, view, teaching, opinion, belief, conclusion, hypothesis **2** = <u>understanding</u>, thought, view, opinion, concept, impression, perception **3** = <u>intention</u>, aim, purpose, object, plan, objective

> ## Word Power
>
> **idea** – It is usually considered correct to say that someone has *the idea of doing something*, rather than *the idea to do something*. For example, you would say *he had the idea of taking a holiday*, not *he had the idea to take a holiday*.

ideal NOUN **1** = <u>epitome</u>, standard, dream, pattern, perfection, last word, paragon **2** = <u>model</u>, prototype, paradigm ● ADJECTIVE = <u>perfect</u>, best, model, classic, supreme, ultimate, archetypal, exemplary ≠ imperfect

ideally = <u>in a perfect world</u>, all things being equal, if you had your way

identical = <u>alike</u>, matching, twin, duplicate, indistinguishable, interchangeable ≠ different

identification 1 = <u>discovery</u>, recognition, determining, establishment, diagnosis, confirmation, divination **2** = <u>recognition</u>, naming, distinguishing, confirmation, pinpointing **3** = <u>connection</u>, relationship, association **4** = <u>understanding</u>, relationship, involvement, unity, sympathy, empathy, rapport, fellow feeling

identify VERB **1** = <u>recognize</u>, place, name, remember, spot, diagnose, make out, pinpoint **2** = <u>establish</u>, spot, confirm, demonstrate, pick out, certify, verify, mark out ● PHRASES **identify something** or **someone with something** or **someone** = <u>equate with</u>, associate with ◆ **identify with someone** = <u>relate to</u>, respond to, feel for, empathize with

identity = <u>individuality</u>, self, character, personality, existence, originality, separateness

idiot = <u>fool</u>, moron, twit (*informal, chiefly Brit.*), chump, imbecile, cretin, simpleton, halfwit, galah (*Austral. & N.Z. informal*), dorba or dorb (*Austral. slang*), bogan (*Austral. slang*)

idle ADJECTIVE 1 = <u>unoccupied</u>, unemployed, redundant, inactive ≠ occupied 2 = <u>unused</u>, inactive, out of order, out of service 3 = <u>lazy</u>, slow, slack, sluggish, lax, negligent, inactive, inert ≠ busy 4 = <u>useless</u>, vain, pointless, unsuccessful, ineffective, worthless, futile, fruitless ≠ useful
● VERB *often with away* = <u>fritter</u>, lounge, potter, loaf, dally, loiter, dawdle, laze

idol 1 = <u>hero</u>, pin-up, favourite, pet, darling, beloved (*slang*), fave (*informal*) 2 = <u>graven image</u>, god, deity

if 1 = <u>provided</u>, assuming, given that, providing, supposing, presuming, on condition that, as long as 2 = <u>when</u>, whenever, every time, any time

ignite 1 = <u>catch fire</u>, burn, burst into flames, inflame, flare up, take fire 2 = <u>set fire to</u>, light, set alight, torch, kindle

ignorance 1 = <u>lack of education</u>, stupidity, foolishness ≠ knowledge 2 *with of*

= <u>unawareness of</u>, inexperience of, unfamiliarity with, innocence of, unconsciousness of

ignorant 1 = <u>uneducated</u>, illiterate ≠ educated 2 = <u>insensitive</u>, rude, crass 3 *with of* = <u>uninformed</u>, unaware of, oblivious to, innocent of, unconscious of, inexperienced of, uninitiated about, unenlightened about ≠ informed

ignore 1 = <u>pay no attention to</u>, neglect, disregard, slight, overlook, scorn, spurn, rebuff ≠ pay attention to 2 = <u>overlook</u>, discount, disregard, reject, neglect, shrug off, pass over, brush aside 3 = <u>snub</u>, slight, rebuff

ill ADJECTIVE 1 = <u>unwell</u>, sick, poorly (*informal*), diseased, weak, crook (*Austral. & N.Z. slang*), ailing, frail ≠ healthy 2 = <u>harmful</u>, bad, damaging, evil, foul, unfortunate, destructive, detrimental ≠ favourable
● NOUN = <u>problem</u>, trouble, suffering, worry, injury, hurt, strain, harm ≠ good
● ADVERB 1 = <u>badly</u>, unfortunately, unfavourably, inauspiciously 2 = <u>hardly</u>, barely, scarcely, just, only just, by no means, at a push ≠ well

illegal = <u>unlawful</u>, banned, forbidden, prohibited, criminal, outlawed, illicit, unlicensed ≠ legal

illicit 1 = illegal, criminal, prohibited, unlawful, illegitimate, unlicensed, unauthorized, felonious ≠ legal **2** = forbidden, improper, immoral, guilty, clandestine, furtive

illness = sickness, disease, infection, disorder, bug (*informal*), ailment, affliction, malady

illuminate 1 = light up, brighten ≠ darken **2** = explain, interpret, make clear, clarify, clear up, enlighten, shed light on, elucidate ≠ obscure

illuminating = informative, revealing, enlightening, helpful, explanatory, instructive ≠ confusing

illusion 1 = delusion, misconception, misapprehension, fancy, fallacy, false impression, false belief **2** = false impression, appearance, impression, deception, fallacy ≠ reality **3** = fantasy, vision, hallucination, trick, spectre, mirage, daydream, apparition

illustrate 1 = demonstrate, emphasize **2** = explain, sum up, summarize, bring home, point up, elucidate

illustrated = pictured, decorated, pictorial

illustration 1 = example, case, instance, sample, specimen, exemplar **2** = picture, drawing, painting, image, print, plate, figure, portrait

image 1 = thought, idea, vision, concept, impression, perception, mental picture, conceptualization **2** = figure of speech **3** = reflection, likeness, mirror image **4** = figure, idol, icon, fetish, talisman **5** = replica, copy, reproduction, counterpart, clone, facsimile, spitting image (*informal*), Doppelgänger **6** = picture, photo, photograph, representation, reproduction, snapshot

imaginary = fictional, made-up, invented, imagined, unreal, hypothetical, fictitious, illusory ≠ real

imagination 1 = creativity, vision, invention, ingenuity, enterprise, originality, inventiveness, resourcefulness **2** = mind's eye, fancy

imaginative = creative, original, inspired, enterprising, clever, ingenious, inventive ≠ unimaginative

imagine 1 = envisage, see, picture, plan, think of, conjure up, envision, visualize **2** = believe, think, suppose, assume, suspect, guess (*informal, chiefly U.S. & Canad.*), take it, reckon

imitate 1 = copy, follow, repeat, echo, emulate, ape, simulate, mirror **2** = do an impression of, mimic, copy

imitation NOUN 1 = <u>replica</u>, fake, reproduction, sham, forgery, counterfeiting, likeness, duplication 2 = <u>copying</u>, resemblance, mimicry 3 = <u>impression</u>, impersonation
● ADJECTIVE = <u>artificial</u>, mock, reproduction, dummy, synthetic, man-made, simulated, sham ≠ real

immaculate 1 = <u>clean</u>, spotless, neat, spruce, squeaky-clean, spick-and-span ≠ dirty 2 = <u>pure</u>, perfect, impeccable, flawless, faultless, above reproach ≠ corrupt 3 = <u>perfect</u>, flawless, impeccable, faultless, unblemished, untarnished, unexceptionable ≠ tainted

immediate 1 = <u>instant</u>, prompt, instantaneous, quick, on-the-spot, split-second ≠ later 2 = <u>nearest</u>, next, direct, close, near ≠ far

immediately = <u>at once</u>, now, instantly, straight away, directly, promptly, right away, without delay

immense = <u>huge</u>, great, massive, vast, enormous, extensive, tremendous, very big ≠ tiny

immerse 1 = <u>engross</u>, involve, absorb, busy, occupy, engage 2 = <u>plunge</u>, dip, submerge, sink, duck, bathe, douse, dunk

immigrant = <u>settler</u>, incomer, alien, stranger, outsider, newcomer, migrant, emigrant

imminent = <u>near</u>, coming, close, approaching, gathering, forthcoming, looming, impending ≠ remote

immoral = <u>wicked</u>, bad, wrong, corrupt, indecent, sinful, unethical, depraved ≠ moral

immortal ADJECTIVE 1 = <u>timeless</u>, eternal, everlasting, lasting, traditional, classic, enduring, perennial ≠ ephemeral 2 = <u>undying</u>, eternal, imperishable, deathless ≠ mortal
● NOUN 1 = <u>hero</u>, genius, great 2 = <u>god</u>, goddess, deity, divine being, immortal being, atua (N.Z.)

immune
● PHRASES **immune from** = exempt from, free from
◆ **immune to** 1 = <u>resistant to</u>, free from, protected from, safe from, not open to, spared from, secure against, invulnerable to 2 = <u>unaffected by</u>, invulnerable to

immunity 1 = <u>exemption</u>, amnesty, indemnity, release, freedom, invulnerability 2 with to = <u>resistance to</u>, protection from, resilience to, inoculation against, immunization from ≠ susceptibility to

impact NOUN 1 = <u>effect</u>, influence, consequences, impression, repercussions, ramifications **2** = <u>collision</u>, contact, crash, knock, stroke, smash, bump, thump

● VERB = <u>hit</u>, strike, crash, clash, crush, ram, smack, collide

impair = <u>worsen</u>, reduce, damage, injure, harm, undermine, weaken, diminish ≠ improve

impaired = <u>damaged</u>, flawed, faulty, defective, imperfect, unsound

impasse = <u>deadlock</u>, stalemate, standstill, dead end, standoff

impatient 1 = <u>cross</u>, annoyed, irritated, prickly, touchy, bad-tempered, intolerant, ill-tempered ≠ easy-going

2 = <u>eager</u>, longing, keen, anxious, hungry, enthusiastic, restless, avid ≠ calm

impeccable = <u>faultless</u>, perfect, immaculate, flawless, squeaky-clean, unblemished, unimpeachable, irreproachable ≠ flawed

impending = <u>looming</u>, coming, approaching, near, forthcoming, imminent, upcoming, in the pipeline

imperative = <u>urgent</u>, essential, pressing, vital, crucial ≠ unnecessary

imperial = <u>royal</u>, regal, kingly, queenly, princely, sovereign, majestic, monarchial

impetus 1 = <u>incentive</u>, push, spur, motivation, impulse,

stimulus, catalyst, goad **2** = <u>force</u>, power, energy, momentum

implant 1 = <u>insert</u>, fix, graft
2 = <u>instil</u>, infuse, inculcate

implement VERB = <u>carry out</u>, effect, carry through, complete, apply, perform, realize, fulfil ≠ hinder

● NOUN = <u>tool</u>, machine, device, instrument, appliance, apparatus, gadget, utensil

implicate VERB = <u>incriminate</u>, involve, embroil, entangle, inculpate ≠ dissociate

● PHRASES **implicate something** or **someone in something** = <u>involve in</u>, associate with

implication NOUN = <u>suggestion</u>, hint, inference, meaning, significance, presumption, overtone, innuendo

● PLURAL NOUN = <u>consequences</u>, result, developments, upshot

implicit 1 = <u>implied</u>, understood, suggested, hinted at, taken for granted, unspoken, inferred, tacit ≠ explicit

2 = <u>inherent</u>, underlying, intrinsic, latent, ingrained, inbuilt

3 = <u>absolute</u>, full, complete, firm, fixed, constant, utter, outright

implied = <u>suggested</u>, indirect, hinted at, implicit, unspoken, tacit, undeclared, unstated

imply 1 = <u>suggest</u>, hint, insinuate, indicate, intimate, signify

2 = <u>involve</u>, mean, entail, require, indicate, point to, signify, presuppose

import VERB = <u>bring in</u>, buy in, ship in, introduce
● NOUN 1 (*Formal*) = <u>significance</u>, concern, value, weight, consequence, substance, moment, magnitude
2 = <u>meaning</u>, implication, significance, sense, intention, substance, drift, thrust

importance 1 = <u>significance</u>, interest, concern, moment, value, weight, import, consequence
2 = <u>prestige</u>, standing, status, rule, authority, influence, distinction, esteem, mana (*N.Z.*)

important 1 = <u>significant</u>, critical, substantial, urgent, serious, far-reaching, momentous, seminal ≠ unimportant
2 = <u>powerful</u>, prominent, commanding, dominant, influential, eminent, high-ranking, authoritative

impose
● PHRASES **impose something on** *or* **upon someone** 1 = <u>levy</u>, introduce, charge, establish, fix, institute, decree, ordain
2 = <u>inflict</u>, force, enforce, visit, press, apply, thrust, saddle (someone) with

imposing = <u>impressive</u>, striking, grand, powerful, commanding, awesome, majestic, dignified

≠ unimposing

imposition 1 = <u>application</u>, introduction, levying
2 = <u>intrusion</u>, liberty, presumption

impossible 1 = <u>not possible</u>, out of the question, impracticable, unfeasible
2 = <u>unachievable</u>, out of the question, vain, unthinkable, inconceivable, far-fetched, unworkable, implausible
● possible 3 = <u>absurd</u>, crazy (*informal*), ridiculous, outrageous, ludicrous, unreasonable, preposterous, farcical

impotence = <u>powerlessness</u>, inability, helplessness, weakness, incompetence, paralysis, frailty, incapacity ≠ powerfulness

impoverish 1 = <u>bankrupt</u>, ruin, beggar, break 2 = <u>deplete</u>, drain, exhaust, diminish, use up, sap, wear out, reduce

impoverished = <u>poor</u>, needy, destitute, bankrupt, poverty-stricken, impecunious, penurious ≠ rich

impress VERB = <u>excite</u>, move, strike, touch, affect, inspire, amaze, overcome
● PHRASES **impress something on** *or* **upon someone** = <u>stress</u>, bring home to, instil in, drum into, knock into, emphasize to, fix in, inculcate in

impression 1 = <u>idea</u>, feeling,

thought, sense, view, assessment, judgment, reaction **2** = <u>effect</u>, influence, impact **3** = <u>imitation</u>, parody, impersonation, send-up (*Brit. informal*), takeoff (*informal*) **4** = <u>mark</u>, imprint, stamp, outline, hollow, dent, indentation

impressive = <u>grand</u>, striking, splendid, good, great (*informal*), fine, powerful, exciting ≠ unimpressive

imprint NOUN = <u>mark</u>, impression, stamp, indentation
● VERB = <u>engrave</u>, print, stamp, impress, etch, emboss

imprison = <u>jail</u>, confine, detain, lock up, put away, intern, incarcerate, send down (*informal*) ≠ free

imprisoned = <u>jailed</u>, confined, locked up, inside (*slang*), in jail, captive, behind bars, incarcerated

imprisonment = <u>confinement</u>, custody, detention, captivity, incarceration

improbable **1** = <u>doubtful</u>, unlikely, dubious, questionable, fanciful, far-fetched, implausible ≠ probable **2** = <u>unconvincing</u>, weak, unbelievable, preposterous ≠ convincing

improper **1** = <u>inappropriate</u>, unfit, unsuitable, out of place, unwarranted, uncalled-for ≠ appropriate **2** = <u>indecent</u>, vulgar, suggestive, unseemly, untoward, risqué, smutty, unbecoming ≠ decent

improve **1** = <u>enhance</u>, better, add to, upgrade, touch up, ameliorate ≠ worsen **2** = <u>get better</u>, pick up, develop, advance

improvement **1** = <u>enhancement</u>, advancement, betterment **2** = <u>advance</u>, development, progress, recovery, upswing

improvise **1** = <u>devise</u>, contrive, concoct, throw together **2** = <u>ad-lib</u>, invent, busk, wing it (*informal*), play it by ear (*informal*), extemporize, speak off the cuff (*informal*)

impulse = <u>urge</u>, longing, wish, notion, yearning, inclination, itch, whim

inaccurate = <u>incorrect</u>, wrong, mistaken, faulty, unreliable, defective, erroneous, unsound ≠ accurate

inadequacy **1** = <u>shortage</u>, poverty, dearth, paucity, insufficiency, meagreness, scantiness **2** = <u>incompetence</u>, inability, deficiency, incapacity, ineffectiveness **3** = <u>shortcoming</u>, failing, weakness, defect, imperfection

inadequate **1** = <u>insufficient</u>, meagre, poor, lacking, scant, sparse, sketchy ≠ adequate **2** = <u>incapable</u>, incompetent, faulty, deficient, unqualified, not up to scratch (*informal*)

≠ capable

inadvertently
= <u>unintentionally</u>, accidentally, by accident, mistakenly, unwittingly, by mistake, involuntarily ≠ deliberately

inaugural = <u>first</u>, opening, initial, maiden, introductory

incarnation = <u>embodiment</u>, manifestation, epitome, type, personification

incense = <u>anger</u>, infuriate, enrage, irritate, madden, inflame, rile (*informal*), make your blood boil (*informal*)

incensed = <u>angry</u>, furious, fuming, infuriated, enraged, maddened, indignant, irate, tooshie (*Austral. slang*), off the air (*Austral. slang*)

incentive = <u>inducement</u>, encouragement, spur, lure, bait, motivation, carrot (*informal*), stimulus ≠ disincentive

incident 1 = <u>disturbance</u>, scene, clash, disorder, confrontation, brawl, fracas, commotion
2 = <u>adventure</u>, drama, excitement, crisis, spectacle
3 = <u>happening</u>, event, affair, business, fact, matter, occasion, episode

incidentally = <u>by the way</u>, in passing, en passant, parenthetically, by the bye

inclination 1 = <u>desire</u>, longing, aspiration, craving, hankering
2 = <u>tendency</u>, liking, disposition, penchant, propensity, predisposition, predilection, proclivity ≠ aversion

incline VERB = <u>predispose</u>, influence, persuade, prejudice, sway, dispose
● NOUN = <u>slope</u>, rise, dip, grade, descent, ascent, gradient

inclined 1 = <u>disposed</u>, given, prone, likely, liable, apt, predisposed 2 = <u>willing</u>, minded, disposed

include 1 = <u>contain</u>, involve, incorporate, cover, consist of, take in, embrace, comprise ≠ exclude
2 = <u>count</u> 3 = <u>add</u>, enter, put in, insert

inclusion = <u>addition</u>, incorporation, introduction, insertion ≠ exclusion

inclusive = <u>comprehensive</u>, general, global, sweeping, blanket, umbrella, across-the-board, all-embracing ≠ limited

income = <u>revenue</u>, earnings, pay, returns, profits, wages, yield, proceeds

incoming 1 = <u>arriving</u>, landing, approaching, entering, returning, homeward ≠ departing 2 = <u>new</u>

incompatible = <u>inconsistent</u>, conflicting, contradictory, incongruous, unsuited, mismatched ≠ compatible

incompetence = <u>ineptitude</u>, inability, inadequacy, incapacity, ineffectiveness, uselessness, unfitness, incapability

incompetent = <u>inept</u>, useless, incapable, floundering, bungling, unfit, ineffectual, inexpert ≠ competent

incomplete = <u>unfinished</u>, partial, wanting, deficient, imperfect, fragmentary, half-pie (*N.Z. informal*) ≠ complete

inconsistency 1 = <u>unreliability</u>, instability, unpredictability, fickleness, unsteadiness 2 = <u>incompatibility</u>, discrepancy, disparity, disagreement, variance, divergence, incongruity

inconsistent 1 = <u>changeable</u>, variable, unpredictable, unstable, erratic, fickle, capricious, unsteady ≠ consistent 2 = <u>incompatible</u>, conflicting, at odds, contradictory, incongruous, discordant, out of step, irreconcilable ≠ compatible

inconvenience NOUN = <u>trouble</u>, difficulty, bother, fuss, disadvantage, disturbance, disruption, nuisance, uphill (*S. African*)

● VERB = <u>trouble</u>, bother, disturb, upset, disrupt, put out, discommode

incorporate 1 = <u>include</u>, contain, take in, embrace, integrate, encompass, assimilate, comprise of 2 = <u>integrate</u>, include, absorb, merge, fuse,

assimilate, subsume 3 = <u>blend</u>, combine, compound, mingle

incorrect = <u>false</u>, wrong, mistaken, flawed, faulty, inaccurate, untrue, erroneous ≠ correct

increase VERB 1 = <u>raise</u>, extend, boost, expand, develop, advance, strengthen, widen ≠ decrease 2 = <u>grow</u>, develop, spread, expand, swell, enlarge, escalate, multiply ≠ shrink

● NOUN = <u>growth</u>, rise, development, gain, expansion, extension, proliferation, enlargement

increasingly = <u>progressively</u>, more and more

incredible 1 (*Informal*) = <u>amazing</u>, wonderful, stunning, extraordinary, overwhelming, astonishing, staggering, sensational (*informal*) 2 = <u>unbelievable</u>, unthinkable, improbable, inconceivable, preposterous, unconvincing, unimaginable, far-fetched

incumbent NOUN = <u>holder</u>, keeper, bearer

● ADJECTIVE (*Formal*) = <u>obligatory</u>, required, necessary, essential, binding, compulsory, mandatory, imperative

incur = <u>sustain</u>, experience, suffer, gain, earn, collect, meet with, provoke

indecent 1 = <u>obscene</u>, lewd,

dirty, inappropriate, rude, crude, filthy, improper ≠ decent
2 = **unbecoming**, unsuitable, vulgar, unseemly, undignified, indecorous ≠ proper

indeed 1 = **certainly**, yes, definitely, surely, truly, undoubtedly, without doubt, indisputably 2 = **really**, actually, in fact, certainly, genuinely, in truth, in actuality

indefinitely = **endlessly**, continually, for ever, ad infinitum

independence = **freedom**, liberty, autonomy, sovereignty, self-rule, self-sufficiency, self-reliance, rangatiratanga (*N.Z.*) ≠ subjugation

independent 1 = **separate**, unattached, uncontrolled, unconstrained ≠ controlled 2 = **self-sufficient**, free, liberated, self-contained, self-reliant, self-supporting 3 = **self-governing**, free, autonomous, liberated, sovereign, self-determining, nonaligned ≠ subject

independently = **separately**, alone, solo, on your own, by yourself, unaided, individually, autonomously

indicate 1 = **show**, suggest, reveal, display, demonstrate, point to, imply, manifest
2 = **imply**, suggest, hint, intimate, signify, insinuate 3 = **point to**, point out, specify, gesture

towards, designate 4 = **register**, show, record, read, express, display, demonstrate

indication = **sign**, mark, evidence, suggestion, symptom, hint, clue, manifestation

indicator = **sign**, mark, measure, guide, signal, symbol, meter, gauge

indict = **charge**, accuse, prosecute, summon, impeach, arraign

indictment = **charge**, allegation, prosecution, accusation, impeachment, summons, arraignment

indifference = **disregard**, apathy, negligence, detachment, coolness, coldness, nonchalance, aloofness ≠ concern

indifferent 1 = **unconcerned**, detached, cold, cool, callous, aloof, unmoved, unsympathetic ≠ concerned 2 = **mediocre**, ordinary, moderate, so-so (*informal*), passable, undistinguished, no great shakes (*informal*), half-pie (*N.Z. informal*) ≠ excellent

indignation = **resentment**, anger, rage, exasperation, pique, umbrage

indirect 1 = **related**, secondary, subsidiary, incidental, unintended 2 = **circuitous**, roundabout, curving, wandering, rambling, deviant, meandering, tortuous

≠ direct

indispensable = essential, necessary, needed, key, vital, crucial, imperative, requisite ≠ dispensable

individual ADJECTIVE
1 = separate, independent, isolated, lone, solitary ≠ collective
2 = unique, special, fresh, novel, exclusive, singular, idiosyncratic, unorthodox ≠ conventional
● NOUN = person, being, human, unit, character, soul, creature

individually = separately, independently, singly, one by one, one at a time

induce 1 = cause, produce, create, effect, lead to, occasion, generate, bring about ≠ prevent
2 = persuade, encourage, influence, convince, urge, prompt, sway, entice ≠ dissuade

indulge VERB 1 = gratify, satisfy, feed, give way to, yield to, pander to, gladden 2 = spoil, pamper, cosset, humour, give in to, coddle, mollycoddle, overindulge
● PHRASES **indulge yourself** = treat yourself, splash out, spoil yourself, luxuriate in something, overindulge yourself

indulgence 1 = luxury, treat, extravagance, favour, privilege
2 = gratification, satisfaction, fulfilment, appeasement, satiation

industrialist = capitalist, tycoon, magnate, manufacturer, captain of industry, big businessman

industry 1 = business, production, manufacturing, trade, commerce 2 = trade, world, business, service, line, field, profession, occupation
3 = diligence, effort, labour, hard work, trouble, activity, application, endeavour

ineffective 1 = unproductive, useless, futile, vain, unsuccessful, pointless, fruitless, ineffectual ≠ effective 2 = inefficient, useless, poor, powerless, unfit, worthless, inept, impotent

inefficient 1 = wasteful, uneconomical, profligate
2 = incompetent, inept, weak, bungling, ineffectual, disorganized ≠ efficient

inequality = disparity, prejudice, difference, bias, diversity, irregularity, unevenness, disproportion

inevitable = unavoidable, inescapable, inexorable, sure, certain, fixed, assured, fated ≠ avoidable

inevitably = unavoidably, naturally, necessarily, surely, certainly, as a result, automatically, consequently

inexpensive = cheap, reasonable, budget, bargain, modest, economical ≠ expensive

inexperienced = new, green, raw, callow, immature, untried, unpractised, unversed ≠ experienced

infamous = notorious, ignominious, disreputable, ill-famed ≠ esteemed

infancy = beginnings, start, birth, roots, seeds, origins, dawn, outset ≠ end

infant = baby, child, babe, toddler, tot, bairn (Scot.), littlie (Austral. informal), ankle-biter (Austral. slang), tacker (Austral. slang)

infect 1 = contaminate 2 = pollute, poison, corrupt, contaminate, taint, defile 3 = affect, move, upset, overcome, stir, disturb

infection = disease, condition, complaint, illness, virus, disorder, corruption, poison

infectious = catching, spreading, contagious, communicable, virulent, transmittable

inferior ADJECTIVE = lower, minor, secondary, subsidiary, lesser, humble, subordinate, lowly ≠ superior
• NOUN = underling, junior, subordinate, lesser, menial, minion

infertility = sterility, barrenness, unproductiveness, infecundity

infiltrate = penetrate, pervade, permeate, percolate, filter through to, make inroads into, sneak into (informal), insinuate yourself

infinite 1 = vast, enormous, immense, countless, measureless 2 = limitless, endless, unlimited, eternal, never-ending, boundless, everlasting, inexhaustible ≠ finite

inflame = enrage, stimulate, provoke, excite, anger, arouse, rouse, infuriate ≠ calm

inflamed = swollen, sore, red, hot, infected, fevered

inflate 1 = blow up, pump up, swell, dilate, distend, bloat, puff up or out ≠ deflate 2 = increase, expand, enlarge ≠ diminish 3 = exaggerate, embroider, embellish, enlarge, amplify, overstate, overestimate, overemphasize

inflated = exaggerated, swollen, overblown

inflation = increase, expansion, extension, swelling, escalation, enlargement

inflict = impose, administer, visit, apply, deliver, levy, wreak, mete or deal out

influence NOUN 1 = control, power, authority, direction, command, domination, supremacy, mastery, mana (N.Z.) 2 = power, authority, pull (informal), importance, prestige, clout (informal), leverage

3 = spell, hold, power, weight, magic, sway, allure, magnetism
● VERB **1** = affect, have an effect on, have an impact on, control, concern, direct, guide, bear upon **2** = persuade, prompt, urge, induce, entice, coax, incite, instigate

influential 1 = important, powerful, telling, leading, inspiring, potent, authoritative, weighty ≠ unimportant **2** = instrumental, important, significant, crucial

influx = arrival, rush, invasion, incursion, inundation, inrush

inform VERB = tell, advise, notify, instruct, enlighten, communicate to, tip someone off
● PHRASES **inform on someone** = betray, denounce, shop (slang, chiefly Brit.), give someone away, incriminate, blow the whistle on (informal), grass on (Brit. slang), double-cross (informal), dob someone in (Austral. & N.Z. slang)

informal 1 = natural, relaxed, casual, familiar, unofficial, laid-back, easy-going, colloquial **2** = relaxed, easy, comfortable, simple, natural, casual, cosy, laid-back (informal) ≠ formal **3** = casual, comfortable, leisure, everyday, simple **4** = unofficial, irregular ≠ official

information = facts, news, report, message, notice, knowledge, data, intelligence, drum (Austral. informal)

informative = instructive, revealing, educational, forthcoming, illuminating, enlightening, chatty, communicative

informed = knowledgeable, up to date, enlightened, learned, expert, familiar, versed, in the picture

infuriate = enrage, anger, provoke, irritate, incense, madden, exasperate, rile ≠ soothe

infuriating = annoying, irritating, provoking, galling, maddening, exasperating, vexatious

ingenious = creative, original, brilliant, clever, bright, shrewd, inventive, crafty ≠ unimaginative

ingredient = component, part, element, feature, piece, unit, item, aspect

inhabit = live in, occupy, populate, reside in, dwell in, abide in

inhabitant = occupant, resident, citizen, local, native, tenant, inmate, dweller

inhabited = populated, peopled, occupied, developed, settled, tenanted, colonized

inhale = breathe in, gasp, draw in, suck in, respire ≠ exhale

inherent = intrinsic, natural, essential, native, fundamental, hereditary, instinctive, innate ≠ extraneous

inherit 1 = be left, come into, be willed, succeed to, fall heir to

inheritance = legacy, heritage, bequest, birthright, patrimony

inhibit 1 = hinder, check, frustrate, curb, restrain, constrain, obstruct, impede ≠ further 2 = prevent, stop, frustrate ≠ allow

inhibited 1 = shy, reserved, guarded, subdued, repressed, constrained, self-conscious, reticent ≠ uninhibited

initial 1 = opening, first, earliest, beginning, primary, maiden, introductory, embryonic ≠ final

initially = at first, first, firstly, originally, primarily, in the beginning, at or in the beginning

initiate VERB 1 = begin, start, open, launch, kick off (informal), embark on, originate, set about 2 = introduce, admit, enlist, enrol, launch, establish, invest, recruit ● NOUN = novice, member, pupil, convert, amateur, newcomer, beginner, trainee ● PHRASES **initiate someone into something** = instruct in, train in, coach in, acquaint with, drill in, make aware of, teach about, tutor in

initiative 1 = advantage, start, lead, upper hand 2 = enterprise, drive, energy, leadership,

ambition, daring, enthusiasm, dynamism

inject 1 = vaccinate, administer, inoculate 2 = introduce, bring in, insert, instil, infuse, breathe

injection 1 = vaccination, shot (informal), jab (informal), dose, booster, immunization, inoculation 2 = introduction, investment, insertion, advancement, dose, infusion

injunction = order, ruling, command, instruction, mandate, precept, exhortation

injure 1 = hurt, wound, harm, damage, smash, crush, mar, shatter, mangulate (Austral. slang) 2 = damage, harm, ruin, wreck, spoil, impair, crool or cruel (Austral. slang) 3 = undermine, damage

injured 1 = hurt, damaged, wounded, broken, cut, crushed, disabled, weakened, crook (Austral. & N.Z. slang)

injury 1 = wound, cut, damage, trauma (Pathology), gash, lesion, laceration 2 = harm, suffering, damage, ill, hurt, disability, misfortune, affliction 3 = wrong, offence, insult, detriment, disservice

injustice 1 = unfairness, discrimination, prejudice, bias, inequality, oppression, intolerance, bigotry ≠ justice 2 = wrong, injury, crime, error, offence, sin, misdeed, transgression

inland = <u>interior</u>, internal, upcountry

inner 1 = <u>inside</u>, internal, interior, inward ≠ outer **2** = <u>central</u>, middle, internal, interior **3** = <u>hidden</u>, deep, secret, underlying, obscure, repressed, unrevealed ≠ obvious

innocence 1 = <u>naiveté</u>, simplicity, inexperience, credulity, gullibility, ingenuousness, artlessness, unworldliness ≠ worldliness **2** = <u>blamelessness</u>, clean hands, uprightness, irreproachability, guiltlessness ≠ guilt **3** = <u>chastity</u>, virtue, purity, modesty, celibacy, continence, maidenhood

innocent 1 = <u>not guilty</u>, in the clear, blameless, clean, honest, uninvolved, irreproachable, guiltless ≠ guilty **2** = <u>naive</u>, open, trusting, simple, childlike, gullible, unsophisticated, unworldly ≠ worldly **3** = <u>harmless</u>, innocuous, inoffensive, well-meant, unobjectionable, well-intentioned

innovation 1 = <u>change</u>, revolution, departure, introduction, variation, transformation, upheaval, alteration **2** = <u>newness</u>, novelty, originality, freshness, modernization, uniqueness

inquest = <u>inquiry</u>, investigation, probe, inquisition

inquire or **enquire** VERB = <u>ask</u>, question, query, quiz
● PHRASES **inquire into something** = <u>investigate</u>, study, examine, research, explore, look into, probe into, make inquiries into

inquiry or **enquiry**
1 = <u>question</u>, query, investigation
2 = <u>investigation</u>, study, review, survey, examination, probe, inspection, exploration
3 = <u>research</u>, investigation, analysis, inspection, exploration, interrogation

insane 1 = <u>mad</u>, crazy, mentally ill, crazed, demented, deranged, out of your mind, off the air (Austral. slang), porangi (N.Z.) ≠ sane **2** = <u>stupid</u>, foolish, daft (informal), irresponsible, irrational, senseless, preposterous, impractical ≠ reasonable

insect = <u>bug</u>, creepy-crawly (Brit. informal), gogga (S. African informal)
► **beetles** ► **butterflies and moths** ► **flies** ► **types of insect**

insecure 1 = <u>unconfident</u>, worried, anxious, afraid, shy, uncertain, unsure, timid ≠ confident **2** = <u>unsafe</u>, exposed, vulnerable, wide-open,

Types of insect

body louse, cootie (*U.S. & N.Z.*),
 or (*N.Z. slang*) kutu
bookworm
caddis worm *or* caseworm
cankerworm
cochineal *or* cochineal insect
cockroach
crab (*louse*)
cricket
earwig, *or* (*Scot. dialect*)
 clipshears, *or* clipshear
flea
grasshopper
katydid
locust
louse *or* (*N.Z.*) kutu
mantis *or* praying mantis

measuring worm, looper, *or*
 inchworm
midge
mosquito
nit
phylloxera
scale insect
silkworm
silverfish
stick insect *or* (*U.S. & Canad.*)
 walking stick
thrips
treehopper
weta (*N.Z.*)
wireworm
woodworm

---

unprotected, defenceless,
unguarded ≠ safe

insecurity = anxiety, fear, worry,
uncertainty ≠ confidence

insert = put, place, position, slip,
slide, slot, thrust, stick in

inside NOUN = interior, contents,
core, nucleus

● **PLURAL NOUN** (*Informal*)
= stomach, guts, belly, bowels,
innards (*informal*), entrails,
viscera, vitals

● **ADJECTIVE 1** = inner, internal,
interior, inward ≠ outside

2 = confidential, private, secret,
internal, exclusive, restricted,
privileged, classified

● **ADVERB** = indoors, in, within,

under cover

insight 1 = understanding,
perception, sense, knowledge,
vision, judgment, awareness,
grasp **2** *with* into
= understanding of, perception
of, awareness of, experience of,
description of, introduction to,
observation of, judgment of

insignificant = unimportant,
minor, irrelevant, petty, trivial,
meaningless, trifling, paltry
≠ important

insist 1 lay down the law, put
your foot down (*informal*)
2 = demand, order, require,
command, dictate, entreat
3 = assert, state, maintain, claim,

declare, repeat, vow, swear

insistence 1 = <u>demand</u>, command, dictate, entreaty, importunity 2 = <u>assertion</u>, claim, statement, declaration, persistence, pronouncement

inspect 1 = <u>examine</u>, check, look at, view, survey, look over, scrutinize, go over *or* through 2 = <u>check</u>, examine, investigate, look at, survey, vet, look over, go over *or* through

inspection 1 = <u>examination</u>, investigation, scrutiny, once-over (*informal*) 2 = <u>check</u>, search, investigation, review, survey, examination, scrutiny, once-over (*informal*)

inspector = <u>examiner</u>, investigator, supervisor, monitor, superintendent, auditor, censor, surveyor

inspiration 1 = <u>imagination</u>, creativity, ingenuity, insight, originality, inventiveness, cleverness 2 = <u>motivation</u>, example, model, boost, spur, incentive, revelation, stimulus ≠ deterrent 3 = <u>influence</u>, spur, stimulus, muse

inspire 1 = <u>motivate</u>, stimulate, encourage, influence, spur, animate, enliven, galvanize ≠ discourage 2 = <u>give rise to</u>, produce, result in, engender

inspired 1 = <u>brilliant</u>, wonderful, impressive, outstanding, thrilling, memorable, dazzling, superlative 2 = <u>stimulated</u>, uplifted, exhilarated, enthused, elated

inspiring = <u>uplifting</u>, exciting, moving, stirring, stimulating, rousing, exhilarating, heartening ≠ uninspiring

instability 1 = <u>uncertainty</u>, insecurity, vulnerability, volatility, unpredictability, fluctuation, impermanence, unsteadiness ≠ stability 2 = <u>imbalance</u>, variability, unpredictability, unsteadiness, changeableness

install 1 = <u>set up</u>, put in, place, position, station, establish, lay, fix 2 = <u>institute</u>, establish, introduce, invest, ordain, inaugurate, induct 3 = <u>settle</u>, position, plant, establish, lodge, ensconce

installation 1 = <u>setting up</u>, fitting, instalment, placing, positioning, establishment 2 = <u>appointment</u>, ordination, inauguration, induction, investiture

instalment 1 = <u>payment</u>, repayment, part payment 2 = <u>part</u>, section, chapter, episode, portion, division

instance NOUN = <u>example</u>, case, occurrence, occasion, sample, illustration
● VERB = <u>name</u>, mention, identify, point out, advance, quote, refer to, point to

instant NOUN 1 = <u>moment</u>,

second, flash, split second, jiffy (*informal*), trice, twinkling of an eye (*informal*) 2 = time, point, hour, moment, stage, occasion, phase, juncture

● ADJECTIVE 1 = immediate, prompt, instantaneous, direct, quick, on-the-spot, split-second 2 = ready-made, fast, convenience, ready-mixed, ready-cooked, precooked

instantly ADVERB = immediately, at once, straight away, now, directly, right away, instantaneously, this minute

instead ADVERB = rather, alternatively, preferably, in preference, in lieu, on second thoughts

● PHRASES **instead of** = in place of, rather than, in preference to, in lieu of, in contrast with

instinct 1 = natural inclination, talent, tendency, faculty, inclination, knack, predisposition, proclivity 2 = talent, skill, gift, capacity, bent, genius, faculty, knack 3 = intuition, impulse

instinctive = natural, inborn, automatic, unconscious, inherent, spontaneous, reflex, innate ≠ acquired

instinctively = intuitively, naturally, automatically, without thinking, involuntarily, by instinct

institute NOUN = establishment, body, centre, school, university,

society, association, college

● VERB = establish, start, found, launch, set up, introduce, fix, organize ≠ end

institution 1 = establishment, body, centre, school, university, society, association, college 2 = custom, practice, tradition, law, rule, procedure, convention, ritual

institutional = conventional, accepted, established, formal, routine, orthodox, procedural

instruct 1 = order, tell, direct, charge, bid, command, mandate, enjoin 2 = teach, school, train, coach, educate, drill, tutor

instruction NOUN 1 = order, ruling, command, rule, demand, regulation, dictate, decree 2 = teaching, schooling, training, grounding, education, coaching, lesson(s), guidance

● PLURAL NOUN = information, rules, advice, directions, recommendations, guidance, specifications

instructor = teacher, coach, guide, adviser, trainer, demonstrator, tutor, mentor

instrument 1 = tool, device, implement, mechanism, appliance, apparatus, gadget, contraption (*informal*) 2 = agent, means, medium, agency, vehicle, mechanism, organ

instrumental = active,

involved, influential, useful, helpful, contributory

insufficient = inadequate, scant, meagre, short, sparse, deficient, lacking ≠ ample

insulate = isolate, protect, screen, defend, shelter, shield, cut off, cushion

insult VERB = offend, abuse, wound, slight, put down, snub, malign, affront ≠ praise
● NOUN 1 = jibe, slight, put-down, abuse, snub, barb, affront, abusive remark 2 = offence, slight, snub, slur, affront, slap in the face (informal), kick in the teeth (informal), insolence

insulting = offensive, rude, abusive, degrading, contemptuous, disparaging, scurrilous, insolent ≠ complimentary

insurance 1 = assurance, cover, security, protection, safeguard, indemnity 2 = protection, security, guarantee, shelter, safeguard, warranty

insure 1 = assure, cover, protect, guarantee, warrant, underwrite, indemnify 2 = protect, cover, safeguard

intact = undamaged, whole, complete, sound, perfect, entire, unscathed, unbroken ≠ damaged

integral = essential, basic, fundamental, necessary, component, constituent, indispensable, intrinsic ≠ inessential

integrate = join, unite, combine, blend, incorporate, merge, fuse, assimilate ≠ separate

integrity 1 = honesty, principle, honour, virtue, goodness, morality, purity, probity ≠ dishonesty 2 = unity, unification, cohesion, coherence, wholeness, soundness, completeness

intellect = intelligence, mind, reason, understanding, sense, brains (informal), judgment

intellectual ADJECTIVE = scholarly, learned, academic, lettered, intelligent, cerebral, erudite, scholastic ≠ stupid
● NOUN = academic, expert, genius, thinker, master, mastermind, maestro, highbrow, fundi (S. African), acca (Austral. slang) ≠ idiot

intelligence 1 = intellect, understanding, brains (informal), sense, knowledge, judgment, wit, perception ≠ stupidity 2 = information, news, facts, report, findings, knowledge, data, notification ≠ misinformation

intelligent = clever, bright, smart, sharp, enlightened, knowledgeable, well-informed, brainy (informal) ≠ stupid

intend = plan, mean, aim, propose, purpose, have in mind or view

intense 1 = <u>extreme</u>, great, severe, fierce, deep, powerful, supreme, acute ≠ mild 2 = <u>fierce</u>, tough 3 = <u>passionate</u>, emotional, fierce, heightened, ardent, fanatical, fervent, heartfelt ≠ indifferent

---

Word Power

intense – Intense is sometimes wrongly used where intensive is meant: the land is under intensive (not intense) cultivation. Intensely is sometimes wrongly used where intently is meant: he listened intently (not intensely).

---

intensify 1 = <u>increase</u>, raise, add to, strengthen, reinforce, widen, heighten, sharpen ≠ decrease 2 = <u>escalate</u>, increase, widen, deepen

intensity 1 = <u>force</u>, strength, fierceness 2 = <u>passion</u>, emotion, fervour, force, strength, fanaticism, ardour, vehemence

intensive = <u>concentrated</u>, thorough, exhaustive, full, demanding, detailed, complete, serious

intent ADJECTIVE = <u>absorbed</u>, intense, fascinated, preoccupied, enthralled, attentive, watchful, engrossed ≠ indifferent

● NOUN = <u>intention</u>, aim, purpose,

intense → interfere

meaning, end, plan, goal, design ≠ chance

intention = <u>aim</u>, plan, idea, goal, end, design, target, wish

inter = <u>bury</u>, lay to rest, entomb, consign to the grave

intercept = <u>catch</u>, stop, block, seize, cut off, interrupt, head off, obstruct

intercourse 1 = <u>sexual intercourse</u>, sex (informal), copulation, coitus, carnal knowledge 2 = <u>contact</u>, communication, commerce, dealings

interest NOUN 1 often plural = <u>hobby</u>, activity, pursuit, entertainment, recreation, amusement, preoccupation, diversion 2 often plural = <u>advantage</u>, good, benefit, profit 3 = <u>stake</u>, investment

● VERB = <u>arouse your curiosity</u>, fascinate, attract, grip, entertain, intrigue, divert, captivate ≠ bore

interested 1 = <u>curious</u>, attracted, excited, drawn, keen, gripped, fascinated, captivated ≠ uninterested 2 = <u>involved</u>, concerned, affected, implicated

interesting = <u>intriguing</u>, absorbing, appealing, attractive, engaging, gripping, entrancing, stimulating ≠ uninteresting

interface = <u>connection</u>, link, boundary, border, frontier

interfere VERB = <u>meddle</u>,

intervene, intrude, butt in, tamper, pry, encroach, stick your oar in (*informal*)
● PHRASES **interfere with something** *or* **someone** = conflict with, check, clash, handicap, hamper, disrupt, inhibit, thwart

interference = intrusion, intervention, meddling, opposition, conflict, obstruction, prying

interim = temporary, provisional, makeshift, acting, caretaker, improvised, stopgap

interior NOUN = inside, centre, heart, middle, depths, core, nucleus
● ADJECTIVE 1 = inside, internal, inner ≠ exterior 2 = mental, emotional, psychological, private, personal, secret, hidden, spiritual

intermediary = mediator, agent, middleman, broker, go-between

intermediate = middle, mid, halfway, in-between (*informal*), midway, intervening, transitional, median

internal 1 = domestic, home, national, local, civic, in-house, intramural 2 = inner, inside, interior ≠ external

international = global, world, worldwide, universal, cosmopolitan, intercontinental

Internet
● PHRASES **the Internet** = the information superhighway, the net (*informal*), the web (*informal*), the World Wide Web, cyberspace

interpret 1 = take, understand, explain, construe 2 = translate, transliterate 3 = explain, make sense of, decode, decipher, elucidate 4 = understand, read, crack, solve, figure out (*informal*), comprehend, decode, deduce 5 = portray, present, perform, render, depict, enact, act out

interpretation 1 = explanation, analysis, exposition, elucidation 2 = performance, portrayal, presentation, reading, rendition 3 = reading, study, review, version, analysis, explanation, examination, evaluation

interpreter = translator

interrogation = questioning, inquiry, examination, grilling (*informal*), cross-examination, inquisition, third degree (*informal*)

interrupt 1 = intrude, disturb, intervene, interfere (with), break in, heckle, butt in, barge in (*informal*) 2 = suspend, stop, end, delay, cease, postpone, shelve, put off

interruption 1 = disruption, break, disturbance, hitch, intrusion 2 = stoppage, pause, suspension

interval 1 = period, spell, space, stretch, pause, span 2 = break, interlude, intermission, rest, gap, pause, respite, lull 3 = delay, gap, hold-up, stoppage 4 = stretch, space

intervene 1 = step in (informal), interfere, mediate, intrude, intercede, arbitrate, take a hand (informal) 2 = interrupt, involve yourself 3 = happen, occur, take place, follow, arise, ensue, befall, materialize

intervention = mediation, interference, intrusion, arbitration, conciliation, agency

interview NOUN 1 = meeting 2 = audience, talk, conference, exchange, dialogue, consultation, press conference
● VERB 1 = examine, talk to 2 = question, interrogate, examine, investigate, pump, grill (informal), quiz, cross-examine

interviewer = questioner, reporter, investigator, examiner, interrogator

intimacy = familiarity, closeness, confidentiality ≠ aloofness

intimate¹ ADJECTIVE 1 = close, dear, loving, near, familiar, thick (informal), devoted, friendly ≠ distant 2 = private, personal, confidential, special, individual, secret, exclusive ≠ public 3 = detailed, minute, full, deep, particular, immediate,

comprehensive, profound 4 = cosy, relaxed, friendly, informal, harmonious, snug, comfy (informal), warm
● NOUN = friend, close friend, crony, cobber (Austral. & N.Z. old-fashioned informal), confidant or confidante, (constant) companion, E hoa (N.Z.) ≠ stranger

intimate² 1 = suggest, indicate, hint, imply, insinuate 2 = announce, state, declare, communicate, make known

intimately 1 = closely, personally, warmly, familiarly, tenderly, affectionately, confidentially, confidingly 2 = fully, very well, thoroughly, in detail, inside out

intimidate = frighten, pressure, threaten, scare, bully, plague, hound, daunt

intimidation = bullying, pressure, threat(s), menaces, coercion, arm-twisting (informal), browbeating, terrorization

intricate = complicated, involved, complex, fancy, elaborate, tangled, tortuous, convoluted ≠ simple

intrigue NOUN 1 = plot, scheme, conspiracy, manoeuvre, collusion, stratagem, chicanery, wile 2 = affair, romance, intimacy, liaison, amour
● VERB 1 = interest, fascinate,

attract, rivet, titillate 2 = **plot**, scheme, manoeuvre, conspire, connive, machinate

intriguing = interesting, fascinating, absorbing, exciting, engaging, gripping, stimulating, compelling

introduce 1 = bring in, establish, set up, start, found, launch, institute, pioneer 2 = **present**, acquaint, make known, familiarize 3 = **suggest**, air, advance, submit, bring up, put forward, broach, moot 4 = **add**, insert, inject, throw in (*informal*), infuse

introduction 1 = **launch**, institution, pioneering, inauguration ≠ elimination 2 = **opening**, prelude, preface, lead-in, preamble, foreword, prologue, intro (*informal*) ≠ conclusion

introductory 1 = **preliminary**, first, initial, inaugural, preparatory ≠ concluding 2 = **starting**, opening, initial

intruder = **trespasser**, invader, prowler, interloper, infiltrator, gate-crasher (*informal*)

intrusion 1 = **interruption**, interference, infringement, trespass, encroachment 2 = **invasion**, breach, infringement, encroachment, infraction, usurpation

intuition 1 = instinct, perception, insight, sixth sense 2 = **feeling**, idea, impression, suspicion, premonition, inkling, presentiment

invade 1 = attack, storm, assault, capture, occupy, seize, raid, overwhelm 2 = **infest**, swarm, overrun, ravage, beset, pervade, permeate

invader = attacker, raider, plunderer, aggressor, trespasser

invalid[1] NOUN = patient, sufferer, convalescent, valetudinarian
• ADJECTIVE = **disabled**, ill, sick, ailing, frail, infirm, bedridden

invalid[2] 1 = **null and void**, void, worthless, inoperative ≠ valid 2 = **unfounded**, false, illogical, irrational, unsound, fallacious ≠ sound

invaluable = **precious**, valuable, priceless, inestimable, worth your or its weight in gold ≠ worthless

invariably = **always**, regularly, constantly, repeatedly, consistently, continually, eternally, habitually

invasion 1 = attack, assault, capture, takeover, raid, offensive, occupation, conquering 2 = **intrusion**, breach, violation, disturbance, disruption, infringement, encroachment, infraction

invent 1 = create, make, produce, design, discover, manufacture, devise, conceive 2 = **make up**, devise, concoct, forge, fake, fabricate, feign, falsify

invention 1 = <u>creation</u>, machine, device, design, instrument, discovery, innovation, gadget 2 = <u>development</u>, design, production, setting up, foundation, construction, creation, discovery 3 = <u>fiction</u>, fantasy, lie, yarn, fabrication, falsehood, untruth 4 = <u>creativity</u>, imagination, initiative, enterprise, genius, ingenuity, originality, inventiveness

inventive = <u>creative</u>, original, innovative, imaginative, inspired, fertile, ingenious, resourceful ≠ uninspired

inventor = <u>creator</u>, maker, author, designer, architect, coiner, originator

inventory = <u>list</u>, record, catalogue, listing, account, roll, file, register

invertebrate ‣ crustaceans ‣ snails, slugs and other gastropods ‣ spiders and other arachnids ‣ types of invertebrate

invest VERB 1 = <u>spend</u>, expend, advance, venture, put in, devote, lay out, sink in 2 = <u>empower</u>, provide, charge, sanction, license, authorize, vest

● PHRASES **invest in something** = <u>buy</u>, get, purchase, pay for, obtain, acquire, procure

investigate = <u>examine</u>, study, research, go into, explore, look into, inspect, probe into

investigation = <u>examination</u>, study, inquiry, review, search, survey, probe, inspection

investigator = <u>examiner</u>, researcher, monitor, detective, analyser, explorer, scrutinizer, inquirer

investment 1 = <u>investing</u>, backing, funding, financing, contribution, speculation, transaction, expenditure 2 = <u>stake</u>, interest, share, concern, portion, ante (*informal*) 3 = <u>buy</u>, asset, acquisition, venture, risk, gamble

invisible = <u>unseen</u>, imperceptible, indiscernible, unseeable ≠ visible

invitation = <u>request</u>, call, invite (*informal*), summons

invite 1 = <u>ask</u> 2 = <u>request</u>, look for, bid for, appeal for 3 = <u>encourage</u>, attract, cause, court, ask for (*informal*), generate, foster, tempt

inviting = <u>tempting</u>, appealing, attractive, welcoming, enticing, seductive, alluring, mouthwatering ≠ uninviting

invoke 1 = <u>apply</u>, use, implement, initiate, resort to, put into effect 2 = <u>call upon</u>, appeal to, pray to, petition, beseech, entreat, supplicate

Types of invertebrate

amoeba or (U.S.) ameba
animalcule or animalculum
arthropod
bardy, bardie, or bardi (Austral.)
bivalve
blue-ringed octopus (Austral.)
Bluff oyster (N.Z.)
box jellyfish or (Austral.) sea wasp
brachiopod or lamp shell
brandling
bryozoan or (colloquial) sea mat
centipede
chiton or coat-of-mail shell
clam
cone (shell)
coral
ctenophore or comb jelly
cunjevoi or cunje (Austral.)
cuttlefish or cuttle
daphnia
earthworm
eelworm
gastropodart
horseleech
jellyfish or (Austral. slang)
  blubber
kina (N.Z.)
lancelet or amphioxus
leech
lugworm, lug, or lobworm
millipede, millepede, or
  milleped
mollusc
mussel
octopus or devilfish
oyster

paper nautilus, nautilus, or
  argonaut
pearly nautilus, nautilus, or
  chambered nautilus
piddock
pipi or ugari (Austral.)
Portuguese man-of-war or
  (Austral.) bluebottle
quahog, hard-shell clam, hard-
  shell, or round clam
ragworm or (U.S.) clamworm
razor-shell or (U.S.) razor clam
red coral or precious coral
roundworm
sandworm or (Austral.)
  pumpworm
scallop
sea anemone
sea cucumber
sea lily
sea mouse
sea squirt
sea urchin
seed oyster
sponge
squid
starfish
tapeworm
tardigrade or water bear
teredo or shipworm
trepang or bêche-de-mer
tube worm
tubifex
tusk shell or tooth shell
worm

involve 1 = <u>entail</u>, mean, require, occasion, imply, give rise to, necessitate 2 = <u>concern</u>, draw in, bear on

involved = <u>complicated</u>, complex, intricate, hard, confused, confusing, elaborate, tangled ≠ straightforward

involvement = <u>connection</u>, interest, association, commitment, attachment

inward 1 = <u>incoming</u>, entering, inbound, ingoing 2 = <u>internal</u>, inner, private, personal, inside, secret, hidden, interior ≠ outward

Ireland = <u>Hibernia</u> (*Latin*)

iron ADJECTIVE 1 = <u>ferrous</u>, ferric 2 = <u>inflexible</u>, hard, strong, tough, rigid, adamant, unconditional, steely ≠ weak

● PHRASES **iron something out** = <u>settle</u>, resolve, sort out, get rid of, reconcile, clear up, put right, straighten out

(*Related Words*)

adjectives: ferric, ferrous

ironic *or* **ironical** 1 = <u>sarcastic</u>, dry, acid, bitter, mocking, wry, satirical, tongue-in-cheek 2 = <u>paradoxical</u>, contradictory, puzzling, baffling, confounding, enigmatic, incongruous

irony 1 = <u>sarcasm</u>, mockery, ridicule, satire, cynicism, derision 2 = <u>paradox</u>, incongruity

irrational = <u>illogical</u>, crazy, absurd, unreasonable,

preposterous, nonsensical ≠ rational

irregular 1 = <u>variable</u>, erratic, occasional, random, casual, shaky, sporadic, haphazard ≠ steady 2 = <u>uneven</u>, rough, ragged, crooked, jagged, bumpy, contorted, lopsided ≠ even 3 = <u>inappropriate</u>, unconventional, unethical, unusual, extraordinary, exceptional, peculiar, unofficial 4 = <u>unofficial</u>, underground, guerrilla, resistance, partisan, rogue, paramilitary, mercenary

irrelevant = <u>unconnected</u>, unrelated, unimportant, inappropriate, peripheral, immaterial, extraneous, beside the point ≠ relevant

irresistible = <u>overwhelming</u>, compelling, overpowering, urgent, compulsive

irresponsible = <u>thoughtless</u>, reckless, careless, unreliable, untrustworthy, shiftless, scatterbrained ≠ responsible

irritate 1 = <u>annoy</u>, anger, bother, needle (*informal*), infuriate, exasperate, nettle, irk ≠ placate 2 = <u>inflame</u>, pain, rub, scratch, scrape, chafe

irritated = <u>annoyed</u>, cross, angry, bothered, put out, exasperated, nettled, vexed, tooshie (*Austral. slang*), hoha (*N.Z.*)

irritating = <u>annoying</u>, trying,

infuriating, disturbing, nagging, troublesome, maddening, irksome ≠ pleasing

irritation 1 = annoyance, anger, fury, resentment, gall, indignation, displeasure, exasperation ≠ pleasure
2 = nuisance, irritant, drag (*informal*), pain in the neck (*informal*), thorn in your flesh

island = isle, atoll, islet, ait or eyot (*dialect*), cay or key
(*Related Words*)
adjective: insular

isolate 1 = separate, break up, cut off, detach, split up, insulate, segregate, disconnect
2 = quarantine

isolated = remote, far, distant, lonely, out-of-the-way, hidden, secluded, inaccessible

isolation = separation, segregation, detachment, solitude, seclusion, remoteness

issue NOUN 1 = topic, point, matter, problem, question, subject, theme 2 = point, question, bone of contention
3 = edition, printing, copy, publication, number, version
4 = children, offspring, babies, kids (*informal*), heirs, descendants, progeny ≠ parent
● VERB = give out, release, publish, announce, deliver, spread, broadcast, distribute
● PHRASES **take issue with**

something *or* someone = disagree with, question, challenge, oppose, dispute, object to, argue with, take exception to

itch VERB 1 = prickle, tickle, tingle
2 = long, ache, crave, pine, hunger, lust, yearn, hanker
● NOUN 1 = irritation, tingling, prickling, itchiness 2 = desire, longing, craving, passion, yen (*informal*), hunger, lust, yearning

item 1 = article, thing, object, piece, unit, component
2 = matter, point, issue, case, question, concern, detail, subject
3 = report, story, piece, account, note, feature, notice, article

itinerary = schedule, programme, route, timetable

J

jab VERB = poke, dig, punch, thrust, tap, stab, nudge, prod
● NOUN = poke, dig, punch, thrust, tap, stab, nudge, prod

jacket = covering, casing, case, cover, skin, shell, coat, wrapping

jackpot = prize, winnings, award, reward, bonanza

jail NOUN = prison, penitentiary (*U.S.*), confinement, dungeon, nick (*Brit. slang*), slammer (*slang*), reformatory, boob (*Austral. slang*)
● VERB = imprison, confine, detain, lock up, put away, intern,

incarcerate, send down

jam NOUN = predicament, tight spot, situation, trouble, hole (slang), fix (informal), mess, pinch
● VERB 1 = pack, force, press, stuff, squeeze, ram, wedge, cram 2 = crowd, throng, crush, mass, surge, flock, swarm, congregate 3 = congest, block, clog, stick, stall, obstruct

jar¹ = pot, container, drum, vase, jug, pitcher, urn, crock

jar² 1 usually with **on** = irritate, annoy, offend, nettle, irk, grate on, get on your nerves (informal) 2 = jolt, rock, shake, bump, rattle, vibrate, convulse

jargon = parlance, idiom, usage, argot

jaw PLURAL NOUN = opening, entrance, mouth
● VERB (Informal) = talk, chat, gossip, chatter, spout, natter

jealous 1 = suspicious, protective, wary, doubtful, sceptical, vigilant, watchful, possessive ≠ trusting 2 = envious, grudging, resentful, green, green with envy, desirous, covetous ≠ satisfied

jealousy = suspicion, mistrust, possessiveness, doubt, spite, resentment, wariness, dubiety

jeer VERB = mock, deride, heckle, barrack, ridicule, taunt, scoff, gibe ≠ cheer
● NOUN = mockery, abuse, ridicule,

taunt, boo, derision, gibe, catcall ≠ applause

jeopardy = danger, risk, peril, vulnerability, insecurity

jerk VERB = jolt, bang, bump, lurch
● NOUN = lurch, movement, thrust, twitch, jolt

jet NOUN = stream, current, spring, flow, rush, flood, burst, spray
● VERB = fly, wing, cruise, soar, zoom

jewel 1 = gemstone, gem, ornament, sparkler (informal), rock (slang) 2 = treasure, wonder, darling, pearl, gem, paragon, pride and joy, taonga (N.Z.)

jewellery = jewels, treasure, gems, trinkets, ornaments, finery, regalia

job 1 = position, work, calling, business, field, career, employment, profession 2 = task, duty, work, venture, enterprise, undertaking, assignment, chore

jobless = unemployed, redundant, out of work, inactive, unoccupied, idle

jog 1 = run, trot, canter, lope 2 = nudge, push, shake, prod 3 = stimulate, stir, prod

join 1 = enrol in, enter, sign up for, enlist in 2 = connect, unite, couple, link, combine, attach, fasten, add ≠ detach

joint ADJECTIVE = shared, mutual, collective, communal, united, joined, allied, combined
● NOUN = junction, connection,

brace, bracket, hinge, intersection, node, nexus

jointly = <u>collectively</u>, together, in conjunction, as one, in common, mutually, in partnership, in league ≠ separately

joke NOUN 1 = <u>jest</u>, gag (*informal*), wisecrack (*informal*), witticism, crack (*informal*), quip, pun, one-liner (*informal*) 2 = <u>laugh</u>, jest, jape 3 = <u>prank</u>, trick, practical joke, lark (*informal*), escapade, jape 4 = <u>laughing stock</u>, clown, buffoon ● VERB = <u>jest</u>, kid (*informal*), mock, tease, taunt, gag, banter, play the fool .

joker = <u>comedian</u>, comic, wit, clown, wag, jester, prankster, buffoon

jolly = <u>happy</u>, cheerful, merry, upbeat (*informal*), playful, cheery, genial, chirpy (*informal*) ≠ miserable

jolt VERB 1 = <u>jerk</u>, push, shake, knock, jar, shove, jog, jostle 2 = <u>surprise</u>, stun, disturb, stagger, startle, perturb, discompose ● NOUN 1 = <u>jerk</u>, start, jump, shake, bump, jar, jog, lurch 2 = <u>surprise</u>, blow, shock, setback, bombshell, bolt from the blue

journal 1 = <u>magazine</u>, publication, gazette, periodical 2 = <u>newspaper</u>, paper, daily, weekly, monthly 3 = <u>diary</u>, record, history, log, notebook, chronicle, annals, yearbook

journalist = <u>reporter</u>, writer,

correspondent, newsman *or* newswoman, commentator, broadcaster, hack (*derogatory*), columnist

journey NOUN 1 = <u>trip</u>, drive, tour, flight, excursion, trek, expedition, voyage 2 = <u>progress</u>, voyage, pilgrimage, odyssey ● VERB = <u>travel</u>, go, move, tour, progress, proceed, wander, trek, go walkabout (*Austral.*)

joy = <u>delight</u>, pleasure, satisfaction, ecstasy, enjoyment, bliss, glee, rapture ≠ sorrow

jubilee = <u>celebration</u>, holiday, festival, festivity

judge NOUN 1 = <u>magistrate</u>, justice, beak (*Brit. slang*), His, Her *or* Your Honour 2 = <u>referee</u>, expert, specialist, umpire, mediator, examiner, connoisseur, assessor 3 = <u>critic</u>, assessor, arbiter ● VERB 1 = <u>adjudicate</u>, referee, umpire, mediate, officiate, arbitrate 2 = <u>evaluate</u>, rate, consider, view, value, esteem 3 = <u>estimate</u>, guess, assess, calculate, evaluate, gauge
Related Words
adjective: judicial

judgment 1 = <u>opinion</u>, view, estimate, belief, assessment, diagnosis, valuation, appraisal 2 = <u>verdict</u>, finding, ruling, decision, sentence, decree, arbitration, adjudication 3 = <u>sense</u>, good sense, understanding, discrimination, perception, wisdom, wit, prudence

judicial = <u>legal</u>, official

jug = <u>container</u>, pitcher, urn, carafe, creamer (*U.S. & Canad.*), vessel, jar, crock

juggle = <u>manipulate</u>, change, alter, modify, manoeuvre

juice 1 = <u>liquid</u>, extract, fluid, liquor, sap, nectar **2** = <u>secretion</u>

juicy 1 = <u>moist</u>, lush, succulent **2** (*Informal*) = <u>interesting</u>, colourful, sensational, vivid, provocative, spicy (*informal*), suggestive, racy

jumble NOUN = <u>muddle</u>, mixture, mess, disorder, confusion, clutter, disarray, mishmash
● VERB = <u>mix</u>, mistake, confuse, disorder, shuffle, muddle, disorganize

jumbo = <u>giant</u>, large, huge, immense, gigantic, oversized ≠ tiny

jump VERB **1** = <u>leap</u>, spring, bound, bounce, hop, skip **2** = <u>vault</u>, hurdle, go over, sail over, hop over **3** = <u>spring</u>, bound, bounce **4** = <u>recoil</u>, start, jolt, flinch, shake, jerk, quake, shudder **5** = <u>increase</u>, rise, climb, escalate, advance, soar, surge, spiral **6** = <u>miss</u>, avoid, skip, omit, evade
● NOUN **1** = <u>leap</u>, spring, skip, bound, hop, vault **2** = <u>rise</u>, increase, upswing, advance, upsurge, upturn, increment

jumped-up = <u>conceited</u>, arrogant, pompous, overbearing, presumptuous, insolent

jumper = <u>sweater</u>, top, jersey, cardigan, woolly, pullover

junior 1 = <u>minor</u>, lower, secondary, lesser, subordinate, inferior **2** = <u>younger</u> ≠ senior

junk = <u>rubbish</u>, refuse, waste, scrap, litter, debris, garbage (*chiefly U.S.*), trash

jurisdiction 1 = <u>authority</u>, power, control, rule, influence, command, mana (*N.Z.*) **2** = <u>range</u>, area, field, bounds, province, scope, sphere, compass

just ADVERB **1** = <u>recently</u>, lately, only now **2** = <u>merely</u>, only, simply, solely **3** = <u>barely</u>, hardly, by a whisker, by the skin of your teeth **4** = <u>exactly</u>, really, quite, completely, totally, perfectly, entirely, truly
● ADJECTIVE **1** = <u>fair</u>, good, legitimate, upright, honest, equitable, conscientious, virtuous ≠ unfair **2** = <u>fitting</u>, due, correct, deserved, appropriate, justified, decent, merited ≠ inappropriate

---

Word Power

just – The expression *just exactly* is considered to be poor style because, since both words mean the same thing, only one or the other is needed. Use *just* – it's *just what they want* – or *exactly* – it's *exactly what they want*, but not both together.

justice 1 = <u>fairness</u>, equity, integrity, honesty, decency, rightfulness, right ≠ injustice **2** = <u>justness</u>, fairness, legitimacy, right, integrity, honesty, legality, rightfulness **3** = <u>judge</u>, magistrate, beak (*Brit. slang*), His, Her *or* Your Honour

justification = <u>reason</u>, grounds, defence, basis, excuse, warrant, rationale, vindication

justify = <u>explain</u>, support, warrant, defend, excuse, uphold, vindicate, exonerate

juvenile NOUN = <u>child</u>, youth, minor, girl, boy, teenager, infant, adolescent ≠ adult
• ADJECTIVE **1** = <u>young</u>, junior, adolescent, immature ≠ adult **2** = <u>immature</u>, childish, infantile, puerile, young, youthful, inexperienced, callow

K

kai (*N.Z. informal*) = <u>food</u>, grub (*slang*), provisions, fare, tucker (*Austral. & N.Z. informal*), refreshment, foodstuffs

kak (*S. African taboo*) **1** = <u>faeces</u>, excrement, manure, dung, droppings, waste matter **2** = <u>rubbish</u>, nonsense, garbage (*informal*), rot, drivel, tripe (*informal*), bizzo (*Austral. slang*), bull's wool (*Austral. & N.Z. slang*)

keen 1 = <u>eager</u>, intense, enthusiastic, passionate, ardent, avid, fervent, impassioned ≠ unenthusiastic **2** = <u>earnest</u>, fierce, intense, vehement, passionate, heightened, ardent, fanatical **3** = <u>sharp</u>, incisive, cutting, edged, razor-like ≠ dull **4** = <u>perceptive</u>, quick, sharp, acute, smart, wise, clever, shrewd ≠ obtuse **5** = <u>intense</u>, strong, fierce, relentless, cut-throat

keep¹ VERB **1** *usually with from* = <u>prevent</u>, restrain, hinder, keep back **2** = <u>hold on to</u>, maintain, retain, save, preserve, nurture, cherish, conserve ≠ lose **3** = <u>store</u>, put, place, house, hold, deposit, stack, stow **4** = <u>carry</u>, stock, sell, supply, handle **5** = <u>support</u>, maintain, sustain, provide for, mind, fund, finance, feed **6** = <u>raise</u>, own, maintain, tend, farm, breed, look after, rear **7** = <u>manage</u>, run, administer, be in charge (of), direct, handle, supervise **8** = <u>delay</u>, detain, hinder, impede, obstruct, set back ≠ release
• NOUN = <u>board</u>, food, maintenance, living, kai (*N.Z. informal*)
• PHRASES **keep something up 1** = <u>continue</u>, make, maintain, carry on, persist in, persevere with **2** = <u>maintain</u>, sustain, perpetuate, retain, preserve,

prolong ♦ **keep up** = keep pace

keep² = tower, castle

keeper = curator, guardian, steward, attendant, caretaker, preserver

keeping NOUN = care, charge, protection, possession, custody, guardianship, safekeeping

• PHRASES **in keeping with** = in agreement with, in harmony with, in accord with, in compliance with, in conformity with, in balance with, in correspondence with, in proportion with

key NOUN 1 = opener, door key, latchkey 2 = answer

• ADJECTIVE = essential, leading, major, main, important, necessary, vital, crucial ≠ minor

kia ora (*N.Z.*) = hello, hi (*informal*), greetings, gidday or g'day (*Austral. & N.Z.*), how do you do?, good morning, good evening, good afternoon

kick VERB 1 = boot, knock, punt 2 (*Informal*) = give up, break, stop, abandon, quit, cease, eschew, leave off

• NOUN (*Informal*) = thrill, buzz (*slang*), tingle, high (*slang*)

• PHRASES **kick off** (*Informal*) = begin, start, open, commence, initiate, get on the road ♦ **kick someone out** (*Informal*) = dismiss, remove, get rid of, expel, eject, evict, sack (*informal*)

kid¹ (*Informal*) = child, baby, teenager, youngster, infant, adolescent, juvenile, toddler, littlie (*Austral. informal*), ankle-biter (*Austral. slang*), tacker (*Austral. slang*)

kid² = tease, joke, trick, fool, pretend, wind up (*Brit. slang*), hoax, delude

kidnap = abduct, capture, seize, snatch (*slang*), hijack, hold to ransom

kill 1 = slay, murder, execute, slaughter, destroy, massacre, butcher, cut down 2 (*Informal*) = destroy, crush, scotch, stop, halt, wreck, shatter, suppress

killer = murderer, slayer, hit man (*slang*), butcher, gunman, assassin, terminator, executioner

killing NOUN = murder, massacre, slaughter, dispatch, manslaughter, elimination, slaying, homicide

• ADJECTIVE (*Informal*) = tiring, taxing, exhausting, punishing, fatiguing, gruelling, sapping, debilitating

• PHRASES **make a killing** (*Informal*) = profit, gain, clean up (*informal*), be lucky, be successful, make a fortune, strike it rich (*informal*), make a bomb (*slang*)

kind¹ 1 = class, sort, type, variety, brand, category, genre 2 = sort, set, type, family, species, breed

Word Power

kind – It is common in informal speech to combine singular and plural in sentences like *children enjoy those kind of stories.* However, this is not acceptable in careful writing, where the plural must be used consistently: *children enjoy those kinds of stories.*

kind² = <u>considerate</u>, kindly, concerned, friendly, generous, obliging, charitable, benign
≠ unkind

kindly ADJECTIVE = <u>benevolent</u>, kind, caring, warm, helpful, pleasant, sympathetic, benign
≠ cruel

● ADVERB = <u>benevolently</u>, politely, generously, thoughtfully, tenderly, lovingly, cordially, affectionately ≠ unkindly

kindness = <u>goodwill</u>, understanding, charity, humanity, compassion, generosity, philanthropy, benevolence
≠ malice

king = <u>ruler</u>, monarch, sovereign, leader, lord, Crown, emperor, head of state

kingdom = <u>country</u>, state, nation, territory, realm

kiss VERB 1 = <u>peck</u> (*informal*), osculate, neck (*informal*)
2 = <u>brush</u>, touch, shave, scrape, graze, glance off, stroke

● NOUN = <u>peck</u> (*informal*), snog (*Brit. slang*), smacker (*slang*), French kiss, osculation

kit NOUN 1 = <u>equipment</u>, materials, tackle, tools, apparatus, paraphernalia 2 = <u>gear</u>, things, stuff, equipment, uniform

● PHRASES **kit something** or **someone out** or **up** = <u>equip</u>, fit, supply, provide with, arm, stock, costume, furnish

knack = <u>skill</u>, art, ability, facility, talent, gift, capacity, trick
≠ ineptitude

kneel = <u>genuflect</u>, stoop

knickers = <u>underwear</u>, smalls, briefs, drawers, panties, bloomers

knife NOUN = <u>blade</u>, carver, cutter
● VERB = <u>cut</u>, wound, stab, slash, thrust, pierce, spear, jab

knit 1 = <u>join</u>, unite, link, tie, bond, combine, bind, weave 2 = <u>heal</u>, unite, join, link, bind, fasten, intertwine 3 = <u>furrow</u>, tighten, knot, wrinkle, crease, screw up, pucker, scrunch up

knob = <u>ball</u>, stud, knot, lump, bump, projection, hump, protrusion

knock VERB 1 = <u>bang</u>, strike, tap, rap, thump, pummel 2 = <u>hit</u>, strike, punch, belt (*informal*), smack, thump, cuff 3 (*Informal*) = <u>criticize</u>, condemn, put down, run down, abuse, slate (*informal*), censure, denigrate

● NOUN 1 = <u>knocking</u>, pounding, beating, tap, bang, banging, rap, thump 2 = <u>bang</u>, blow, impact, jar, collision, jolt, smash 3 = <u>blow</u>, hit, punch, crack, clip, slap, bash, smack 4 (*Informal*) = <u>setback</u>, check, defeat, blow, reverse, disappointment, hold-up, hitch

● PHRASES **knock about or around** = <u>wander</u>, travel, roam, rove, range, drift, stray, ramble, go walkabout (*Austral.*) ◆ **knock about or around with someone** = <u>mix with</u>, associate with, mingle with, consort with, hobnob with, socialize with, accompany ◆ **knock off** (*Informal*) = <u>stop work</u>, get out, call it a day (*informal*), finish work, clock off, clock out ◆ **knock someone about or around** = <u>hit</u>, attack, beat, strike, abuse, injure, assault, batter ◆ **knock someone down** = <u>run over</u>, hit, run down, knock over, mow down ◆ **knock something down** = <u>demolish</u>, destroy, flatten, tear down, level, fell, dismantle, bulldoze ◆ **knock something off** (*Slang*) = <u>steal</u>, take, nick (*slang, chiefly Brit.*), thieve, rob, pinch

knockout 1 = <u>killer blow</u>, coup de grâce (*French*), KO or K.O. (*slang*) 2 (*Informal*) = <u>success</u>, hit, winner, triumph, smash, sensation, smash hit ≠ failure

knot NOUN = <u>connection</u>, tie, bond, joint, loop, ligature

● VERB = <u>tie</u>, secure, bind, loop, tether

know 1 = <u>have knowledge of</u>, see, understand, recognize, perceive, be aware of, be conscious of **2** = <u>be acquainted with</u>, recognize, be familiar with, be friends with, be friendly with, have knowledge of, have dealings with, socialize with ≠ be unfamiliar with **3** *sometimes with* **about** *or of* = <u>be familiar with</u>, understand, comprehend, have knowledge of, be acquainted with, feel certain of, have dealings in, be versed in ≠ ignorant of

know-how (*Informal*) = <u>expertise</u>, ability, skill, knowledge, facility, talent, command, capability

knowing = <u>meaningful</u>, significant, expressive, enigmatic, suggestive

knowledge 1 = <u>understanding</u>, sense, judgment, perception, awareness, insight, grasp, appreciation **2** = <u>learning</u>, education, intelligence, instruction, wisdom, scholarship, enlightenment, erudition ≠ ignorance **3** = <u>acquaintance</u>, intimacy, familiarity ≠ unfamiliarity

knowledgeable 1 = <u>well-</u>

<u>informed</u>, conversant, au fait (*French*), experienced, aware, familiar, in the know (*informal*), cognizant 2 = <u>intelligent</u>, learned, educated, scholarly, erudite

known = <u>famous</u>, well-known, celebrated, noted, acknowledged, recognized, avowed ≠ unknown

kopje or **koppie** (*S. African*) = <u>hill</u>, down (*archaic*), fell, mount, hilltop, knoll, hillock, brae (*Scot.*)

L

label NOUN = <u>tag</u>, ticket, tab, marker, sticker
● VERB = <u>tag</u>, mark, stamp, ticket, tab

labour NOUN 1 = <u>workers</u>, employees, workforce, labourers, hands 2 = <u>work</u>, effort, employment, toil, industry 3 = <u>childbirth</u>, birth, delivery, parturition
● VERB 1 = <u>work</u>, toil, strive, work hard, sweat (*informal*), slave, endeavour, slog away (*informal*) ≠ rest 2 = <u>struggle</u>, work, strain, work hard, strive, grapple, toil, make an effort
3 = <u>overemphasize</u>, stress, elaborate, exaggerate, strain, dwell on, overdo, go on about 4 *usually with* **under** = <u>be disadvantaged by</u>, suffer from, be a victim of, be burdened by

Labour = <u>left-wing</u>, Democrat (*U.S.*)

laboured = <u>difficult</u>, forced, strained, heavy, awkward

labourer = <u>worker</u>, manual worker, hand, blue-collar worker, drudge, navvy (*Brit. informal*)

lace NOUN 1 = <u>netting</u>, net, filigree, meshwork, openwork 2 = <u>cord</u>, tie, string, lacing, shoelace, bootlace
● VERB 1 = <u>fasten</u>, tie, tie up, do up, secure, bind, thread 2 = <u>mix</u>, drug, doctor, add to, spike, contaminate, fortify, adulterate 3 = <u>intertwine</u>, interweave, entwine, twine, interlink

lack NOUN = <u>shortage</u>, want, absence, deficiency, need, inadequacy, scarcity, dearth ≠ abundance
● VERB = <u>miss</u>, want, need, require, not have, be without, be short of, be in need of ≠ have

lad = <u>boy</u>, kid (*informal*), guy (*informal*), youth, fellow, youngster, juvenile, nipper (*informal*)

laden = <u>loaded</u>, burdened, full, charged, weighed down, encumbered

lady 1 = <u>gentlewoman</u>, duchess, noble, dame, baroness, countess, aristocrat, viscountess 2 = <u>woman</u>, female, girl, damsel, charlie (*Austral. slang*), chook (*Austral. slang*), wahine (*N.Z.*)

lag = hang back, delay, trail, linger, loiter, straggle, dawdle, tarry

laid-back = relaxed, calm, casual, easy-going, unflappable (*informal*), unhurried, free and easy ≠ tense

lake = pond, pool, reservoir, loch (*Scot.*), lagoon, mere, lough (*Irish*), tarn

lame 1 = disabled, handicapped, crippled, limping, hobbling, game **2** = unconvincing, poor, pathetic, inadequate, thin, weak, feeble, unsatisfactory

lament VERB = bemoan, grieve, mourn, weep over, complain about, regret, wail about, deplore
● NOUN **1** = complaint, moan, wailing, lamentation **2** = dirge, requiem, elegy, threnody

land NOUN **1** = ground, earth, dry land, terra firma **2** = soil, ground, earth, clay, dirt, sod, loam **3** = countryside, farmland **4** (*Law*) = property, grounds, estate, real estate, realty, acreage **5** = country, nation, region, state, district, territory, province, kingdom
● VERB **1** = arrive, dock, put down, moor, alight, touch down, disembark, come to rest **2** (*Informal*) = gain, get, win, secure, acquire
● PHRASES **land up** = end up, turn up, wind up, finish up, fetch up (*informal*)
(Related Words)
adjective: terrestrial

landlord 1 = owner, landowner, proprietor, freeholder, lessor, landholder **2** = innkeeper, host, hotelier

landmark 1 = feature, spectacle, monument **2** = milestone, turning point, watershed, critical point

landscape = scenery, country, view, land, scene, prospect, countryside, outlook

landslide = landslip, avalanche, rockfall

lane = road, street, track, path, way, passage, trail, pathway

language 1 = tongue, dialect, vernacular, patois **2** = speech, communication, expression, speaking, talk, talking, discourse, parlance

languish 1 = decline, fade away, wither away, flag, weaken, wilt ≠ flourish **2** (*Literary*) = waste away, suffer, rot, be abandoned, be neglected ≠ thrive **3** *often with* **for** = pine, long, desire, hunger, yearn, hanker

lap¹ = circuit, tour, leg, stretch, circle, orbit, loop

lap² VERB **1** = ripple, wash, splash, swish, gurgle, slosh, purl, plash **2** = drink, sip, lick, swallow, gulp, sup
● PHRASES **lap something up**

= <u>relish</u>, like, enjoy, delight in, savour, revel in, wallow in, accept eagerly

lapse NOUN 1 = <u>decline</u>, fall, drop, deterioration 2 = <u>mistake</u>, failing, fault, failure, error, slip, negligence, omission 3 = <u>interval</u>, break, gap, pause, interruption, lull, breathing space, intermission • VERB 1 = <u>slip</u>, fall, decline, sink, drop, slide, deteriorate, degenerate 2 = <u>end</u>, stop, run out, expire, terminate

lapsed = <u>expired</u>, ended, finished, run out, invalid, out of date, discontinued

large ADJECTIVE 1 = <u>big</u>, great, huge, heavy, massive, vast, enormous, tall ≠ small 2 = <u>massive</u>, great, big, huge, enormous, considerable, substantial ≠ small • PHRASES **at large 1** = <u>in general</u>, generally, chiefly, mainly, as a whole, in the main 2 = <u>free</u>, on the run, fugitive, at liberty, on the loose, unchained, unconfined ◆ **by and large** = <u>on the whole</u>, generally, mostly, in general, all things considered, predominantly, in the main, all in all

largely = <u>mainly</u>, generally, chiefly, mostly, principally, primarily, predominantly, by and large

large-scale = <u>wide-ranging</u>, global, sweeping, broad, wide, vast, extensive, wholesale

lash[1] VERB 1 = <u>pound</u>, beat, strike, hammer, drum, smack (*dialect*) 2 = <u>censure</u>, attack, blast, put down, criticize, slate (*informal*, *chiefly Brit.*), scold, tear into (*informal*) 3 = <u>whip</u>, beat, thrash, birch, flog, scourge • NOUN = <u>blow</u>, hit, strike, stroke, stripe, swipe (*informal*)

lash[2] = <u>fasten</u>, tie, secure, bind, strap, make fast

last[1] ADJECTIVE 1 = <u>most recent</u>, latest, previous 2 = <u>hindmost</u>, final, at the end, remotest, furthest behind, most distant, rearmost ≠ foremost 3 = <u>final</u>, closing, concluding, ultimate ≠ first • ADVERB = <u>in</u> or <u>at the end</u>, after, behind, in the rear, bringing up the rear • PHRASES **the last word** 1 = <u>final decision</u>, final say, final statement, conclusive comment 2 = <u>leading</u>, finest, cream, supreme, elite, foremost, pre-eminent, unsurpassed

> ### Word Power
>
> **last** – Since *last* can mean either *after all others* or *most recent*, it is better to avoid using this word where ambiguity might arise, as in *her last novel*. *Final* or *latest* should be used as alternatives in such contexts to avoid any possible confusion.

last² = <u>continue</u>, remain, survive, carry on, endure, persist, keep on, abide ≠ end

lasting = <u>continuing</u>, long-term, permanent, enduring, remaining, abiding, long-standing, perennial ≠ passing

latch NOUN = <u>fastening</u>, catch, bar, lock, hook, bolt, hasp
● VERB = <u>fasten</u>, bar, secure, bolt, make fast

late ADJECTIVE 1 = <u>overdue</u>, delayed, last-minute, belated, tardy, behind time, behindhand ≠ early 2 = <u>dead</u>, deceased, departed, passed on, former, defunct ≠ alive 3 = <u>recent</u>, new, advanced, fresh ≠ old
● ADVERB = <u>behind time</u>, belatedly, tardily, behindhand, dilatorily ≠ early

lately = <u>recently</u>, of late, just now, in recent times, not long ago, latterly

later ADVERB = <u>afterwards</u>, after, eventually, in time, subsequently, later on, thereafter, in a while
● ADJECTIVE = <u>subsequent</u>, next, following, ensuing

latest = <u>up-to-date</u>, current, fresh, newest, modern, most recent, up-to-the-minute

latitude = <u>scope</u>, liberty, freedom, play, space, licence, leeway, laxity

latter PRONOUN = <u>second</u>, last,

last-mentioned, second-mentioned
● ADJECTIVE = <u>last</u>, ending, closing, final, concluding ≠ earlier

> ### Word Power
>
> **latter** – *The latter should only be used to specify the second of two items, for example in* if I had to choose between the hovercraft and the ferry, I would opt for the latter. *Where there are three or more items, the last can be referred to as the last-named, but not the latter.*

laugh VERB = <u>chuckle</u>, giggle, snigger, cackle, chortle, guffaw, titter, be in stitches
● NOUN 1 = <u>chortle</u>, giggle, chuckle, snigger, guffaw, titter 2 (*Informal*) = <u>joke</u>, scream (*informal*), hoot (*informal*), lark, prank 3 (*Informal*) = <u>clown</u>, character (*informal*), scream (*informal*), entertainer, card (*informal*), joker, hoot (*informal*)
● PHRASES **laugh something off** = <u>disregard</u>, ignore, dismiss, overlook, shrug off, minimize, brush aside, make light of

laughter = <u>amusement</u>, entertainment, humour, glee, fun, mirth, hilarity, merriment

launch VERB 1 = <u>propel</u>, fire, dispatch, discharge, project, send

off, set in motion, send into orbit **2** = **begin**, start, open, initiate, introduce, found, set up, originate
● PHRASES **launch into something** = <u>start</u> enthusiastically, begin, initiate, embark on, instigate, inaugurate, embark upon

laurel
● PHRASES **rest on your laurels** = <u>sit back</u>, relax, take it easy, relax your efforts

lavatory = <u>toilet</u>, bathroom, loo (*Brit. informal*), privy, cloakroom (*Brit.*), urinal, latrine, washroom, dunny (*Austral. & N.Z. old-fashioned informal*), bogger (*Austral. slang*), brasco (*Austral. slang*)

lavish ADJECTIVE **1** = <u>grand</u>, magnificent, splendid, abundant, copious, profuse ≠ stingy **2** = <u>extravagant</u>, wild, excessive, exaggerated, wasteful, prodigal, unrestrained, immoderate ≠ thrifty **3** = <u>generous</u>, free, liberal, bountiful, open-handed, unstinting, munificent ≠ stingy
● VERB = <u>shower</u>, pour, heap, deluge, dissipate ≠ stint

law 1 = <u>constitution</u>, code, legislation, charter **2** = <u>statute</u>, act, bill, rule, order, command, regulation, resolution **3** = <u>principle</u>, code, canon, precept, axiom, kaupapa (*N.Z.*) **4** = <u>the legal profession</u>, the bar,

barristers
(*Related Words*)
adjectives: legal, judicial

lawsuit = <u>case</u>, action, trial, suit, proceedings, dispute, prosecution, legal action

lawyer = <u>legal adviser</u>, attorney, solicitor, counsel, advocate, barrister, counsellor, legal representative

lay¹ VERB **1** = <u>place</u>, put, set, spread, plant, leave, deposit, put down **2** = <u>devise</u>, plan, design, prepare, work out, plot, hatch, contrive **3** = <u>produce</u>, bear, deposit **4** = <u>arrange</u>, prepare, make, organize, position, set out, devise, put together **5** = <u>attribute</u>, assign, allocate, allot, ascribe, impute **6** = <u>put forward</u>, offer, present, advance, lodge, submit, bring forward ♦ = <u>bet</u>, stake, venture, gamble, chance, risk, hazard, wager
● PHRASES **lay someone off** = <u>dismiss</u>, fire (*informal*), release, sack (*informal*), pay off, discharge, let go, make redundant ♦ **lay someone out** (*Informal*) = <u>knock out</u>, fell, floor, knock unconscious, knock for six ♦ **lay something out 1** = <u>arrange</u>, order, design, display, exhibit, put out, spread out **2** (*Informal*) = <u>spend</u>, pay, invest, fork out (*slang*), expend, shell out (*informal*), disburse

Word Power

lay – In standard English, the verb *to lay* (meaning 'to put something somewhere') always needs an object, for example *the Queen laid a wreath*. By contrast, the verb *to lie* is always used without an object, for example *he was just lying there*.

lay² 1 = <u>nonclerical</u>, secular, non-ordained 2 = <u>nonspecialist</u>, amateur, unqualified, untrained, inexpert, nonprofessional

layer = <u>tier</u>, level, seam, stratum

layout = <u>arrangement</u>, design, outline, format, plan, formation

lazy 1 = <u>idle</u>, inactive, indolent, slack, negligent, inert, workshy, slothful ≠ industrious
2 = <u>lethargic</u>, languorous, slow-moving, languid, sleepy, sluggish, drowsy, somnolent ≠ quick

leach = <u>extract</u>, strain, drain, filter, seep, percolate

lead VERB 1 = <u>go in front (of)</u>, head, be in front, be at the head (of), walk in front (of) 2 = <u>guide</u>, conduct, steer, escort, precede, usher, pilot, show the way
3 = <u>connect to</u>, link, open onto 4 = <u>be ahead (of)</u>, be first, exceed, be winning, excel, surpass, come first, transcend 5 = <u>command</u>, rule, govern, preside over, head, control, manage, direct 6 = <u>live</u>,

have, spend, experience, pass, undergo 7 = <u>result in</u>, cause, produce, contribute, generate, bring about, bring on, give rise to 8 = <u>cause</u>, prompt, persuade, move, draw, influence, motivate, prevail

● NOUN 1 = <u>first place</u>, winning position, primary position, vanguard 2 = <u>advantage</u>, start, edge, margin, winning margin 3 = <u>example</u>, direction, leadership, guidance, model, pattern 4 = <u>clue</u>, suggestion, hint, indication, pointer, tip-off 5 = <u>leading role</u>, principal, protagonist, title role, principal part 6 = <u>leash</u>, line, cord, rein, tether

● ADJECTIVE = <u>main</u>, prime, top, leading, first, head, chief, premier
● PHRASES **lead someone on** = <u>entice</u>, tempt, lure, mislead, draw on, seduce, deceive, beguile
◆ **lead up to something** = <u>introduce</u>, prepare for, pave the way for

leader = <u>principal</u>, president, head, chief, boss (*informal*), director, manager, chairman, baas (*S. African*) ≠ follower

leadership 1 = <u>authority</u>, control, influence, command, premiership, captaincy, governance, headship 2 = <u>guidance</u>, government, authority, management, direction, supervision, domination, superintendency

leading = <u>principal</u>, top, major, main, first, highest, greatest, chief ≠ minor

leaf NOUN 1 = <u>frond</u>, blade, cotyledon 2 = <u>page</u>, sheet, folio

● PHRASES **leaf through something** (with *book, magazine* etc. as object) = <u>skim</u>, glance, scan, browse, look through, dip into, flick through, flip through

leaflet = <u>booklet</u>, notice, brochure, circular, flyer, tract, pamphlet, handout

leafy = <u>green</u>, shaded, shady, verdant

league 1 = <u>association</u>, union, alliance, coalition, group, corporation, partnership, federation 2 (*Informal*) = <u>class</u>, group, level, category

leak VERB 1 = <u>escape</u>, pass, spill, release, drip, trickle, ooze, seep 2 = <u>disclose</u>, tell, reveal, pass on, give away, make public, divulge, let slip

● NOUN 1 = <u>leakage</u>, discharge, drip, seepage, percolation 2 = <u>hole</u>, opening, crack, puncture, aperture, chink, crevice, fissure 3 = <u>disclosure</u>, exposé, exposure, admission, revelation, uncovering, betrayal, unearthing

lean¹ VERB 1 = <u>bend</u>, tip, slope, incline, tilt, heel, slant 2 = <u>rest</u>, prop, be supported, recline, repose 3 = <u>tend</u>, prefer, favour, incline, be prone to, be disposed to

● PHRASES **lean on someone** = <u>depend on</u>, trust, rely on, cling to, count on, have faith in

lean² = <u>thin</u>, slim, slender, skinny, angular, trim, spare, gaunt ≠ fat

leaning = <u>tendency</u>, bias, inclination, bent, disposition, penchant, propensity, predilection

leap VERB = <u>jump</u>, spring, bound, bounce, hop, skip

● NOUN 1 = <u>jump</u>, spring, bound, vault 2 = <u>rise</u>, change, increase, soaring, surge, escalation, upsurge, upswing

● PHRASES **leap at something** = <u>accept eagerly</u>, seize on, jump at

learn 1 = <u>master</u>, grasp, pick up, take in, familiarize yourself with 2 = <u>discover</u>, hear, understand, find out about, become aware, discern, ascertain, come to know 3 = <u>memorize</u>, commit to memory, learn by heart, learn by rote, learn parrot-fashion, get off pat

learned = <u>scholarly</u>, academic, intellectual, versed, well-informed, erudite, highbrow, well-read ≠ uneducated

learner = <u>student</u>, novice,

beginner, apprentice, neophyte, tyro ≠ expert

learning = knowledge, study, education, scholarship, enlightenment

lease = hire, rent, let, loan, charter, rent out, hire out

least = smallest, meanest, fewest, lowest, tiniest, minimum, slightest, minimal

leave VERB 1 = depart from, withdraw from, go from, escape from, quit, flee, exit, pull out of ≠ arrive 2 = quit, give up, get out of, resign from, drop out of 3 = give up, abandon, dump (informal), drop, surrender, ditch (informal), chuck (informal), discard ≠ stay with 4 = entrust, commit, delegate, refer, hand over, assign, consign, allot 5 = bequeath, will, transfer, endow, confer, hand down 6 = forget, leave behind, mislay 7 = cause, produce, result in, generate, deposit
● NOUN 1 = holiday, break, vacation, time off, sabbatical, leave of absence, furlough 2 = permission, freedom, sanction, liberty, concession, consent, allowance, warrant ≠ refusal 3 = departure, parting, withdrawal, goodbye, farewell, retirement, leave-taking, adieu ≠ arrival
● PHRASES **leave something** or

someone out = omit, exclude, miss out, forget, reject, ignore, overlook, neglect

lecture NOUN 1 = talk, address, speech, lesson, instruction, presentation, discourse, sermon 2 = telling-off (informal), rebuke, reprimand, talking-to (informal), scolding, dressing-down (informal), reproof
● VERB 1 = talk, speak, teach, address, discourse, spout, expound, hold forth 2 = tell off (informal), berate, scold, reprimand, censure, castigate, admonish, reprove

lees = sediment, grounds, deposit, dregs

left 1 = left-hand, port, larboard (Nautical) 2 (of politics) = socialist, radical, left-wing, leftist

left-wing = socialist, communist, red (informal), radical, revolutionary, militant, Bolshevik, Leninist

leg NOUN 1 = limb, member, shank, lower limb, pin (informal), stump (informal) 2 = support, prop, brace, upright 3 = stage, part, section, stretch, lap, segment, portion
● PHRASES **pull someone's leg** (Informal) = tease, trick, fool, kid (informal), wind up (Brit. slang), hoax, make fun of, lead up the garden path

legacy = bequest, inheritance,

gift, estate, heirloom

legal 1 = <u>judicial</u>, judiciary, forensic, juridical, jurisdictive 2 = <u>lawful</u>, allowed, sanctioned, constitutional, valid, legitimate, authorized, permissible

legend 1 = <u>myth</u>, story, tale, fiction, saga, fable, folk tale, folk story 2 = <u>celebrity</u>, star, phenomenon, genius, prodigy, luminary, megastar (*informal*) 3 = <u>inscription</u>, title, caption, device, motto, rubric

legendary 1 = <u>famous</u>, celebrated, well-known, acclaimed, renowned, famed, immortal, illustrious ≠ unknown 2 = <u>mythical</u>, fabled, traditional, romantic, fabulous, fictitious, storybook, apocryphal ≠ factual

legion 1 = <u>army</u>, company, force, division, troop, brigade 2 = <u>multitude</u>, host, mass, drove, number, horde, myriad, throng

legislation 1 = <u>law</u>, act, ruling, rule, bill, measure, regulation, charter 2 = <u>lawmaking</u>, regulation, prescription, enactment

legislative = <u>law-making</u>, judicial, law-giving

legislator = <u>lawmaker</u>, lawgiver

legislature = <u>parliament</u>, congress, senate, assembly, chamber

legitimate ADJECTIVE 1 = <u>lawful</u>, legal, genuine, authentic, authorized, rightful, kosher (*informal*), dinkum (*Austral. & N.Z. informal*), licit ≠ unlawful 2 = <u>reasonable</u>, correct, sensible, valid, warranted, logical, justifiable, well-founded ≠ unreasonable

● VERB = <u>legitimize</u>, allow, permit, sanction, authorize, legalize, pronounce lawful

leisure = <u>spare</u>, free, rest, ease, relaxation, recreation ≠ work

lekker (*S. African slang*) = <u>delicious</u>, tasty, luscious, palatable, delectable, mouthwatering, scrumptious (*informal*), appetizing, yummo (*Austral. slang*)

lemon

(Related Words)

adjectives: citric, citrous

> **shades of yellow**

lend VERB 1 = <u>loan</u>, advance, sub (*Brit. informal*) 2 = <u>give</u>, provide, add, supply, grant, confer, bestow, impart

● PHRASES **lend itself to something** = <u>be appropriate for</u>, suit, be suitable for, be appropriate to, be serviceable for

length NOUN 1 = <u>distance</u>, reach, measure, extent, span, longitude 2 = <u>duration</u>, term, period, space, stretch, span, expanse 3 = <u>piece</u>, measure, section, segment, portion

• PHRASES **at length** 1 = <u>at last</u>, finally, eventually, in time, in the end, at long last 2 = <u>for a long time</u>, completely, fully, thoroughly, for hours, in detail, for ages, in depth

lengthen 1 = <u>extend</u>, continue, increase, stretch, expand, elongate ≠ shorten 2 = <u>protract</u>, extend, prolong, draw out, spin out, make longer ≠ cut down

lengthy 1 = <u>protracted</u>, long, prolonged, tedious, drawn-out, interminable, long-winded, long-drawn-out 2 = <u>very long</u>, rambling, interminable, long-winded, wordy, discursive, extended ≠ brief

lesbian = <u>homosexual</u>, gay, les (slang), sapphic, lesbo (slang)

less DETERMINER = <u>smaller</u>, shorter, not so much
• PREPOSITION = <u>minus</u>, without, lacking, excepting, subtracting

Word Power

less – *Less* should not be confused with *fewer*. *Less* refers strictly only to quantity and not to number: *there is less water than before*. *Fewer* means smaller in number: *there are fewer people than before*.

lessen 1 = <u>reduce</u>, lower, diminish, decrease, ease, narrow,

minimize ≠ increase 2 = <u>grow less</u>, diminish, decrease, contract, ease, shrink

lesser = <u>lower</u>, secondary, subsidiary, inferior, less important ≠ greater

lesson 1 = <u>class</u>, schooling, period, teaching, coaching, session, instruction, lecture 2 = <u>example</u>, warning, message, moral, deterrent 3 = <u>Bible reading</u>, reading, text, Bible passage, Scripture passage

let VERB 1 = <u>allow</u>, permit, authorize, give the go-ahead, give permission 2 = <u>lease</u>, hire, rent, rent out, hire out, sublease
• PHRASES **let on** (Informal) 1 = <u>reveal</u>, disclose, say, tell, admit, give away, divulge, let slip ♦ **let someone down** = <u>disappoint</u>, fail, abandon, desert, disillusion, fall short, leave stranded, leave in the lurch ♦ **let someone off** = <u>excuse</u>, release, discharge, pardon, spare, forgive, exempt, exonerate ♦ **let something or someone in** = <u>admit</u>, include, receive, welcome, greet, take in, incorporate, give access to ♦ **let something down** = <u>deflate</u>, empty, exhaust, flatten, puncture ♦ **let something off** 1 = <u>fire</u>, explode, set off, discharge, detonate 2 = <u>emit</u>, release, leak,

exude, give off ♦ **let something out** 1 = <u>release</u>, discharge 2 = <u>emit</u>, make, produce, give vent to ♦ **let up** = <u>stop</u>, diminish, decrease, subside, relax, ease (up), moderate, lessen

lethal = <u>deadly</u>, terminal, fatal, dangerous, devastating, destructive, mortal, murderous ≠ harmless

letter 1 = <u>message</u>, line, note, communication, dispatch, missive, epistle 2 = <u>character</u>, mark, sign, symbol

level NOUN = <u>position</u>, standard, degree, grade, standing, stage, rank, status
● ADJECTIVE 1 = <u>equal</u>, balanced, at the same height 2 = <u>horizontal</u>, even, flat, smooth, uniform ≠ slanted 3 = <u>even</u>, tied, equal, drawn, neck and neck, all square, level pegging
● VERB 1 = <u>equalize</u>, balance, even up 2 = <u>destroy</u>, devastate, demolish, flatten, knock down, pull down, tear down, bulldoze ≠ build 3 = <u>direct</u>, point, turn, train, aim, focus 4 = <u>flatten</u>, plane, smooth, even off *or* out
● PHRASES **on the level** (*Informal*) = <u>honest</u>, genuine, straight, fair, square, dinkum (*Austral. & N.Z. informal*), above board

lever NOUN = <u>handle</u>, bar
● VERB = <u>prise</u>, force

leverage 1 = <u>influence</u>, authority, pull (*informal*), weight, clout (*informal*) 2 = <u>force</u>, hold, pull, strength, grip, grasp

levy NOUN = <u>tax</u>, fee, toll, tariff, duty, excise, exaction
● VERB = <u>impose</u>, charge, collect, demand, exact

liability 1 = <u>disadvantage</u>, burden, drawback, inconvenience, handicap, nuisance, hindrance, millstone 2 = <u>responsibility</u>, accountability, culpability, answerability

liable 1 = <u>likely</u>, tending, inclined, disposed, prone, apt 2 = <u>vulnerable</u>, subject, exposed, prone, susceptible, open, at risk of 3 = <u>responsible</u>, accountable, answerable, obligated

> ### Word Power
>
> **liable** – In the past, it was considered incorrect to use *liable* to mean 'probable' or 'likely', as in *it's liable to happen soon*. However, this usage is now generally considered acceptable.

liaison 1 = <u>contact</u>, communication, connection, interchange 2 = <u>intermediary</u>, contact, hook-up 3 = <u>affair</u>, romance, intrigue, fling, love affair, amour, entanglement

liar = <u>falsifier</u>, perjurer, fibber, fabricator

libel NOUN = defamation, misrepresentation, denigration, smear, calumny, aspersion
• VERB = defame, smear, slur, blacken, malign, denigrate, revile, vilify

liberal 1 = tolerant, open-minded, permissive, indulgent, easy-going, broad-minded ≠ intolerant 2 = progressive, radical, reformist, libertarian, forward-looking, free-thinking ≠ conservative 3 = abundant, generous, handsome, lavish, ample, rich, plentiful, copious ≠ limited 4 = generous, kind, charitable, extravagant, open-hearted, bountiful, magnanimous, open-handed ≠ stingy

liberate = free, release, rescue, save, deliver, let out, set free, let loose ≠ imprison

liberty NOUN = independence, sovereignty, liberation, autonomy, immunity, self-determination, emancipation, self-government ≠ restraint
• PHRASES **at liberty** 1 = free, escaped, unlimited, at large, not confined, untied, on the loose, unchained 2 = able, free, allowed, permitted, entitled, authorized
♦ **take liberties** or **a liberty** = not show enough respect, show disrespect, act presumptuously, behave too

familiarly, behave impertinently

licence NOUN 1 = certificate, document, permit, charter, warrant 2 = permission, the right, authority, leave, sanction, liberty, immunity, entitlement ≠ denial 3 = freedom, creativity, latitude, independence, liberty, deviation, leeway, free rein ≠ restraint 4 = laxity, excess, indulgence, irresponsibility, licentiousness, immoderation ≠ moderation
• PHRASES **under licence** = with permission, under a charter, under warrant, under a permit, with authorization, under a patent

license = permit, sanction, allow, warrant, authorize, empower, certify, accredit ≠ forbid

lick VERB 1 = taste, lap, tongue 2 (*Informal*) = beat, defeat, overcome, rout, outstrip, outdo, trounce, vanquish 3 (*of flames*) = flicker, touch, flick, dart, ripple, play over
• NOUN 1 = dab, bit, touch, stroke 2 (*Informal*) = pace, rate, speed, clip (*informal*)

lie¹ NOUN 1 = falsehood, deceit, fabrication, fib, fiction, invention, deception, untruth
• VERB = fib, fabricate, falsify, prevaricate, not tell the truth, equivocate, dissimulate, tell untruths

- **PHRASES give the lie to something** = <u>disprove</u>, expose, discredit, contradict, refute, negate, invalidate, rebut

lie² 1 = <u>recline</u>, rest, lounge, sprawl, stretch out, loll, repose 2 = <u>be placed</u>, be, rest, exist, be situated 3 = <u>be situated</u>, sit, be located, be positioned 4 = <u>be buried</u>, remain, rest, be, be entombed

life 1 = <u>being</u>, existence, vitality, sentience 2 = <u>existence</u>, being, lifetime, time, days, span 3 = <u>way of life</u>, situation, conduct, behaviour, life style 4 = <u>liveliness</u>, energy, spirit, vitality, animation, vigour, verve, zest 5 = <u>biography</u>, story, history, profile, confessions, autobiography, memoirs, life story

(Related Words)

adjectives: animate, vital

lifelong = <u>long-lasting</u>, enduring, lasting, persistent, long-standing, perennial

lifetime = <u>existence</u>, time, day(s), span

lift VERB 1 = <u>raise</u>, pick up, hoist, draw up, elevate, uplift, heave up, upraise ≠ lower 2 = <u>revoke</u>, end, remove, withdraw, stop, cancel, terminate, rescind ≠ impose 3 = <u>disappear</u>, clear, vanish, disperse, dissipate, rise, be dispelled

- **NOUN** 1 = <u>boost</u>, encouragement, stimulus, pick-me-up, fillip, shot in the arm

(informal), gee-up ≠ blow 2 = <u>elevator</u> (chiefly U.S.), hoist, paternoster 3 = <u>ride</u>, run, drive, hitch (informal)

- **PHRASES lift off** = <u>take off</u>, be launched, blast off, take to the air

light¹ NOUN 1 = <u>brightness</u>, illumination, luminosity, shining, glow, glare, gleam, brilliance ≠ dark 2 = <u>lamp</u>, torch, candle, flare, beacon, lantern, taper 3 = <u>match</u>, spark, flame, lighter 4 = <u>aspect</u>, context, angle, point of view, interpretation, viewpoint, slant, standpoint

- **ADJECTIVE** 1 = <u>bright</u>, brilliant, shining, illuminated, luminous, well-lit, lustrous, well-illuminated ≠ dark 2 = <u>pale</u>, fair, faded, blonde, blond, bleached, pastel, light-coloured ≠ dark

- **VERB** 1 = <u>illuminate</u>, light up, brighten ≠ darken 2 = <u>ignite</u>, inflame, kindle, touch off, set alight ≠ put out

- **PHRASES light up** 1 = <u>cheer</u>, shine, blaze, sparkle, animate, brighten, lighten, irradiate 2 = <u>shine</u>, flash, beam, blaze, sparkle, flare, glare, gleam

light² ADJECTIVE 1 = <u>insubstantial</u>, thin, slight, portable, buoyant, airy, flimsy, underweight ≠ heavy 2 = <u>weak</u>, soft, gentle, moderate, slight, mild, faint, indistinct ≠ strong 3 = <u>digestible</u>, modest, frugal ≠ substantial

4 = insignificant, small, slight, petty, trivial, trifling, inconsequential, inconsiderable ≠ serious 5 = light-hearted, funny, entertaining, amusing, witty, humorous, frivolous, unserious ≠ serious 6 = nimble, graceful, deft, agile, sprightly, lithe, limber, lissom ≠ clumsy

• PHRASES **light on** *or* **upon something** 1 = settle, land, perch, alight 2 = come across, find, discover, encounter, stumble on, hit upon, happen upon

lighten[1] = brighten, illuminate, light up, irradiate, become light

lighten[2] 1 = ease, relieve, alleviate, allay, reduce, lessen, mitigate, assuage ≠ intensify 2 = cheer, lift, revive, brighten, perk up, buoy up ≠ depress

lightly 1 = moderately, thinly, slightly, sparsely, sparingly ≠ heavily 2 = gently, softly, slightly, faintly, delicately ≠ forcefully 3 = carelessly, breezily, thoughtlessly, flippantly, frivolously, heedlessly ≠ seriously 4 = easily, simply, readily, effortlessly, unthinkingly, without thought, flippantly, heedlessly ≠ with difficulty

lightweight 1 = thin, fine, delicate, sheer, flimsy, gossamer, diaphanous, filmy 2 = unimportant, shallow, trivial, insignificant, slight, petty,

worthless, trifling ≠ significant

like[1] = similar to, same as, equivalent to, parallel to, identical to, alike, corresponding to, comparable to ≠ different

> ### Word Power
>
> **like** – The use of *like* to mean 'such as' was in the past considered undesirable in formal writing, but has now become acceptable, for example in *I enjoy team sports like football and rugby*. However, the common use of *look like* and *seem like* to mean 'look or seem as if' is thought by many people to be incorrect or nonstandard. You might say *it looks as if* (or *as though*) *he's coming*, but it is still wise to avoid *it looks like he's coming*, particularly in formal or written contexts.

like[2] 1 = enjoy, love, delight in, go for, relish, savour, revel in, be fond of ≠ dislike 2 = admire, approve of, appreciate, prize, take to, esteem, cherish, hold dear ≠ dislike 3 = wish, want, choose, prefer, desire, fancy, care, feel inclined

likelihood = probability, chance, possibility, prospect

likely 1 = inclined, disposed, prone, liable, tending, apt 2 = probable, expected, anticipated, odds-on, on the cards, to be expected **3** = <u>plausible</u>, possible, reasonable, credible, feasible, believable

liken = <u>compare</u>, match, relate, parallel, equate, set beside

likewise = <u>similarly</u>, the same, in the same way, in similar fashion, in like manner

liking = <u>fondness</u>, love, taste, weakness, preference, affection, inclination, penchant ≠ dislike

limb 1 = <u>part</u>, member, arm, leg, wing, extremity, appendage **2** = <u>branch</u>, spur, projection, offshoot, bough

limelight = <u>publicity</u>, recognition, fame, the spotlight, attention, prominence, stardom, public eye

limit NOUN **1** = <u>end</u>, ultimate, deadline, breaking point, extremity **2** = <u>boundary</u>, edge, border, frontier, perimeter
● VERB = <u>restrict</u>, control, check, bound, confine, curb, restrain, ration

limitation 1 = <u>restriction</u>, control, check, curb, restraint, constraint **2** = <u>weakness</u>, failing, qualification, reservation, defect, flaw, shortcoming, imperfection

limited 1 = <u>restricted</u>, controlled, checked, bounded, confined, curbed, constrained, finite ≠ unlimited

limp[1] VERB = <u>hobble</u>, stagger, stumble, shuffle, hop, falter, shamble, totter
● NOUN = <u>lameness</u>, hobble

limp[2] = <u>floppy</u>, soft, slack, drooping, flabby, pliable, flaccid ≠ stiff

line NOUN **1** = <u>stroke</u>, mark, score, band, scratch, slash, streak, stripe **2** = <u>wrinkle</u>, mark, crease, furrow, crow's foot **3** = <u>row</u>, queue, rank, file, column, convoy, procession **4** = <u>string</u>, cable, wire, rope, thread, cord **5** = <u>trajectory</u>, way, course, track, channel, direction, route, path **6** = <u>boundary</u>, limit, edge, border, frontier, partition, borderline **7** = <u>occupation</u>, work, calling, business, job, area, trade, field
● VERB **1** = <u>border</u>, edge, bound, fringe **2** = <u>mark</u>, crease, furrow, rule, score
● PHRASES **in line for** = <u>due for</u>, shortlisted for, in the running for

lined 1 = <u>wrinkled</u>, worn, furrowed, wizened **2** = <u>ruled</u>, feint

line-up = <u>arrangement</u>, team, row, selection, array

linger = <u>stay</u>, remain, stop, wait, delay, hang around, idle, dally

link NOUN **1** = <u>connection</u>, relationship, association, tie-up, affinity **2** = <u>relationship</u>, association, bond, connection, attachment, affinity **3** = <u>component</u>, part, piece, element, constituent

● VERB 1 = <u>associate</u>, relate, identify, connect, bracket 2 = <u>connect</u>, join, unite, couple, tie, bind, attach, fasten ≠ separate

lip 1 = <u>edge</u>, rim, brim, margin, brink 2 (*Slang*) = <u>impudence</u>, insolence, impertinence, cheek (*informal*), effrontery, backchat (*informal*), brass neck (*informal*)

liquid NOUN = <u>fluid</u>, solution, juice, sap

● ADJECTIVE 1 = <u>fluid</u>, running, flowing, melted, watery, molten, runny, aqueous 2 (*of assets*) = <u>convertible</u>, disposable, negotiable, realizable

liquor 1 = <u>alcohol</u>, drink, spirits, booze (*informal*), hard stuff (*informal*), strong drink 2 = <u>juice</u>, stock, extract, broth

list¹ NOUN = <u>inventory</u>, record, series, roll, index, register, catalogue, directory

● VERB = <u>itemize</u>, record, enter, register, catalogue, enumerate, note down, tabulate

list² VERB = <u>lean</u>, tip, incline, tilt, heel over, careen

● NOUN = <u>tilt</u>, leaning, slant, cant

listen 1 = <u>hear</u>, attend, pay attention, lend an ear, prick up your ears 2 = <u>pay attention</u>, observe, obey, mind, heed, take notice, take note of, take heed of

literacy = <u>education</u>, learning, knowledge

literal 1 = <u>exact</u>, close, strict, accurate, faithful, verbatim, word for word 2 = <u>actual</u>, real, true, simple, plain, genuine, bona fide, unvarnished

literally = <u>exactly</u>, really, closely, actually, truly, precisely, strictly, faithfully

literary = <u>well-read</u>, learned, formal, intellectual, scholarly, erudite, bookish

literate = <u>educated</u>, informed, knowledgeable

literature = <u>writings</u>, letters, compositions, lore, creative writing

➤ Shakespeare

litigation = <u>lawsuit</u>, case, action, prosecution

litter NOUN 1 = <u>rubbish</u>, refuse, waste, junk, debris, garbage (*chiefly U.S.*), trash, muck 2 = <u>brood</u>, young, offspring, progeny

● VERB 1 = <u>clutter</u>, mess up, clutter up, be scattered about, disorder, disarrange, derange 2 = <u>scatter</u>, spread, shower, strew

little ADJECTIVE 1 = <u>small</u>, minute, short, tiny, wee, compact, miniature, diminutive ≠ big 2 = <u>young</u>, small, junior, infant, immature, undeveloped, babyish

● ADVERB 1 = <u>hardly</u>, barely, scarcely ≠ much 2 = <u>rarely</u>, seldom, scarcely, not often, infrequently, hardly ever ≠ always

• NOUN = bit, touch, spot, trace, hint, particle, fragment, speck ≠ lot

• PHRASES **a little** = to a small extent, slightly, to some extent, to a certain extent, to a small degree

live[1] 1 = dwell, board, settle, lodge, occupy, abide, inhabit, reside 2 = exist, last, prevail, live, have being, breathe, persist, be alive 3 = survive, get along, make a living, make ends meet, subsist, eke out a living, support yourself, maintain yourself 4 = thrive, flourish, prosper, have fun, enjoy yourself, live life to the full

live[2] 1 = living, alive, breathing, animate 2 = active, unexploded 3 = topical, important, pressing, current, hot, burning, controversial, prevalent

livelihood = occupation, work, employment, living, job, bread and butter (informal)

lively 1 = animated, spirited, quick, keen, active, alert, dynamic, vigorous ≠ dull 2 = vivid, strong, striking, bright, exciting, stimulating, bold, colourful ≠ dull 3 = enthusiastic, strong, keen, stimulating, eager, formidable, vigorous, animated

living NOUN = lifestyle, ways, situation, conduct, behaviour, customs, lifestyle, way of life

• ADJECTIVE 1 = alive, existing, moving, active, breathing, animate ≠ dead 2 = current, present, active, contemporary, in use, extant ≠ obsolete

lizard ▸ reptiles

load VERB 1 = fill, stuff, pack, pile, stack, heap, cram, freight 2 = make ready, charge, prime

• NOUN 1 = cargo, delivery, haul, shipment, batch, freight, consignment 2 = oppression, charge, worry, trouble, weight, responsibility, burden, onus

• PHRASES **load someone down** = burden, worry, oppress, weigh down, saddle with, encumber, snow under

loaded 1 = tricky, charged, sensitive, delicate, manipulative, emotive, insidious, artful 2 = biased, weighted, rigged, distorted 3 (Slang) = rich, wealthy, affluent, well off, flush (informal), well-heeled (informal), well-to-do, moneyed

loaf[1] 1 = lump, block, cake, cube, slab 2 (Slang) = head, mind, sense, common sense, nous (Brit. slang), gumption (Brit. informal)

loaf[2] = idle, hang around, take it easy, lie around, loiter, laze, lounge around

loan NOUN = advance, credit, overdraft

• VERB = lend, advance, let out

loathe = hate, dislike, despise, detest, abhor, abominate

loathing = <u>hatred</u>, hate, disgust, aversion, revulsion, antipathy, repulsion, abhorrence

lobby VERB = <u>campaign</u>, press, pressure, push, influence, promote, urge, persuade
● NOUN **1** = <u>pressure group</u>, group, camp, faction, lobbyists, interest group, special-interest group, ginger group **2** = <u>corridor</u>, passage, entrance, porch, hallway, foyer, entrance hall, vestibule

lobola (*S. African*) = <u>dowry</u>, portion, marriage settlement, dot (*archaic*)

local ADJECTIVE **1** = <u>community</u>, regional **2** = <u>confined</u>, limited, restricted
● NOUN = <u>resident</u>, native, inhabitant

locate 1 = <u>find</u>, discover, detect, come across, track down, pinpoint, unearth, pin down **2** = <u>place</u>, put, set, position, seat, site, establish, settle

location = <u>place</u>, point, setting, position, situation, spot, venue, locale

lock¹ VERB **1** = <u>fasten</u>, close, secure, shut, bar, seal, bolt **2** = <u>unite</u>, join, link, engage, clench, entangle, interlock, entwine **3** = <u>embrace</u>, press, grasp, clutch, hug, enclose, clasp, encircle
● NOUN = <u>fastening</u>, catch, bolt, clasp, padlock

● PHRASES **lock someone up** = <u>imprison</u>, jail, confine, cage, detain, shut up, incarcerate, send down (*informal*)

lock² = <u>strand</u>, curl, tuft, tress, ringlet

lodge NOUN **1** = <u>cabin</u>, shelter, cottage, hut, chalet, gatehouse **2** = <u>society</u>, group, club, section, wing, chapter, branch
● VERB **1** = <u>register</u>, enter, file, submit, put on record **2** = <u>stay</u>, room, board, reside **3** = <u>stick</u>, remain, implant, come to rest, imbed

lodging often plural = <u>accommodation</u>, rooms, apartments, quarters, digs (*Brit. informal*), shelter, residence, abode

lofty 1 = <u>noble</u>, grand, distinguished, renowned, elevated, dignified, illustrious, exalted ≠ humble **2** = <u>high</u>, raised, towering, soaring, elevated ≠ low **3** = <u>haughty</u>, proud, arrogant, patronizing, condescending, disdainful, supercilious ≠ modest

log NOUN **1** = <u>stump</u>, block, branch, chunk, trunk **2** = <u>record</u>, account, register, journal, diary, logbook
● VERB = <u>record</u>, enter, note, register, chart, put down, set down

logic = <u>reason</u>, reasoning, sense,

good sense

logical 1 = <u>rational</u>, clear, reasoned, sound, consistent, valid, coherent, well-organized ≠ illogical 2 = <u>reasonable</u>, sensible, natural, wise, plausible ≠ unlikely

lone = <u>solitary</u>, single, one, only, sole, unaccompanied

loneliness = <u>solitude</u>, isolation, desolation, seclusion

lonely 1 = <u>solitary</u>, alone, isolated, abandoned, lone, withdrawn, single, forsaken ≠ accompanied 2 = <u>desolate</u>, deserted, remote, isolated, out-of-the-way, secluded, uninhabited, godforsaken ≠ crowded

lonesome (Chiefly U.S. & Canad.) = <u>lonely</u>, gloomy, dreary, desolate, forlorn, friendless, companionless

long¹ 1 = <u>elongated</u>, extended, stretched, lengthy, far-reaching, spread out ≠ short 2 = <u>prolonged</u>, sustained, lengthy, lingering, protracted, interminable, spun out, long-drawn-out ≠ brief

long² = <u>desire</u>, want, wish, burn, pine, lust, crave, yearn

longing = <u>desire</u>, hope, wish, burning, urge, ambition, hunger, yen (informal) ≠ indifference

long-standing = <u>established</u>, fixed, enduring, abiding, long-lasting, long-established, time-honoured

look VERB 1 = <u>see</u>, view, consider, watch, eye, study, survey, examine 2 = <u>search</u>, seek, hunt, forage, fossick (Austral. & N.Z.) 3 = <u>consider</u>, contemplate 4 = <u>face</u>, overlook 5 = <u>hope</u>, expect, await, anticipate, reckon on 6 = <u>seem</u>, appear, look like, strike you as

● NOUN 1 = <u>glimpse</u>, view, glance, observation, sight, examination, gaze, inspection 2 = <u>appearance</u>, bearing, air, style, aspect, manner, expression, impression

◆ PHRASES **look after something** or **someone** = <u>take care of</u>, mind, protect, tend, guard, nurse, care for, supervise ◆ **look down on** or **upon someone** = <u>disdain</u>, despise, scorn, sneer at, spurn, contemn (formal) ◆ **look forward to something** = <u>anticipate</u>, expect, look for, wait for, await, hope for, long for ◆ **look out for something** = <u>be careful of</u>, beware, watch out for, pay attention to, be wary of, keep an eye out for ◆ **look someone up** = <u>visit</u>, call on, drop in on (informal), look in on ◆ **look something up** = <u>research</u>, find, search for, hunt for, track down, seek out ◆ **look up** = <u>improve</u>, develop, advance, pick up, progress, get better, perk up (informal), perk up ◆ **look up to someone** = <u>respect</u>, honour, admire, esteem, revere, defer to, think highly of

lookout 1 = <u>watchman</u>, guard, sentry, sentinel 2 = <u>watch</u>, guard, vigil 3 = <u>watchtower</u>, post, observatory, observation post 4 (*Informal*) = <u>concern</u>, business, worry

loom = <u>appear</u>, emerge, hover, take shape, threaten, bulk, menace, come into view

loop NOUN = <u>curve</u>, ring, circle, twist, curl, spiral, coil, twirl
● VERB = <u>twist</u>, turn, roll, knot, curl, spiral, coil, wind round

loophole = <u>let-out</u>, escape, excuse

loose ADJECTIVE 1 = <u>free</u>, detached, insecure, unfettered, unrestricted, untied, unattached, unfastened 2 = <u>slack</u>, easy, relaxed, sloppy, loose-fitting ≠ tight 3 (*Old-fashioned*) = <u>promiscuous</u>, fast, abandoned, immoral, dissipated, profligate, debauched, dissolute ≠ chaste 4 = <u>vague</u>, random, inaccurate, rambling, imprecise, ill-defined, indistinct, inexact ≠ precise
● VERB = <u>free</u>, release, liberate, detach, unleash, disconnect, set free, untie ≠ fasten

loosen VERB = <u>untie</u>, undo, release, separate, detach, unloose
● PHRASES **loosen up** = <u>relax</u>, chill (*slang*), soften, unwind, go easy (*informal*), hang loose,

outspan (*S. African*), ease up or off

loot VERB = <u>plunder</u>, rob, raid, sack, rifle, ravage, ransack, pillage
● NOUN = <u>plunder</u>, goods, prize, haul, spoils, booty, swag (*slang*)

lord NOUN 1 = <u>peer</u>, nobleman, count, duke, gentleman, earl, noble, baron 2 = <u>ruler</u>, leader, chief, master, governor, commander, superior, liege
● PHRASES **lord it over someone** = <u>boss around</u> or about (*informal*), order around, threaten, bully, menace, intimidate, hector, bluster ◆ **the Lord** or **Our Lord** = <u>Jesus Christ</u>, God, Christ, Messiah, Jehovah, the Almighty

lose 1 = <u>be defeated</u>, be beaten, lose out, come to grief 2 = <u>mislay</u>, drop, forget, be deprived of, lose track of, misplace 3 = <u>forfeit</u>, miss, yield, be deprived of, pass up (*informal*)

loser = <u>failure</u>, flop (*informal*), also-ran, no-hoper (*Austral. slang*), dud (*informal*), non-achiever

loss NOUN 1 = <u>losing</u>, waste, squandering, forfeiture ≠ gain 2 *sometimes plural* = <u>deficit</u>, debt, deficiency, debit, depletion ≠ gain 3 = <u>damage</u>, cost, injury, hurt, harm ≠ advantage
● PHRASES **at a loss** = <u>confused</u>, puzzled, baffled, bewildered, helpless, stumped, perplexed,

mystified

lost = missing, disappeared, vanished, wayward, misplaced, mislaid

lot NOUN **1** = bunch (*informal*), group, crowd, crew, set, band, quantity, assortment **2** = destiny, situation, circumstances, fortune, chance, accident, fate, doom

● PHRASES **a lot** or **lots** **1** = plenty, scores, masses (*informal*), load(s) (*informal*), wealth, piles (*informal*), a great deal, stack(s) **2** = often, regularly, a great deal, frequently, a good deal

lotion = cream, solution, balm, salve, liniment, embrocation

lottery 1 = raffle, draw, lotto (*Brit., N.Z., & S. African*), sweepstake **2** = gamble, chance, risk, hazard, toss-up (*informal*)

loud 1 = noisy, booming, roaring, thundering, forte (*Music*), resounding, deafening, thunderous ≠ quiet **2** = garish, bold, glaring, flamboyant, brash, flashy, lurid, gaudy ≠ sombre

loudly = noisily, vigorously, vehemently, vociferously, uproariously, lustily, shrilly, fortissimo (*Music*)

lounge VERB = relax, loaf, sprawl, lie about, take it easy, loiter, loll, laze, outspan (*S. African*)

● NOUN = sitting room, living room, parlour, drawing room,

front room, reception room, television room

love VERB **1** = adore, care for, treasure, cherish, prize, worship, be devoted to, dote on ≠ hate **2** = enjoy, like, appreciate, relish, delight in, savour, take pleasure in, have a soft spot for ≠ dislike

● NOUN **1** = passion, affection, warmth, attachment, intimacy, devotion, tenderness, adoration, aroha (*N.Z.*) ≠ hatred **2** = liking, taste, bent for, weakness for, relish for, enjoyment, devotion to, penchant for **3** = beloved, dear, dearest, lover, darling, honey, sweetheart, truelove ≠ enemy **4** = sympathy, understanding, pity, humanity, warmth, mercy, sorrow, kindness, aroha (*N.Z.*)

● PHRASES **make love** = have sexual intercourse, have sex, go to bed, sleep together, do it (*informal*), mate, have sexual relations, have it off (*slang*)

love affair = romance, relationship, affair, intrigue, liaison, amour

lovely 1 = beautiful, appealing, attractive, charming, pretty, handsome, good-looking, exquisite ≠ ugly **2** = wonderful, pleasing, nice, pleasant, engaging, marvellous, delightful, enjoyable ≠ horrible

lover = sweetheart, beloved, loved one, flame (*informal*), mistress, admirer, suitor, woman friend

loving 1 = <u>affectionate</u>, dear, devoted, tender, fond, doting, amorous, warm-hearted ≠ cruel **2** = <u>tender</u>, kind, caring, warm, gentle, sympathetic, considerate

low 1 = <u>small</u>, little, short, stunted, squat ≠ tall **2** = <u>inferior</u>, bad, poor, inadequate, unsatisfactory, deficient, second-rate, shoddy, half-pie (*N.Z. informal*), bodger or bodgie (*Austral. slang*) **3** = <u>quiet</u>, soft, gentle, whispered, muted, subdued, hushed, muffled ≠ loud **4** = <u>dejected</u>, depressed, miserable, fed up, moody, gloomy, glum, despondent ≠ happy **5** = <u>coarse</u>, common, rough, crude, rude, vulgar, undignified, disreputable **6** = <u>ill</u>, weak, frail, stricken, debilitated ≠ strong

lower ADJECTIVE 1 = <u>subordinate</u>, under, smaller, junior, minor, secondary, lesser, inferior **2** = <u>reduced</u>, cut, diminished, decreased, lessened, curtailed ≠ increased

● VERB **1** = <u>drop</u>, sink, depress, let down, submerge, take down, let fall ≠ raise **2** = <u>lessen</u>, cut, reduce, diminish, slash, decrease, prune, minimize ≠ increase

low-key = <u>subdued</u>, quiet, restrained, muted, understated, toned down

loyal = <u>faithful</u>, true, devoted, dependable, constant, staunch, trustworthy, trusty ≠ disloyal

loyalty = <u>faithfulness</u>, commitment, devotion, allegiance, fidelity, homage, obedience, constancy

luck NOUN 1 = <u>good fortune</u>, success, advantage, prosperity, blessing, windfall, godsend, serendipity **2** = <u>fortune</u>, lot, stars, chance, accident, fate, destiny, twist of fate

● PHRASES **in luck** = <u>fortunate</u>, successful, favoured, well-off, jammy (*Brit. slang*) ◆ **out of luck** = <u>unfortunate</u>, cursed, unlucky, unsuccessful

luckily = <u>fortunately</u>, happily, opportunely

lucky = <u>fortunate</u>, successful, favoured, charmed, blessed, jammy (*Brit. slang*), serendipitous ≠ unlucky

lucrative = <u>profitable</u>, rewarding, productive, fruitful, well-paid, advantageous, remunerative

ludicrous = <u>ridiculous</u>, crazy, absurd, preposterous, silly, laughable, farcical, outlandish ≠ sensible

luggage = <u>baggage</u>, things, cases, bags, gear, suitcases, paraphernalia, impedimenta

lull NOUN = <u>respite</u>, pause, quiet, silence, calm, hush, let-up

(informal)
● **VERB** = <u>calm</u>, soothe, subdue, quell, allay, pacify, tranquillize

lumber¹ **VERB** (Brit. informal) = <u>burden</u>, land, load, saddle, encumber
● **NOUN** (Brit.) = <u>junk</u>, refuse, rubbish, trash, clutter, jumble

lumber² = <u>plod</u>, shuffle, shamble, trudge, stump, waddle, trundle

lumbering = <u>awkward</u>, heavy, hulking, ponderous, ungainly

lump **NOUN** 1 = <u>piece</u>, ball, block, mass, chunk, hunk, nugget
2 = <u>swelling</u>, growth, bump, tumour, bulge, hump, protrusion
● **VERB** = <u>group</u>, throw, mass, combine, collect, pool, consolidate, conglomerate

lunatic **NOUN** = <u>madman</u>, maniac, psychopath, nutcase (slang)
● **ADJECTIVE** = <u>mad</u>, crazy, insane, irrational, daft, deranged, crackpot (informal), crackbrained, off the air (Austral. slang)

lunge **VERB** = <u>pounce</u>, charge, dive, leap, plunge, thrust
● **NOUN** = <u>thrust</u>, charge, pounce, spring, swing, jab

lurch 1 = <u>tilt</u>, roll, pitch, list, rock, lean, heel 2 = <u>stagger</u>, reel, stumble, weave, sway, totter

lure **VERB** = <u>tempt</u>, draw, attract, invite, trick, seduce, entice, allure
● **NOUN** = <u>temptation</u>, attraction, incentive, bait, carrot (informal), inducement, enticement, allurement

lurk = <u>hide</u>, sneak, prowl, lie in wait, slink, skulk, conceal yourself

lush 1 = <u>abundant</u>, green, flourishing, dense, rank, verdant
2 = <u>luxurious</u>, grand, elaborate, lavish, extravagant, sumptuous, plush (informal), ornate

lust **NOUN** 1 = <u>lechery</u>, sensuality, lewdness, lasciviousness
2 = <u>desire</u>, longing, passion, appetite, craving, greed, thirst
● **PHRASES** **lust for** or **after someone** = <u>desire</u>, want, crave, yearn for, covet, hunger for or after ♦ **lust for** or **after something** = <u>desire</u>, crave, yearn for, covet

luxurious = <u>sumptuous</u>, expensive, comfortable, magnificent, splendid, lavish, plush (informal), opulent

---

Word Power

luxurious – Luxurious is sometimes wrongly used where luxuriant is meant: he had a luxuriant (not luxurious) moustache; the walls were covered with a luxuriant growth of wisteria.

---

luxury 1 = <u>opulence</u>, splendour, richness, extravagance, affluence, hedonism, a bed of roses, the life of Riley ≠ poverty

2 = extravagance, treat, extra, indulgence, frill ≠ necessity

lying NOUN = dishonesty, perjury, deceit, misrepresentation, mendacity, untruthfulness
● **ADJECTIVE** = deceitful, false, deceiving, treacherous, dishonest, two-faced, mendacious, perfidious ≠ truthful

lyrical = enthusiastic, inspired, poetic, impassioned, effusive, rhapsodic

M

machine 1 = appliance, device, apparatus, engine, tool, instrument, mechanism, gadget **2** = system, structure, organization, machinery, setup (informal)

machinery = equipment, gear, instruments, apparatus, technology, tackle, tools, gadgetry

macho = manly, masculine, chauvinist, virile

mad 1 = insane, crazy (informal), nuts (slang), raving, unstable, psychotic, demented, deranged, off the air (Austral. slang) ≠ sane **2** = foolish, absurd, wild, stupid, daft (informal), irrational, senseless, preposterous ≠ sensible **3** (Informal) = angry, furious, incensed, enraged, livid

(informal), berserk, berko (Austral. slang), tooshie (Austral. slang), off the air (Austral. slang) ≠ calm **4** = enthusiastic, wild, crazy (informal), ardent, fanatical, avid, impassioned, infatuated ≠ nonchalant **5** = frenzied, wild, excited, frenetic, uncontrolled, unrestrained

madden = infuriate, irritate, incense, enrage, upset, annoy, inflame, drive you crazy ≠ calm

madly 1 (Informal) = passionately, wildly, desperately, intensely, to distraction, devotedly **2** = foolishly, wildly, absurdly, ludicrously, irrationally, senselessly **3** = energetically, wildly, furiously, excitedly, recklessly, speedily, like mad (informal) **4** = insanely, frantically, hysterically, crazily, deliriously, distractedly, frenziedly

madness 1 = insanity, mental illness, delusion, mania, dementia, distraction, aberration, psychosis **2** = foolishness, nonsense, folly, absurdity, idiocy, wildness, daftness (informal), foolhardiness

magazine = journal, publication, supplement, rag (informal), issue, glossy (informal), pamphlet, periodical

magic NOUN **1** = sorcery, wizardry, witchcraft,

enchantment, black art, necromancy **2** = conjuring, illusion, trickery, sleight of hand, legerdemain, prestidigitation **3** = charm, power, glamour, fascination, magnetism, enchantment, allurement
● ADJECTIVE = miraculous, entrancing, charming, fascinating, marvellous, magical, enchanting, bewitching

magician 1 = conjuror, illusionist, prestidigitator **2** = sorcerer, witch, wizard, illusionist, warlock, necromancer, enchanter *or* enchantress

magistrate = judge, justice, justice of the peace, J.P.

magnetic = attractive, irresistible, seductive, captivating, charming, fascinating, charismatic, hypnotic ≠ repulsive

magnificent 1 = splendid, impressive, imposing, glorious, gorgeous, majestic, regal, sublime ≠ ordinary **2** = brilliant, fine, excellent, outstanding, superb, splendid

magnify 1 = enlarge, increase, boost, expand, intensify, blow up (*informal*), heighten, amplify ≠ reduce **2** = make worse, exaggerate, intensify, worsen, exacerbate, increase, inflame **3** = exaggerate, overstate, inflate, overplay, overemphasize ≠ understate

magnitude 1 = importance, consequence, significance, moment, note, weight, greatness ≠ unimportance **2** = immensity, size, extent, enormity, volume, vastness ≠ smallness **3** = intensity, amplitude

maid 1 = servant, chambermaid, housemaid, menial, maidservant, female servant, domestic (*archaic*), parlourmaid **2** (*Literary*) = girl, maiden, lass, damsel, lassie (*informal*), wench

maiden NOUN (*Literary*) = girl, maid, lass, damsel, virgin, lassie (*informal*), wench
● ADJECTIVE **1** = first, initial, inaugural, introductory **2** = unmarried, unwed

mail NOUN = letters, post, correspondence
● VERB = post, send, forward, e-mail, dispatch

main ADJECTIVE = chief, leading, head, central, essential, primary, principal, foremost ≠ minor
● PLURAL NOUN **1** = pipeline, channel, pipe, conduit, duct **2** = cable, line, electricity supply, mains supply
● PHRASES **in the main** = on the whole, generally, mainly, mostly, in general, for the most part

mainly = chiefly, mostly, largely, principally, primarily, on the whole, predominantly, in the main

mainstream = conventional, general, established, received, accepted, current, prevailing, orthodox ≠ unconventional

maintain 1 = continue, retain, preserve, sustain, carry on, keep up, prolong, perpetuate ≠ end 2 = assert, state, claim, insist, declare, contend, profess, avow ≠ disavow 3 = look after, care for, take care of, conserve, keep in good condition

maintenance 1 = upkeep, keeping, care, repairs, conservation, nurture, preservation 2 = allowance, support, keep, alimony 3 = continuation, carrying-on, perpetuation, prolongation

majestic = grand, magnificent, impressive, superb, splendid, regal, stately, monumental ≠ modest

majesty = grandeur, glory, splendour, magnificence, nobility ≠ triviality

major 1 = important, critical, significant, great, serious, crucial, outstanding, notable 2 = main, higher, greater, bigger, leading, chief, senior, supreme ≠ minor

majority 1 = most, mass, bulk, best part, better part, lion's share, preponderance, greater number 2 = adulthood, maturity, age of consent, seniority, manhood *or* womanhood

---

Word Power

majority – *The majority of* should always refer to a countable number of things or people. If you are talking about an amount or quantity, rather than a countable number, use *most of*, as in *most of the harvest was saved* (not *the majority of the harvest was saved*).

---

make VERB 1 = produce, cause, create, effect, lead to, generate, bring about, give rise to 2 = perform, do, effect, carry out, execute 3 = force, cause, compel, drive, require, oblige, induce, constrain 4 = create, build, produce, manufacture, form, fashion, construct, assemble 5 = earn, get, gain, net, win, clear, obtain, bring in 6 = amount to, total, constitute, add up to, count as, tot up to (*informal*)

● NOUN = brand, sort, style, model, kind, type, variety, marque

● PHRASES **make for something** = head for, aim for, head towards, be bound for ◆ **make it** (*Informal*) = succeed, prosper, arrive (*informal*), get on, crack it (*informal*) ◆ **make off** = flee, clear out (*informal*), bolt, take to your heels, run away *or* off ◆ **make something up** = invent, create, construct, compose, frame, coin, devise, originate ♦ **make up** = settle your differences, bury the hatchet, call it quits, declare a truce, be friends again ♦ **make up for something** = compensate for, make amends for, atone for, balance out, offset, make recompense for ♦ **make up something 1** = form, account for, constitute, compose, comprise **2** = complete, supply, fill, round off

maker = manufacturer, producer, builder, constructor

makeshift = temporary, provisional, substitute, expedient, stopgap

make-up 1 = cosmetics, paint (informal), powder, face (informal), greasepaint (Theatre) **2** = nature, character, constitution, temperament, disposition **3** = structure, organization, arrangement, construction, assembly, constitution, format, composition

making NOUN = creation, production, manufacture, construction, assembly, composition, fabrication
● PLURAL NOUN = beginnings, potential, capacity, ingredients

male = masculine, manly, macho, virile ≠ female

malicious = spiteful, malevolent, resentful, vengeful, rancorous, ill-disposed, ill-natured

≠ benevolent

mammal ➤ bats ➤ carnivores ➤ marsupials ➤ monkeys, apes and other primates ➤ rodents ➤ sea mammals ➤ whales and dolphins

Extinct mammals	
apeman	mastodon
aurochs	megathere
australopithecine	quagga
eohippus	sabre-toothed
glyptodont	tiger *or* cat
mammoth	tarpan

mammoth = colossal, huge, giant, massive, enormous, immense, gigantic, monumental ≠ tiny

man NOUN **1** = male, guy (informal), fellow (informal), gentleman, bloke (Brit. informal), chap (Brit. informal), dude (U.S. informal), geezer (informal) **2** = human, human being, person, individual, soul **3** = mankind, humanity, people, human race, humankind, Homo sapiens
● VERB = staff, people, crew, occupy, garrison

mana (N.Z.) = authority, influence, power, might, standing, status, importance, eminence

manage 1 = be in charge of, run, handle, direct, conduct, command, administer, supervise **2** = organize, use, handle, regulate **3** = <u>cope</u>, survive, succeed, carry on, make do, get by (*informal*), muddle through **4** = <u>perform</u>, do, achieve, carry out, undertake, cope with, accomplish, contrive **5** = <u>control</u>, handle, manipulate

management
1 = <u>administration</u>, control, running, operation, handling, direction, command, supervision **2** = <u>directors</u>, board, executive(s), administration, employers

manager = <u>supervisor</u>, head, director, executive, boss (*informal*), governor, administrator, organizer, baas (*S. African*)

mandate = <u>command</u>, order, commission, instruction, decree, directive, edict

mandatory = <u>compulsory</u>, required, binding, obligatory, requisite ≠ optional

manhood = <u>manliness</u>, masculinity, virility

manifest ADJECTIVE = <u>obvious</u>, apparent, patent, evident, clear, glaring, noticeable, blatant ≠ concealed

● VERB = <u>display</u>, show, reveal, express, demonstrate, expose, exhibit ≠ conceal

manifestation 1 = <u>sign</u>, symptom, indication, mark, example, evidence, proof, testimony **2** = <u>display</u>, show,

exhibition, expression, demonstration

manipulate 1 = <u>influence</u>, control, direct, negotiate, exploit, manoeuvre **2** = <u>work</u>, use, operate, handle

mankind = <u>people</u>, man, humanity, human race, humankind, Homo sapiens

> *Word Power*
>
> **mankind** – Some people object to the use of *mankind* to refer to all human beings on the grounds that it is sexist. A preferable term is *humankind*, which refers to both men and women.

manly = <u>virile</u>, masculine, strong, brave, bold, strapping, vigorous, courageous ≠ effeminate

man-made = <u>artificial</u>, manufactured, mock, synthetic, ersatz

manner NOUN **1** = <u>style</u>, way, fashion, method, custom, mode **2** = <u>behaviour</u>, air, bearing, conduct, aspect, demeanour **3** = <u>type</u>, form, sort, kind, variety, brand, category

● PLURAL NOUN **1** = <u>conduct</u>, behaviour, demeanour **2** = <u>politeness</u>, courtesy, etiquette, refinement, decorum, p's and q's **3** = <u>protocol</u>, customs, social graces

mannered = <u>affected</u>, artificial,

pretentious, stilted, arty-farty (*informal*) ≠ natural

manoeuvre VERB 1 = <u>scheme</u>, wangle (*informal*), machinate 2 = <u>manipulate</u>, arrange, organize, set up, engineer, fix, orchestrate, contrive
● NOUN 1 = <u>stratagem</u>, scheme, trick, tactic, intrigue, dodge, ploy, ruse 2 *often plural* = <u>movement</u>, operation, exercise, war game

mansion = <u>residence</u>, manor, hall, villa, seat

mantle 1 = <u>covering</u>, screen, curtain, blanket, veil, shroud, canopy, pall 2 = <u>cloak</u>, wrap, cape, hood, shawl

manual ADJECTIVE 1 = <u>physical</u>, human 2 = <u>hand-operated</u>, hand, non-automatic
● NOUN = <u>handbook</u>, guide, instructions, bible

manufacture VERB 1 = <u>make</u>, build, produce, construct, create, turn out, assemble, put together 2 = <u>concoct</u>, make up, invent, devise, fabricate, think up, cook up (*informal*), trump up
● NOUN = <u>making</u>, production, construction, assembly, creation

manufacturer = <u>maker</u>, producer, builder, creator, industrialist, constructor

many DETERMINER = <u>numerous</u>, various, countless, abundant, myriad, innumerable, manifold, umpteen (*informal*)
● PRONOUN = <u>a lot</u>, lots (*informal*), plenty, scores, heaps (*informal*)

mar 1 = <u>harm</u>, damage, hurt, spoil, stain, taint, tarnish 2 = <u>ruin</u>, spoil, scar, flaw, impair, detract from, deform, blemish ≠ improve

march VERB 1 = <u>parade</u>, walk, file, pace, stride, swagger 2 = <u>walk</u>, strut, storm, sweep, stride, flounce
● NOUN 1 = <u>walk</u>, trek, slog, yomp (*Brit. informal*), routemarch 2 = <u>progress</u>, development, advance, evolution, progression

margin = <u>edge</u>, side, border, boundary, verge, brink, rim, perimeter

marginal 1 = <u>insignificant</u>, small, minor, slight, minimal, negligible 2 = <u>borderline</u>, bordering, on the edge, peripheral

marijuana = <u>cannabis</u>, pot (*slang*), dope (*slang*), grass (*slang*), hemp, dagga (*S. African*)

marine = <u>nautical</u>, maritime, naval, seafaring, seagoing

mariner = <u>sailor</u>, seaman, sea dog, seafarer, salt

marital = <u>matrimonial</u>, nuptial, conjugal, connubial

maritime 1 = <u>nautical</u>, marine, naval, oceanic, seafaring 2 = <u>coastal</u>, seaside, littoral

mark NOUN 1 = <u>spot</u>, stain, streak, smudge, line, scratch, scar, blot 2 = <u>characteristic</u>, feature, standard, quality, measure, stamp, attribute, criterion 3 = <u>indication</u>, sign, symbol, token **4** = <u>brand</u>, impression, label, device, flag, symbol, token, emblem **5** = <u>target</u>, goal, aim, purpose, object, objective

● VERB **1** = <u>scar</u>, scratch, stain, streak, blot, smudge, blemish **2** = <u>label</u>, identify, brand, flag, stamp, characterize **3** = <u>grade</u>, correct, assess, evaluate, appraise **4** = <u>distinguish</u>, show, illustrate, exemplify, denote **5** = <u>observe</u>, mind, note, notice, attend to, pay attention to, pay heed to

marked = <u>noticeable</u>, clear, decided, striking, obvious, prominent, patent, distinct ≠ imperceptible

markedly = <u>noticeably</u>, clearly, obviously, considerably, distinctly, decidedly, strikingly, conspicuously

market NOUN = <u>fair</u>, mart, bazaar, souk (Arabic)

● VERB = <u>sell</u>, promote, retail, peddle, vend

maroon = <u>abandon</u>, leave, desert, strand, leave high and dry (informal)

marriage = <u>wedding</u>, match, nuptials, wedlock, matrimony

Related Words

adjectives: conjugal, marital, nuptial

marry 1 = <u>tie the knot</u> (informal), wed, get hitched (slang) **2** = <u>unite</u>, join, link, bond, ally, merge, knit, unify

marsh = <u>swamp</u>, bog, slough,

fen, quagmire, morass

marshal 1 = <u>conduct</u>, take, lead, guide, steer, escort, shepherd, usher **2** = <u>arrange</u>, group, order, line up, organize, deploy, array, draw up

marsupial ▸ marsupials

martial = <u>military</u>, belligerent, warlike, bellicose

marvel VERB = <u>be amazed</u>, wonder, gape, be awed

● NOUN **1** = <u>wonder</u>, phenomenon, miracle, portent **2** = <u>genius</u>, prodigy

marvellous = <u>excellent</u>, great (informal), wonderful, brilliant, amazing, extraordinary, superb, spectacular, booshit (Austral. slang), exo (Austral. slang), sik (Austral. slang) ≠ terrible

masculine = <u>male</u>, manly, mannish, manlike, virile

mask NOUN = <u>façade</u>, disguise, front, cover, screen, veil, guise, camouflage

● VERB = <u>disguise</u>, hide, conceal, obscure, cover (up), screen, blanket, veil

mass NOUN **1** = <u>lot</u>, collection, load, pile, quantity, bunch, stack, heap **2** = <u>piece</u>, block, lump, chunk, hunk **3** = <u>size</u>, matter, weight, extent, bulk, magnitude, greatness

● ADJECTIVE = <u>large-scale</u>, general, widespread, extensive, universal, wholesale, indiscriminate

● VERB = <u>gather</u>, assemble,

Marsupials

bandicoot

Bennett's tree kangaroo *or* tcharibeena

bettong

bilby, rabbit(-eared) bandicoot, long-eared bandicoot, dalgyte, *or* dalgite

bobuck *or* mountain (brushtail) possum

boodie (rat), burrowing rat-kangaroo, Lesueur's rat-kangaroo, tungoo, *or* tungo

boongary *or* Lumholtz's tree kangaroo

bridled nail-tail wallaby *or* merrin

brush-tail(ed) possum

burramys *or* (mountain) pygmy possum

crest-tailed marsupial mouse, Cannings' little dog, *or* mulgara

crescent nail-tail wallaby *or* wurrung

cuscus

dasyurid, dasyure, native cat, marsupial cat, *or* wild cat

dibbler

diprotodon

dunnart

fluffy glider *or* yellow-bellied glider

flying phalanger, flying squirrel, glider, *or* pongo

green ringtail possum *or* toolah

hare-wallaby

honey mouse, honey possum, noolbenger, *or* tait

jerboa, jerboa pouched mouse, jerboa kangaroo, *or* kultarr

kangaroo *or* (*Austral. informal*) roo

koala (bear) *or* (*Austral.*) native bear

kowari

larapinta *or* Darling Downs dunnart

marlu

marsupial mole

marsupial mouse

munning

ningaui

northern native cat *or* satanellus

numbat *or* banded anteater

opossum *or* possum

pademelon *or* paddymelon

phalanger

pitchi-pitchi *or* wuhl-wuhl

platypus, duck-billed platypus, *or* duckbill

potoroo

pygmy glider, feather glider, *or* flying mouse

quokka

quoll

rat kangaroo

squirrel glider

sugar glider

tammar, damar, *or* dama

Tasmanian devil *or* ursine dasyure

thylacine, Tasmanian wolf, *or* Tasmanian tiger

tiger cat *or* spotted native cat

tree kangaroo

tuan, phascogale, *or* wambenger

wallaby

wallaroo, uroo, *or* biggada

warabi

wombat *or* (*Austral.*) badger

yapok

yallara

accumulate, collect, rally, swarm, throng, congregate

massacre NOUN = <u>slaughter</u>, murder, holocaust, carnage, extermination, annihilation, butchery, blood bath

• VERB = <u>slaughter</u>, kill, murder, butcher, wipe out, exterminate, mow down, cut to pieces

massage NOUN = <u>rub-down</u>, manipulation

• VERB = <u>rub down</u>, manipulate, knead **2** = <u>manipulate</u>, alter, distort, doctor, cook (*informal*), fix (*informal*), rig, fiddle (*informal*)

massive = <u>huge</u>, big, enormous, immense, hefty, gigantic, monumental, mammoth ≠ tiny

master NOUN **1** = <u>lord</u>, ruler, commander, chief, director, manager, boss (*informal*), head, baas (*S. African*) ≠ servant **2** = <u>expert</u>, maestro, ace (*informal*), genius, wizard, virtuoso, doyen, past master, fundi (*S. African*) ≠ amateur **3** = <u>teacher</u>, tutor, instructor ≠ student

• ADJECTIVE = <u>main</u>, principal, chief, prime, foremost, predominant ≠ lesser

• VERB **1** = <u>learn</u>, understand, pick up, grasp, get the hang of (*informal*), know inside out, know backwards **2** = <u>overcome</u>, defeat, conquer, tame, triumph over, vanquish ≠ give in to

masterly = <u>skilful</u>, expert, crack (*informal*), supreme, world-class, consummate, first-rate, masterful

mastermind VERB = <u>plan</u>, manage, direct, organize, devise, conceive

• NOUN = <u>organizer</u>, director, manager, engineer, brain(s) (*informal*), architect, planner

masterpiece = <u>classic</u>, tour de force (*French*), pièce de résistance (*French*), magnum opus, jewel

mastery 1 = <u>understanding</u>, skill, know-how, expertise, prowess, finesse, proficiency, virtuosity **2** = <u>control</u>, command, domination, superiority, supremacy, upper hand, ascendancy, mana (*N.Z.*), whip hand

match NOUN **1** = <u>game</u>, test, competition, trial, tie, contest, fixture, bout **2** = <u>marriage</u>, pairing, alliance, partnership **3** = <u>equal</u>, rival, peer, counterpart

• VERB **1** = <u>correspond with</u>, go with, fit with, harmonize with **2** = <u>correspond</u>, agree, accord, square, coincide, tally, conform, match up **3** = <u>rival</u>, equal, compete with, compare with, emulate, measure up to

matching = <u>identical</u>, like, twin, equivalent, corresponding, coordinating ≠ different

mate NOUN **1** (*Informal*) = <u>friend</u>, pal (*informal*), companion, buddy (*informal*), comrade, chum (*informal*), mucker (*Brit. informal*), crony, cobber (*Austral. & N.Z. old-fashioned informal*), E hoa (*N.Z.*) 2 = **partner**, lover, companion, spouse, consort, helpmeet, husband *or* wife 3 = **assistant**, subordinate, apprentice, helper, accomplice, sidekick (*informal*) 4 = **colleague**, associate, companion

● VERB = **pair**, couple, breed

material NOUN 1 = **substance**, matter, stuff 2 = **cloth**, fabric, textile 3 = **information**, details, facts, notes, evidence, particulars, data, info (*informal*)

● ADJECTIVE 1 = **physical**, solid, substantial, concrete, bodily, tangible, palpable, corporeal 2 = **relevant**, important, significant, essential, vital, serious, meaningful, applicable

materially = **significantly**, much, greatly, essentially, seriously, gravely, substantially ≠ insignificantly

maternal = **motherly**, protective, nurturing, maternalistic

maternity = **motherhood**, parenthood, motherliness

matted = **tangled**, knotted, unkempt, knotty, tousled, ratty, uncombed

matter NOUN 1 = **situation**, concern, business, question, event, subject, affair, incident 2 = **substance**, material, body, stuff

● VERB = **be important**, make a difference, count, be relevant, make any difference, carry weight, cut any ice (*informal*), be of account

matter-of-fact = **unsentimental**, plain, sober, down-to-earth, mundane, prosaic, deadpan, unimaginative

mature VERB = **develop**, grow up, bloom, blossom, come of age, age

● ADJECTIVE 1 = **matured**, seasoned, ripe, mellow 2 = **grown-up**, adult, of age, fully fledged, full-grown ≠ immature

maturity 1 = **adulthood**, puberty, coming of age, pubescence, manhood *or* womanhood ≠ immaturity 2 = **ripeness**

maul 1 = **mangle**, claw, lacerate, tear, mangulate (*Austral. slang*) 2 = **ill-treat**, abuse, batter, molest, manhandle

maverick NOUN = **rebel**, radical, dissenter, individualist, protester, eccentric, heretic, nonconformist ≠ traditionalist

● ADJECTIVE = **rebel**, radical, dissenting, individualistic, eccentric, heretical, iconoclastic, nonconformist

maximum ADJECTIVE = **greatest**,

highest, supreme, paramount, utmost, most, topmost ≠ minimal
● NOUN = top, peak, ceiling, utmost, upper limit ≠ minimum

maybe = perhaps, possibly, perchance (*archaic*)

mayhem = chaos, trouble, violence, disorder, destruction, confusion, havoc, fracas

maze = web, confusion, tangle, labyrinth, imbroglio, complex network

meadow = field, pasture, grassland, lea (*poetic*)

mean¹ 1 = signify, indicate, represent, express, stand for, convey, spell out, symbolize **2** = imply, suggest, intend, hint at, insinuate **3** = intend, want, plan, expect, design, aim, wish, think

> ### Word Power
>
> **mean** – In standard British English, *mean* should not be followed by *for* when expressing intention. *I didn't mean this to happen* is acceptable, but not *I didn't mean for this to happen.*

mean² 1 = miserly, stingy, parsimonious, niggardly, mercenary, penny-pinching, ungenerous, tight-fisted, snoep (*S. African informal*) ≠ generous **2** = dishonourable, petty, shameful, shabby, vile, callous, sordid, despicable, scungy (*Austral. & N.Z.*) ≠ honourable

mean³ NOUN = average, middle, balance, norm, midpoint
● ADJECTIVE = average, middle, standard

meaning 1 = significance, message, substance, drift, connotation, gist **2** = definition, sense

meaningful = significant, important, material, useful, relevant, valid, worthwhile, purposeful ≠ trivial

meaningless = nonsensical, senseless, inconsequential, inane ≠ worthwhile

means PLURAL NOUN **1** = method, way, process, medium, agency, instrument, mode **2** = money, funds, capital, income, resources, fortune, wealth, affluence
● PHRASES **by all means** = certainly, surely, of course, definitely, doubtlessly ◆ **by no means** = in no way, definitely not, not in the least, on no account

meantime or **meanwhile** = at the same time, simultaneously, concurrently

meanwhile or **meantime** = for now, in the interim

measure VERB = quantify, determine, assess, weigh, calculate, evaluate, compute, gauge
● NOUN **1** = quantity, share, amount, allowance, portion,

quota, ration, allotment
2 = <u>action</u>, act, step, procedure, means, control, initiative, manoeuvre **3** = <u>gauge</u>, rule, scale, metre, ruler, yardstick **4** = <u>law</u>, act, bill, legislation, resolution, statute

measured 1 = <u>steady</u>, even, slow, regular, dignified, stately, solemn, leisurely **2** = <u>considered</u>, reasoned, studied, calculated, deliberate, sober, well-thought-out

measurement = <u>calculation</u>, assessment, evaluation, valuation, computation, calibration, mensuration

meat = <u>food</u>, flesh, kai (*N.Z. informal*)

mechanical 1 = <u>automatic</u>, automated, mechanized, power-driven, motor-driven ≠ manual **2** = <u>unthinking</u>, routine, automatic, instinctive, involuntary, impersonal, cursory, perfunctory ≠ conscious

mechanism 1 = <u>process</u>, way, means, system, operation, agency, method, technique **2** = <u>machine</u>, device, tool, instrument, appliance, apparatus, contrivance

mediate = <u>intervene</u>, step in (*informal*), intercede, referee, umpire, reconcile, arbitrate, conciliate

mediation = <u>arbitration</u>, intervention, reconciliation,

conciliation, intercession

mediator = <u>negotiator</u>, arbitrator, referee, umpire, intermediary, middleman, arbiter, peacemaker

medicine = <u>remedy</u>, drug, cure, prescription, medication, nostrum, medicament

mediocre = <u>second-rate</u>, average, ordinary, indifferent, middling, pedestrian, inferior, so-so (*informal*), half-pie (*N.Z. informal*) ≠ excellent

meditation = <u>reflection</u>, thought, study, musing, pondering, contemplation, rumination, cogitation

medium ADJECTIVE = <u>average</u>, mean, middle, middling, fair, intermediate, midway, mediocre ≠ extraordinary
● NOUN **1** = <u>spiritualist</u>, seer, clairvoyant, fortune teller, channeller **2** = <u>middle</u>, mean, centre, average, compromise, midpoint

meet 1 = <u>encounter</u>, come across, run into, happen on, find, contact, confront, bump into (*informal*) ≠ avoid **2** = <u>gather</u>, collect, assemble, get together, come together, muster, convene, congregate ≠ disperse **3** = <u>fulfil</u>, match (up to), answer, satisfy, discharge, comply with, come up to, conform to ≠ fall short of **4** = <u>experience</u>, face, suffer, bear, go through, encounter, endure, undergo **5** = <u>converge</u>, join, cross, touch, connect, come together, link up, intersect ≠ diverge

meeting 1 = <u>conference</u>, gathering, assembly, congress, session, convention, get-together (*informal*), reunion, hui (*N.Z.*) **2** = <u>encounter</u>, introduction, confrontation, engagement, rendezvous, tryst, assignation

melancholy ADJECTIVE = <u>sad</u>, depressed, miserable, gloomy, glum, mournful, despondent, dispirited ≠ happy
● NOUN = <u>sadness</u>, depression, misery, gloom, sorrow, unhappiness, despondency, dejection ≠ happiness

mellow ADJECTIVE **1** = <u>full-flavoured</u>, rich, sweet, delicate **2** = <u>ripe</u>, mature, ripened ≠ unripe
● VERB **1** = <u>relax</u>, improve, settle, calm, mature, soften, sweeten **2** = <u>season</u>, develop, improve, ripen

melody 1 = <u>tune</u>, song, theme, air, music, strain **2** = <u>tunefulness</u>, harmony, musicality, euphony, melodiousness

melt 1 = <u>dissolve</u>, run, soften, fuse, thaw, defrost, liquefy, unfreeze **2** *often with* **away** = <u>disappear</u>, fade, vanish, dissolve, disperse, evaporate, evanesce **3** = <u>soften</u>, relax, disarm, mollify

member = <u>representative</u>, associate, supporter, fellow, subscriber, comrade, disciple

membership 1 = <u>participation</u>, belonging, fellowship, enrolment **2** = <u>members</u>, body, associates, fellows

memoir = <u>account</u>, life, record, journal, essay, biography, narrative, monograph

memoirs = <u>autobiography</u>, diary, life story, experiences, memories, journals, recollections, reminiscences

memorable = <u>noteworthy</u>, celebrated, historic, striking, famous, significant, remarkable, notable ≠ forgettable

memorandum = <u>note</u>, minute, message, communication, reminder, memo, jotting

memorial NOUN = <u>monument</u>, shrine, plaque, cenotaph
● ADJECTIVE = <u>commemorative</u>, remembrance, monumental

memory 1 = <u>recall</u>, mind, retention, ability to remember, powers of recall, powers of retention **2** = <u>recollection</u>, reminder, reminiscence, impression, echo, remembrance **3** = <u>commemoration</u>, respect, honour, recognition, tribute, remembrance, observance

menace NOUN **1** (*Informal*) = <u>nuisance</u>, plague, pest, annoyance, troublemaker

2 = <u>threat</u>, warning, intimidation, ill-omen, ominousness

● VERB = <u>bully</u>, threaten, intimidate, terrorize, frighten, scare

menacing = <u>threatening</u>, frightening, forbidding, looming, intimidating, ominous, louring *or* lowering ≠ encouraging

mend VERB **1** = <u>repair</u>, fix, restore, renew, patch up, renovate, refit, retouch **2** = <u>darn</u>, repair, patch, stitch, sew **3** = <u>heal</u>, improve, recover, get better, be all right, be cured, recuperate, pull through **4** = <u>improve</u>, reform, correct, revise, amend, rectify, ameliorate, emend

● PHRASES **on the mend** = <u>convalescent</u>, improving, recovering, getting better, recuperating

mental 1 = <u>intellectual</u>, rational, theoretical, cognitive, brain, conceptual, cerebral **2** (*Informal*) = <u>insane</u>, mad, disturbed, unstable, mentally ill, psychotic, unbalanced, deranged

mentality = <u>attitude</u>, character, personality, psychology, make-up, outlook, disposition, cast of mind

mentally = <u>psychologically</u>, intellectually, inwardly

mention VERB = <u>refer to</u>, point out, bring up, state, reveal, declare, disclose, intimate

● NOUN **1** *often with of* = <u>reference</u> to, observation, indication, remark on, allusion to **2** = <u>acknowledgment</u>, recognition, tribute, citation, honourable mention

mentor = <u>guide</u>, teacher, coach, adviser, tutor, instructor, counsellor, guru

menu = <u>bill of fare</u>, tariff (*chiefly Brit.*), set menu, table d'hôte, carte du jour (*French*)

merchandise = <u>goods</u>, produce, stock, products, commodities, wares

merchant = <u>tradesman</u>, dealer, trader, broker, retailer, supplier, seller, salesman

mercy 1 = <u>compassion</u>, pity, forgiveness, grace, kindness, clemency, leniency, forbearance ≠ cruelty **2** = <u>blessing</u>, boon, godsend

mere 1 = <u>simple</u>, nothing more than, common, plain, pure **2** = <u>bare</u>, slender, trifling, meagre, just, only, basic, no more than

merge 1 = <u>combine</u>, blend, fuse, amalgamate, unite, join, mix, mingle ≠ separate **2** = <u>join</u>, unite, combine, fuse ≠ separate **3** = <u>melt</u>, blend, mingle

merger = <u>union</u>, fusion, consolidation, amalgamation, combination, coalition, incorporation

merit NOUN = <u>advantage</u>, value, quality, worth, strength, asset, virtue, strong point

● **VERB** = <u>deserve</u>, warrant, be entitled to, earn, have a right to, be worthy of

merry 1 = <u>cheerful</u>, happy, carefree, jolly, festive, joyous, convivial, blithe ≠ gloomy 2 (*Brit. informal*) = <u>tipsy</u>, happy, mellow, tiddly (*slang, chiefly Brit.*), squiffy (*Brit. informal*)

mesh NOUN = <u>net</u>, netting, network, web, tracery

● **VERB** = <u>engage</u>, combine, connect, knit, coordinate, interlock, dovetail, harmonize

mess NOUN 1 = <u>untidiness</u>, disorder, confusion, chaos, litter, clutter, disarray, jumble 2 = <u>shambles</u>, difficulty, dilemma, plight, hole (*informal*), fix (*informal*), jam (*informal*), muddle, pickle (*informal*), uphill (*S. African*)

● **PHRASES mess about** *or* **around** = <u>potter about</u>, dabble, amuse yourself, fool about *or* around, muck about *or* around (*informal*), play about *or* around, trifle ◆ **mess something up** 1 = <u>botch</u>, muck something up (*Brit. slang*), muddle something up 2 = <u>dirty</u>, pollute, clutter, disarrange, dishevel ◆ **mess with something** *or* **someone** = <u>interfere</u>, play, fiddle (*informal*), tamper, tinker, meddle

message 1 = <u>communication</u>,

note, bulletin, word, letter, dispatch, memorandum, communiqué 2 = <u>point</u>, meaning, idea, moral, theme, import, purport

messenger = <u>courier</u>, runner, carrier, herald, envoy, go-between, emissary, delivery boy

messy 1 = <u>disorganized</u>, sloppy (*informal*), untidy 2 = <u>dirty</u> 3 = <u>untidy</u>, disordered, chaotic, muddled, cluttered, shambolic, disorganized ≠ tidy 4 = <u>dishevelled</u>, ruffled, untidy, rumpled, bedraggled, tousled, uncombed 5 = <u>confusing</u>, difficult, complex, confused, tangled, chaotic, tortuous

metaphor = <u>figure of speech</u>, image, symbol, analogy, conceit (*literary*), allegory, trope, figurative expression

method 1 = <u>manner</u>, process, approach, technique, way, system, style, procedure 2 = <u>orderliness</u>, planning, order, system, purpose, pattern, organization, regularity

midday = <u>noon</u>, twelve o'clock, noonday

middle NOUN = <u>centre</u>, heart, midst, halfway point, midpoint, midsection

● **ADJECTIVE** 1 = <u>central</u>, medium, mid, intervening, halfway, intermediate, median 2 = <u>intermediate</u>, intervening

middle-class = bourgeois, traditional, conventional

middling 1 = mediocre, all right, indifferent, so-so (informal), unremarkable, tolerable, run-of-the-mill, passable, half-pie (N.Z. informal) 2 = moderate, medium, average, fair, ordinary, modest, adequate

midnight = twelve o'clock, middle of the night, dead of night, the witching hour

midst

PHRASES **in the midst of** = among, during, in the middle of, surrounded by, amidst, in the thick of

midway ADJECTIVE OR ADVERB = halfway, in the middle of, part-way, equidistant, at the midpoint, betwixt and between

might NOUN = power, force, energy, strength, vigour

● PHRASES **with all your might** = forcefully, vigorously, mightily, manfully, lustily

mighty = powerful, strong, strapping, robust, sturdy, forceful, lusty ≠ weak

migrant NOUN = wanderer, immigrant, traveller, rover, nomad, emigrant, itinerant, drifter

● ADJECTIVE = itinerant, wandering, drifting, roving, travelling, shifting, immigrant, transient

migrate = move, travel, journey, wander, trek, voyage, roam, emigrate

migration = wandering, journey, voyage, travel, movement, trek, emigration, roving

mild 1 = gentle, calm, easy-going, meek, placid, docile, peaceable, equable ≠ harsh 2 = temperate, warm, calm, moderate, tranquil, balmy ≠ cold 3 = bland, thin, smooth, tasteless, insipid, flavourless

militant = aggressive, active, vigorous, assertive, combative ≠ peaceful

military ADJECTIVE = warlike, armed, soldierly, martial

● NOUN = armed forces, forces, services, army

milk = exploit, pump, take advantage of

Related Words

adjective: lactic

mill NOUN 1 = grinder, crusher, quern 2 = factory, works, plant, workshop, foundry

● VERB = grind, pound, crush, powder, grate

● PHRASES **mill about** or **around** = swarm, crowd, stream, surge, throng

mimic VERB = imitate, do (informal), take off (informal), ape, parody, caricature, impersonate

● NOUN = imitator, impressionist, copycat (informal), impersonator, caricaturist

mince 1 = cut, grind, crumble, dice, hash, chop up 2 = tone down, spare, moderate, weaken, soften

mincing = affected, camp (*informal*), precious, pretentious, dainty, sissy, effeminate, foppish

mind NOUN 1 = memory, recollection, remembrance, powers of recollection 2 = intelligence, reason, reasoning, understanding, sense, brain(s) (*informal*), wits, intellect 3 = intention, wish, desire, urge, fancy, leaning, notion, inclination 4 = sanity, reason, senses, judgment, wits, marbles (*informal*), rationality, mental balance
• VERB 1 = take offence at, dislike, care about, object to, resent, disapprove of, be bothered by, be affronted by 2 = be careful, watch, take care, be wary, be cautious, be on your guard 3 = look after, watch, protect, tend, guard, take care of, attend to, keep an eye on 4 = pay attention to, mark, note, listen to, observe, obey, heed, take heed of
Related Words
adjective: mental

mine NOUN 1 = pit, deposit, shaft, colliery, excavation 2 = source, store, fund, stock, supply, reserve, treasury, wealth
• VERB = dig up, extract, quarry, unearth, excavate, hew, dig for

miner = coalminer, pitman (*Brit.*), collier (*Brit.*)

mingle 1 = mix, combine, blend, merge, unite, join, interweave, intermingle ≠ separate 2 = associate, consort, socialize, rub shoulders (*informal*), hobnob, fraternize, hang about *or* around ≠ dissociate

miniature = small, little, minute, tiny, toy, scaled-down, diminutive, minuscule ≠ giant

minimal = minimum, smallest, least, slightest, token, nominal, negligible, least possible

minimize 1 = reduce, decrease, shrink, diminish, prune, curtail, miniaturize ≠ increase 2 = play down, discount, belittle, disparage, decry, underrate, deprecate, make light *or* little of ≠ praise

minimum ADJECTIVE = lowest, smallest, least, slightest, minimal, least possible ≠ maximum
• NOUN = lowest, least, lowest level, nadir

minister NOUN = clergyman, priest, vicar, parson, preacher, pastor, cleric, rector
• VERB often with **to** = attend, serve, tend, take care of, cater to, pander to, administer to

ministry 1 = department, office, bureau, government department 2 = administration, council 3 = the priesthood, the church, the cloth, holy orders

minor = <u>small</u>, lesser, slight, petty, trivial, insignificant, unimportant, inconsequential ≠ major

mint = <u>make</u>, produce, strike, cast, stamp, punch, coin

minute¹ NOUN = <u>moment</u>, second, bit, flash, instant, tick (*Brit. informal*), sec (*informal*), short time

● PLURAL NOUN = <u>record</u>, notes, proceedings, transactions, transcript, memorandum

minute² 1 = <u>small</u>, little, tiny, miniature, microscopic, diminutive, microscopic, infinitesimal ≠ huge 2 = <u>precise</u>, close, detailed, critical, exact, meticulous, exhaustive, painstaking ≠ imprecise

miracle = <u>wonder</u>, phenomenon, sensation, marvel, amazing achievement, astonishing feat

miraculous = <u>wonderful</u>, amazing, extraordinary, incredible, astonishing, unbelievable, phenomenal, astounding ≠ ordinary

mirror NOUN = <u>looking-glass</u>, glass (*Brit.*), reflector

● VERB = <u>reflect</u>, follow, copy, echo, emulate

miscarriage = <u>failure</u>, error, breakdown, mishap, perversion

misconduct = <u>immorality</u>, wrongdoing, mismanagement,

malpractice, impropriety

miserable 1 = <u>sad</u>, depressed, gloomy, forlorn, dejected, despondent, sorrowful, wretched ≠ happy 2 = <u>pathetic</u>, sorry, shameful, despicable, deplorable, lamentable ≠ respectable

misery 1 = <u>unhappiness</u>, distress, despair, grief, suffering, depression, gloom, torment ≠ happiness 2 (*Brit. informal*) = <u>moaner</u>, pessimist, killjoy, spoilsport, prophet of doom, wet blanket (*informal*), sourpuss (*informal*), wowser (*Austral. & N.Z. slang*)

misfortune 1 *often plural* = <u>bad luck</u>, adversity, hard luck, ill luck, infelicity 2 = <u>mishap</u>, trouble, disaster, reverse, tragedy, setback, calamity, affliction ≠ good luck

misguided = <u>unwise</u>, mistaken, misplaced, deluded, ill-advised, imprudent, injudicious

mislead = <u>deceive</u>, fool, delude, take someone in (*informal*), misdirect, misinform, hoodwink, misguide

misleading = <u>confusing</u>, false, ambiguous, deceptive, evasive, disingenuous ≠ straightforward

miss VERB 1 = <u>fail to notice</u>, overlook, pass over 2 = <u>long for</u>, yearn for, pine for, long to see, ache for, feel the loss of, regret the absence of 3 = <u>not go to</u>, skip, cut, omit, be absent from, fail to attend, skive off (*informal*), play truant from, bludge (*Austral. & N.Z. informal*) **4** = <u>avoid</u>, beat, escape, skirt, duck, cheat, bypass, dodge

• NOUN = <u>mistake</u>, failure, error, blunder, omission, oversight

missile = <u>projectile</u>, weapon, shell, rocket

missing = <u>lost</u>, misplaced, not present, astray, unaccounted for, mislaid

mission = <u>task</u>, job, commission, duty, undertaking, quest, assignment, vocation

missionary = <u>evangelist</u>, preacher, apostle

mist = <u>fog</u>, cloud, steam, spray, film, haze, vapour, smog

mistake NOUN **1** = <u>error</u>, blunder, oversight, slip, gaffe (*informal*), miscalculation, faux pas **2** = <u>oversight</u>, error, slip, fault, howler (*informal*), erratum

• VERB **1** = <u>confuse with</u>, take for, mix up with **2** = <u>misunderstand</u>, misinterpret, misjudge, misread, misconstrue, misapprehend

mistaken 1 = <u>wrong</u>, incorrect, misguided, wide of the mark ≠ correct **2** = <u>inaccurate</u>, false, faulty, erroneous, unsound ≠ accurate

mistress = <u>lover</u>, girlfriend, concubine, kept woman, paramour

misunderstand

1 = <u>misinterpret</u>, misread,

mistake, misjudge, misconstrue, misapprehend, be at cross-purposes with **2** = <u>miss the point</u>, get the wrong end of the stick

misunderstanding = <u>mistake</u>, error, mix-up, misconception, misinterpretation, misjudgment

misuse NOUN **1** = <u>waste</u>, squandering **2** = <u>abuse</u> **3** = <u>misapplication</u>, abuse, illegal use, wrong use **4** = <u>perversion</u>, desecration **5** = <u>misapplication</u>

• VERB **1** = <u>abuse</u>, misapply, prostitute **2** = <u>waste</u>, squander, embezzle, misappropriate

mix VERB **1** = <u>combine</u>, blend, merge, join, cross, fuse, mingle, jumble **2** = <u>socialize</u>, associate, hang out (*informal*), mingle, circulate, consort, hobnob, fraternize **3** often with **up** = <u>combine</u>, marry, blend, integrate, amalgamate, coalesce, meld

• NOUN = <u>mixture</u>, combination, blend, fusion, compound, assortment, alloy, medley

• PHRASES **mix something up 1** = <u>confuse</u>, scramble, muddle, confound **2** = <u>blend</u>, beat, mix, stir, fold

mixed 1 = <u>varied</u>, diverse, different, differing, cosmopolitan, assorted, jumbled, disparate ≠ homogeneous **2** = <u>combined</u>, blended, united, compound, composite, mingled, amalgamated ≠ pure

mixed-up = confused, disturbed, puzzled, bewildered, at sea, upset, distraught, muddled

mixture 1 = blend, mix, variety, fusion, assortment, brew, jumble, medley 2 = composite, compound 3 = cross, combination, blend 4 = concoction, compound, blend, brew, amalgam

mix-up = confusion, mistake, misunderstanding, mess, tangle, muddle

moan VERB 1 = groan, sigh, sob, whine, lament 2 (*Informal*) = grumble, complain, groan, whine, carp, grouse, whinge (*informal*), bleat

• NOUN 1 = groan, sigh, sob, lament, wail, grunt, whine 2 (*Informal*) = complaint, protest, grumble, whine, grouse, gripe (*informal*), grouch (*informal*)

mob NOUN 1 = crowd, mass, host, drove, flock, swarm, horde 2 (*Slang*) = gang, group, set, lot, crew (*informal*)

• VERB = surround, besiege, jostle, fall on, set upon, crowd around, swarm around

mobile = movable, moving, travelling, wandering, portable, itinerant, peripatetic

mobilize 1 = rally, organize, stimulate, excite, prompt,

marshal, activate, awaken 2 = deploy, prepare, ready, rally, assemble, call up, marshal, muster

mock VERB 1 = laugh at, tease, ridicule, taunt, scorn, sneer, scoff, deride ≠ respect

• ADJECTIVE = imitation, pretended, artificial, fake, false, dummy, sham, feigned ≠ genuine

mocking = scornful, scoffing, satirical, contemptuous, sarcastic, sardonic, disrespectful, disdainful

mode 1 = method, way, system, form, process, style, technique, manner 2 = fashion, style, trend, rage, vogue, look, craze

model NOUN 1 = representation, image, copy, miniature, dummy, replica, imitation, duplicate 2 = pattern, example, standard, original, ideal, prototype, paradigm, archetype 3 = sitter, subject, poser

• VERB 1 = show off (*informal*), wear, display, sport 2 = shape, form, design, fashion, carve, mould, sculpt

moderate ADJECTIVE 1 = mild, reasonable, controlled, limited, steady, modest, restrained, middle-of-the-road ≠ extreme 2 = average, middling, fair, ordinary, indifferent, mediocre, so-so (*informal*), passable, half-pie (*N.Z. informal*)

• VERB 1 = soften, control, temper, regulate, curb, restrain, subdue, lessen 2 = <u>lessen</u>, ease ≠ intensify

modern 1 = <u>current</u>, contemporary, recent, present-day, latter-day 2 = <u>up-to-date</u>, fresh, new, novel, newfangled ≠ old-fashioned

modest 1 = <u>moderate</u>, small, limited, fair, ordinary, middling, meagre, frugal 2 = <u>unpretentious</u>, reserved, retiring, shy, coy, reticent, self-effacing, demure

modesty = <u>reserve</u>, humility, shyness, reticence, timidity, diffidence, coyness, bashfulness ≠ conceit

modification = <u>change</u>, variation, qualification, adjustment, revision, alteration, refinement

modify 1 = <u>change</u>, reform, convert, alter, adjust, adapt, revise, remodel 2 = <u>tone down</u>, lower, qualify, ease, moderate, temper, soften, restrain

mogul = <u>tycoon</u>, baron, magnate, big shot (*informal*), big noise (*informal*), big hitter (*informal*), heavy hitter (*informal*), V.I.P.

moist = <u>damp</u>, wet, soggy, humid, clammy, dewy

moisture = <u>damp</u>, water, liquid, dew, wetness

molecule = <u>particle</u>, jot, speck

moment 1 = <u>instant</u>, second, flash, twinkling, split second, jiffy (*informal*), trice 2 = <u>time</u>, point, stage, juncture

momentous = <u>significant</u>, important, vital, critical, crucial, historic, pivotal, fateful ≠ unimportant

momentum = <u>impetus</u>, force, power, drive, push, energy, strength, thrust

monarch = <u>ruler</u>, king *or* queen, sovereign, tsar, potentate, emperor *or* empress, prince *or* princess

monarchy 1 = <u>sovereignty</u>, autocracy, kingship, royalism, monocracy 2 = <u>kingdom</u>, empire, realm, principality

monastery = <u>abbey</u>, convent, priory, cloister, nunnery, friary

monetary = <u>financial</u>, money, economic, capital, cash, fiscal, budgetary, pecuniary

money = <u>cash</u>, capital, currency, hard cash, readies (*informal*), riches, silver, coin

monitor VERB = <u>check</u>, follow, watch, survey, observe, keep an eye on, keep track of, keep tabs on

● NOUN 1 = <u>guide</u>, observer, supervisor, invigilator 2 = <u>prefect</u> (*Brit.*), head girl, head boy, senior boy, senior girl

monk (*Loosely*) = <u>friar</u>, brother
(*Related Words*)
adjective: monastic

monkey 1 = <u>simian</u>, ape, primate 2 = <u>rascal</u>, horror, devil, rogue, imp, tyke, scallywag, scamp, nointer (*Austral. slang*)

(Related Words)

adjective: simian

> **monkeys, apes and other primates**

monster NOUN 1 = giant, mammoth, titan, colossus, monstrosity 2 = brute, devil, beast, demon, villain, fiend

• ADJECTIVE = huge, massive, enormous, tremendous, immense, gigantic, mammoth, colossal

monstrous 1 = outrageous, shocking, foul, intolerable, disgraceful, scandalous, inhuman, diabolical ≠ decent 2 = huge, massive, enormous, tremendous, immense, mammoth, colossal, prodigious ≠ tiny 3 = unnatural, horrible, hideous, grotesque, gruesome, frightful, freakish, fiendish ≠ normal

monument = memorial, cairn, marker, shrine, tombstone, mausoleum, commemoration, headstone

monumental 1 = important, significant, enormous, historic, memorable, awesome, majestic,

---

Monkeys, apes and other primates

baboon	loris
Barbary ape	macaque
bushbaby *or* galago	mandrill
capuchin	mangabey
chacma	marmoset
chimpanzee *or* chimp	mona
colobus	monkey *or* (*archaic*) jackanapes
douroucouli	orang-outang, orang-utan, *or* orang
flying lemur *or* colugo	proboscis monkey
gelada	rhesus monkey
gibbon	saki
gorilla	siamang
green monkey	sifaka
grivet	spider monkey
guenon	squirrel monkey
guereza	tamarin
howler monkey	tarsier
indris *or* indri	vervet
langur	
lemur	

unforgettable ≠ unimportant
2 (*Informal*) = immense, great, massive, staggering, colossal ≠ tiny

mood = state of mind, spirit, humour, temper, disposition, frame of mind

moody 1 = changeable, volatile, unpredictable, erratic, fickle, temperamental, impulsive, mercurial ≠ stable **2** = sulky, irritable, temperamental, touchy, ill-tempered, tooshie (*Austral. slang*) ≠ cheerful **3** = gloomy, sad, sullen, glum, morose ≠ cheerful **4** = sad, gloomy, melancholy, sombre

moon NOUN = satellite
● VERB = idle, drift, loaf, languish, waste time, daydream, mope
(*Related Words*)
adjective: lunar

moor[1] = moorland, fell (*Brit.*), heath

moor[2] = tie up, secure, anchor, dock, lash, berth, make fast

mop NOUN **1** = squeegee, sponge, swab **2** = mane, shock, mass, tangle, mat, thatch
● VERB = clean, wash, wipe, sponge, swab

moral ADJECTIVE = good, just, right, principled, decent, noble, ethical, honourable ≠ immoral
● NOUN = lesson, meaning, point, message, teaching, import, significance, precept
● PLURAL NOUN = morality, standards, conduct, principles, behaviour, manners, habits, ethics

morale = confidence, heart, spirit, self-esteem, team spirit, esprit de corps

morality 1 = virtue, justice, morals, honour, integrity, goodness, honesty, decency **2** = ethics, conduct, principles, morals, manners, philosophy, mores **3** = rights and wrongs, ethics

moratorium = postponement, freeze, halt, suspension, standstill

more ADJECTIVE = extra, additional, new, other, added, further, new-found, supplementary
● ADVERB **1** = to a greater extent, longer, better, further, some more **2** = moreover, also, in addition, besides, furthermore, what's more, on top of that, to boot

moreover = furthermore, also, further, in addition, too, as well, besides, additionally

morning 1 = before noon, forenoon, morn (*poetic*), a.m. **2** = dawn, sunrise, first light, daybreak, break of day

mortal ADJECTIVE **1** = human, worldly, passing, fleshly, temporal, transient, ephemeral, perishable **2** = fatal, killing, terminal, deadly, destructive, lethal, murderous, death-dealing
● NOUN = human being, being, man, woman, person, human, individual, earthling

mortality 1 = <u>humanity</u>,
transience, impermanence,
corporeality, impermanency
2 = <u>death</u>, dying, fatality

mostly 1 = <u>mainly</u>, largely,
chiefly, principally, primarily, on
the whole, predominantly
2 = <u>generally</u>, usually, on the
whole, as a rule

moth

Related Words

young: caterpillar
enthusiast: lepidopterist

➤ **butterflies and moths**

mother NOUN = <u>female parent</u>,
mum (*Brit. informal*), ma
(*informal*), mater, dam, mummy
(*Brit. informal*), foster mother,
biological mother
• VERB = <u>nurture</u>, raise, protect,
tend, nurse, rear, care for, cherish
• ADJECTIVE = <u>native</u>, natural,
innate, inborn

Related Words

adjective: maternal

motherly = <u>maternal</u>, loving,
caring, comforting, sheltering,
protective, affectionate

motif 1 = <u>design</u>, shape,
decoration, ornament 2 = <u>theme</u>,
idea, subject, concept, leitmotif

motion NOUN 1 = <u>movement</u>,
mobility, travel, progress, flow,
locomotion 2 = <u>proposal</u>,
suggestion, recommendation,
proposition, submission
• VERB = <u>gesture</u>, direct, wave,

signal, nod, beckon, gesticulate

motivate 1 = <u>inspire</u>, drive,
stimulate, move, cause, prompt,
stir, induce 2 = <u>stimulate</u>, drive,
inspire, stir, arouse, galvanize,
incentivize

motivation = <u>incentive</u>,
inspiration, motive, stimulus, reason,
spur, inducement, incitement

motive = <u>reason</u>, ground(s),
purpose, object, incentive,
inspiration, stimulus, rationale

motto = <u>saying</u>, slogan, maxim,
rule, adage, proverb, dictum,
precept

mould¹ NOUN 1 = <u>cast</u>, shape,
pattern 2 = <u>design</u>, style, fashion,
build, form, kind, shape, pattern
3 = <u>nature</u>, character, sort, kind,
quality, type, stamp, calibre
• VERB 1 = <u>shape</u>, make, work,
form, create, model, fashion,
construct 2 = <u>influence</u>, make,
form, control, direct, affect, shape

mould² = <u>fungus</u>, blight, mildew

mound 1 = <u>heap</u>, pile, drift, stack,
rick 2 = <u>hill</u>, bank, rise, dune,
embankment, knoll, hillock, kopje
or koppie (*S. African*)

mount VERB 1 = <u>increase</u>, build,
grow, swell, intensify, escalate,
multiply ≠ decrease
2 = <u>accumulate</u>, increase, collect,
gather, build up, pile up, amass
3 = <u>ascend</u>, scale, climb (up), go
up, clamber up ≠ descend 4 = <u>get</u>
<u>(up) on</u>, jump on, straddle, climb

onto, hop on to, bestride, get on the back of ≠ get off **5** = display, present, prepare, put on, organize, put on display

● NOUN **1** = horse, steed (literary) **2** = backing, setting, support, stand, base, frame

mountain 1 = peak, mount, horn, ridge, fell (Brit.), berg (S. African), alp, pinnacle **2** = heap, mass, masses, pile, a great deal, ton, stack, abundance

mourn 1 often with **for** = grieve for, lament, weep for, wail for **2** = bemoan, rue, deplore, bewail

mourning 1 = grieving, grief, bereavement, weeping, woe, lamentation **2** = black, sackcloth and ashes, widow's weeds

mouth 1 = lips, jaws, gob (slang, esp. Brit.), maw, cakehole (Brit. slang) **2** = entrance, opening, gateway, door, aperture, orifice **3** = opening **4** = inlet, outlet, estuary, firth, outfall, debouchment

(Related Words)

adjective: oral

move VERB **1** = transfer, change, switch, shift, transpose **2** = go, advance, progress, shift, proceed, stir, budge, make a move **3** = relocate, leave, remove, quit, migrate, emigrate, decamp, up sticks (Brit. informal) **4** = drive, cause, influence, persuade, shift, inspire, prompt, induce ≠ discourage **5** = touch, affect,

excite, impress, stir, disquiet **6** = propose, suggest, urge, recommend, request, advocate, submit, put forward

● NOUN **1** = action, step, manoeuvre **2** = ploy, action, measure, step, initiative, stroke, tactic, manoeuvre **3** = transfer, posting, shift, removal, relocation **4** = turn, go, play, chance, shot (informal), opportunity

movement 1 = group, party, organization, grouping, front, faction **2** = campaign, drive, push, crusade **3** = move, action, motion, manoeuvre **4** = activity, moving, stirring, bustle **5** = advance, progress, flow **6** = transfer, transportation, displacement **7** = development, change, variation, fluctuation **8** = progression, progress **9** (Music) = section, part, division, passage

movie = film, picture, feature, flick (slang)

moving 1 = emotional, touching, affecting, inspiring, stirring, poignant ≠ unemotional **2** = mobile, running, active, going, operational, in motion, driving, kinetic ≠ stationary

mow VERB = cut, crop, trim, shear, scythe

● PHRASES **mow something or someone down** = massacre, butcher, slaughter, cut down, shoot down, cut to pieces

much ADVERB 1 = greatly, a lot, considerably, decidedly, exceedingly, appreciably ≠ hardly 2 = often, a lot, routinely, a great deal, many times, habitually, on many occasions, customarily

● DETERMINER = great, a lot of, plenty of, considerable, substantial, piles of (informal), ample, abundant ≠ little

● PRONOUN = a lot, plenty, a great deal, lots (informal), loads (informal), tons (informal), heaps (informal) ≠ little

muck 1 = dirt, mud, filth, ooze, sludge, mire, slime, gunge (informal), kak (S. African informal) 2 = manure, dung, ordure

mud = dirt, clay, ooze, silt, sludge, mire, slime

muddle NOUN = confusion, mess, disorder, chaos, tangle, mix-up, disarray, predicament

● VERB 1 = jumble, disorder, scramble, tangle, mix up 2 = confuse, bewilder, daze, confound, perplex, disorient, stupefy, befuddle

muddy 1 = boggy, swampy, marshy, quaggy 2 = dirty, soiled, grimy, mucky, mud-caked, bespattered

mug¹ = cup, pot, beaker, tankard

mug² (Informal) 1 = face,

features, countenance, visage 2 = fool, sucker (slang), chump (informal), simpleton, easy or soft touch (slang), dorba or dorb (Austral. slang), bogan (Austral. slang)

mug³ VERB = attack, assault, beat up, rob, set about or upon

● PHRASES **mug up (on) something** = study, cram (informal), bone up on (informal), swot up on (Brit. informal)

multiple = many, several, various, numerous, sundry, manifold, multitudinous

multiply 1 = increase, extend, expand, spread, build up, proliferate ≠ decrease 2 = reproduce, breed, propagate

multitude 1 = great number, host, army, mass, horde, myriad 2 = crowd, host, mass, mob, swarm, horde, throng

mundane 1 = ordinary, routine, commonplace, banal, everyday, day-to-day, prosaic, humdrum ≠ extraordinary 2 = earthly, worldly, secular, mortal, terrestrial, temporal ≠ spiritual

municipal = civic, public, local, council, district, urban, metropolitan

murder NOUN = killing, homicide, massacre, assassination, slaying, bloodshed, carnage, butchery

● VERB = kill, massacre, slaughter, assassinate, eliminate (slang), butcher, slay, bump off (*slang*)

murderer = <u>killer</u>, assassin, slayer, butcher, slaughterer, cut-throat, hit man (*slang*)

murderous = <u>deadly</u>, savage, brutal, cruel, lethal, ferocious, cut-throat, bloodthirsty

murky 1 = <u>dark</u>, gloomy, grey, dull, dim, cloudy, misty, overcast ≠ bright 2 = <u>dark</u>, cloudy

murmur VERB = <u>mumble</u>, whisper, mutter

• NOUN = <u>whisper</u>, drone, purr

muscle NOUN 1 = <u>tendon</u>, sinew 2 = <u>strength</u>, might, power, weight, stamina, brawn

• PHRASES **muscle in** (*Informal*) = <u>impose yourself</u>, encroach, butt in, force your way in

muscular = <u>strong</u>, powerful, athletic, strapping, robust, vigorous, sturdy, sinewy

muse = <u>ponder</u>, consider, reflect, contemplate, deliberate, brood, meditate, mull over

music ► musical expressions and tempo instructions

musical = <u>melodious</u>, lyrical, harmonious, melodic, tuneful, dulcet, sweet-sounding, euphonious ≠ discordant

must = <u>necessity</u>, essential, requirement, fundamental, imperative, requisite, prerequisite, sine qua non (*Latin*)

muster VERB 1 = <u>summon up</u>, marshal 2 = <u>rally</u>, gather,

assemble, marshal, mobilize, call together 3 = <u>assemble</u>, convene

• NOUN = <u>assembly</u>, meeting, collection, gathering, rally, convention, congregation, roundup, hui (*N.Z.*), runanga (*N.Z.*)

mutation 1 = <u>anomaly</u>, variation, deviant, freak of nature 2 = <u>change</u>, variation, evolution, transformation, modification, alteration, metamorphosis, transfiguration

mute 1 = <u>close-mouthed</u>, silent 2 = <u>silent</u>, dumb, unspoken, tacit, wordless, voiceless, unvoiced 3 = <u>dumb</u>, speechless, voiceless

mutter = <u>grumble</u>, complain, murmur, rumble, whine, mumble, grouse, bleat

mutual = <u>shared</u>, common, joint, returned, reciprocal, interchangeable, requited

---

Word Power

mutual – Mutual is sometimes used, as in *a mutual friend*, to mean 'common to or shared by two or more people'. This use has sometimes been frowned on in the past because it does not reflect the two-way relationship contained in the origins of the word, which comes from Latin *mutuus* meaning 'reciprocal'. However, this usage is very common and is now generally regarded as acceptable.

Musical expressions and tempo instructions

instruction	meaning
accelerando	with increasing speed
adagio	slowly
agitato	in an agitated manner
allegretto	fairly quickly or briskly
allegro	quickly, in a brisk, lively manner
amoroso	lovingly
andante	at a moderately slow tempo
andantino	slightly faster than andante
assai	(in combination) very
cantabile	in a singing style
con	(in combination) with
con amore	lovingly
con brio	vigorously
con moto	quickly
crescendo	gradual increase in loudness
diminuendo	gradual decrease in loudness
dolce	gently and sweetly
doloroso	in a sorrowful manner
espressivo	expressively
forte	loud or loudly
fortissimo	very loud
furioso	in a frantically rushing manner
giocoso	merry
grave	solemn and slow
grazioso	graceful
largo	slowly and broadly
larghetto	slowly and broadly, but less so than largo
legato	smoothly and connectedly
leggiero	light
lento	slowly
maestoso	majestically
mezzo	(in combination) moderately
moderato	at a moderate tempo
molto	(in combination) very

Musical expressions and tempo instructions (continued)

instruction	meaning
non troppo *or* non tanto	(in combination) not too much
pianissimo	very quietly
piano	softly
più	(in combination) more
pizzicato	(in music for stringed instruments) to be plucked with the finger
poco *or* un poco	(in combination) a little
pomposo	in a pompous manner
presto	very fast
prestissimo	faster than presto
quasi	(in combination) almost, as if
rallentando	becoming slower
rubato	with a flexible tempo
scherzando	in jocular style
semplice	simple and unforced
sforzando	with strong initial attack
sostenuto	in a smooth and sustained manner
sotto voce	extremely quiet
staccato	(of notes) short, clipped, and separate
strepitoso	noisy
stringendo	with increasing speed
tanto	(in combination) too much
troppo	(in combination) too much
vivace	in a brisk lively manner

myriad NOUN = <u>multitude</u>, host, army, swarm, horde
● ADJECTIVE = <u>innumerable</u>, countless, untold, incalculable, immeasurable, multitudinous

mysterious 1 = <u>strange</u>, puzzling, secret, weird, perplexing, uncanny, mystifying, arcane ≠ clear 2 = <u>secretive</u>, enigmatic, evasive, discreet, covert, reticent, furtive, inscrutable

mystery = <u>puzzle</u>, problem, question, secret, riddle, enigma, conundrum, teaser

mystic *or* **mystical** = <u>supernatural</u>, mysterious, transcendental, occult, metaphysical, paranormal, inscrutable, otherworldly

myth 1 = <u>legend</u>, story, fiction, saga, fable, allegory, fairy story, folk tale 2 = <u>illusion</u>, story, fancy, fantasy, imagination, invention, delusion, superstition

mythology = <u>legend</u>, folklore, tradition, lore

N

nab = <u>catch</u>, arrest, apprehend, seize, grab, capture, collar (*informal*), snatch

nag[1] VERB = <u>scold</u>, harass, badger, pester, worry, plague, hassle (*informal*), upbraid
● NOUN = <u>scold</u>, complainer, grumbler, virago, shrew, tartar, moaner, harpy

nag[2] = <u>horse</u> (*U.S.*), hack

nagging 1 = <u>continuous</u>, persistent, continual, niggling, repeated, constant, endless, perpetual 2 = <u>scolding</u>, shrewish

nail NOUN 1 = <u>tack</u>, spike, rivet, hobnail, brad (*technical*) 2 = <u>fingernail</u>, toenail, talon, thumbnail, claw
● VERB 1 = <u>fasten</u>, fix, secure, attach, pin, hammer, tack 2 (*informal*) = <u>catch</u>, arrest, capture, apprehend, trap, snare, ensnare, entrap

naive *or* **naïve** = <u>gullible</u>,

trusting, credulous, unsuspicious, green, simple, innocent, callow ≠ worldly

naked = <u>nude</u>, stripped, exposed, bare, undressed, starkers (*informal*), stark-naked, unclothed ≠ dressed

name NOUN = <u>title</u>, nickname, designation, term, handle (*slang*), epithet, sobriquet, moniker *or* monicker (*slang*)
● VERB 1 = <u>call</u>, christen, baptize, dub, term, style, label, entitle 2 = <u>nominate</u>, choose, select, appoint, specify, designate

namely = <u>specifically</u>, to wit, viz.

nap[1] NOUN = <u>sleep</u>, rest, kip (*Brit. slang*), siesta, catnap, forty winks (*informal*)
● VERB = <u>sleep</u>, rest, drop off (*informal*), doze, kip (*Brit. slang*), snooze (*informal*), nod off (*informal*), catnap

nap[2] NOUN = <u>pile</u>, down, fibre, weave, grain

napkin = <u>serviette</u>, cloth

narcotic NOUN = <u>drug</u>, anaesthetic, painkiller, sedative, opiate, tranquillizer, anodyne, analgesic
● ADJECTIVE = <u>sedative</u>, calming, hypnotic, analgesic, soporific, painkilling

narrative = <u>story</u>, report, history, account, statement, tale, chronicle

narrator = <u>storyteller</u>, writer,

author, reporter, commentator, chronicler

narrow ADJECTIVE 1 = <u>thin</u>, fine, slim, slender, tapering, attenuated ≠ broad 2 = <u>limited</u>, restricted, confined, tight, close, meagre, constricted ≠ wide 3 = <u>insular</u>, prejudiced, partial, dogmatic, intolerant, narrow-minded, small-minded, illiberal ≠ broad-minded
● VERB 1 = <u>restrict</u>, limit, reduce, constrict 2 = <u>get narrower</u>, taper, shrink, tighten, constrict

narrowly = <u>just</u>, barely, only just, scarcely, by the skin of your teeth

nasty 1 = <u>unpleasant</u>, ugly, disagreeable ≠ pleasant 2 = <u>spiteful</u>, mean, offensive, vicious, unpleasant, vile, malicious, despicable ≠ pleasant 3 = <u>disgusting</u>, unpleasant, offensive, vile, distasteful, obnoxious, objectionable, disagreeable, festy (Austral. slang), yucko (Austral. slang) 4 = <u>serious</u>, bad, dangerous, critical, severe, painful

nation 1 = <u>country</u>, state, realm 2 = <u>public</u>, people, society

national ADJECTIVE = <u>nationwide</u>, public, widespread, countrywide
● NOUN = <u>citizen</u>, subject, resident, native, inhabitant

nationalism = <u>patriotism</u>, loyalty to your country, chauvinism, jingoism, allegiance

nationality 1 = <u>citizenship</u>, birth

2 = <u>race</u>, nation

nationwide = <u>national</u>, general, widespread, countrywide

native ADJECTIVE = <u>mother</u>, indigenous, vernacular
● NOUN = <u>inhabitant</u>, national, resident, citizen, countryman, aborigine (often offensive), dweller

natural 1 = <u>logical</u>, valid, legitimate 2 = <u>normal</u>, common, regular, usual, ordinary, typical, everyday ≠ abnormal 3 = <u>innate</u>, native, characteristic, inherent, instinctive, intuitive, inborn, essential 4 = <u>unaffected</u>, open, genuine, spontaneous, unpretentious, unsophisticated, dinkum (Austral. & N.Z. informal), ingenuous, real ≠ affected 5 = <u>pure</u>, plain, organic, whole, unrefined ≠ processed

naturally 1 = <u>of course</u>, certainly 2 = <u>typically</u>, simply, normally, spontaneously

nature 1 = <u>creation</u>, world, earth, environment, universe, cosmos, natural world 2 = <u>quality</u>, character, make-up, constitution, essence, complexion 3 = <u>temperament</u>, character, personality, disposition, outlook, mood, humour, temper 4 = <u>kind</u>, sort, style, type, variety, species, category, description

naughty 1 = <u>disobedient</u>, bad, mischievous, badly behaved, wayward, wicked, impish, refractory ≠ **good 2** = <u>obscene</u>, vulgar, improper, lewd, risqué, smutty, ribald ≠ clean

nausea = <u>sickness</u>, vomiting, retching, squeamishness, queasiness, biliousness

naval = <u>nautical</u>, marine, maritime

navigation = <u>sailing</u>, voyaging, seamanship, helmsmanship

navy = <u>fleet</u>, flotilla, armada

near 1 = <u>close</u>, neighbouring, nearby, adjacent, adjoining ≠ far **2** = <u>imminent</u>, forthcoming, approaching, looming, impending, upcoming, nigh, in the offing ≠ far-off

nearby = <u>neighbouring</u>, adjacent, adjoining

nearly 1 = <u>practically</u>, almost, virtually, just about, as good as, well-nigh **2** = <u>almost</u>, approaching, roughly, just about, approximately

neat 1 = <u>tidy</u>, trim, orderly, spruce, shipshape, spick-and-span ≠ untidy **2** = <u>methodical</u>, tidy, systematic, fastidious ≠ disorganized **3** = <u>smart</u>, trim, tidy, spruce, dapper, natty (*informal*), well-groomed, well-turned out **4** = <u>graceful</u>, elegant, adept, nimble, adroit, efficient ≠ clumsy **5** = <u>clever</u>, efficient, handy, apt, well-judged ≠ inefficient **6** = <u>cool</u>, great

(*informal*), excellent, brilliant, superb, fantastic (*informal*), tremendous, fabulous (*informal*), booshit (*Austral. slang*), exo (*Austral. slang*), sik (*Austral. slang*) ≠ terrible **7** (*of alcoholic drinks*) = <u>undiluted</u>, straight, pure, unmixed

neatly 1 = <u>tidily</u>, smartly, systematically, methodically, fastidiously **2** = <u>smartly</u>, elegantly, tidily, nattily **3** = <u>gracefully</u>, expertly, efficiently, adeptly, skilfully, nimbly, adroitly, dexterously **4** = <u>cleverly</u>, efficiently

necessarily 1 = <u>automatically</u>, naturally, definitely, undoubtedly, certainly **2** = <u>inevitably</u>, of necessity, unavoidably, incontrovertibly, nolens volens (*Latin*)

necessary 1 = <u>needed</u>, required, essential, vital, compulsory, mandatory, imperative, indispensable ≠ unnecessary **2** = <u>inevitable</u>, certain, unavoidable, inescapable ≠ avoidable

necessity NOUN **1** = <u>essential</u>, need, requirement, fundamental, requisite, prerequisite, sine qua non (*Latin*), desideratum **2** = <u>inevitability</u>, certainty ● PLURAL NOUN = <u>essentials</u>, needs, requirements, fundamentals

need VERB **1** = <u>want</u>, miss, require,

lack, have to have, demand
2 = <u>require</u>, want, demand, call for, entail, necessitate 3 = <u>have to</u>, be obliged to
● NOUN 1 = <u>requirement</u>, demand, essential, necessity, requisite, desideratum 2 = <u>necessity</u>, call, demand, obligation
3 = <u>emergency</u>, want, necessity, urgency, exigency 4 = <u>poverty</u>, deprivation, destitution, penury

needed = necessary, wanted, required, lacked, called for, desired

needle = <u>irritate</u>, provoke, annoy, harass, taunt, nag, goad, rile

needless = <u>unnecessary</u>, pointless, gratuitous, useless, unwanted, redundant, superfluous, groundless ≠ essential

needy = <u>poor</u>, deprived, disadvantaged, impoverished, penniless, destitute, poverty-stricken, underprivileged ≠ wealthy

negative ADJECTIVE
1 = <u>pessimistic</u>, cynical, unwilling, gloomy, jaundiced, uncooperative ≠ optimistic
2 = <u>dissenting</u>, contradictory, refusing, denying, rejecting, opposing, resisting, contrary ≠ assenting
● NOUN = <u>denial</u>, no, refusal, rejection, contradiction

neglect VERB 1 = <u>disregard</u>,
ignore, fail to look after ≠ look after 2 = <u>shirk</u>, forget, overlook, omit, evade, pass over, skimp, be remiss in or about 3 = <u>fail</u>, forget, omit
● NOUN 1 = <u>negligence</u>, inattention ≠ care 2 = <u>shirking</u>, failure, oversight, carelessness, dereliction, slackness, laxity

neglected 1 = <u>uncared-for</u>, abandoned, underestimated, disregarded, undervalued, unappreciated 2 = <u>run down</u>, derelict, overgrown, uncared-for

negligence = <u>carelessness</u>, neglect, disregard, dereliction, slackness, inattention, laxity, thoughtlessness

negotiate 1 = <u>bargain</u>, deal, discuss, debate, mediate, hold talks, cut a deal, conciliate
2 = <u>arrange</u>, work out, bring about, transact 3 = <u>get round</u>, clear, pass, cross, get over, get past, surmount

negotiation 1 = <u>bargaining</u>, debate, discussion, transaction, dialogue, mediation, arbitration, wheeling and dealing (informal)
2 = <u>arrangement</u>, working out, transaction, bringing about

negotiator = <u>mediator</u>, ambassador, diplomat, delegate, intermediary, moderator, honest broker

neighbourhood 1 = <u>district</u>, community, quarter, region, locality, locale **2** = <u>vicinity</u>, environs

neighbouring = <u>nearby</u>, next, near, bordering, surrounding, connecting, adjacent, adjoining ≠ remote

neighbourly = <u>helpful</u>, kind, friendly, obliging, harmonious, considerate, sociable, hospitable

nerve NOUN **1** = <u>bravery</u>, courage, bottle (*Brit. slang*), resolution, daring, guts (*informal*), pluck, grit **2** (*Informal*) = <u>impudence</u>, cheek (*informal*), audacity, boldness, temerity, insolence, impertinence, brazenness

● PLURAL NOUN **1** = <u>tension</u>, stress, strain, anxiety, butterflies (in your stomach) (*informal*), nervousness, cold feet (*informal*), worry

● PHRASES **nerve yourself** = <u>brace yourself</u>, prepare yourself, steel yourself, fortify yourself, gear yourself up, gee yourself up

nervous = <u>apprehensive</u>, anxious, uneasy, edgy, worried, tense, fearful, uptight (*informal*), toey (*Austral. slang*) ≠ calm

nest NOUN = <u>refuge</u>, retreat, haunt, den, hideaway

nestle = <u>snuggle</u>, cuddle, huddle, curl up, nuzzle

nestling = <u>chick</u>, fledgling, baby bird

net[1] NOUN = <u>mesh</u>, netting, network, web, lattice, openwork

● VERB = <u>catch</u>, bag, capture, trap, entangle, ensnare, enmesh

net[2] or **nett** ADJECTIVE = <u>after taxes</u>, final, clear, take-home

● VERB = <u>earn</u>, make, clear, gain, realize, bring in, accumulate, reap

network 1 = <u>web</u>, system, arrangement, grid, lattice **2** = <u>maze</u>, warren, labyrinth

neurotic = <u>unstable</u>, nervous, disturbed, abnormal, obsessive, compulsive, manic, unhealthy ≠ rational

neutral 1 = <u>unbiased</u>, impartial, disinterested, even-handed, uninvolved, nonpartisan, unprejudiced, nonaligned ≠ biased **2** = <u>expressionless</u>, dull **3** = <u>uncontroversial</u> or noncontroversial, inoffensive **4** = <u>colourless</u>

never 1 = <u>at no time</u>, not once, not ever ≠ always **2** = <u>under no circumstances</u>, not at all, on no account, not ever

---

Word Power

never – *Never* is sometimes used in informal speech and writing as an emphatic form of *not*, with simple past tenses of certain verbs: *I never said that* – and in very informal speech as a denial in place of *did not*: *he says I hit him, but I never*. These uses of *never* should be avoided in careful writing.

nevertheless = <u>even so</u>, still, however, yet, regardless, nonetheless, notwithstanding, in spite of that

new 1 = <u>modern</u>, recent, contemporary, up-to-date, latest, current, original, fresh ≠ old-fashioned **2** = <u>brand new</u> **3** = <u>extra</u>, more, added, new-found, supplementary **4** = <u>unfamiliar</u>, strange **5** = <u>renewed</u>, changed, improved, restored, altered, revitalized

newcomer 1 = <u>new arrival</u>, stranger **2** = <u>beginner</u>, novice, new arrival, parvenu, Johnny-come-lately (*informal*)

news = <u>information</u>, latest (*informal*), report, story, exposé, intelligence, rumour, revelation

next ADJECTIVE **1** = <u>following</u>, later, succeeding, subsequent **2** = <u>adjacent</u>, closest, nearest, neighbouring, adjoining
• ADVERB = <u>afterwards</u>, then, later, following, subsequently, thereafter

nice 1 = <u>pleasant</u>, delightful, agreeable, good, attractive, charming, pleasurable, enjoyable ≠ unpleasant **2** = <u>kind</u>, helpful, obliging, considerate ≠ unkind **3** = <u>likable</u> or <u>likeable</u>, friendly, engaging, charming, pleasant, agreeable **4** = <u>polite</u>, courteous, well-mannered ≠ vulgar **5** = <u>precise</u>, fine, careful, strict,

subtle, delicate, meticulous, fastidious ≠ vague

nicely 1 = <u>pleasantly</u>, well, delightfully, attractively, charmingly, agreeably, acceptably, pleasurably ≠ unpleasantly **2** = <u>kindly</u>, politely, thoughtfully, amiably, courteously

niche 1 = <u>recess</u>, opening, corner, hollow, nook, alcove **2** = <u>position</u>, calling, place, slot (*informal*), vocation, pigeonhole (*informal*)

nick VERB **1** (*Slang*) = <u>steal</u>, pinch (*informal*), swipe (*slang*), pilfer **2** = <u>cut</u>, mark, score, chip, scratch, scar, notch, dent
• NOUN = <u>cut</u>, mark, scratch, chip, scar, notch, dent

nickname = <u>pet name</u>, label, diminutive, epithet, sobriquet, moniker or monicker (*slang*)

night = <u>darkness</u>, dark, night-time

(Related Words)
adjective: nocturnal

nightly ADJECTIVE = <u>nocturnal</u>, night-time
• ADVERB = <u>every night</u>, nights (*informal*), each night, night after night

nightmare 1 = <u>bad dream</u>, hallucination **2** = <u>ordeal</u>, trial, hell, horror, torture, torment, tribulation, purgatory

nil 1 = <u>nothing</u>, love, zero

2 = <u>zero</u>, nothing, none, naught

nip¹ VERB **1** = <u>pop</u>, go, run, rush, dash **2** = <u>bite</u> **3** = <u>pinch</u>, squeeze, tweak

• PHRASES **nip something in the bud** = <u>thwart</u>, check, frustrate

nip² = <u>dram</u>, shot (*informal*), drop, sip, draught, mouthful, snifter (*informal*)

nirvana = <u>paradise</u>, peace, joy, bliss, serenity, tranquillity

no INTERJECTION = <u>not at all</u>, certainly not, of course not, absolutely not, never, no way, nay ≠ yes

• NOUN = <u>refusal</u>, rejection, denial, negation ≠ consent

noble ADJECTIVE **1** = <u>worthy</u>, generous, upright, honourable, virtuous, magnanimous ≠ despicable **2** = <u>dignified</u>, great, imposing, impressive, distinguished, splendid, stately ≠ lowly **3** = <u>aristocratic</u>, lordly, titled, patrician, blue-blooded, highborn ≠ humble

• NOUN = <u>lord</u>, peer, aristocrat, nobleman ≠ commoner

nobody PRONOUN = <u>no-one</u>

• NOUN = <u>nonentity</u>, lightweight (*informal*), zero, cipher ≠ celebrity

nod VERB **1** = <u>incline</u>, bow **2** = <u>signal</u>, indicate, motion, gesture **3** = <u>salute</u>, acknowledge

• NOUN **1** = <u>signal</u>, sign, motion, gesture, indication **2** = <u>salute</u>,

greeting, acknowledgment

noise = <u>sound</u>, row, racket, clamour, din, uproar, commotion, hubbub ≠ silence, calm

noisy 1 = <u>rowdy</u>, strident, boisterous, vociferous, uproarious, clamorous ≠ quiet **2** = <u>loud</u>, piercing, deafening, tumultuous, ear-splitting, cacophonous, clamorous ≠ quiet

nominal 1 = <u>titular</u>, formal, purported, in name only, supposed, so-called, theoretical, professed **2** = <u>token</u>, small, symbolic, minimal, trivial, trifling, insignificant, inconsiderable

nominate 1 = <u>propose</u>, suggest, recommend, put forward **2** = <u>appoint</u>, name, choose, select, elect, assign, designate

nomination 1 = <u>proposal</u>, suggestion, recommendation **2** = <u>appointment</u>, election, selection, designation, choice

nominee = <u>candidate</u>, applicant, entrant, contestant, aspirant, runner

none 1 = <u>not any</u>, nothing, zero, not one, nil **2** = <u>no-one</u>, nobody, not one

nonetheless = <u>nevertheless</u>, however, yet, even so, despite that, in spite of that

non-existent *or* **nonexistent** = <u>imaginary</u>, fictional, mythical, unreal, hypothetical, illusory ≠ real

nonsense 1 = <u>rubbish</u>, hot air (*informal*), twaddle, drivel, tripe (*informal*), gibberish, claptrap (*informal*), double Dutch (*Brit. informal*), bizzo (*Austral. slang*), bull's wool (*Austral. & N.Z. slang*) ≠ sense 2 = <u>idiocy</u>, stupidity

non-stop or **nonstop** ADJECTIVE = <u>continuous</u>, constant, relentless, uninterrupted, endless, unbroken, interminable, incessant ≠ occasional

● ADVERB = <u>continuously</u>, constantly, endlessly, relentlessly, perpetually, incessantly, ceaselessly, interminably

noon NOUN = <u>midday</u>, high noon, noonday, twelve noon, noontide

● ADJECTIVE = <u>midday</u>, noonday, noontide

norm = <u>standard</u>, rule, pattern, average, par, criterion, benchmark, yardstick

normal 1 = <u>usual</u>, common, standard, average, natural, regular, ordinary, typical ≠ unusual 2 = <u>sane</u>, reasonable, rational, well-adjusted, compos mentis (*Latin*), in your right mind, mentally sound

normally 1 = <u>usually</u>, generally, commonly, regularly, typically, ordinarily, as a rule, habitually 2 = <u>as usual</u>, naturally, properly, conventionally, in the usual way

north ADJECTIVE = <u>northern</u>, polar, arctic, boreal, northerly

● ADVERB = <u>northward(s)</u>, in a northerly direction

nose NOUN = <u>snout</u>, bill, beak, hooter (*slang*), proboscis

● VERB = <u>ease forward</u>, push, edge, shove, nudge

Related Words
adjective: nasal

nostalgia = <u>reminiscence</u>, longing, pining, yearning, remembrance, homesickness, wistfulness

nostalgic = <u>sentimental</u>, longing, emotional, homesick, wistful, maudlin, regretful

notable ADJECTIVE 1 = <u>remarkable</u>, striking, unusual, extraordinary, outstanding, memorable, uncommon, conspicuous ≠ imperceptible 2 = <u>prominent</u>, famous ≠ unknown

● NOUN = <u>celebrity</u>, big name, dignitary, luminary, personage, V.I.P.

notably = <u>remarkably</u>, unusually, extraordinarily, noticeably, strikingly, singularly, outstandingly, uncommonly

notch NOUN 1 = <u>level</u> (*Informal*), step, degree, grade 2 = <u>cut</u>, nick, incision, indentation, mark, score, cleft

● VERB = <u>cut</u>, mark, score, nick, scratch, indent

note NOUN 1 = <u>message</u>, letter, communication, memo, memorandum, epistle **2** = <u>record</u>, reminder, memo, memorandum, jotting, minute **3** = <u>annotation</u>, comment, remark **4** = <u>document</u>, form, record, certificate **5** = <u>symbol</u>, mark, sign, indication, token **6** = <u>tone</u>, touch, trace, hint, sound

● VERB **1** = <u>notice</u>, see, observe, perceive **2** = <u>bear in mind</u>, be aware, take into account **3** = <u>mention</u>, record, mark, indicate, register, remark **4** = <u>write down</u>, record, scribble, set down, jot down

notebook = <u>notepad</u>, exercise book, journal, diary

noted = <u>famous</u>, celebrated, distinguished, well-known, prominent, acclaimed, notable, renowned ≠ unknown

nothing 1 = <u>nought</u>, zero, nil, not a thing, zilch (slang) **2** = <u>a trifle</u> **3** = <u>nobody</u>, cipher, nonentity **4** = <u>void</u>, emptiness, nothingness, nullity

notice VERB = <u>observe</u>, see, note, spot, distinguish, perceive, detect, discern ≠ overlook

● NOUN **1** = <u>notification</u>, warning, advice, intimation, news, communication, announcement, instruction **2** = <u>attention</u>, interest, note, regard, consideration, observation, scrutiny, heed ≠ oversight **3** = <u>the sack</u> (informal), dismissal, the boot

(slang), the push (slang), marching orders (informal)

noticeable = <u>obvious</u>, clear, striking, plain, evident, manifest, conspicuous, perceptible

notify = <u>inform</u>, tell, advise, alert to, announce, warn, make known to

notion 1 = <u>idea</u>, view, opinion, belief, concept, impression, sentiment, inkling **2** = <u>whim</u>, wish, desire, fancy, impulse, inclination, caprice

notorious = <u>infamous</u>, disreputable, opprobrious

notoriously = <u>infamously</u>, disreputably

notwithstanding = <u>despite</u>, in spite of, regardless of

nought or (Archaic or literary) **naught** = <u>zero</u>, nothing, nil

nourish 1 = <u>feed</u>, supply, sustain, nurture **2** = <u>encourage</u>, support, maintain, promote, sustain, foster

nourishing = <u>nutritious</u>, beneficial, wholesome, nutritive

novel[1] = <u>story</u>, tale, fiction, romance, narrative

novel[2] = <u>new</u>, different, original, fresh, unusual, innovative, uncommon ≠ ordinary

novelist > WORD POWER SUPPLEMENT novelists

novelty 1 = <u>newness</u>, originality, freshness, innovation, surprise, uniqueness, strangeness, unfamiliarity **2** = <u>curiosity</u>, rarity, oddity, wonder **3** = <u>trinket</u>, souvenir, memento, bauble, trifle, knick-knack

novice = beginner, pupil, amateur, newcomer, trainee, apprentice, learner, probationer ≠ expert

now ADVERB 1 = nowadays, at the moment 2 = immediately, promptly, instantly, at once, straightaway

● PHRASES **now and then** or **again** = occasionally, sometimes, from time to time, on and off, intermittently, infrequently, sporadically

nowadays = now, today, at the moment, in this day and age

nucleus = centre, heart, focus, basis, core, pivot, kernel, nub

nude = naked, stripped, bare, undressed, stark-naked, disrobed, unclothed, unclad ≠ dressed

nudge VERB 1 = push, touch, dig, jog, prod, elbow, shove, poke 2 = prompt, influence, persuade, spur, prod, coax

● NOUN 1 = push, touch, dig, elbow, bump, shove, poke, jog 2 = prompting, push, encouragement, prod

nuisance = trouble, problem, trial, drag (*informal*), bother, pest, irritation, hassle (*informal*) ≠ benefit

numb ADJECTIVE 1 = unfeeling, dead, frozen, paralysed, insensitive, deadened, immobilized, torpid ≠ sensitive 2 = stupefied, deadened, unfeeling

● VERB 1 = stun, knock out, paralyse, daze 2 = deaden, freeze, dull, paralyse, immobilize, benumb

number NOUN 1 = numeral, figure, character, digit, integer 2 = amount, quantity, collection, aggregate ≠ shortage 3 = crowd, horde, multitude, throng 4 = group, set, band, crowd, gang 5 = issue, copy, edition, imprint, printing

● VERB 1 = amount to, come to, total, add up to 2 = calculate, account, reckon, compute, enumerate ≠ guess 3 = include, count

numerous = many, several, countless, lots, abundant, plentiful, innumerable, copious ≠ few

nurse 1 = look after, treat, tend, care for, take care of, minister to 2 = harbour, have, maintain, preserve, entertain, cherish 3 = breast-feed, feed, nurture, nourish, suckle, wet-nurse

nursery = crèche, kindergarten, playgroup

nurture VERB = bring up, raise, look after, rear, care for, develop ≠ neglect

● NOUN = upbringing, training, education, instruction, rearing, development

nut 1 (*Slang*) = <u>madman</u>, psycho (*slang*), crank (*informal*), lunatic, maniac, nutcase (*slang*) **2** (*Slang*) = <u>head</u>, skull

nutrition = <u>food</u>, nourishment, sustenance, nutriment

oath 1 = <u>promise</u>, bond, pledge, vow, word, affirmation, avowal **2** = <u>swear word</u>, curse, obscenity, blasphemy, expletive, four-letter word, profanity

obedience = <u>compliance</u>, respect, reverence, observance, subservience, submissiveness, docility ≠ disobedience

obey 1 = <u>submit to</u>, surrender (to), give way to, bow to, give in to, yield to, do what you are told by ≠ disobey **2** = <u>carry out</u>, follow, implement, act upon, carry through ≠ disregard **3** = <u>abide by</u>, keep, follow, comply with, observe, heed, conform to, keep to

object¹ 1 = <u>thing</u>, article, body, item, entity **2** = <u>purpose</u>, aim, end, point, plan, idea, goal, design **3** = <u>target</u>, victim, focus, recipient

object² 1 *with to* = <u>protest against</u>, oppose, argue against, draw the line at, take exception to, cry out against, complain against, expostulate against ≠ accept **2** = <u>disagree</u>, demur, remonstrate, express disapproval ≠ agree

objection = <u>protest</u>, opposition, complaint, doubt, dissent, outcry, protestation, scruple ≠ agreement

objective NOUN = <u>purpose</u>, aim, goal, end, plan, hope, idea, target
● ADJECTIVE **1** = <u>factual</u>, real **2** = <u>unbiased</u>, detached, fair, open-minded, impartial, impersonal, disinterested, even-handed ≠ subjective

objectively = <u>impartially</u>, neutrally, fairly, justly, without prejudice, dispassionately, with an open mind, equitably

obligation 1 = <u>duty</u>, compulsion **2** = <u>task</u>, job, duty, work, charge, role, function, mission **3** = <u>responsibility</u>, duty, liability, accountability, answerability

oblige 1 = <u>compel</u>, make, force, require, bind, constrain, necessitate, impel **2** = <u>help</u>, assist, benefit, please, humour, accommodate, indulge, gratify ≠ bother

obliged 1 = <u>forced</u>, required, bound, compelled, duty-bound **2** = <u>grateful</u>, in (someone's) debt, thankful, indebted, appreciative, beholden

obliging = <u>accommodating</u>, kind, helpful, willing, polite, cooperative, agreeable, considerate ≠ unhelpful

obscene → obstacle

obscene 1 = <u>indecent</u>, dirty, offensive, filthy, improper, immoral, pornographic, lewd ≠ decent 2 = <u>offensive</u>, shocking, evil, disgusting, outrageous, revolting, sickening, vile

obscure ADJECTIVE 1 = <u>unknown</u>, little-known, humble, unfamiliar, out-of-the-way, lowly, unheard-of, undistinguished ≠ famous 2 = <u>abstruse</u>, complex, confusing, mysterious, vague, unclear, ambiguous, enigmatic ≠ straightforward 3 = <u>unclear</u>, uncertain, confused, mysterious, doubtful, indeterminate ≠ well-known 4 = <u>indistinct</u>, vague, blurred, dark, faint, dim, gloomy, murky ≠ clear
● VERB 1 = <u>obstruct</u>, hinder 2 = <u>hide</u>, screen, mask, disguise, conceal, veil, cloak, camouflage ≠ expose

observation 1 = <u>watching</u>, study, survey, review, investigation, monitoring, examination, inspection 2 = <u>comment</u>, thought, note, statement, opinion, remark, explanation, reflection 3 = <u>remark</u>, comment, statement, reflection, utterance 4 = <u>observance of</u>, compliance with, honouring of, fulfilment of, carrying out of

observe 1 = <u>watch</u>, study, view, look at, check, survey, monitor, keep an eye on (*informal*) 2 = <u>notice</u>, see, note, discover, spot, regard, witness, distinguish 3 = <u>remark</u>, say, comment, state, note, reflect, mention, opine 4 = <u>comply with</u>, keep, follow, respect, carry out, honour, discharge, obey ≠ disregard

observer 1 = <u>witness</u>, viewer, spectator, looker-on, watcher, onlooker, eyewitness, bystander 2 = <u>commentator</u>, reporter, special correspondent 3 = <u>monitor</u>, watchdog, supervisor, scrutineer

obsessed = <u>absorbed</u>, dominated, gripped, haunted, distracted, hung up (*slang*), preoccupied ≠ indifferent

obsession = <u>preoccupation</u>, thing (*informal*), complex, hang-up (*informal*), mania, phobia, fetish, fixation

obsessive = <u>compulsive</u>, gripping, consuming, haunting, irresistible, neurotic, besetting, uncontrollable

obsolete = <u>outdated</u>, old, passé, old-fashioned, discarded, extinct, out of date, archaic ≠ up-to-date

obstacle 1 = <u>obstruction</u>, block, barrier, hurdle, snag, impediment, blockage, hindrance 2 = <u>hindrance</u>, bar, difficulty, barrier, handicap, hurdle, hitch, drawback, uphill (*S. African*)

≠ **help**

obstruct 1 = <u>block</u>, close, bar, plug, barricade, stop up, bung up (*informal*) 2 = <u>hold up</u>, stop, check, block, restrict, slow down, hamper, hinder 3 = <u>impede</u>, hamper, hold back, thwart, hinder ≠ help 4 = <u>obscure</u>, screen, cover

obtain 1 = <u>get</u>, gain, acquire, land, net, pick up, secure, procure ≠ lose 2 = <u>achieve</u>, get, gain, accomplish, attain 3 (*Formal*) = <u>prevail</u>, hold, exist, be the case, abound, predominate, be in force, be current

obvious = <u>clear</u>, plain, apparent, evident, distinct, manifest, noticeable, conspicuous ≠ unclear

obviously 1 = <u>clearly</u>, of course, without doubt, assuredly 2 = <u>plainly</u>, patently, undoubtedly, evidently, manifestly, markedly, without doubt, unquestionably

occasion NOUN 1 = <u>time</u>, moment, point, stage, instance, juncture 2 = <u>function</u>, event, affair, do (*informal*), happening, experience, gathering, celebration 3 = <u>opportunity</u>, chance, time, opening, window 4 = <u>reason</u>, cause, call, ground(s), excuse, incentive, motive, justification
● VERB (*Formal*) = <u>cause</u>, produce, lead to, inspire, result in,

generate, prompt, provoke

occasional = <u>infrequent</u>, odd, rare, irregular, sporadic, intermittent, few and far between, periodic ≠ constant

occasionally = <u>sometimes</u>, at times, from time to time, now and then, irregularly, now and again, periodically, once in a while ≠ constantly

occult NOUN = <u>magic</u>, witchcraft, sorcery, wizardry, enchantment, black art, necromancy
● ADJECTIVE = <u>supernatural</u>, magical, mysterious, psychic, mystical, unearthly, esoteric, uncanny

occupant = <u>occupier</u>, resident, tenant, inmate, inhabitant, incumbent, dweller, lessee

occupation 1 = <u>job</u>, calling, business, line (of work), trade, career, employment, profession 2 = <u>hobby</u>, pastime, diversion, relaxation, leisure pursuit, (leisure) activity 3 = <u>invasion</u>, seizure, conquest, incursion, subjugation 4 = <u>occupancy</u>, residence, holding, control, possession, tenure, tenancy

occupied 1 = <u>in use</u>, taken, full, engaged, unavailable 2 = <u>inhabited</u>, peopled, lived-in, settled, tenanted ≠ uninhabited 3 = <u>busy</u>, engaged, employed, working, active, hard at work, rushed off your feet

occupy 1 = <u>inhabit</u>, own, live in, dwell in, reside in, abide in ≠ vacate **2** = <u>invade</u>, take over, capture, seize, conquer, overrun, annex, colonize ≠ withdraw **3** = <u>hold</u>, control, dominate, possess **4** = <u>take up</u>, consume, tie up, use up, monopolize **5** *often passive* = <u>engage</u>, involve, employ, divert, preoccupy, engross **6** = <u>fill</u>, take up, cover, fill up, pervade, permeate, extend over

occur VERB **1** = <u>happen</u>, take place, come about, turn up (*informal*), crop up (*informal*), transpire (*informal*), befall **2** = <u>exist</u>, appear, be found, develop, turn up, be present, manifest itself, present itself

● PHRASES **occur to someone** = <u>come to mind</u>, strike someone, dawn on someone, spring to mind, cross someone's mind, enter someone's head, suggest itself to someone

---

Word Power

occur – It is usually regarded as incorrect to talk of pre-arranged events *occurring* or *happening*. For this meaning a synonym such as *take place* would be more appropriate: *the wedding took place* (not *occurred* or *happened*) *in the afternoon*.

---

occurrence 1 = <u>incident</u>, happening, event, fact, matter, affair, circumstance, episode **2** = <u>existence</u>, instance, appearance, manifestation, materialization

odd 1 = <u>peculiar</u>, strange, unusual, extraordinary, bizarre, offbeat, freakish **2** = <u>unusual</u>, strange, rare, extraordinary, remarkable, bizarre, peculiar, irregular ≠ normal **3** = <u>occasional</u>, various, random, casual, irregular, periodic, sundry, incidental ≠ regular **4** = <u>spare</u>, remaining, extra, surplus, solitary, leftover, unmatched, unpaired ≠ matched

odds PLURAL NOUN **1** = <u>probability</u>, chances, likelihood

● PHRASES **at odds 1** = <u>in conflict</u>, arguing, quarrelling, at loggerheads, at daggers drawn **2** = <u>at variance</u>, conflicting, contrary to, at odds, out of line, out of step, at sixes and sevens (*informal*) ◆ **odds and ends** = <u>scraps</u>, bits, remains, fragments, debris, remnants, bits and pieces, bric-a-brac

odour = <u>smell</u>, scent, perfume, fragrance, stink, bouquet, aroma, stench

odyssey = <u>journey</u>, tour, trip, quest, trek, expedition, voyage, crusade

off ADVERB = <u>away</u>, out, apart,

elsewhere, aside, hence, from here

● ADJECTIVE 1 = <u>absent</u>, gone, unavailable 2 = <u>cancelled</u>, abandoned, postponed, shelved 3 = <u>bad</u>, rotten, rancid, mouldy, turned, spoiled, sour, decayed

offence 1 = <u>crime</u>, sin, fault, violation, wrongdoing, trespass, felony, misdemeanour 2 = <u>outrage</u>, shock, anger, trouble, bother, resentment, irritation, hassle (*informal*) 3 = <u>insult</u>, slight, hurt, outrage, injustice, snub, affront, indignity

offend 1 = <u>distress</u>, upset, outrage, wound, slight, insult, annoy, snub ≠ please 2 = <u>break the law</u>, sin, err, do wrong, fall, go astray

offended = <u>upset</u>, hurt, bothered, disturbed, distressed, outraged, stung, put out (*informal*), tooshie (*Austral. slang*)

offender = <u>criminal</u>, convict, crook, villain, culprit, sinner, delinquent, felon

offensive ADJECTIVE
1 = <u>insulting</u>, rude, abusive, degrading, contemptuous, disparaging, objectionable, disrespectful ≠ respectful 2 = <u>disgusting</u>, gross, foul, unpleasant, revolting, vile, repellent, obnoxious, festy (*Austral. slang*), yucko (*Austral.*

slang) ≠ pleasant 3 = <u>attacking</u>, threatening, aggressive, striking, hostile, invading, combative ≠ defensive

● NOUN = <u>attack</u>, charge, campaign, strike, push (*informal*), assault, raid, drive

offer VERB 1 = <u>provide</u>, present, furnish, afford ≠ withhold 2 = <u>volunteer</u>, come forward, offer your services 3 = <u>propose</u>, suggest, advance, submit 4 = <u>give</u>, show, bring, provide, render, impart 5 = <u>put up for sale</u>, sell 6 = <u>bid</u>, submit, propose, tender, proffer

● NOUN 1 = <u>proposal</u>, suggestion, proposition, submission 2 = <u>bid</u>, tender, bidding price

offering 1 = <u>contribution</u>, gift, donation, present, subscription, hand-out 2 = <u>sacrifice</u>, tribute, libation, burnt offering

office 1 = <u>place of work</u>, workplace, base, workroom, place of business 2 = <u>branch</u>, department, division, section, wing, subdivision, subsection 3 = <u>post</u>, place, role, situation, responsibility, function, occupation

officer 1 = <u>official</u>, executive, agent, representative, appointee, functionary, office-holder, office bearer 2 = <u>police officer</u>, detective, PC, police constable, police man, police woman

official ADJECTIVE 1 = <u>authorized</u>, formal, sanctioned, licensed, proper, legitimate, authentic, certified ≠ unofficial 2 = <u>formal</u>, bureaucratic, ceremonial, solemn, ritualistic

● NOUN = <u>officer</u>, executive, agent, representative, bureaucrat, appointee, functionary, office-holder

offset = <u>cancel out</u>, balance, set off, make up for, compensate for, counteract, neutralize, counterbalance

offspring 1 = <u>child</u>, baby, kid (*informal*), youngster, infant, successor, babe, toddler, littlie (*Austral. informal*), ankle-biter (*Austral. slang*), tacker (*Austral. slang*) ≠ parent 2 = <u>children</u>, young, family, issue, stock, heirs, descendants, brood

often = <u>frequently</u>, generally, commonly, repeatedly, time and again, habitually, not infrequently ≠ never

oil VERB = <u>lubricate</u>, grease

● NOUN 1 = <u>lubricant</u>, grease, lubrication, fuel oil 2 = <u>lotion</u>, cream, balm, salve, liniment, embrocation, solution

oily = <u>greasy</u>, slimy, fatty, slippery, oleaginous

OK *or* **okay** ADJECTIVE (*Informal*) 1 = <u>all right</u>, fine, fitting, in order, permitted, suitable, acceptable,

allowable ≠ unacceptable 2 = <u>fine</u>, good, average, fair, all right, acceptable, adequate, satisfactory ≠ unsatisfactory 3 = <u>well</u>, all right, safe, sound, healthy, unharmed, uninjured

● INTERJECTION = <u>all right</u>, right, yes, agreed, very good, roger, very well, ya (*S. African*), righto (*Brit. informal*), yebo (*S. African informal*)

● VERB = <u>approve</u>, allow, agree to, permit, sanction, endorse, authorize, rubber-stamp (*informal*)

● NOUN = <u>authorization</u>, agreement, sanction, approval, go-ahead (*informal*), blessing, permission, consent

old 1 = <u>aged</u>, elderly, ancient, mature, venerable, antiquated, senile, decrepit ≠ young 2 = <u>former</u>, earlier, past, previous, prior, one-time, erstwhile 3 = <u>long-standing</u>, established, fixed, enduring, long-lasting, long-established, time-honoured 4 = <u>stale</u>, worn-out, banal, threadbare, trite, overused, timeworn

old-fashioned 1 = <u>out of date</u>, dated, outdated, unfashionable, outmoded, passé, old hat, behind the times ≠ up-to-date 2 = <u>oldfangled</u>, square (*informal*), outdated, unfashionable, obsolescent

ominous = <u>threatening</u>, sinister, grim, fateful, foreboding, unpromising, portentous, inauspicious ≠ promising

omission 1 = <u>exclusion</u>, removal, elimination, deletion, excision ≠ inclusion 2 = <u>gap</u>, space, exclusion, lacuna 3 = <u>failure</u>, neglect, negligence, oversight, carelessness, dereliction, slackness, laxity

omit 1 = <u>leave out</u>, drop, exclude, eliminate, skip ≠ include 2 = <u>forget</u>, overlook, neglect, pass over, lose sight of

once ADVERB 1 = <u>on one occasion</u>, one time, one single time 2 = <u>at one time</u>, previously, formerly, long ago, once upon a time

● CONJUNCTION = <u>as soon as</u>, when, after, the moment, immediately, the instant

● PHRASES **at once** 1 = <u>immediately</u>, now, straight away, directly, promptly, instantly, right away, forthwith 2 = <u>simultaneously</u>, together, at the same time, concurrently

one-sided 1 = <u>unequal</u>, unfair, uneven, unjust, unbalanced, lopsided, ill-matched ≠ equal 2 = <u>biased</u>, prejudiced, weighted, unfair, partial, distorted, partisan, slanted ≠ unbiased

ongoing = <u>in progress</u>, developing, progressing, evolving, unfolding, unfinished

onlooker = <u>spectator</u>, witness, observer, viewer, looker-on, watcher, eyewitness, bystander

only ADJECTIVE = <u>sole</u>, one, single, individual, exclusive, unique, lone, solitary

● ADVERB 1 = <u>just</u>, simply, purely, merely 2 = <u>hardly</u>, just, barely, only just, scarcely, at a push

onset = <u>beginning</u>, start, birth, outbreak, inception, commencement ≠ end

onslaught = <u>attack</u>, charge, campaign, strike, assault, raid, invasion, offensive ≠ retreat

onward or **onwards** = <u>forward</u>, on, forwards, ahead, beyond, in front, forth

ooze[1] 1 = <u>seep</u>, well, escape, leak, drain, filter, drip, trickle 2 = <u>emit</u>, release, leak, drip, dribble, give off, pour forth 3 = <u>exude</u>, emit

ooze[2] = <u>mud</u>, clay, dirt, silt, sludge, mire, slime, alluvium

open VERB 1 = <u>unfasten</u>, unlock ≠ close 2 = <u>unwrap</u>, uncover, undo, unravel, untie ≠ wrap 3 = <u>uncork</u> 4 = <u>unfold</u>, spread (out), expand, unfurl, unroll ≠ fold 5 = <u>clear</u>, unblock ≠ block 6 = <u>undo</u>, unbutton, unfasten ≠ fasten 7 = <u>begin business</u> 8 = <u>start</u>, begin, launch, trigger, kick off (*informal*), initiate,

commence, get going ≠ end
9 = <u>begin</u>, start, commence ≠ end
● ADJECTIVE **1** = <u>unclosed</u>,
unlocked, ajar, unfastened,
yawning ≠ closed **2** = <u>unsealed</u>,
unstoppered ≠ unopened
3 = <u>extended</u>, unfolded, stretched
out, unfurled, straightened out,
unrolled ≠ shut **4** = <u>frank</u>, direct,
straightforward, sincere,
transparent, honest, candid,
truthful ≠ sly **5** = <u>receptive</u>,
sympathetic, responsive,
amenable **6** = <u>unresolved</u>,
unsettled, undecided, debatable,
moot, arguable **7** = <u>clear</u>,
passable, unhindered,
unimpeded, navigable,
unobstructed ≠ obstructed
8 = <u>available</u>, to hand, accessible,
handy, at your disposal
9 = <u>general</u>, public, free, universal,
blanket, across-the-board,
unrestricted, overarching
≠ restricted **10** = <u>vacant</u>, free,
available, empty, unoccupied,
unfilled

open-air = <u>outdoor</u>, outside,
out-of-door(s), alfresco

opening ADJECTIVE = <u>first</u>,
earliest, beginning, premier,
primary, initial, maiden, inaugural
● NOUN **1** = <u>beginning</u>, start,
launch, dawn, outset, initiation,
inception, commencement
≠ ending **2** = <u>hole</u>, space, tear,
crack, gap, slot, puncture,

aperture ≠ blockage
3 = <u>opportunity</u>, chance, time,
moment, occasion, look-in
(*informal*) **4** = <u>job</u>, position, post,
situation, opportunity, vacancy

openly = <u>frankly</u>, plainly,
honestly, overtly, candidly,
unreservedly, unhesitatingly,
forthrightly ≠ privately

open-minded = <u>unprejudiced</u>,
liberal, balanced, objective,
reasonable, tolerant, impartial,
receptive ≠ narrow-minded

operate 1 = <u>manage</u>, run, direct,
handle, supervise, be in charge of
2 = <u>function</u>, work, act **3** = <u>run</u>,
work, use, control, manoeuvre
4 = <u>work</u>, go, run, perform,
function ≠ break down

operation = <u>performance</u>,
action, movement, motion

operational = <u>working</u>, going,
running, ready, functioning,
operative, viable, functional
≠ inoperative

operative ADJECTIVE = <u>in force</u>,
effective, functioning, active, in
effect, operational, in operation
≠ inoperative
● NOUN **1** = <u>worker</u>, employee,
labourer, workman, artisan (*U.S.
& Canad.*) **2** = <u>spy</u>, undercover
agent, mole, nark (*Brit., Austral., &
N.Z. slang*)

operator = <u>worker</u>, driver,
mechanic, operative, conductor,

technician, handler

opinion 1 = <u>belief</u>, feeling, view, idea, theory, conviction, point of view, sentiment 2 = <u>estimation</u>, view, impression, assessment, judgment, appraisal, considered opinion

opponent 1 = <u>adversary</u>, rival, enemy, competitor, challenger, foe, contestant, antagonist ≠ ally 2 = <u>opposer</u>, dissident, objector ≠ supporter

opportunity = <u>chance</u>, opening, time, turn, moment, possibility, occasion, slot

oppose = <u>be against</u>, fight (against), block, take on, counter, contest, resist, combat ≠ support

opposed 1 with to = <u>against</u>, hostile, adverse, in opposition, averse, antagonistic, (dead) set against 2 = <u>contrary</u>, conflicting, clashing, counter, adverse, contradictory, dissentient

opposing 1 = <u>conflicting</u>, different, contrasting, opposite, differing, contrary, contradictory, incompatible 2 = <u>rival</u>, conflicting, competing, enemy, opposite, hostile

opposite PREPOSITION = <u>facing</u>, face to face with, across from, eyeball to eyeball (informal)
● ADJECTIVE 1 = <u>facing</u>, other, opposing 2 = <u>different</u>, conflicting, contrasted,

contrasting, unlike, contrary, dissimilar, divergent ≠ alike 3 = <u>rival</u>, conflicting, opposing, competing
● NOUN = <u>reverse</u>, contrary, converse, antithesis, contradiction, inverse, obverse

opposition 1 = <u>hostility</u>, resistance, resentment, disapproval, obstruction, animosity, antagonism, antipathy ≠ support 2 = <u>opponent(s)</u>, competition, rival(s), enemy, competitor(s), other side, challenger(s), foe

oppress 1 = <u>subjugate</u>, abuse, suppress, wrong, master, overcome, subdue, persecute ≠ liberate 2 = <u>depress</u>, burden, discourage, torment, harass, afflict, sadden, vex

oppression = <u>persecution</u>, control, abuse, injury, injustice, cruelty, domination, repression ≠ justice

oppressive 1 = <u>tyrannical</u>, severe, harsh, cruel, brutal, authoritarian, unjust, repressive ≠ merciful 2 = <u>stifling</u>, close, sticky, stuffy, humid, sultry, airless, muggy

opt VERB = <u>choose</u>, decide, prefer, select, elect ≠ reject
● PHRASES opt for something or someone = <u>choose</u>, pick, select, adopt, go for, designate,

decide on, plump for

optimistic 1 = <u>hopeful</u>, positive, confident, encouraged, cheerful, rosy, buoyant, sanguine ≠ pessimistic **2** = <u>encouraging</u>, promising, bright, good, reassuring, rosy, heartening, auspicious ≠ discouraging

optimum *or* **optimal** = <u>ideal</u>, best, highest, finest, perfect, supreme, peak, outstanding ≠ worst

option = <u>choice</u>, alternative, selection, preference, freedom of choice, power to choose

optional = <u>voluntary</u>, open, discretionary, possible, extra, elective ≠ compulsory

opus = <u>work</u>, piece, production, creation, composition, work of art, brainchild, oeuvre (*French*)

oral = <u>spoken</u>, vocal, verbal, unwritten

orange

> ### Shades of orange
> amber   peach
> burnt sienna   tangerine
> ochre   terracotta

orbit NOUN **1** = <u>path</u>, course, cycle, circle, revolution, rotation, trajectory, sweep **2** = <u>sphere of influence</u>, reach, range, influence, province, scope, domain, compass

● VERB = <u>circle</u>, ring, go round,

revolve around, encircle, circumscribe, circumnavigate

orchestrate 1 = <u>organize</u>, plan, run, set up, arrange, put together, marshal, coordinate **2** = <u>score</u>, set, arrange, adapt

ordain 1 = <u>appoint</u>, name, commission, select, invest, nominate, anoint, consecrate **2** (*Formal*) = <u>order</u>, will, rule, demand, require, direct, command, dictate

ordeal = <u>hardship</u>, trial, difficulty, test, suffering, nightmare, torture, agony ≠ pleasure

order VERB **1** = <u>command</u>, instruct, direct, charge, demand, require, bid, compel ≠ forbid **2** = <u>decree</u>, rule, demand, prescribe, pronounce, ordain ≠ ban **3** = <u>request</u>, ask (for), book, seek, reserve, apply for, solicit, send away for **4** = <u>arrange</u>, group, sort, position, line up, organize, catalogue, sort out ≠ disarrange

● NOUN **1** = <u>instruction</u>, ruling, demand, direction, command, dictate, decree, mandate **2** = <u>request</u>, booking, demand, commission, application, reservation, requisition **3** = <u>sequence</u>, grouping, series, structure, chain, arrangement, line-up, array **4** = <u>organization</u>, system, method, pattern, symmetry, regularity, neatness, tidiness ≠ chaos **5** = <u>peace</u>, control, law, quiet, calm, discipline, law and order, tranquillity **6** = <u>society</u>, company, group, club, community, association, institute, organization **7** = <u>class</u>, set, rank, grade, caste **8** = <u>kind</u>, group, class, family, sort, type, variety, category

orderly 1 = <u>well-behaved</u>, controlled, disciplined, quiet, restrained, law-abiding, peaceable ≠ disorderly **2** = <u>well-organized</u>, regular, in order, organized, precise, neat, tidy, systematic ≠ disorganized

ordinary 1 = <u>usual</u>, standard, normal, common, regular, typical, conventional, routine **2** = <u>commonplace</u>, plain, modest, humble, mundane, banal, unremarkable, run-of-the-mill ≠ extraordinary

organ 1 = <u>body part</u>, part of the body, element, biological structure **2** = <u>newspaper</u>, medium, voice, vehicle, gazette, mouthpiece

organic 1 = <u>natural</u>, biological, living, live, animate **2** = <u>systematic</u>, ordered, structured, organized, integrated, orderly, methodical

organism = <u>creature</u>, being, thing, body, animal, structure, beast, entity

organization 1 = <u>group</u>, company, party, body, association, band, institution, corporation **2** = <u>management</u>, running, planning, control, operation, handling, structuring, administration **3** = <u>structure</u>, form, pattern, make-up, arrangement, construction, format, formation

organize 1 = <u>arrange</u>, run, plan, prepare, set up, devise, put together, take care of, jack up (*N.Z. informal*) ≠ disrupt **2** = <u>put in order</u>, arrange, group, list, file, index, classify, inventory ≠ muddle

orient *or* **orientate 1** = <u>adjust</u>, adapt, alter, accustom, align, familiarize, acclimatize **2** = <u>get your bearings</u>, establish your location

orientation 1 = <u>inclination</u>, tendency, disposition, predisposition, predilection, proclivity, partiality **2** = <u>induction</u>, introduction, adjustment, settling in, adaptation, assimilation, familiarization, acclimatization **3** = <u>position</u>, situation, location, bearings, direction, arrangement, whereabouts

origin 1 = <u>beginning</u>, start, birth, launch, foundation, creation, emergence, onset ≠ end **2** = <u>root</u>, source, basis, base, seed, foundation, nucleus, derivation

original ADJECTIVE 1 = <u>first</u>, earliest, initial 2 = <u>initial</u>, first, starting, opening, primary, introductory ≠ final 3 = <u>new</u>, fresh, novel, unusual, unprecedented, innovative, unfamiliar, seminal ≠ unoriginal 4 = <u>creative</u>, inspired, imaginative, artistic, fertile, ingenious, visionary, inventive

● NOUN = <u>prototype</u>, master, pattern ≠ copy

originally = <u>initially</u>, first, firstly, at first, primarily, to begin with, in the beginning

originate 1 = <u>begin</u>, start, emerge, come, happen, rise, appear, spring ≠ end 2 = <u>invent</u>, create, design, launch, introduce, institute, generate, pioneer

ornament NOUN 1 = <u>decoration</u>, trimming, accessory, festoon, trinket, bauble, knick-knack 2 = <u>embellishment</u>, decoration, embroidery, elaboration, adornment, ornamentation

● VERB = <u>decorate</u>, adorn, array, do up (*informal*), embellish, festoon, beautify, prettify

orthodox 1 = <u>established</u>, official, accepted, received, common, traditional, normal, usual ≠ unorthodox

2 = <u>conformist</u>, conservative, traditional, strict, devout, observant ≠ nonconformist

orthodoxy 1 = <u>doctrine</u>, teaching, opinion, principle, belief, convention, creed, dogma 2 = <u>conformity</u>, received wisdom, traditionalism, conventionality ≠ nonconformity

other 1 = <u>additional</u>, more, further, new, added, extra, fresh, spare 2 = <u>different</u>, alternative, contrasting, distinct, diverse, dissimilar, separate, alternative

otherwise 1 = <u>or else</u>, or, if not, or then 2 = <u>apart from that</u>, in other ways, in (all) other respects 3 = <u>differently</u>, any other way, contrarily

ounce = <u>shred</u>, bit, drop, trace, scrap, grain, fragment, atom

oust = <u>expel</u>, turn out, dismiss, exclude, exile, throw out, displace, topple

out ADJECTIVE 1 = <u>not in</u>, away, elsewhere, outside, gone, abroad, from home, absent

2 = <u>extinguished</u>, ended, finished, dead, exhausted, expired, used up, at an end ≠ alight 3 = <u>in bloom</u>, opening, open, flowering, blooming, in flower, in full bloom

4 = <u>available</u>, on sale, in the shops, to be had, purchasable

5 = <u>revealed</u>, exposed, common knowledge, public knowledge, (out) in the open ≠ kept secret

● VERB = <u>expose</u>

outbreak 1 = <u>eruption</u>, burst,

explosion, epidemic, rash,
outburst, flare-up, upsurge
2 = <u>onset</u>, beginning, outset,
opening, dawn, commencement

outburst = <u>explosion</u>, fit, surge,
outbreak, flare-up, eruption,
spasm, outpouring

outcome = <u>result</u>, end,
consequence, conclusion, payoff
(*informal*), upshot

outcry = <u>protest</u>, complaint,
objection, dissent, outburst,
clamour, uproar, commotion

outdated = <u>old-fashioned</u>,
dated, obsolete, out of date,
passé, archaic, unfashionable,
antiquated ≠ modern

outdoor = <u>open-air</u>, outside, out-
of-door(s), alfresco ≠ indoor

outer **1** = <u>external</u>, outside,
outward, exterior, exposed,
outermost ≠ inner **2** = <u>surface</u>
3 = <u>outlying</u>, distant, provincial,
out-of-the-way, peripheral, far-
flung ≠ central

outfit **1** = <u>costume</u>, dress,
clothes, clothing, suit, get-up
(*informal*), kit, ensemble
2 (*Informal*) = <u>group</u>, company,
team, party, unit, crowd, squad,
organization

outgoing **1** = <u>leaving</u>, former,
previous, retiring, withdrawing,
prior, departing, outbound
≠ incoming **2** = <u>sociable</u>, open,
social, warm, friendly,

expansive, affable, extrovert
≠ reserved

outgoings = <u>expenses</u>, costs,
payments, expenditure,
overheads, outlay

outing = <u>journey</u>, run, trip, tour,
expedition, excursion, spin
(*informal*), jaunt

outlaw VERB **1** = <u>ban</u>, bar, veto,
forbid, exclude, prohibit, disallow,
proscribe ≠ legalise **2** = <u>banish</u>,
put a price on (someone's) head
● NOUN (*History*) = <u>bandit</u>,
criminal, thief, robber, fugitive,
outcast, felon, highwayman

outlet **1** = <u>shop</u>, store,
supermarket, market, boutique,
emporium, hypermarket
2 = <u>channel</u>, release, medium,
avenue, vent, conduit **3** = <u>pipe</u>,
opening, channel, exit, duct

outline VERB **1** = <u>summarize</u>,
draft, plan, trace, sketch (in), sum
up, encapsulate, delineate
2 = <u>silhouette</u>, etch
● NOUN **1** = <u>summary</u>, review,
résumé, rundown, synopsis,
précis, thumbnail sketch,
recapitulation **2** = <u>shape</u>, lines,
form, figure, profile, silhouette,
configuration, contour(s)

outlook **1** = <u>attitude</u>, opinion,
position, approach, mood,
perspective, point of view, stance
2 = <u>prospect(s)</u>, future,
expectations, forecast, prediction,

out of date 1 = <u>old-fashioned</u>, dated, outdated, obsolete, démodé (*French*), antiquated, outmoded, passé ≠ modern **2** = <u>invalid</u>, expired, lapsed, void, null and void

output = <u>production</u>, manufacture, manufacturing, yield, productivity

outrage VERB = <u>offend</u>, shock, upset, wound, insult, infuriate, incense, madden

● NOUN = <u>indignation</u>, shock, anger, rage, fury, hurt, resentment, scorn

outrageous 1 = <u>atrocious</u>, shocking, terrible, offensive, appalling, cruel, savage, horrifying ≠ mild **2** = <u>unreasonable</u>, unfair, steep (*informal*), shocking, extravagant, scandalous, preposterous, unwarranted ≠ reasonable

outright ADJECTIVE **1** = <u>absolute</u>, complete, total, perfect, sheer, thorough, unconditional, unqualified **2** = <u>definite</u>, clear, certain, flat, absolute, black-and-white, straightforward, unequivocal

● ADVERB **1** = <u>openly</u>, frankly, plainly, overtly, candidly, unreservedly, unhesitatingly, forthrightly **2** = <u>absolutely</u>, completely, totally, fully,

entirely, thoroughly, wholly, utterly

outset = <u>beginning</u>, start, opening, onset, inauguration, inception, commencement, kickoff (*informal*) ≠ finish

outside NOUN = <u>exterior</u>, face, front, covering, skin, surface, shell, coating

● ADJECTIVE **1** = <u>external</u>, outer, exterior, outward, extraneous ≠ inner **2** = <u>remote</u>, small, unlikely, slight, slim, distant, faint, marginal

● ADVERB = <u>outdoors</u>, out of the house, out-of-doors

Word Power

outside – The use of *outside of* and *inside of*, although fairly common, is generally thought to be incorrect or nonstandard: *She waits outside* (not *outside of*) *the school.*

---

outsider = <u>stranger</u>, incomer, visitor, newcomer, intruder, interloper, odd one out

outskirts = <u>edge</u>, boundary, suburbs, fringe, perimeter, periphery, suburbia, environs

outspan (*S. African*) = <u>relax</u>, chill out (*slang, chiefly U.S.*), take it easy, loosen up, put your feet up

outspoken = <u>forthright</u>, open, frank, straightforward, blunt, explicit, upfront (*informal*), unequivocal ≠ reserved

outstanding 1 = <u>excellent</u>, good, great, important, special, fine, brilliant, impressive, booshit (*Austral. slang*), exo (*Austral. slang*), sik (*Austral. slang*) ≠ mediocre 2 = <u>unpaid</u>, remaining, due, pending, payable, unsettled, uncollected 3 = <u>undone</u>, left, omitted, unfinished, unfulfilled, unperformed

outward = <u>apparent</u>, seeming, surface, ostensible ≠ inward

outwardly = <u>apparently</u>, externally, seemingly, it seems that, on the surface, it appears that, ostensibly, on the face of it

outweigh = <u>override</u>, cancel (out), eclipse, offset, compensate for, supersede, neutralize, counterbalance

oval = <u>elliptical</u>, egg-shaped, ovoid

ovation = <u>applause</u>, hand, cheers, praise, tribute, acclaim, clapping, accolade ≠ derision

over PREPOSITION 1 = <u>above</u>, on top of 2 = <u>on top of</u>, on, across, upon 3 = <u>across</u>, (looking) onto 4 = <u>more than</u>, above, exceeding, in excess of, upwards of 5 = <u>about</u>, regarding, relating to, concerning, apropos of

● ADVERB 1 = <u>above</u>, overhead, in the sky, on high, aloft, up above

2 = <u>extra</u>, more, further, beyond, additional, in addition, surplus, in excess

● ADJECTIVE = <u>finished</u>, done (with), through, ended, closed, past, completed, complete

(*Related Words*)
prefixes: hyper-, super-

overall ADJECTIVE = <u>total</u>, full, whole, general, complete, entire, global, comprehensive

● ADVERB = <u>in general</u>, generally, mostly, all things considered, on average, on the whole, predominantly, in the main

overcome VERB 1 = <u>defeat</u>, beat, conquer, master, overwhelm, subdue, rout, overpower 2 = <u>conquer</u>, beat, master, subdue, triumph over, vanquish

● ADJECTIVE = <u>overwhelmed</u>, moved, affected, emotional, choked, speechless, bowled over (*informal*), at a loss for words

overdue 1 = <u>delayed</u>, belated, late, behind schedule, tardy, unpunctual, behindhand ≠ early 2 = <u>unpaid</u>, owing

overflow VERB = <u>spill over</u>, well over, run over, pour over, bubble over, brim over

● NOUN 1 = <u>flood</u>, spilling over 2 = <u>surplus</u>, extra, excess, overspill, overabundance, additional people *or* things

overhaul VERB 1 = <u>check</u>, service,

maintain, examine, restore, tune (up), repair, go over **2** = <u>overtake</u>, pass, leave behind, catch up with, get past, outstrip, get ahead of, outdistance

● NOUN = <u>check</u>, service, examination, going-over (*informal*), inspection, once-over (*informal*), checkup, reconditioning

overhead ADJECTIVE = <u>raised</u>, suspended, elevated, aerial, overhanging

● ADVERB = <u>above</u>, in the sky, on high, aloft, up above
≠ underneath

overheads = <u>running costs</u>, expenses, outgoings, operating costs

overlook 1 = <u>look over or out on</u>, have a view of **2** = <u>miss</u>, forget, neglect, omit, disregard, pass over ≠ notice **3** = <u>ignore</u>, excuse, forgive, pardon, disregard, condone, turn a blind eye to, wink at

overpower 1 = <u>overcome</u>, master, overwhelm, overthrow, subdue, quell, subjugate, prevail over **2** defeat, crush, triumph over, vanquish **3** = <u>overwhelm</u>, overcome, bowl over (*informal*), stagger

override 1 = <u>outweigh</u>, eclipse, supersede, take precedence over, prevail over **2** = <u>overrule</u>, cancel,

overturn, repeal, rescind, annul, nullify, countermand **3** = <u>ignore</u>, reject, discount, overlook, disregard, pass over, take no notice of

overrun 1 = <u>overwhelm</u>, attack, assault, occupy, raid, invade, penetrate, rout **2** = <u>spread over</u>, overwhelm, choke, swamp, infest, inundate, permeate, swarm over **3** = <u>exceed</u>, go beyond, surpass, overshoot, run over *or* on

overshadow 1 = <u>spoil</u>, ruin, mar, wreck, blight, crool *or* cruel (*Austral. slang*), mess up, put a damper on **2** = <u>outshine</u>, eclipse, surpass, dwarf, tower above, leave *or* put in the shade

overt = <u>open</u>, obvious, plain, public, manifest, blatant, observable, undisguised
≠ hidden

overtake 1 = <u>pass</u>, leave behind, overhaul, catch up with, get past, outdistance, go by *or* past **2** = <u>outdo</u>, top, exceed, eclipse, surpass, outstrip, get the better of, outclass **3** = <u>befall</u>, hit, happen to, catch off guard, catch unawares **4** = <u>engulf</u>, overwhelm, hit, strike, swamp, envelop, swallow up

overthrow VERB = <u>defeat</u>, overcome, conquer, bring down, oust, topple, rout, overpower
≠ uphold

overturn

● NOUN = <u>downfall</u>, fall, defeat, collapse, destruction, ousting, undoing, unseating ≠ preservation

overturn 1 = <u>tip over</u>, topple, upturn, capsize, upend, keel over, overbalance 2 = <u>knock over</u> or <u>down</u>, upturn, tip over, upend 3 = <u>reverse</u>, change, cancel, abolish, overthrow, set aside, repeal, quash 4 = <u>overthrow</u>, defeat, destroy, overcome, bring down, oust, topple, depose

overweight = <u>fat</u>, heavy, stout, hefty, plump, bulky, chunky, chubby ≠ underweight

overwhelm 1 = <u>overcome</u>, devastate, stagger, bowl over (*informal*), knock (someone) for six (*informal*), sweep (someone) off his or her feet, take (someone's) breath away 2 = <u>destroy</u>, defeat, overcome, crush, massacre, conquer, wipe out, overthrow

overwhelming

1 = <u>overpowering</u>, strong, powerful, towering, stunning, crushing, devastating, shattering ≠ negligible 2 = <u>vast</u>, huge, massive, enormous, tremendous, immense, very large ≠ insignificant

owe = <u>be in debt (to)</u>, be in arrears (to), be overdrawn (by), be obligated or indebted (to)

owing to = <u>because of</u>, thanks to, as a result of, on account of, by reason of

own ADJECTIVE = <u>personal</u>, special, private, individual, particular, exclusive

● VERB = <u>possess</u>, have, keep, hold, enjoy, retain, be in possession of, have to your name

owner = <u>possessor</u>, holder, proprietor, titleholder, landlord or landlady

ownership = <u>possession</u>, occupation, tenure, dominion

P

pace NOUN 1 = <u>speed</u>, rate, tempo, velocity 2 = <u>step</u>, walk, stride, tread, gait 3 = <u>footstep</u>, step, stride

● VERB = <u>stride</u>, walk, pound, patrol, tread, march up and down

pack VERB 1 = <u>package</u>, load, store, bundle, stow 2 = <u>cram</u>, crowd, press, fill, stuff, jam, ram, compress

● NOUN 1 = <u>packet</u>, box, package, carton 2 = <u>bundle</u>, parcel, load, burden, rucksack, knapsack, back pack, kitbag 3 = <u>group</u>, crowd, company, band, troop, gang, bunch, mob

● PHRASES **pack someone off** = <u>send away</u>, dismiss, send

packing (*informal*) ◆ **pack
something in 1** (*Brit. informal*)
= resign from, leave, give up, quit
(*informal*), chuck (*informal*), jack
in (*informal*) **2** = stop, give up,
kick (*informal*), cease, chuck
(*informal*)

package NOUN **1** = parcel, box,
container, packet, carton
2 = collection, lot, unit,
combination, compilation
● VERB = pack, box, parcel (up)

packet 1 = container, box,
package, carton **2** = package,
parcel **3** (*Slang*) = a fortune, a
bomb (*Brit. slang*), a pile
(*informal*), a small fortune, a tidy
sum (*informal*), a king's ransom
(*informal*)

pact = agreement, alliance,
treaty, deal, understanding,
bargain, covenant

pad¹ NOUN **1** = wad, dressing,
pack, padding, compress,
wadding **2** = cushion, filling,
stuffing, pillow, bolster,
upholstery **3** = notepad, block,
notebook, jotter, writing pad
4 (*Slang*) = home, flat, apartment,
place **5** = paw, foot, sole
● VERB = pack, fill, protect, stuff,
cushion

pad² = sneak, creep, steal, go
barefoot

padding 1 = filling, stuffing,
packing, wadding **2** = waffle

(*informal*, *chiefly Brit.*), hot air
(*informal*), verbiage, wordiness,
verbosity

paddle¹ NOUN = oar, scull
● VERB = row, pull, scull

paddle² = wade, splash (about),
slop

pagan ADJECTIVE = heathen,
infidel, polytheistic, idolatrous
● NOUN = heathen, infidel,
polytheist, idolater

page¹ = folio, side, leaf, sheet

page² VERB = call, summon, send
for
● NOUN **1** = attendant, pageboy
2 = servant, attendant, squire,
pageboy

pain NOUN **1** = suffering,
discomfort, hurt, irritation,
tenderness, soreness **2** = ache,
stinging, aching, cramp, throb,
throbbing, pang, twinge
3 = sorrow, suffering, torture,
distress, despair, misery, agony,
sadness
● PLURAL NOUN = trouble, effort,
care, bother, diligence
● VERB **1** = distress, hurt, torture,
grieve, torment, sadden, agonize,
cut to the quick **2** = hurt

painful 1 = sore, smarting,
aching, tender ≠ painless
2 = distressing, unpleasant,
grievous, distasteful, agonizing,
disagreeable ≠ pleasant
3 = difficult, arduous, trying, hard,

troublesome, laborious ≠ easy

painfully = <u>distressingly</u>, clearly, sadly, unfortunately, dreadfully

paint NOUN = <u>colouring</u>, colour, stain, dye, tint, pigment, emulsion

● VERB 1 = <u>colour</u>, cover, coat, stain, whitewash, daub, distemper, apply paint to 2 = <u>depict</u>, draw, portray, picture, represent, sketch

pair NOUN 1 = <u>set</u> 2 = <u>couple</u>, brace, duo

● VERB = <u>team</u>, match (up), join, couple, twin, bracket

---

Word Power

pair – Like other collective nouns, *pair* takes a singular or a plural verb according to whether it is seen as a unit or as a collection of two things: *the pair are said to dislike each other*; *a pair of good shoes is essential*.

---

pal (*Informal*) = <u>friend</u>, companion, mate (*informal*), buddy (*informal*), comrade, chum (*informal*), crony, cobber (*Austral. & N.Z. old-fashioned informal*), E hoa (*N.Z.*)

pale ADJECTIVE 1 = <u>light</u>, soft, faded, subtle, muted, bleached, pastel, light-coloured 2 = <u>dim</u>, weak, faint, feeble, thin, wan, watery 3 = <u>white</u>, pasty, bleached, wan, colourless, pallid, ashen

≠ rosy-cheeked

● VERB = <u>become pale</u>, blanch, whiten, go white, lose colour

pamper = <u>spoil</u>, indulge, pet, cosset, coddle, mollycoddle

pamphlet = <u>booklet</u>, leaflet, brochure, circular, tract

pan¹ NOUN = <u>pot</u>, container, saucepan

● VERB 1 (*Informal*) = <u>criticize</u>, knock, slam (*slang*), censure, tear into (*informal*) 2 = <u>sift out</u>, look for, search for

pan² = <u>move along</u> or <u>across</u>, follow, track, sweep

panic NOUN = <u>fear</u>, alarm, terror, anxiety, hysteria, fright, trepidation, a flap (*informal*)

● VERB 1 = <u>go to pieces</u>, become hysterical, lose your nerve 2 = <u>alarm</u>, scare, unnerve

panorama 1 = <u>view</u>, prospect, vista 2 = <u>survey</u>, perspective, overview, overall picture

pant = <u>puff</u>, blow, breathe, gasp, wheeze, heave

pants 1 (*Brit.*) = <u>underpants</u>, briefs, drawers, knickers, panties, boxer shorts, broekies (*S. African*), underdaks (*Austral. slang*) 2 (*U.S.*) = <u>trousers</u>, slacks

paper NOUN 1 = <u>newspaper</u>, daily, journal, gazette 2 = <u>essay</u>, article, treatise, dissertation 3 = <u>examination</u>, test, exam 4 = <u>report</u>

● **PLURAL NOUN 1** = <u>letters</u>, records, documents, file, diaries, archive, paperwork, dossier
2 = <u>documents</u>, records, certificates, identification, deeds, identity papers, I.D. (*informal*)

● **VERB 1** = <u>wallpaper</u>, hang

parade NOUN **1** = <u>procession</u>, march, pageant, cavalcade
2 = <u>show</u>, display, spectacle

● **VERB 1** = <u>march</u>, process, promenade **2** = <u>flaunt</u>, display, exhibit, show off (*informal*)
3 = <u>strut</u>, show off (*informal*), swagger, swank

paradigm = <u>model</u>, example, pattern, ideal

paradise 1 = <u>heaven</u>, Promised Land, Happy Valley (*Islam*), Elysian fields **2** = <u>bliss</u>, delight, heaven, felicity, utopia

paradox = <u>contradiction</u>, puzzle, anomaly, enigma, oddity

paragraph = <u>section</u>, part, item, passage, clause, subdivision

parallel NOUN **1** = <u>equivalent</u>, counterpart, match, equal, twin, analogue ≠ opposite
2 = <u>similarity</u>, comparison, analogy, resemblance, likeness
≠ difference

● **ADJECTIVE 1** = <u>matching</u>, corresponding, like, similar, resembling, analogous
≠ different **2** = <u>equidistant</u>, alongside, side by side

≠ divergent

paralyse 1 = <u>disable</u>, cripple, lame, incapacitate **2** = <u>freeze</u>, stun, numb, petrify, halt, immobilize **3** = <u>immobilize</u>, freeze, halt, disable, cripple, incapacitate, bring to a standstill

paralysis 1 = <u>immobility</u>, palsy
2 = <u>standstill</u>, breakdown, stoppage, halt

parameter (*Informal*) usually *plural* = <u>limit</u>, restriction, framework, limitation, specification

paramount = <u>principal</u>, prime, first, chief, main, primary, supreme, cardinal ≠ secondary

paranoid (*Informal*)
= <u>suspicious</u>, worried, nervous, fearful, antsy (*informal*)
2 = <u>obsessive</u>, disturbed, manic, neurotic, mentally ill, psychotic, deluded, paranoiac

parasite = <u>sponger</u> (*informal*), leech, hanger-on, scrounger (*informal*), bloodsucker (*informal*), quandong (*Austral. slang*)

parcel NOUN = <u>package</u>, case, box, pack, bundle

● **VERB** often with **up** = <u>wrap</u>, pack, package, tie up, do up, gift-wrap, box up, fasten together

pardon VERB **1** = <u>forgive</u>, excuse
≠ condemn **2** = <u>acquit</u>, let off (*informal*), exonerate, absolve

≠ punish

● **NOUN 1** = <u>forgiveness</u>, absolution ≠ condemnation **2** = <u>acquittal</u>, amnesty, exoneration ≠ punishment

parent = <u>father</u> or <u>mother</u>, sire, progenitor, procreator, old (Austral. & N.Z. informal), patriarch

parish 1 = <u>district</u>, community **2** = <u>community</u>, flock, church, congregation

park 1 = <u>recreation ground</u>, garden, playground, pleasure garden, playpark, domain (N.Z.), forest park (N.Z.) **2** = <u>parkland</u>, grounds, estate, lawns, woodland, grassland **3** = <u>field</u>, pitch, playing field

parliament 1 = <u>assembly</u>, council, congress, senate, convention, legislature **2** = <u>sitting</u>

parliamentary = <u>governmental</u>, legislative, law-making

parlour or (U.S.) **parlor 1** (Old-fashioned) = <u>sitting room</u>, lounge, living room, drawing room, front room **2** = <u>establishment</u>, shop, store, salon

parody NOUN = <u>takeoff</u> (informal), satire, caricature, send-up (Brit. informal), spoof (informal), skit, burlesque

● **VERB** = <u>take off</u> (informal), caricature, send up (Brit.

informal), burlesque, satirize, do a takeoff of (informal)

parrot = <u>repeat</u>, echo, imitate, copy, mimic

parry 1 = <u>evade</u>, avoid, dodge, sidestep **2** = <u>ward off</u>, block, deflect, repel, rebuff, repulse

parson = <u>clergyman</u>, minister, priest, vicar, preacher, pastor, cleric, churchman

part NOUN 1 = <u>piece</u>, share, proportion, percentage, bit, section, scrap, portion ≠ entirety **2** often plural = <u>region</u>, area, district, neighbourhood, quarter, vicinity **3** = <u>component</u>, bit, unit, constituent **4** = <u>branch</u>, division, office, section, wing, subdivision, subsection **5** = <u>organ</u>, member, limb (Theatre) = <u>role</u>, representation, persona, portrayal, depiction, character part **7** (Theatre) = <u>lines</u>, words, script, dialogue **8** = <u>side</u>, behalf

● **VERB 1** = <u>divide</u>, separate, break, tear, split, rend, detach, sever ≠ join **2** = <u>part company</u>, separate, split up ≠ meet

● **PHRASES in good part** = <u>good-naturedly</u>, well, cheerfully, without offence

partial 1 = <u>incomplete</u>, unfinished, imperfect, uncompleted ≠ complete **2** = <u>biased</u>, prejudiced, discriminatory, partisan, unfair, one-sided, unjust ≠ unbiased

partially = partly, somewhat, in part, not wholly, fractionally, incompletely

participant = participator, member, player, contributor, stakeholder

participate = take part, be involved, perform, join, partake ≠ refrain from

participation = taking part, contribution, involvement, sharing in, joining in, partaking

particle = bit, piece, scrap, grain, shred, mite, jot, speck

particular ADJECTIVE 1 = specific, special, exact, precise, distinct, peculiar ≠ general 2 = special, exceptional, notable, uncommon, marked, unusual, remarkable, singular 3 = fussy, demanding, fastidious, choosy (informal), picky (informal), finicky, pernickety (informal) ≠ indiscriminate

• NOUN usually plural = detail, fact, feature, item, circumstance, specification

particularly 1 = specifically, expressly, explicitly, especially, in particular, distinctly 2 = especially, notably, unusually, exceptionally, singularly, uncommonly

parting 1 = farewell, goodbye 2 = division, breaking, split,

separation, rift, rupture

partisan ADJECTIVE = prejudiced, one-sided, biased, partial, sectarian ≠ unbiased

• NOUN 1 = supporter, devotee, adherent, upholder ≠ opponent 2 = underground fighter, guerrilla, freedom fighter, resistance fighter

partition NOUN 1 = screen, wall, barrier 2 = division, separation, segregation

• VERB = separate, screen, divide

partly = partially, somewhat, slightly ≠ completely

Word Power

partly – Partly and partially are to some extent interchangeable, but partly should be used when referring to a part or parts of something: the building is partly (not partially) made of stone, while partially is preferred for the meaning to some extent: his mother is partially (not partly) sighted.

---

partner 1 = spouse, consort, significant other (U.S. informal), mate, husband or wife 2 = companion, ally, colleague, associate, mate, comrade 3 = associate, colleague, collaborator

partnership 1 = cooperation, alliance, sharing, union,

connection, participation, copartnership **2** = <u>company</u>, firm, house, interest, society, cooperative

party 1 = <u>faction</u>, set, side, league, camp, clique, coterie **2** = <u>get-together</u> (*informal*), celebration, do (*informal*), gathering, function, reception, festivity, social gathering **3** = <u>group</u>, team, band, company, unit, squad, crew, gang

pass VERB **1** = <u>go by</u> or past, overtake, drive past, lap, leave behind, pull ahead of ≠ stop **2** = <u>go</u>, move, travel, progress, flow, proceed **3** = <u>run</u>, move, stroke **4** = <u>give</u>, hand, send, transfer, deliver, convey **5** = <u>be left</u>, come, be bequeathed, be inherited by **6** = <u>kick</u>, hit, loft, head, lob **7** = <u>elapse</u>, progress, go by, lapse, wear on, go past, tick by **8** = <u>end</u>, go, cease, blow over **9** = <u>spend</u>, fill, occupy, while away **10** = <u>exceed</u>, beat, overtake, go beyond, surpass, outstrip, outdo **11** = <u>be successful in</u>, qualify (in), succeed (in), graduate (in), get through, do, gain a pass in ≠ fail **12** = <u>approve</u>, accept, decree, enact, ratify, ordain, legislate (for) ≠ ban

● NOUN **1** = <u>licence</u>, ticket, permit, passport, warrant, authorization **2** = <u>gap</u>, route, canyon, gorge, ravine

● PHRASES **pass away** or **on** (*Euphemistic*) = <u>die</u>, pass on, expire, pass over, snuff it (*informal*), kick the bucket (*slang*), shuffle off this mortal coil, cark it (*Austral. & N.Z. informal*) ◆ **pass out** (*Informal*) = <u>faint</u>, black out (*informal*), lose consciousness, become unconscious ◆ **pass something over** = <u>disregard</u>, ignore, not dwell on ◆ **pass something up** (*Informal*) = <u>miss</u>, let slip, decline, neglect, forgo, abstain from, give (something) a miss (*informal*)

Word Power

pass – The past participle of *pass* is sometimes wrongly spelt *past*: *the time for recriminations has passed* (not *past*).

---

passage 1 = <u>corridor</u>, hall, lobby, vestibule **2** = <u>alley</u>, way, close (*Brit.*), course, road, channel, route, path **3** = <u>extract</u>, reading, piece, section, text, excerpt, quotation **4** = <u>journey</u>, crossing, trip, trek, voyage **5** = <u>safe-conduct</u>, right to travel, freedom to travel, permission to travel

passenger = <u>traveller</u>, rider, fare, commuter, fare payer

passer-by = <u>bystander</u>, witness, observer, viewer, spectator, looker-on, watcher, onlooker

passing 1 = <u>momentary</u>, fleeting, short-lived, transient, ephemeral, brief, temporary, transitory **2** = <u>superficial</u>, short, quick, glancing, casual, summary, cursory, perfunctory

passion 1 = <u>love</u>, desire, lust, infatuation, ardour **2** = <u>emotion</u>, feeling, fire, heat, excitement, intensity, warmth, zeal ≠ indifference **3** = <u>mania</u>, enthusiasm, obsession, bug (*informal*), craving, fascination, craze **4** = <u>rage</u>, fit, storm, anger, fury, outburst, frenzy, paroxysm

passionate 1 = <u>emotional</u>, eager, strong, intense, fierce, ardent, fervent, heartfelt ≠ unemotional **2** = <u>loving</u>, erotic, hot, ardent, amorous, lustful ≠ cold

passive 1 = <u>submissive</u>, compliant, receptive, docile, quiescent, uninvolved **2** = <u>inactive</u>, inactive ≠ active

past NOUN **1** = <u>former times</u>, long ago, days gone by, the olden days ≠ future **2** = <u>background</u>, life, history, past life, life story, career to date

● ADJECTIVE **1** = <u>former</u>, early, previous, ancient, bygone, olden ≠ future **2** = <u>previous</u>, former, one-time, ex- **3** = <u>last</u>, previous **4** = <u>over</u>, done, ended, finished, gone

● PREPOSITION **1** = <u>after</u>, beyond, later than **2** = <u>by</u>, across, in front of

● ADVERB = <u>on</u>, by, along

> ## Word Power
>
> **past** – The past participle of *pass* is sometimes wrongly spelt *past: the time for recriminations has passed* (not *past*).

paste NOUN **1** = <u>adhesive</u>, glue, cement, gum **2** = <u>purée</u>, pâté, spread

● VERB = <u>stick</u>, glue, cement, gum

pastel = <u>pale</u>, light, soft, delicate, muted ≠ bright

pastime = <u>activity</u>, game, entertainment, hobby, recreation, amusement, diversion

pastor = <u>clergyman</u>, minister, priest, vicar, parson, rector, curate, churchman

pastoral 1 = <u>ecclesiastical</u>, priestly, ministerial, clerical **2** = <u>rustic</u>, country, rural, bucolic

pasture = <u>grassland</u>, grass, meadow, grazing

pat VERB = <u>stroke</u>, touch, tap, pet, caress, fondle

● NOUN = <u>tap</u>, stroke, clap

patch NOUN **1** = <u>spot</u>, bit, scrap, shred, small piece **2** = <u>plot</u>, area, ground, land, tract **3** = <u>reinforcement</u>, piece of fabric, piece of cloth, piece of material, piece sewn on

● **VERB** *often with* **up** = mend, cover, repair, reinforce, stitch (up), sew (up)

patent NOUN = copyright, licence, franchise, registered trademark
● **ADJECTIVE** = obvious, apparent, evident, clear, glaring, manifest

path 1 = way, road, walk, track, trail, avenue, footpath, berm (*N.Z.*) 2 = route, way, course, direction 3 = course, way, road, route

pathetic = sad, moving, touching, affecting, distressing, tender, poignant, plaintive ≠ funny

patience 1 = forbearance, tolerance, serenity, restraint, calmness, sufferance ≠ impatience 2 = endurance, resignation, submission, fortitude, long-suffering, perseverance, stoicism, constancy

patient NOUN = sick person, case, sufferer, invalid
● **ADJECTIVE** 1 = forbearing, understanding, forgiving, mild, tolerant, indulgent, lenient, even-tempered ≠ impatient 2 = long-suffering, resigned, calm, enduring, philosophical, persevering, stoical, submissive

patriot = nationalist, loyalist, chauvinist

patriotic = nationalistic, loyal, chauvinistic, jingoistic

patriotism = nationalism, jingoism

patrol VERB = police, guard, keep watch (on), inspect, safeguard, keep guard (on)
● NOUN = guard, watch, watchman, sentinel, patrolman

patron 1 = supporter, friend, champion, sponsor, backer, helper, benefactor, philanthropist 2 = customer, client, buyer, frequenter, shopper, habitué

patronage = support, promotion, sponsorship, backing, help, aid, assistance

pattern 1 = order, plan, system, method, sequence 2 = design, arrangement, motif, figure, device, decoration 3 = plan, design, original, guide, diagram, stencil, template

pause VERB = stop briefly, delay, break, wait, rest, halt, cease, interrupt ≠ continue
● NOUN = stop, break, interval, rest, gap, halt, respite, lull ≠ continuance

pave = cover, floor, surface, concrete, tile

paw (*Informal*) = manhandle, grab, maul, molest, handle roughly

pay VERB 1 = reward, compensate, reimburse, recompense, requite, remunerate 2 = spend, give, fork out (*informal*), remit, shell out (*informal*) 3 = settle 4 = bring in, earn, return, net, yield **5** = <u>be profitable</u>, make money, make a return **6** = <u>benefit</u>, repay, be worthwhile **7** = <u>give</u>, extend, present with, grant, hand out, bestow

● NOUN = <u>wages</u>, income, payment, earnings, fee, reward, salary, allowance

● PHRASES **pay off** = <u>succeed</u>, work, be effective ◆ **pay something off** = <u>settle</u>, clear, square, discharge, pay in full

payable = <u>due</u>, outstanding, owed, owing

payment 1 = <u>remittance</u>, advance, deposit, premium, instalment **2** = <u>settlement</u>, paying, discharge, remittance **3** = <u>wages</u>, fee, reward, hire, remuneration

peace 1 = <u>truce</u>, ceasefire, treaty, armistice ≠ war **2** = <u>stillness</u>, rest, quiet, silence, calm, hush, tranquillity, seclusion **3** = <u>serenity</u>, calm, composure, contentment, repose, equanimity, peacefulness, harmoniousness **4** = <u>harmony</u>, accord, agreement, concord

peaceful 1 = <u>at peace</u>, friendly, harmonious, amicable, nonviolent ≠ hostile **2** = <u>peace-loving</u>, conciliatory, peaceable, unwarlike ≠ belligerent **3** = <u>calm</u>, still, quiet, tranquil, restful ≠ agitated **4** = <u>serene</u>, placid,

undisturbed

peak NOUN **1** = <u>high point</u>, crown, climax, culmination, zenith, acme **2** = <u>point</u>, top, tip, summit, brow, crest, pinnacle, apex

● VERB = <u>culminate</u>, climax, come to a head

peasant = <u>rustic</u>, countryman

peck VERB **1** = <u>pick</u>, hit, strike, tap, poke, jab, prick **2** = <u>kiss</u>, plant a kiss, give someone a smacker, give someone a peck *or* kiss

● NOUN = <u>kiss</u>, smacker, osculation (*rare*)

peculiar 1 = <u>odd</u>, strange, unusual, bizarre, funny, extraordinary, curious, weird ≠ ordinary **2** = <u>special</u>, particular, unique, characteristic ≠ common

peddle = <u>sell</u>, trade, push (*informal*), market, hawk, flog (*slang*)

pedestrian NOUN = <u>walker</u>, foot-traveller ≠ driver

● ADJECTIVE = <u>dull</u>, ordinary, boring, commonplace, mundane, mediocre, banal, prosaic, half-pie (*N.Z. informal*) ≠ exciting

pedigree ADJECTIVE = <u>purebred</u>, thoroughbred, full-blooded

● NOUN = <u>lineage</u>, family, line, race, stock, blood, breed, descent

peel NOUN = <u>rind</u>, skin, peeling

● VERB = <u>skin</u>, scale, strip, pare, shuck, flake off, take the skin *or* rind off

peep VERB = peek, look, eyeball (*slang*), sneak a look, steal a look

● NOUN = look, glimpse, peek, look-see (*slang*)

peer[1] = squint, look, spy, gaze, scan, inspect, peep, peek

peer[2] 1 = noble, lord, aristocrat, nobleman 2 = equal, like, fellow, contemporary, compeer

peg NOUN = pin, spike, rivet, skewer, dowel, spigot

● VERB = fasten, join, fix, secure, attach

pen[1] = write (down), draft, compose, pencil, draw up, scribble, take down, inscribe

pen[2] NOUN = enclosure, pound, fold, cage, coop, hutch, sty

● VERB = enclose, confine, cage, fence in, coop up, hedge in, shut up *or* in

penalty = punishment, price, fine, handicap, forfeit

pending ADJECTIVE

1 = undecided, unsettled, in the balance, undetermined

2 = forthcoming, imminent, prospective, impending, in the wind

● PREPOSITION = awaiting, until, waiting for, till

penetrate 1 = pierce, enter, go through, bore, stab, prick

2 = grasp, work out, figure out (*informal*), comprehend, fathom, decipher, suss (out) (*slang*), get to the bottom of

penetrating 1 = sharp, harsh, piercing, carrying, piping, loud, strident, shrill ≠ sweet

2 = pungent 3 = piercing

4 = intelligent, quick, sharp, keen, acute, shrewd, astute, perceptive ≠ dull 5 = perceptive, sharp, keen ≠ unperceptive

penetration 1 = piercing, entry, entrance, puncturing, incision

2 = entry, entrance

pension = allowance, benefit, welfare, annuity, superannuation

pensioner = senior citizen, retired person, retiree (*U.S.*), old-age pensioner, O.A.P.

people PLURAL NOUN 1 = persons, individuals, folk (*informal*), men and women, humanity, mankind, mortals, the human race

2 = nation, public, community, subjects, population, residents, citizens, folk 3 = race, tribe

4 = family, parents, relations, relatives, folk, folks (*informal*), clan, kin

● VERB = inhabit, occupy, settle, populate, colonize

pepper NOUN = seasoning, flavour, spice

● VERB 1 = pelt, hit, shower, blitz, rake, bombard, assail, strafe

2 = sprinkle, spot, scatter, dot, fleck, intersperse, speck, spatter

perceive 1 = <u>see</u>, notice, note, identify, discover, spot, observe, recognize 2 = <u>understand</u>, gather, see, learn, realize, grasp, comprehend, suss (out) (*slang*) 3 = <u>consider</u>, believe, judge, suppose, rate, deem, adjudge

perception 1 = <u>awareness</u>, understanding, sense, impression, feeling, idea, notion, consciousness 2 = <u>understanding</u>, intelligence, observation, discrimination, insight, sharpness, cleverness, keenness

perch VERB 1 = <u>sit</u>, rest, balance, settle 2 = <u>place</u>, put, rest, balance 3 = <u>land</u>, alight, roost
● NOUN = <u>resting place</u>, post, branch, pole

perennial 1 = <u>continual</u>, lasting, constant, enduring, persistent, abiding, recurrent, incessant

perfect ADJECTIVE 1 = <u>faultless</u>, correct, pure, impeccable, exemplary, flawless, foolproof ≠ deficient 2 = <u>excellent</u>, ideal, supreme, superb, splendid, sublime, superlative 3 = <u>immaculate</u>, impeccable, flawless, spotless, unblemished ≠ flawed 4 = <u>complete</u>, absolute, sheer, utter, consummate, unmitigated ≠ partial 5 = <u>exact</u>, true, accurate, precise, correct, faithful, unerring

● VERB = <u>improve</u>, develop, polish, refine ≠ mar

> ## Word Power
>
> **perfect** – For most of its meanings, the adjective *perfect* describes an absolute state, so that something either is or is not *perfect*, and cannot be referred to in terms of degree – thus, one thing should not be described as *more perfect* or *less perfect* than another thing. However, when *perfect* is used in the sense of 'excellent in all respects', *more* and *most* are acceptable, for example *the next day the weather was even more perfect*.

perfection = <u>excellence</u>, integrity, superiority, purity, wholeness, sublimity, exquisiteness, faultlessness

perfectly 1 = <u>completely</u>, totally, absolutely, quite, fully, altogether, thoroughly, wholly ≠ partially 2 = <u>flawlessly</u>, ideally, wonderfully, superbly, supremely, impeccably, faultlessly ≠ badly

perform 1 = <u>do</u>, achieve, carry out, complete, fulfil, accomplish, execute, pull off 2 = <u>fulfil</u>, carry out, execute, discharge 3 = <u>present</u>, act (out), stage, play, produce, represent, put on, enact 4 = <u>appear on stage</u>, act 5 = <u>function</u>, go, work, run, operate, handle, respond, behave

performance 1 = <u>presentation</u>, playing, acting (out), staging, production, exhibition, rendering, portrayal 2 = <u>show</u>, appearance, concert, gig (informal), recital 3 = <u>work</u>, acts, conduct, exploits, feats 4 = <u>carrying out</u>, practice, achievement, execution, completion, accomplishment, fulfilment

performer = <u>artiste</u>, player, Thespian, trouper, actor or actress

perfume 1 = <u>fragrance</u>, scent 2 = <u>scent</u>, smell, fragrance, bouquet, aroma, odour

perhaps = <u>maybe</u>, possibly, it may be, it is possible (that), conceivably, perchance (archaic), feasibly, happen (Northern English dialect)

peril 1 = <u>danger</u>, risk, threat, hazard, menace, jeopardy, perilousness 2 often plural = <u>pitfall</u>, problem, risk, hazard ≠ safety

perimeter = <u>boundary</u>, edge, border, bounds, limit, margin, confines, periphery ≠ centre

period = <u>time</u>, term, season, space, run, stretch, spell, phase

periodic = <u>recurrent</u>, regular, repeated, occasional, cyclical, sporadic, intermittent

peripheral 1 = <u>secondary</u>, minor, marginal, irrelevant,

unimportant, incidental, inessential 2 = <u>outermost</u>, outside, external, outer, exterior

perish 1 = <u>die</u>, be killed, expire, pass away, lose your life, cark it (Austral. & N.Z. slang) 2 = <u>be destroyed</u>, fall, decline, collapse, disappear, vanish 3 = <u>rot</u>, waste away, decay, disintegrate, decompose, moulder

perk (Brit. informal) = <u>bonus</u>, benefit, extra, plus, fringe benefit, perquisite

permanent 1 = <u>lasting</u>, constant, enduring, persistent, eternal, abiding, perpetual, everlasting ≠ temporary 2 = <u>long-term</u>, established, secure, stable, steady ≠ temporary

permission = <u>authorization</u>, sanction, licence, approval, leave, go-ahead (informal), liberty, consent ≠ prohibition

permit VERB 1 = <u>allow</u>, grant, sanction, let, entitle, license, authorize, consent to ≠ forbid 2 = <u>enable</u>, let, allow, cause
● NOUN = <u>licence</u>, pass, document, certificate, passport, visa, warrant, authorization ≠ prohibition

perpetual 1 = <u>everlasting</u>, permanent, endless, eternal, lasting, perennial, infinite, never-ending ≠ temporary 2 = <u>continual</u>, repeated, constant, endless, continuous, persistent, recurrent, never-ending ≠ brief

perpetuate = maintain, preserve, keep going, immortalize ≠ end

persecute 1 = victimize, torment, oppress, pick on, ill-treat, maltreat ≠ mollycoddle 2 = harass, bother, annoy, tease, hassle (*informal*), badger, pester ≠ leave alone

persist 1 = continue, last, remain, carry on, keep up, linger 2 = persevere, continue, go on, carry on, keep on, keep going, press on, not give up

persistence = determination, resolution, grit, endurance, tenacity, perseverance, doggedness, pertinacity

persistent 1 = continuous, constant, repeated, endless, perpetual, continual, never-ending, incessant ≠ occasional 2 = determined, dogged, steady, stubborn, persevering, tireless, tenacious, steadfast ≠ irresolute

person NOUN = individual, being, body, human, soul, creature, mortal, man or woman
- PHRASES **in person**
1 = personally, yourself 2 = in the flesh, actually, physically, bodily

personal 1 = own, special, private, individual, particular, peculiar 2 = individual, special,

particular, exclusive 3 = private 4 = offensive, nasty, insulting, disparaging, derogatory

personality 1 = nature, character, make-up, identity, temperament, disposition, individuality 2 = character, charm, attraction, charisma, magnetism 3 = celebrity, star, notable, household name, famous name, personage, megastar (*informal*)

personally 1 = in your opinion, in your book, for your part, from your own viewpoint, in your own view 2 = by yourself, alone, independently, solely, on your own 3 = individually, specially, subjectively, individualistically 4 = privately, in private, off the record

personnel = employees, people, staff, workers, workforce, human resources, helpers

perspective 1 = outlook, attitude, context, angle, frame of reference 2 = objectivity, proportion, relation, relativity, relative importance

persuade 1 = talk (someone) into, urge, influence, win (someone) over, induce, sway, entice, coax ≠ dissuade 2 = cause, lead, move, influence, motivate, induce, incline, dispose 3 = convince, satisfy, assure, cause to believe

persuasion 1 = <u>urging</u>, inducement, wheedling, enticement, cajolery 2 = <u>belief</u>, views, opinion, party, school, side, camp, faith

persuasive = <u>convincing</u>, telling, effective, sound, compelling, influential, valid, credible ≠ unconvincing

pervasive = <u>widespread</u>, general, common, extensive, universal, prevalent, ubiquitous, rife

perverse 1 = <u>stubborn</u>, contrary, dogged, troublesome, rebellious, wayward, intractable, wilful ≠ cooperative 2 = <u>ill-natured</u>, cross, surly, fractious, churlish, ill-tempered, stroppy (*Brit. slang*), peevish ≠ good-natured 3 = <u>abnormal</u>, unhealthy, improper, deviant

pervert VERB 1 = <u>distort</u>, abuse, twist, misuse, warp, misrepresent, falsify 2 = <u>corrupt</u>, degrade, deprave, debase, debauch, lead astray

● NOUN = <u>deviant</u>, degenerate, sicko (*informal*), weirdo or weirdie (*informal*)

pessimistic = <u>gloomy</u>, dark, despairing, bleak, depressed, cynical, hopeless, glum ≠ optimistic

pest 1 = <u>infection</u>, bug, insect, plague, epidemic, blight, scourge, pestilence, gogga (*S. African informal*) 2 = <u>nuisance</u>, trial, pain (*informal*), drag (*informal*), bother, irritation, annoyance, bane

pet ADJECTIVE = <u>favourite</u>, favoured, dearest, cherished, fave (*informal*), dear to your heart

● NOUN = <u>favourite</u>, treasure, darling, jewel, idol

● VERB 1 = <u>fondle</u>, pat, stroke, caress 2 = <u>pamper</u>, spoil, indulge, cosset, baby, dote on, coddle, mollycoddle 3 (*Informal*) = <u>cuddle</u>, kiss, snog (*Brit. slang*), smooch (*informal*), neck (*informal*), canoodle (*slang*)

petition NOUN 1 = <u>appeal</u>, round robin, list of signatures 2 = <u>entreaty</u>, appeal, suit, application, request, prayer, plea, solicitation

● VERB = <u>appeal</u>, plead, ask, pray, beg, solicit, beseech, entreat

petty 1 = <u>trivial</u>, insignificant, little, small, slight, trifling, negligible, unimportant ≠ important 2 = <u>small-minded</u>, mean, shabby, spiteful, ungenerous, mean-minded ≠ broad-minded

phantom = <u>spectre</u>, ghost, spirit, shade (*literary*), spook (*informal*), apparition, wraith, phantasm

phase NOUN = <u>stage</u>, time, point,

position, step, development, period, chapter

● PHRASES **phase something in** = introduce, incorporate, ease in, start ◆ **phase something out** = eliminate, close, remove, withdraw, pull out, wind up, run down, terminate

phenomenal = extraordinary, outstanding, remarkable, fantastic, unusual, marvellous, exceptional, miraculous ≠ unremarkable

phenomenon 1 = occurrence, happening, fact, event, incident, circumstance, episode 2 = wonder, sensation, exception, miracle, marvel, prodigy, rarity

---

Word Power

phenomenon – Although *phenomena* is often treated as a singular, this is not grammatically correct. *Phenomenon* is the singular form of this word, and *phenomena* the plural; so *several new phenomena were recorded in his notes* is correct, but *that is an interesting phenomena* is not.

---

philosopher = thinker, theorist, sage, wise man, logician, metaphysician

philosophical or **philosophic** 1 = theoretical, abstract, wise, rational, logical,

---

thoughtful, sagacious ≠ practical 2 = stoical, calm, composed, cool, collected, serene, tranquil, unruffled ≠ emotional

philosophy 1 = thought, knowledge, thinking, reasoning, wisdom, logic, metaphysics 2 = outlook, values, principles, convictions, thinking, beliefs, doctrine, ideology

phone NOUN 1 = telephone, blower (*informal*) 2 = call, ring (*informal, chiefly Brit.*), tinkle (*Brit. informal*)

● VERB = call, telephone, ring (up) (*informal, chiefly Brit.*), give someone a call, give someone a ring (*informal, chiefly Brit.*), make a call, give someone a tinkle (*Brit. informal*), get on the blower (*informal*)

photograph NOUN = picture, photo (*informal*), shot, print, snap (*informal*), snapshot, transparency

● VERB = take a picture of, record, film, shoot, snap (*informal*), take (someone's) picture

photographic 1 = pictorial, visual, graphic, cinematic, filmic 2 = accurate, exact, precise, faithful, retentive

phrase NOUN = expression, saying, remark, construction, quotation, maxim, idiom, adage

● VERB = express, say, word, put,

voice, communicate, convey, put into words

physical 1 = <u>corporal</u>, fleshly, bodily, corporeal 2 = <u>earthly</u>, fleshly, mortal, incarnate 3 = <u>material</u>, real, substantial, natural, solid, tangible, palpable

physician = <u>doctor</u>, doc (*informal*), medic (*informal*), general practitioner, medical practitioner, doctor of medicine, G.P., M.D.

pick VERB 1 = <u>select</u>, choose, identify, elect, nominate, specify, opt for, single out ≠ reject 2 = <u>gather</u>, pull, collect, take in, harvest, pluck, garner 3 = <u>provoke</u>, start, cause, stir up, incite, instigate 4 = <u>open</u>, force, crack (*informal*), break into, break open

● NOUN 1 = <u>choice</u>, decision, option, selection, preference 2 = <u>best</u>, prime, finest, elect, elite, cream, jewel in the crown, crème de la crème (*French*)

● PHRASES **pick on someone** 1 = <u>torment</u>, bully, bait, tease, get at (*informal*), badger, persecute, hector 2 = <u>choose</u>, select, prefer, elect, single out, fix on, settle upon ◆ **pick something** *or* **someone out** = <u>identify</u>, recognize, distinguish, perceive, discriminate, make someone or something out, tell someone or something apart ◆ **pick**

something *or* **someone up** 1 = <u>lift</u>, raise, gather, take up, grasp, uplift 2 = <u>collect</u>, get, call for ◆ **pick something up** 1 = <u>learn</u>, master, acquire, get the hang of (*informal*), become proficient in 2 = <u>obtain</u>, get, find, buy, discover, purchase, acquire, locate ◆ **pick up** 1 = <u>improve</u>, recover, rally, get better, bounce back, make progress, perk up, turn the corner 2 = <u>recover</u>, improve, rally, get better, mend, turn the corner, be on the mend, take a turn for the better

picket VERB = <u>blockade</u>, boycott, demonstrate outside

● NOUN 1 = <u>demonstration</u>, strike, blockade 2 = <u>protester</u>, demonstrator, picketer 3 = <u>lookout</u>, watch, guard, patrol, sentry, sentinel 4 = <u>stake</u>, post, pale, paling, upright, stanchion

pickle VERB = <u>preserve</u>, marinade, steep

● NOUN 1 = <u>chutney</u>, relish, piccalilli 2 (*Informal*) = <u>predicament</u>, fix (*informal*), difficulty, bind (*informal*), jam (*informal*), dilemma, scrape (*informal*), hot water (*informal*), uphill (*S. African*)

pick-up = <u>improvement</u>, recovery, rise, rally, strengthening, revival, upturn, change for the better

picnic = <u>excursion</u>, barbecue,

barbie (*informal*), cookout (*U.S. & Canad.*), alfresco meal, clambake (*U.S. & Canad.*), outdoor meal, outing

picture NOUN **1** = representation, drawing, painting, portrait, image, print, illustration, sketch **2** = photograph, photo, still, shot, image, print, frame, slide **3** = film, movie (*U.S. informal*), flick (*slang*), feature film, motion picture **4** = idea, vision, concept, impression, notion, visualization, mental picture, mental image **5** = description, impression, explanation, report, account, image, sketch, depiction **6** = personification, embodiment, essence, epitome

● VERB **1** = imagine, see, envision, visualize, conceive of, fantasize about, conjure up an image of **2** = represent, show, draw, paint, illustrate, sketch, depict **3** = show, photograph, capture on film

picturesque 1 = interesting, pretty, beautiful, attractive, charming, scenic, quaint ≠ unattractive **2** = vivid, striking, graphic, colourful, memorable ≠ dull

piece 1 = bit, slice, part, block, quantity, segment, portion, fragment **2** = component, part, section, bit, unit, segment, constituent, module **3** = item, report, story, study, review, article

4 = composition, work, production, opus **5** = work of art, work, creation **6** = share, cut (*informal*), slice, percentage, quantity, portion, quota, fraction

pier 1 = jetty, wharf, quay, promenade, landing place **2** = pillar, support, post, column, pile, upright, buttress

pierce = penetrate, stab, spike, enter, bore, drill, puncture, prick

piercing 1 (*of sound*) = penetrating, sharp, loud, shrill, high-pitched, ear-splitting ≠ low **2** = perceptive, sharp, keen, alert, penetrating, shrewd, perspicacious, quick-witted ≠ unperceptive **3** = sharp, acute, severe, intense, painful, stabbing, excruciating, agonizing **4** (*of weather*) = cold, biting, freezing, bitter, arctic, wintry, nippy

pig 1 = hog, sow, boar, swine, porker **2** (*Informal*) = slob, glutton **3** (*Informal*) = brute, monster, scoundrel, rogue, swine, rotter, boor

pigment = colour, colouring, paint, stain, dye, tint, tincture

pile¹ NOUN **1** = heap, collection, mountain, mass, stack, mound, accumulation, hoard **2** (*Informal*) *often plural* = lot(s), mountain(s), load(s) (*informal*), oceans, wealth, great deal, stack(s), abundance **3** = mansion, building, residence, manor, country house, seat, big house, stately home

● VERB 1 = **load**, stuff, pack, stack, charge, heap, cram, lade 2 = **crowd**, pack, rush, climb, flood, stream, crush, squeeze

● PHRASES **pile up** = **accumulate**, collect, gather (up), build up, amass

pile² = **foundation**, support, post, column, beam, upright, pillar

pile³ = **nap**, fibre, down, hair, fur, plush

pile-up (*Informal*) = **collision**, crash, accident, smash, smash-up (*informal*), multiple collision

pilgrim = **traveller**, wanderer, devotee, wayfarer

pilgrimage = **journey**, tour, trip, mission, expedition, excursion

pill = **tablet**, capsule, pellet

pillar 1 = **support**, post, column, prop, shaft, upright, pier, stanchion 2 = **supporter**, leader, mainstay, leading light (*informal*), upholder

pilot NOUN 1 = **airman**, flyer, aviator, aeronaut 2 = **helmsman**, navigator, steersman

● VERB 1 = **fly**, operate, be at the controls of 2 = **navigate**, drive, direct, guide, handle, conduct, steer 3 = **direct**, conduct, steer

● ADJECTIVE = **trial**, test, model, sample, experimental

pin NOUN 1 = **tack**, nail, needle,

safety pin 2 = **peg**, rod, brace, bolt

● VERB 1 = **fasten**, stick, attach, join, fix, secure, nail, clip 2 = **hold fast**, hold down, constrain, immobilize, pinion

● PHRASES **pin someone down** = **force**, pressure, compel, put pressure on, pressurize, nail someone down, make someone commit themselves ◆ **pin something down** = **determine**, identify, locate, name, specify, pinpoint

pinch VERB 1 = **nip**, press, squeeze, grasp, compress 2 = **hurt**, crush, squeeze, pain, cramp 3 (*Brit. informal*) = **steal**, lift (*informal*), nick (*slang, chiefly Brit.*), swipe (*slang*), knock off (*slang*), pilfer, purloin, filch

● NOUN 1 = **nip**, squeeze 2 = **dash**, bit, mite, jot, speck, soupçon (*French*) 3 = **emergency**, crisis, difficulty, plight, scrape (*informal*), strait, uphill (*S. African*), predicament

pine VERB = **waste**, decline, sicken, fade, languish

● PHRASES **pine for something or someone** 1 = **long**, ache, crave, yearn, eat your heart out over 2 = **hanker after**, crave, wish for, yearn, thirst for, hunger for

pink NOUN or ADJECTIVE = **rosy**, rose, salmon, flushed, reddish, roseate

> **shades of red**

pinnacle 1 = <u>summit</u>, top, height, peak **2** = <u>height</u>, top, crown, crest, zenith, apex, vertex

pinpoint 1 = <u>identify</u>, discover, define, distinguish, put your finger on **2** = <u>locate</u>, find, identify, zero in on

pioneer NOUN **1** = <u>founder</u>, leader, developer, innovator, trailblazer **2** = <u>settler</u>, explorer, colonist
• VERB = <u>develop</u>, create, establish, start, discover, institute, invent, initiate

pipe NOUN **1** = <u>tube</u>, drain, canal, pipeline, line, main, passage, cylinder
• VERB = <u>convey</u>, channel, conduct
• PHRASES **pipe down** (*Informal*) = <u>be quiet</u>, shut up (*informal*), hush, stop talking, quieten down, shush, shut your mouth, hold your tongue

pipeline = <u>tube</u>, passage, pipe, conduit, duct

pirate NOUN **1** = <u>buccaneer</u>, raider, marauder, corsair, freebooter
• VERB = <u>copy</u>, steal, reproduce, bootleg, appropriate, poach, crib (*informal*), plagiarize

pit NOUN **1** = <u>coal mine</u>, mine, shaft, colliery, mine shaft **2** = <u>hole</u>, depression, hollow, crater, trough, cavity, abyss, chasm
• VERB = <u>scar</u>, mark, dent, indent, pockmark

pitch NOUN **1** = <u>sports field</u>, ground, stadium, arena, park, field of play **2** = <u>tone</u>, sound, key, frequency, timbre, modulation **3** = <u>level</u>, point, degree, summit, extent, height, intensity, high point **4** = <u>talk</u>, patter, spiel (*informal*)
• VERB **1** = <u>throw</u>, cast, toss, hurl, fling, chuck (*informal*), sling, lob (*informal*) **2** = <u>fall</u>, drop, plunge, dive, tumble, topple, plummet, fall headlong **3** = <u>set up</u>, raise, settle, put up, erect **4** = <u>toss (about)</u>, roll, plunge, lurch
• PHRASES **pitch in** = <u>help</u>, contribute, participate, join in, cooperate, chip in (*informal*), get stuck in (*Brit. informal*), lend a hand

pitfall *usually plural* = <u>danger</u>, difficulty, peril, catch, trap, hazard, drawback, snag, uphill (*S. African*)

pity NOUN **1** = <u>compassion</u>, charity, sympathy, kindness, fellow feeling ≠ mercilessness **2** = <u>shame</u>, sin (*informal*), misfortune, bummer (*slang*), crying shame **3** = <u>mercy</u>, kindness, clemency, forbearance
• VERB = <u>feel sorry for</u>, feel for, sympathize with, grieve for, weep for, bleed for, have compassion for

pivotal = <u>crucial</u>, central, vital, critical, decisive

place NOUN 1 = <u>spot</u>, point, position, site, area, location, venue, whereabouts 2 = <u>region</u>, quarter, district, neighbourhood, vicinity, locality, locale, dorp (S. African) 3 = <u>position</u>, point, spot, location 4 = <u>space</u>, position, seat, chair 5 = <u>rank</u>, standing, position, footing, station, status, grade, niche 6 = <u>situation</u>, position, circumstances, shoes (informal) 7 = <u>job</u>, position, post, situation, office, employment, appointment 8 = <u>home</u>, house, room, property, accommodation, pad (slang), residence, dwelling 9 (In this context, the construction is always negative) = <u>duty</u>, right, job, charge, concern, role, affair, responsibility

● VERB 1 = <u>lay (down)</u>, put (down), set (down), stand, position, rest, station, stick (informal) 2 = <u>put</u>, lay, set, invest, pin 3 = <u>classify</u>, class, group, put, order, sort, rank, arrange 4 = <u>entrust to</u>, give to, assign to, appoint to, allocate to, find a home for 5 = <u>identify</u>, remember, recognize, pin someone down, put your finger on, put a name to

● PHRASES **take place** = <u>happen</u>, occur, go on, go down (U.S. & Canad.), arise, come about, crop up, transpire (informal)

plague NOUN 1 = <u>disease</u>, infection, epidemic, pestilence

2 = <u>infestation</u>, invasion, epidemic, influx, host, swarm, multitude

● VERB 1 = <u>torment</u>, trouble, torture 2 = <u>pester</u>, trouble, bother, annoy, tease, harry, harass, hassle

plain ADJECTIVE 1 = <u>unadorned</u>, simple, basic, severe, bare, stark, austere, spartan ≠ ornate 2 = <u>clear</u>, obvious, patent, evident, visible, distinct, understandable, manifest ≠ hidden 3 = <u>straightforward</u>, open, direct, frank, blunt, outspoken, honest, downright ≠ roundabout 4 = <u>ugly</u>, unattractive, homely (U.S. & Canad.), unlovely, unprepossessing, not beautiful, no oil painting (informal), ill-favoured ≠ attractive 5 = <u>ordinary</u>, common, simple, everyday, commonplace, unaffected, unpretentious ≠ sophisticated

● NOUN = <u>flatland</u>, plateau, prairie, grassland, steppe, veld

plan NOUN 1 = <u>scheme</u>, system, design, programme, proposal, strategy, method, suggestion 2 = <u>diagram</u>, map, drawing, chart, representation, sketch, blueprint, layout

● VERB 1 = <u>devise</u>, arrange, scheme, plot, draft, organize, outline, formulate 2 = <u>intend</u>, aim, mean, propose, purpose 3 = <u>design</u>, outline, draw up a plan of

plane NOUN 1 = <u>aeroplane</u>, aircraft, jet, airliner, jumbo jet 2 = <u>flat surface</u>, the flat, horizontal, level surface 3 = <u>level</u>, position, stage, condition, standard, degree, rung, echelon

• ADJECTIVE = <u>level</u>, even, flat, regular, smooth, horizontal

• VERB = <u>skim</u>, sail, skate, glide

plant¹ NOUN 1 = <u>flower</u>, bush, vegetable, herb, weed, shrub

• VERB 1 = <u>sow</u>, scatter, transplant, implant, put in the ground 2 = <u>seed</u>, sow, implant 3 = <u>place</u>, put, set, fix 4 = <u>hide</u>, put, place, conceal 5 = <u>place</u>, put, establish, found, fix, insert

plant² 1 = <u>factory</u>, works, shop, yard, mill, foundry 2 = <u>machinery</u>, equipment, gear, apparatus

plaster NOUN 1 = <u>mortar</u>, stucco, gypsum, plaster of Paris 2 = <u>bandage</u>, dressing, sticking plaster, Elastoplast®, adhesive plaster

• VERB = <u>cover</u>, spread, coat, smear, overlay, daub

plastic = <u>pliant</u>, soft, flexible, supple, pliable, ductile, mouldable ≠ rigid

plate NOUN 1 = <u>platter</u>, dish, dinner plate, salver, trencher (*archaic*) 2 = <u>helping</u>, course, serving, dish, portion, platter, plateful 3 = <u>layer</u>, panel, sheet, slab

4 = <u>illustration</u>, picture, photograph, print, engraving, lithograph

• VERB = <u>coat</u>, gild, laminate, cover, overlay

plateau 1 = <u>upland</u>, table, highland, tableland 2 = <u>levelling off</u>, level, stage, stability

platform 1 = <u>stage</u>, stand, podium, rostrum, dais, soapbox 2 = <u>policy</u>, programme, principle, objective(s), manifesto, party line

plausible 1 = <u>believable</u>, possible, likely, reasonable, credible, probable, persuasive, conceivable ≠ unbelievable 2 = <u>glib</u>, smooth, specious, smooth-talking, smooth-tongued

play VERB 1 = <u>amuse yourself</u>, have fun, sport, fool, romp, revel, trifle, entertain yourself 2 = <u>take part in</u>, be involved in, engage in, participate in, compete in 3 = <u>compete against</u>, challenge, take on, oppose, contend against 4 = <u>perform</u>, carry out 5 = <u>act</u>, portray, represent, perform, act the part of 6 = <u>perform on</u>, strum, make music on

• NOUN 1 = <u>amusement</u>, pleasure, leisure, games, sport, fun, entertainment, relaxation 2 = <u>drama</u>, show, piece, comedy, tragedy, farce, soapie (*Austral. slang*), pantomime

• PHRASES **play on** or **upon something** = <u>take advantage of</u>, abuse, exploit, impose on, trade on, capitalize on ◆ **play something down** = minimize, make light of, gloss over, talk down, underrate, underplay, pooh-pooh (*informal*), soft-pedal (*informal*) ◆ **play something up** = emphasize, highlight, underline, stress, accentuate ◆ **play up 1** (*Brit. informal*) = hurt, be painful, bother you, trouble you, be sore, pain you **2** (*Brit. informal*) = malfunction, not work properly, be on the blink (*slang*) **3** (*Brit. informal*) = be awkward, misbehave, give trouble, be disobedient, be stroppy (*Brit. slang*)

playboy = womanizer, philanderer, rake, lady-killer (*informal*), roué, ladies' man

player 1 = sportsman or sportswoman, competitor, participant, contestant **2** = musician, artist, performer, virtuoso, instrumentalist **3** = performer, entertainer, Thespian, trouper, actor or actress

plea 1 = appeal, request, suit, prayer, petition, entreaty, intercession, supplication **2** = excuse, defence, explanation, justification

plead = appeal, ask, request, beg, petition, implore, beseech, entreat

pleasant 1 = pleasing, nice, fine, lovely, amusing, delightful, enjoyable, agreeable, lekker (*S. African slang*) ≠ horrible **2** = friendly, nice, agreeable, likable or likeable, engaging, charming, amiable, genial ≠ disagreeable

please = delight, entertain, humour, amuse, suit, satisfy, indulge, gratify ≠ annoy

pleased = happy, delighted, contented, satisfied, thrilled, glad, gratified, over the moon (*informal*)

pleasing 1 = enjoyable, satisfying, charming, delightful, gratifying, agreeable, pleasurable ≠ unpleasant **2** = likable or likeable, engaging, charming, delightful, agreeable ≠ disagreeable

pleasure 1 = happiness, delight, satisfaction, enjoyment, bliss, gratification, gladness, delectation ≠ displeasure **2** = amusement, joy ≠ duty

pledge NOUN 1 = promise, vow, assurance, word, undertaking, warrant, oath, covenant **2** = guarantee, security, deposit, bail, collateral, pawn, surety ● **VERB** = promise, vow, swear, contract, engage, give your word, give your oath

plentiful = abundant, liberal, generous, lavish, ample, overflowing, copious, bountiful ≠ scarce

plenty 1 = abundance, wealth,

prosperity, fertility, profusion, affluence, plenitude, fruitfulness **2** *usually with* **of** = lots of (*informal*), enough, a great deal of, masses of, piles of (*informal*), stacks of, heaps of (*informal*), an abundance of

plight = difficulty, condition, state, situation, trouble, predicament

plot¹ NOUN **1** = plan, scheme, intrigue, conspiracy, cabal, stratagem, machination **2** = story, action, subject, theme, outline, scenario, narrative, story line
● VERB **1** = plan, scheme, conspire, intrigue, manoeuvre, contrive, collude, machinate **2** = devise, design, lay, conceive, hatch, contrive, concoct, cook up (*informal*) **3** = chart, mark, map, locate, calculate, outline

plot² = patch, lot, area, ground, parcel, tract, allotment

plough VERB = turn over, dig, till, cultivate
● PHRASES **plough through something** = forge, cut, drive, press, push, plunge, wade

ploy = tactic, move, trick, device, scheme, manoeuvre, dodge, ruse

pluck VERB **1** = pull out *or* off, pick, draw, collect, gather, harvest **2** = tug, catch, snatch, clutch, jerk, yank, tweak, pull at **3** = strum, pick, finger, twang
● NOUN = courage, nerve, bottle

(*Brit. slang*), guts (*informal*), grit, bravery, backbone, boldness

plug NOUN **1** = stopper, cork, bung, spigot **2** (*Informal*) = mention, advertisement, advert (*Brit. informal*), push, publicity, hype
● VERB **1** = seal, close, stop, fill, block, stuff, pack, cork **2** (*Informal*) = mention, push, promote, publicize, advertise, build up, hype
● PHRASES **plug away** (*Informal*) = slog away, labour, toil away, grind away (*informal*), peg away, plod away

plum = choice, prize, first-class

plumb VERB = delve into, explore, probe, go into, penetrate, gauge, unravel, fathom
● ADVERB = exactly, precisely, bang, slap, spot-on (*Brit. informal*)

plummet 1 = drop, fall, crash, nose-dive, descend rapidly **2** = plunge, fall, drop, crash, tumble, nose-dive, descend rapidly

plump = chubby, fat, stout, round, tubby, dumpy, roly-poly, rotund ≠ scrawny

plunder VERB **1** = loot, strip, sack, rob, raid, rifle, ransack, pillage **2** = steal, rob, take, nick (*informal*), pinch, embezzle, pilfer, thieve
● NOUN **1** = pillage **2** = loot, spoils, booty, swag (*slang*), ill-gotten gains

plunge VERB **1** = descend, fall,

drop, crash, pitch, sink, dive, tumble **2** = <u>hurtle</u>, charge, career, jump, tear, rush, drive, dash **3** = <u>submerge</u>, dip **4** = <u>throw</u>, cast, pitch, propel **5** = <u>fall steeply</u>, drop, crash (*informal*), slump, plummet, take a nosedive (*informal*)

● **NOUN 1** = <u>dive</u>, jump, duck, descent **2** = <u>fall</u>, crash (*informal*), slump, drop, tumble

plus PREPOSITION = <u>and</u>, with, added to, coupled with

● **NOUN** (*Informal*) = <u>advantage</u>, benefit, asset, gain, extra, bonus, good point

● **ADJECTIVE** = <u>additional</u>, added, extra, supplementary, add-on

> ### Word Power
>
> **plus** – When you have a sentence with more than one subject linked by *and*, this makes the subject plural and means it should take a plural verb: *the doctor and all the nurses were* (not *was*) *waiting for the patient*. However, where the subjects are linked by *plus*, *together with*, or *along with*, the number of the verb remains just as it would have been if the extra subjects had not been mentioned. Therefore you would say *the doctor, together with all the nurses, was* (not *were*) *waiting for the patient*.

plush = <u>luxurious</u>, luxury, lavish,

rich, sumptuous, opulent, de luxe

ply = <u>work at</u>, follow, exercise, pursue, carry on, practise

pocket NOUN = <u>pouch</u>, bag, sack, compartment, receptacle

● **ADJECTIVE** = <u>small</u>, compact, miniature, portable, little

● **VERB** = <u>steal</u>, take, lift (*informal*), appropriate, pilfer, purloin, filch

pod = <u>shell</u>, case, hull, husk, shuck

podium = <u>platform</u>, stand, stage, rostrum, dais

poem = <u>verse</u>, song, lyric, rhyme, sonnet, ode, verse composition

poet = <u>bard</u>, rhymer, lyricist, lyric poet, versifier, elegist

> **WORD POWER SUPPLEMENT poets**

poetic 1 = <u>figurative</u>, creative, lyric, symbolic, lyrical **2** = <u>lyrical</u>, lyric, elegiac, metrical

poetry = <u>verse</u>, poems, rhyme, rhyming, verse composition

poignant = <u>moving</u>, touching, sad, bitter, intense, painful, distressing, pathetic

point NOUN **1** = <u>essence</u>, meaning, subject, question, heart, import, drift, thrust **2** = <u>purpose</u>, aim, object, end, reason, goal, intention, objective **3** = <u>aspect</u>, detail, feature, quality, particular, respect, item, characteristic **4** = <u>place</u>, area, position, site, spot, location, locality, locale **5** = <u>moment</u>, time, stage, period, phase, instant, juncture, moment in time 6 = **stage**, level, position, condition, degree, pitch, circumstance, extent 7 = **end**, tip, sharp end, top, spur, spike, apex, prong 8 = **score**, tally, mark 9 = **pinpoint**, mark, spot, dot, fleck

• VERB 1 = **aim**, level, train, direct 2 = **indicate**, show, signal, point to, gesture towards 3 = **face**, look, direct

• PHRASES **point at** or **to something** or **someone** = **indicate**, point out, specify, designate, gesture towards

pointed 1 = **sharp**, edged, acute, barbed 2 = **cutting**, telling, biting, sharp, keen, acute, penetrating, pertinent

pointer 1 = **hint**, tip, suggestion, recommendation, caution, direct piece of information, piece of advice 2 = **indicator**, hand, guide, needle, arrow

pointless = **senseless**, meaningless, futile, fruitless, stupid, silly, useless, absurd ≠ worthwhile

poised 1 = **ready**, waiting, prepared, standing by, all set 2 = **composed**, calm, together (informal), collected, dignified, self-confident, self-possessed ≠ agitated

poison NOUN = **toxin**, venom, bane (archaic)

• VERB 1 = **murder**, kill, give someone poison, administer poison to 2 = **contaminate**, foul, infect, spoil, pollute, blight, taint, befoul 3 = **corrupt**, colour, undermine, bias, sour, pervert, warp, taint

poisonous 1 = **toxic**, fatal, deadly, lethal, mortal, virulent, noxious, venomous 2 = **evil**, malicious, corrupting, pernicious, baleful

poke VERB 1 = **jab**, push, stick, dig, stab, thrust, shove, nudge 2 = **protrude**, stick, thrust, jut
• NOUN = **jab**, dig, thrust, nudge, prod

pole = **rod**, post, support, staff, bar, stick, stake, paling

police NOUN = **the law** (informal), police force, constabulary, fuzz (slang), boys in blue (informal), the Old Bill (slang), rozzers (slang)

• VERB = **control**, patrol, guard, watch, protect, regulate

policy 1 = **procedure**, plan, action, practice, scheme, code, custom 2 = **line**, rules, approach

polish NOUN 1 = **varnish**, wax, glaze, lacquer, japan 2 = **sheen**, finish, glaze, gloss, brightness, lustre 3 = **style**, class (informal), finish, breeding, grace, elegance, refinement, finesse

• VERB 1 = **shine**, wax, smooth, rub, buff, brighten, burnish

2 *often with* **up** = perfect, improve, enhance, refine, finish, brush up, touch up

polished 1 = elegant, sophisticated, refined, polite, cultivated, suave, well-bred ≠ unsophisticated **2** = accomplished, professional, masterly, fine, expert, skilful, adept, superlative ≠ amateurish **3** = shining, bright, smooth, gleaming, glossy, burnished ≠ dull

polite 1 = mannerly, civil, courteous, gracious, respectful, well-behaved, complaisant, well-mannered ≠ rude **2** = refined, cultured, civilized, decorous, sophisticated, elegant, genteel, well-bred ≠ uncultured

politic = wise, diplomatic, sensible, prudent, advisable, expedient, judicious

political = governmental, government, state, parliamentary, constitutional, administrative, legislative, ministerial

politician = statesman *or* stateswoman, representative, senator (*U.S.*), congressman (*U.S.*), Member of Parliament, legislator, public servant, congresswoman (*U.S.*)

politics 1 = affairs of state, government, public affairs, civics **2** = political beliefs, party politics,

political allegiances, political leanings, political sympathies **3** = political science, statesmanship, civics, statecraft

poll NOUN **1** = survey, figures, count, sampling, returns, ballot, tally, census **2** = election, vote, voting, referendum, ballot, plebiscite

● VERB **1** = question, interview, survey, sample, ballot, canvass **2** = gain, return, record, register, tally

pollute 1 = contaminate, dirty, poison, soil, foul, infect, spoil, stain ≠ decontaminate **2** = defile, corrupt, sully, deprave, debase, profane, desecrate, dishonour ≠ honour

pollution 1 = contamination, dirtying, corruption, taint, foulness, defilement, uncleanness **2** = waste, poisons, dirt, impurities

pond = pool, tarn, small lake, fish pond, duck pond, millpond

ponder = think about, consider, reflect on, contemplate, deliberate about, muse on, brood on, meditate on

pool¹ 1 = swimming pool, lido, swimming bath(s) (*Brit.*), bathing pool (*archaic*) **2** = pond, lake, mere, tarn **3** = puddle, drop, patch

pool² NOUN 1 = <u>supply</u>, reserve, fall-back 2 = <u>kitty</u>, bank, fund, stock, store, pot, jackpot, stockpile
● VERB = <u>combine</u>, share, merge, put together, amalgamate, lump together, join forces on

poor 1 = <u>impoverished</u>, broke (*informal*), hard up (*informal*), short, needy, penniless, destitute, poverty-stricken ≠ rich 2 = <u>unfortunate</u>, unlucky, hapless, pitiful, luckless, wretched, ill-starred, pitiable ≠ fortunate 3 = <u>inferior</u>, unsatisfactory, mediocre, second-rate, rotten (*informal*), low-grade, below par, substandard, half-pie (*N.Z. informal*), bodger or bodgie (*Austral. slang*) ≠ excellent 4 = <u>meagre</u>, inadequate, insufficient, lacking, incomplete, scant, deficient, skimpy ≠ ample

poorly ADVERB = <u>badly</u>, incompetently, inadequately, unsuccessfully, insufficiently, unsatisfactorily, inexpertly ≠ well
● ADJECTIVE (*Informal*) = <u>ill</u>, sick, unwell, crook (*Austral. & N.Z. informal*), seedy (*informal*), below par, off colour, under the weather (*informal*), feeling rotten (*informal*) ≠ healthy

pop NOUN = <u>bang</u>, report, crack, noise, burst, explosion
● VERB 1 = <u>burst</u>, crack, snap, bang, explode, go off (with a bang) 2 = <u>put</u>, insert, push, stick, slip, thrust, tuck, shove

pope = <u>Holy Father</u>, pontiff, His Holiness, Bishop of Rome, Vicar of Christ

popular 1 = <u>well-liked</u>, liked, in, accepted, favourite, approved, in favour, fashionable ≠ unpopular 2 = <u>common</u>, general, prevailing, current, conventional, universal, prevalent ≠ rare

popularity 1 = <u>favour</u>, esteem, acclaim, regard, approval, vogue 2 = <u>currency</u>, acceptance, circulation, vogue, prevalence

populate 1 = <u>inhabit</u>, people, live in, occupy, reside in, dwell in (*formal*) 2 = <u>settle</u>, occupy, pioneer, colonize

population = <u>inhabitants</u>, people, community, society, residents, natives, folk, occupants

pore = <u>opening</u>, hole, outlet, orifice

pornography = <u>obscenity</u>, porn (*informal*), dirt, filth, indecency, smut

port = <u>harbour</u>, haven, anchorage, seaport

portable = <u>light</u>, compact, convenient, handy, manageable, movable, easily carried

porter¹ (*Chiefly Brit.*) = <u>doorman</u>,

caretaker, janitor, concierge, gatekeeper

porter² 1 = <u>baggage attendant</u>, carrier, bearer, baggage-carrier

portion 1 = <u>part</u>, bit, piece, section, scrap, segment, fragment, chunk 2 = <u>helping</u>, serving, piece, plateful 3 = <u>share</u>, allowance, lot, measure, quantity, quota, ration, allocation

portrait 1 = <u>picture</u>, painting, image, photograph, representation, likeness 2 = <u>description</u>, profile, portrayal, depiction, characterization, thumbnail sketch

portray 1 = <u>play</u>, take the role of, act the part of, represent, personate (*rare*) 2 = <u>describe</u>, present, depict, evoke, delineate, put in words 3 = <u>represent</u>, draw, paint, illustrate, sketch, figure, picture, depict 4 = <u>characterize</u>, represent, depict

portrayal 1 = <u>performance</u>, interpretation, characterization 2 = <u>depiction</u>, picture, representation, sketch, rendering 3 = <u>description</u>, account, representation 4 = <u>characterization</u>, representation, depiction

pose VERB 1 = <u>position yourself</u>, sit, model, arrange yourself 2 = <u>put on airs</u>, posture, show off (*informal*)

● NOUN 1 = <u>posture</u>, position, bearing, attitude, stance 2 = <u>act</u>, façade, air, front, posturing, pretence, mannerism, affectation

● PHRASES **pose as something** or **someone** = <u>impersonate</u>, pretend to be, profess to be, masquerade as, pass yourself off as

posh (*Informal, chiefly Brit.*) 1 = <u>smart</u>, grand, stylish, luxurious, classy (*slang*), swish (*informal, chiefly Brit.*), up-market, swanky (*informal*) 2 = <u>upper-class</u>, high-class

position NOUN 1 = <u>location</u>, place, point, area, post, situation, station, spot 2 = <u>posture</u>, attitude, arrangement, pose, stance 3 = <u>status</u>, place, standing, footing, station, rank, reputation, importance 4 = <u>job</u>, place, post, opening, office, role, situation, duty 5 = <u>place</u>, standing, rank, status 6 = <u>attitude</u>, view, perspective, point of view, opinion, belief, stance, outlook

● VERB = <u>place</u>, put, set, stand, arrange, locate, lay out

positive 1 = <u>beneficial</u>, useful, practical, helpful, progressive, productive, worthwhile, constructive ≠ harmful 2 = <u>certain</u>, sure, convinced, confident, satisfied, assured, free

from doubt ≠ uncertain
3 = <u>definite</u>, real, clear, firm,
certain, express, absolute,
decisive ≠ inconclusive
4 (*Informal*) = <u>absolute</u>, complete,
perfect, right (*Brit. informal*), real,
total, sheer, utter

positively 1 = <u>definitely</u>, surely,
firmly, certainly, absolutely,
emphatically, unquestionably,
categorically **2** = <u>really</u>,
completely, simply, plain
(*informal*), absolutely, thoroughly,
utterly, downright

possess 1 = <u>own</u>, have, hold, be
in possession of, be the owner of,
have in your possession **2** = <u>be
endowed with</u>, have, enjoy,
benefit from, be possessed of, be
gifted with **3** = <u>seize</u>, hold,
control, dominate, occupy, take
someone over, have power over,
have mastery over

possession NOUN = <u>ownership</u>,
control, custody, hold, hands,
tenure
  ● PLURAL NOUN = <u>property</u>, things,
effects, estate, assets, belongings,
chattels

possibility 1 = <u>feasibility</u>,
likelihood, potentiality,
practicability, workableness
2 = <u>likelihood</u>, chance, risk, odds,
prospect, liability, probability
3 *often plural* = <u>potential</u>,
promise, prospects, talent,
capabilities, potentiality

possible 1 = <u>feasible</u>, viable,
workable, achievable,
practicable, attainable, doable,
realizable ≠ unfeasible **2** = <u>likely</u>,
potential, anticipated, probable,
odds-on, on the cards
≠ improbable **3** = <u>conceivable</u>,
likely, credible, plausible,
hypothetical, imaginable,
believable, thinkable
≠ inconceivable **4** = <u>aspiring</u>,
would-be, promising, hopeful,
prospective, wannabe (*informal*)

Word Power

possible – Although it is very
common to talk about
something's being *very possible*
or *more possible*, many people
object to such uses, claiming
that *possible* describes an
absolute state, and therefore
something can only be either
possible or *not possible*. If you
want to refer to different
degrees of probability, a word
such as *likely* or *easy* may be
more appropriate than *possible*,
for example *it is very likely that
he will resign* (not *very possible*).

possibly = <u>perhaps</u>, maybe,
perchance (*archaic*)

post[1] NOUN **1** = <u>mail</u>, collection,
delivery, postal service, snail mail
(*informal*) **2** = <u>correspondence</u>,
letters, cards, mail
  ● VERB = <u>send (off)</u>, forward, mail,

get off, transmit, dispatch, consign

● PHRASES **keep someone posted** = notify, brief, advise, inform, report to, keep someone informed, keep someone up to date, apprise

post² NOUN 1 = job, place, office, position, situation, employment, appointment, assignment **2** = position, place, base, beat, station

● VERB = station, assign, put, place, position, situate, put on duty

post³ NOUN = support, stake, pole, column, shaft, upright, pillar, picket

● VERB = put something up, display, affix, pin something up

poster = notice, bill, announcement, advertisement, sticker, placard, public notice

postpone = put off, delay, suspend, adjourn, shelve, defer, put back, put on the back burner (informal) ≠ go ahead with

posture NOUN = bearing, set, attitude, stance, carriage, disposition

● VERB = show off (informal), pose, affect, put on airs

pot = container, bowl, pan, vessel, basin, cauldron, skillet

potent 1 = powerful, commanding, dynamic, dominant, influential, authoritative **2** = strong, powerful, mighty, vigorous, forceful ≠ weak

potential ADJECTIVE 1 = possible, future, likely, promising, probable **2** = hidden, possible, inherent, dormant, latent

● NOUN = ability, possibilities, capacity, capability, aptitude, wherewithal, potentiality

potter usually with **around** or **about** = mess about, tinker, dabble, footle (informal)

pottery = ceramics, terracotta, crockery, earthenware, stoneware

pounce = attack, strike, jump, leap, swoop

pound¹ = enclosure, yard, pen, compound, kennels

pound² **1** sometimes with **on** = beat, strike, hammer, batter, thrash, thump, clobber (slang), pummel **2** = crush, powder, pulverize **3** = pulsate, beat, pulse, throb, palpitate **4** = stomp, tramp, march, thunder (informal)

pour 1 = let flow, spill, splash, dribble, drizzle, slop (informal), slosh (informal), decant **2** = flow, stream, run, course, rush, emit, cascade, gush **3** = rain, pelt (down), teem, bucket down (informal) **4** = stream, crowd, flood, swarm, gush, throng, teem

Word Power

pour – The spelling of *pour* (as in *she poured cream on her strudel*) should be carefully distinguished from that of *pore over* or *through* (as in *she pored over the manuscript*).

pout VERB = <u>sulk</u>, glower, look petulant, pull a long face
● NOUN = <u>sullen look</u>, glower, long face

poverty 1 = <u>pennilessness</u>, want, need, hardship, insolvency, privation, penury, destitution ≠ wealth 2 = <u>scarcity</u>, lack, absence, want, deficit, shortage, deficiency, inadequacy ≠ abundance

powder NOUN = <u>dust</u>, talc, fine grains, loose particles
● VERB = <u>dust</u>, cover, scatter, sprinkle, strew, dredge

power 1 = <u>control</u>, authority, influence, command, dominance, domination, mastery, dominion, mana (N.Z.) 2 = <u>ability</u>, capacity, faculty, property, potential, capability, competence, competency ≠ inability 3 = <u>authority</u>, right, licence, privilege, warrant, prerogative, authorization 4 = <u>strength</u>, might, energy, muscle, vigour, potency, brawn ≠ weakness 5 = <u>forcefulness</u>, force, strength, punch (*informal*), intensity, potency, eloquence, persuasiveness

powerful 1 = <u>influential</u>, dominant, controlling, commanding, prevailing, authoritative ≠ powerless 2 = <u>strong</u>, strapping, mighty, vigorous, potent, energetic, sturdy ≠ weak 3 = <u>persuasive</u>, convincing, telling, moving, striking, storming, dramatic, impressive

powerless 1 = <u>defenceless</u>, vulnerable, dependent, subject, tied, ineffective, unarmed 2 = <u>weak</u>, disabled, helpless, incapable, frail, feeble, debilitated, impotent ≠ strong

practical 1 = <u>functional</u>, realistic, pragmatic ≠ impractical 2 = <u>empirical</u>, real, applied, actual, hands-on, in the field, experimental, factual ≠ theoretical 3 = <u>sensible</u>, ordinary, realistic, down-to-earth, matter-of-fact, businesslike, hard-headed ≠ impractical 4 = <u>feasible</u>, possible, viable, workable, practicable, doable ≠ impractical 5 = <u>useful</u>, ordinary, appropriate, sensible, everyday, functional, utilitarian, serviceable 6 = <u>skilled</u>, experienced, efficient, accomplished, proficient ≠ inexperienced

Word Power

practical – A distinction is usually made between *practical* and *practicable*. Practical refers to a person, idea, project, etc., as being more concerned with or relevant to practice than theory: *he is a very practical person; the idea had no practical application*. Practicable refers to a project or idea as being capable of being done or put into effect: *the plan was expensive, yet practicable*.

practically 1 = <u>almost</u>, nearly, essentially, virtually, basically, fundamentally, all but, just about **2** = <u>sensibly</u>, reasonably, matter-of-factly, realistically, rationally, pragmatically

practice 1 = <u>custom</u>, way, system, rule, method, tradition, habit, routine, tikanga (*N.Z.*) **2** = <u>training</u>, study, exercise, preparation, drill, rehearsal, repetition **3** = <u>profession</u>, work, business, career, occupation, pursuit, vocation **4** = <u>business</u>, company, office, firm, enterprise, partnership, outfit (*informal*) **5** = <u>use</u>, experience, action, operation, application, enactment

practise 1 = <u>rehearse</u>, study, prepare, perfect, repeat, go through, go over, refine **2** = <u>do</u>, train, exercise, drill **3** = <u>carry out</u>, follow, apply, perform, observe, engage in **4** = <u>work at</u>, pursue, carry on

practised = <u>skilled</u>, trained, experienced, seasoned, able, expert, accomplished, proficient ≠ inexperienced

pragmatic = <u>practical</u>, sensible, realistic, down-to-earth, utilitarian, businesslike, hard-headed ≠ idealistic

praise VERB **1** = <u>acclaim</u>, approve of, honour, cheer, admire, applaud, compliment, congratulate ≠ criticize **2** = <u>give thanks to</u>, bless, worship, adore, glorify, exalt

● NOUN **1** = <u>approval</u>, acclaim, tribute, compliment, congratulations, eulogy, commendation, approbation ≠ criticism **2** = <u>thanks</u>, glory, worship, homage, adoration

pray 1 = <u>say your prayers</u>, offer a prayer, recite the rosary **2** = <u>beg</u>, ask, plead, petition, request, solicit, implore, beseech

prayer 1 = <u>supplication</u>, devotion **2** = <u>orison</u>, litany, invocation, intercession **3** = <u>plea</u>, appeal, request, petition, entreaty, supplication

preach 1 *often with* **to** = <u>deliver a sermon</u>, address, evangelize, preach a sermon **2** = <u>urge</u>, teach, champion, recommend, advise, counsel, advocate, exhort

preacher = <u>clergyman</u>, minister, parson, missionary, evangelist

precarious 1 = <u>insecure</u>, dangerous, tricky, risky, dodgy (*Brit., Austral., & N.Z. informal*), unsure, hazardous, shaky ≠ secure 2 = <u>dangerous</u>, shaky, insecure, unsafe, unreliable ≠ stable

precaution 1 = <u>safeguard</u>, insurance, protection, provision, safety measure 2 = <u>forethought</u>, care, caution, prudence, providence, wariness

precede 1 = <u>go before</u>, antedate 2 = <u>go ahead of</u>, lead, head, go before 3 = <u>preface</u>, introduce, go before

precedent = <u>instance</u>, example, standard, model, pattern, prototype, paradigm, antecedent

precinct = <u>area</u>, quarter, section, sector, district, zone

precious 1 = <u>valuable</u>, expensive, fine, prized, dear, costly, invaluable, priceless ≠ worthless 2 = <u>loved</u>, prized, dear, treasured, darling, beloved, adored, cherished 3 = <u>affected</u>, artificial, twee (*Brit. informal*), overrefined, overnice

precipitate VERB 1 = <u>quicken</u>,

trigger, accelerate, advance, hurry, speed up, bring on, hasten 2 = <u>throw</u>, launch, cast, hurl, fling, let fly
● ADJECTIVE 1 = <u>hasty</u>, rash, reckless, impulsive, precipitous, impetuous, heedless 2 = <u>sudden</u>, quick, brief, rushing, rapid, unexpected, swift, abrupt

precise 1 = <u>exact</u>, specific, particular, express, correct, absolute, accurate, explicit ≠ vague 2 = <u>strict</u>, particular, exact, formal, careful, stiff, rigid, meticulous ≠ inexact

precisely 1 = <u>exactly</u>, squarely, correctly, absolutely, strictly, accurately, plumb (*informal*), square on 2 = <u>just so</u>, yes, absolutely, exactly, quite so, you bet (*informal*), without a doubt, indubitably 3 = <u>just</u>, entirely, absolutely, altogether, exactly, in all respects 4 = <u>word for word</u>, literally, exactly, to the letter

precision = <u>exactness</u>, care, accuracy, particularity, meticulousness, preciseness

predecessor 1 = <u>previous job holder</u>, precursor, forerunner, antecedent 2 = <u>ancestor</u>, forebear, antecedent, forefather, tupuna *or* tipuna (*N.Z.*)

predicament = <u>fix</u> (*informal*), situation, spot (*informal*), hole (*slang*), mess, jam (*informal*), dilemma, pinch

predict = <u>foretell</u>, forecast, divine, prophesy, augur, portend

predictable = <u>likely</u>, expected, sure, certain, anticipated, reliable, foreseeable ≠ unpredictable

prediction = <u>prophecy</u>, forecast, prognosis, divination, prognostication, augury

predominantly = <u>mainly</u>, largely, chiefly, mostly, generally, principally, primarily, for the most part

prefer 1 = <u>like better</u>, favour, go for, pick, fancy, opt for, incline towards, be partial to 2 = <u>choose</u>, opt for, pick, desire, would rather, would sooner, incline towards

---

Word Power

prefer – Normally, *to* (not *than*) is used after *prefer* and *preferable*. Therefore, you would say *I prefer skating to skiing*, and *a small income is preferable to no income at all*. However, when expressing a preference between two activities stated as infinitive verbs, for example *to skate* and *to ski*, use *than*, as in *I prefer to skate than to ski*.

---

preferable = <u>better</u>, best, chosen, preferred, recommended, favoured, superior, more suitable ≠ undesirable

preferably = <u>ideally</u>, if possible, rather, sooner, by choice, in *or* for preference

preference 1 = <u>liking</u>, wish, taste, desire, leaning, bent, bias, inclination 2 = <u>first choice</u>, choice, favourite, pick, option, selection 3 = <u>priority</u>, first place, precedence, favouritism, favoured treatment

pregnant 1 = <u>expectant</u>, expecting (*informal*), with child, in the club (*Brit. slang*), big or heavy with child 2 = <u>meaningful</u>, pointed, charged, significant, telling, loaded, expressive, eloquent

prejudice NOUN
1 = <u>discrimination</u>, injustice, intolerance, bigotry, unfairness, chauvinism, narrow-mindedness
2 = <u>bias</u>, preconception, partiality, preconceived notion, prejudgment
● VERB 1 = <u>bias</u>, influence, colour, poison, distort, slant, predispose
2 = <u>harm</u>, damage, hurt, injure, mar, undermine, spoil, impair, crool or cruel (*Austral. slang*)

prejudiced = <u>biased</u>, influenced, unfair, one-sided, bigoted, intolerant, opinionated, narrow-minded ≠ unbiased

preliminary ADJECTIVE 1 = <u>first</u>, opening, trial, initial, test, pilot, prior, introductory 2 = <u>qualifying</u>, eliminating

● NOUN = <u>introduction</u>, opening, beginning, start, prelude, preface, overture, preamble

prelude 1 = <u>introduction</u>, beginning, start 2 = <u>overture</u>, opening, introduction, introductory movement

premature 1 = <u>early</u>, untimely, before time, unseasonable 2 = <u>hasty</u>, rash, too soon, untimely, ill-timed, overhasty

premier NOUN = <u>head of government</u>, prime minister, chancellor, chief minister, P.M.

● ADJECTIVE = <u>chief</u>, leading, first, highest, head, main, prime, primary

premiere = <u>first night</u>, opening, debut

premise = <u>assumption</u>, proposition, argument, hypothesis, assertion, supposition, presupposition, postulation

premises = <u>building(s)</u>, place, office, property, site, establishment

premium NOUN 1 = <u>fee</u>, charge, payment, instalment 2 = <u>surcharge</u>, extra charge, additional fee or charge 3 = <u>bonus</u>, reward, prize, perk (Brit. informal), bounty, perquisite

● PHRASES **at a premium** = <u>in great demand</u>, rare, scarce, in

short supply, hard to come by

preoccupation 1 = <u>obsession</u>, fixation, bee in your bonnet 2 = <u>absorption</u>, abstraction, daydreaming, immersion, reverie, absent-mindedness, engrossment, woolgathering

preoccupied 1 = <u>absorbed</u>, lost, wrapped up, immersed, engrossed, rapt 2 = <u>lost in thought</u>, distracted, oblivious, absent-minded

preparation 1 = <u>groundwork</u>, preparing, getting ready 2 usually plural = <u>arrangement</u>, plan, measure, provision 3 = <u>mixture</u>, medicine, compound, concoction

prepare 1 = <u>make or get ready</u>, arrange, jack up (N.Z. informal) 2 = <u>train</u>, guide, prime, direct, brief, discipline, put someone in the picture 3 = <u>make</u>, cook, put together, get, produce, assemble, muster, concoct 4 = <u>get ready</u> 5 = <u>practise</u>, get ready, train, exercise, warm up, get into shape

prepared 1 = <u>willing</u>, inclined, disposed 2 = <u>ready</u>, set 3 = <u>fit</u>, primed, in order, arranged, in readiness

prescribe 1 = <u>specify</u>, order, direct, stipulate, write a prescription for 2 = <u>ordain</u>, set, order, rule, recommend, dictate, lay down, decree

prescription 1 = <u>instruction</u>,

direction, formula, script
(*informal*), recipe 2 = medicine,
drug, treatment, preparation,
cure, mixture, dose, remedy

presence NOUN 1 = being,
existence, residence, attendance,
showing up, occupancy,
inhabitance 2 = personality,
bearing, appearance, aspect, air,
carriage, aura, poise

● PHRASES **presence of mind**
= level-headedness, assurance,
composure, poise, cool (*slang*),
wits, countenance, coolness

present[1] ADJECTIVE 1 = current,
existing, immediate,
contemporary, present-day,
existent 2 = here, there, near,
ready, nearby, at hand ≠ absent
3 = in existence, existing, existent,
extant

● PHRASES **the present** = now,
today, the time being, here and
now, the present moment

present[2] NOUN = gift, offering,
grant, donation, hand-out,
endowment, boon, gratuity,
bonsela (*S. African*), koha (*N.Z.*)

● VERB 1 = give, award, hand over,
grant, hand out, confer, bestow
2 = put on, stage, perform, give,
show, render 3 = launch, display,
parade, exhibit, unveil
4 = introduce, make known,
acquaint someone with

presentation 1 = giving, award,
offering, donation, bestowal,

conferral 2 = appearance, look,
display, packaging, arrangement,
layout 3 = performance,
production, show

presently 1 = at present,
currently, now, today, these days,
nowadays, at the present time, in
this day and age 2 = soon,
shortly, directly, before long,
momentarily (*U.S. & Canad.*), by
and by, in a jiffy (*informal*)

preservation 1 = upholding,
support, maintenance
2 = protection, safety,
maintenance, conservation,
salvation, safeguarding,
safekeeping

preserve VERB 1 = maintain,
keep, continue, sustain, keep up,
prolong, uphold, conserve ≠ end
2 = protect, keep, save, maintain,
defend, shelter, shield, care for
≠ attack

● NOUN = area, department, field,
territory, province, arena, sphere

preside = officiate, chair,
moderate, be chairperson

president ▸ WORD POWER
SUPPLEMENT **presidents**

press 1 = push (down), depress,
lean on, press down, force down
2 = push, squeeze, jam, thrust,
ram, wedge, shove 3 = hug,
squeeze, embrace, clasp, crush,
hold close, fold in your arms
4 = urge, beg, petition, exhort,

implore, pressurize, entreat
5 = <u>plead</u>, present, lodge, submit, tender, advance insistently
6 = <u>steam</u>, iron, smooth, flatten
7 = <u>compress</u>, grind, reduce, mill, crush, pound, squeeze, tread
8 = <u>crowd</u>, push, gather, surge, flock, herd, swarm, seethe

pressing = <u>urgent</u>, serious, vital, crucial, imperative, important, high-priority, importunate ≠ unimportant

pressure 1 = <u>force</u>, crushing, squeezing, compressing, weight, compression **2** = <u>power</u>, influence, force, constraint, sway, compulsion, coercion **3** = <u>stress</u>, demands, strain, heat, load, burden, urgency, hassle (*informal*), uphill (*S. African*)

prestige = <u>status</u>, standing, credit, reputation, honour, importance, fame, distinction, mana (*N.Z.*)

prestigious = <u>celebrated</u>, respected, prominent, great, important, esteemed, notable, renowned ≠ unknown

presumably = <u>it would seem</u>, probably, apparently, seemingly, on the face of it, in all probability, in all likelihood

presume 1 = <u>believe</u>, think, suppose, assume, guess (*informal, chiefly U.S. & Canad.*), take for granted, infer, conjecture

2 = <u>dare</u>, venture, go so far as, take the liberty, make so bold as

pretend 1 = <u>feign</u>, affect, assume, allege, fake, simulate, profess, sham **2** = <u>make believe</u>, suppose, imagine, act, make up

pretty ADJECTIVE = <u>attractive</u>, beautiful, lovely, charming, fair, good-looking, bonny, comely ≠ plain

● **ADVERB** (*Informal*) = <u>fairly</u>, rather, quite, kind of (*informal*), somewhat, moderately, reasonably

prevail 1 = <u>win</u>, succeed, triumph, overcome, overrule, be victorious **2** = <u>be widespread</u>, abound, predominate, be current, be prevalent, exist generally

prevailing 1 = <u>widespread</u>, general, established, popular, common, current, usual, ordinary **2** = <u>predominating</u>, ruling, main, existing, principal

prevalent = <u>common</u>, established, popular, general, current, usual, widespread, universal ≠ rare

prevent = <u>stop</u>, avoid, frustrate, hamper, foil, inhibit, avert, thwart ≠ help

prevention = <u>elimination</u>, safeguard, precaution, thwarting, avoidance, deterrence

preview = <u>sample</u>, sneak preview, trailer, taster, foretaste, advance showing

previous 1 = <u>earlier</u>, former, past, prior, preceding, erstwhile ≠ later **2** = <u>preceding</u>, past, prior, foregoing

previously = <u>before</u>, earlier, once, in the past, formerly, hitherto, beforehand

prey 1 = <u>quarry</u>, game, kill **2** = <u>victim</u>, target, mug (Brit. slang), dupe, fall guy (informal)
 ➤ **birds of prey**

price NOUN **1** = <u>cost</u>, value, rate, charge, figure, worth, damage (informal), amount **2** = <u>consequences</u>, penalty, cost, result, toll, forfeit
 ● VERB = <u>evaluate</u>, value, estimate, rate, cost, assess

priceless = <u>valuable</u>, expensive, precious, invaluable, dear, costly ≠ worthless

prick VERB = <u>pierce</u>, stab, puncture, punch, lance, jab, perforate
 ● NOUN = <u>puncture</u>, hole, wound, perforation, pinhole

prickly 1 = <u>spiny</u>, barbed, thorny,

Birds of prey

accipiter	kestrel
Australian goshawk or chicken hawk	kite
	lammergeier, lammergeyer,
bald eagle	bearded vulture, or (archaic)
barn owl	ossifrage
buzzard	lanner
caracara	merlin
condor	mopoke or (N.Z.) ruru
duck hawk	osprey, fish eagle, or (archaic)
eagle	ossifrage
eagle-hawk or wedge-tailed eagle	owl
falcon or (N.Z.) bush-hawk or	peregrine falcon
karearea	saker
falconet	screech owl
golden eagle	sea eagle, erne, or ern
goshawk	secretary bird
gyrfalcon or gerfalcon	snowy owl
harrier	sparrowhawk
hawk	tawny owl
hobby	turkey buzzard or vulture
honey buzzard	vulture

bristly 2 = <u>itchy</u>, sharp, smarting, stinging, crawling, tingling, scratchy

pride 1 = <u>satisfaction</u>, achievement, fulfilment, delight, content, pleasure, joy, gratification 2 = <u>self-respect</u>, honour, ego, dignity, self-esteem, self-image, self-worth 3 = <u>conceit</u>, vanity, arrogance, pretension, hubris, self-importance, egotism, self-love ≠ humility

priest = <u>clergyman</u>, minister, father, divine, vicar, pastor, cleric, curate

primarily 1 = <u>chiefly</u>, largely, generally, mainly, essentially, mostly, principally, fundamentally 2 = <u>at first</u>, originally, initially, in the first place, in the beginning, first and foremost, at or from the start

primary = <u>chief</u>, main, first, highest, greatest, prime, principal, cardinal ≠ subordinate

prime ADJECTIVE 1 = <u>main</u>, leading, chief, central, major, key, primary, supreme 2 = <u>best</u>, top, select, highest, quality, choice, excellent, first-class
● NOUN = <u>peak</u>, flower, bloom, height, heyday, zenith
● VERB 1 = <u>inform</u>, tell, train, coach, brief, fill in (informal), notify, clue in (informal) 2 = <u>prepare</u>, set up, load, equip, get ready, make

ready

prime minister ▸ WORD POWER SUPPLEMENT prime ministers

primitive 1 = <u>early</u>, first, earliest, original, primary, elementary, primordial, primeval ≠ modern 2 = <u>crude</u>, simple, rough, rudimentary, unrefined ≠ elaborate

prince = <u>ruler</u>, lord, monarch, sovereign, crown prince, liege, prince regent, crowned head

princely 1 = <u>substantial</u>, considerable, large, huge, massive, enormous, sizable or sizeable 2 = <u>regal</u>, royal, imperial, noble, sovereign, majestic

princess = <u>ruler</u>, lady, monarch, sovereign, liege, crowned head, crowned princess, dynast

principal ADJECTIVE = <u>main</u>, leading, chief, prime, first, key, essential, primary ≠ minor
● NOUN 1 = <u>headmaster</u> or <u>headmistress</u>, head (informal), dean, head teacher, rector, master or mistress 2 = <u>star</u>, lead, leader, prima ballerina, leading man or lady, coryphée 3 = <u>capital</u>, money, assets, working capital

principally = <u>mainly</u>, largely, chiefly, especially, mostly, primarily, above all, predominantly

principle NOUN 1 = <u>morals</u>, standards, ideals, honour, virtue, ethics, integrity, conscience, kaupapa (*N.Z.*) 2 = **rule**, law, truth, precept

● PHRASES **in principle** 1 = <u>in general</u> 2 = <u>in theory</u>, ideally, on paper, theoretically, in an ideal world, en principe (*French*)

> ### Word Power
> **principle** – Principle and principal are often confused: *the principal* (not *principle*) *reason for his departure; the plan was approved in principle* (not *principal*).

print VERB 1 = <u>run off</u>, publish, copy, reproduce, issue, engrave 2 = <u>publish</u>, release, issue, disseminate 3 = <u>mark</u>, impress, stamp, imprint

● NOUN 1 = <u>photograph</u>, photo, snap 2 = <u>picture</u>, plate, etching, engraving, lithograph, woodcut, linocut 3 = <u>copy</u>, photo (*informal*), picture, reproduction, replica

prior ADJECTIVE = <u>earlier</u>, previous, former, preceding, foregoing, pre-existing, pre-existent

● PHRASES **prior to** = <u>before</u>, preceding, earlier than, in advance of, previous to

priority 1 = <u>prime concern</u> 2 = <u>precedence</u>, preference, primacy, predominance 3 = <u>supremacy</u>, rank, precedence, seniority, right of way, pre-

eminence

prison = <u>jail</u>, confinement, nick (*Brit. slang*), cooler (*slang*), jug (*slang*), dungeon, clink (*slang*), gaol, boob (*Austral. slang*)

prisoner 1 = <u>convict</u>, con (*slang*), lag (*slang*), jailbird 2 = <u>captive</u>, hostage, detainee, internee

privacy = <u>seclusion</u>, isolation, solitude, retirement, retreat

private 1 = <u>exclusive</u>, individual, privately owned, own, special, reserved ≠ public 2 = <u>secret</u>, confidential, covert, unofficial, clandestine, off the record, hush-hush (*informal*) ≠ public 3 = <u>personal</u>, individual, secret, intimate, undisclosed, unspoken, innermost, unvoiced 4 = <u>secluded</u>, secret, separate, isolated, sequestered ≠ busy 5 = <u>solitary</u>, reserved, retiring, withdrawn, discreet, secretive, self-contained, reclusive ≠ sociable

privilege = <u>right</u>, due, advantage, claim, freedom, liberty, concession, entitlement

privileged = <u>special</u>, advantaged, favoured, honoured, entitled, elite

prize[1] NOUN 1 = <u>reward</u>, cup, award, honour, medal, trophy, accolade 2 = <u>winnings</u>, haul, jackpot, stakes, purse

● ADJECTIVE = champion, best, winning, top, outstanding, award-winning, first-rate

prize² = value, treasure, esteem, cherish, hold dear

prize³ or **prise** 1 = force, pull, lever 2 = drag, force, draw, wring, extort

probability 1 = likelihood, prospect, chance, odds, expectation, liability, likeliness 2 = chance, odds, possibility, likelihood

probable = likely, possible, apparent, reasonable to think, credible, plausible, feasible, presumable ≠ unlikely

probably = likely, perhaps, maybe, possibly, presumably, most likely, doubtless, perchance (archaic)

probation = trial period, trial, apprenticeship

probe VERB 1 often with **into** = examine, go into, investigate, explore, search, look into, analyze, dissect 2 = explore, examine, poke, prod, feel around
● NOUN = investigation, study, inquiry, analysis, examination, exploration, scrutiny, scrutinization

problem 1 = difficulty, trouble, dispute, plight, obstacle, dilemma, headache (informal), complication 2 = puzzle,

question, riddle, enigma, conundrum, poser

problematic = tricky, puzzling, doubtful, dubious, debatable, problematical ≠ clear

procedure = method, policy, process, course, system, action, practice, strategy

proceed 1 = begin, go ahead 2 = continue, go on, progress, carry on, go ahead, press on ≠ discontinue 3 = go on, continue, progress, carry on, go ahead, move on, move forward, press on ≠ stop 4 = arise, come, issue, result, spring, flow, stem, derive

proceeding = action, process, procedure, move, act, step, measure, deed

proceeds = income, profit, revenue, returns, products, gain, earnings, yield

process NOUN 1 = procedure, means, course, system, action, performance, operation, measure 2 = development, growth, progress, movement, advance, evolution, progression 3 = method, system, practice, technique, procedure
● VERB = handle, manage, action, deal with, fulfil

procession = parade, train, march, file, cavalcade, cortege

proclaim 1 = announce, declare,

advertise, publish, indicate, herald, circulate, profess ≠ keep secret **2** = <u>pronounce</u>, announce, declare

prod VERB **1** = <u>poke</u>, push, dig, shove, nudge, jab **2** = <u>prompt</u>, move, urge, motivate, spur, stimulate, rouse, incite
● NOUN **1** = <u>poke</u>, push, dig, shove, nudge, jab **2** = <u>prompt</u>, signal, cue, reminder, stimulus

prodigy 1 = <u>genius</u>, talent, wizard, mastermind, whizz (*informal*)

produce VERB **1** = <u>cause</u>, effect, generate, bring about, give rise to **2** = <u>make</u>, create, develop, manufacture, construct, invent, fabricate **3** = <u>create</u>, develop, write, turn out, compose, originate, churn out (*informal*) **4** = <u>yield</u>, provide, grow, bear, give, supply, afford, render **5** = <u>bring forth</u>, bear, deliver, breed, give birth to, beget, bring into the world **6** = <u>show</u>, provide, present, advance, demonstrate, offer, come up with, exhibit **7** = <u>display</u>, show, present, proffer **8** = <u>present</u>, stage, direct, put on, do, show, mount, exhibit
● NOUN = <u>fruit and vegetables</u>, goods, food, products, crops, yield, harvest, greengrocery (*Brit.*)

producer 1 = <u>director</u>, promoter, impresario **2** = <u>maker</u>, manufacturer, builder, creator, fabricator **3** = <u>grower</u>, farmer

product 1 = <u>goods</u>, produce, creation, commodity, invention, merchandise, artefact **2** = <u>result</u>, consequence, effect, outcome, upshot

production 1 = <u>producing</u>, making, manufacture, manufacturing, construction, formation, fabrication **2** = <u>creation</u>, development, fashioning, composition, origination **3** = <u>management</u>, administration, direction **4** = <u>presentation</u>, staging, mounting

productive 1 = <u>fertile</u>, rich, prolific, plentiful, fruitful, fecund ≠ barren **2** = <u>creative</u>, inventive **3** = <u>useful</u>, rewarding, valuable, profitable, effective, worthwhile, beneficial, constructive ≠ useless

productivity = <u>output</u>, production, capacity, yield, efficiency, work rate

profess 1 = <u>claim</u>, allege, pretend, fake, make out, purport, feign **2** = <u>state</u>, admit, announce, declare, confess, assert, proclaim, affirm

professed 1 = <u>supposed</u>, would-be, alleged, so-called, pretended, purported, self-styled, ostensible **2** = <u>declared</u>, confirmed, confessed, proclaimed, self-confessed, avowed, self-acknowledged

profession = occupation, calling, business, career, employment, office, position, sphere

professional ADJECTIVE
1 = qualified, trained, skilled, white-collar **2** = expert, experienced, skilled, masterly, efficient, competent, adept, proficient ≠ amateurish
● NOUN = expert, master, pro (*informal*), specialist, guru, adept, maestro, virtuoso, fundi (*S. African*)

professor = don (*Brit.*), fellow (*Brit.*), prof (*informal*)

profile 1 = outline, lines, form, figure, silhouette, contour, side view **2** = biography, sketch, vignette, characterization, thumbnail sketch

profit NOUN **1** often plural = earnings, return, revenue, gain, yield, proceeds, receipts, takings ≠ loss **2** = benefit, good, use, value, gain, advantage, advancement ≠ disadvantage
● VERB **1** = make money, gain, earn **2** = benefit, help, serve, gain, promote, be of advantage to

profitable 1 = money-making, lucrative, paying, commercial, worthwhile, cost-effective, fruitful, remunerative
2 = beneficial, useful, rewarding, valuable, productive, worthwhile,

fruitful, advantageous ≠ useless

profound 1 = sincere, acute, intense, great, keen, extreme, heartfelt, deeply felt ≠ insincere
2 = wise, learned, deep, penetrating, philosophical, sage, abstruse, sagacious ≠ uninformed

programme 1 = schedule, plan, agenda, timetable, listing, list, line-up, calendar **2** = course, curriculum, syllabus **3** = show, performance, production, broadcast, episode, presentation, transmission, telecast

progress NOUN
1 = development, growth, advance, gain, improvement, breakthrough, headway ≠ regression **2** = movement forward, passage, advancement, course, advance, headway ≠ movement backward
● VERB **1** = move on, continue, travel, advance, proceed, go forward, make headway ≠ move back **2** = develop, improve, advance, grow, gain ≠ get behind
● PHRASES **in progress** = going on, happening, continuing, being done, occurring, taking place, proceeding, under way

progression 1 = progress, advance, advancement, gain, headway, furtherance, movement forward **2** = sequence, course, series, chain, cycle, string, succession

progressive → promote

progressive 1 = enlightened, liberal, modern, advanced, radical, revolutionary, avant-garde, reformist **2** = growing, continuing, increasing, developing, advancing, ongoing

prohibit 1 = forbid, ban, veto, outlaw, disallow, proscribe, debar ≠ permit **2** = prevent, restrict, stop, hamper, hinder, impede ≠ allow

prohibition = ban, boycott, embargo, bar, veto, prevention, exclusion, injunction

project NOUN **1** = scheme, plan, job, idea, campaign, operation, activity, venture **2** = assignment, task, homework, piece of research

● VERB **1** = forecast, expect, estimate, predict, reckon, calculate, gauge, extrapolate **2** = stick out, extend, stand out, bulge, protrude, overhang, jut

projection = forecast, estimate, reckoning, calculation, estimation, computation, extrapolation

proliferation = multiplication, increase, spread, expansion

prolific 1 = productive, creative, fertile, inventive, copious **2** = fruitful, fertile, abundant, luxuriant, profuse, fecund ≠ unproductive

prolong = lengthen, continue, perpetuate, draw out, extend, delay, stretch out, spin out ≠ shorten

prominence 1 = fame, name, reputation, importance, celebrity, distinction, prestige, eminence **2** = conspicuousness, markedness

prominent 1 = famous, leading, top, important, main, distinguished, well-known, notable ≠ unknown **2** = noticeable, obvious, outstanding, pronounced, conspicuous, eye-catching, obtrusive ≠ inconspicuous

promise VERB **1** = guarantee, pledge, vow, swear, contract, assure, undertake, warrant **2** = seem likely, look like, show signs of, augur, betoken

● NOUN **1** = guarantee, word, bond, vow, commitment, pledge, undertaking, assurance **2** = potential, ability, talent, capacity, capability, aptitude

promising 1 = encouraging, likely, bright, reassuring, hopeful, favourable, rosy, auspicious ≠ unpromising **2** = talented, able, gifted, rising

promote 1 = help, back, support, aid, forward, encourage, advance, boost ≠ impede **2** = advertise, sell, hype, publicize, push, plug (informal) **3** = raise, upgrade, elevate, exalt ≠ demote

promotion 1 = <u>rise</u>, upgrading, move up, advancement, elevation, exaltation, preferment **2** = <u>publicity</u>, advertising, plugging (*informal*) **3** = <u>encouragement</u>, support, boosting, advancement, furtherance

prompt VERB **1** = <u>cause</u>, occasion, provoke, give rise to, elicit **2** = <u>remind</u>, assist, cue, help out
● ADJECTIVE = <u>immediate</u>, quick, rapid, instant, timely, early, swift, speedy ≠ slow
● ADVERB (*Informal*) = <u>exactly</u>, sharp, promptly, on the dot, punctually

promptly 1 = <u>immediately</u>, swiftly, directly, quickly, at once, speedily **2** = <u>punctually</u>, on time, spot on (*informal*), bang on (*informal*), on the dot, on the button (*U.S.*), on the nail

prone 1 = <u>liable</u>, given, subject, inclined, tending, bent, disposed, susceptible ≠ disinclined **2** = <u>face down</u>, flat, horizontal, prostrate, recumbent ≠ face up

pronounce 1 = <u>say</u>, speak, sound, articulate, enunciate **2** = <u>declare</u>, announce, deliver, proclaim, decree, affirm

pronounced = <u>noticeable</u>, decided, marked, striking, obvious, evident, distinct, definite

≠ imperceptible

proof NOUN = <u>evidence</u>, demonstration, testimony, confirmation, verification, corroboration, authentication, substantiation
● ADJECTIVE = <u>impervious</u>, strong, resistant, impenetrable, repellent

prop VERB **1** = <u>lean</u>, place, set, stand, position, rest, lay, balance **2** *often with* **up** = <u>support</u>, sustain, hold up, brace, uphold, bolster, buttress
● NOUN **1** = <u>support</u>, stay, brace, mainstay, buttress, stanchion **2** = <u>mainstay</u>, support, sustainer, anchor, backbone, cornerstone, upholder

propaganda = <u>information</u>, advertising, promotion, publicity, hype, disinformation

propel 1 = <u>drive</u>, launch, force, send, shoot, push, thrust, shove ≠ stop **2** = <u>impel</u>, drive, push, prompt, spur, motivate ≠ hold back

proper 1 = <u>real</u>, actual, genuine, true, bona fide, dinkum (*Austral. & N.Z. informal*) **2** = <u>correct</u>, accepted, established, appropriate, right, formal, conventional, precise ≠ improper **3** = <u>polite</u>, right, becoming, seemly, fitting, fit, mannerly, suitable ≠ unseemly

properly 1 = <u>correctly</u>, rightly,

fittingly, appropriately, accurately, suitably, aptly ≠ incorrectly **2** = politely, decently, respectably ≠ badly

property 1 = possessions, goods, effects, holdings, capital, riches, estate, assets **2** = land, holding, estate, real estate, freehold **3** = quality, feature, characteristic, attribute, trait, hallmark

prophecy 1 = prediction, forecast, prognostication, augury **2** = second sight, divination, augury, telling the future, soothsaying

prophet or **prophetess** = soothsayer, forecaster, diviner, oracle, seer, sibyl, prophesier

proportion NOUN **1** = part, share, amount, division, percentage, segment, quota, fraction **2** = relative amount, relationship, ratio **3** = balance, harmony, correspondence, symmetry, concord, congruity
● PLURAL NOUN = dimensions, size, volume, capacity, extent, expanse

proportional or **proportionate** = correspondent, corresponding, even, balanced, consistent, compatible, equitable, in proportion ≠ disproportionate

proposal = suggestion, plan, programme, scheme, offer, project, bid, recommendation

propose 1 = put forward, present, suggest, advance, submit **2** = intend, mean, plan, aim, design, scheme, have in mind **3** = nominate, name, present, recommend **4** = offer marriage, pop the question (informal), ask for someone's hand (in marriage)

proposition NOUN **1** = task, problem, activity, job, affair, venture, undertaking **2** = theory, idea, argument, concept, thesis, hypothesis, theorem, premiss **3** = proposal, plan, suggestion, scheme, bid, recommendation **4** = advance, pass (informal), proposal, overture, improper suggestion, come-on (informal)
● VERB = make a pass at, solicit, accost, make an improper suggestion to

proprietor or **proprietress** = owner, titleholder, landlord or landlady

prosecute (Law) = take someone to court, try, sue, indict, arraign, put someone on trial, litigate, bring someone to trial

prospect NOUN **1** = likelihood, chance, possibility, hope, promise, odds, expectation, probability **2** = idea, outlook **3** = view, landscape, scene, sight, outlook, spectacle, vista
● PLURAL NOUN = possibilities,

chances, future, potential,
expectations, outlook, scope
● VERB = <u>look</u>, search, seek, dowse

prospective 1 = <u>potential</u>,
possible **2** = <u>expected</u>, coming,
future, likely, intended,
anticipated, forthcoming,
imminent

prospectus = <u>catalogue</u>, list,
programme, outline, syllabus,
synopsis

prosper = <u>succeed</u>, advance,
progress, thrive, get on, do well,
flourish

prosperity = <u>success</u>, riches,
plenty, fortune, wealth, luxury,
good fortune, affluence
≠ poverty

prosperous 1 = <u>wealthy</u>, rich,
affluent, well-off, well-heeled
(*informal*), well-to-do, moneyed
≠ poor **2** = <u>successful</u>, booming,
thriving, flourishing, doing well
≠ unsuccessful

prostitute NOUN = <u>whore</u>,
hooker (*U.S. slang*), pro (*slang*),
tart (*informal*), call girl, harlot,
streetwalker, loose woman
● VERB = <u>cheapen</u>, sell out,
pervert, degrade, devalue,
squander, demean, debase

protagonist 1 = <u>supporter</u>,
champion, advocate, exponent
2 = <u>leading character</u>, principal,
central character, hero *or* heroine

protect = <u>keep someone safe</u>,

defend, support, save, guard,
preserve, look after, shelter
≠ endanger

protection 1 = <u>safety</u>, care,
defence, protecting, security,
custody, safeguard, aegis
2 = <u>safeguard</u>, cover, guard,
shelter, screen, barrier, shield,
buffer **3** = <u>armour</u>, cover, screen,
barrier, shelter, shield

protective 1 = <u>protecting</u>
2 = <u>caring</u>, defensive, motherly,
fatherly, maternal, vigilant,
watchful, paternal

protector 1 = <u>defender</u>,
champion, guard, guardian,
patron, bodyguard **2** = <u>guard</u>,
screen, protection, shield, pad,
cushion, buffer

protest VERB **1** = <u>object</u>,
demonstrate, oppose, complain,
disagree, cry out, disapprove,
demur **2** = <u>assert</u>, insist, maintain,
declare, affirm, profess, attest,
avow
● NOUN **1** = <u>demonstration</u>, march,
rally, sit-in, demo (*informal*), hikoi
(*N.Z.*) **2** = <u>objection</u>, complaint,
dissent, outcry, protestation,
remonstrance

protocol = <u>code of behaviour</u>,
manners, conventions, customs,
etiquette, propriety, decorum

prototype = <u>original</u>, model,
first, example, standard

protracted = <u>extended</u>,

prolonged, drawn-out, spun out, dragged out, long-drawn-out

proud 1 = <u>satisfied</u>, pleased, content, thrilled, glad, gratified, joyful, well-pleased ≠ dissatisfied 2 = <u>conceited</u>, arrogant, lordly, imperious, overbearing, haughty, snobbish, self-satisfied ≠ humble

prove 1 = <u>turn out</u>, come out, end up 2 = <u>verify</u>, establish, determine, show, confirm, demonstrate, justify, substantiate ≠ disprove

proven = <u>established</u>, proved, confirmed, tested, reliable, definite, verified, attested

provide VERB 1 = <u>supply</u>, give, distribute, outfit, equip, donate, furnish, dispense ≠ withhold 2 = <u>give</u>, bring, add, produce, present, serve, afford, yield

● PHRASES **provide for someone** = <u>support</u>, care for, keep, maintain, sustain, take care of, fend for ♦ **provide for something** = <u>take precautions</u> against, plan for, prepare for, anticipate, plan ahead for, forearm for

provided often with **that** = <u>if</u>, given, on condition, as long as

provider 1 = <u>supplier</u>, giver, source, donor 2 = <u>breadwinner</u>, supporter, earner, wage earner

providing often with **that** = <u>on condition that</u>, given that, as long as

province 1 = <u>region</u>, section, district, zone, patch, colony, domain 2 = <u>area</u>, business, concern, responsibility, line, role, department, field

➤ WORD POWER SUPPLEMENT
Canadian provinces

➤ WORD POWER SUPPLEMENT
South African provinces and provincial capitals

provincial ADJECTIVE 1 = <u>regional</u>, state, local, county, district, territorial, parochial 2 = <u>rural</u>, country, local, rustic, homespun, hick (informal, chiefly U.S. & Canad.), backwoods ≠ urban 3 = <u>parochial</u>, insular, narrow-minded, unsophisticated, limited, narrow, small-town (chiefly U.S.), inward-looking ≠ cosmopolitan

provision NOUN 1 = <u>supplying</u>, giving, providing, supply, delivery, distribution, catering, presentation 2 = <u>condition</u>, term, requirement, demand, rider, restriction, qualification, clause ● PLURAL NOUN = <u>food</u>, supplies, stores, fare, rations, foodstuff, kai (N.Z. informal), victuals, edibles

provisional 1 = <u>temporary</u>, interim ≠ permanent 2 = <u>conditional</u>, limited, qualified, contingent, tentative ≠ definite

provocation 1 = <u>cause</u>, reason, grounds, motivation, stimulus,

incitement 2 = offence,
challenge, insult, taunt, injury,
dare, grievance, annoyance

provocative = offensive,
provoking, insulting, stimulating,
annoying, galling, goading

provoke 1 = anger, annoy,
irritate, infuriate, hassle
(*informal*), aggravate (*informal*),
incense, enrage ≠ pacify
2 = rouse, cause, produce,
promote, occasion, prompt, stir,
induce ≠ curb

prowess 1 = skill, ability, talent,
expertise, genius, excellence,
accomplishment, mastery
≠ inability 2 = bravery, daring,
courage, heroism, mettle, valour,
fearlessness, valiance ≠ cowardice

proximity = nearness, closeness

proxy = representative, agent,
deputy, substitute, factor,
delegate

prudent 1 = cautious, careful,
wary, discreet, vigilant ≠ careless
2 = wise, politic, sensible, shrewd,
discerning, judicious ≠ unwise
3 = thrifty, economical, sparing,
careful, canny, provident, frugal,
far-sighted ≠ extravagant

prune 1 = cut, trim, clip, dock,
shape, shorten, snip 2 = reduce,
cut, cut back, trim, cut down, pare
down, make reductions in

psyche = soul, mind, self, spirit,
personality, individuality, anima,

wairua (*N.Z.*)

psychiatrist = psychotherapist,
analyst, therapist, psychologist,
shrink (*slang*), psychoanalyst,
headshrinker (*slang*)

psychic ADJECTIVE
1 = supernatural, mystic, occult
2 = mystical, spiritual, magical,
other-worldly, paranormal,
preternatural 3 = psychological,
emotional, mental, spiritual, inner,
psychiatric, cognitive
● NOUN = clairvoyant, fortune
teller

psychological 1 = mental,
emotional, intellectual, inner,
cognitive, cerebral 2 = imaginary,
psychosomatic, irrational, unreal,
all in the mind

psychology 1 = behaviourism,
study of personality, science of
mind 2 (*Informal*) = way of
thinking, attitude, behaviour,
temperament, mentality, thought
processes, mental processes,
what makes you tick

pub *or* **public house** = tavern,
bar, inn, saloon

public NOUN = people, society,
community, nation, everyone,
citizens, electorate, populace
● ADJECTIVE 1 = civic, government,
state, national, local, official,
community, social 2 = general,
popular, national, shared,
common, widespread, universal,

collective 3 = <u>open</u>, accessible, communal, unrestricted ≠ private 4 = <u>well-known</u>, leading, important, respected, famous, celebrated, recognized, distinguished 5 = <u>known</u>, open, obvious, acknowledged, plain, patent, overt ≠ secret

publication 1 = <u>pamphlet</u>, newspaper, magazine, issue, title, leaflet, brochure, periodical 2 = <u>announcement</u>, publishing, broadcasting, reporting, declaration, disclosure, proclamation, notification

publicity 1 = <u>advertising</u>, press, promotion, hype, boost, plug (*informal*) 2 = <u>attention</u>, exposure, fame, celebrity, fuss, public interest, limelight, notoriety

publish 1 = <u>put out</u>, issue, produce, print 2 = <u>announce</u>, reveal, spread, advertise, broadcast, disclose, proclaim, circulate

pudding = <u>dessert</u>, afters (*Brit. informal*), sweet, pud (*informal*)

puff VERB 1 = <u>smoke</u>, draw, drag (*slang*), suck, inhale, pull at *or* on 2 = <u>breathe heavily</u>, pant, exhale, blow, gasp, gulp, wheeze, fight for breath

● NOUN 1 = <u>drag</u>, pull (*slang*), moke 2 = <u>blast</u>, breath, whiff, draught, gust

pull VERB 1 = <u>draw</u>, haul, drag, trail, tow, tug, jerk, yank ≠ push 2 = <u>extract</u>, pick, remove, gather, take out, pluck, uproot, draw out ≠ insert 3 (*Informal*) = <u>attract</u>, draw, bring in, tempt, lure, interest, entice, pull in ≠ repel 4 = <u>strain</u>, tear, stretch, rip, wrench, dislocate, sprain

● NOUN 1 = <u>tug</u>, jerk, yank, twitch, heave ≠ shove 2 = <u>puff</u>, drag (*slang*), inhalation 3 (*Informal*) = <u>influence</u>, power, weight, muscle, clout (*informal*), kai (*N.Z. informal*)

● PHRASES **pull out (of)** 1 = <u>withdraw</u>, quit 2 = <u>leave</u>, abandon, get out, quit, retreat from, depart, evacuate ◆ **pull someone up** = <u>reprimand</u>, rebuke, admonish, read the riot act to, tell someone off (*informal*), reprove, bawl someone out (*informal*), tear someone off a strip (*Brit. informal*) ◆ **pull something off** (*Informal*) = <u>succeed in</u>, manage, carry out, accomplish ◆ **pull something out** = <u>produce</u>, draw, bring out, draw out ◆ **pull up** = <u>stop</u>, halt, brake

pulp NOUN 1 = <u>paste</u>, mash, mush 2 = <u>flesh</u>, meat, soft part

● ADJECTIVE = <u>cheap</u>, lurid, trashy, rubbishy

● VERB = <u>crush</u>, squash, mash,

pulverize

pulse NOUN = beat, rhythm, vibration, beating, throb, throbbing, pulsation
• VERB = beat, throb, vibrate, pulsate

pump 1 = supply, send, pour, inject 2 = interrogate, probe, quiz, cross-examine

punch[1] VERB = hit, strike, box, smash, belt (*informal*), sock (*slang*), swipe (*informal*), bop (*informal*)
• NOUN 1 = blow, hit, sock (*slang*), jab, swipe (*informal*), bop (*informal*), wallop (*informal*)
2 (*Informal*) = effectiveness, bite, impact, drive, vigour, verve, forcefulness

punch[2] = pierce, cut, bore, drill, stamp, puncture, prick, perforate

punctuate = interrupt, break, pepper, sprinkle, intersperse

puncture NOUN 1 = flat tyre, flat, flattie (*N.Z.*) 2 = hole, opening, break, cut, nick, leak, slit
• VERB = pierce, cut, nick, penetrate, prick, rupture, perforate, bore a hole

punish = discipline, correct, castigate, chastise, sentence, chasten, penalize

punishing = hard, taxing, wearing, tiring, exhausting, gruelling, strenuous, arduous

≠ easy

punishment 1 = penalizing, discipline, correction, retribution, chastening, chastisement
2 = penalty, penance

punitive = retaliatory, in reprisal, retaliative

punt VERB = bet, back, stake, gamble, lay, wager
• NOUN = bet, stake, gamble, wager

punter 1 = gambler, better, backer 2 (*Informal*) = person, man in the street

pupil 1 = student, schoolboy *or* schoolgirl, schoolchild ≠ teacher
2 = learner, novice, beginner, disciple ≠ instructor

puppet 1 = marionette, doll, glove puppet, finger puppet
2 = pawn, tool, instrument, mouthpiece, stooge, cat's-paw

purchase VERB = buy, pay for, obtain, get, score (*slang*), gain, pick up, acquire ≠ sell
• NOUN 1 = acquisition, buy, investment, property, gain, asset, possession 2 = grip, hold, support, leverage, foothold

pure 1 = unmixed, real, simple, natural, straight, genuine, neat, authentic ≠ adulterated
2 = clean, wholesome, sanitary, spotless, sterilized, squeaky-clean, untainted, uncontaminated

≠ contaminated **3** = <u>complete</u>, total, perfect, absolute, sheer, patent, utter, outright ≠ qualified **4** = <u>innocent</u>, modest, good, moral, impeccable, righteous, virtuous, squeaky-clean ≠ corrupt

purely = <u>absolutely</u>, just, only, completely, simply, entirely, exclusively, merely

purge VERB **1** = <u>rid</u>, clear, cleanse, strip, empty, void **2** = <u>get rid of</u>, remove, expel, wipe out, eradicate, do away with, exterminate

● NOUN = <u>removal</u>, elimination, expulsion, eradication, ejection

purity 1 = <u>cleanness</u>, cleanliness, wholesomeness, pureness, faultlessness, immaculateness ≠ impurity **2** = <u>innocence</u>, virtue, integrity, honesty, decency, virginity, chastity, chasteness ≠ immorality

purple ▶ shades of purple

purport = <u>claim</u>, allege, assert, profess

purpose NOUN **1** = <u>reason</u>, point, idea, aim, object, intention **2** = <u>aim</u>, end, plan, hope, goal, wish, desire, object **3** = <u>determination</u>, resolve, will, resolution, ambition, persistence, tenacity, firmness

● PHRASES **on purpose** = <u>deliberately</u>, purposely, intentionally, knowingly, designedly

> ### Word Power
>
> **purpose** – The two concepts *purposeful* and *on purpose* should be carefully distinguished. *On purpose* and *purposely* have roughly the same meaning, and imply that a person's action is deliberate, rather than accidental. However, *purposeful* and its related adverb *purposefully* refer to the way that someone acts as being full of purpose or determination.

purposely = <u>deliberately</u>, expressly, consciously, intentionally, knowingly, with intent, on purpose ≠ accidentally

purse NOUN **1** = <u>pouch</u>, wallet, money-bag **2** (*U.S.*) = <u>handbag</u>, bag, shoulder bag, pocket book,

Shades of purple

amethyst	heather	magenta	puce
aubergine	indigo	mauve	Tyrian purple
burgundy	lavender	mulberry	violet
claret	lilac	plum	wine

clutch bag **3** = <u>funds</u>, means, money, resources, treasury, wealth, exchequer

● **VERB** = <u>pucker</u>, contract, tighten, pout, press together

pursue 1 = <u>engage in</u>, perform, conduct, carry on, practise **2** = <u>try for</u>, seek, desire, search for, aim for, work towards, strive for **3** = <u>continue</u>, maintain, carry on, keep on, persist in, proceed in, persevere in **4** = <u>follow</u>, track, hunt, chase, dog, shadow, tail (*informal*), hound ≠ flee

pursuit 1 = <u>quest</u>, seeking, search, aim of, aspiration for, striving towards **2** = <u>pursuing</u>, seeking, search, hunt, chase, trailing **3** = <u>occupation</u>, activity, interest, line, pleasure, hobby, pastime

push VERB 1 = <u>shove</u>, force, press, thrust, drive, knock, sweep, plunge ≠ pull **2** = <u>press</u>, operate, depress, squeeze, activate, hold down **3** = <u>make or force your way</u>, move, shoulder, inch, squeeze, thrust, elbow, shove **4** = <u>urge</u>, encourage, persuade, spur, press, incite, impel ≠ discourage

● **NOUN 1** = <u>shove</u>, thrust, butt, elbow, nudge ≠ pull **2** (*Informal*) = <u>drive</u>, go (*informal*), energy, initiative, enterprise, ambition, vitality, vigour

● **PHRASES the push** (*Informal*,

chiefly Brit.) = <u>dismissal</u>, the sack (*informal*), discharge, the boot (*slang*), your cards (*informal*)

put VERB 1 = <u>place</u>, leave, set, position, rest, deposit, plant, lay **2** = <u>express</u>, state, word, phrase, utter

● **PHRASES put someone off 1** = <u>discourage</u>, intimidate, deter, daunt, dissuade, demoralize, scare off, dishearten **2** = <u>disconcert</u>, confuse, unsettle, throw (*informal*), dismay, perturb, faze, discomfit ◆ **put someone up 1** = <u>accommodate</u>, house, board, lodge, quarter, take someone in, billet **2** = <u>nominate</u>, put forward, offer, present, propose, recommend, submit ◆ **put something across** or **over** = <u>communicate</u>, explain, convey, make clear, get across, make yourself understood ◆ **put something off** = <u>postpone</u>, delay, defer, adjourn, hold over, put on the back burner (*informal*), take a rain check on (*U.S. & Canad. informal*) ◆ **put something up 1** = <u>build</u>, raise, set up, construct, erect, fabricate **2** = <u>offer</u>, present, mount, put forward

puzzle VERB = <u>perplex</u>, confuse, baffle, stump, bewilder, confound, mystify, faze

● **NOUN 1** = <u>problem</u>, riddle,

question, conundrum, poser
2 = <u>mystery</u>, problem, paradox, enigma, conundrum

puzzling = <u>perplexing</u>, baffling, bewildering, involved, enigmatic, incomprehensible, mystifying, abstruse ≠ simple

quake = <u>shake</u>, tremble, quiver, move, rock, shiver, shudder, vibrate

qualification 1 = <u>eligibility</u>, quality, ability, skill, fitness, attribute, capability, aptitude **2** = <u>condition</u>, proviso, requirement, rider, reservation, limitation, modification, caveat

qualified 1 = <u>capable</u>, trained, experienced, seasoned, able, fit, expert, chartered ≠ untrained **2** = <u>restricted</u>, limited, provisional, conditional, reserved, bounded, adjusted, moderated ≠ unconditional

qualify 1 = <u>certify</u>, equip, empower, train, prepare, fit, ready, permit ≠ disqualify **2** = <u>restrict</u>, limit, reduce, ease, moderate, regulate, diminish, temper

quality 1 = <u>standard</u>, standing, class, condition, rank, grade, merit, classification **2** = <u>excellence</u>, status, merit,

position, value, worth, distinction, virtue **3** = <u>characteristic</u>, feature, attribute, point, side, mark, property, aspect **4** = <u>nature</u>, character, make, sort, kind

quantity 1 = <u>amount</u>, lot, total, sum, part, number **2** = <u>size</u>, measure, mass, volume, length, capacity, extent, bulk

> ### Word Power
>
> **quantity** – The use of a plural noun after *quantity of*, as in *a large quantity of bananas*, used to be considered incorrect, the objection being that the word *quantity* should only be used to refer to an uncountable amount, which was grammatically regarded as a singular concept. Nowadays, however, most people consider the use of *quantity* with a plural noun to be acceptable.

quarrel NOUN = <u>disagreement</u>, fight, row, argument, dispute, controversy, breach, contention, biffo (*Austral. slang*) ≠ accord

● VERB = <u>disagree</u>, fight, argue, row, clash, dispute, differ, fall out (*informal*) ≠ get on *or* along (with)

quarry = <u>prey</u>, victim, game, goal, aim, prize, objective

quarter NOUN **1** = <u>district</u>, region, neighbourhood, place, part, side,

area, zone 2 = **mercy**, pity, compassion, charity, sympathy, tolerance, kindness, forgiveness
● PLURAL NOUN = **lodgings**, rooms, chambers, residence, dwelling, barracks, abode, habitation
● VERB = **accommodate**, house, lodge, place, board, post, station, billet

quash 1 = **annul**, overturn, reverse, cancel, overthrow, revoke, overrule, rescind 2 = **suppress**, crush, put down, beat, overthrow, squash, subdue, repress

queen 1 = **sovereign**, ruler, monarch, leader, Crown, princess, majesty, head of state 2 = **leading light**, star, favourite, celebrity, darling, mistress, big name

queer 1 = **strange**, odd, funny, unusual, extraordinary, curious, weird, peculiar ≠ normal 2 = **faint**, dizzy, giddy, queasy, light-headed

---

Word Power

queer – Although the term *queer* meaning 'gay' is still considered derogatory when used by non-gays, it is now being used by gay people themselves as a positive term in certain contexts, such as *queer politics, queer cinema*. Nevertheless, many gay people would not wish to have the term applied to them, nor would they use it of themselves.

---

query NOUN 1 = **question**, inquiry, problem 2 = **doubt**, suspicion, objection
● VERB 1 = **question**, challenge, doubt, suspect, dispute, object to, distrust, mistrust 2 = **ask**, inquire *or* enquire, question

quest 1 = **search**, hunt, mission, enterprise, crusade 2 = **expedition**, journey, adventure

question NOUN 1 = **inquiry**, enquiry, query, investigation, examination, interrogation ≠ answer 2 = **difficulty**, problem, doubt, argument, dispute, controversy, query, contention 3 = **issue**, point, matter, subject, problem, debate, proposal, theme
● VERB 1 = **interrogate**, cross-examine, interview, examine, probe, quiz, ask questions 2 = **dispute**, challenge, doubt, suspect, oppose, query, mistrust, disbelieve ≠ accept
● PHRASES out of the question = **impossible**, unthinkable, inconceivable, not on (*informal*), hopeless, unimaginable, unworkable, unattainable

questionable = **dubious**, suspect, doubtful, controversial, suspicious, dodgy (*Brit., Austral., & N.Z. informal*), debatable, moot ≠ indisputable

queue = **line**, row, file, train,

series, chain, string, column

quick 1 = <u>fast</u>, swift, speedy, express, cracking (*Brit. informal*), smart, rapid, fleet ≠ slow **2** = <u>brief</u>, passing, hurried, flying, fleeting, summary, lightning, short-lived ≠ long **3** = <u>immediate</u>, instant, prompt, sudden, abrupt, instantaneous **4** = <u>excitable</u>, passionate, irritable, touchy, irascible, testy ≠ calm **5** = <u>intelligent</u>, bright (*informal*), alert, sharp, acute, smart, clever, shrewd ≠ stupid

quicken 1 = <u>speed up</u>, hurry, accelerate, hasten, gee up (*informal*) **2** = <u>stimulate</u>, inspire, arouse, excite, revive, incite, energize, invigorate

quickly 1 = <u>swiftly</u>, rapidly, hurriedly, fast, hastily, briskly, apace ≠ slowly **2** = <u>soon</u>, speedily, as soon as possible, momentarily (*U.S.*), instantaneously, pronto (*informal*), a.s.a.p. (*informal*) **3** = <u>immediately</u>, at once, directly, promptly, abruptly, without delay

quiet ADJECTIVE **1** = <u>soft</u>, low, muted, lowered, whispered, faint, suppressed, stifled ≠ loud **2** = <u>peaceful</u>, silent, hushed, soundless, noiseless ≠ noisy **3** = <u>calm</u>, peaceful, tranquil, mild, serene, placid, restful ≠ exciting **4** = <u>still</u>, calm, peaceful, tranquil ≠ troubled **5** = <u>undisturbed</u>, isolated, secluded, private,

sequestered, unfrequented ≠ crowded **6** = <u>silent</u> **7** = <u>reserved</u>, retiring, shy, gentle, mild, sedate, meek ≠ excitable ● NOUN = <u>peace</u>, rest, tranquillity, ease, silence, solitude, serenity, stillness ≠ noise

quietly 1 = <u>noiselessly</u>, silently **2** = <u>softly</u>, inaudibly, in an undertone, under your breath **3** = <u>calmly</u>, serenely, placidly, patiently, mildly **4** = <u>silently</u>, mutely

quilt = <u>bedspread</u>, duvet, coverlet, eiderdown, counterpane, continental quilt (*Austral.*), continental quilt

quip = <u>joke</u>, sally, jest, riposte, wisecrack (*informal*), retort, pleasantry, gibe

quirky = <u>odd</u>, unusual, eccentric, idiosyncratic, peculiar, offbeat

quit 1 = <u>resign (from)</u>, leave, retire (from), pull out (of), step down (from) (*informal*), abdicate **2** = <u>stop</u>, give up, cease, end, drop, abandon, halt, discontinue ≠ continue **3** = <u>leave</u>, depart from, go out of, go away from, pull out from

quite 1 = <u>somewhat</u>, rather, fairly, reasonably, relatively, moderately **2** = <u>absolutely</u>, perfectly, completely, totally, fully, entirely, wholly

quiz NOUN = <u>examination</u>, questioning, interrogation, interview, investigation, grilling (*informal*), cross-examination, cross-questioning

● VERB = <u>question</u>, ask, interrogate, examine, investigate

quota = <u>share</u>, allowance, ration, part, limit, slice, quantity, portion

quotation 1 = <u>passage</u>, quote (*informal*), excerpt, reference, extract, citation 2 (*Commerce*) = <u>estimate</u>, price, tender, rate, cost, charge, figure, quote (*informal*)

quote 1 = <u>repeat</u>, recite, recall 2 = <u>refer to</u>, cite, give, name, detail, relate, mention, instance

R

race¹ NOUN 1 = <u>competition</u>, contest, chase, dash, pursuit 2 = <u>contest</u>, competition, rivalry

● VERB 1 = <u>compete against</u>, run against 2 = <u>compete</u>, run, contend, take part in a race 3 = <u>run</u>, fly, career, speed, tear, dash, hurry, dart

race² 1 = <u>people</u>, nation, blood, stock, type, folk, tribe

racial = <u>ethnic</u>, ethnological, national, folk, genetic, tribal, genealogical

rack NOUN = <u>frame</u>, stand, structure, framework

● VERB = <u>torture</u>, torment, afflict, oppress, harrow, crucify, agonize, pain

---

Word Power

rack – The use of the spelling *wrack* rather than *rack* in sentences such as *she was wracked by grief* or *the country was wracked by civil war* is very common, but is thought by many people to be incorrect.

---

racket 1 = <u>noise</u>, row, fuss, disturbance, outcry, clamour, din, pandemonium 2 = <u>fraud</u>, scheme

radiate 1 = <u>emit</u>, spread, send out, pour, shed, scatter 2 = <u>shine</u>, be diffused 3 = <u>show</u>, display, demonstrate, exhibit, emanate, give off *or* out 4 = <u>spread out</u>, diverge, branch out

radical ADJECTIVE 1 = <u>extreme</u>, complete, entire, sweeping, severe, thorough, drastic 2 = <u>revolutionary</u>, extremist, fanatical 3 = <u>fundamental</u>, natural, basic, profound, innate, deep-seated ≠ superficial

● NOUN = <u>extremist</u>, revolutionary, militant, fanatic ≠ conservative

rage NOUN 1 = <u>fury</u>, temper, frenzy, rampage, tantrum, foulie (*Australia. slang*) ≠ calmness 2 = <u>anger</u>, passion, madness, wrath, ire 3 = <u>craze</u>, fashion, enthusiasm, vogue, fad (*informal*), latest thing

● VERB = <u>be furious</u>, blow up (*informal*), fume, lose it (*informal*), seethe, lose the plot (*informal*), go ballistic (*slang, chiefly U.S.*), lose your temper ≠ stay calm

ragged 1 = tatty, worn, torn, run-down, shabby, seedy, scruffy, in tatters ≠ smart 2 = rough, rugged, unfinished, uneven, jagged, serrated

raid VERB 1 = steal from, plunder, pillage, sack 2 = attack, invade, assault 3 = make a search of, search, bust (*informal*), make a raid on, make a swoop on
● NOUN 1 = attack, invasion, foray, sortie, incursion, sally, inroad 2 = bust (*informal*), swoop 3 = robbery, sacking

raider = attacker, thief, robber, plunderer, invader, marauder

railing = fence, rails, barrier, paling, balustrade

rain NOUN 1 = rainfall, fall, showers, deluge, drizzle, downpour, raindrops, cloudburst
● VERB 1 = pour, pelt (down), teem, bucket down (*informal*), drizzle, come down in buckets (*informal*) 2 = fall, shower, be dropped, sprinkle, be deposited

rainy = wet, damp, drizzly, showery ≠ dry

raise 1 = lift, elevate, uplift, heave 2 = set upright, lift, elevate 3 = increase, intensify, heighten, advance, boost, strengthen, enhance, enlarge ≠ reduce 4 = make louder, heighten, amplify, louden 5 = collect, gather, obtain 6 = cause, start, produce, create, occasion, provoke, originate, engender 7 = put forward, suggest, introduce, advance, broach, moot 8 = bring up, develop, rear, nurture 9 = build, construct, put up, erect ≠ demolish

rake[1] 1 = gather, collect, remove 2 = search, comb, scour, scrutinize, fossick (*Austral. & N.Z.*)

rake[2] = libertine, playboy, swinger (*slang*), lecher, roué, debauchee ≠ puritan

rally NOUN 1 = gathering, convention, meeting, congress, assembly, hui (*N.Z.*) 2 = recovery, improvement, revival, recuperation ≠ relapse
● VERB 1 = gather together, unite, regroup, reorganize, reassemble 2 = recover, improve, revive, get better, recuperate ≠ get worse

ram 1 = hit, force, drive into, crash, impact, smash, dash, butt 2 = cram, force, stuff, jam, thrust

ramble NOUN 1 = walk, tour, stroll, hike, roaming, roving, saunter
● VERB 1 = walk, range, wander, stroll, stray, roam, rove, saunter, go walkabout (*Austral.*) 2 often with on = walk, babble, rabbit (on) (*Brit. informal*), waffle (*informal, chiefly Brit.*), witter on (*informal*)

ramp = <u>slope</u>, incline, gradient, rise

rampage VERB = <u>go berserk</u>, storm, rage, run riot, run amok
• PHRASES **on the rampage** = <u>berserk</u>, wild, violent, raging, out of control, amok, riotous, berko (*Austral. slang*)

rampant 1 = <u>widespread</u>, prevalent, rife, uncontrolled, unchecked, unrestrained, profuse, spreading like wildfire
2 (*Heraldry*) = <u>upright</u>, standing, rearing, erect

random ADJECTIVE 1 = <u>chance</u>, casual, accidental, incidental, haphazard, fortuitous, hit or miss, adventitious ≠ planned 2 = <u>casual</u>
• PHRASES **at random** = <u>haphazardly</u>, randomly, arbitrarily, by chance, willy-nilly, unsystematically

randy (*Informal*) = <u>lustful</u>, hot, turned-on (*slang*), aroused, horny (*slang*), amorous, lascivious

range NOUN 1 = <u>series</u>, variety, selection, assortment, lot, collection, gamut 2 = <u>limits</u>, reach 3 = <u>scope</u>, area, bounds, province, orbit, radius
• VERB 1 = <u>vary</u>, run, reach, extend, stretch 2 = <u>roam</u>, wander, rove, ramble, traverse

rank¹ NOUN 1 = <u>status</u>, level, position, grade, order, sort, type, division 2 = <u>class</u>, caste 3 = <u>row</u>, line, file, column, group, range, series, tier
• VERB 1 = <u>order</u>, dispose
2 = <u>arrange</u>, sort, line up, array, align

rank² 1 = <u>absolute</u>, complete, total, gross, sheer, utter, thorough, blatant 2 = <u>foul</u>, bad, offensive, disgusting, revolting, stinking, noxious, rancid, festy (*Austral. slang*) 3 = <u>abundant</u>, lush, luxuriant, dense, profuse

ransom = <u>payment</u>, money, price, payoff

rant = <u>shout</u>, roar, yell, rave, cry, declaim

rap VERB = <u>hit</u>, strike, knock, crack, tap
• NOUN 1 = <u>blow</u>, knock, crack, tap, clout (*informal*) 2 (*Slang*) = <u>rebuke</u>, blame, responsibility, punishment

rape VERB = <u>sexually assault</u>, violate, abuse, ravish, force, outrage
• NOUN = <u>sexual assault</u>, violation, ravishment, outrage

rapid 1 = <u>sudden</u>, prompt, speedy, express, swift ≠ gradual
2 = <u>quick</u>, fast, hurried, swift, brisk, hasty ≠ slow

rapidly = <u>quickly</u>, fast, swiftly, briskly, promptly, hastily, hurriedly, speedily

rare 1 = <u>uncommon</u>, unusual, few, strange, scarce, singular, sparse, infrequent ≠ common

2 = superb, great, fine, excellent, superlative, choice, peerless

rarely = seldom, hardly, hardly ever, infrequently ≠ often

> ### Word Power
> **rarely** – Since the meaning of *rarely* is 'hardly ever', the combination *rarely ever* is repetitive and should be avoided in careful writing, even though you may sometimes hear this phrase used in informal speech.

raring (in construction *raring to do something*) = eager, impatient, longing, ready, keen, desperate, enthusiastic

rarity 1 = curio, find, treasure, gem, collector's item 2 = uncommonness, scarcity, infrequency, unusualness, shortage, strangeness, sparseness

rash[1] = reckless, hasty, impulsive, imprudent, careless, ill-advised, foolhardy, impetuous ≠ cautious

rash[2] 1 = outbreak of spots, (skin) eruption 2 = spate, series, wave, flood, plague, outbreak

rate NOUN 1 = speed, pace, tempo, velocity, frequency 2 = degree, standard, scale, proportion, ratio 3 = charge,

price, cost, fee, figure

● VERB 1 = evaluate, consider, rank, reckon, value, measure, estimate, count 2 = deserve, merit, be entitled to, be worthy of

● PHRASES at any rate = in any case, anyway, anyhow, at all events

rather 1 = preferably, sooner, more readily, more willingly 2 = to some extent, quite, a little, fairly, relatively, somewhat, moderately, to some degree

> ### Word Power
> **rather** – It is acceptable to use either *would rather* or *had rather* in sentences such as *I would rather* (or *had rather*) *see a film than a play*. Had rather, however, is less common than *would rather*, and sounds a little old-fashioned nowadays.

ratify = approve, establish, confirm, sanction, endorse, uphold, authorize, affirm ≠ annul

rating = position, placing, rate, order, class, degree, rank, status

ratio = proportion, rate, relation, percentage, fraction

ration NOUN = allowance, quota, allotment, helping, part, share, measure, portion

● VERB = limit, control, restrict,

budget

rational = <u>sensible</u>, sound, wise, reasonable, intelligent, realistic, logical, sane ≠ insane

rationale = <u>reason</u>, grounds, theory, principle, philosophy, logic, motivation, raison d'être (French)

rattle 1 = <u>clatter</u>, bang, jangle 2 = <u>shake</u>, jolt, vibrate, bounce, jar 3 (Informal) = <u>fluster</u>, shake, upset, disturb, disconcert, perturb, faze

ravage VERB = <u>destroy</u>, ruin, devastate, spoil, demolish, ransack, lay waste, despoil
● PLURAL NOUN = <u>damage</u>, destruction, devastation, ruin, havoc, ruination, spoliation

rave 1 = <u>rant</u>, rage, roar, go mad (informal), babble, be delirious 2 (Informal) = <u>enthuse</u>, praise, gush, be mad about (informal), be wild about (informal)

raving = <u>mad</u>, wild, crazy, hysterical, insane, irrational, crazed, delirious, berko (Austral. slang), off the air (Austral. slang)

raw 1 = <u>unrefined</u>, natural, crude, unprocessed, basic, rough, coarse, unfinished ≠ refined 2 = <u>uncooked</u>, natural, fresh ≠ cooked 3 = <u>inexperienced</u>, new, green, immature, callow ≠ experienced 4 = <u>chilly</u>, biting,

cold, freezing, bitter, piercing, parky (Brit. informal)

ray = <u>beam</u>, bar, flash, shaft, gleam

re = <u>concerning</u>, about, regarding, with regard to, with reference to, apropos

---

> ## Word Power
>
> **re** – In contexts such as *re your letter, your remarks have been noted* or *he spoke to me re your complaint*, *re* is common in business or official correspondence. In spoken and in general written English *with reference to* is preferable in the former case and *about* or *concerning* in the latter. Even in business correspondence, the use of *re* is often restricted to the letter heading.

---

reach VERB 1 = <u>arrive at</u>, get to, make, attain 2 = <u>attain</u>, get to 3 = <u>touch</u>, grasp, extend to, stretch to, contact 4 = <u>contact</u>, get in touch with, get through to, communicate with, get hold of
● NOUN 1 = <u>grasp</u>, range, distance, stretch, capacity, extent, extension, scope 2 = <u>jurisdiction</u>, power, influence

react = <u>respond</u>, act, proceed, behave

reaction 1 = <u>response</u>, answer, reply 2 = <u>counteraction</u>, backlash, recoil 3 = <u>conservatism</u>, the right

> ### Word Power
>
> **reaction** – Some people say
> that *reaction* should always refer
> to an instant response to
> something (as in *his reaction
> was one of amazement*), and
> that this word should not be
> used to refer to a considered
> response given in the form of a
> statement (as in *the Minister
> gave his reaction to the court's
> decision*). Use *response* instead.

reactionary ADJECTIVE
= <u>conservative</u>, right-wing
● NOUN = <u>conservative</u>, die-hard,
right-winger ≠ radical

read 1 = <u>scan</u>, study, look at, pore
over, peruse 2 = <u>understand</u>,
interpret, comprehend, construe,
decipher, see, discover
3 = <u>register</u>, show, record, display,
indicate

readily 1 = <u>willingly</u>, freely,
quickly, gladly, eagerly
≠ reluctantly 2 = <u>promptly</u>,
quickly, easily, smoothly,
effortlessly, speedily,
unhesitatingly ≠ with difficulty

readiness 1 = <u>willingness</u>,
eagerness, keenness
2 = <u>promptness</u>, facility, ease,
dexterity, adroitness

reading 1 = <u>perusal</u>, study,
examination, inspection, scrutiny

2 = <u>learning</u>, education,
knowledge, scholarship, erudition
3 = <u>recital</u>, performance, lesson,
sermon 4 = <u>interpretation</u>,
version, impression, grasp

ready 1 = <u>prepared</u>, set, primed,
organized ≠ unprepared
2 = <u>completed</u>, arranged
3 = <u>mature</u>, ripe, mellow, ripened,
seasoned 4 = <u>willing</u>, happy, glad,
disposed, keen, eager, inclined,
prone ≠ reluctant 5 = <u>prompt</u>,
smart, quick, bright, sharp, keen,
alert, clever ≠ slow 6 = <u>available</u>,
handy, present, near, accessible,
convenient ≠ unavailable

real 1 = <u>true</u>, genuine, sincere,
factual, dinkum (*Austral. & N.Z.
informal*), unfeigned 2 = <u>genuine</u>,
authentic, dinkum (*Austral. & N.Z.
informal*) ≠ fake 3 = <u>proper</u>, true,
valid 4 = <u>true</u>, actual 5 = <u>typical</u>,
true, genuine, sincere, dinkum
(*Austral. & N.Z. informal*),
unfeigned 6 = <u>complete</u>, total,
perfect, utter, thorough

realistic 1 = <u>practical</u>, real,
sensible, common-sense, down-
to-earth, matter-of-fact, level-
headed ≠ impractical
2 = <u>attainable</u>, sensible
3 = <u>lifelike</u>, true to life, authentic,
true, natural, genuine, faithful

reality 1 = <u>fact</u>, truth, realism,
validity, verity, actuality 2 = <u>truth</u>,
fact, actuality

realization 1 = <u>awareness</u>, understanding, recognition, perception, grasp, conception, comprehension, cognizance **2** = <u>achievement</u>, accomplishment, fulfilment

realize 1 = <u>become aware of</u>, understand, take in, grasp, comprehend, get the message **2** = <u>fulfil</u>, achieve, accomplish, make real **3** = <u>achieve</u>, do, effect, complete, perform, fulfil, accomplish, carry out *or* through

really 1 = <u>certainly</u>, genuinely, positively, surely **2** = <u>truly</u>, actually, in fact, indeed, in actuality

realm 1 = <u>field</u>, world, area, province, sphere, department, branch, territory **2** = <u>kingdom</u>, country, empire, land, domain, dominion

reap 1 = <u>get</u>, gain, obtain, acquire, derive **2** = <u>collect</u>, gather, bring in, harvest, garner, cut

rear¹ NOUN 1 = <u>back part</u>, back ≠ front **2** = <u>back</u>, end, tail, rearguard, tail end
• **ADJECTIVE** = <u>back</u>, hind, last, following ≠ front

rear² 1 = <u>bring up</u>, raise, educate, train, foster, nurture **2** = <u>breed</u>, keep **3** = <u>rise</u>, tower, soar, loom

reason NOUN 1 = <u>cause</u>, grounds, purpose, motive, goal, aim, object, intention **2** = <u>sense</u>, mind,

understanding, judgment, logic, intellect, sanity, rationality ≠ emotion
• **VERB** = <u>deduce</u>, conclude, work out, make out, infer, think
• **PHRASES reason with someone** = <u>persuade</u>, bring round, urge, win over, prevail upon (*informal*), talk into *or* out of

---

Word Power

reason – Many people object to the expression *the reason is because*, on the grounds that it is repetitive. It is therefore advisable to use either *this is because* or *the reason is that*.

---

reasonable 1 = <u>sensible</u>, sound, practical, wise, logical, sober, plausible, sane ≠ irrational **2** = <u>fair</u>, just, right, moderate, equitable, tenable ≠ unfair **3** = <u>within reason</u>, fit, proper ≠ impossible **4** = <u>low</u>, cheap, competitive, moderate, modest, inexpensive **5** = <u>average</u>, fair, moderate, modest, O.K. *or* okay (*informal*)

reassure = <u>encourage</u>, comfort, hearten, gee up, restore confidence to, put *or* set your mind at rest

rebate = <u>refund</u>, discount, reduction, bonus, allowance, deduction

rebel NOUN 1 = <u>revolutionary</u>, insurgent, secessionist, revolutionist 2 = <u>nonconformist</u>, dissenter, heretic, apostate, schismatic

● VERB 1 = <u>revolt</u>, resist, rise up, mutiny 2 = <u>defy</u>, dissent, disobey

● ADJECTIVE = <u>rebellious</u>, revolutionary, insurgent, insurrectionary

rebellion 1 = <u>resistance</u>, rising, revolution, revolt, uprising, mutiny 2 = <u>nonconformity</u>, defiance, heresy, schism

rebellious 1 = <u>defiant</u>, difficult, resistant, unmanageable, refractory ≠ obedient 2 = <u>revolutionary</u>, rebel, disorderly, unruly, insurgent, disloyal, seditious, mutinous ≠ obedient

rebound 1 = <u>bounce</u>, ricochet, recoil 2 = <u>misfire</u>, backfire, recoil, boomerang

rebuff VERB = <u>reject</u>, refuse, turn down, cut, slight, snub, spurn, knock back (slang) ≠ encourage

● NOUN = <u>rejection</u>, snub, knock-back, slight, refusal, repulse, cold shoulder, slap in the face (informal) ≠ encouragement

rebuke VERB = <u>scold</u>, censure, reprimand, castigate, chide, dress down (informal), admonish, tell off (informal) ≠ praise

● NOUN = <u>scolding</u>, censure, reprimand, row, dressing down (informal), telling-off (informal), admonition ≠ praise

recall VERB 1 = <u>recollect</u>, remember, evoke, call to mind 2 = <u>call back</u> 3 = <u>annul</u>, withdraw, cancel, repeal, revoke, retract, countermand

● NOUN 1 = <u>recollection</u>, memory, remembrance 2 = <u>annulment</u>, withdrawal, repeal, cancellation, retraction, rescindment

recede = <u>fall back</u>, withdraw, retreat, return, retire, regress

receipt 1 = <u>sales slip</u>, proof of purchase, counterfoil 2 = <u>receiving</u>, delivery, reception, acceptance

receive 1 = <u>get</u>, accept, be given, pick up, collect, obtain, acquire, take 2 = <u>experience</u>, suffer, bear, encounter, sustain, undergo 3 = <u>greet</u>, meet, admit, welcome, entertain, accommodate

recent = <u>new</u>, modern, up-to-date, late, current, fresh, novel, present-day ≠ old

recently = <u>not long ago</u>, newly, lately, currently, freshly, of late, latterly

reception 1 = <u>party</u>, gathering, get-together, social gathering, function, celebration, festivity, soirée 2 = <u>response</u>, reaction, acknowledgment, treatment, welcome, greeting

recess 1 = <u>break</u>, rest, holiday, interval, vacation, respite, intermission **2** = <u>alcove</u>, corner, bay, hollow, niche, nook

recession = <u>depression</u>, drop, decline, slump ≠ boom

recipe = <u>directions</u>, instructions, ingredients

recital 1 = <u>performance</u>, rendering, rehearsal, reading **2** = <u>account</u>, telling, statement, relation, narrative **3** = <u>recitation</u>

recite = <u>perform</u>, deliver, repeat, declaim

reckless = <u>careless</u>, wild, rash, precipitate, hasty, mindless, headlong, thoughtless ≠ cautious

reckon 1 (*Informal*) = <u>think</u>, believe, suppose, imagine, assume, guess (*informal, chiefly U.S. & Canad.*) **2** = <u>consider</u>, rate, account, judge, regard, count, esteem, deem **3** = <u>count</u>, figure, total, calculate, compute, add up, tally, number

reckoning = <u>count</u>, estimate, calculation, addition

reclaim 1 = <u>retrieve</u>, regain **2** = <u>regain</u>, salvage, recapture

recognition 1 = <u>identification</u>, recollection, discovery, remembrance **2** = <u>acceptance</u>, admission, allowance, confession

recognize 1 = <u>identify</u>, know, place, remember, spot, notice,

recall, recollect **2** = <u>acknowledge</u>, allow, accept, admit, grant, concede ≠ ignore **3** = <u>appreciate</u>, respect, notice

recollection = <u>memory</u>, recall, impression, remembrance, reminiscence

recommend 1 = <u>advocate</u>, suggest, propose, approve, endorse, commend ≠ disapprove of **2** = <u>put forward</u>, approve, endorse, commend, praise **3** = <u>advise</u>, suggest, advance, propose, counsel, advocate, prescribe, put forward

recommendation 1 = <u>advice</u>, proposal, suggestion, counsel **2** = <u>commendation</u>, reference, praise, sanction, approval, endorsement, advocacy, testimonial

reconcile 1 = <u>resolve</u>, settle, square, adjust, compose, rectify, put to rights **2** = <u>reunite</u>, bring back together, conciliate **3** = <u>make peace between</u>, reunite, propitiate

reconciliation = <u>reunion</u>, conciliation, pacification, reconcilement ≠ separation

reconsider = <u>rethink</u>, review, revise, think again, reassess

reconstruct 1 = <u>rebuild</u>, restore, recreate, remake, renovate, remodel, regenerate **2** = <u>build up a picture of</u>, build up, piece together, deduce

record NOUN 1 = <u>document</u>, file, register, log, report, account, entry, journal 2 = <u>evidence</u>, trace, documentation, testimony, witness 3 = <u>disc</u>, single, album, LP, vinyl 4 = <u>background</u>, history, performance, career

● VERB 1 = <u>set down</u>, minute, note, enter, document, register, log, chronicle 2 = <u>make a recording of</u>, video, tape, video-tape, tape-record 3 = <u>register</u>, show, indicate, give evidence of

recorder = <u>chronicler</u>, archivist, historian, clerk, scribe, diarist

recording = <u>record</u>, video, tape, disc

recount = <u>tell</u>, report, describe, relate, repeat, depict, recite, narrate

recover 1 = <u>get better</u>, improve, get well, recuperate, heal, revive, mend, convalesce ≠ relapse 2 = <u>rally</u> 3 = <u>save</u>, rescue, retrieve, salvage, reclaim ≠ abandon 4 = <u>recoup</u>, restore, get back, regain, retrieve, reclaim, redeem, recapture ≠ lose

recovery 1 = <u>improvement</u>, healing, revival, mending, recuperation, convalescence 2 = <u>retrieval</u>, repossession, reclamation, restoration

recreation = <u>leisure</u>, play, sport, fun, entertainment, relaxation, enjoyment, amusement

recruit VERB 1 = <u>gather</u>, obtain, engage, procure 2 = <u>assemble</u>, raise, levy, muster, mobilize 3 = <u>enlist</u>, draft, enrol ≠ dismiss

● NOUN = <u>beginner</u>, trainee, apprentice, novice, convert, initiate, helper, learner

recur = <u>happen again</u>, return, repeat, persist, revert, reappear, come again

recycle = <u>reprocess</u>, reuse, salvage, reclaim, save

red NOUN or ADJECTIVE 1 = <u>crimson</u>, scarlet, ruby, vermilion, cherry, coral, carmine 2 = <u>flushed</u>, embarrassed, blushing, florid, shamefaced 3 (of hair) = <u>chestnut</u>, reddish, flame-coloured, sandy, Titian, carroty

● PHRASES in the red (Informal) = <u>in debt</u>, insolvent, in arrears, overdrawn ◆ see red (Informal) = <u>lose your temper</u>, lose it (informal), go mad (informal), crack up (informal), lose the plot (informal), go ballistic (slang, chiefly U.S.), fly off the handle (informal), blow your top

➤ shades of red

redeem 1 = <u>reinstate</u>, absolve, restore to favour 2 = <u>make up for</u>, compensate for, atone for, make amends for 3 = <u>buy back</u>, recover, regain, retrieve, reclaim, repurchase 4 = <u>save</u>, free, deliver,

Shades of red

auburn	flesh	raspberry
baby pink	foxy	rose
burgundy	fuchsia	roseate
burnt sienna	ginger	rosy
cardinal red	henna	ruby
carmine	liver	russet
carnation	magenta	rust
carroty	maroon	sandy
cerise	mulberry	scarlet
cherry	old rose	strawberry
chestnut	oxblood	tea rose
cinnabar	oyster pink	terracotta
copper *or* coppery	peach	Titian
coral	pink	vermilion
crimson	plum	wine
damask	poppy	
flame	puce	

liberate, ransom, emancipate

redemption 1 = <u>compensation</u>, amends, reparation, atonement **2** = <u>salvation</u>, release, rescue, liberation, emancipation, deliverance

redress VERB **1** = <u>make amends for</u>, make up for, compensate for **2** = <u>put right</u>, balance, correct, adjust, regulate, rectify, even up
● NOUN = <u>amends</u>, payment, compensation, reparation, atonement, recompense

reduce 1 = <u>lessen</u>, cut, lower, moderate, weaken, diminish, decrease, cut down ≠ increase **2** = <u>degrade</u>, downgrade, break,

humble, bring low ≠ promote

redundancy 1 = <u>layoff</u>, sacking, dismissal **2** = <u>unemployment</u>, the sack (*informal*), the axe (*informal*), joblessness

redundant = <u>superfluous</u>, extra, surplus, unnecessary, unwanted, inessential, supernumerary ≠ essential

reel 1 = <u>stagger</u>, rock, roll, pitch, sway, lurch **2** = <u>whirl</u>, spin, revolve, swirl

refer VERB = <u>direct</u>, point, send, guide
● PHRASES **refer to something** *or* **someone 1** = <u>allude to</u>,

mention, cite, speak of, bring up
2 = <u>relate to</u>, concern, apply to, pertain to, be relevant to
3 = <u>consult</u>, go, apply, turn to, look up

> ### Word Power
>
> **refer** – It is usually unnecessary to add *back* to the verb *refer*, since the sense of *back* is already contained in the *re-* part of this word. For example, you might say *This refers to* (not *refers back to*) *what has already been said*. Refer back is only considered acceptable when used to mean 'return a document or question to the person it came from for further consideration', as in *he referred the matter back to me*.

referee NOUN = <u>umpire</u>, judge, ref (*informal*), arbiter, arbitrator, adjudicator
• VERB = <u>umpire</u>, judge, mediate, adjudicate, arbitrate

reference 1 = <u>allusion</u>, note, mention, quotation **2** = <u>citation</u>
3 = <u>testimonial</u>, recommendation, credentials, endorsement, character reference

referendum = <u>public vote</u>, popular vote, plebiscite

refine 1 = <u>purify</u>, process, filter, cleanse, clarify, distil **2** = <u>improve</u>,
perfect, polish, hone

refined 1 = <u>purified</u>, processed, pure, filtered, clean, clarified, distilled ≠ unrefined **2** = <u>cultured</u>, polished, elegant, polite, cultivated, civilized, well-bred ≠ coarse **3** = <u>discerning</u>, fine, sensitive, delicate, precise, discriminating, fastidious

reflect 1 = <u>show</u>, reveal, display, indicate, demonstrate, manifest
2 = <u>throw back</u>, return, mirror, echo, reproduce **3** = <u>consider</u>, think, muse, ponder, meditate, ruminate, cogitate, wonder

reflection 1 = <u>image</u>, echo, mirror image **2** = <u>consideration</u>, thinking, thought, idea, opinion, observation, musing, meditation

reflective = <u>thoughtful</u>, contemplative, meditative, pensive

reform NOUN = <u>improvement</u>, amendment, rehabilitation, betterment
• VERB **1** = <u>improve</u>, correct, restore, amend, mend, rectify
2 = <u>mend your ways</u>, go straight (*informal*), shape up (*informal*), turn over a new leaf, clean up your act (*informal*), pull your socks up (*Brit. informal*)

refrain¹ = <u>stop</u>, avoid, cease, renounce, abstain, leave off, desist, forbear

refrain² = <u>chorus</u>, tune, melody

refresh 1 = <u>revive</u>, freshen, revitalize, stimulate, brace, enliven, invigorate **2** = <u>stimulate</u>, prompt, renew, jog

refreshing 1 = <u>new</u>, original, novel **2** = <u>stimulating</u>, fresh, bracing, invigorating ≠ tiring

refreshment = <u>food and drink</u>, drinks, snacks, titbits, kai (N.Z. informal)

refuge 1 = <u>protection</u>, shelter, asylum **2** = <u>haven</u>, retreat, sanctuary, hide-out

refugee = <u>exile</u>, émigré, displaced person, escapee

refund NOUN = <u>repayment</u>, reimbursement, return

● VERB = <u>repay</u>, return, restore, pay back, reimburse

refurbish = <u>renovate</u>, restore, repair, clean up, overhaul, revamp, mend, do up (informal)

refusal = <u>rejection</u>, denial, rebuff, knock-back (slang)

refuse¹ 1 = <u>decline</u>, reject, turn down, say no to **2** = <u>deny</u>, decline, withhold ≠ allow

refuse² = <u>rubbish</u>, waste, junk (informal), litter, garbage, trash

regain 1 = <u>recover</u>, get back, retrieve, recapture, win back, take back, recoup **2** = <u>get back to</u>, return to, reach again

regal = <u>royal</u>, majestic, kingly or queenly, noble, princely, magnificent

regard VERB **1** = <u>consider</u>, see, rate, view, judge, think of, esteem, deem **2** = <u>look at</u>, view, eye, watch, observe, clock (Brit. slang), check out (informal), gaze at

● NOUN **1** = <u>respect</u>, esteem, thought, concern, care, consideration **2** = <u>look</u>, gaze, scrutiny, stare, glance

● PLURAL NOUN = <u>good wishes</u>, respects, greetings, compliments, best wishes

● PHRASES **as regards** = <u>concerning</u>, regarding, relating to, pertaining to

> ## Word Power
>
> **regard** – The word *regard* in the expression *with regard to* is singular, and has no *s* at the end. People often make the mistake of saying *with regards to*, perhaps being influenced by the phrase *as regards*.

regarding = <u>concerning</u>, about, on the subject of, re, respecting, as regards, with reference to, in or with regard to

regardless 1 = <u>in spite of everything</u>, anyway, nevertheless, in any case **2** *with of* = <u>irrespective of</u>, heedless of, unmindful of

regime 1 = <u>government</u>, rule, management, leadership, reign **2** = <u>plan</u>, course, system, policy, programme, scheme, regimen

region = <u>area</u>, place, part, quarter, section, sector, district, territory

➤ WORD POWER SUPPLEMENT
administrative regions

regional = <u>local</u>, district, provincial, parochial, zonal

register NOUN = <u>list</u>, record, roll, file, diary, catalogue, log, archives
• VERB 1 = <u>enrol</u>, enlist, list, note, enter 2 = <u>record</u>, catalogue, chronicle 3 = <u>indicate</u>, show 4 = <u>show</u>, mark, indicate, manifest 5 = <u>express</u>, show, reveal, display, exhibit

regret VERB 1 = <u>be or feel sorry about</u>, rue, deplore, bemoan, repent (of), bewail ≠ be satisfied with 2 = <u>mourn</u>, miss, grieve for or over
• NOUN 1 = <u>remorse</u>, compunction, bitterness, repentance, contrition, penitence 2 = <u>sorrow</u> ≠ satisfaction

regular 1 = <u>frequent</u> 2 = <u>normal</u>, common, usual, ordinary, typical, routine, customary, habitual ≠ infrequent 3 = <u>steady</u>, consistent 4 = <u>even</u>, level, balanced, straight, flat, fixed, smooth, uniform ≠ uneven

regulate 1 = <u>control</u>, run, rule, manage, direct, guide, handle, govern 2 = <u>moderate</u>, control, modulate, fit, tune, adjust

regulation 1 = <u>rule</u>, order, law, dictate, decree, statute, edict, precept 2 = <u>control</u>, government, management, direction, supervision

rehearsal = <u>practice</u>, rehearsing, run-through, preparation, drill

rehearse = <u>practise</u>, prepare, run through, go over, train, repeat, drill, recite

reign VERB 1 = <u>be supreme</u>, prevail, predominate, hold sway 2 = <u>rule</u>, govern, be in power, influence, command
• NOUN = <u>rule</u>, power, control, command, monarchy, dominion

---

Word Power

reign – The words rein and reign should not be confused; note the correct spellings in he gave full rein to his feelings (not reign); and it will be necessary to rein in public spending (not reign in).

---

rein = <u>control</u>, harness, bridle, hold, check, brake, curb, restraint

reincarnation = <u>rebirth</u>, transmigration of souls

reinforce 1 = <u>support</u>, strengthen, fortify, toughen, stress, prop, supplement, emphasize 2 = <u>increase</u>, extend, add to, strengthen, supplement

reinforcement NOUN

1 = <u>strengthening</u>, increase, fortification, augmentation 2 = <u>support</u>, stay, prop, brace, buttress

● PLURAL NOUN = <u>reserves</u>, support, auxiliaries, additional *or* fresh troops

reinstate = <u>restore</u>, recall, re-establish, return

reiterate (*Formal*) = <u>repeat</u>, restate, say again, do again

reject VERB 1 = <u>rebuff</u>, jilt, turn down, spurn, refuse, say no to, repulse ≠ accept 2 = <u>deny</u>, exclude, veto, relinquish, renounce, disallow, forsake, disown ≠ approve 3 = <u>discard</u>, decline, eliminate, scrap, jettison, throw away *or* out ≠ accept

● NOUN 1 = <u>castoff</u>, second, discard ≠ treasure 2 = <u>failure</u>, loser, flop

rejection 1 = <u>denial</u>, veto, dismissal, exclusion, disowning, thumbs down, renunciation, repudiation ≠ approval 2 = <u>rebuff</u>, refusal, knock-back (*slang*), kick in the teeth (*slang*), brushoff (*slang*) ≠ acceptance

rejoice = <u>be glad</u>, celebrate, be happy, glory, be overjoyed, exult ≠ lament

rejoin = <u>reply</u>, answer, respond, retort, riposte

relate VERB = <u>tell</u>, recount, report, detail, describe, recite, narrate

● PHRASES **relate to something** *or* **someone** 1 = <u>concern</u>, refer to, apply to, have to do with, pertain to, be relevant to 2 = <u>connect with</u>, associate with, link with, couple with, join with, correlate to

related 1 = <u>associated</u>, linked, joint, connected, affiliated, akin, interconnected ≠ unconnected 2 = <u>akin</u>, kindred ≠ unrelated

relation NOUN 1 = <u>similarity</u>, link, bearing, bond, comparison, correlation, connection 2 = <u>relative</u>, kin, kinsman *or* kinswoman

● PLURAL NOUN 1 = <u>dealings</u>, relationship, affairs, contact, connections, interaction, intercourse 2 = <u>family</u>, relatives, tribe, clan, kin, kindred, kinsmen, kinsfolk, ainga (*N.Z.*)

relationship 1 = <u>association</u>, bond, connection, affinity, rapport, kinship 2 = <u>affair</u>, romance, liaison, amour, intrigue 3 = <u>connection</u>, link, parallel, similarity, tie-up, correlation

relative NOUN = <u>relation</u>, kinsman *or* kinswoman, member of your *or* his family

● ADJECTIVE 1 = <u>comparative</u> 2 = <u>corresponding</u> 3 *with* **to** = <u>in proportion to</u>, proportionate to

relatively = <u>comparatively</u>, rather, somewhat

relax 1 = be or feel at ease, chill
out (slang, chiefly U.S.), take it
easy, lighten up (slang), outspan
(S. African) ≠ be alarmed 2 = calm
down, calm, unwind 3 = make
less tense, rest 4 = lessen, reduce,
ease, relieve, weaken, loosen, let
up, slacken ≠ tighten
5 = moderate, ease, relieve,
weaken, slacken ≠ tighten up

relaxation = leisure, rest, fun,
pleasure, recreation, enjoyment

relay = broadcast, carry, spread,
communicate, transmit, send out

release VERB 1 = set free, free,
discharge, liberate, drop, loose,
undo, extricate ≠ imprison
2 = acquit, let go, let off,
exonerate, absolve 3 = issue,
publish, make public, make
known, launch, distribute, put
out, circulate ≠ withhold
● NOUN 1 = liberation, freedom,
liberty, discharge, emancipation,
deliverance ≠ imprisonment
2 = acquittal, exemption,
absolution, exoneration 3 = issue,
publication, proclamation

relegate = demote, degrade,
downgrade

relentless 1 = merciless, fierce,
cruel, ruthless, unrelenting,
implacable, remorseless, pitiless
≠ merciful 2 = unremitting,
persistent, unrelenting, incessant,
nonstop, unrelieved

relevant = significant, appropriate,
related, fitting, to the point, apt,
pertinent, apposite ≠ irrelevant

reliable 1 = dependable,
trustworthy, sure, sound, true,
faithful, staunch ≠ unreliable
2 = safe, dependable 3 = definitive,
sound, dependable, trustworthy

reliance 1 = dependency,
dependence 2 = trust,
confidence, belief, faith

relic = remnant, vestige,
memento, trace, fragment,
souvenir, keepsake

relief 1 = ease, release, comfort,
cure, remedy, solace, deliverance,
mitigation 2 = rest, respite,
relaxation, break, breather
(informal) 3 = aid, help, support,
assistance, succour

relieve 1 = ease, soothe,
alleviate, relax, comfort, calm,
cure, soften ≠ intensify 2 = help,
support, aid, sustain, assist, succour

religion = belief, faith, theology,
creed
➤ **religion**

religious 1 = spiritual, holy,
sacred, devotional
2 = conscientious, faithful, rigid,
meticulous, scrupulous,
punctilious

relinquish (Formal) = give up,
leave, drop, abandon, surrender,
let go, renounce, forsake

relish VERB 1 = enjoy, like, savour,

Religion

Religions

animism
Babi or Babism
Baha'ism
Buddhism
Christianity
Confucianism
druidism
heliolatry
Hinduism or Hindooism
Islam
Jainism
Judaism
Macumba
Manichaeism or Manicheism
Mithraism or Mithraicism
Orphism

paganism
Rastafarianism
Ryobu Shinto
Santeria
Satanism
Scientology ®
shamanism
Shango
Shembe
Shinto
Sikhism
Taoism
voodoo or voodooism
Yezidis
Zoroastrianism or Zoroastrism

Religious festivals

Advent
Al Hijrah
Ascension Day
Ash Wednesday
Baisakhi
Bodhi Day
Candlemas
Chanukah or Hanukkah
Ching Ming
Christmas
Corpus Christi
Day of Atonement
Dhammacakka
Diwali
Dragon Boat Festival
Dussehra
Easter
Eid ul-Adha or Id-ul-Adha
Eid ul-Fitr or Id-ul-Fitr

Epiphany
Feast of Tabernacles
Good Friday
Guru Nanak's Birthday
Hirja
Hola Mohalla
Holi
Janamashtami
Lailat ul-Barah
Lailat ul-Isra Wal Mi'raj
Lailat ul-Qadr
Lent
Mahashivaratri
Maundy Thursday
Michaelmas
Moon Festival
Palm Sunday
Passion Sunday
Passover

Religious festivals (continued)	
Pentecost	Sexagesima
Pesach	Shavuot
Purim	Shrove Tuesday
Quadragesima	Sukkoth *or* Succoth
Quinquagesima	Trinity
Raksha Bandhan	Wesak
Ramadan	Whitsun
Rama Naumi	Winter Festival
Rogation	Yom Kippur
Rosh Hashanah	Yuan Tan
Septuagesima	

revel in ≠ dislike 2 = <u>look forward to</u>, fancy, delight in

● NOUN 1 = <u>enjoyment</u>, liking, love, taste, fancy, penchant, fondness, gusto ≠ distaste

2 = <u>condiment</u>, seasoning, sauce

reluctance = <u>unwillingness</u>, dislike, loathing, distaste, aversion, disinclination, repugnance

reluctant = <u>unwilling</u>, hesitant, loath, disinclined, unenthusiastic ≠ willing

Word Power

reluctant – *Reticent* is quite commonly used nowadays as a synonym of *reluctant* and followed by *to* and a verb. In careful writing it is advisable to avoid this use, since many people would regard it as mistaken.

rely on 1 = <u>depend on</u>, lean on

2 = <u>be confident of</u>, bank on, trust, count on, bet on

remain 1 = <u>stay</u>, continue, go on, stand, dwell 2 = <u>stay behind</u>, wait, delay ≠ go 3 = <u>continue</u>, be left, linger

remainder = <u>rest</u>, remains, balance, excess, surplus, remnant, residue, leavings

remains 1 = <u>remnants</u>, leftovers, rest, debris, residue, dregs, leavings 2 = <u>corpse</u>, body, carcass, cadaver 3 = <u>relics</u>

remark VERB 1 = <u>comment</u>, say, state, reflect, mention, declare, observe, pass comment

2 = <u>notice</u>, note, observe, perceive, see, mark, make out, espy

● NOUN = <u>comment</u>, observation, reflection, statement, utterance

remarkable = <u>extraordinary</u>, striking, outstanding, wonderful,

rare, unusual, surprising, notable
≠ ordinary

remedy NOUN = <u>cure</u>, treatment, medicine, nostrum

• VERB = <u>put right</u>, rectify, fix, correct, set to rights

remember 1 = <u>recall</u>, think back to, recollect, reminisce about, call to mind ≠ forget 2 = <u>bear in mind</u>, keep in mind 3 = <u>look back (on)</u>, commemorate

remembrance
1 = <u>commemoration</u>, memorial
2 = <u>souvenir</u>, token, reminder, monument, memento, keepsake
3 = <u>memory</u>, recollection, thought, recall, reminiscence

remind 1 = <u>jog your memory</u>, prompt, make you remember

reminiscent = <u>suggestive</u>, evocative, similar

remnant = <u>remainder</u>, remains, trace, fragment, end, rest, residue, leftovers

remorse = <u>regret</u>, shame, guilt, grief, sorrow, anguish, repentance, contrition

remote 1 = <u>distant</u>, far, isolated, out-of-the-way, secluded, inaccessible, in the middle of nowhere ≠ nearby 2 = <u>far</u>, distant 3 = <u>slight</u>, small, outside, unlikely, slim, faint, doubtful, dubious ≠ strong 4 = <u>aloof</u>, cold, reserved, withdrawn, distant, abstracted, detached, uncommunicative

≠ outgoing

removal 1 = <u>extraction</u>, withdrawal, uprooting, eradication, dislodgment, taking away or off or out 2 = <u>dismissal</u>, expulsion, elimination, ejection 3 = <u>move</u>, transfer, departure, relocation, flitting (*Scot. & Northern English dialect*)

remove 1 = <u>take out</u>, withdraw, extract ≠ insert 2 = <u>take off</u> ≠ put on 3 = <u>erase</u>, eliminate, take out 4 = <u>dismiss</u>, eliminate, get rid of, discharge, abolish, expel, throw out, oust ≠ appoint 5 = <u>get rid of</u>, erase, eradicate, expunge 6 = <u>take away</u>, detach, displace ≠ put back 7 = <u>delete</u>, get rid of, erase, excise 8 = <u>move</u>, depart, relocate, flit (*Scot. & Northern English dialect*)

renaissance or **renascence** = <u>rebirth</u>, revival, restoration, renewal, resurgence, reappearance, reawakening

rend (*Literary*) = <u>tear</u>, rip, separate, wrench, rupture

render 1 = <u>make</u>, cause to become, leave 2 = <u>provide</u>, give, pay, present, supply, submit, tender, hand out 3 = <u>represent</u>, portray, depict, do, give, play, act, perform

renew 1 = <u>recommence</u>, continue, extend, repeat, resume, reopen, recreate, reaffirm

2 = <u>reaffirm</u>, resume, recommence 3 = <u>replace</u>, refresh, replenish, restock 4 = <u>restore</u>, repair, overhaul, mend, refurbish, renovate, refit, modernize

renounce 1 = <u>disown</u>, quit, forsake, recant, forswear, abjure 2 = <u>disclaim</u>, deny, give up, relinquish, waive, abjure ≠ assert

renovate = <u>restore</u>, repair, refurbish, do up (*informal*), renew, overhaul, refit, modernize

renowned = <u>famous</u>, noted, celebrated, well-known, distinguished, esteemed, notable, eminent ≠ unknown

rent¹ VERB 1 = <u>hire</u>, lease 2 = <u>let</u>, lease
● NOUN = <u>hire</u>, rental, lease, fee, payment

rent² 1 = <u>tear</u>, split, rip, slash, slit, gash, hole 2 = <u>opening</u>, hole

repair VERB 1 = <u>mend</u>, fix, restore, heal, patch, renovate, patch up ≠ damage 2 = <u>put right</u>, make up for, compensate for, rectify, redress
● NOUN 1 = <u>mend</u>, restoration, overhaul 2 = <u>darn</u>, mend, patch 3 = <u>condition</u>, state, form, shape (*informal*)

repay = <u>pay back</u>, refund, settle up, return, square, compensate, reimburse, recompense

repeal VERB = <u>abolish</u>, reverse, revoke, annul, recall, cancel,

invalidate, nullify ≠ pass
● NOUN = <u>abolition</u>, cancellation, annulment, invalidation, rescindment ≠ passing

repeat VERB 1 = <u>reiterate</u>, restate 2 = <u>retell</u>, echo, replay, reproduce, rerun, reshow
● NOUN 1 = <u>repetition</u>, echo, reiteration 2 = <u>rerun</u>, replay, reshowing

> ### Word Power
>
> **repeat** – Since the sense of *again* is already contained within the *re-* part of the word *repeat*, it is unnecessary to say that something is *repeated again*.

repeatedly = <u>over and over</u>, often, frequently, many times

repel 1 = <u>drive off</u>, fight, resist, parry, hold off, rebuff, ward off, repulse ≠ submit to 2 = <u>disgust</u>, offend, revolt, sicken, nauseate, gross out (*U.S. slang*) ≠ delight

repertoire = <u>range</u>, list, stock, supply, store, collection, repertory

repetition 1 = <u>recurrence</u>, repeating, echo 2 = <u>repeating</u>, replication, restatement, reiteration, tautology

replace 1 = <u>take the place of</u>, follow, succeed, oust, take over from, supersede, supplant 2 = <u>substitute</u>, change, exchange, switch, swap **3** = <u>put back</u>, restore

replacement 1 = <u>replacing</u>
2 = <u>successor</u>, double, substitute,
stand-in, proxy, surrogate,
understudy

replica 1 = <u>reproduction</u>, model,
copy, imitation, facsimile, carbon
copy ≠ original **2** = <u>duplicate</u>,
copy, carbon copy

replicate = <u>copy</u>, reproduce,
recreate, mimic, duplicate,
reduplicate

reply VERB **1** = <u>answer</u>, respond,
retort, counter, rejoin, retaliate,
reciprocate

● NOUN = <u>answer</u>, response,
reaction, counter, retort,
retaliation, counterattack,
rejoinder

report VERB **1** = <u>inform of</u>,
communicate, recount **2** *often*
with *on* = <u>communicate</u>, tell,
state, detail, describe, relate,
broadcast, pass on **3** = <u>present</u>
<u>yourself</u>, come, appear, arrive,
turn up

● NOUN **1** = <u>article</u>, story, piece,
write-up **2** = <u>account</u>, record,
statement, communication,
description, narrative **3** *often*
plural = <u>news</u>, word **4** = <u>bang</u>,
sound, crack, noise, blast, boom,
explosion, discharge **5** = <u>rumour</u>,
talk, buzz, gossip, hearsay

reporter = <u>journalist</u>, writer,
correspondent, hack (*derogatory*),

pressman, journo (*slang*)

represent 1 = <u>act for</u>, speak for
2 = <u>stand for</u>, serve as
3 = <u>express</u>, correspond to,
symbolize, mean **4** = <u>exemplify</u>,
embody, symbolize, typify,
personify, epitomize **5** = <u>depict</u>,
show, describe, picture, illustrate,
outline, portray, denote

representation 1 = <u>picture</u>,
model, image, portrait,
illustration, likeness **2** = <u>portrayal</u>,
depiction, account, description

representative NOUN
1 = <u>delegate</u>, member, agent,
deputy, proxy, spokesman *or*
spokeswoman **2** = <u>agent</u>,
salesman, rep, commercial
traveller

● ADJECTIVE **1** = <u>typical</u>,
characteristic, archetypal,
exemplary ≠ uncharacteristic
2 = <u>symbolic</u>

repress 1 = <u>control</u>, suppress,
hold back, bottle up, check, curb,
restrain, inhibit ≠ release **2** = <u>hold</u>
<u>back</u>, suppress, stifle **3** = <u>subdue</u>,
abuse, wrong, persecute, quell,
subjugate, maltreat ≠ liberate

repression 1 = <u>subjugation</u>,
control, constraint, domination,
tyranny, despotism
2 = <u>suppression</u>, crushing,
quashing **3** = <u>inhibition</u>, control,
restraint, bottling up

reprieve VERB = <u>grant a stay of</u>

execution to, pardon, let off the hook (*slang*)

● NOUN = stay of execution, amnesty, pardon, remission, deferment, postponement of punishment

reproduce 1 = copy, recreate, replicate, duplicate, match, mirror, echo, imitate 2 = print, copy 3 (*Biology*) = breed, procreate, multiply, spawn, propagate

reproduction 1 = copy, picture, print, replica, imitation, duplicate, facsimile ≠ original 2 (*Biology*) = breeding, increase, generation, multiplication

reptile ➤ reptiles

Republican ADJECTIVE = right-wing, Conservative

● NOUN = right-winger, Conservative

reputation = name, standing, character, esteem, stature, renown, repute

request VERB 1 = ask for, appeal for, put in for, demand, desire 2 = invite, entreat 3 = seek, ask (for), solicit

● NOUN 1 = appeal, call, demand, plea, desire, entreaty, suit 2 = asking, plea

require 1 = need, crave, want, miss, lack, wish, desire 2 = order, demand, command, compel, exact, oblige, call upon, insist upon 3 = ask

> ### Word Power
>
> **require** – The use of *require to* as in *I require to see the manager* or *you require to complete a special form* is thought by many people to be incorrect. Useful alternatives are: *I need to see the manager* and *you are required to complete a special form.*

requirement = necessity, demand, stipulation, want, need, must, essential, prerequisite

rescue VERB 1 = save, get out, release, deliver, recover, liberate ≠ desert 2 = salvage, deliver, redeem

● NOUN = saving, salvage, deliverance, release, recovery, liberation, salvation, redemption

research NOUN = investigation, study, analysis, examination, probe, exploration

● VERB = investigate, study, examine, explore, probe, analyse

resemblance = similarity, correspondence, parallel, likeness, kinship, sameness, similitude ≠ dissimilarity

resemble = be like, look like, mirror, parallel, be similar to, bear a resemblance to

resent = be bitter about, object to, grudge, begrudge, take exception to, take offence at ≠ be

Reptiles

adder
agama
agamid
alligator
amphisbaena
anaconda or (Caribbean) camoodi
asp
bandy-bandy
black snake or red-bellied black snake
blind snake
blue tongue
boa
boa constrictor
box turtle
brown snake or (Austral.) mallee snake
bull snake or gopher snake
bushmaster
carpet snake or python
cayman or caiman
chameleon
chuckwalla
cobra
constrictor
copperhead
coral snake
crocodile
death adder or deaf adder
diamondback, diamondback terrapin, or diamondback turtle
diamond snake or diamond python
elapid
fer-de-lance

frill-necked lizard, frilled lizard, bicycle lizard, cycling lizard, or (Austral. informal) frillie
gaboon viper
garter snake
gecko
giant tortoise
Gila monster
glass snake
goanna, bungarra (Austral.), or go (Austral. informal)
grass snake
green turtle
harlequin snake
hawksbill or hawksbill turtle
hognose snake or puff adder
horned toad or lizard
horned viper
iguana
jew lizard, bearded lizard, or bearded dragon
king cobra or hamadryad
king snake
Komodo dragon or Komodo lizard
krait
leatherback or (Brit.) leathery turtle
lizard
loggerhead or loggerhead turtle
mamba
massasauga
milk snake
monitor
mud turtle
ngarara (N.Z.)

Reptiles (continued)

perentie or perenty	snake
pit viper	snapping turtle
puff adder	soft-shelled turtle
python	taipan
rat snake	terrapin
rattlesnake or (U.S. & Canad. informal) rattler	tiger snake
rock snake, rock python, amethystine python, or Schneider python	tokay
	tortoise
	tree snake
saltwater crocodile or (Austral. informal) saltie	tuatara or (technical) sphenodon (N.Z.)
sand lizard	turtle
sand viper	viper
sea snake	wall lizard
sidewinder	water moccasin, moccasin, or cottonmouth
skink	water snake
slowworm or blindworm	whip snake
smooth snake	

content with

resentment = <u>bitterness</u>, indignation, ill feeling, ill will, grudge, animosity, pique, rancour

reservation 1 often plural = <u>doubt</u>, scruples, hesitancy 2 = <u>reserve</u>, territory, preserve, sanctuary

reserve VERB 1 = <u>book</u>, prearrange, engage 2 = <u>put by</u>, secure 3 = <u>keep</u>, hold, save, store, retain, set aside, stockpile, hoard
● NOUN 1 = <u>store</u>, fund, savings, stock, supply, reservoir, hoard, cache 2 = <u>park</u>, reservation,

preserve, sanctuary, tract, forest park (N.Z.) 3 = <u>shyness</u>, silence, restraint, constraint, reticence, secretiveness, taciturnity
4 = <u>reservation</u>, doubt, delay, uncertainty, indecision, hesitancy, vacillation, irresolution
● ADJECTIVE = <u>substitute</u>, extra, spare, secondary, fall-back, auxiliary

reserved 1 = <u>uncommunicative</u>, retiring, silent, shy, restrained, secretive, reticent, taciturn
≠ uninhibited 2 = <u>set aside</u>, taken, kept, held, booked, retained, engaged, restricted

reservoir 1 = <u>lake</u>, pond, basin
2 = <u>store</u>, stock, source, supply,
reserves, pool

reside (*Formal*) = <u>live</u>, lodge,
dwell, stay, abide ≠ visit

residence = <u>home</u>, house,
dwelling, place, flat, lodging,
abode, habitation

resident 1 = <u>inhabitant</u>, citizen,
local ≠ nonresident 2 = <u>tenant</u>,
occupant, lodger 3 = <u>guest</u>,
lodger

residue = <u>remainder</u>, remains,
remnant, leftovers, rest, extra,
excess, surplus

resign VERB 1 = <u>quit</u>, leave, step
down (*informal*), vacate, abdicate,
give *or* hand in your notice
2 = <u>give up</u>, abandon, yield,
surrender, relinquish, renounce,
forsake, forgo
● PHRASES **resign yourself to
something** = <u>accept</u>, succumb
to, submit to, give in to, yield to,
acquiesce to

resignation 1 = <u>leaving</u>,
departure, abandonment,
abdication 2 = <u>acceptance</u>,
patience, submission,
compliance, endurance, passivity,
acquiescence, sufferance
≠ resistance

resigned = <u>stoical</u>, patient,
subdued, long-suffering,
compliant, unresisting

resist 1 = <u>oppose</u>, battle against,

combat, defy, stand up to, hinder
≠ accept 2 = <u>refrain from</u>, avoid,
keep from, forgo, abstain from,
forbear ≠ indulge in
3 = <u>withstand</u>, be proof against

resistance 1 = <u>opposition</u>,
hostility, aversion 2 = <u>fighting</u>,
fight, battle, struggle, defiance,
obstruction, impediment,
hindrance

resistant 1 = <u>opposed</u>, hostile,
unwilling, intractable,
antagonistic, intransigent
2 = <u>impervious</u>, hard, strong,
tough, unaffected

resolution 1 = <u>declaration</u>
2 = <u>decision</u>, resolve, intention,
aim, purpose, determination,
intent 3 = <u>determination</u>,
purpose, resolve, tenacity,
perseverance, willpower,
firmness, steadfastness

resolve VERB 1 = <u>work out</u>,
answer, clear up, crack, fathom
2 = <u>decide</u>, determine, agree,
purpose, intend, fix, conclude
● NOUN 1 = <u>determination</u>,
resolution, willpower, firmness,
steadfastness, resoluteness
≠ indecision 2 = <u>decision</u>,
resolution, objective, purpose,
intention

resort 1 = <u>holiday centre</u>, spot,
retreat, haunt, tourist centre
2 = <u>recourse to</u>, reference to

resound 1 = <u>echo</u>, resonate,

reverberate, re-echo 2 = **ring**

resounding = <u>echoing</u>, full, ringing, powerful, booming, reverberating, resonant, sonorous

resource NOUN 1 = <u>facility</u> 2 = <u>means</u>, course, resort, device, expedient

● PLURAL NOUN 1 = <u>funds</u>, holdings, money, capital, riches, assets, wealth 2 = <u>reserves</u>, supplies, stocks

respect VERB 1 = <u>think highly of</u>, value, honour, admire, esteem, look up to, defer to, have a good or high opinion of, <u>show consideration for</u>, honour, observe, heed 3 = <u>abide by</u>, follow, observe, comply with, obey, heed, keep to, adhere to ≠ disregard

● NOUN 1 = <u>regard</u>, honour, recognition, esteem, admiration, estimation ≠ contempt 2 = <u>consideration</u>, kindness, deference, tact, thoughtfulness, considerateness 3 = <u>particular</u>, way, point, matter, sense, detail, feature, aspect

respectable 1 = <u>honourable</u>, good, decent, worthy, upright, honest, reputable, estimable ≠ disreputable 2 = <u>decent</u>, neat, spruce 3 = <u>reasonable</u>, considerable, substantial, fair, ample, appreciable, sizable or sizeable ≠ small

respective = <u>specific</u>, own, individual, particular, relevant

respite = <u>pause</u>, break, rest, relief, halt, interval, recess, lull

respond 1 = <u>answer</u>, return, reply, counter, retort, rejoin ≠ remain silent 2 often with **to** = <u>reply to</u>, answer 3 = <u>react</u>, retaliate, reciprocate

response = <u>answer</u>, return, reply, reaction, feedback, retort, counterattack, rejoinder

responsibility 1 = <u>duty</u>, business, job, role, task, accountability, answerability 2 = <u>fault</u>, blame, liability, guilt, culpability 3 = <u>obligation</u>, duty, liability, charge, care 4 = <u>authority</u>, power, importance, mana (N.Z.) 5 = <u>job</u>, task, function, role 6 = <u>level-headedness</u>, rationality, dependability, trustworthiness, conscientiousness, sensibleness

responsible 1 = <u>to blame</u>, guilty, at fault, culpable 2 = <u>in charge</u>, in control, in authority 3 = <u>accountable</u>, liable, answerable ≠ unaccountable 4 = <u>sensible</u>, reliable, rational, dependable, trustworthy, level-headed ≠ unreliable

responsive = <u>sensitive</u>, open, alive, susceptible, receptive, reactive, impressionable ≠ unresponsive

rest[1] VERB 1 = <u>relax</u>, take it easy, sit down, be at ease, put your feet up, outspan (*S. African*) ≠ work 2 = <u>stop</u>, have a break, break off, take a breather (*informal*), halt, cease ≠ keep going 3 = <u>place</u>, repose, sit, lean, prop 4 = <u>be placed</u>, sit, lie, be supported, recline

● NOUN 1 = <u>relaxation</u>, repose, leisure ≠ work 2 = <u>pause</u>, break, stop, halt, interval, respite, lull, interlude 3 = <u>refreshment</u>, release, relief, ease, comfort, cure, remedy, solace 4 = <u>inactivity</u> 5 = <u>support</u>, stand, base, holder, prop 6 = <u>calm</u>, tranquillity, stillness

rest[2] = <u>remainder</u>, remains, excess, remnants, others, balance, surplus, residue

restaurant = <u>café</u>, diner (*chiefly U.S. & Canad.*), bistro, cafeteria, tearoom, eatery *or* eaterie

restless 1 = <u>unsettled</u>, nervous, edgy, fidgeting, on edge, restive, jumpy, fidgety ≠ relaxed 2 = <u>moving</u>, wandering, unsettled, unstable, roving, transient, nomadic ≠ settled

restoration 1 = <u>reinstatement</u>, return, revival, restitution, re-establishment, replacement ≠ abolition 2 = <u>repair</u>, reconstruction, renewal, renovation, revitalization

≠ demolition

restore 1 = <u>reinstate</u>, re-establish, reintroduce ≠ abolish 2 = <u>revive</u>, build up, strengthen, refresh, revitalize ≠ make worse 3 = <u>re-establish</u>, replace, reinstate, give back 4 = <u>repair</u>, refurbish, renovate, reconstruct, fix (up), renew, rebuild, mend ≠ demolish 5 = <u>return</u>, replace, recover, bring back, send back, hand back

restrain 1 = <u>hold back</u>, control, check, contain, restrict, curb, hamper, hinder ≠ encourage 2 = <u>control</u>, inhibit

restrained 1 = <u>controlled</u>, moderate, self-controlled, calm, mild, undemonstrative ≠ hot-headed 2 = <u>unobtrusive</u>, discreet, subdued, tasteful, quiet ≠ garish

restraint 1 = <u>limitation</u>, limit, check, ban, embargo, curb, rein, interdict ≠ freedom 2 = <u>self-control</u>, self-discipline, self-restraint, self-possession ≠ self-indulgence 3 = <u>constraint</u>, limitation, inhibition, control, restriction

restrict 1 = <u>limit</u>, regulate, curb, ration ≠ widen 2 = <u>hamper</u>, handicap, restrain, inhibit

restriction 1 = <u>control</u>, rule, regulation, curb, restraint, confinement 2 = <u>limitation</u>, handicap, inhibition

result NOUN 1 = <u>consequence</u>,

effect, outcome, end result, product, sequel, upshot ≠ cause
2 = <u>outcome</u>, end

● VERB = <u>arise</u>, follow, issue, happen, appear, develop, spring, derive

resume = <u>begin again</u>, continue, go on with, proceed with, carry on, reopen, restart ≠ discontinue

résumé = <u>summary</u>, synopsis, précis, rundown, recapitulation

resumption = <u>continuation</u>, carrying on, reopening, renewal, restart, resurgence, re-establishment

resurgence = <u>revival</u>, return, renaissance, resurrection, resumption, rebirth, re-emergence

resurrect 1 = <u>revive</u>, renew, bring back, reintroduce
2 = <u>restore to life</u>, raise from the dead

resurrection 1 = <u>revival</u>, restoration, renewal, resurgence, return, renaissance, rebirth, reappearance ≠ killing off
2 *usually caps* = <u>raising</u> or <u>rising from the dead</u>, return from the dead ≠ demise

retain 1 = <u>maintain</u>, reserve, preserve, keep up, continue to have **2** = <u>keep</u>, save ≠ let go

retaliate = <u>pay someone back</u>, hit back, strike back, reciprocate, take revenge, get even with

(*informal*), get your own back (*informal*) ≠ turn the other cheek

retaliation = <u>revenge</u>, repayment, vengeance, reprisal, an eye for an eye, reciprocation, requital, counterblow

retard = <u>slow down</u>, check, arrest, delay, handicap, hinder, impede, set back ≠ speed up

retire 1 = <u>stop working</u>, give up work **2** = <u>withdraw</u>, leave, exit, go away, depart **3** = <u>go to bed</u>, turn in (*informal*), hit the sack (*slang*), hit the hay (*slang*)

retirement = <u>withdrawal</u>, retreat, privacy, solitude, seclusion

retiring = <u>shy</u>, reserved, quiet, timid, unassuming, self-effacing, bashful, unassertive ≠ outgoing

retort VERB = <u>reply</u>, return, answer, respond, counter, come back with, riposte

● NOUN = <u>reply</u>, answer, response, comeback, riposte, rejoinder

retreat VERB = <u>withdraw</u>, back off, draw back, leave, go back, depart, fall back, pull back ≠ advance

● NOUN **1** = <u>flight</u>, retirement, departure, withdrawal, evacuation ≠ advance **2** = <u>refuge</u>, haven, shelter, sanctuary, hideaway, seclusion

retrieve 1 = <u>get back</u>, regain, recover, restore, recapture

2 = redeem, save, win back, recoup

retrospect = hindsight, review, re-examination ≠ foresight

return VERB 1 = come back, go back, retreat, turn back, revert, reappear ≠ depart 2 = put back, replace, restore, reinstate ≠ keep 3 = give back, repay, refund, pay back, reimburse, recompense ≠ keep 4 = recur, repeat, persist, revert, happen again, reappear, come again 5 = elect, choose, vote in

● NOUN 1 = reappearance ≠ departure 2 = restoration, reinstatement, re-establishment ≠ removal 3 = recurrence, repetition, reappearance, reversion, persistence 4 = profit, interest, gain, income, revenue, yield, proceeds, takings 5 = statement, report, form, list, account, summary

revamp = renovate, restore, overhaul, refurbish, do up (*informal*), recondition

reveal 1 = make known, disclose, give away, make public, tell, announce, proclaim, let out ≠ keep secret 2 = show, display, exhibit, unveil, uncover, manifest, unearth, unmask ≠ hide

revel VERB = celebrate, carouse, live it up (*informal*), make merry

● NOUN often plural

= merrymaking, party, celebration, spree, festivity, carousal

revelation 1 = disclosure, news, announcement, publication, leak, confession, divulgence 2 = exhibition, publication, exposure, unveiling, uncovering, unearthing, proclamation

revenge NOUN = retaliation, vengeance, reprisal, retribution, an eye for an eye

● VERB = avenge, repay, take revenge for, get your own back for (*informal*)

revenue = income, returns, profits, gain, yield, proceeds, receipts, takings ≠ expenditure

revere = be in awe of, respect, honour, worship, reverence, exalt, look up to, venerate ≠ despise

reverse VERB 1 (*Law*) = change, cancel, overturn, overthrow, undo, repeal, quash, revoke ≠ implement 2 = turn round, turn over, turn upside down, upend 3 = transpose, change, move, exchange, transfer, switch, shift, alter 4 = go backwards, retreat, back up, turn back, move backwards, back ≠ go forward

● NOUN 1 = opposite, contrary, converse, inverse 2 = misfortune, blow, failure, disappointment, setback, hardship, reversal, adversity 3 = back, rear, other

side, wrong side, underside
≠ front

● ADJECTIVE = opposite, contrary, converse

revert 1 = go back, return, come back, resume 2 = return

Word Power

revert – Since the concept *back* is already contained in the *re-* part of the word *revert*, it is unnecessary to say that someone *reverts back* to a particular type of behaviour.

---

review NOUN 1 = survey, study, analysis, examination, scrutiny 2 = critique, commentary, evaluation, notice, criticism, judgment 3 = inspection, parade, march past 4 = magazine, journal, periodical, zine (*informal*)

● VERB 1 = reconsider, revise, rethink, reassess, re-examine, re-evaluate, think over 2 = assess, study, judge, evaluate, criticize 3 = inspect, check, survey, examine, vet 4 = look back on, remember, recall, reflect on, recollect

reviewer = critic, judge, commentator

revise 1 = change, review 2 = edit, correct, alter, update, amend, rework, redo, emend 3 = study, go over, run through,

cram (*informal*), swot up on (*Brit. informal*)

revision 1 = emendation, updating, correction 2 = change, amendment 3 = studying, cramming (*informal*), swotting (*Brit. informal*), homework

revival 1 = resurgence ≠ decline 2 = reawakening, renaissance, renewal, resurrection, rebirth, revitalization

revive 1 = revitalize, restore, renew, rekindle, invigorate, reanimate 2 = bring round, awaken 3 = come round, recover 4 = refresh ≠ exhaust

revolt NOUN 1 = uprising, rising, revolution, rebellion, mutiny, insurrection, insurgency

● VERB 1 = rebel, rise up, resist, mutiny 2 = disgust, sicken, repel, repulse, nauseate, gross out (*U.S. slang*), turn your stomach, make your flesh creep

revolting = disgusting, foul, horrible, sickening, horrid, repellent, repulsive, nauseating, yucko (*Austral. slang*) ≠ delightful

revolution 1 = revolt, rising, coup, rebellion, uprising, mutiny, insurgency 2 = transformation, shift, innovation, upheaval, reformation, sea change 3 = rotation, turn, cycle, circle, spin, lap, circuit, orbit

revolutionary ADJECTIVE

1 = <u>rebel</u>, radical, extremist, subversive, insurgent ≠ reactionary 2 = <u>innovative</u>, new, different, novel, radical, progressive, drastic, groundbreaking ≠ conventional

● NOUN = <u>rebel</u>, insurgent, revolutionist ≠ reactionary

revolve 1 = <u>go round</u>, circle, orbit 2 = <u>rotate</u>, turn, wheel, spin, twist, whirl

reward NOUN 1 = <u>punishment</u>, retribution, comeuppance (*slang*), just deserts 2 = <u>payment</u>, return, prize, wages, compensation, bonus, premium, repayment ≠ penalty

● VERB = <u>compensate</u>, pay, repay, recompense, remunerate ≠ penalize

rewarding = <u>satisfying</u>, fulfilling, valuable, profitable, productive, worthwhile, beneficial, enriching ≠ unrewarding

rhetoric 1 = <u>hyperbole</u>, bombast, wordiness, verbosity, grandiloquence, magniloquence 2 = <u>oratory</u>, eloquence, public speaking, speech-making, elocution, declamation, grandiloquence, whaikorero (*N.Z.*)

rhetorical = <u>high-flown</u>, bombastic, verbose, oratorical, grandiloquent, declamatory, artyfarty (*informal*), magniloquent

rhyme = <u>poem</u>, song, verse, ode

rhythm 1 = <u>beat</u>, swing, accent, pulse, tempo, cadence, lilt 2 = <u>metre</u>, time

rich 1 = <u>wealthy</u>, affluent, well-off, loaded (*slang*), prosperous, well-heeled (*informal*), well-to-do, moneyed ≠ poor 2 = <u>well-stocked</u>, full, productive, ample, abundant, plentiful, copious, well-supplied ≠ scarce 3 = <u>full-bodied</u>, sweet, fatty, tasty, creamy, luscious, succulent ≠ bland 4 = <u>fruitful</u>, productive, fertile, prolific ≠ barren 5 = <u>abounding</u>, luxurious, lush, abundant

riches 1 = <u>wealth</u>, assets, plenty, fortune, substance, treasure, affluence ≠ poverty 2 = <u>resources</u>, treasures

richly 1 = <u>elaborately</u>, lavishly, elegantly, splendidly, exquisitely, expensively, luxuriously, gorgeously 2 = <u>fully</u>, well, thoroughly, amply, appropriately, properly, suitably

rid VERB = <u>free</u>, clear, deliver, relieve, purge, unburden, make free, disencumber

● PHRASES **get rid of something** *or* **someone** = <u>dispose of</u>, throw away *or* out, dump, remove, eliminate, expel, eject

riddle¹ 1 = <u>puzzle</u>, problem, conundrum, poser 2 = <u>enigma</u>, question, secret, mystery, puzzle, conundrum, teaser, problem

riddle² 1 = <u>pierce</u>, pepper, puncture, perforate, honeycomb 2 = <u>pervade</u>, fill, spread through

riddled = <u>filled</u>, spoilt, pervaded, infested, permeated

ride VERB 1 = <u>control</u>, handle, manage 2 = <u>travel</u>, be carried, go, move

● NOUN = <u>journey</u>, drive, trip, lift, outing, jaunt

ridicule VERB = <u>laugh at</u>, mock, make fun of, sneer at, jeer at, deride, poke fun at, chaff

● NOUN = <u>mockery</u>, scorn, derision, laughter, jeer, chaff, gibe, raillery

ridiculous = <u>laughable</u>, stupid, silly, absurd, ludicrous, farcical, comical, risible ≠ sensible

rife = <u>widespread</u>, rampant, general, common, universal, frequent, prevalent, ubiquitous

rifle = <u>ransack</u>, rob, burgle, loot, strip, sack, plunder, pillage

rift 1 = <u>breach</u>, division, split, separation, falling out (*informal*), disagreement, quarrel 2 = <u>split</u>, opening, crack, gap, break, fault, flaw, cleft

rig VERB 1 = <u>fix</u>, engineer (*informal*), arrange, manipulate, tamper with, gerrymander 2 (*Nautical*) = <u>equip</u>, fit out, kit out, outfit, supply, furnish

● PHRASES **rig something up** = <u>set up</u>, build, construct, put up, arrange, assemble, put together, erect

right ADJECTIVE 1 = <u>correct</u>, true, genuine, accurate, exact, precise, valid, factual, dinkum (*Austral. & N.Z. informal*) ≠ wrong 2 = <u>proper</u>, done, becoming, seemly, fitting, fit, appropriate, suitable ≠ inappropriate 3 = <u>just</u>, good, fair, moral, proper, ethical, honest, equitable ≠ unfair

● ADVERB 1 = <u>correctly</u>, truly, precisely, exactly, genuinely, accurately ≠ wrongly 2 = <u>suitably</u>, fittingly, appropriately, properly, aptly ≠ improperly 3 = <u>exactly</u>, squarely, precisely 4 = <u>directly</u>, straight, precisely, exactly, unswervingly, without deviation, by the shortest route, in a beeline 5 = <u>straight</u>, directly, quickly, promptly, straightaway ≠ indirectly

● NOUN 1 = <u>prerogative</u>, business, power, claim, authority, due, freedom, licence 2 = <u>justice</u>, truth, fairness, legality, righteousness, lawfulness ≠ injustice

● VERB = <u>rectify</u>, settle, fix, correct, sort out, straighten, redress, put right

right away = <u>immediately</u>, now, directly, instantly, at once, straightaway, forthwith, pronto (*informal*)

righteous = <u>virtuous</u>, good, just, fair, moral, pure, ethical, upright ≠ wicked

rigid 1 = <u>strict</u>, set, fixed, exact, rigorous, stringent ≠ flexible 2 = <u>inflexible</u>, uncompromising, unbending 3 = <u>stiff</u>, inflexible, inelastic ≠ pliable

rigorous = <u>strict</u>, hard, demanding, tough, severe, exacting, harsh, stern ≠ soft

rim 1 = <u>edge</u>, lip, brim 2 = <u>border</u>, edge, trim 3 = <u>margin</u>, border, verge, brink

ring[1] 1 = <u>phone</u>, call, telephone, buzz (informal, chiefly Brit.) 2 = <u>chime</u>, sound, toll, reverberate, clang, peal 3 = <u>reverberate</u>
 • NOUN 1 = <u>call</u>, phone call, buzz (informal, chiefly Brit.) 2 = <u>chime</u>, knell, peal

Word Power

ring – *Rang* is the past tense of the verb *ring*, as in *he rang the bell*. *Rung* is the past participle, as in *he has already rung the bell*, and care should be taken not to use it as if it were a variant form of the past tense.

ring[2] NOUN 1 = <u>circle</u>, round, band, circuit, loop, hoop, halo 2 = <u>arena</u>, enclosure, circus, rink 3 = <u>gang</u>, group, association, band, circle, mob, syndicate, cartel

 • VERB = <u>encircle</u>, surround, enclose, girdle, gird

rinse VERB = <u>wash</u>, clean, dip, splash, cleanse, bathe
 • NOUN = <u>wash</u>, dip, splash, bath

riot NOUN 1 = <u>disturbance</u>, disorder, confusion, turmoil, upheaval, strife, turbulence, lawlessness 2 = <u>display</u>, show, splash, extravaganza, profusion 3 = <u>laugh</u>, joke, scream (informal), hoot (informal), lark
 • VERB = <u>rampage</u>, run riot, go on the rampage
 • PHRASES **run riot** 1 = <u>rampage</u>, go wild, be out of control 2 = <u>grow profusely</u>, spread like wildfire

rip VERB 1 = <u>tear</u>, cut, split, burst, rend, slash, claw, slit 2 = <u>be torn</u>, tear, split, burst
 • NOUN = <u>tear</u>, cut, hole, split, rent, slash, slit, gash
 • PHRASES **rip someone off** (Slang) = <u>cheat</u>, rob, con (informal), skin (slang), fleece, defraud, swindle

ripe 1 = <u>ripened</u>, seasoned, ready, mature, mellow ≠ unripe 2 = <u>right</u>, suitable 3 = <u>mature</u> 4 = <u>suitable</u>, timely, ideal, favourable, auspicious, opportune ≠ unsuitable

rip-off or **ripoff** (Slang) = <u>cheat</u>, con (informal), scam (slang), trick (informal), fraud, theft, swindle

rise VERB 1 = <u>get up</u>, stand up, get to your feet 2 = <u>arise</u> 3 = <u>go up</u>, climb, ascend ≠ descend

4 = <u>loom</u>, tower 5 = <u>get steeper</u>, ascend, go uphill, slope upwards ≠ drop 6 = <u>increase</u>, mount ≠ decrease 7 = <u>grow</u>, go up, intensify 8 = <u>rebel</u>, revolt, mutiny 9 = <u>advance</u>, progress, get on, prosper

● NOUN 1 = <u>upward slope</u>, incline, elevation, ascent, kopje or koppie (S. African) 2 = <u>increase</u>, upturn, upswing, upsurge ≠ decrease 3 = <u>pay increase</u>, raise (U.S.), increment 4 = <u>advancement</u>, progress, climb, promotion

● PHRASES **give rise to something** = <u>cause</u>, produce, effect, result in, bring about

risk NOUN 1 = <u>danger</u>, chance, possibility, hazard 2 = <u>gamble</u>, chance, speculation, leap in the dark 3 = <u>peril</u>, jeopardy

● VERB 1 = <u>stand a chance of</u> 2 = <u>dare</u>, endanger, jeopardize, imperil, venture, gamble, hazard

risky = <u>dangerous</u>, hazardous, unsafe, perilous, uncertain, dodgy (Brit., Austral., & N.Z. informal), dicey (informal), chiefly Brit.), chancy (informal) ≠ safe

rite = <u>ceremony</u>, custom, ritual, practice, procedure, observance

ritual NOUN 1 = <u>ceremony</u>, rite, observance 2 = <u>custom</u>, tradition, routine, convention, practice, procedure, habit, protocol, tikanga (N.Z.)

● ADJECTIVE = <u>ceremonial</u>, conventional, routine, customary, habitual

rival NOUN 1 = <u>opponent</u>, competitor, contender, contestant, adversary ≠ supporter

● VERB = <u>compete with</u>, match, equal, compare with, come up to, be a match for

● ADJECTIVE = <u>competing</u>, conflicting, opposing

rivalry = <u>competition</u>, opposition, conflict, contest, contention

river 1 = <u>stream</u>, brook, creek, waterway, tributary, burn (Scot.) 2 = <u>flow</u>, rush, flood, spate, torrent

riveting = <u>enthralling</u>, gripping, fascinating, absorbing, captivating, hypnotic, engrossing, spellbinding

road 1 = <u>roadway</u>, highway, motorway, track, route, path, lane, pathway 2 = <u>way</u>, path

roam = <u>wander</u>, walk, range, travel, stray, ramble, prowl, rove

roar VERB 1 = <u>thunder</u> 2 = <u>guffaw</u>, laugh heartily, hoot, split your sides (informal) 3 = <u>cry</u>, shout, yell, howl, bellow, bawl, bay

● NOUN 1 = <u>guffaw</u>, hoot 2 = <u>cry</u>,

shout, yell, howl, outcry, bellow

rob 1 = steal from, hold up, mug (*informal*) 2 = raid, hold up, loot, plunder, burgle, pillage 3 = dispossess, con (*informal*), cheat, defraud 4 = deprive, do out of (*informal*)

robber = thief, raider, burglar, looter, fraud, cheat, bandit, plunderer

robbery 1 = burglary, raid, hold-up, rip-off (*slang*), stick-up (*slang, chiefly U.S.*) 2 = theft, stealing, mugging (*informal*), plunder, swindle, pillage, larceny

robe = gown, costume, habit

robot = machine, automaton, android, mechanical man

robust = strong, tough, powerful, fit, healthy, strapping, hardy, vigorous ≠ weak

rock¹ = stone, boulder

rock² 1 = sway, pitch, swing, reel, toss, lurch, roll 2 = shock, surprise, shake, stun, astonish, stagger, astound

rocky¹ = rough, rugged, stony, craggy

rocky² = unstable, shaky, wobbly, rickety, unsteady

rod 1 = stick, bar, pole, shaft, cane 2 = staff, baton, wand

rodent ▸ rodents

rogue 1 = scoundrel, crook (*informal*), villain, fraud, blackguard, skelm (*S. African*),

rorter (*Austral. slang*) 2 = scamp, rascal, scally (*Northwest English dialect*), nointer (*Austral. slang*)

role 1 = job, part, position, post, task, duty, function, capacity 2 = part, character, representation, portrayal

roll VERB 1 = turn, wheel, spin, go round, revolve, rotate, whirl, swivel 2 = trundle, go, move 3 = flow, run, course 4 *often with up* = wind, bind, wrap, swathe, envelop, furl, enfold 5 = level, even, press, smooth, flatten 6 = toss, rock, lurch, reel, tumble, sway

● NOUN 1 = rumble, boom, roar, thunder, reverberation 2 = register, record, list, index, census 3 = turn, spin, rotation, cycle, wheel, revolution, reel, whirl

romance 1 = love affair, relationship, affair, attachment, liaison, amour 2 = excitement, colour, charm, mystery, glamour, fascination 3 = story, tale, fantasy, legend, fairy tale, love story, melodrama

romantic ADJECTIVE 1 = loving, tender, passionate, fond, sentimental, amorous, icky (*informal*) ≠ unromantic 2 = idealistic, unrealistic, impractical, dreamy, starry-eyed ≠ realistic 3 = exciting, fascinating, mysterious, colourful,

Rodents

agouti	kangaroo rat
beaver	kiore (N.Z.)
capybara	lemming
cavy	Māori rat or (N.Z.) kiore
chinchilla	marmot
chipmunk	mouse
coypu or nutria	muskrat or musquash
desert rat	paca
dormouse	pack rat
fieldmouse	porcupine
flying squirrel	rat
gerbil, gerbille, or jerbil	red squirrel or chickaree
gopher or pocket gopher	spinifex hopping mouse or
gopher or ground squirrel	(Austral.) dargawarra
grey squirrel	springhaas
groundhog or woodchuck	squirrel
guinea pig or cavy	suslik or souslik
hamster	viscacha or vizcacha
harvest mouse	vole
hedgehog	water rat
house mouse	water vole or water rat
jerboa	

glamorous ≠ unexciting
● NOUN = idealist, dreamer, sentimentalist

romp VERB = frolic, sport, have fun, caper, cavort, frisk, gambol
● NOUN = frolic, lark (informal), caper

room 1 = chamber, office, apartment 2 = space, area, capacity, extent, expanse
3 = opportunity, scope, leeway, chance, range, occasion, margin

root¹ NOUN 1 = stem, tuber, rhizome
2 = source, cause, heart, bottom, base, seat, seed, foundation
● PLURAL NOUN = sense of belonging, origins, heritage, birthplace, home, family, cradle
● PHRASES **root something** or **someone out** = get rid of, remove, eliminate, abolish, eradicate, do away with, weed out, exterminate

root² = dig, burrow, ferret

rope NOUN = cord, line, cable, strand, hawser

● PHRASES **know the ropes** = <u>be experienced</u>, be knowledgeable, be an old hand ◆ **rope someone in** or **into something** (Brit.) = <u>persuade</u>, involve, engage, enlist, talk into, inveigle

rosy ADJECTIVE 1 = <u>glowing</u>, blooming, radiant, ruddy, healthy-looking ≠ pale 2 = <u>promising</u>, encouraging, bright, optimistic, hopeful, cheerful, favourable, auspicious ≠ gloomy

● NOUN = <u>pink</u>, red

➤ **shades of red**

rot VERB 1 = <u>decay</u>, spoil, deteriorate, perish, decompose, moulder, go bad, putrefy 2 = <u>crumble</u> 3 = <u>deteriorate</u>, decline, waste away

● NOUN 1 = <u>decay</u>, decomposition, corruption, mould, blight, canker, putrefaction 2 (Informal) = <u>nonsense</u>, rubbish, drivel, twaddle, garbage (chiefly U.S.), trash, tripe (informal), claptrap (informal), bizzo (Austral. slang), bull's wool (Austral. & N.Z. slang)

Related Words

adjective: putrid

rotate 1 = <u>revolve</u>, turn, wheel, spin, reel, go round, swivel, pivot 2 = <u>follow in sequence</u>, switch, alternate, take turns

rotation 1 = <u>revolution</u>, turning, turn, wheel, spin, spinning, reel,

orbit 2 = <u>sequence</u>, switching, cycle, succession, alternation

rotten 1 = <u>decaying</u>, bad, rank, corrupt, sour, stinking, perished, festering, festy (Austral. slang) ≠ fresh 2 = <u>crumbling</u>, perished 3 (Informal) = <u>despicable</u>, mean, base, dirty, nasty, contemptible 4 (Informal) = <u>inferior</u>, poor, inadequate, duff (Brit. informal), unsatisfactory, lousy (slang), substandard, crummy (slang), bodger or bodgie (Austral. slang) 5 = <u>corrupt</u>, immoral, crooked (informal), dishonest, dishonourable, perfidious ≠ honourable

rough ADJECTIVE 1 = <u>uneven</u>, broken, rocky, irregular, jagged, bumpy, stony, craggy ≠ even 2 = <u>boisterous</u>, hard, tough, arduous 3 = <u>ungracious</u>, blunt, rude, coarse, brusque, uncouth, impolite, uncivil ≠ refined 4 = <u>unpleasant</u>, hard, difficult, tough, uncomfortable ≠ easy 5 = <u>approximate</u>, estimated ≠ exact 6 = <u>vague</u>, general, sketchy, imprecise, inexact 7 = <u>basic</u>, crude, unfinished, incomplete, imperfect, rudimentary, sketchy, unrefined ≠ complete 8 = <u>stormy</u>, wild, turbulent, choppy, squally ≠ calm 9 = <u>harsh</u>, tough, nasty, cruel, unfeeling ≠ gentle

● NOUN = <u>outline</u>, draft, mock-up,

preliminary sketch

● PHRASES **rough and ready**
1 = <u>makeshift</u>, crude, provisional, improvised, sketchy, stopgap
2 = <u>unrefined</u>, shabby, untidy, unkempt, unpolished, ill-groomed ◆ **rough something out** = <u>outline</u>, plan, draft, sketch

round NOUN 1 = <u>series</u>, session, cycle, sequence, succession
2 = <u>stage</u>, turn, level, period, division, session, lap 3 = <u>sphere</u>, ball, band, ring, circle, disc, globe, orb 4 = <u>course</u>, tour, circuit, beat, series, schedule, routine

● ADJECTIVE 1 = <u>spherical</u>, rounded, curved, circular, cylindrical, rotund, globular
2 = <u>plump</u>, full, ample, fleshy, rotund, full-fleshed

● VERB = <u>go round</u>, circle, skirt, flank, bypass, encircle, turn

● PHRASES **round something** or **someone up** = <u>gather</u>, muster, group, drive, collect, rally, herd, marshal

roundabout 1 = <u>indirect</u>, devious, tortuous, circuitous, evasive, discursive ≠ direct
2 = <u>oblique</u>, implied, indirect, circuitous

roundup = <u>muster</u>, collection, rally, assembly, herding

rouse 1 = <u>wake up</u>, call, wake, awaken 2 = <u>excite</u>, move, stir, provoke, anger, animate, agitate, inflame 3 = <u>stimulate</u>, provoke, incite

rousing = <u>lively</u>, moving, spirited, exciting, inspiring, stirring, stimulating ≠ dull

rout VERB = <u>defeat</u>, beat, overthrow, thrash, destroy, crush, conquer, wipe the floor with (*informal*)

● NOUN = <u>defeat</u>, beating, overthrow, thrashing, pasting (*slang*), debacle, drubbing

route 1 = <u>way</u>, course, road, direction, path, journey, itinerary
2 = <u>beat</u>, circuit

> ### Word Power
>
> **route** — When adding -*ing* to the verb *route* to form the present participle, it is more conventional, and clearer, to keep the final *e* from the end of the verb stem: *routeing*. The spelling *routing* in this sense is also possible, but keeping the *e* distinguishes it from *routing*, which is the participle formed from the verb *rout* meaning 'to defeat'.

routine NOUN = <u>procedure</u>, programme, order, practice, method, pattern, custom

● ADJECTIVE 1 = <u>usual</u>, standard, normal, customary, ordinary, typical, everyday, habitual ≠ unusual 2 = <u>boring</u>, dull, predictable, tedious, tiresome, humdrum

row¹ NOUN = line, bank, range, series, file, string, column

• PHRASES **in a row** = consecutively, running, in turn, one after the other, successively, in sequence

row² NOUN (Informal) 1 = quarrel, dispute, argument, squabble, tiff, trouble, brawl 2 = disturbance, noise, racket, uproar, commotion, rumpus, tumult

• VERB = quarrel, fight, argue, dispute, squabble, wrangle

royal 1 = regal, kingly, queenly, princely, imperial, sovereign 2 = splendid, grand, impressive, magnificent, majestic, stately

rub VERB 1 = stroke, massage, caress 2 = polish, clean, shine, wipe, scour 3 = chafe, scrape, grate, abrade

• NOUN 1 = massage, caress, kneading 2 = polish, stroke, shine, wipe

• PHRASES **rub something out** = erase, remove, cancel, wipe out, delete, obliterate, efface

rubbish 1 = waste, refuse, scrap, junk (informal), litter, garbage (chiefly U.S.), trash, lumber 2 = nonsense, garbage (chiefly U.S.), twaddle, rot, trash, hot air (informal), tripe (informal), claptrap (informal), bizzo (Austral. slang), bull's wool (Austral. & N.Z.

slang)

rude 1 = impolite, insulting, cheeky, abusive, disrespectful, impertinent, insolent, impudent ≠ polite 2 = uncivilized, rough, coarse, brutish, boorish, uncouth, loutish, graceless ≠ vulgar ≠ refined 4 = unpleasant, sharp, sudden, harsh, startling, abrupt 5 = roughly-made, simple, rough, raw, crude, primitive, makeshift, artless ≠ well-made

rue (Literary) = regret, mourn, lament, repent, be sorry for, kick yourself for

ruffle 1 = disarrange, disorder, mess up, rumple, tousle, dishevel 2 = annoy, upset, irritate, agitate, nettle, fluster, peeve (informal) ≠ calm

rugged 1 = rocky, broken, rough, craggy, difficult, ragged, irregular, uneven ≠ even 2 = strong-featured, rough-hewn, weather-beaten ≠ delicate 3 = well-built, strong, tough, robust, sturdy 4 = tough, strong, robust, muscular, sturdy, burly, husky (informal), brawny ≠ delicate

ruin VERB 1 = destroy, devastate, wreck, defeat, smash, crush, demolish, lay waste ≠ create 2 = bankrupt, break, impoverish, beggar, pauperize 3 = spoil, damage, mess up, blow (slang), screw up (informal), botch, make

a mess of, crool or cruel (*Austral. slang*) ≠ **improve**
● NOUN 1 = **bankruptcy**, insolvency, destitution 2 = **disrepair**, decay, disintegration, ruination, wreckage 3 = **destruction**, fall, breakdown, defeat, collapse, wreck, undoing, downfall ≠ **preservation**

rule NOUN 1 = **regulation**, law, direction, guideline, decree 2 = **precept**, principle, canon, maxim, tenet, axiom 3 = **custom**, procedure, practice, routine, tradition, habit, convention 4 = **government**, power, control, authority, command, regime, reign, jurisdiction, mana (*N.Z.*)
● VERB 1 = **govern**, control, direct, have power over, command over, have charge of 2 = **reign**, govern, be in power, be in authority 3 = **decree**, decide, judge, settle, pronounce 4 = **be prevalent**, prevail, predominate, be customary, preponderate
● PHRASES **as a rule** = **usually**, generally, mainly, normally, on the whole, ordinarily ◆ **rule someone out** = **exclude**, eliminate, disqualify, ban, reject, dismiss, prohibit, leave out ◆ **rule something out** = **reject**, exclude, eliminate

ruler 1 = **governor**, leader, lord, commander, controller, monarch,

sovereign, head of state 2 = **measure**, rule, yardstick

ruling ADJECTIVE 1 = **governing**, reigning, controlling, commanding 2 = **predominant**, dominant, prevailing, preponderant, chief, main, principal, pre-eminent ≠ **minor**
● NOUN = **decision**, verdict, judgment, decree, adjudication, pronouncement

rumour 1 = **story**, news, report, talk, word, whisper, buzz, gossip

run VERB 1 = **race**, rush, dash, hurry, sprint, bolt, gallop, hare (*Brit. informal*) ≠ **dawdle** 2 = **flee**, escape, take off (*informal*), bolt, beat it (*slang*), leg it (*informal*), take flight, do a runner (*slang*) ≠ **stay** 3 = **take part**, compete 4 = **continue**, go, stretch, reach, extend, proceed ≠ **stop** 5 = (*Chiefly U.S. & Canad.*) = **compete**, stand, contend, be a candidate, put yourself up for, take part 6 = **manage**, lead, direct, be in charge of, head, control, operate, handle 7 = **go**, work, operate, perform, function 8 = **perform**, carry out 9 = **work**, go, operate, function 10 = **pass**, go, move, roll, glide, skim 11 = **flow**, pour, stream, go, leak, spill, discharge, gush 12 = **publish**, feature, display, print 13 = **melt**, dissolve, liquefy, go soft 14 = **smuggle**, traffic in, bootleg
● NOUN 1 = **race**, rush, dash, sprint,

gallop, jog, spurt **2** = <u>ride</u>, drive, trip, spin (*informal*), outing, excursion, jaunt **3** = <u>sequence</u>, period, stretch, spell, course, season, series, string **4** = <u>enclosure</u>, pen, coop
● PHRASES **run away** = <u>flee</u>, escape, bolt, abscond, do a runner (*slang*), make a run for it, scram (*informal*), fly the coop (*U.S. & Canad. informal*) ◆ **run into someone** = <u>meet</u>, encounter, bump into, run across, come across *or* upon ◆ **run into something 1** = <u>be beset by</u>, encounter, come across *or* upon, face, experience **2** = <u>collide with</u>, hit, strike ◆ **run out 1** = <u>be used up</u>, dry up, give out, fail, finish, be exhausted **2** = <u>expire</u>, end, terminate ◆ **run over something** = <u>exceed</u>, overstep, go over the top of, go over the limit of **2** = <u>review</u>, check, go through, go over, run through, rehearse ◆ **run over something** *or* **someone** = <u>knock down</u>, hit, run down, knock over ◆ **run something** *or* **someone down 1** = <u>criticize</u>, denigrate, belittle, knock (*informal*), rubbish (*informal*), slag (off) (*slang*), disparage, decry **2** = <u>downsize</u>, cut, reduce, trim, decrease, cut back, curtail **3** = <u>knock down</u>, hit, run into, run over, knock over

run-down *or* **rundown**
1 = <u>exhausted</u>, weak, drained, weary, unhealthy, worn-out, debilitated, below par ≠ fit **2** = <u>dilapidated</u>, broken-down, shabby, worn-out, seedy, ramshackle, decrepit

runner 1 = <u>athlete</u>, sprinter, jogger **2** = <u>messenger</u>, courier, errand boy, dispatch bearer

running NOUN **1** = <u>management</u>, control, administration, direction, leadership, organization, supervision **2** = <u>working</u>, performance, operation, functioning, maintenance
● ADJECTIVE **1** = <u>continuous</u>, constant, perpetual, uninterrupted, incessant **2** = <u>in succession</u>, unbroken **3** = <u>flowing</u>, moving, streaming, coursing

rupture NOUN = <u>break</u>, tear, split, crack, rent, burst, breach, fissure
● VERB = <u>break</u>, separate, tear, split, crack, burst, sever

rural 1 = <u>agricultural</u>, country **2** = <u>rustic</u>, country, pastoral, sylvan ≠ urban

rush VERB **1** = <u>hurry</u>, run, race, shoot, fly, career, speed, tear ≠ dawdle **2** = <u>push</u>, hurry, press, hustle **3** = <u>attack</u>, storm, charge at
● NOUN **1** = <u>dash</u>, charge, race, scramble, stampede **2** = <u>hurry</u>, haste, hustle **3** = <u>surge</u>, flow, gush **4** = <u>attack</u>, charge, assault,

onslaught

● ADJECTIVE = <u>hasty</u>, fast, quick, hurried, rapid, urgent, swift ≠ leisurely

rust NOUN 1 = <u>corrosion</u>, oxidation 2 = <u>mildew</u>, must, mould, rot, blight

● VERB = <u>corrode</u>, oxidize

rusty 1 = <u>corroded</u>, rusted, oxidized, rust-covered 2 = <u>out of practice</u>, weak, stale, unpractised 3 = <u>reddish-brown</u>, chestnut, reddish, russet, coppery, rust-coloured

▸ **shades of red**

ruthless = <u>merciless</u>, harsh, cruel, brutal, relentless, callous, heartless, remorseless ≠ merciful

S

sabotage VERB = <u>damage</u>, destroy, wreck, disable, disrupt, subvert, incapacitate, vandalize

● NOUN = <u>damage</u>, destruction, wrecking

sack[1] NOUN 1 = <u>bag</u>, pocket, sac, pouch, receptacle 2 = <u>dismissal</u>, discharge, the boot (*slang*), the axe (*informal*), the push (*slang*)

● VERB (*Informal*) = <u>dismiss</u>, fire (*informal*), axe (*informal*), discharge, kiss off (*slang, chiefly U.S. & Canad.*), give (someone) the push

(*informal*)

sack[2] VERB = <u>plunder</u>, loot, pillage, strip, rob, raid, ruin

● NOUN = <u>plundering</u>, looting, pillage

sacred 1 = <u>holy</u>, hallowed, blessed, divine, revered, sanctified ≠ secular 2 = <u>religious</u>, holy, ecclesiastical, hallowed ≠ unconsecrated 3 = <u>inviolable</u>, protected, sacrosanct, hallowed, inalienable, unalterable

sacrifice VERB 1 = <u>offer</u>, offer up, immolate 2 = <u>give up</u>, abandon, relinquish, lose, surrender, let go, do without, renounce

● NOUN 1 = <u>offering</u>, oblation 2 = <u>surrender</u>, loss, giving up, rejection, abdication, renunciation, repudiation, forswearing

sad 1 = <u>unhappy</u>, down, low, blue, depressed, melancholy, mournful, dejected ≠ happy 2 = <u>tragic</u>, moving, upsetting, depressing, dismal, pathetic, poignant, harrowing 3 = <u>deplorable</u>, bad, sorry, terrible, unfortunate, regrettable, lamentable, wretched ≠ good

sadden = <u>upset</u>, depress, distress, grieve, make sad, deject

saddle = <u>burden</u>, load, lumber (*Brit. informal*), encumber

sadness = <u>unhappiness</u>, sorrow, grief, depression, the blues,

misery, melancholy, poignancy
≠ **happiness**

safe ADJECTIVE 1 = <u>protected</u>,
secure, impregnable, out of
danger, safe and sound, in safe
hands, out of harm's way
≠ **endangered** 2 = <u>all right</u>, intact,
unscathed, unhurt, unharmed,
undamaged, O.K. or okay
(*informal*) 3 = <u>risk-free</u>, sound,
secure, certain, impregnable
● NOUN = <u>strongbox</u>, vault, coffer,
repository, deposit box, safe-
deposit box

safeguard VERB = <u>protect</u>,
guard, defend, save, preserve,
look after, keep safe
● NOUN = <u>protection</u>, security,
defence, guard

safely = <u>in safety</u>, with impunity,
without risk, safe and sound

safety 1 = <u>security</u>, protection,
safeguards, precautions, safety
measures, impregnability
≠ **risk** 2 = <u>shelter</u>, haven,
protection, cover, retreat, asylum,
refuge, sanctuary

sag 1 = <u>sink</u>, bag, droop, fall,
slump, dip, give way, hang loosely
2 = <u>drop</u>, sink, slump, flop, droop,
loll 3 = <u>decline</u>, tire, flag, weaken,
wilt, wane, droop

saga 1 = <u>carry-on</u> (*informal*,
chiefly Brit.), performance
(*informal*), pantomime (*informal*)
2 = <u>epic</u>, story, tale, narrative, yarn

sage NOUN = <u>wise man</u>,
philosopher, guru, master, elder,
tohunga (*N.Z.*)
● ADJECTIVE = <u>wise</u>, sensible,
judicious, sagacious, sapient

sail NOUN = <u>sheet</u>, canvas
● VERB 1 = <u>go by water</u>, cruise,
voyage, ride the waves, go by sea
2 = <u>set sail</u>, embark, get under
way, put to sea, put off, leave
port, hoist sail, cast or weigh
anchor 3 = <u>pilot</u>, steer 4 = <u>glide</u>,
sweep, float, fly, wing, soar, drift,
skim

sailor = <u>mariner</u>, marine,
seaman, sea dog, seafarer

sake NOUN = <u>purpose</u>, interest,
reason, end, aim, objective,
motive
● PHRASES **for someone's sake**
= <u>in someone's interests</u>, to
someone's advantage, on
someone's account, for the
benefit of, for the good of, for the
welfare of, out of respect for, out
of consideration for

salary = <u>pay</u>, income, wage, fee,
payment, wages, earnings,
allowance

sale 1 = <u>selling</u>, marketing,
dealing, transaction, disposal
2 = <u>auction</u>, fair, mart, bazaar

salt NOUN = <u>seasoning</u>
● ADJECTIVE = <u>salty</u>, saline,
brackish, briny

salute VERB 1 = <u>greet</u>, welcome, acknowledge, address, hail, mihi (N.Z.) 2 = <u>honour</u>, acknowledge, recognize, pay tribute or homage to

● NOUN = <u>greeting</u>, recognition, salutation, address

salvage = <u>save</u>, recover, rescue, get back, retrieve, redeem

salvation = <u>saving</u>, rescue, recovery, salvage, redemption, deliverance ≠ ruin

same 1 = <u>identical</u>, similar, alike, equal, twin, corresponding, duplicate ≠ different 2 = <u>the very same</u>, one and the same, selfsame 3 = <u>aforementioned</u>, aforesaid 4 = <u>unchanged</u>, consistent, constant, unaltered, invariable, unvarying, changeless ≠ altered

---

Word Power

same – The use of *same* as in *if you send us your order for the materials, we will deliver same tomorrow* is common in business and official English. In general English, however, this use of the word is best avoided, as it may sound rather stilted: *may I borrow your book? I will return it* (not *same*) *tomorrow.*

---

sample NOUN 1 = <u>specimen</u>, example, model, pattern, instance 2 = <u>cross section</u>

● VERB = <u>test</u>, try, experience, taste, inspect

● ADJECTIVE = <u>test</u>, trial, specimen, representative

sanction VERB = <u>permit</u>, allow, approve, endorse, authorize ≠ forbid

● NOUN 1 often plural = <u>ban</u>, boycott, embargo, exclusion, penalty, coercive measures ≠ permission 2 = <u>permission</u>, backing, authority, approval, authorization, O.K. or okay (informal), stamp or seal of approval ≠ ban

sanctuary 1 = <u>protection</u>, shelter, refuge, haven, retreat, asylum 2 = <u>reserve</u>, park, preserve, reservation, national park, tract, nature reserve, conservation area

sane 1 = <u>rational</u>, all there (informal), of sound mind, compos mentis (Latin), in your right mind, mentally sound ≠ insane 2 = <u>sensible</u>, sound, reasonable, balanced, judicious, level-headed ≠ foolish

sap¹ 1 = <u>juice</u>, essence, vital fluid, lifeblood 2 (Slang) = <u>fool</u>, jerk (slang, chiefly U.S. & Canad.), idiot, wally (slang), twit (informal), simpleton, ninny, dorba or dorb (Austral. slang), bogan (Austral. slang)

sap² = <u>weaken</u>, drain, undermine,

exhaust, deplete

satanic = <u>evil</u>, demonic, hellish, black, wicked, devilish, infernal, fiendish ≠ godly

satire 1 = <u>mockery</u>, irony, ridicule 2 = <u>parody</u>, mockery, caricature, lampoon, burlesque

satisfaction 1 = <u>fulfilment</u>, pleasure, achievement, relish, gratification, pride ≠ dissatisfaction
2 = <u>contentment</u>, content, comfort, pleasure, happiness, enjoyment, satiety, repletion ≠ discontent

satisfactory = <u>adequate</u>, acceptable, good enough, average, fair, all right, sufficient, passable ≠ unsatisfactory

satisfy 1 = <u>content</u>, please, indulge, gratify, pander to, assuage, pacify, quench ≠ dissatisfy 2 = <u>convince</u>, persuade, assure, reassure ≠ dissuade 3 = <u>comply with</u>, meet, fulfil, answer, serve, fill, observe, obey ≠ fail to meet

saturate 1 = <u>flood</u>, overwhelm, swamp, overrun 2 = <u>soak</u>, steep, drench, imbue, suffuse, wet through, waterlog, souse

saturated = <u>soaked</u>, soaking (wet), drenched, sodden, dripping, waterlogged, sopping (wet), wet through

sauce = <u>dressing</u>, dip, relish, condiment

savage ADJECTIVE 1 = <u>cruel</u>, brutal, vicious, fierce, harsh, ruthless, ferocious, sadistic ≠ gentle 2 = <u>wild</u>, fierce, ferocious, unbroken, feral, untamed, undomesticated ≠ tame 3 = <u>primitive</u>, undeveloped, uncultivated, uncivilized 4 = <u>uncultivated</u>, rugged, unspoilt, uninhabited, rough, uncivilized ≠ cultivated
● NOUN = <u>lout</u>, yob (*Brit. slang*), barbarian, yahoo, hoon (*Austral. & N.Z.*), boor, cougan (*Austral. slang*), scozza (*Austral. slang*), bogan (*Austral. slang*)
● VERB = <u>maul</u>, tear, claw, attack, mangle, lacerate, mangulate (*Austral. slang*)

save 1 = <u>rescue</u>, free, release, deliver, recover, get out, liberate, salvage ≠ endanger 2 = <u>keep</u>, reserve, set aside, store, collect, gather, hold, hoard ≠ spend 3 = <u>protect</u>, keep, guard, preserve, look after, safeguard, salvage, conserve 4 = <u>put aside</u>, keep, reserve, collect, retain, set aside, put by

saving NOUN = <u>economy</u>, discount, reduction, bargain
● PLURAL NOUN = <u>nest egg</u>, fund, store, reserves, resources

saviour = <u>rescuer</u>, deliverer, defender, protector, liberator, redeemer, preserver

Saviour = Christ, Jesus, the Messiah, the Redeemer

savour VERB 1 = relish, delight in, revel in, luxuriate in 2 = enjoy, appreciate, relish, delight in, revel in, luxuriate in

● NOUN = flavour, taste, smell, relish, smack, tang, piquancy

say VERB 1 = state, declare, remark, announce, maintain, mention, assert, affirm 2 = speak, utter, voice, express, pronounce 3 = suggest, express, imply, communicate, disclose, give away, convey, divulge 4 = suppose, supposing, imagine, assume, presume 5 = estimate, suppose, guess, conjecture, surmise

● NOUN 1 = influence, power, control, authority, weight, clout (informal), mana (N.Z.) 2 = chance to speak, vote, voice

saying = proverb, maxim, adage, dictum, axiom, aphorism

scale[1] = flake, plate, layer, lamina

scale[2] NOUN 1 = degree, size, range, extent, dimensions, scope, magnitude, breadth 2 = system of measurement, measuring system 3 = ranking, ladder, hierarchy, series, sequence, progression 4 = ratio, proportion

● VERB = climb up, mount, ascend, surmount, clamber up, escalade

scan 1 = glance over, skim, look over, eye, check, examine, check out (informal), run over 2 = survey, search, investigate, sweep, scour, scrutinize

scandal 1 = disgrace, crime, offence, sin, embarrassment, wrongdoing, dishonourable behaviour, discreditable behaviour 2 = gossip, talk, rumours, dirt, slander, tattle, aspersion 3 = shame, disgrace, stigma, infamy, opprobrium 4 = outrage, shame, insult, disgrace, injustice, crying shame

scant = inadequate, meagre, sparse, little, minimal, barely sufficient ≠ adequate

scapegoat = fall guy, whipping boy

scar NOUN 1 = mark, injury, wound, blemish 2 = trauma, suffering, pain, torture, anguish

● VERB = mark, disfigure, damage, mar, mutilate, blemish, deface

scarce 1 = in short supply, insufficient ≠ plentiful 2 = rare, few, uncommon, few and far between, infrequent ≠ common

scarcely 1 = hardly, barely 2 (Often used ironically) = by no means, hardly, definitely not

Word Power

scarcely – Since *scarcely*, *hardly*, and *barely* already have negative force, it is unnecessary to use another negative word with them. Therefore, say *he had hardly had time to think* (not *he hadn't hardly had time to think*); and *there was scarcely any bread left* (not *there was scarcely no bread left*). When *scarcely*, *hardly*, and *barely* are used at the beginning of a sentence, as in *scarcely had I arrived*, the following clause should start with *when*: *scarcely had I arrived when I was asked to chair a meeting*. The word *before* can be used in place of *when* in this context, but the word *than* used in the same way is considered incorrect by many people, though this use is becoming increasingly common.

scare VERB = <u>frighten</u>, alarm, terrify, panic, shock, startle, intimidate, dismay
● NOUN 1 = <u>fright</u>, shock, start
2 = <u>panic</u>, hysteria 3 = <u>alert</u>, warning, alarm

scared = <u>afraid</u>, alarmed, frightened, terrified, shaken, startled, fearful, petrified

scary (*Informal*) = <u>frightening</u>, alarming, terrifying, chilling, horrifying, spooky (*informal*), creepy (*informal*), spine-chilling

scatter 1 = <u>throw about</u>, spread, sprinkle, strew, shower, fling, diffuse, disseminate ≠ gather
2 = <u>disperse</u>, dispel, disband, dissipate ≠ assemble

scenario 1 = <u>situation</u> 2 = <u>story line</u>, résumé, outline, summary, synopsis

scene 1 = <u>act</u>, part, division, episode 2 = <u>setting</u>, set, background, location, backdrop
3 = <u>site</u>, place, setting, area, position, spot, locality
4 (*Informal*) = <u>world</u>, business, environment, arena 5 = <u>view</u>, prospect, panorama, vista, landscape, outlook 6 = <u>fuss</u>, to-do, row, performance, exhibition, carry-on (*informal*, *chiefly Brit.*), tantrum, commotion

scenery 1 = <u>landscape</u>, view, surroundings, terrain, vista
2 (*Theatre*) = <u>set</u>, setting, backdrop, flats, stage set

scenic = <u>picturesque</u>, beautiful, spectacular, striking, panoramic

scent NOUN 1 = <u>fragrance</u>, smell, perfume, bouquet, aroma, odour
2 = <u>trail</u>, track, spoor
● VERB = <u>smell</u>, sense, detect, sniff, discern, nose out

scented = <u>fragrant</u>, perfumed, aromatic, sweet-smelling, odoriferous

sceptic 1 = <u>doubter</u>, cynic,

disbeliever 2 = <u>agnostic</u>, doubter, unbeliever, doubting Thomas

sceptical = <u>doubtful</u>, cynical, dubious, unconvinced, disbelieving, incredulous, mistrustful ≠ convinced

scepticism = <u>doubt</u>, suspicion, disbelief, cynicism, incredulity

schedule NOUN 1 = <u>plan</u>, programme, agenda, calendar, timetable

● VERB = <u>plan</u>, set up, book, programme, arrange, organize

scheme NOUN 1 = <u>plan</u>, programme, strategy, system, project, proposal, tactics 2 = <u>plot</u>, ploy, ruse, intrigue, conspiracy, manoeuvre, subterfuge, stratagem

● VERB = <u>plot</u>, plan, intrigue, manoeuvre, conspire, contrive, collude, machinate

scheming = <u>calculating</u>, cunning, sly, tricky, wily, artful, conniving, underhand ≠ straightforward

scholar 1 = <u>intellectual</u>, academic, savant, acca (*Austral. slang*) 2 = <u>student</u>, pupil, learner, schoolboy or schoolgirl

scholarly = <u>learned</u>, academic, intellectual, lettered, erudite, scholastic, bookish ≠ uneducated

scholarship 1 = <u>grant</u>, award, payment, endowment, fellowship, bursary 2 = <u>learning</u>,

education, knowledge, erudition, book-learning

school NOUN 1 = <u>academy</u>, college, institution, institute, seminary 2 = <u>group</u>, set, circle, faction, followers, disciples, devotees, denomination

● VERB = <u>train</u>, coach, discipline, educate, drill, tutor, instruct

science = <u>discipline</u>, body of knowledge, branch of knowledge

scientific = <u>systematic</u>, accurate, exact, precise, controlled, mathematical

scientist = <u>researcher</u>, inventor, boffin (*informal*), technophile

scoff[1] = <u>scorn</u>, mock, laugh at, ridicule, knock (*informal*), despise, sneer, jeer

scoff[2] = <u>gobble (up)</u>, wolf, devour, bolt, guzzle, gulp down, gorge yourself on

scoop VERB = <u>win</u>, get, land, gain, achieve, earn, secure, obtain

● NOUN 1 = <u>ladle</u>, spoon, dipper 2 = <u>exclusive</u>, exposé, revelation, sensation

● PHRASES **scoop something** or **someone up** = <u>gather up</u>, lift, pick up, take up, sweep up or away ♦ **scoop something out** 1 = <u>take out</u>, empty, spoon out, bail or bale out 2 = <u>dig</u>, shovel, excavate, gouge, hollow out

scope 1 = <u>opportunity</u>, room, freedom, space, liberty, latitude

2 = <u>range</u>, capacity, reach, area, outlook, orbit, span, sphere

scorch = <u>burn</u>, sear, roast, wither, shrivel, parch, singe

scorching = <u>burning</u>, boiling, baking, flaming, roasting, searing, fiery, red-hot

score VERB **1** = <u>gain</u>, win, achieve, make, get, attain, notch up (*informal*), chalk up (*informal*) **2** (*Music*) = <u>arrange</u>, set, orchestrate, adapt **3** = <u>cut</u>, scratch, mark, slash, scrape, graze, gouge, deface

● NOUN **1** = <u>rating</u>, mark, grade, percentage **2** = <u>points</u>, result, total, outcome **3** = <u>composition</u>, soundtrack, arrangement, orchestration **4** = <u>grievance</u>, wrong, injury, injustice, grudge

● PLURAL NOUN = <u>lots</u>, loads, many, millions, hundreds, masses, swarms, multitudes

● PHRASES **score something out** *or* **through** = <u>cross out</u>, delete, strike out, cancel, obliterate

scorn NOUN = <u>contempt</u>, disdain, mockery, derision, sarcasm, disparagement ≠ respect

● VERB = <u>despise</u>, reject, disdain, slight, be above, spurn, deride, flout ≠ respect

scour[1] = <u>scrub</u>, clean, polish, rub, buff, abrade

scour[2] = <u>search</u>, hunt, comb, ransack

scout NOUN = <u>vanguard</u>, lookout, precursor, outrider, reconnoitrer, advance guard

● VERB = <u>reconnoitre</u>, investigate, watch, survey, observe, spy, probe, recce (*slang*)

scramble VERB **1** = <u>struggle</u>, climb, crawl, swarm, scrabble **2** = <u>strive</u>, rush, contend, vie, run, push, jostle **3** = <u>jumble</u>, mix up, muddle, shuffle

● NOUN **1** = <u>clamber</u>, ascent **2** = <u>race</u>, competition, struggle, rush, confusion, commotion, melee *or* mêlée

scrap[1] NOUN **1** = <u>piece</u>, fragment, bit, grain, particle, portion, part, crumb **2** = <u>waste</u>, junk, off cuts

● PLURAL NOUN = <u>leftovers</u>, remains, bits, leavings

● VERB = <u>get rid of</u>, drop, abandon, ditch (*slang*), discard, write off, jettison, throw away *or* out ≠ bring back

scrap[2] (*Informal*) NOUN = <u>fight</u>, battle, row, argument, dispute, disagreement, quarrel, squabble, biffo (*Austral. slang*)

● VERB = <u>fight</u>, argue, row, squabble, wrangle

scrape VERB **1** = <u>rake</u>, sweep, drag, brush **2** = <u>grate</u>, grind, scratch, squeak, rasp **3** = <u>graze</u>, skin, scratch, bark, scuff, rub **4** = <u>clean</u>, remove, scour

● NOUN (*Informal*) = <u>predicament</u>, difficulty, fix (*informal*), mess, dilemma, plight, tight spot, awkward situation

scratch VERB 1 = <u>rub</u>, scrape, claw at 2 = <u>mark</u>, cut, score, damage, grate, graze, etch, lacerate

● NOUN = <u>mark</u>, scrape, graze, blemish, gash, laceration, claw mark

● PHRASES **up to scratch** (*Informal*) = <u>adequate</u>, acceptable, satisfactory, sufficient, up to standard

scream VERB = <u>cry</u>, yell, shriek, screech, bawl, howl

● NOUN = <u>cry</u>, yell, howl, shriek, screech, yelp

screen NOUN = <u>cover</u>, guard, shade, shelter, shield, partition, cloak, canopy

● VERB 1 = <u>broadcast</u>, show, put on, present, air, cable, beam, transmit 2 = <u>cover</u>, hide, conceal, shade, mask, veil, cloak 3 = <u>investigate</u>, test, check, examine, scan 4 = <u>process</u>, sort, examine, filter, scan, evaluate, gauge, sift 5 = <u>protect</u>, guard, shield, defend, shelter

screw NOUN = <u>nail</u>, pin, tack, rivet, fastener, spike

● VERB 1 = <u>fasten</u>, fix, attach, bolt, clamp, rivet 2 = <u>turn</u>, twist, tighten 3 (*Informal*) = <u>cheat</u>, do (*slang*), rip (someone) off (*slang*), skin (*slang*), trick, con, sting (*informal*), fleece 4 (*Informal*) often with **out of** = <u>squeeze</u>, wring, extract, wrest

● PHRASES **screw something up** 1 = <u>contort</u>, wrinkle, distort, pucker 2 (*Informal*) = <u>bungle</u>, botch, mess up, spoil, mishandle, make a mess of (*slang*), make a hash of (*informal*), crool or cruel (*Austral. slang*)

scribble = <u>scrawl</u>, write, jot, dash off

script NOUN 1 = <u>text</u>, lines, words, book, copy, dialogue, libretto 2 = <u>handwriting</u>, writing, calligraphy, penmanship

● VERB = <u>write</u>, draft

scripture = <u>The Bible</u>, The Gospels, The Scriptures, The Good Book, Holy Scripture, Holy Writ, Holy Bible

scrub 1 = <u>scour</u>, clean, polish, rub, wash, cleanse, buff 2 (*Informal*) = <u>cancel</u>, drop, give up, abolish, forget about, call off, delete

scrutiny = <u>examination</u>, study, investigation, search, analysis, inspection, exploration, perusal

sculpture NOUN = <u>statue</u>, figure, model, bust, effigy, figurine, statuette

● VERB = <u>carve</u>, form, model, fashion, shape, mould, sculpt, chisel

sea NOUN 1 = <u>ocean</u>, the deep, the waves, main 2 = <u>mass</u>, army, host, crowd, mob, abundance, swarm, horde

● PHRASES **at sea** = <u>bewildered</u>, lost, confused, puzzled, baffled, perplexed, mystified, flummoxed

(*Related Words*)

adjectives: marine, maritime

sea bird ▸ *sea birds*

seal VERB = <u>settle</u>, clinch, conclude, consummate, finalize

● NOUN 1 = <u>sealant</u>, sealer, adhesive 2 = <u>authentication</u>, stamp, confirmation, ratification, insignia, imprimatur

seam 1 = <u>joint</u>, closure 2 = <u>layer</u>, vein, stratum, lode

sea mammal

Sea mammals

dugong	seal
elephant seal	sea lion
harp seal	walrus *or*
manatee	(*archaic*) sea
sea cow	horse

sear = <u>wither</u>, burn, scorch, sizzle

search VERB = <u>examine</u>, investigate, explore, inspect, comb, scour, ransack, scrutinize, fossick (*Austral. & N.Z.*)

● NOUN = <u>hunt</u>, look, investigation, examination, pursuit, quest, inspection, exploration

● PHRASES **search for something** *or* **someone** = <u>look</u>

Sea birds

albatross *or* (*informal*) gooney bird	man-of-war bird *or* frigate bird
auk	oystercatcher
black-backed gull	petrel
coot	razorbill *or* razor-billed auk
cormorant	scoter
fairy penguin, little penguin, *or* (*N.Z.*) korora	sea eagle, erne, *or* ern
fish hawk	seagull
fulmar	shearwater
gannet	short-tailed shearwater, (Tasmanian) mutton bird, *or* (*N.Z.*) titi
guillemot	skua
gull *or* (*archaic or dialect*) cob(b)	storm petrel, stormy petrel, *or* Mother Carey's chicken
herring gull	wandering albatross
kittiwake	

for, hunt for, pursue

searching = <u>keen</u>, sharp, probing, close, intent, piercing, penetrating, quizzical ≠ superficial

searing 1 = <u>acute</u>, intense, shooting, severe, painful, stabbing, piercing, gut-wrenching 2 = <u>cutting</u>, biting, bitter, harsh, barbed, hurtful, caustic

season NOUN = <u>period</u>, time, term, spell

• VERB = <u>flavour</u>, salt, spice, enliven, pep up

seasoned = <u>experienced</u>, veteran, practised, hardened, time-served ≠ inexperienced

seasoning = <u>flavouring</u>, spice, salt and pepper, condiment

seat NOUN 1 = <u>chair</u>, bench, stall, stool, pew, settle 2 = <u>membership</u>, place, constituency, chair, incumbency 3 = <u>centre</u>, place, site, heart, capital, situation, source, hub 4 = <u>mansion</u>, house, residence, abode, ancestral hall

• VERB 1 = <u>sit</u>, place, settle, set, fix, locate, install 2 = <u>hold</u>, take, accommodate, sit, contain, cater for

second[1] ADJECTIVE 1 = <u>next</u>, following, succeeding, subsequent 2 = <u>additional</u>, other, further, extra, alternative

3 = <u>inferior</u>, secondary, subordinate, lower, lesser

• NOUN = <u>supporter</u>, assistant, aide, colleague, backer, helper, right-hand man

• VERB = <u>support</u>, back, endorse, approve, go along with

second[2] = <u>moment</u>, minute, instant, flash, sec (informal), jiffy (informal), trice

secondary 1 = <u>subordinate</u>, minor, lesser, lower, inferior, unimportant ≠ main 2 = <u>resultant</u>, contingent, derived, indirect ≠ original

second-hand = <u>used</u>, old, hand-me-down (informal), nearly new

secondly = <u>next</u>, second, moreover, furthermore, also, in the second place

secrecy 1 = <u>mystery</u>, stealth, concealment, furtiveness, secretiveness, clandestineness, covertness 2 = <u>confidentiality</u>, privacy 3 = <u>privacy</u>, silence, seclusion

secret ADJECTIVE 1 = <u>undisclosed</u>, unknown, confidential, underground, undercover, unrevealed ≠ concealed, hidden, disguised ≠ unconcealed 3 = <u>undercover</u>, furtive ≠ open 4 = <u>secretive</u>, reserved, close ≠ frank 5 = <u>mysterious</u>, cryptic, abstruse, occult, clandestine, arcane ≠ straightforward

● NOUN = private affair

● PHRASES in secret = secretly, surreptitiously, slyly

secretive = reticent, reserved, close, deep, uncommunicative, tight-lipped ≠ open

secretly = in secret, privately, surreptitiously, quietly, covertly, furtively, stealthily, clandestinely

sect = group, division, faction, party, camp, denomination, schism

section 1 = part, piece, portion, division, slice, passage, segment, fraction 2 = district, area, region, sector, zone

sector 1 = part, division 2 = area, part, region, district, zone, quarter

secular = worldly, lay, earthly, civil, temporal, nonspiritual ≠ religious

secure VERB 1 = obtain, get, acquire, score (slang), gain, procure ≠ lose 2 = attach, stick, fix, bind, fasten ≠ detach

● ADJECTIVE 1 = safe, protected, immune, unassailable ≠ unprotected 2 = fast, firm, fixed, stable, steady, fastened, immovable ≠ insecure 3 = confident, sure, easy, certain, assured, reassured ≠ uneasy

security 1 = precautions, defence, safeguards, protection, safety measures 2 = assurance,

confidence, conviction, certainty, reliance, sureness, positiveness ≠ insecurity 3 = pledge, insurance, guarantee, hostage, collateral, pawn, gage, surety 4 = protection, safety, custody, refuge, sanctuary, safekeeping ≠ vulnerability

sediment = dregs, grounds, residue, lees, deposit

seduce 1 = tempt, lure, entice, mislead, deceive, beguile, lead astray, inveigle 2 = corrupt, deprave, dishonour, debauch, deflower

seductive = tempting, inviting, attractive, enticing, provocative, alluring, bewitching

see VERB 1 = perceive, spot, notice, sight, witness, observe, distinguish, glimpse 2 = understand, get, follow, realize, appreciate, grasp, comprehend, fathom 3 = find out, learn, discover, determine, verify, ascertain 4 = consider, decide, reflect, deliberate, think over 5 = make sure, ensure, guarantee, make certain, see to it 6 = accompany, show, escort, lead, walk, usher 7 = speak to, receive, interview, consult, confer with 8 = meet, come across, happen on, bump into, run across, chance on 9 = go out with, court, date (informal, chiefly U.S.), go steady with (informal)

● PHRASES **seeing as** = <u>since</u>, as, in view of the fact that, inasmuch as

> ### Word Power
>
> **see** – It is common to hear *seeing as how*, as in *seeing as how the bus is always late, I don't need to hurry*. However, the use of *how* here is considered incorrect or nonstandard, and should be avoided.

seed NOUN 1 = <u>grain</u>, pip, germ, kernel, egg, embryo, spore, ovum 2 = <u>beginning</u>, start, germ 3 = <u>origin</u>, source, nucleus 4 (*Chiefly Bible*) = <u>offspring</u>, children, descendants, issue, progeny

● PHRASES **go** *or* **run to seed** = <u>decline</u>, deteriorate, degenerate, decay, go downhill (*informal*), let yourself go, go to pot

seek 1 = <u>look for</u>, pursue, search for, be after, hunt 2 = <u>try</u>, attempt, aim, strive, endeavour, essay, aspire to

seem = <u>appear</u>, give the impression of being, look

seep = <u>ooze</u>, well, leak, soak, trickle, exude, permeate

seethe 1 = <u>be furious</u>, rage, fume, simmer, see red (*informal*), be livid, go ballistic (*slang, chiefly U.S.*) 2 = <u>boil</u>, bubble, foam, fizz, froth

segment = <u>section</u>, part, piece, division, slice, portion, wedge

segregate = <u>set apart</u>, divide, separate, isolate, discriminate against, dissociate ≠ unite

segregation = <u>separation</u>, discrimination, apartheid, isolation

seize 1 = <u>grab</u>, grip, grasp, take, snatch, clutch, snap up, pluck ≠ let go 2 = <u>take by storm</u>, take over, acquire, occupy, conquer 3 = <u>capture</u>, catch, arrest, apprehend, take captive ≠ release

seizure 1 = <u>attack</u>, fit, spasm, convulsion, paroxysm 2 = <u>taking</u>, grabbing, annexation, confiscation, commandeering 3 = <u>capture</u>, arrest, apprehension

seldom = <u>rarely</u>, not often, infrequently, hardly ever ≠ often

select VERB = <u>choose</u>, take, pick, opt for, decide on, single out, adopt, settle upon ≠ reject

● ADJECTIVE 1 = <u>choice</u>, special, excellent, superior, first-class, hand-picked, top-notch (*informal*) ≠ ordinary 2 = <u>exclusive</u>, elite, privileged, cliquish ≠ indiscriminate

selection 1 = <u>choice</u>, choosing, pick, option, preference 2 = <u>anthology</u>, collection, medley, choice

selective = <u>particular</u>,

discriminating, careful, discerning, tasteful, fastidious ≠ indiscriminate

selfish = <u>self-centred</u>, self-interested, greedy, ungenerous, egoistic or egoistical, egotistic or egotistical ≠ unselfish

sell VERB 1 = <u>trade</u>, exchange, barter ≠ buy 2 = <u>deal in</u>, market, trade in, stock, handle, retail, peddle, traffic in ≠ buy
● PHRASES **sell out of something** = <u>run out of</u>, be out of stock of

seller = <u>dealer</u>, merchant, vendor, agent, retailer, supplier, purveyor, salesman or saleswoman

send VERB 1 = <u>dispatch</u>, forward, direct, convey, remit 2 = <u>propel</u>, hurl, fling, shoot, fire, cast, let fly
● PHRASES **send something or someone up** (Brit. informal) = <u>mock</u>, mimic, parody, spoof (informal), imitate, take off (informal), make fun of, lampoon

send-off = <u>farewell</u>, departure, leave-taking, valediction

senior 1 = <u>higher ranking</u>, superior ≠ subordinate 2 = <u>the elder</u>, major (Brit.) ≠ junior

sensation 1 = <u>feeling</u>, sense, impression, perception, awareness, consciousness 2 = <u>excitement</u>, thrill, stir, furore, commotion

sensational 1 = <u>amazing</u>, dramatic, thrilling, astounding ≠ dull 2 = <u>shocking</u>, exciting, melodramatic, shock-horror (facetious) ≠ unexciting 3 (Informal) = <u>excellent</u>, superb, mean (slang), impressive, smashing (informal), fabulous (informal), marvellous, out of this world (informal), boshit (Austral. slang), exo (Austral. slang), sik (Austral. slang) ≠ ordinary

sense NOUN 1 = <u>faculty</u> 2 = <u>feeling</u>, impression, perception, awareness, consciousness, atmosphere, aura 3 = <u>understanding</u>, awareness 4 sometimes plural = <u>intelligence</u>, reason, understanding, brains (informal), judgment, wisdom, wit(s), common sense ≠ foolishness 5 = <u>meaning</u>, significance, import, implication, drift, gist
● VERB = <u>perceive</u>, feel, understand, pick up, realize, be aware of, discern, get the impression ≠ be unaware of

sensibility often plural = <u>feelings</u>, emotions, sentiments, susceptibilities, moral sense

sensible 1 = <u>wise</u>, practical, prudent, shrewd, judicious ≠ foolish 2 = <u>intelligent</u>, practical, rational, sound, realistic, sage, shrewd, down-to-earth ≠ senseless

sensitive 1 = <u>thoughtful</u>, kindly, concerned, patient, attentive, tactful, unselfish 2 = <u>delicate</u>, tender 3 = <u>susceptible to</u>, responsive, easily affected by 4 = <u>touchy</u>, oversensitive, easily upset, easily offended, easily hurt ≠ insensitive 5 = <u>precise</u>, fine, acute, keen, responsive ≠ imprecise

sensitivity 1 = <u>susceptibility</u>, responsiveness, receptiveness, sensitiveness 2 = <u>consideration</u>, patience, thoughtfulness 3 = <u>touchiness</u>, oversensitivity 4 = <u>responsiveness</u>, precision, keenness, acuteness

sensual 1 = <u>sexual</u>, erotic, raunchy (*slang*), lewd, lascivious, lustful, lecherous 2 = <u>physical</u>, bodily, voluptuous, animal, luxurious, fleshly, carnal

sentence NOUN 1 = <u>punishment</u>, condemnation 2 = <u>verdict</u>, order, ruling, decision, judgment, decree
● VERB 1 = <u>condemn</u>, doom 2 = <u>convict</u>, condemn, penalize

sentiment 1 = <u>feeling</u>, idea, view, opinion, attitude, belief, judgment 2 = <u>sentimentality</u>, emotion, tenderness, romanticism, sensibility, emotionalism, mawkishness

sentimental = <u>romantic</u>, touching, emotional, nostalgic, maudlin, weepy (*informal*), slushy (*informal*), schmaltzy (*slang*) ≠ unsentimental

separate ADJECTIVE
1 = <u>unconnected</u>, individual, particular, single, divorced, isolated, detached, disconnected ≠ connected 2 = <u>individual</u>, independent, apart, distinct ≠ joined
● VERB 1 = <u>divide</u>, detach, disconnect, disjoin ≠ combine 2 = <u>come apart</u>, split, come away ≠ connect 3 = <u>sever</u>, break apart, split in two, divide in two ≠ join 4 = <u>split up</u>, part, divorce, break up, part company, get divorced, be estranged 5 = <u>distinguish</u>, mark, single out, set apart ≠ link

separated 1 = <u>estranged</u>, parted, separate, apart, disunited 2 = <u>disconnected</u>, parted, divided, separate, disassociated, disunited, sundered

separately 1 = <u>alone</u>, apart, not together, severally ≠ together 2 = <u>individually</u>, singly

separation 1 = <u>division</u>, break, dissociation, disconnection, disunion 2 = <u>split-up</u>, parting, split, divorce, break-up, rift

sequel 1 = <u>follow-up</u>, continuation, development 2 = <u>consequence</u>, result, outcome, conclusion, end, upshot

sequence = <u>succession</u>, course, series, order, chain, cycle, arrangement, progression

series 1 = <u>sequence</u>, course, chain, succession, run, set, order, train **2** = <u>drama</u>, serial, soap (*informal*), sitcom (*informal*), soap opera, soapie (*Austral. slang*), situation comedy

serious 1 = <u>grave</u>, bad, critical, dangerous, acute, severe **2** = <u>important</u>, crucial, urgent, pressing, worrying, significant, grim, momentous ≠ unimportant **3** = <u>thoughtful</u>, detailed, careful, deep, profound, in-depth **4** = <u>deep</u>, sophisticated **5** = <u>solemn</u>, earnest, grave, sober, staid, humourless, unsmiling ≠ light-hearted **6** = <u>sincere</u>, earnest, genuine, honest, in earnest ≠ insincere

seriously 1 = <u>truly</u>, in earnest, all joking aside **2** = <u>badly</u>, severely, gravely, critically, acutely, dangerously

seriousness 1 = <u>importance</u>, gravity, urgency, significance **2** = <u>solemnity</u>, gravity, earnestness, gravitas

sermon = <u>homily</u>, address

servant = <u>attendant</u>, domestic, slave, maid, help, retainer, skivvy (*chiefly Brit.*)

serve 1 = <u>work for</u>, help, aid, assist, be in the service of **2** = <u>perform</u>, do, complete, fulfil, discharge **3** = <u>be adequate</u>, do,

suffice, suit, satisfy, be acceptable, answer the purpose **4** = <u>present</u>, provide, supply, deliver, set out, dish up

service NOUN **1** = <u>facility</u>, system, resource, utility, amenity **2** = <u>ceremony</u>, worship, rite, observance **3** = <u>work</u>, labour, employment, business, office, duty **4** = <u>check</u>, maintenance check

● VERB = <u>overhaul</u>, check, maintain, tune (up), go over, fine tune

session = <u>meeting</u>, hearing, sitting, period, conference, congress, discussion, assembly

set¹ VERB **1** = <u>put</u>, place, lay, position, rest, plant, station, stick **2** = <u>arrange</u>, decide (upon), settle, establish, determine, fix, schedule, appoint **3** = <u>assign</u>, give, allot, prescribe **4** = <u>harden</u>, stiffen, solidify, cake, thicken, crystallize, congeal **5** = <u>go down</u>, sink, dip, decline, disappear, vanish, subside **6** = <u>prepare</u>, lay, spread, arrange, make ready

● ADJECTIVE **1** = <u>established</u>, planned, decided, agreed, arranged, rigid, definite, inflexible **2** = <u>strict</u>, rigid, stubborn, inflexible ≠ flexible **3** = <u>conventional</u>, traditional, stereotyped, unspontaneous

● NOUN **1** = <u>scenery</u>, setting, scene, stage set **2** = <u>position</u>, bearing,

attitude, carriage, posture
● PHRASES **be set on** *or* **upon**
something = be determined to,
be intent on, be bent on, be
resolute about ◆ **set**
something up 1 = arrange,
organize, prepare, prearrange
2 = establish, begin, found,
institute, initiate **3** = build, raise,
construct, put up, assemble, put
together, erect **4** = assemble, put
up

set² 1 = series, collection,
assortment, batch, compendium,
ensemble **2** = group, company,
crowd, circle, band, gang, faction,
clique

setback = hold-up, check,
defeat, blow, reverse,
disappointment, hitch,
misfortune

setting = surroundings, site,
location, set, scene, background,
context, backdrop

settle 1 = resolve, work out, put
an end to, straighten out **2** = pay,
clear, square (up), discharge
3 = move to, take up residence in,
live in, dwell in, inhabit, reside in,
set up home in, put down roots
in **4** = colonize, populate, people,
pioneer **5** = land, alight, descend,
light, come to rest **6** = calm,
quiet, relax, relieve, reassure,
soothe, lull, quell ≠ disturb

settlement 1 = agreement,

arrangement, working out,
conclusion, establishment,
confirmation **2** = payment,
clearing, discharge **3** = colony,
community, outpost,
encampment, kainga *or* kaika
(*N.Z.*)

settler = colonist, immigrant,
pioneer, frontiersman

set-up (*Informal*)
= arrangement, system, structure,
organization, conditions, regime

sever 1 = cut, separate, split,
part, divide, detach, disconnect,
cut in two ≠ join **2** = discontinue,
terminate, break off, put an end
to, dissociate ≠ continue

several ADJECTIVE = some, a few,
a number of, a handful of
● PRONOUN = various, different,
diverse, sundry

severe 1 = serious, critical,
terrible, desperate, extreme,
awful, drastic, catastrophic
2 = acute, intense, violent,
piercing, harrowing, unbearable,
agonizing, insufferable **3** = strict,
hard, harsh, cruel, rigid, drastic,
oppressive, austere ≠ lenient
4 = grim, serious, grave,
forbidding, stern, unsmiling,
tight-lipped ≠ genial **5** = plain,
simple, austere, classic, restrained,
Spartan, unadorned, unfussy
≠ fancy

severely 1 = seriously, badly,

extremely, gravely, acutely
2 = <u>strictly</u>, harshly, sternly, sharply

severity = <u>strictness</u>, harshness, toughness, hardness, sternness, severeness

sew = <u>stitch</u>, tack, seam, hem

sex 1 = <u>gender</u> **2** (*Informal*) = <u>lovemaking</u>, sexual relations, copulation, fornication, coitus, coition

sexual 1 = <u>carnal</u>, erotic, intimate **2** = <u>sexy</u>, erotic, sensual, arousing, naughty, provocative, seductive, sensuous

sexuality = <u>desire</u>, lust, eroticism, sensuality, sexiness (*informal*), carnality

sexy = <u>erotic</u>, sensual, seductive, arousing, naughty, provocative, sensuous, suggestive

shabby 1 = <u>tatty</u>, worn, ragged, scruffy, tattered, threadbare ≠ smart **2** = <u>run-down</u>, seedy, mean, dilapidated **3** = <u>mean</u>, low, rotten (*informal*), cheap, dirty, despicable, contemptible, scurvy ≠ fair

shack = <u>hut</u>, cabin, shanty, whare (*N.Z.*)

shade NOUN 1 = <u>hue</u>, tone, colour, tint **2** = <u>shadow</u> **3** = <u>dash</u>, trace, hint, suggestion **4** = <u>nuance</u>, difference, degree **5** = <u>screen</u>, covering, cover, blind, curtain, shield, veil, canopy **6** (*Literary*)

= <u>ghost</u>, spirit, phantom, spectre, apparition, kehua (*N.Z.*)

● VERB **1** = <u>darken</u>, shadow, cloud, dim **2** = <u>cover</u>, protect, screen, hide, shield, conceal, obscure, veil

shadow NOUN 1 = <u>silhouette</u>, shape, outline, profile **2** = <u>shade</u>, dimness, darkness, gloom, cover, dusk

● VERB **1** = <u>shade</u>, screen, shield, darken, overhang **2** = <u>follow</u>, tail (*informal*), trail, stalk

shady 1 = <u>shaded</u>, cool, dim ≠ sunny **2** (*Informal*) = <u>crooked</u>, dodgy (*Brit., Austral., & N.Z. informal*), unethical, suspect, suspicious, dubious, questionable, shifty ≠ honest

shaft 1 = <u>tunnel</u>, hole, passage, burrow, passageway, channel **2** = <u>handle</u>, staff, pole, rod, stem, baton, shank **3** = <u>ray</u>, beam, gleam

shake VERB 1 = <u>jiggle</u>, agitate **2** = <u>tremble</u>, shiver, quake, quiver **3** = <u>rock</u>, totter **4** = <u>wave</u>, wield, flourish, brandish **5** = <u>upset</u>, shock, frighten, disturb, distress, rattle (*informal*), unnerve, traumatize

● NOUN = <u>vibration</u>, trembling, quaking, jerk, shiver, shudder, jolt, tremor

Shakespeare ▸ Shakespeare

shaky 1 = <u>unstable</u>, weak, precarious, rickety ≠ stable

Shakespeare

Character	Play
Sir Andrew Aguecheek	Twelfth Night
Antonio	The Merchant of Venice
Antony	Antony and Cleopatra, Julius Caesar
Ariel	The Tempest
Aufidius	Coriolanus
Autolycus	The Winter's Tale
Banquo	Macbeth
Bassanio	The Merchant of Venice
Beatrice	Much Ado About Nothing
Sir Toby Belch	Twelfth Night
Benedick	Much Ado About Nothing
Bolingbroke	Richard II
Bottom	A Midsummer Night's Dream
Brutus	Julius Caesar
Caliban	The Tempest
Casca	Julius Caesar
Cassio	Othello
Cassius	Julius Caesar
Claudio	Much Ado About Nothing, Measure for Measure
Claudius	Hamlet
Cleopatra	Antony and Cleopatra
Cordelia	King Lear
Coriolanus	Coriolanus
Cressida	Troilus and Cressida
Demetrius	A Midsummer Night's Dream
Desdemona	Othello
Dogberry	Much Ado About Nothing
Edmund	King Lear
Enobarbus	Antony and Cleopatra
Falstaff	Henry IV Parts I and II, The Merry Wives of Windsor
Ferdinand	The Tempest
Feste	Twelfth Night
Fluellen	Henry V
Fool	King Lear

Shakespeare *(continued)*

Character	Play
Guildenstern	Hamlet
Hamlet	Hamlet
Helena	All's Well that Ends Well, A Midsummer Night's Dream
Hermia	A Midsummer Night's Dream
Hero	Much Ado About Nothing
Hotspur	Henry IV Part I
Iago	Othello
Jaques	As You Like It
John of Gaunt	Richard II
Juliet	Romeo and Juliet
Julius Caesar	Julius Caesar
Katharina *or* Kate	The Taming of the Shrew
Kent	King Lear
Laertes	Hamlet
Lear	King Lear
Lysander	A Midsummer Night's Dream
Macbeth	Macbeth
Lady Macbeth	Macbeth
Macduff	Macbeth
Malcolm	Macbeth
Malvolio	Twelfth Night
Mercutio	Romeo and Juliet
Miranda	The Tempest
Oberon	A Midsummer Night's Dream
Octavius	Antony and Cleopatra
Olivia	Twelfth Night
Ophelia	Hamlet
Orlando	As You Like It
Orsino	Twelfth Night
Othello	Othello
Pandarus	Troilus and Cressida
Perdita	The Winter's Tale
Petruchio	The Taming of the Shrew
Pistol	Henry IV Part II, Henry V, The Merry Wives of Windsor

Shakespeare (continued)	
Character	*Play*
Polonius	Hamlet
Puck	A Midsummer Night's Dream
Mistress Quickly	The Merry Wives of Windsor
Regan	King Lear
Romeo	Romeo and Juliet
Rosalind	As You Like It
Rosencrantz	Hamlet
Sebastian	The Tempest, Twelfth Night
Shylock	The Merchant of Venice
Thersites	Troilus and Cressida
Timon	Timon of Athens
Titania	A Midsummer Night's Dream
Touchstone	As You Like It
Troilus	Troilus and Cressida
Tybalt	Romeo and Juliet
Viola	Twelfth Night

2 = <u>unsteady</u>, faint, trembling, faltering, quivery **3** = <u>uncertain</u>, suspect, dubious, questionable, iffy (*informal*) ≠ reliable

shallow = <u>superficial</u>, surface, empty, slight, foolish, trivial, meaningless, frivolous ≠ deep

sham NOUN = <u>fraud</u>, imitation, hoax, pretence, forgery, counterfeit, humbug, impostor ≠ the real thing
● ADJECTIVE = <u>false</u>, artificial, bogus, pretended, mock, imitation, simulated, counterfeit ≠ real

shambles 1 = <u>chaos</u>, mess, disorder, confusion, muddle,

havoc, disarray, madhouse
2 = <u>mess</u>, jumble, untidiness

shame NOUN **1** = <u>embarrassment</u>, humiliation, ignominy, mortification, abashment ≠ shamelessness **2** = <u>disgrace</u>, scandal, discredit, smear, disrepute, reproach, dishonour, infamy ≠ honour
● VERB **1** = <u>embarrass</u>, disgrace, humiliate, humble, mortify, abash ≠ make proud **2** = <u>dishonour</u>, degrade, stain, smear, blot, debase, defile ≠ honour

shameful = <u>disgraceful</u>, outrageous, scandalous, mean, low, base, wicked, dishonourable

≠ admirable

shape NOUN 1 = <u>appearance</u>, form, aspect, guise, likeness, semblance 2 = <u>form</u>, profile, outline, lines, build, figure, silhouette, configuration 3 = <u>pattern</u>, model, frame, mould 4 = <u>condition</u>, state, health, trim, fettle

● VERB 1 = <u>form</u>, make, produce, create, fashion, mould 2 = <u>mould</u>, form, make, fashion, model, frame

share NOUN 1 = <u>part</u>, portion, quota, ration, lot, due, contribution, allowance

● VERB 1 = <u>divide</u>, split, distribute, assign 2 = <u>go halves on</u>, go fifty-fifty on (*informal*)

shark ▶ **sharks**

sharp ADJECTIVE 1 = <u>keen</u>, jagged, serrated ≠ blunt 2 = <u>quick-witted</u>, clever, astute, knowing, quick, bright, alert, penetrating ≠ dim 3 = <u>cutting</u>, biting, bitter, harsh, barbed, hurtful, caustic ≠ gentle

4 = <u>sudden</u>, marked, abrupt, extreme, distinct ≠ gradual 5 = <u>clear</u>, distinct, well-defined, crisp ≠ indistinct 6 = <u>sour</u>, tart, pungent, hot, acid, acrid, piquant ≠ bland 7 = <u>acute</u>, severe, intense, painful, shooting, stabbing, piercing, gut-wrenching

● ADVERB = <u>promptly</u>, precisely, exactly, on time, on the dot, punctually ≠ approximately

sharpen = <u>make sharp</u>, hone, whet, grind, edge

shatter 1 = <u>smash</u>, break, burst, crack, crush, pulverize

2 = <u>destroy</u>, ruin, wreck, demolish, torpedo

shattered 1 = <u>devastated</u>, crushed, gutted (*slang*)

2 (*Informal*) = <u>exhausted</u>, drained, worn out, done in (*informal*), all in (*slang*), knackered (*slang*), tired out, ready to drop

shave 1 = <u>trim</u>, crop 2 = <u>scrape</u>, trim, shear, pare

shed¹ = <u>hut</u>, shack, outhouse,

Sharks

angel shark, angelfish, *or* monkfish	nurse shark
basking shark *or* sailfish	porbeagle *or* mackerel shark
blue pointer	requiem shark
dogfish *or* (*Austral.*) dog shark	shovelhead
gummy (shark)	thrasher *or* thresher shark
hammerhead	tiger shark
mako	tope
	whale shark

whare (*N.Z.*)

shed [2] 1 = drop, spill, scatter
2 = cast off, discard, moult, slough
off 3 = give out, cast, emit, give,
radiate

sheen = shine, gleam, gloss,
polish, brightness, lustre

sheer 1 = total, complete,
absolute, utter, pure, downright,
out-and-out, unmitigated
≠ moderate 2 = steep, abrupt,
precipitous ≠ gradual 3 = fine,
thin, transparent, see-through,
gossamer, diaphanous, gauzy
≠ thick

sheet 1 = page, leaf, folio, piece
of paper 2 = plate, piece, panel,
slab 3 = coat, film, layer, surface,
stratum, veneer, overlay, lamina
4 = expanse, area, stretch, sweep,
covering, blanket

shell NOUN 1 = husk, case, pod
2 = carapace 3 = frame, structure,
hull, framework, chassis
● VERB = bomb, bombard, attack,
blitz, strafe
● PHRASES **shell something out**
(with money or a specified sum
of money as object) = pay out,
fork out (*slang*), give, hand over

shelter NOUN 1 = cover, screen
2 = protection, safety, refuge,
cover 3 = refuge, haven,
sanctuary, retreat, asylum
● VERB 1 = take shelter, hide, seek
refuge, take cover 2 = protect,

shield, harbour, safeguard, cover,
hide, guard, defend ≠ endanger

sheltered 1 = screened,
covered, protected, shielded,
secluded ≠ exposed
2 = protected, screened, shielded,
quiet, isolated, secluded,
cloistered

shelve = postpone, defer, freeze,
suspend, put aside, put on ice,
put on the back burner
(*informal*), take a rain check on
(*U.S. & Canad. informal*)

shepherd NOUN = drover,
stockman, herdsman, grazier
● VERB = guide, conduct, steer,
herd, usher
(Related Words)
adjective: pastoral

shield NOUN = protection, cover,
defence, screen, guard, shelter,
safeguard
● VERB = protect, cover, screen,
guard, defend, shelter, safeguard

shift VERB 1 = move, move
around, budge 2 = remove, move,
displace, relocate, rearrange,
reposition
● NOUN 1 = change, shifting,
displacement 2 = move,
rearrangement

shimmer VERB = gleam, twinkle,
glisten, scintillate
● NOUN = gleam, iridescence

shine VERB 1 = gleam, flash,
beam, glow, sparkle, glitter, glare,

radiate **2** = <u>polish</u>, buff, burnish, brush **3** = <u>be outstanding</u>, stand out, excel, be conspicuous
● **NOUN 1** = <u>polish</u>, gloss, sheen, lustre **2** = <u>brightness</u>, light, sparkle, radiance

shining = <u>bright</u>, brilliant, gleaming, beaming, sparkling, shimmering, radiant, luminous

shiny = <u>bright</u>, gleaming, glossy, glistening, polished, lustrous

ship = <u>vessel</u>, boat, craft

shiver VERB = <u>shudder</u>, shake, tremble, quake, quiver
● **NOUN** = <u>tremble</u>, shudder, quiver, trembling, flutter, tremor

shock NOUN **1** = <u>upset</u>, blow, trauma, bombshell, turn (*informal*), distress, disturbance **2** = <u>impact</u>, blow, clash, collision **3** = <u>start</u>, scare, fright, turn, jolt
● VERB **1** = <u>shake</u>, stun, stagger, jolt, stupefy **2** = <u>horrify</u>, appal, disgust, revolt, sicken, nauseate, scandalize

shocking 1 (*Informal*) = <u>terrible</u>, appalling, dreadful, bad, horrendous, ghastly, deplorable, abysmal **2** = <u>appalling</u>, outrageous, disgraceful, disgusting, dreadful, horrifying, revolting, sickening ≠ wonderful

shoot VERB **1** = <u>open fire on</u>, blast (*slang*), hit, kill, plug (*slang*), bring down **2** = <u>fire</u>, launch, discharge, project, hurl, fling, propel, emit

3 = <u>speed</u>, race, rush, charge, fly, tear, dash, barrel (along) (*informal, chiefly U.S. & Canad.*)
● **NOUN** = <u>sprout</u>, branch, bud, sprig, offshoot

shop = <u>store</u>, supermarket, boutique, emporium, hypermarket, dairy (*N.Z.*)

shore = <u>beach</u>, coast, sands, strand (*poetic*), seashore

short ADJECTIVE **1** = <u>brief</u>, fleeting, momentary ≠ long **2** = <u>concise</u>, brief, succinct, summary, compressed, terse, laconic, pithy ≠ lengthy **3** = <u>small</u>, little, squat, diminutive, petite, dumpy ≠ tall **4** = <u>abrupt</u>, sharp, terse, curt, brusque, impolite, discourteous, uncivil ≠ polite **5** = <u>scarce</u>, wanting, low, limited, lacking, scant, deficient ≠ plentiful
● ADVERB = <u>abruptly</u>, suddenly, without warning ≠ gradually

shortage = <u>deficiency</u>, want, lack, scarcity, dearth, paucity, insufficiency ≠ abundance

shortcoming = <u>failing</u>, fault, weakness, defect, flaw, imperfection

shorten 1 = <u>cut</u>, reduce, decrease, diminish, lessen, curtail, abbreviate, abridge ≠ increase **2** = <u>turn up</u>

shortly 1 = <u>soon</u>, presently, before long, in a little while

shot 1 = <u>discharge</u>, gunfire, crack,

blast, explosion, bang
2 = <u>ammunition</u>, bullet, slug, pellet, projectile, lead, ball **3** = <u>marksman</u>, shooter, markswoman **4** (*Informal*) = <u>strike</u>, throw, lob **5** = <u>attempt</u>, go (*informal*), try, turn, effort, stab (*informal*), endeavour

shoulder 1 = <u>bear</u>, carry, take on, accept, assume, be responsible for **2** = <u>push</u>, elbow, shove, jostle, press

shout VERB = <u>cry (out)</u>, call (out), yell, scream, roar, bellow, bawl, holler (*informal*)

● NOUN = <u>cry</u>, call, yell, scream, roar, bellow

● PHRASES **shout someone down** = <u>drown out</u>, overwhelm, drown, silence

shove VERB = <u>push</u>, thrust, elbow, drive, press, propel, jostle, impel

● NOUN = <u>push</u>, knock, thrust, elbow, bump, nudge, jostle

● PHRASES **shove off** (*Informal*) = <u>go away</u>, leave, clear off (*informal*), depart, push off (*informal*), scram (*informal*)

shovel 1 = <u>move</u>, scoop, dredge, load, heap **2** = <u>stuff</u>, ladle

show VERB **1** = <u>indicate</u>, demonstrate, prove, reveal, display, point out, manifest, testify to ≠ <u>disprove</u> **2** = <u>display</u>, exhibit, lead, conduct, accompany, direct, escort

4 = <u>demonstrate</u>, describe, explain, teach, illustrate, instruct **5** = <u>be visible</u> ≠ be invisible **6** = <u>express</u>, display, reveal, indicate, register, demonstrate, manifest ≠ hide **7** = <u>turn up</u>, appear, attend **8** = <u>broadcast</u>, transmit, air, beam, relay, televise, put on the air

● NOUN **1** = <u>display</u>, sight, spectacle, array **2** = <u>exhibition</u>, fair, display, parade, pageant **3** = <u>appearance</u>, display, pose, parade **4** = <u>pretence</u>, appearance, illusion, affectation **5** = <u>programme</u>, broadcast, presentation, production **6** = <u>entertainment</u>, production, presentation

● PHRASES **show off** (*Informal*) = <u>boast</u>, brag, blow your own trumpet, swagger ◆ **show someone up** (*Informal*) = <u>embarrass</u>, let down, mortify, put to shame ◆ **show something off** = <u>exhibit</u>, display, parade, demonstrate, flaunt ◆ **show something up** = <u>reveal</u>, expose, highlight, lay bare

showdown (*Informal*) = <u>confrontation</u>, clash, face-off (*slang*)

shower NOUN = <u>deluge</u>

● VERB **1** = <u>cover</u>, dust, spray, sprinkle **2** = <u>inundate</u>, heap, lavish, pour, deluge

show-off (*Informal*)
= <u>exhibitionist</u>, boaster, poseur, braggart

shred 1 = <u>strip</u>, bit, piece, scrap, fragment, sliver, tatter
2 = <u>particle</u>, trace, scrap, grain, atom, jot, iota

shrewd = <u>astute</u>, clever, sharp, keen, smart, calculating, intelligent, cunning ≠ naive

shriek VERB = <u>scream</u>, cry, yell, screech, squeal
• NOUN = <u>scream</u>, cry, yell, screech, squeal

shrink = <u>decrease</u>, dwindle, lessen, grow *or* get smaller, contract, narrow, diminish, shorten ≠ grow

shroud NOUN 1 = <u>winding sheet</u>, grave clothes 2 = <u>covering</u>, veil, mantle, screen, pall
• VERB = <u>conceal</u>, cover, screen, hide, blanket, veil, cloak, envelop

shudder VERB = <u>shiver</u>, shake, tremble, quake, quiver, convulse
• NOUN = <u>shiver</u>, tremor, quiver, spasm

shuffle 1 = <u>shamble</u>, stagger, stumble, dodder 2 = <u>scuffle</u>, drag, scrape 3 = <u>rearrange</u>, jumble, mix, disorder, disarrange

shun = <u>avoid</u>, steer clear of, keep away from

shut VERB = <u>close</u>, secure, fasten, seal, slam ≠ open
• ADJECTIVE = <u>closed</u>, fastened, sealed, locked ≠ open
• PHRASES **shut down** = <u>stop work</u>, halt work, close down

shuttle = <u>go back and forth</u>, commute, go to and fro, alternate

shy ADJECTIVE 1 = <u>timid</u>, self-conscious, bashful, retiring, shrinking, coy, self-effacing, diffident ≠ confident
2 = <u>cautious</u>, wary, hesitant, suspicious, distrustful, chary ≠ reckless
• VERB *sometimes with* **off** *or* **away** = <u>recoil</u>, flinch, draw back, start, balk

sick 1 = <u>unwell</u>, ill, poorly (*informal*), diseased, crook (*Austral. & N.Z. informal*), ailing, under the weather, indisposed ≠ well 2 = <u>nauseous</u>, ill, queasy, nauseated 3 = <u>tired</u>, bored, fed up, weary, jaded 4 (*Informal*) = <u>morbid</u>, sadistic, black, macabre, ghoulish

sicken 1 = <u>disgust</u>, revolt, nauseate, repel, gross out (*U.S. slang*), turn your stomach 2 = <u>fall ill</u>, take sick, ail

sickening = <u>disgusting</u>, revolting, offensive, foul, distasteful, repulsive, nauseating, loathsome, yucko (*Austral. slang*) ≠ delightful

sickness 1 = <u>illness</u>, disorder, ailment, disease, complaint, bug (*informal*), affliction, malady
2 = <u>nausea</u>, queasiness

3 = vomiting

side NOUN 1 = border, margin, boundary, verge, flank, rim, perimeter, edge ≠ middle 2 = face, surface, facet 3 = party, camp, faction, cause 4 = point of view, viewpoint, position, opinion, angle, slant, standpoint 5 = team, squad, line-up 6 = aspect, feature, angle, facet
• ADJECTIVE = subordinate, minor, secondary, subsidiary, lesser, marginal, incidental, ancillary ≠ main
• PHRASES **side with someone** = support, agree with, stand up for, favour, go along with, take the part of, ally yourself with

sidewalk (U.S. & Canad.) = pavement, footpath (Austral. & N.Z.)

sideways ADVERB 1 = indirectly, obliquely 2 = to the side, laterally
• ADJECTIVE = sidelong, oblique

sift 1 = part, filter, strain, separate, sieve 2 = examine, investigate, go through, research, analyse, work over, scrutinize

sight NOUN 1 = vision, eyes, eyesight, seeing, eye 2 = spectacle, show, scene, display, exhibition, vista, pageant 3 = view, range of vision, visibility 4 (Informal) = eyesore, mess, monstrosity
• VERB = spot, see, observe, distinguish, perceive, make out,

discern, behold

(Related Words)
adjectives: optical, visual

sign NOUN 1 = symbol, mark, device, logo, badge, emblem 2 = figure 3 = notice, board, warning, placard 4 = indication, evidence, mark, signal, symptom, hint, proof, gesture 5 = omen, warning, portent, foreboding, augury, auspice
• VERB 1 = gesture, indicate, signal, beckon, gesticulate 2 = autograph, initial, inscribe

signal NOUN 1 = flare, beam, beacon 2 = cue, sign, prompting, reminder 3 = sign, gesture, indication, mark, note, expression, token
• VERB = gesture, sign, wave, indicate, motion, beckon, gesticulate

significance = importance, consequence, moment, weight

significant 1 = important, serious, material, vital, critical, momentous, weighty, noteworthy ≠ insignificant 2 = meaningful, expressive, eloquent, indicative, suggestive ≠ meaningless

signify = indicate, mean, suggest, imply, intimate, be a sign of, denote, connote

silence NOUN 1 = quiet, peace, calm, hush, lull, stillness ≠ noise 2 = reticence, dumbness,

taciturnity, muteness ≠ speech
● **VERB** = quieten, still, quiet, cut off, stifle, cut short, muffle, deaden ≠ make louder

silent 1 = mute, dumb, speechless, wordless, voiceless ≠ noisy 2 = uncommunicative, quiet, taciturn 3 = quiet, still, hushed, soundless, noiseless, muted ≠ loud

silently 1 = quietly, in silence, soundlessly, noiselessly, inaudibly, without a sound 2 = mutely, in silence, wordlessly

silhouette NOUN = outline, form, shape, profile
● **VERB** = outline, etch

silly 1 = stupid, ridiculous, absurd, daft, inane, senseless, idiotic, fatuous ≠ clever 2 = foolish, stupid, unwise, rash, irresponsible, thoughtless, imprudent ≠ sensible

similar 1 = alike, resembling, comparable ≠ different 2 **with to** = like, comparable to, analogous to, close to

---

Word Power

similar – As should not be used after *similar* – so *Wilson held a similar position to Jones* is correct, but not *Wilson held a similar position as Jones*; and *the system is similar to the one in France* is correct, but not *the system is similar as in France*.

---

similarity = resemblance, likeness, sameness, agreement, correspondence, analogy, affinity, closeness ≠ difference

simmer VERB 1 = bubble, boil gently, seethe 2 = fume, seethe, smoulder, rage, be angry
● **PHRASES simmer down** (*Informal*) = calm down, control yourself, cool off *or* down

simple 1 = uncomplicated, clear, plain, understandable, lucid, recognizable, comprehensible, intelligible ≠ complicated 2 = easy, straightforward, not difficult, effortless, painless, uncomplicated, undemanding 3 = plain, natural, classic, unfussy, unembellished 4 = pure, mere, sheer, unalloyed 5 = artless, innocent, naive, natural, sincere, unaffected, childlike, unsophisticated ≠ sophisticated 6 = unpretentious, modest, humble, homely, unfussy, unembellished ≠ fancy

simplicity
1 = straightforwardness, ease, clarity, clearness ≠ complexity 2 = plainness, restraint, purity, lack of adornment ≠ elaborateness

simplify = make simpler, streamline, disentangle, dumb

down, reduce to essentials

simply 1 = just, only, merely, purely, solely **2** = totally, really, completely, absolutely, wholly, utterly **3** = clearly, straightforwardly, directly, plainly, intelligibly **4** = plainly, naturally, modestly, unpretentiously **5** = without doubt, surely, certainly, definitely, beyond question

simulate = pretend, act, feign, affect, put on, sham

simultaneous = coinciding, concurrent, contemporary, coincident, synchronous, happening at the same time

simultaneously = at the same time, together, concurrently

sin NOUN **1** = wickedness, evil, crime, error, transgression, iniquity **2** = crime, offence, error, wrongdoing, misdeed, transgression, act of evil, guilt
● VERB = transgress, offend, lapse, err, go astray, do wrong

sincere = honest, genuine, real, true, serious, earnest, frank, candid, dinkum (*Austral. & N.Z. informal*) ≠ false

sincerely = honestly, truly, genuinely, seriously, earnestly, wholeheartedly, in earnest

sincerity = honesty, truth, candour, frankness, seriousness, genuineness

sing 1 = croon, carol, chant, warble, yodel, pipe **2** = trill, chirp, warble

> ### Word Power
>
> **sing** – *Sang* is the past tense of the verb *sing*, as in *she sang sweetly*. *Sung* is the past participle, as in *we have sung our song*, and care should be taken not to use it as if it were a variant form of the past tense.

singer = vocalist, crooner, minstrel, soloist, chorister, balladeer

single ADJECTIVE **1** = one, sole, lone, solitary, only, only one **2** = individual, separate, distinct **3** = unmarried, free, unattached, unwed **4** = separate, individual, exclusive, undivided, unshared **5** = simple, unmixed, unblended
● PHRASES **single something** or **someone out** = pick, choose, select, separate, distinguish, fix on, set apart, pick on or out

singly = one by one, individually, one at a time, separately

singular 1 = single, individual **2** = remarkable, outstanding, exceptional, notable, eminent, noteworthy ≠ ordinary **3** = unusual, odd, strange, extraordinary, curious, peculiar, eccentric, queer ≠ conventional

sinister = threatening, evil, menacing, dire, ominous, malign, disquieting ≠ reassuring

sink 1 = go down, founder, go under, submerge, capsize **2** = slump, drop **3** = fall, drop, slip, plunge, subside, abate **4** = drop, fall **5** = stoop, be reduced to, lower yourself **6** = decline, fade, fail, flag, weaken, diminish, decrease, deteriorate ≠ improve **7** = dig, bore, drill, drive, excavate

sip VERB = drink, taste, sample, sup
• NOUN = swallow, drop, taste, thimbleful

sit 1 = take a seat, perch, settle down **2** = place, set, put, position, rest, lay, settle, deposit **3** = be a member of, serve on, have a seat on, preside on **4** = convene, meet, assemble, officiate

site NOUN **1** = area, plot **2** = location, place, setting, point, position, situation, spot
• VERB = locate, put, place, set, position, establish, install, situate

situation 1 = position, state, case, condition, circumstances, equation, plight, state of affairs **2** = scenario, state of affairs **3** = location, place, setting, position, site, spot

---

> ### Word Power
>
> **situation** – It is common to hear the word *situation* used in sentences such as *the company is in a crisis situation*. This use of *situation* is considered bad style and the word should be left out, since it adds nothing to the sentence's meaning.

size NOUN = dimensions, extent, range, amount, mass, volume, proportions, bulk
• PHRASES **size something or someone up** (*Informal*) = assess, evaluate, appraise, take stock of

sizeable or **sizable** = large, considerable, substantial, goodly, decent, respectable, largish

sizzle = hiss, spit, crackle, fry, frizzle

skeleton = bones, bare bones

sketch NOUN = drawing, design, draft, delineation
• VERB = draw, outline, represent, draft, depict, delineate, rough out

skilful = expert, skilled, masterly, able, professional, clever, practised, competent ≠ clumsy

skill = expertise, ability, proficiency, art, technique, facility, talent, craft ≠ clumsiness

skilled = expert, professional, able, masterly, skilful, proficient ≠ unskilled

skim 1 = <u>remove</u>, separate, cream
2 = <u>glide</u>, fly, coast, sail, float
3 *usually with **over** or **through***
= <u>scan</u>, glance, run your eye over

skin NOUN **1** = <u>hide</u>, pelt, fell
2 = <u>peel</u>, rind, husk, casing,
outside, crust **3** = <u>film</u>, coating
● VERB **1** = <u>peel</u> **2** = <u>scrape</u>, flay

skinny = <u>thin</u>, lean, scrawny,
emaciated, undernourished ≠ fat

skip 1 = <u>hop</u>, dance, bob, trip,
bounce, caper, prance, frisk
2 = <u>miss out</u>, omit, leave out,
overlook, pass over, eschew, give
(something) a miss

skirt 1 = <u>border</u>, edge, flank
2 *often with **around** or **round***
= <u>go round</u>, circumvent **3** *often
with **around** or **round*** = <u>avoid</u>,
evade, steer clear of, circumvent

sky = <u>heavens</u>, firmament, rangi
(N.Z.)

Related Words
adjective: celestial

slab = <u>piece</u>, slice, lump, chunk,
wedge, portion

slack ADJECTIVE **1** = <u>limp</u>, relaxed,
loose, lax **2** = <u>loose</u>, baggy ≠ taut
3 = <u>slow</u>, quiet, inactive, dull,
sluggish, slow-moving ≠ busy
4 = <u>negligent</u>, lazy, lax, idle,
inactive, slapdash, neglectful,
slipshod ≠ strict
● VERB = <u>shirk</u>, idle, dodge, skive
(*Brit. slang*), bludge (*Austral. &
N.Z. informal*)

● NOUN **1** = <u>surplus</u>, excess, glut,
surfeit, superabundance,
superfluity **2** = <u>room</u>, excess,
leeway, give (*informal*)

slam 1 = <u>bang</u>, crash, smash
2 = <u>throw</u>, dash, hurl, fling

slant VERB **1** = <u>slope</u>, incline, tilt,
list, bend, lean, heel, cant **2** = <u>bias</u>,
colour, twist, angle, distort
● NOUN **1** = <u>slope</u>, incline, tilt,
gradient, camber **2** = <u>bias</u>,
emphasis, prejudice, angle, point
of view, one-sidedness

slanting = <u>sloping</u>, angled,
inclined, tilted, tilting, bent,
diagonal, oblique

slap VERB = <u>smack</u>, beat, clap, cuff,
swipe, spank, clobber (*slang*),
wallop (*informal*)
● NOUN = <u>smack</u>, blow, cuff, swipe,
spank

slash VERB **1** = <u>cut</u>, slit, gash,
lacerate, score, rend, rip, hack
2 = <u>reduce</u>, cut, decrease, drop,
lower, moderate, diminish, cut
down
● NOUN = <u>cut</u>, slit, gash, rent, rip,
incision, laceration

slate (*Informal, chiefly Brit.*)
= <u>criticize</u>, censure, rebuke, scold,
tear into (*informal*)

slaughter VERB **1** = <u>kill</u>, murder,
massacre, destroy, execute,
assassinate **2** = <u>butcher</u>, kill, slay,
massacre
● NOUN = <u>slaying</u>, killing, murder,

massacre, bloodshed, carnage, butchery

slave NOUN 1 = <u>servant</u>, serf, vassal 2 = <u>drudge</u>, skivvy (*chiefly Brit.*)

● VERB = <u>toil</u>, drudge, slog

slavery = <u>enslavement</u>, servitude, subjugation, captivity, bondage ≠ freedom

slay 1 (*Archaic or literary*) = <u>kill</u>, slaughter, massacre, butcher 2 = <u>murder</u>, kill, massacre, slaughter, mow down

sleaze (*Informal*) = <u>corruption</u>, fraud, dishonesty, bribery, extortion, venality, unscrupulousness

sleek = <u>glossy</u>, shiny, lustrous, smooth ≠ shaggy

sleep NOUN = <u>slumber(s)</u>, nap, doze, snooze (*informal*), hibernation, siesta, forty winks (*informal*), zizz (*Brit. informal*)

● VERB = <u>slumber</u>, doze, snooze (*informal*), hibernate, take a nap, catnap, drowse

sleepy = <u>drowsy</u>, sluggish, lethargic, heavy, dull, inactive ≠ wide-awake

slender 1 = <u>slim</u>, narrow, slight, lean, willowy ≠ chubby 2 = <u>faint</u>, slight, remote, slim, thin, tenuous ≠ strong 3 = <u>meagre</u>, little, small, scant, scanty ≠ large

slice NOUN = <u>piece</u>, segment, portion, wedge, sliver, helping, share, cut

● VERB = <u>cut</u>, divide, carve, sever, dissect, bisect

slick ADJECTIVE 1 = <u>skilful</u>, deft, adroit, dexterous, professional, polished ≠ clumsy 2 = <u>glib</u>, smooth, plausible, polished, specious

● VERB = <u>smooth</u>, sleek, plaster down

slide = <u>slip</u>, slither, glide, skim, coast

slight ADJECTIVE 1 = <u>small</u>, minor, insignificant, trivial, feeble, trifling, meagre, unimportant ≠ large 2 = <u>slim</u>, small, delicate, spare, fragile, lightly-built ≠ sturdy

● VERB = <u>snub</u>, insult, ignore, affront, scorn, disdain ≠ compliment

● NOUN = <u>insult</u>, snub, affront, rebuff, slap in the face (*informal*), (the) cold shoulder ≠ compliment

slightly = <u>a little</u>, a bit, somewhat

slim ADJECTIVE 1 = <u>slender</u>, slight, trim, thin, narrow, lean, svelte, willowy ≠ chubby 2 = <u>slight</u>, remote, faint, slender ≠ strong

● VERB = <u>lose weight</u>, diet ≠ put on weight

sling 1 (*Informal*) = <u>throw</u>, cast, toss, hurl, fling, chuck (*informal*), lob (*informal*), heave 2 = <u>hang</u>, suspend

slip VERB 1 = <u>fall</u>, skid 2 = <u>slide</u>, slither 3 = <u>sneak</u>, creep, steal
• NOUN = <u>mistake</u>, failure, error, blunder, lapse, omission, oversight
• PHRASES **give someone the slip** = <u>escape from</u>, get away from, evade, elude, lose (someone), flee, dodge ◆ **slip up** = <u>make a mistake</u>, blunder, err, miscalculate

slippery 1 = <u>smooth</u>, icy, greasy, glassy, slippy (*informal*, *dialect*), unsafe 2 = <u>untrustworthy</u>, tricky, cunning, dishonest, devious, crafty, evasive, shifty

slit VERB = <u>cut (open)</u>, rip, slash, knife, pierce, lance, gash
• NOUN 1 = <u>cut</u>, gash, incision, tear, rent 2 = <u>opening</u>, split

slogan = <u>catch phrase</u>, motto, tag-line, catchword

slope NOUN = <u>inclination</u>, rise, incline, tilt, slant, ramp, gradient
• VERB = <u>slant</u>, incline, drop away, fall, rise, lean, tilt
• PHRASES **slope off** (*Informal*) = <u>slink away</u>, slip away, creep away

sloping = <u>slanting</u>, leaning, inclined, oblique

sloppy 1 (*Informal*) = <u>careless</u>, slovenly, slipshod, messy, untidy 2 (*Informal*) = <u>sentimental</u>, soppy (*Brit. informal*), slushy (*informal*), gushing, mawkish, icky (*informal*)

slot NOUN 1 = <u>opening</u>, hole, groove, vent, slit, aperture 2 (*Informal*) = <u>place</u>, time, space, opening, position, vacancy
• VERB = <u>fit</u>, insert

slow ADJECTIVE 1 = <u>unhurried</u>, sluggish, leisurely, lazy, ponderous, dawdling, laggard, lackadaisical ≠ quick
2 = <u>prolonged</u>, protracted, long-drawn-out, lingering, gradual 3 = <u>late</u>, behind, tardy 4 = <u>stupid</u>, dim, dense, thick, retarded, dozy (*Brit. informal*), obtuse, braindead (*informal*) ≠ bright
• VERB 1 often with **down** = <u>decelerate</u>, brake 2 often with **down** = <u>delay</u>, hold up, handicap, retard ≠ speed up

> ### Word Power
> **slow** – While not as unkind as *thick* and *stupid*, words like *slow* and *backward*, when used to talk about a person's mental abilities, are both unhelpful and likely to cause offence. It is preferable to say that a person has *special educational needs* or *learning difficulties*.

slowly = <u>gradually</u>, unhurriedly ≠ quickly

slug ➤ snails, slugs and other gastropods

sluggish = <u>inactive</u>, slow, lethargic, heavy, dull, inert,

Snails, slugs and other gastropods	
abalone or ear shell	periwinkle or winkle
conch	slug
cowrie or cowry	snail
limpet	triton
murex	wentletrap
nudibranch or sea slug	whelk
ormer or sea-ear	

indolent, torpid ≠ energetic

slum = <u>hovel</u>, ghetto, shanty

slump VERB 1 = <u>fall</u>, sink, plunge, crash, collapse, slip ≠ increase 2 = <u>sag</u>, hunch, droop, slouch, loll

● NOUN 1 = <u>fall</u>, drop, decline, crash, collapse, reverse, downturn, trough ≠ increase 2 = <u>recession</u>, depression, stagnation, inactivity, hard or bad times

slur = <u>insult</u>, stain, smear, affront, innuendo, calumny, insinuation, aspersion

sly ADJECTIVE 1 = <u>roguish</u>, knowing, arch, mischievous, impish 2 = <u>cunning</u>, scheming, devious, secret, clever, subtle, wily, crafty ≠ open

● PHRASES on the sly = <u>secretly</u>, privately, covertly, surreptitiously, on the quiet

smack VERB 1 = <u>slap</u>, hit, strike, clap, cuff, swipe, spank 2 = <u>drive</u>, hit, strike

● NOUN = <u>slap</u>, blow, cuff, swipe, spank

● ADVERB (Informal) = <u>directly</u>, right, straight, squarely, precisely, exactly, slap (informal)

small 1 = <u>little</u>, minute, tiny, mini, miniature, minuscule, diminutive, petite ≠ big 2 = <u>young</u>, little, junior, wee, juvenile, youthful, immature 3 = <u>unimportant</u>, minor, trivial, insignificant, little, petty, trifling, negligible ≠ important 4 = <u>modest</u>, humble, unpretentious ≠ grand

smart ADJECTIVE 1 = <u>chic</u>, trim, neat, stylish, elegant, spruce, snappy, natty (informal) ≠ scruffy 2 = <u>clever</u>, bright, intelligent, quick, sharp, keen, acute, shrewd ≠ stupid 3 = <u>brisk</u>, quick, lively, vigorous

● VERB = <u>sting</u>, burn, hurt

smash VERB 1 = <u>break</u>, crush, shatter, crack, demolish, pulverize 2 = <u>shatter</u>, break, disintegrate, crack, splinter 3 = <u>collide</u>, crash, meet head-on, clash, come into collision 4 = <u>destroy</u>, ruin, wreck, trash (slang), lay waste

● NOUN = <u>collision</u>, crash, accident

smashing (*Informal, chiefly Brit.*)
= <u>excellent</u>, mean (*slang*), great
(*informal*), wonderful, brilliant
(*informal*), cracking (*Brit.
informal*), superb, fantastic
(*informal*), boshit (*Austral.
slang*), exo (*Austral. slang*), sik
(*Austral. slang*) ≠ awful

smear VERB 1 = <u>spread over</u>,
daub, rub on, cover, coat, bedaub
2 = <u>slander</u>, malign, blacken,
besmirch 3 = <u>smudge</u>, soil, dirty,
stain, sully

● NOUN 1 = <u>smudge</u>, daub, streak,
blot, blotch, splotch 2 = <u>slander</u>,
libel, defamation, calumny

smell NOUN 1 = <u>odour</u>, scent,
fragrance, perfume, bouquet,
aroma 2 = <u>stink</u>, stench, pong
(*Brit. informal*), fetor

● VERB 1 = <u>stink</u>, reek, pong (*Brit.
informal*) 2 = <u>sniff</u>, scent

smile VERB = <u>grin</u>, beam, smirk,
twinkle, grin from ear to ear

● NOUN = <u>grin</u>, beam, smirk

smooth ADJECTIVE 1 = <u>even</u>, level,
flat, plane, flush, horizontal
≠ uneven 2 = <u>sleek</u>, polished,
shiny, glossy, silky, velvety
≠ rough 3 = <u>mellow</u>, pleasant,
mild, agreeable 4 = <u>flowing</u>,
steady, regular, uniform, rhythmic
5 = <u>easy</u>, effortless, well-ordered
6 = <u>suave</u>, slick, persuasive,
urbane, glib, facile, unctuous,

smarmy (*Brit. informal*)

● VERB 1 = <u>flatten</u>, level, press,
plane, iron 2 = <u>ease</u>, facilitate
≠ hinder

smother 1 = <u>extinguish</u>, put out,
stifle, snuff 2 = <u>suffocate</u>, choke,
strangle, stifle 3 = <u>suppress</u>, stifle,
repress, hide, conceal, muffle

smug = <u>self-satisfied</u>, superior,
complacent, conceited

snack = <u>light meal</u>, bite,
refreshment(s)

snag NOUN = <u>difficulty</u>, hitch,
problem, obstacle, catch,
disadvantage, complication,
drawback

● VERB = <u>catch</u>, tear, rip

snail ➤ snails, slugs and
other gastropods

snake = <u>serpent</u>

Related Words

adjective: serpentine

➤ reptiles

snap VERB 1 = <u>break</u>, crack,
separate 2 = <u>pop</u>, click, crackle
3 = <u>speak sharply</u>, bark, lash out
at, jump down (someone's) throat
(*informal*) 4 = <u>bite at</u>, bite, nip

● ADJECTIVE = <u>instant</u>, immediate,
sudden, spur-of-the-moment

● PHRASES **snap something up**
= <u>grab</u>, seize, take advantage of,
pounce upon

snare NOUN = <u>trap</u>, net, wire, gin,
noose

● VERB = <u>trap</u>, catch, net, wire,

seize, entrap

snatch VERB **1** = <u>grab</u>, grip, grasp, clutch **2** = <u>steal</u>, take, nick (*slang, chiefly Brit.*), pinch (*informal*), lift (*informal*), pilfer, filch, thieve **3** = <u>win</u> **4** = <u>save</u>, recover, get out, salvage

• NOUN = <u>bit</u>, part, fragment, piece, snippet

sneak VERB **1** = <u>slink</u>, slip, steal, pad, skulk **2** = <u>slip</u>, smuggle, spirit

• NOUN = <u>informer</u>, betrayer, telltale, Judas, accuser, stool pigeon, nark (*Brit., Austral., & N.Z. slang*), fizgig (*Austral. slang*)

sneaking 1 = <u>nagging</u>, worrying, persistent, uncomfortable **2** = <u>secret</u>, private, hidden, unexpressed, unvoiced, undivulged

sneer VERB **1** = <u>scorn</u>, mock, ridicule, laugh, jeer, disdain, deride **2** = <u>say contemptuously</u>, snigger

• NOUN = <u>scorn</u>, ridicule, mockery, derision, jeer, gibe

sniff 1 = <u>breathe in</u>, inhale **2** = <u>smell</u>, scent **3** = <u>inhale</u>, breathe in, suck in, draw in

snub VERB = <u>insult</u>, slight, put down, humiliate, cut (*informal*), rebuff, cold-shoulder

• NOUN = <u>insult</u>, put-down, affront, slap in the face

so = <u>therefore</u>, thus, hence, consequently, then, as a result,

accordingly, thence

soak VERB **1** = <u>steep</u> **2** = <u>wet</u>, damp, saturate, drench, moisten, suffuse, wet through, waterlog **3** = <u>penetrate</u>, permeate, seep

• PHRASES **soak something up** = <u>absorb</u>, suck up, assimilate

soaking = <u>soaked</u>, dripping, saturated, drenched, sodden, streaming, sopping, wet through

soar 1 = <u>rise</u>, increase, grow, mount, climb, go up, rocket, escalate **2** = <u>fly</u>, wing, climb, ascend ≠ plunge **3** = <u>tower</u>, climb, go up

sob VERB = <u>cry</u>, weep, howl, shed tears

• NOUN = <u>cry</u>, whimper, howl

sober 1 = <u>abstinent</u>, temperate, abstemious, moderate ≠ drunk **2** = <u>serious</u>, cool, grave, reasonable, steady, composed, rational, solemn ≠ frivolous **3** = <u>plain</u>, dark, sombre, quiet, subdued, drab ≠ bright

so-called = <u>alleged</u>, supposed, professed, pretended, self-styled

social ADJECTIVE **1** = <u>communal</u>, community, collective, group, public, general, common **2** = <u>organized</u>, gregarious

• NOUN = <u>get-together</u> (*informal*), party, gathering, function, reception, social gathering

society 1 = <u>the community</u>, people, the public, humanity, civilization, mankind **2** = <u>culture</u>, community, population **3** = <u>organization</u>, group, club, union, league, association, institute, circle **4** = <u>upper classes</u>, gentry, elite, high society, beau monde **5** (*Old-fashioned*) = <u>companionship</u>, company, fellowship, friendship

sofa = <u>couch</u>, settee, divan, chaise longue

soft 1 = <u>velvety</u>, smooth, silky, feathery, downy, fleecy ≠ rough **2** = <u>yielding</u>, elastic ≠ hard **3** = <u>soggy</u>, swampy, marshy, boggy **4** = <u>squashy</u>, sloppy, mushy, spongy, gelatinous, pulpy **5** = <u>pliable</u>, flexible, supple, malleable, plastic, elastic, bendable, mouldable **6** = <u>quiet</u>, gentle, murmured, muted, dulcet, soft-toned ≠ loud **7** = <u>lenient</u>, easy-going, lax, indulgent, permissive, spineless, overindulgent ≠ harsh **8** = <u>kind</u>, tender, sentimental, compassionate, sensitive, gentle, tenderhearted, touchy-feely (*informal*) **9** (*Informal*) = <u>easy</u>, comfortable, undemanding, cushy (*informal*) **10** = <u>pale</u>, light, subdued, pastel, bland, mellow ≠ bright **11** = <u>dim</u>, faint, dimmed ≠ bright **12** = <u>mild</u>, temperate, balmy

soften 1 = <u>melt</u>, tenderize **2** = <u>lessen</u>, moderate, temper, ease, cushion, subdue, allay, mitigate

soil[1] **1** = <u>earth</u>, ground, clay, dust, dirt **2** = <u>territory</u>, country, land

soil[2] = <u>dirty</u>, foul, stain, pollute, tarnish, sully, defile, besmirch ≠ clean

soldier = <u>fighter</u>, serviceman, trooper, warrior, man-at-arms, squaddie *or* squaddy (*Brit. slang*)

sole = <u>only</u>, one, single, individual, alone, exclusive, solitary

solely = <u>only</u>, completely, entirely, exclusively, alone, merely

solemn 1 = <u>serious</u>, earnest, grave, sober, sedate, staid ≠ cheerful **2** = <u>formal</u>, grand, grave, dignified, ceremonial, stately, momentous ≠ informal

solid 1 = <u>firm</u>, hard, compact, dense, concrete ≠ unsubstantial **2** = <u>strong</u>, stable, sturdy, substantial, unshakable ≠ unstable **3** = <u>reliable</u>, dependable, upstanding, worthy, upright, trusty ≠ unreliable **4** = <u>sound</u>, real, reliable, good, genuine, dinkum (*Austral. & N.Z. informal*) ≠ unsound

solidarity = <u>unity</u>, unification, accord, cohesion, team spirit, unanimity, concordance, like-mindedness, kotahitanga (*N.Z.*)

solitary 1 = <u>unsociable</u>, reclusive, unsocial, isolated, lonely, cloistered, lonesome, friendless ≠ sociable **2** = <u>lone</u>, alone **3** = <u>isolated</u>, remote, out-of-the-way, hidden, unfrequented ≠ busy

solution 1 = <u>answer</u>, key, result, explanation **2** (*Chemistry*) = <u>mixture</u>, mix, compound, blend, solvent

solve = <u>answer</u>, work out, resolve, crack, clear up, unravel, decipher, suss (out) (*slang*)

sombre 1 = <u>gloomy</u>, sad, sober, grave, dismal, mournful, lugubrious, joyless ≠ cheerful **2** = <u>dark</u>, dull, gloomy, sober, drab ≠ bright

somebody = <u>celebrity</u>, name, star, notable, household name, dignitary, luminary, personage ≠ nobody

somehow = <u>one way or another</u>, come what may, come hell or high water (*informal*), by fair means or foul, by hook or (by) crook, by some means or other

sometimes = <u>occasionally</u>, at times, now and then ≠ always

song = <u>ballad</u>, air, tune, carol, chant, chorus, anthem, number, waiata (*N.Z.*)

soon = <u>before long</u>, shortly, in the near future

soothe 1 = <u>calm</u>, still, quiet, hush, appease, lull, pacify, mollify ≠ upset **2** = <u>relieve</u>, ease, alleviate, assuage ≠ irritate

soothing 1 = <u>calming</u>, relaxing, peaceful, quiet, calm, restful **2** = <u>emollient</u>, palliative

sophisticated 1 = <u>complex</u>, advanced, complicated, subtle, delicate, elaborate, refined, intricate ≠ simple **2** = <u>cultured</u>, refined, cultivated, worldly, cosmopolitan, urbane ≠ unsophisticated

sophistication = <u>poise</u>, worldliness, savoir-faire, urbanity, finesse, worldly wisdom

sore 1 = <u>painful</u>, smarting, raw, tender, burning, angry, sensitive, irritated **2** = <u>annoyed</u>, cross, angry, pained, hurt, upset, stung, irritated, tooshie (*Austral. slang*), hoha (*N.Z.*) **3** = <u>annoying</u>, troublesome **4** (*Literary*) = <u>urgent</u>, desperate, extreme, dire, pressing, critical, acute

sorrow NOUN **1** = <u>grief</u>, sadness, woe, regret, distress, misery, mourning, anguish ≠ joy **2** = <u>hardship</u>, trial, tribulation, affliction, trouble, woe, misfortune ≠ good fortune

● VERB **1** = <u>grieve</u>, mourn, lament, be sad, bemoan, agonize, bewail ≠ rejoice

sorry 1 = <u>regretful</u>, apologetic, contrite, repentant, remorseful, penitent, shamefaced, conscience-stricken

≠ unapologetic 2 = <u>sympathetic</u>, moved, full of pity, compassionate, commiserative ≠ unsympathetic 3 = <u>wretched</u>, miserable, pathetic, mean, poor, sad, pitiful, deplorable

sort NOUN 1 = <u>kind</u>, type, class, make, order, style, quality, nature

● VERB = <u>arrange</u>, group, order, rank, divide, grade, classify, categorize

Word Power

sort – It is common in informal speech to combine singular and plural in sentences like *these sort of distinctions are becoming blurred*. This is not acceptable in careful writing, where the plural must be used consistently: *these sorts of distinctions are becoming blurred*.

soul 1 = <u>spirit</u>, essence, life, vital force, wairua (*N.Z.*) 2 = <u>embodiment</u>, essence, epitome, personification, quintessence, type 3 = <u>person</u>, being, individual, body, creature, man *or* woman

sound¹ NOUN 1 = <u>noise</u>, din, report, tone, reverberation 2 = <u>idea</u>, impression, drift 3 = <u>cry</u>, noise, peep, squeak 4 = <u>tone</u>, music, note

● VERB 1 = <u>toll</u>, set off 2 = <u>resound</u>, echo, go off, toll, set off, chime, reverberate, clang 3 = <u>seem</u>, seem to be, appear to be

(Related Words)

adjectives: sonic, acoustic

sound² 1 = <u>fit</u>, healthy, perfect, intact, unhurt, uninjured, unimpaired ≠ frail 2 = <u>sturdy</u>, strong, solid, stable 3 = <u>sensible</u>, wise, reasonable, right, correct, proper, valid, rational ≠ irresponsible 4 = <u>deep</u>, unbroken, undisturbed, untroubled ≠ troubled

sour 1 = <u>sharp</u>, acid, tart, bitter, pungent, acetic ≠ sweet 2 = <u>rancid</u>, turned, gone off, curdled, gone bad, off ≠ fresh 3 = <u>bitter</u>, tart, acrimonious, embittered, disagreeable, ill-tempered, waspish, ungenerous ≠ good-natured

source 1 = <u>cause</u>, origin, derivation, beginning, author 2 = <u>informant</u>, authority 3 = <u>origin</u>, fount

souvenir = <u>keepsake</u>, reminder, memento

sovereign ADJECTIVE

1 = <u>supreme</u>, ruling, absolute, royal, principal, imperial, kingly *or* queenly 2 = <u>excellent</u>, efficient, effectual

● NOUN = <u>monarch</u>, ruler, king *or* queen, chief, potentate, emperor *or* empress, prince *or* princess

sovereignty = <u>supreme power</u>,

domination, supremacy, primacy, kingship, rangatiratanga (N.Z.)

sow = scatter, plant, seed, implant

space 1 = room, capacity, extent, margin, scope, play, expanse, leeway 2 = period, interval, time, while, span, duration 3 = outer space, the universe, the galaxy, the solar system, the cosmos 4 = blank, gap, interval

spacious = roomy, large, huge, broad, extensive, ample, expansive, capacious ≠ limited

span NOUN 1 = period, term, duration, spell 2 = extent, reach, spread, length, distance, stretch
● VERB = extend across, cross, bridge, cover, link, traverse

spar = argue, row, squabble, scrap (informal), wrangle, bicker

spare ADJECTIVE 1 = back-up, reserve, second, extra, additional, auxiliary 2 = extra, surplus, leftover, over, free, odd, unwanted, unused ≠ necessary 3 = free, leisure, unoccupied 4 = thin, lean, meagre, gaunt, wiry ≠ plump
● VERB 1 = afford, give, grant, do without, part with, manage without, let someone have 2 = have mercy on, pardon, leave, let off (informal), go easy on (informal), save (from harm) ≠ show no mercy to

sparing = economical, frugal, thrifty, saving, careful, prudent ≠ lavish

spark NOUN 1 = flicker, flash, gleam, glint, flare 2 = trace, hint, scrap, atom, jot, vestige
● VERB often with off = start, stimulate, provoke, trigger (off), set off, precipitate

sparkle VERB = glitter, flash, shine, gleam, shimmer, twinkle, dance, glint
● NOUN 1 = glitter, flash, gleam, flicker, brilliance, twinkle, glint 2 = vivacity, life, spirit, dash, vitality, élan, liveliness

spate = flood, flow, torrent, rush, deluge, outpouring

speak 1 = talk, say something 2 = articulate, say, pronounce, utter, tell, state, talk, express 3 = converse, talk, chat, discourse, confer, commune, exchange views, korero (N.Z.) 4 = lecture, address an audience

speaker = orator, public speaker, lecturer, spokesperson, spokesman or spokeswoman

spearhead = lead, head, pioneer, launch, set off, initiate, set in motion

special 1 = exceptional, important, significant, particular, unique, unusual, extraordinary, memorable ≠ ordinary 2 = specific, particular, distinctive, individual, appropriate, precise ≠ general

specialist = <u>expert</u>, authority, professional, master, consultant, guru, buff (*informal*), connoisseur, fundi (*S. African*)

speciality = <u>forte</u>, métier, specialty, bag (*slang*), pièce de résistance (*French*)

species = <u>kind</u>, sort, type, group, class, variety, breed, category

specific 1 = <u>particular</u>, special, characteristic, distinguishing ≠ general **2** = <u>precise</u>, exact, explicit, definite, express, clear-cut, unequivocal ≠ vague **3** = <u>peculiar</u>, appropriate, individual, particular, unique

specification = <u>requirement</u>, detail, particular, stipulation, condition, qualification

specify = <u>state</u>, designate, stipulate, name, detail, mention, indicate, define

specimen 1 = <u>sample</u>, example, model, type, pattern, instance, representative, exemplification **2** = <u>example</u>, model, type

spectacle 1 = <u>show</u>, display, exhibition, event, performance, extravaganza, pageant **2** = <u>sight</u>, wonder, scene, phenomenon, curiosity, marvel

spectacular ADJECTIVE = <u>impressive</u>, striking, dramatic, stunning (*informal*), grand, magnificent, splendid, dazzling ≠ unimpressive

● NOUN = <u>show</u>, display, spectacle

spectator = <u>onlooker</u>, observer, viewer, looker-on, watcher, bystander ≠ participant

spectre = <u>ghost</u>, spirit, phantom, vision, apparition, wraith, kehua (*N.Z.*)

speculate 1 = <u>conjecture</u>, consider, wonder, guess, surmise, theorize, hypothesize **2** = <u>gamble</u>, risk, venture, hazard

speculation 1 = <u>theory</u>, opinion, hypothesis, conjecture, guess, surmise, guesswork, supposition **2** = <u>gamble</u>, risk, hazard

speculative = <u>hypothetical</u>, academic, theoretical, notional, conjectural, suppositional

speech 1 = <u>communication</u>, talk, conversation, discussion, dialogue **2** = <u>diction</u>, pronunciation, articulation, delivery, fluency, inflection, intonation, elocution **3** = <u>language</u>, tongue, jargon, dialect, idiom, parlance, articulation, diction **4** = <u>talk</u>, address, lecture, discourse, homily, oration, spiel (*informal*), whaikorero (*N.Z.*)

speed NOUN **1** = <u>rate</u>, pace **2** = <u>swiftness</u>, rush, hurry, haste, rapidity, quickness ≠ slowness

● **VERB 1** = <u>race</u>, rush, hurry, zoom, career, tear, barrel (along) (*informal, chiefly U.S. & Canad.*), gallop ≠ crawl **2** = <u>help</u>, advance, aid, boost, assist, facilitate, expedite ≠ hinder

> ### Word Power
>
> **speed** – The past tense of *speed up* is *speeded up* (not *sped up*), for example *I speeded up to overtake the lorry.* The past participle is also *speeded up*, for example *I had already speeded up when I spotted the police car.*

speedy = <u>quick</u>, fast, rapid, swift, express, immediate, prompt, hurried ≠ slow

spell¹ = <u>indicate</u>, mean, signify, point to, imply, augur, portend

spell² **1** = <u>incantation</u>, charm, makutu (*N.Z.*) **2** = <u>enchantment</u>, magic, fascination, glamour, allure, bewitchment

spell³ = <u>period</u>, time, term, stretch, course, season, interval, bout

spend **1** = <u>pay out</u>, fork out (*slang*), expend, disburse ≠ save **2** = <u>pass</u>, fill, occupy, while away **3** = <u>use up</u>, waste, squander, empty, drain, exhaust, consume, run through ≠ save

sphere **1** = <u>ball</u>, globe, orb, globule, circle **2** = <u>field</u>, department, function, territory, capacity, province, patch, scope

spice **1** = <u>seasoning</u> **2** = <u>excitement</u>, zest, colour, pep, zing (*informal*), piquancy

spicy **1** = <u>hot</u>, seasoned, aromatic, savoury, piquant **2** (*Informal*) = <u>risqué</u>, racy, ribald, hot (*informal*), suggestive, titillating, indelicate

spider ➤ **spiders and other arachnids**

(*Related Words*)

fear of: arachnophobia

spike **NOUN** = <u>point</u>, stake, spine,

> ### Spiders and other arachnids
>
> | | |
> |---|---|
> | black widow | red-back (spider) |
> | chigger, chigoe, *or* (*U.S. &* *Canad.*) redbug | spider |
> | | spider mite |
> | chigoe, chigger, jigger, *or* sand flea | tarantula |
> | | tick |
> | harvestman *or* (*U.S. & Canad.*) daddy-longlegs | trap-door spider |
> | | whip scorpion |
> | katipo | wolf spider *or* hunting spider |
> | mite | |

barb, prong

● VERB = impale, spit, spear, stick

spill 1 = tip over, overturn, capsize, knock over 2 = shed, discharge, disgorge 3 = slop, flow, pour, run, overflow

spin VERB = revolve, turn, rotate, reel, whirl, twirl, gyrate, pirouette 2 = reel, swim, whirl

● NOUN 1 = drive, ride, joy ride (*informal*) 2 = revolution, roll, whirl, gyration

● PHRASES **spin something out** = prolong, extend, lengthen, draw out, drag out, delay, amplify

spine 1 = backbone, vertebrae, spinal column, vertebral column 2 = barb, spur, needle, spike, ray, quill

spiral ADJECTIVE = coiled, winding, whorled, helical

● NOUN = coil, helix, corkscrew, whorl

spirit NOUN 1 = soul, life 2 = life force, vital spark, mauri (*N.Z.*) 3 = ghost, phantom, spectre, apparition, atua (*N.Z.*), kehua (*N.Z.*) 4 = courage, guts (*informal*), grit, backbone, spunk (*informal*), gameness 5 = liveliness, energy, vigour, life, force, fire, enthusiasm, animation 6 = attitude, character, temper, outlook, temperament, disposition 7 = heart, sense, nature, soul, core, substance,

essence, quintessence 8 = intention, meaning, purpose, purport, gist 9 = feeling, atmosphere, character, tone, mood, tenor, ambience

● PLURAL NOUN = mood, feelings, morale, temper, disposition, state of mind, frame of mind

spirited = lively, energetic, animated, active, feisty (*informal, chiefly U.S. & Canad.*), vivacious, mettlesome ≠ lifeless

spiritual 1 = nonmaterial, immaterial, incorporeal ≠ material 2 = sacred, religious, holy, divine, devotional

spit VERB 1 = expectorate 2 = eject, throw out

● NOUN = saliva, dribble, spittle, drool, slaver

spite NOUN = malice, malevolence, ill will, hatred, animosity, venom, spleen, spitefulness ≠ kindness

● VERB = annoy, hurt, injure, harm, vex ≠ benefit

● PHRASES **in spite of** = despite, regardless of, notwithstanding, (even) though

splash VERB 1 = paddle, plunge, bathe, dabble, wade, wallow 2 = scatter, shower, spray, sprinkle, wet, spatter, slop 3 = spatter, mark, stain, speck, speckle

● NOUN 1 = dash, touch, spattering

2 = spot, burst, patch, spurt

3 = blob, spot, smudge, stain, smear, fleck, speck

splendid 1 = excellent, wonderful, marvellous, great (*informal*), cracking (*Brit. informal*), fantastic (*informal*), first-class, glorious, booshit (*Austral. slang*), exo (*Austral. slang*), sik (*Austral. slang*) ≠ poor 2 = magnificent, grand, impressive, rich, superb, costly, gorgeous, lavish ≠ squalid

splendour = magnificence, grandeur, show, display, spectacle, richness, nobility, pomp ≠ squalor

splinter NOUN = sliver, fragment, chip, flake

● VERB = shatter, split, fracture, disintegrate

split VERB 1 = break, crack, burst, open, give way, come apart, come undone 2 = cut, break, crack, snap, chop 3 = divide, separate, disunite, disband, cleave 4 = diverge, separate, branch, fork, part 5 = tear, rend, rip 6 = share out, divide, distribute, halve, allocate, partition, allot, apportion

● NOUN 1 = division, breach, rift, rupture, discord, schism, estrangement, dissension

2 = separation, break-up, split-up

3 = crack, tear, rip, gap, rent, breach, slit, fissure

● ADJECTIVE 1 = divided

2 = broken, cracked, fractured, ruptured, cleft

spoil VERB 1 = ruin, destroy, wreck, damage, injure, harm, mar, trash (*slang*), crool *or* cruel (*Austral. slang*) ≠ improve 2 = overindulge, indulge, pamper, cosset, coddle, mollycoddle ≠ deprive 3 = indulge, pamper, satisfy, gratify, pander to 4 = go bad, turn, go off (*Brit. informal*), rot, decay, decompose, curdle, addle

● PLURAL NOUN = booty, loot, plunder, prey, swag (*slang*)

spoken = verbal, voiced, expressed, uttered, oral, said, told, unwritten

spokesperson = speaker, official, spokesman *or* spokeswoman, voice, spin doctor (*informal*), mouthpiece

sponsor VERB = back, fund, finance, promote, subsidize, patronize

● NOUN = backer, patron, promoter

spontaneous = unplanned, impromptu, unprompted, willing, natural, voluntary, instinctive, impulsive ≠ planned

sport NOUN 1 = game, exercise, recreation, play, amusement, diversion, pastime 2 = fun, joking, teasing, banter, jest, badinage

● VERB (*Informal*) = <u>wear</u>, display, flaunt, exhibit, flourish, show off, vaunt

sporting = <u>fair</u>, sportsmanlike, game (*informal*) ≠ unfair

sporty = <u>athletic</u>, outdoor, energetic

spot NOUN 1 = <u>mark</u>, stain, speck, scar, blot, smudge, blemish, speckle 2 = <u>pimple</u>, pustule, zit (*slang*) 3 = <u>place</u>, site, point, position, scene, location 4 (*Informal*) = <u>predicament</u>, trouble, difficulty, mess, plight, hot water (*informal*), quandary, tight spot

● VERB 1 = <u>see</u>, observe, catch sight of, sight, recognize, detect, make out, discern 2 = <u>mark</u>, stain, soil, dirty, fleck, spatter, speckle, splodge

spotlight NOUN = <u>attention</u>, limelight, public eye, fame

● VERB = <u>highlight</u>, draw attention to, accentuate

spotted = <u>speckled</u>, dotted, flecked, mottled, dappled

spouse = <u>partner</u>, mate, husband *or* wife, consort, significant other (*U.S. informal*)

sprawl = <u>loll</u>, slump, lounge, flop, slouch

spray[1] NOUN 1 = <u>droplets</u>, fine mist, drizzle 2 = <u>aerosol</u>, sprinkler, atomizer

● VERB = <u>scatter</u>, shower, sprinkle, diffuse

spray[2] = <u>sprig</u>, floral arrangement, branch, corsage

spread VERB 1 = <u>open (out)</u>, extend, stretch, unfold, sprawl, unroll 2 = <u>extend</u>, open, stretch 3 = <u>grow</u>, increase, expand, widen, escalate, proliferate, multiply, broaden 4 = <u>circulate</u>, broadcast, propagate, disseminate, make known ≠ suppress 5 = <u>diffuse</u>, cast, shed, radiate

● NOUN 1 = <u>increase</u>, development, advance, expansion, proliferation, dissemination, dispersal 2 = <u>extent</u>, span, stretch, sweep

spree = <u>fling</u>, binge (*informal*), orgy

spring NOUN = <u>flexibility</u>, bounce, resilience, elasticity, buoyancy

● VERB 1 = <u>jump</u>, bound, leap, bounce, vault 2 often with *from* = <u>originate</u>, come, derive, start, issue, proceed, arise, stem

Related Words
adjective: vernal

sprinkle = <u>scatter</u>, dust, strew, pepper, shower, spray, powder, dredge

sprinkling = <u>scattering</u>, dusting, few, dash, handful, sprinkle

sprint = <u>run</u>, race, shoot, tear, dash, dart, hare (*Brit. informal*)

sprout 1 = <u>germinate</u>, bud,

shoot, spring 2 = <u>grow</u>, develop, ripen

spur VERB = <u>incite</u>, drive, prompt, urge, stimulate, animate, prod, prick

• NOUN = <u>stimulus</u>, incentive, impetus, motive, impulse, inducement, incitement

• PHRASES **on the spur of the moment** = <u>on impulse</u>, impulsively, on the spot, impromptu, without planning

spurn = <u>reject</u>, slight, scorn, rebuff, snub, despise, disdain, repulse ≠ accept

spy NOUN = <u>undercover agent</u>, mole, nark (Brit., Austral., & N.Z. slang)

• VERB = <u>catch sight of</u>, spot, notice, observe, glimpse, espy

squabble VERB = <u>quarrel</u>, fight, argue, row, dispute, wrangle, bicker

• NOUN = <u>quarrel</u>, fight, row, argument, dispute, disagreement, tiff

squad = <u>team</u>, group, band, company, force, troop, crew, gang

squander = <u>waste</u>, spend, fritter away, blow (slang), misuse, expend, misspend ≠ save

square ADJECTIVE = <u>fair</u>, straight, genuine, ethical, honest, on the level (informal), kosher (informal), dinkum (Austral. & N.Z. informal), above board

• VERB often with **with** = <u>agree</u>, match, fit, correspond, tally, reconcile

squash 1 = <u>crush</u>, press, flatten, mash, smash, distort, pulp, compress 2 = <u>suppress</u>, quell, silence, crush, annihilate 3 = <u>embarrass</u>, put down, shame, degrade, mortify

squeeze VERB 1 = <u>press</u>, crush, squash, pinch 2 = <u>clutch</u>, press, grip, crush, pinch, squash, compress, wring 3 = <u>cram</u>, press, crowd, force, stuff, pack, jam, ram 4 = <u>hug</u>, embrace, cuddle, clasp, enfold

• NOUN 1 = <u>press</u>, grip, clasp, crush, pinch, squash, wring 2 = <u>crush</u>, jam, squash, press, crowd, congestion 3 = <u>hug</u>, embrace, clasp

stab VERB = <u>pierce</u>, stick, wound, knife, thrust, spear, jab, transfix

• NOUN 1 (Informal) = <u>attempt</u>, go, try, endeavour 2 = <u>twinge</u>, prick, pang, ache

stability = <u>firmness</u>, strength, soundness, solidity, steadiness ≠ instability

stable 1 = <u>secure</u>, lasting, strong, sound, fast, sure, established, permanent ≠ insecure 2 = <u>well-balanced</u>, balanced, sensible, reasonable, rational 3 = <u>solid</u>, firm, fixed, substantial, durable, well-made, well-built, immovable

≠ unstable

stack NOUN 1 = <u>pile</u>, heap, mountain, mass, load, mound 2 = <u>lot</u>, mass, load (*informal*), ton (*informal*), heap (*informal*), great amount

● VERB = <u>pile</u>, heap up, load, assemble, accumulate, amass

staff 1 = <u>workers</u>, employees, personnel, workforce, team 2 = <u>stick</u>, pole, rod, crook, cane, stave, wand, sceptre

stage = <u>step</u>, leg, phase, point, level, period, division, lap

stagger 1 = <u>totter</u>, reel, sway, lurch, wobble 2 = <u>astound</u>, amaze, stun, shock, shake, overwhelm, astonish, confound

stain NOUN 1 = <u>mark</u>, spot, blot, blemish, discoloration, smirch 2 = <u>stigma</u>, shame, disgrace, slur, dishonour 3 = <u>dye</u>, colour, tint

● VERB 1 = <u>mark</u>, soil, discolour, dirty, tinge, spot, blot, blemish 2 = <u>dye</u>, colour, tint

stake[1] = <u>pole</u>, post, stick, pale, paling, picket, palisade

stake[2] NOUN 1 = <u>bet</u>, ante, wager

● VERB 1 = <u>bet</u>, gamble, wager, chance, risk, venture, hazard 2 = <u>interest</u>, share, involvement, concern, investment

stale 1 = <u>old</u>, hard, dry, decayed ≠ fresh 2 = <u>musty</u>, fusty 3 = <u>tasteless</u>, flat, sour 4 = <u>unoriginal</u>, banal, trite,

stereotyped, worn-out, threadbare, hackneyed, overused ≠ original

stalk = <u>pursue</u>, follow, track, hunt, shadow, haunt

stall VERB 1 = <u>play for time</u>, delay, hedge, temporize 2 = <u>stop dead</u>, jam, seize up, catch, stick, stop short

● NOUN = <u>stand</u>, table, counter, booth, kiosk

stalwart 1 = <u>loyal</u>, faithful, firm, true, dependable, steadfast 2 = <u>strong</u>, strapping, sturdy, stout ≠ puny

stamina = <u>staying power</u>, endurance, resilience, force, power, energy, strength

stammer = <u>stutter</u>, falter, pause, hesitate, stumble over your words

stamp NOUN = <u>imprint</u>, mark, brand, signature, earmark, hallmark

● VERB 1 = <u>print</u>, mark, impress 2 = <u>trample</u>, step, tread, crush 3 = <u>identify</u>, mark, brand, label, reveal, show to be, categorize

● PHRASES **stamp something out** = <u>eliminate</u>, destroy, eradicate, crush, suppress, put down, scotch, quell

stance 1 = <u>attitude</u>, stand, position, viewpoint, standpoint 2 = <u>posture</u>, carriage, bearing, deportment

stand VERB 1 = <u>be upright</u>, be erect, be vertical 2 = <u>get to your feet</u>, rise, stand up, straighten up 3 = <u>be located</u>, be, sit, be positioned, be situated *or* located 4 = <u>be valid</u>, continue, exist, prevail, remain valid 5 = <u>put</u>, place, position, set, mount 6 = <u>sit</u>, mellow 7 = <u>resist</u>, tolerate, stand up to 8 = <u>tolerate</u>, bear, abide, stomach, endure, brook 9 = <u>take</u>, bear, handle, endure, put up with (*informal*), countenance

● NOUN 1 = <u>position</u>, attitude, stance, opinion, determination 2 = <u>stall</u>, booth, kiosk, table

● PHRASES **stand by** = <u>be prepared</u>, wait ◆ **stand for something** 1 = <u>represent</u>, mean, signify, denote, indicate, symbolize, betoken 2 (*Informal*) = <u>tolerate</u>, bear, endure, put up with, brook ◆ **stand in for someone** = <u>be a substitute for</u>, represent, cover for, take the place of, deputize for ◆ **stand up for something** *or* **someone** = <u>support</u>, champion, defend, uphold, stick up for (*informal*)

standard NOUN 1 = <u>level</u>, grade 2 = <u>criterion</u>, measure, guideline, example, model, average, norm, gauge 3 *often plural* = <u>principles</u>, ideals, morals, ethics 4 = <u>flag</u>, banner, ensign

● ADJECTIVE 1 = <u>usual</u>, normal, customary, average, basic, regular, typical, orthodox ≠ unusual 2 = <u>accepted</u>, official, established, approved, recognized, definitive, authoritative ≠ unofficial

stand-in = <u>substitute</u>, deputy, replacement, reserve, surrogate, understudy, locum, stopgap

standing NOUN 1 = <u>status</u>, position, footing, rank, reputation, eminence, repute 2 = <u>duration</u>, existence, continuance

● ADJECTIVE 1 = <u>permanent</u>, lasting, fixed, regular 2 = <u>upright</u>, erect, vertical

staple = <u>principal</u>, chief, main, key, basic, fundamental, predominant

star NOUN 1 = <u>heavenly body</u>, celestial body 2 = <u>celebrity</u>, big name, megastar (*informal*), name, luminary 3 = <u>leading man</u> *or* <u>lady</u>, hero *or* heroine, principal, main attraction

● VERB = <u>play the lead</u>, appear, feature, perform

● ADJECTIVE = <u>leading</u>, major, celebrated, brilliant, well-known, prominent

Related Words

adjectives: astral, stellar

stare = <u>gaze</u>, look, goggle, watch, gape, eyeball (*slang*), gawp (*Brit. slang*), gawk

stark ADJECTIVE 1 = plain, harsh, basic, grim, straightforward, blunt 2 = sharp, clear, striking, distinct, clear-cut 3 = austere, severe, plain, bare, harsh 4 = bleak, grim, barren, hard 5 = absolute, pure, sheer, utter, downright, out-and-out, unmitigated

● ADVERB = absolutely, quite, completely, entirely, altogether, wholly, utterly

start VERB 1 = set about, begin, proceed, embark upon, take the first step, make a beginning ≠ stop 2 = begin, arise, originate, issue, appear, commence ≠ end 3 = set in motion, initiate, instigate, open, trigger, originate, get going, kick-start ≠ stop 4 = establish, begin, found, create, launch, set up, institute, pioneer ≠ terminate 5 = start up, activate, get something going ≠ turn off 6 = jump, shy, jerk, flinch, recoil

● NOUN 1 = beginning, outset, opening, birth, foundation, dawn, onset, initiation ≠ end 2 = jump, spasm, convulsion

startle = surprise, shock, frighten, scare, make (someone) jump

starving = hungry, starved, ravenous, famished

state NOUN 1 = country, nation, land, republic, territory, federation, commonwealth, kingdom 2 = government, ministry, administration, executive, regime, powers-that-be 3 = condition, shape 4 = frame of mind, condition, spirits, attitude, mood, humour 5 = ceremony, glory, grandeur, splendour, majesty, pomp 6 = circumstances, situation, position, predicament

● VERB = say, declare, specify, present, voice, express, assert, utter

➤ WORD POWER SUPPLEMENT
Australian states and territories
➤ WORD POWER SUPPLEMENT
US states

stately = grand, majestic, dignified, royal, august, noble, regal, lofty ≠ lowly

statement 1 = announcement, declaration, communication, communiqué, proclamation 2 = account, report

station NOUN 1 = railway station, stop, stage, halt, terminal, train station, terminus 2 = headquarters, base, depot 3 = position, rank, status, standing, post, situation 4 = post, place, location, position, situation

● VERB = assign, post, locate, set, establish, install

stature 1 = height, build, size 2 = importance, standing, prestige, rank, prominence, eminence

status 1 = <u>position</u>, rank, grade
2 = <u>prestige</u>, standing, authority, influence, weight, honour, importance, fame, mana (*N.Z.*)
3 = <u>state of play</u>, development, progress, condition, evolution

staunch = <u>loyal</u>, faithful, stalwart, firm, sound, true, trusty, steadfast

stay VERB 1 = <u>remain</u>, continue to be, linger, stop, wait, halt, pause, abide ≠ go 2 *often with at* = <u>lodge</u>, visit, sojourn, put up at, be accommodated at
3 = <u>continue</u>, remain, go on, survive, endure
● NOUN 1 = <u>visit</u>, stop, holiday, stopover, sojourn
2 = <u>postponement</u>, delay, suspension, stopping, halt, deferment

steady 1 = <u>continuous</u>, regular, constant, consistent, persistent, unbroken, uninterrupted, incessant ≠ irregular 2 = <u>stable</u>, fixed, secure, firm, safe ≠ unstable
3 = <u>regular</u>, established
4 = <u>dependable</u>, sensible, reliable, secure, calm, supportive, sober, level-headed ≠ undependable

steal 1 = <u>take</u>, nick (*slang, chiefly Brit.*), pinch (*informal*), lift (*informal*), embezzle, pilfer, misappropriate, purloin 2 = <u>copy</u>, take, appropriate, pinch

(*informal*) 3 = <u>sneak</u>, slip, creep, tiptoe, slink

stealth = <u>secrecy</u>, furtiveness, slyness, sneakiness, unobtrusiveness, stealthiness, surreptitiousness

steep[1] 1 = <u>sheer</u>, precipitous, abrupt, vertical ≠ gradual
2 = <u>sharp</u>, sudden, abrupt, marked, extreme, distinct
3 (*Informal*) = <u>high</u>, exorbitant, extreme, unreasonable, overpriced, extortionate ≠ reasonable

steep[2] = <u>soak</u>, immerse, marinate (*Cookery*), submerge, drench, moisten, souse

steeped = <u>saturated</u>, pervaded, permeated, filled, infused, imbued, suffused

steer 1 = <u>drive</u>, control, direct, handle, pilot 2 = <u>direct</u>, lead, guide, conduct, escort

stem[1] NOUN = <u>stalk</u>, branch, trunk, shoot, axis
● PHRASES **stem from something** = <u>originate from</u>, be caused by, derive from, arise from

stem[2] = <u>stop</u>, hold back, staunch, check, dam, curb

step NOUN 1 = <u>pace</u>, stride, footstep 2 = <u>footfall</u> 3 = <u>move</u>, measure, action, means, act, deed, expedient 4 = <u>stage</u>, point, phase
5 = <u>level</u>, rank, degree
● VERB = <u>walk</u>, pace, tread, move

● PHRASES **step in** (*Informal*) = <u>intervene</u>, take action, become involved ◆ **step something up** = <u>increase</u>, intensify, raise

stereotype NOUN = <u>formula</u>, pattern

● VERB = <u>categorize</u>, typecast, pigeonhole, standardize

sterile 1 = <u>germ-free</u>, sterilized, disinfected, aseptic ≠ unhygienic 2 = <u>barren</u>, infertile, unproductive, childless ≠ fertile

sterling = <u>excellent</u>, sound, fine, superlative

stern 1 = <u>strict</u>, harsh, hard, grim, rigid, austere, inflexible ≠ lenient 2 = <u>severe</u>, serious, forbidding ≠ friendly

stick¹ 1 = <u>twig</u>, branch 2 = <u>cane</u>, staff, pole, rod, crook, baton 3 (*Slang*) = <u>abuse</u>, criticism, flak (*informal*), fault-finding

stick² VERB 1 (*Informal*) = <u>put</u>, place, set, lay, deposit 2 = <u>poke</u>, dig, stab, thrust, pierce, penetrate, spear, prod 3 = <u>fasten</u>, fix, bind, hold, bond, attach, glue, paste 4 = <u>adhere</u>, cling, become joined, become welded 5 = <u>stay</u>, remain, linger, persist 6 (*Slang*) = <u>tolerate</u>, take, stand, stomach, abide

● PHRASES **stick out** = <u>protrude</u>, stand out, jut out, show, project, bulge, obtrude ◆ **stick up for someone** (*Informal*) = <u>defend</u>, support, champion, stand up for

sticky 1 = <u>adhesive</u>, gummed, adherent 2 = <u>gooey</u>, tacky (*informal*), viscous, glutinous, gummy, icky (*informal*), gluey, clinging 3 (*Informal*) = <u>difficult</u>, awkward, tricky, embarrassing, nasty, delicate, unpleasant, barro (*Austral. slang*) 4 = <u>humid</u>, close, sultry, oppressive, sweltering, clammy, muggy

stiff 1 = <u>inflexible</u>, rigid, unyielding, hard, firm, tight, solid, tense ≠ flexible 2 = <u>formal</u>, constrained, forced, unnatural, stilted, unrelaxed ≠ informal 3 = <u>vigorous</u>, great, strong 4 = <u>severe</u>, strict, harsh, hard, heavy, extreme, drastic 5 = <u>difficult</u>, hard, tough, exacting, arduous

stifle 1 = <u>suppress</u>, repress, stop, check, silence, restrain, hush, smother 2 = <u>restrain</u>, suppress, repress, smother

stigma = <u>disgrace</u>, shame, dishonour, stain, slur, smirch

still ADJECTIVE 1 = <u>motionless</u>, stationary, calm, peaceful, serene, tranquil, undisturbed, restful ≠ moving 2 = <u>silent</u>, quiet, hushed ≠ noisy

● VERB = <u>quieten</u>, calm, settle, quiet, silence, soothe, hush, lull ≠ get louder

● ADVERB = <u>however</u>, but, yet, nevertheless, notwithstanding

stimulate = <u>encourage</u>, inspire, prompt, fire, spur, provoke, arouse, rouse

stimulating = <u>exciting</u>, inspiring, stirring, rousing, provocative, exhilarating ≠ boring

stimulus = <u>incentive</u>, spur, encouragement, impetus, inducement, goad, incitement, fillip

sting 1 = <u>hurt</u>, burn, wound 2 = <u>smart</u>, burn, pain, hurt, tingle

stink VERB = <u>reek</u>, pong (Brit. informal)

• NOUN = <u>stench</u>, pong (Brit. informal), foul smell, fetor

stint NOUN = <u>term</u>, time, turn, period, share, shift, stretch, spell

• VERB = <u>be mean</u>, hold back, be sparing, skimp on, be frugal

stipulate = <u>specify</u>, agree, require, contract, settle, covenant, insist upon

stir VERB 1 = <u>mix</u>, beat, agitate 2 = <u>stimulate</u>, move, excite, spur, provoke, arouse, awaken, rouse ≠ inhibit 3 = <u>spur</u>, drive, prompt, stimulate, prod, urge, animate, prick

• NOUN = <u>commotion</u>, excitement, activity, disorder, fuss, disturbance, bustle, flurry

stock NOUN 1 = <u>shares</u>, holdings, securities, investments, bonds, equities 2 = <u>property</u>, capital, assets, funds 3 = <u>goods</u>, merchandise, wares, range, choice, variety, selection, commodities 4 = <u>supply</u>, store, reserve, fund, stockpile, hoard 5 = <u>livestock</u>, cattle, beasts, domestic animals

• VERB 1 = <u>sell</u>, supply, handle, keep, trade in, deal in 2 = <u>fill</u>, supply, provide with, equip, furnish, fit out

• ADJECTIVE 1 = <u>hackneyed</u>, routine, banal, trite, overused 2 = <u>regular</u>, usual, ordinary, conventional, customary

stomach NOUN 1 = <u>belly</u>, gut (informal), abdomen, tummy (informal), puku (N.Z.) 2 = <u>tummy</u>, pot 3 = <u>inclination</u>, taste, desire, appetite, relish

• VERB = <u>bear</u>, take, tolerate, endure, swallow, abide

Related Words
adjective: gastric

stone 1 = <u>masonry</u>, rock 2 = <u>rock</u>, pebble 3 = <u>pip</u>, seed, pit, kernel

stoop VERB 1 = <u>hunch</u> 2 = <u>bend</u>, lean, bow, duck, crouch

• NOUN = <u>slouch</u>, bad posture, round-shoulderedness

stop VERB 1 = <u>quit</u>, cease, refrain, put an end to, discontinue, desist ≠ start 2 = <u>prevent</u>, cut short, arrest, restrain, hold back, hinder, repress, impede ≠ facilitate 3 = <u>end</u>, conclude, finish, terminate ≠ continue 4 = <u>cease</u>, shut down, discontinue, desist ≠ continue 5 = <u>halt</u>, pause ≠ keep going 6 = <u>pause</u>, wait, rest, take a break, have a breather (*informal*), stop briefly 7 = <u>stay</u>, rest, lodge

• NOUN 1 = <u>halt</u>, standstill 2 = <u>station</u>, stage, depot, terminus 3 = <u>stay</u>, break, rest

store NOUN 1 = <u>shop</u>, outlet, market, mart 2 = <u>supply</u>, stock, reserve, fund, quantity, accumulation, stockpile, hoard 3 = <u>repository</u>, warehouse, depository, storeroom

• VERB 1 *often with* **away** *or* **up** = <u>put by</u>, save, hoard, keep, reserve, deposit, garner, stockpile 2 = <u>put away</u>, put in storage, put in store 3 = <u>keep</u>, hold, preserve, maintain, retain, conserve

storm NOUN 1 = <u>tempest</u>, hurricane, gale, blizzard, squall 2 = <u>outburst</u>, row, outcry, furore, outbreak, turmoil, disturbance, strife

• VERB 1 = <u>rush</u>, stamp, flounce, fly 2 = <u>rage</u>, rant, thunder, rave, bluster 3 = <u>attack</u>, charge, rush, assault, assail

stormy 1 = <u>wild</u>, rough, raging, turbulent, windy, blustery, inclement, squally 2 = <u>rough</u>, wild, turbulent, raging 3 = <u>angry</u>, heated, fierce, passionate, fiery, impassioned

story 1 = <u>tale</u>, romance, narrative, history, legend, yarn 2 = <u>anecdote</u>, account, tale, report 3 = <u>report</u>, news, article, feature, scoop, news item

stout 1 = <u>fat</u>, big, heavy, overweight, plump, bulky, burly, fleshy ≠ slim 2 = <u>strong</u>, strapping, muscular, robust, sturdy, stalwart, brawny, able-bodied ≠ puny 3 = <u>brave</u>, bold, courageous, fearless, resolute, gallant, intrepid, valiant ≠ timid

straight ADJECTIVE 1 = <u>direct</u> ≠ indirect 2 = <u>level</u>, even, right, square, true, smooth, aligned, horizontal ≠ crooked 3 = <u>frank</u>, plain, straightforward, blunt, outright, honest, candid, forthright ≠ evasive 4 = <u>successive</u>, consecutive, continuous, running, solid, nonstop ≠ discontinuous 5 (*Slang*) = <u>conventional</u>, conservative, bourgeois ≠ fashionable 6 = <u>honest</u>, just, fair, reliable, respectable, upright, honourable, law-abiding ≠ dishonest 7 = <u>undiluted</u>, pure, neat, unadulterated, unmixed 8 = <u>in order</u>, organized, arranged, neat, tidy, orderly, shipshape ≠ untidy

• ADVERB 1 = <u>directly</u>, precisely, exactly, unswervingly, by the shortest route, in a beeline 2 = <u>immediately</u>, directly, promptly, instantly, at once, straight away, without delay, forthwith

straight away = immediately, now, at once, directly, instantly, right away

straighten = neaten, arrange, tidy (up), order, put in order

straightforward 1 (*Chiefly Brit.*) = simple, easy, uncomplicated, routine, elementary, easy-peasy (*slang*) ≠ complicated **2** = honest, open, direct, genuine, sincere, candid, truthful, forthright, dinkum (*Austral. & N.Z. informal*) ≠ devious

strain¹ NOUN **1** = pressure, stress, demands, burden **2** = stress, anxiety **3** = worry, effort, struggle ≠ ease **4** = burden, tension **5** = injury, wrench, sprain, pull
● VERB **1** = stretch, tax, overtax **2** = strive, struggle, endeavour, labour, go for it (*informal*), bend over backwards (*informal*), give it your best shot (*informal*), knock yourself out (*informal*) ≠ relax **3** = sieve, filter, sift, purify

strain² **1** = trace, suggestion, tendency, streak **2** = breed, family, race, blood, descent, extraction, ancestry, lineage

strained 1 = tense, difficult, awkward, embarrassed, stiff, uneasy ≠ relaxed **2** = forced, put on, false, artificial, unnatural ≠ natural

strait NOUN *often plural* = channel, sound, narrows
● PLURAL NOUN = difficulty, dilemma, plight, hardship, uphill (*S. African*), predicament, extremity

strand = filament, fibre, thread, string

stranded 1 = beached, grounded, marooned, ashore, shipwrecked, aground **2** = helpless, abandoned, high and dry

strange 1 = odd, curious, weird, wonderful, extraordinary, bizarre, peculiar, abnormal ≠ ordinary **2** = unfamiliar, new, unknown, foreign, novel, alien, exotic, untried ≠ familiar

stranger 1 = unknown person **2** = newcomer, incomer, foreigner, guest, visitor, alien, outlander

strangle 1 = throttle, choke, asphyxiate, strangulate **2** = suppress, inhibit, subdue, stifle, repress, overpower, quash, quell

strap NOUN = tie, thong, belt
● VERB = fasten, tie, secure, bind, lash, buckle

strapping = well-built, big, powerful, robust, sturdy, husky (*informal*), brawny

strategic 1 = tactical, calculated, deliberate, planned, politic, diplomatic 2 = <u>crucial</u>, important, key, vital, critical, decisive, cardinal

strategy 1 = <u>policy</u>, procedure, approach, scheme 2 = <u>plan</u>, approach, scheme

stray VERB 1 = <u>wander</u>, go astray, drift 2 = <u>drift</u>, wander, roam, meander, rove 3 = <u>digress</u>, diverge, deviate, get off the point
● ADJECTIVE 1 = <u>lost</u>, abandoned, homeless, roaming, vagrant
2 = <u>random</u>, chance, accidental

streak NOUN 1 = <u>band</u>, line, strip, stroke, layer, slash, vein, stripe
2 = <u>trace</u>, touch, element, strain, dash, vein
● VERB = <u>speed</u>, fly, tear, flash, sprint, dart, zoom, whizz (informal)

stream NOUN 1 = <u>river</u>, brook, burn (Scot.), beck, tributary, bayou, rivulet 2 = <u>flow</u>, current, rush, run, course, drift, surge, tide
● VERB 1 = <u>flow</u>, run, pour, issue, flood, spill, cascade, gush
2 = <u>rush</u>, fly, speed, tear, flood, pour

streamlined = <u>efficient</u>, organized, rationalized, slick, smooth-running

street = <u>road</u>, lane, avenue, terrace, row, roadway

strength 1 = <u>might</u>, muscle, brawn ≠ weakness 2 = <u>will</u>, resolution, courage, character, nerve, determination, pluck, stamina 3 = <u>health</u>, fitness, vigour
4 = <u>mainstay</u> 5 = <u>toughness</u>, soundness, robustness, sturdiness
6 = <u>force</u>, power, intensity ≠ weakness 7 = <u>potency</u>, effectiveness, efficacy 8 = <u>strong point</u>, skill, asset, advantage, talent, forte, speciality ≠ failing

strengthen 1 = <u>fortify</u>, harden, toughen, consolidate, stiffen, gee up, brace up ≠ weaken
2 = <u>reinforce</u>, support, intensify, bolster, buttress 3 = <u>bolster</u>, harden, reinforce 4 = <u>heighten</u>, intensify 5 = <u>make stronger</u>, build up, invigorate, restore, give strength to 6 = <u>support</u>, brace, reinforce, consolidate, harden, bolster, augment, buttress
7 = <u>become stronger</u>, intensify, gain strength

stress VERB 1 = <u>emphasize</u>, underline, dwell on 2 = <u>place the emphasis on</u>, emphasize, give emphasis to, lay emphasis upon
● NOUN 1 = <u>emphasis</u>, significance, force, weight 2 = <u>strain</u>, pressure, worry, tension, burden, anxiety, trauma 3 = <u>accent</u>, beat, emphasis, accentuation

stretch VERB 1 = <u>extend</u>, cover, spread, reach, put forth, unroll
2 = <u>last</u>, continue, go on, carry on, reach 3 = <u>expand</u> 4 = <u>pull</u>, distend, strain, tighten, draw out, elongate

• NOUN 1 = <u>expanse</u>, area, tract, spread, distance, extent

2 = <u>period</u>, time, spell, stint, term, space

strict 1 = <u>severe</u>, harsh, stern, firm, stringent ≠ easy-going

2 = <u>stern</u>, firm, severe, harsh, authoritarian 3 = <u>exact</u>, accurate, precise, close, true, faithful, meticulous, scrupulous

4 = <u>absolute</u>, total, utter

strife = <u>conflict</u>, battle, clash, quarrel, friction, discord, dissension

strike NOUN = <u>walkout</u>, industrial action, mutiny, revolt

• VERB 1 = <u>walk out</u>, down tools, revolt, mutiny 2 = <u>hit</u>, smack, thump, beat, knock, punch, hammer, slap 3 = <u>drive</u>, hit, smack, wallop (informal)

4 = <u>collide with</u>, hit, run into, bump into 5 = <u>knock</u>, smack, thump, beat 6 = <u>affect</u>, touch, devastate, overwhelm, leave a mark on 7 = <u>attack</u>, assault someone, set upon someone, lay into someone (informal)

8 = <u>occur to</u>, hit, come to, register (informal), dawn on or upon

9 = <u>seem to</u>, appear to, look to, give the impression to

10 = <u>move</u>, touch, hit, affect, overcome, stir, disturb, perturb

striking = <u>impressive</u>, dramatic, outstanding, noticeable, conspicuous, jaw-dropping

≠ unimpressive

string 1 = <u>cord</u>, twine, fibre

2 = <u>series</u>, line, row, file, sequence, succession, procession

3 = <u>sequence</u>, run, series, chain, succession

stringent = <u>strict</u>, tough, rigorous, tight, severe, rigid, inflexible ≠ lax

strip[1] 1 = <u>undress</u>, disrobe, unclothe 2 = <u>plunder</u>, rob, loot, empty, sack, ransack, pillage, divest

strip[2] 1 = <u>piece</u>, shred, band, belt

2 = <u>stretch</u>, area, tract, expanse, extent

strive = <u>try</u>, labour, struggle, attempt, toil, go all out (informal), bend over backwards (informal), do your best

stroke VERB = <u>caress</u>, rub, fondle, pet

• NOUN 1 = <u>apoplexy</u>, fit, seizure, attack, collapse 2 = <u>blow</u>, hit, knock, pat, thump, swipe

stroll VERB = <u>walk</u>, ramble, amble, promenade, saunter

• NOUN = <u>walk</u>, promenade, constitutional, ramble, breath of air

strong 1 = <u>powerful</u>, muscular, tough, athletic, strapping, hardy, sturdy, burly ≠ weak 2 = <u>fit</u>, robust, lusty 3 = <u>durable</u>, substantial, sturdy, heavy-duty, well-built, hard-wearing ≠ flimsy

4 = <u>extreme</u>, radical, drastic, strict, harsh, rigid, forceful, uncompromising **5** = <u>decisive</u>, firm, forceful, decided, determined, resolute, incisive **6** = <u>persuasive</u>, convincing, compelling, telling, sound, effective, potent, weighty **7** = <u>keen</u>, deep, acute, fervent, zealous, vehement **8** = <u>intense</u>, deep, passionate, ardent, fierce, fervent, vehement, fervid **9** = <u>staunch</u>, firm, fierce, ardent, enthusiastic, passionate, fervent **10** = <u>distinct</u>, marked, clear, unmistakable ≠ slight **11** = <u>bright</u>, brilliant, dazzling, bold ≠ dull

stronghold 1 = <u>bastion</u>, fortress, bulwark **2** = <u>refuge</u>, haven, retreat, sanctuary, hide-out

structure NOUN
1 = <u>arrangement</u>, form, make-up, design, organization, construction, formation, configuration **2** = <u>building</u>, construction, erection, edifice
● VERB = <u>arrange</u>, organize, design, shape, build up, assemble

struggle VERB **1** = <u>strive</u>, labour, toil, work, strain, go all out (*informal*), give it your best shot (*informal*), exert yourself **2** = <u>fight</u>, battle, wrestle, grapple, compete, contend
● NOUN **1** = <u>effort</u>, labour, toil, work, pains, scramble, exertion

2 = <u>fight</u>, battle, conflict, clash, contest, brush, combat, tussle, biffo (*Austral. slang*)

strut = <u>swagger</u>, parade, peacock, prance

stubborn = <u>obstinate</u>, dogged, inflexible, persistent, intractable, tenacious, recalcitrant, unyielding ≠ compliant

stuck 1 = <u>fastened</u>, fast, fixed, joined, glued, cemented **2** (*Informal*) = <u>baffled</u>, stumped, beaten

student 1 = <u>undergraduate</u>, scholar **2** = <u>pupil</u>, scholar, schoolchild, schoolboy or schoolgirl **3** = <u>learner</u>, trainee, apprentice, disciple

studied = <u>planned</u>, deliberate, conscious, intentional, premeditated ≠ unplanned

studio = <u>workshop</u>, workroom, atelier

study VERB **1** = <u>learn</u>, cram (*informal*), swot (up) (*Brit. informal*), read up, mug up (*Brit. slang*) **2** = <u>examine</u>, survey, look at, scrutinize **3** = <u>contemplate</u>, read, examine, consider, go into, pore over
● NOUN **1** = <u>examination</u>, investigation, analysis, consideration, inspection, scrutiny, contemplation **2** = <u>piece of research</u>, survey, report, review, inquiry, investigation

3 = <u>learning</u>, lessons, school work, reading, research, swotting (*Brit. informal*)

stuff NOUN **1** = <u>things</u>, gear, possessions, effects, equipment, objects, tackle, kit **2** = <u>substance</u>, material, essence, matter
- VERB **1** = <u>shove</u>, force, push, squeeze, jam, ram **2** = <u>cram</u>, fill, pack, crowd

stuffing = <u>wadding</u>, filling, packing

stumble VERB **1** = <u>trip</u>, fall, slip, reel, stagger, falter, lurch **2** = <u>totter</u>, reel, lurch, wobble
- PHRASES **stumble across** *or* **on** *or* **upon something** *or* **someone** = <u>discover</u>, find, come across, chance upon

stump NOUN = <u>tail end</u>, end, remnant, remainder
- VERB = <u>baffle</u>, confuse, puzzle, bewilder, perplex, mystify, flummox, nonplus

stun 1 = <u>overcome</u>, shock, confuse, astonish, stagger, bewilder, astound, overpower **2** = <u>daze</u>, knock out, stupefy, numb, benumb

stunning (*Informal*) = <u>wonderful</u>, beautiful, impressive, striking, lovely, spectacular, marvellous, splendid ≠ unimpressive

stunt = <u>feat</u>, act, trick, exploit, deed

stunted = <u>undersized</u>, little, small, tiny, diminutive

stupid 1 = <u>unintelligent</u>, thick, simple, slow, dim, dense, simple-minded, moronic ≠ intelligent **2** = <u>silly</u>, foolish, daft (*informal*), rash, pointless, senseless, idiotic, fatuous ≠ sensible **3** = <u>senseless</u>, dazed, groggy, insensate, semiconscious

sturdy 1 = <u>robust</u>, hardy, powerful, athletic, muscular, lusty, brawny ≠ puny **2** = <u>substantial</u>, solid, durable, well-made, well-built ≠ flimsy

style NOUN **1** = <u>manner</u>, way, method, approach, technique, mode **2** = <u>elegance</u>, taste, chic, flair, polish, sophistication, panache, élan **3** = <u>design</u>, form, cut **4** = <u>type</u>, sort, kind, variety, category, genre **5** = <u>fashion</u>, trend, mode, vogue, rage **6** = <u>luxury</u>, ease, comfort, elegance, grandeur, affluence
- VERB **1** = <u>design</u>, cut, tailor, fashion, shape, arrange, adapt **2** = <u>call</u>, name, term, label, entitle, dub, designate

stylish = <u>smart</u>, chic, fashionable, trendy (*Brit. informal*), modish, dressy (*informal*), voguish ≠ scruffy

subdue 1 = <u>overcome</u>, defeat, master, break, control, crush, conquer, tame **2** = <u>moderate</u>, suppress, soften, mellow, tone down, quieten down ≠ arouse

subdued 1 = <u>quiet</u>, serious, sad, chastened, dejected, downcast, crestfallen, down in the mouth ≠ lively **2** = <u>hushed</u>, soft, quiet, muted ≠ loud

subject NOUN **1** = <u>topic</u>, question, issue, matter, point, business, affair, object **2** = <u>citizen</u>, resident, native, inhabitant, national **3** = <u>dependant</u>, subordinate

● ADJECTIVE = <u>subordinate</u>, dependent, satellite, inferior, obedient

● VERB = <u>put through</u>, expose, submit, lay open

● PHRASES **subject to 1** = <u>liable to</u>, open to, exposed to, vulnerable to, prone to, susceptible to **2** = <u>bound by</u> **3** = <u>dependent on</u>, contingent on, controlled by, conditional on

subjective = <u>personal</u>, prejudiced, biased, nonobjective ≠ objective

sublime = <u>noble</u>, glorious, high, great, grand, elevated, lofty, exalted ≠ lowly

submerge 1 = <u>flood</u>, swamp, engulf, overflow, inundate, deluge **2** = <u>immerse</u>, plunge, duck **3** = <u>sink</u>, plunge, go under water **4** = <u>overwhelm</u>, swamp, engulf, deluge

submission 1 = <u>surrender</u>, yielding, giving in, cave-in

(*informal*), capitulation **2** = <u>presentation</u>, handing in, entry, tendering **3** = <u>compliance</u>, obedience, meekness, resignation, deference, passivity, docility

submit 1 = <u>surrender</u>, yield, give in, agree, endure, tolerate, comply, succumb **2** = <u>present</u>, hand in, tender, put forward, table, proffer

subordinate NOUN = <u>inferior</u>, junior, assistant, aide, second, attendant ≠ superior

● ADJECTIVE = <u>inferior</u>, lesser, lower, junior, subject, minor, secondary, dependent ≠ superior

subscribe 1 = <u>support</u>, advocate, endorse **2** = <u>contribute</u>, give, donate

subscription (*Chiefly Brit.*) = <u>membership fee</u>, dues, annual payment

subsequent = <u>following</u>, later, succeeding, after, successive, ensuing ≠ previous

subsequently = <u>later</u>, afterwards

subside 1 = <u>decrease</u>, diminish, lessen, ease, wane, ebb, abate, slacken ≠ increase **2** = <u>collapse</u>, sink, cave in, drop, lower, settle

subsidiary NOUN = <u>branch</u>, division, section, office, department, wing, subdivision, subsection

● ADJECTIVE = <u>secondary</u>, lesser,

subordinate, minor, supplementary, auxiliary, ancillary ≠ main

subsidy = <u>aid</u>, help, support, grant, assistance, allowance

substance 1 = <u>material</u>, body, stuff, fabric 2 = <u>importance</u>, significance, concreteness 3 = <u>meaning</u>, main point, gist, import, significance, essence 4 = <u>wealth</u>, means, property, assets, resources, estate

substantial = <u>big</u>, significant, considerable, large, important, ample, sizable *or* sizeable ≠ small

substitute VERB = <u>replace</u>, exchange, swap, change, switch, interchange

● NOUN = <u>replacement</u>, reserve, surrogate, deputy, sub, proxy, locum

● ADJECTIVE = <u>replacement</u>, reserve, surrogate, second, alternative, fall-back, proxy

---

Word Power

substitute – Although *substitute* and *replace* have the same meaning, the structures they are used in are different. You replace A *with* B, while you substitute B *for* A. Accordingly, *he replaced the worn tyre with a new one*, and *he substituted a new tyre for the worn one* are both correct ways of saying the same thing.

---

subtle 1 = <u>faint</u>, slight, implied, delicate, understated ≠ obvious 2 = <u>crafty</u>, cunning, sly, shrewd, ingenious, devious, wily, artful ≠ straightforward 3 = <u>muted</u>, soft, subdued, low-key, toned down 4 = <u>fine</u>, minute, narrow, tenuous, hair-splitting

subtlety 1 = <u>fine point</u>, refinement, sophistication, delicacy 2 = <u>skill</u>, ingenuity, cleverness, deviousness, craftiness, artfulness, slyness, wiliness

subversive ADJECTIVE = <u>seditious</u>, riotous, treasonous ● NOUN = <u>dissident</u>, terrorist, saboteur, fifth columnist

succeed 1 = <u>triumph</u>, win, prevail 2 = <u>work out</u>, work, be successful 3 = <u>make it</u> (*informal*), do well, be successful, triumph, thrive, flourish, make good, prosper ≠ fail 4 = <u>take over from</u>, assume the office of 5 *with* **to** = <u>take over</u>, assume, attain, come into, inherit, accede to, come into possession of 6 = <u>follow</u>, come after, follow after ≠ precede

success 1 = <u>victory</u>, triumph ≠ failure 2 = <u>prosperity</u>, fortune, luck, fame 3 = <u>hit</u> (*informal*), winner, smash (*informal*), triumph, sensation ≠ flop (*informal*) 4 = <u>big name</u>, star, hit (*informal*), celebrity, sensation, megastar (informal) ≠ nobody

successful 1 = <u>triumphant</u>, victorious, lucky, fortunate 2 = <u>thriving</u>, profitable, rewarding, booming, flourishing, fruitful ≠ unprofitable 3 = <u>top</u>, prosperous, wealthy

successfully = <u>well</u>, favourably, with flying colours, victoriously

succession 1 = <u>series</u>, run, sequence, course, order, train, chain, cycle 2 = <u>taking over</u>, assumption, inheritance, accession

successive = <u>consecutive</u>, following, in succession

succumb 1 often with **to** = <u>surrender</u>, yield, submit, give in, cave in (informal), capitulate ≠ beat 2 with **to** (with an illness as object) = <u>catch</u>, fall ill with

suck 1 = <u>drink</u>, sip, draw 2 = <u>take</u>, draw, pull, extract

sudden 1 = <u>quick</u>, rapid, unexpected, swift, hurried, abrupt, hasty ≠ gradual

suddenly = <u>abruptly</u>, all of a sudden, unexpectedly

sue (Law) = <u>take (someone) to court</u>, prosecute, charge, summon, indict

suffer 1 = <u>be in pain</u>, hurt, ache 2 = <u>be affected</u>, have trouble with, be afflicted, be troubled with 3 = <u>undergo</u>, experience, sustain, bear, go through, endure

4 = <u>tolerate</u>, stand, put up with (informal), bear, endure

suffering = <u>pain</u>, distress, agony, misery, ordeal, discomfort, torment, hardship

suffice = <u>be enough</u>, do, be sufficient, be adequate, serve, meet requirements

sufficient = <u>adequate</u>, enough, ample, satisfactory ≠ insufficient

suggest 1 = <u>recommend</u>, propose, advise, advocate, prescribe 2 = <u>indicate</u> 3 = <u>hint at</u>, imply, intimate 4 = <u>bring to mind</u>, evoke

suggestion

1 = <u>recommendation</u>, proposal, proposition, plan, motion 2 = <u>hint</u>, insinuation, intimation 3 = <u>trace</u>, touch, hint, breath, indication, whisper, intimation

suit NOUN 1 = <u>outfit</u>, costume, ensemble, dress, clothing, habit 2 = <u>lawsuit</u>, case, trial, proceeding, cause, action, prosecution

● VERB 1 = <u>be acceptable to</u>, please, satisfy, do, gratify 2 = <u>agree with</u>, become, match, go with, harmonize with

suitable 1 = <u>appropriate</u>, right, fitting, fit, becoming, satisfactory, apt, befitting ≠ inappropriate 2 = <u>seemly</u>, fitting, becoming, proper, correct ≠ unseemly 3 = <u>suited</u>, appropriate, in keeping with ≠ out of keeping

4 = <u>pertinent</u>, relevant, applicable, fitting, appropriate, to the point, apt ≠ irrelevant
5 = <u>convenient</u>, timely, appropriate, well-timed, opportune ≠ inopportune

suite = <u>rooms</u>, apartment

sum 1 = <u>amount</u>, quantity, volume 2 = <u>calculation</u>, figures, arithmetic, mathematics, maths (*Brit. informal*), tally, math (*U.S. informal*), arithmetical problem 3 = <u>total</u>, aggregate 4 = <u>totality</u>, whole

summarize = <u>sum up</u>, condense, encapsulate, epitomize, abridge, précis

summary = <u>synopsis</u>, résumé, précis, review, outline, rundown, abridgment

summit 1 = <u>peak</u>, top, tip, pinnacle, apex, head ≠ base 2 = <u>height</u>, pinnacle, peak, zenith, acme ≠ depths

summon 1 = <u>send for</u>, call, bid, invite 2 *often with* **up** = <u>gather</u>, muster, draw on

sumptuous = <u>luxurious</u>, grand, superb, splendid, gorgeous, lavish, opulent ≠ plain

sunny 1 = <u>bright</u>, clear, fine, radiant, sunlit, summery, unclouded ≠ dull 2 = <u>cheerful</u>, happy, cheery, buoyant, joyful, light-hearted ≠ gloomy

sunset = <u>nightfall</u>, dusk,

eventide, close of (the) day

superb 1 = <u>splendid</u>, excellent, magnificent, fine, grand, superior, marvellous, world-class, booshit (*Austral. slang*), exo (*Austral. slang*), sik (*Austral. slang*) ≠ inferior 2 = <u>magnificent</u>, superior, marvellous, exquisite, superlative ≠ terrible

superficial 1 = <u>shallow</u>, frivolous, empty-headed, silly, trivial ≠ serious 2 = <u>hasty</u>, cursory, perfunctory, hurried, casual, sketchy, desultory, slapdash ≠ thorough 3 = <u>slight</u>, surface, external, on the surface, exterior ≠ profound

superintendent = <u>supervisor</u>, director, manager, chief, governor, inspector, controller, overseer

superior ADJECTIVE 1 = <u>better</u>, higher, greater, grander, surpassing, unrivalled ≠ inferior 2 = <u>first-class</u>, excellent, first-rate, choice, exclusive, exceptional, de luxe, booshit (*Austral. slang*), exo (*Austral. slang*), sik (*Austral. slang*) ≠ average 3 = <u>supercilious</u>, patronizing, condescending, haughty, disdainful, lordly, lofty, pretentious

● NOUN = <u>boss</u>, senior, director, manager, chief (*informal*), principal, supervisor, baas (*S. African*) ≠ subordinate

> ### *Word Power*
> **superior** – *Superior* should
> not be used with *than*: *he is a*
> *better* (not *a better*) *poet than*
> *his brother*; *his poetry is superior*
> *to* (not *than*) *his brother's*.

superiority = <u>supremacy</u>, lead,
advantage, excellence,
ascendancy, predominance

supernatural = <u>paranormal</u>,
unearthly, uncanny, ghostly,
psychic, mystic, miraculous,
occult

supervise 1 = <u>observe</u>, guide,
monitor, oversee, keep an eye on
2 = <u>oversee</u>, run, manage, control,
direct, handle, look after,
superintend

supervision
= <u>superintendence</u>, direction,
control, charge, care,
management, guidance

supervisor = <u>boss</u> (*informal*),
manager, chief, inspector,
administrator, foreman, overseer,
baas (*S. African*)

supplement VERB 1 = <u>add to</u>,
reinforce, augment, extend
● NOUN 1 = <u>pull-out</u>, insert
2 = <u>appendix</u>, add-on, postscript
3 = <u>addition</u>, extra

supply VERB 1 = <u>provide</u>, give,
furnish, produce, stock, grant,
contribute, yield 2 = <u>furnish</u>,

provide, equip, endow
● NOUN = <u>store</u>, fund, stock,
source, reserve, quantity, hoard,
cache
● PLURAL NOUN = <u>provisions</u>,
necessities, stores, food, materials,
equipment, rations

support VERB 1 = <u>help</u>, back,
champion, second, aid, defend,
assist, side with ≠ oppose
2 = <u>provide for</u>, maintain, look
after, keep, fund, finance, sustain
≠ live off 3 = <u>bear out</u>, confirm,
verify, substantiate, corroborate
≠ refute 4 = <u>bear</u>, carry, sustain,
prop (up), reinforce, hold, brace,
buttress
● NOUN 1 = <u>furtherance</u>, backing,
promotion, assistance,
encouragement 2 = <u>help</u>, loyalty
≠ opposition 3 = <u>aid</u>, help,
benefits, relief, assistance
4 = <u>prop</u>, post, foundation, brace,
pillar 5 = <u>supporter</u>, prop,
mainstay, tower of strength,
second, backer ≠ antagonist
6 = <u>upkeep</u>, maintenance, keep,
subsistence, sustenance

supporter = <u>follower</u>, fan,
advocate, friend, champion,
sponsor, patron, helper
≠ opponent

supportive = <u>helpful</u>,
encouraging, understanding,
sympathetic

suppose 1 = <u>imagine</u>, consider,
conjecture, postulate,

hypothesize 2 = think, imagine, expect, assume, guess (*informal*, *chiefly U.S. & Canad.*), presume, conjecture

supposed 1 *usually with to* = meant, expected, required, obliged 2 = presumed, alleged, professed, accepted, assumed

supposedly = presumably, allegedly, ostensibly, theoretically, hypothetically ≠ actually

suppress 1 = stamp out, stop, check, crush, conquer, subdue, put an end to, overpower ≠ encourage 2 = check, inhibit, subdue, stop, quell 3 = restrain, stifle, contain, silence, conceal, curb, repress, smother

suppression 1 = elimination, crushing, check, quashing 2 = inhibition, blocking, restraint, smothering

supremacy = domination, sovereignty, sway, mastery, primacy, predominance, supreme power

supreme 1 = paramount ≠ least 2 = chief, leading, principal, highest, head, top, prime, foremost ≠ lowest 3 = ultimate, highest, greatest

supremo (*Brit. informal*) = head, leader, boss (*informal*), director, master, governor, commander, principal, baas (*S. African*)

sure 1 = certain, positive,

decided, convinced, confident, assured, definite ≠ uncertain 2 = inevitable, guaranteed, bound, assured, inescapable ≠ unsure 3 = reliable, accurate, dependable, undoubted, undeniable, foolproof, infallible, unerring ≠ unreliable

surely 1 = it must be the case that 2 = undoubtedly, certainly, definitely, without doubt, unquestionably, indubitably, doubtlessly

surface NOUN 1 = covering, face, exterior, side, top, veneer 2 = façade
● VERB 1 = emerge, come up, come to the surface 2 = appear, emerge, arise, come to light, crop up (*informal*), transpire, materialize

surge NOUN 1 = rush, flood 2 = flow, wave, rush, roller, gush, outpouring 3 = tide, swell, billowing 4 = rush, wave, storm, torrent, eruption
● VERB 1 = rush, pour, rise, gush 2 = roll, rush, heave 3 = sweep, rush, storm

surpass = outdo, beat, exceed, eclipse, excel, transcend, outstrip, outshine

surpassing = supreme, extraordinary, outstanding, exceptional, unrivalled, incomparable, matchless

surplus NOUN 1 = <u>excess</u>, surfeit ≠ shortage

● ADJECTIVE = <u>extra</u>, spare, excess, remaining, odd, superfluous ≠ insufficient

surprise NOUN 1 = <u>shock</u>, revelation, jolt, bombshell, eye-opener (*informal*) 2 = <u>amazement</u>, astonishment, wonder, incredulity

● VERB 1 = <u>amaze</u>, astonish, stun, startle, stagger, take aback 2 = <u>catch unawares</u> or off-guard, spring upon

surprised = <u>amazed</u>, astonished, speechless, thunderstruck

surprising = <u>amazing</u>, remarkable, incredible, astonishing, unusual, extraordinary, unexpected, staggering

surrender VERB 1 = <u>give in</u>, yield, submit, give way, succumb, cave in (*informal*), capitulate ≠ resist 2 = <u>give up</u>, abandon, relinquish, yield, concede, part with, renounce, waive

● NOUN = <u>submission</u>, cave-in (*informal*), capitulation, resignation, renunciation, relinquishment

surround = <u>enclose</u>, ring, encircle, encompass, envelop, hem in

surrounding ADJECTIVE = <u>nearby</u>, neighbouring

● PLURAL NOUN = <u>environment</u>, setting, background, location, milieu

surveillance = <u>observation</u>, watch, scrutiny, supervision, inspection

survey NOUN 1 = <u>poll</u>, study, research, review, inquiry, investigation 2 = <u>examination</u>, inspection, scrutiny 3 = <u>valuation</u>, estimate, assessment, appraisal

● VERB 1 = <u>interview</u>, question, poll, research, investigate 2 = <u>look over</u>, view, examine, observe, contemplate, inspect, eyeball (*slang*), scrutinize 3 = <u>measure</u>, estimate, assess, appraise

survive 1 = <u>remain alive</u>, last, live on, endure 2 = <u>continue</u>, last, live on 3 = <u>live longer than</u>, outlive, outlast

susceptible 1 = <u>responsive</u>, sensitive, receptive, impressionable, suggestible ≠ unresponsive 2 *usually with to* = <u>liable</u>, inclined, prone, given, subject, vulnerable, disposed ≠ resistant

suspect VERB 1 = <u>believe</u>, feel, guess, consider, suppose, speculate ≠ know 2 = <u>distrust</u>, doubt, mistrust ≠ trust

● ADJECTIVE = <u>dubious</u>, doubtful, questionable, iffy (*informal*) ≠ innocent

suspend 1 = <u>postpone</u>, put off, cease, interrupt, shelve, defer, cut short, discontinue ≠ continue 2 = <u>hang</u>, attach, dangle

suspension = <u>postponement</u>, break, breaking off, interruption, abeyance, deferment, discontinuation

suspicion 1 = <u>distrust</u>, scepticism, mistrust, doubt, misgiving, qualm, wariness, dubiety 2 = <u>idea</u>, notion, hunch, guess, impression 3 = <u>trace</u>, touch, hint, suggestion, shade, streak, tinge, soupçon (*French*)

suspicious 1 = <u>distrustful</u>, sceptical, doubtful, unbelieving, wary ≠ trusting 2 = <u>suspect</u>, dubious, questionable, doubtful, dodgy (*Brit., Austral., & N.Z. informal*), fishy (*informal*) ≠ beyond suspicion

sustain 1 = <u>maintain</u>, continue, keep up, prolong, protract 2 = <u>suffer</u>, experience, undergo, feel, bear, endure, withstand 3 = <u>help</u>, aid, assist 4 = <u>keep alive</u>, nourish, provide for 5 = <u>support</u>, bear, uphold

sustained = <u>continuous</u>, constant, steady, prolonged, perpetual, unremitting, nonstop ≠ periodic

swallow 1 = <u>eat</u>, consume, devour, swig (*informal*) 2 = <u>gulp</u>, drink

swamp NOUN = <u>bog</u>, marsh, quagmire, slough, fen, mire, morass, pakihi (*N.Z.*)

● VERB 1 = <u>flood</u>, engulf, submerge, inundate 2 = <u>overload</u>, overwhelm, inundate

swap *or* **swop** = <u>exchange</u>, trade, switch, interchange, barter

swarm NOUN = <u>multitude</u>, crowd, mass, army, host, flock, herd, horde

● VERB 1 = <u>crowd</u>, flock, throng, mass, stream 2 = <u>teem</u>, crawl, abound, bristle

swathe NOUN = <u>area</u>, section, tract

● VERB = <u>wrap</u>, drape, envelop, cloak, shroud, bundle up

sway VERB 1 = <u>move from side to side</u>, rock, roll, swing, bend, lean 2 = <u>influence</u>, affect, guide, persuade, induce

● NOUN = <u>power</u>, control, influence, authority, clout (*informal*)

swear 1 = <u>curse</u>, blaspheme, be foul-mouthed 2 = <u>vow</u>, promise, testify, attest 3 = <u>declare</u>, assert, affirm

swearing = <u>bad language</u>, cursing, profanity, blasphemy, foul language

sweat NOUN 1 = <u>perspiration</u> 2 (*Informal*) = <u>panic</u>, anxiety, worry, distress, agitation

● VERB 1 = <u>perspire</u>, glow

2 (*Informal*) = **worry**, fret, agonize, torture yourself

sweep VERB 1 = **brush**, clean 2 = **clear**, remove, brush, clean 3 = **sail**, pass, fly, tear, zoom, glide, skim

● NOUN 1 = **movement**, move, swing, stroke 2 = **extent**, range, stretch, scope

sweeping 1 = **indiscriminate**, blanket, wholesale, exaggerated, overstated, unqualified 2 = **wide-ranging**, global, comprehensive, wide, broad, extensive, all-inclusive, all-embracing ≠ limited

sweet ADJECTIVE 1 = **sugary**, cloying, saccharine, icky (*informal*) ≠ sour 2 = **fragrant**, aromatic ≠ stinking 3 = **fresh**, clean, pure 4 = **melodious**, musical, harmonious, mellow, dulcet ≠ harsh 5 = **charming**, kind, agreeable ≠ nasty 6 = **delightful**, appealing, cute, winning, engaging, lovable, likable *or* likeable ≠ unpleasant

● NOUN 1 *usually plural* = **confectionery**, candy (*U.S.*), lolly (*Austral. & N.Z.*), bonbon 2 (*Brit.*) = **dessert**, pudding

sweetheart 1 = **dearest**, beloved, sweet, angel, treasure, honey, dear, sweetie (*informal*) 2 = **love**, boyfriend *or* girlfriend, beloved, lover, darling

swell VERB 1 = **increase**, rise, grow, mount, expand, accelerate, escalate, multiply ≠ decrease 2 = **expand**, increase, grow, rise, balloon, enlarge, bulge, dilate ≠ shrink

● NOUN 1 = **wave**, surge, billow

swelling = **enlargement**, lump, bump, bulge, inflammation, protuberance, distension

swift 1 = **quick**, prompt, rapid 2 = **fast**, quick, rapid, hurried, speedy ≠ slow

swiftly 1 = **quickly**, rapidly, speedily 2 = **fast**, promptly, hurriedly

swing VERB 1 = **brandish**, wave, shake, flourish, wield, dangle 2 = **sway**, rock, wave, veer, oscillate 3 *usually with* **round** = **turn**, swivel, curve, rotate, pivot 4 = **hit out**, strike, swipe, lash out at, slap 5 = **hang**, dangle, suspend

● NOUN 1 = **swaying**, sway 2 = **fluctuation**, change, shift, switch, variation

swirl = **whirl**, churn, spin, twist, eddy

switch NOUN 1 = **control**, button, lever, on/off device 2 = **change**, shift, reversal

● VERB 1 = **change**, shift, divert, deviate 2 = **exchange**, swap, substitute

swollen = **enlarged**, bloated, inflamed, puffed up, distended

swoop 1 = **pounce**, attack,

charge, rush, descend **2** = **drop**, plunge, dive, sweep, descend, pounce, stoop

symbol 1 = <u>metaphor</u>, image, sign, representation, token **2** = <u>representation</u>, sign, figure, mark, image, token, logo, badge

symbolic 1 = <u>representative</u>, emblematic, allegorical **2** = <u>representative</u>, figurative

sympathetic 1 = <u>caring</u>, kind, understanding, concerned, interested, warm, pitying, supportive ≠ uncaring **2** = <u>like-minded</u>, compatible, agreeable, friendly, congenial, companionable ≠ uncongenial

sympathy 1 = <u>compassion</u>, understanding, pity, commiseration, aroha (*N.Z.*) ≠ indifference **2** = <u>affinity</u>, agreement, rapport, fellow feeling ≠ opposition

symptom 1 = <u>sign</u>, mark, indication, warning **2** = <u>manifestation</u>, sign, indication, mark, evidence, expression, proof, token

synthetic = <u>artificial</u>, fake, man-made ≠ real

system 1 = <u>arrangement</u>, structure, organization, scheme, classification **2** = <u>method</u>, practice, technique, procedure, routine

systematic = <u>methodical</u>, organized, efficient, orderly ≠ unmethodical

T

table NOUN 1 = <u>counter</u>, bench, stand, board, surface, work surface **2** = <u>list</u>, chart, tabulation, record, roll, register, diagram, itemization
● **VERB** (*Brit.*) = <u>submit</u>, propose, put forward, move, suggest, enter, file, lodge

taboo NOUN 1 = <u>prohibition</u>, ban, restriction, anathema, interdict, proscription, tapu (*N.Z.*)
● **ADJECTIVE** = <u>forbidden</u>, banned, prohibited, unacceptable, outlawed, anathema, proscribed, unmentionable ≠ permitted

tack NOUN 1 = <u>nail</u>, pin, drawing pin
● **VERB 1** = <u>fasten</u>, fix, attach, pin, nail, affix **2** (*Brit.*) = <u>stitch</u>, sew, hem, bind, baste
● **PHRASES tack something on to something** = <u>append</u>, add, attach, tag

tackle VERB 1 = <u>deal with</u>, set about, get stuck into (*informal*), come or get to grips with **2** = <u>undertake</u>, attempt, embark upon, get stuck into (*informal*), have a go or stab at (*informal*) **3** = <u>intercept</u>, stop, challenge
● **NOUN 1** = <u>block</u>, challenge

2 = rig, apparatus

tactic NOUN = policy, approach, move, scheme, plans, method, manoeuvre, ploy

● PLURAL NOUN = strategy, campaigning, manoeuvres, generalship

tactical = strategic, shrewd, smart, diplomatic, cunning ≠ impolitic

tag NOUN = label, tab, note, ticket, slip, identification, marker, flap

● VERB = label, mark

tail NOUN 1 = extremity, appendage, brush, rear end, hindquarters, hind part 2 = train, end, trail, tailpiece

● VERB (Informal) = follow, track, shadow, trail, stalk

● PHRASES turn tail = run away, flee, run off, retreat, cut and run, take to your heels

tailor NOUN = outfitter, couturier, dressmaker, seamstress, clothier, costumier

● VERB = adapt, adjust, modify, style, fashion, shape, alter, mould

taint = spoil, ruin, contaminate, damage, stain, corrupt, pollute, tarnish ≠ purify

take VERB 1 = grip, grab, seize, catch, grasp, clasp, take hold of 2 = carry, bring, bear, transport, ferry, haul, convey, fetch ≠ send 3 = accompany, lead, bring, guide, conduct, escort, convoy,

usher 4 = remove, draw, pull, fish, withdraw, extract 5 = steal, appropriate, pocket, pinch (informal), misappropriate, purloin ≠ return 6 = capture, seize, take into custody, lay hold of ≠ release 7 = tolerate, stand, bear, stomach, endure, abide, put up with (informal), withstand ≠ avoid 8 = require, need, involve, demand, call for, entail, necessitate 9 = understand, follow, comprehend, get, see, grasp, apprehend 10 = regard as, believe to be, consider to be, perceive to be, presume to be 11 = have room for, hold, contain, accommodate, accept

● PHRASES take off 1 = lift off, take to the air 2 (Informal) = depart, go, leave, disappear, abscond, decamp, slope off ◆ take someone in = deceive, fool, con (informal), trick, cheat, mislead, dupe, swindle ◆ take someone off (Informal) = parody, imitate, mimic, mock, caricature, send up (Brit. informal), lampoon, satirize ◆ take something in = understand, absorb, grasp, digest, comprehend, assimilate, get the hang of (informal) ◆ take something up 1 = start, begin, engage in, adopt, become involved in 2 = occupy, absorb, consume, use up, cover, fill, waste, squander

takeover = merger, coup, incorporation

tale = story, narrative, anecdote, account, legend, saga, yarn (*informal*), fable

talent = ability, gift, aptitude, capacity, genius, flair, knack

talented = gifted, able, expert, master, masterly, brilliant, ace (*informal*)

talk VERB 1 = speak, chat, chatter, converse, communicate, natter 2 = discuss, confer, negotiate, parley, confabulate, korero (*N.Z.*) 3 = inform, grass (*Brit. slang*), tell all, give the game away, blab, let the cat out of the bag
• NOUN = speech, lecture, presentation, report, address, discourse, sermon, symposium, whaikorero (*N.Z.*)

talking-to (*Informal*) = reprimand, lecture, rebuke, scolding, criticism, reproach, ticking-off (*informal*), dressing-down (*informal*) ≠ praise

tall 1 = lofty, big, giant, long-legged, lanky, leggy 2 = high, towering, soaring, steep, elevated, lofty ≠ short 3 (*Informal*) = implausible, incredible, far-fetched, exaggerated, absurd, unbelievable, preposterous, cock-and-bull (*informal*) ≠ plausible 4 = difficult, hard, demanding,

unreasonable, well-nigh impossible

tally NOUN = record, score, total, count, reckoning, running total
• VERB = agree, match, accord, fit, square, coincide, correspond, conform ≠ disagree

tame ADJECTIVE 1 = domesticated, docile, broken, gentle, obedient, amenable, tractable ≠ wild 2 = submissive, meek, compliant, subdued, manageable, obedient, docile, unresisting ≠ stubborn 3 = unexciting, boring, dull, bland, uninspiring, humdrum, uninteresting, insipid ≠ exciting
• VERB 1 = domesticate, train, break in, house-train ≠ make fiercer 2 = subdue, suppress, master, discipline, humble, conquer, subjugate ≠ arouse

tangible = definite, real, positive, material, actual, concrete, palpable, perceptible ≠ intangible

tangle NOUN 1 = knot, twist, web, jungle, coil, entanglement 2 = mess, jam, fix (*informal*), confusion, complication, mix-up, shambles, entanglement
• VERB = twist, knot, mat, coil, mesh, entangle, interweave, ravel ≠ disentangle
• PHRASES **tangle with someone** = come into conflict with, come up against, cross swords with, dispute with,

contend with, contest with, lock horns with

tantrum = <u>outburst</u>, temper, hysterics, fit, flare-up, foulie (*Austral. slang*)

tap[1] VERB = <u>knock</u>, strike, pat, rap, beat, touch, drum
● NOUN = <u>knock</u>, pat, rap, touch, drumming

tap[2] NOUN = <u>valve</u>, stopcock
● VERB = <u>listen in on</u>, monitor, bug (*informal*), spy on, eavesdrop on, wiretap
● PHRASES **on tap 1** (*Informal*) = <u>available</u>, ready, standing by, to hand, on hand, at hand, in reserve **2** = <u>on draught</u>, cask-conditioned, from barrels, not bottled *or* canned

tape NOUN = <u>binding</u>, strip, band, string, ribbon
● VERB **1** = <u>record</u>, video, tape-record, make a recording of **2** *sometimes with* **up** = <u>bind</u>, secure, stick, seal, wrap

target 1 = <u>mark</u>, goal **2** = <u>goal</u>, aim, objective, end, mark, object, intention, ambition **3** = <u>victim</u>, butt, prey, scapegoat

tariff 1 = <u>tax</u>, duty, toll, levy, excise **2** = <u>price list</u>, schedule

tarnish VERB **1** = <u>damage</u>, taint, blacken, sully, smirch ≠ enhance **2** = <u>stain</u>, discolour, darken, blot, blemish ≠ brighten
● NOUN = <u>stain</u>, taint,

discoloration, spot, blot, blemish

tart[1] = <u>pie</u>, pastry, pasty, tartlet, patty

tart[2] = <u>sharp</u>, acid, sour, bitter, pungent, tangy, piquant, vinegary ≠ sweet

tart[3] (*Informal*) = <u>slut</u>, prostitute, whore, call girl, trollop, floozy (*slang*)

task NOUN = <u>job</u>, duty, assignment, exercise, mission, enterprise, undertaking, chore
● PHRASES **take someone to task** = <u>criticize</u>, blame, censure, rebuke, reprimand, reproach, scold, tell off (*informal*)

taste NOUN **1** = <u>flavour</u>, savour, relish, smack, tang ≠ blandness **2** = <u>bit</u>, bite, mouthful, sample, dash, spoonful, morsel, titbit **3** = <u>liking</u>, preference, penchant, fondness, partiality, fancy, appetite, inclination ≠ dislike **4** = <u>refinement</u>, style, judgment, discrimination, appreciation, elegance, sophistication, discernment ≠ lack of judgment
● VERB **1** = <u>have a flavour of</u>, smack of, savour of **2** = <u>sample</u>, try, test, sip, savour **3** = <u>distinguish</u>, perceive, discern, differentiate **4** = <u>experience</u>, know, undergo, partake of, encounter, meet with ≠ miss

tasty = <u>delicious</u>, luscious, palatable, delectable, savoury, full-flavoured, scrumptious (*informal*), appetizing, lekker (*S. African slang*), yummo (*Austral. slang*) ≠ bland

taunt VERB = jeer, mock, tease, ridicule, provoke, insult, torment, deride

● NOUN = jeer, dig, insult, ridicule, teasing, provocation, derision, sarcasm

tavern = inn, bar, pub (*informal*, *chiefly Brit.*), public house, hostelry, alehouse (*archaic*)

tax NOUN = charge, duty, toll, levy, tariff, excise, tithe

● VERB 1 = charge, rate, assess 2 = strain, stretch, try, test, load, burden, exhaust, weaken

teach VERB = instruct, train, coach, inform, educate, drill, tutor, enlighten

● VERB = show, train

teacher = instructor, coach, tutor, guide, trainer, lecturer, mentor, educator

team NOUN 1 = side, squad 2 = group, company, set, body, band, gang, line-up, bunch

● PHRASES **team up** = join, unite, work together, cooperate, couple, link up, get together, band together

tear VERB 1 = rip, split, rend, shred, rupture 2 = run 3 = scratch, cut (open), gash, lacerate, injure, mangle, cut to pieces, cut to

ribbons, mangulate (*Austral. slang*) 4 = pull apart, claw, lacerate, mutilate, mangle, mangulate (*Austral. slang*) 5 = rush, run, charge, race, fly, speed, dash, hurry

● NOUN = hole, split, rip, rent, snag, rupture

tears PLURAL NOUN = crying, weeping, sobbing, wailing, blubbering

● PHRASES **in tears** = weeping, crying, sobbing, blubbering

tease 1 = mock, provoke, torment, taunt, goad, pull someone's leg (*informal*), make fun of 2 = tantalize, lead on, flirt with, titillate

technical = scientific, technological, skilled, specialist, specialized, hi-tech or high-tech

technique 1 = method, way, system, approach, means, style, manner, procedure 2 = skill, performance, craft, touch, execution, artistry, craftsmanship, proficiency

tedious = boring, dull, dreary, monotonous, drab, tiresome, laborious, humdrum ≠ exciting

teenager = youth, minor, adolescent, juvenile, girl, boy

telephone NOUN = phone, mobile (phone), handset, dog and bone (*slang*)

● VERB = call, phone, ring (*chiefly*

Brit.), dial

telescope NOUN = glass, scope (*informal*), spyglass

● VERB = shorten, contract, compress, shrink, condense, abbreviate, abridge ≠ lengthen

television = TV, telly (*Brit. informal*), small screen (*informal*), the box (*Brit. informal*), the tube (*slang*)

tell VERB 1 = inform, notify, state to, reveal to, express to, disclose to, proclaim to, divulge 2 = describe, relate, recount, report, portray, chronicle, narrate 3 = instruct, order, command, direct, bid 4 = distinguish, discriminate, discern, differentiate, identify 5 = have or take effect, register, weigh, count, take its toll, carry weight, make its presence felt

● PHRASES **tell someone off** = reprimand, rebuke, scold, lecture, censure, reproach, berate, chide

telling = effective, significant, considerable, marked, striking, powerful, impressive, influential ≠ unimportant

temper NOUN 1 = irritability, irascibility, passion, resentment, petulance, surliness, hot-headedness ≠ good humour 2 = frame of mind, nature, mind, mood, constitution, humour,

temperament, disposition 3 = rage, fury, bad mood, passion, tantrum, foulie (*Austral. slang*) 4 = self-control, composure, cool (*slang*), calmness, equanimity ≠ anger

● VERB 1 = moderate, restrain, tone down, soften, soothe, lessen, mitigate, assuage ≠ intensify 2 = strengthen, harden, toughen, anneal ≠ soften

temperament 1 = nature, character, personality, make-up, constitution, bent, humour, temper 2 = moods, anger, volatility, petulance, excitability, moodiness, hot-headedness

temple = shrine, church, sanctuary, house of God

temporarily = briefly, for the time being, momentarily, fleetingly, pro tem

temporary 1 = impermanent, transitory, brief, fleeting, interim, short-lived, momentary, ephemeral ≠ permanent 2 = short-term, acting, interim, supply, stand-in, fill-in, caretaker, provisional

tempt 1 = attract, allure 2 = entice, lure, lead on, invite, seduce, coax ≠ discourage

temptation 1 = enticement, lure, inducement, pull, seduction, allurement, tantalization 2 = appeal, attraction

tempting = <u>inviting</u>, enticing, seductive, alluring, attractive, mouthwatering, appetizing ≠ uninviting

tenant = <u>leaseholder</u>, resident, renter, occupant, inhabitant, occupier, lodger, boarder

tend¹ = <u>be inclined</u>, be liable, have a tendency, be apt, be prone, lean, incline, gravitate

tend² 1 = <u>take care of</u>, look after, keep, attend, nurture, watch over ≠ neglect 2 = <u>maintain</u>, take care of, nurture, cultivate, manage ≠ neglect

tendency = <u>inclination</u>, leaning, liability, disposition, propensity, susceptibility, proclivity, proneness

tender¹ 1 = <u>gentle</u>, loving, kind, caring, sympathetic, affectionate, compassionate, considerate ≠ harsh 2 = <u>vulnerable</u>, young, sensitive, raw, youthful, inexperienced, immature, impressionable ≠ experienced 3 = <u>sensitive</u>, painful, sore, raw, bruised, inflamed

tender² NOUN = <u>offer</u>, bid, estimate, proposal, submission
● VERB = <u>offer</u>, present, submit, give, propose, volunteer, hand in, put forward

tense ADJECTIVE 1 = <u>strained</u>, uneasy, stressful, fraught, charged, difficult, worrying,

exciting 2 = <u>nervous</u>, edgy, strained, anxious, apprehensive, uptight (*informal*), on edge, jumpy ≠ calm 3 = <u>rigid</u>, strained, taut, stretched, tight ≠ relaxed
● VERB = <u>tighten</u>, strain, brace, stretch, flex, stiffen ≠ relax

tension 1 = <u>strain</u>, stress, nervousness, pressure, anxiety, unease, apprehension, suspense ≠ calmness 2 = <u>friction</u>, hostility, unease, antagonism, antipathy, enmity 3 = <u>rigidity</u>, tightness, stiffness, pressure, stress, stretching, tautness

tentative 1 = <u>unconfirmed</u>, provisional, indefinite, test, trial, pilot, preliminary, experimental ≠ confirmed 2 = <u>hesitant</u>, cautious, uncertain, doubtful, faltering, unsure, timid, undecided ≠ confident

term NOUN 1 = <u>word</u>, name, expression, title, label, phrase 2 = <u>period</u>, time, spell, while, season, interval, span, duration
● PLURAL NOUN 1 = <u>conditions</u>, particulars, provisions, provisos, stipulations, qualifications, specifications 2 = <u>relationship</u>, standing, footing, relations, status
● VERB = <u>call</u>, name, label, style, entitle, tag, dub, designate

terminal ADJECTIVE 1 = <u>fatal</u>, deadly, lethal, killing, mortal, incurable, inoperable, untreatable 2 = <u>final</u>, last, closing, finishing, concluding, ultimate, terminating ≠ initial

● NOUN = <u>terminus</u>, station, depot, end of the line

terminate 1 = <u>end</u>, stop, conclude, finish, complete, discontinue ≠ begin 2 = <u>cease</u>, end, close, finish 3 = <u>abort</u>, end

terrain = <u>ground</u>, country, land, landscape, topography, going

terrestrial = <u>earthly</u>, worldly, global

terrible 1 = <u>awful</u>, shocking, terrifying, horrible, dreadful, horrifying, fearful, horrendous 2 (*Informal*) = <u>bad</u>, awful, dreadful, dire, abysmal, poor, rotten (*informal*) ≠ wonderful 3 = <u>serious</u>, desperate, severe, extreme, dangerous, insufferable ≠ mild

terribly 1 = <u>very much</u>, very, dreadfully, seriously, extremely, desperately, thoroughly, decidedly 2 = <u>extremely</u>, very, dreadfully, desperately, thoroughly, decidedly, awfully (*informal*)

terrific 1 (*Informal*) = <u>excellent</u>, wonderful, brilliant, amazing, outstanding, superb, fantastic (*informal*), magnificent, booshit (*Austral. slang*), exo (*Austral. slang*), sik (*Austral. slang*), ka pai (*N.Z.*) ≠ awful 2 = <u>intense</u>, great, huge, enormous, tremendous,

fearful, gigantic

terrified = <u>frightened</u>, scared, petrified, alarmed, panic-stricken, horror-struck

terrify = <u>frighten</u>, scare, alarm, terrorize

territory = <u>district</u>, area, land, region, country, zone, province, patch

> WORD POWER SUPPLEMENT
New Zealand territories

terror 1 = <u>fear</u>, alarm, dread, fright, panic, anxiety 2 = <u>nightmare</u>, monster, bogeyman, devil, fiend, bugbear

test VERB 1 = <u>check</u>, investigate, assess, research, analyse, experiment with, try out, put something to the test 2 = <u>examine</u>, put someone to the test

● NOUN 1 = <u>trial</u>, research, check, investigation, analysis, assessment, examination, evaluation 2 = <u>examination</u>, paper, assessment, evaluation

testament 1 = <u>proof</u>, evidence, testimony, witness, demonstration, tribute 2 = <u>will</u>, last wishes

testify = <u>bear witness</u>, state, swear, certify, assert, affirm, attest, corroborate ≠ disprove

testimony 1 = <u>evidence</u>, statement, submission, affidavit, deposition 2 = <u>proof</u>, evidence, demonstration, indication, support, manifestation, verification, corroboration

testing = difficult, demanding, taxing, challenging, searching, tough, exacting, rigorous ≠ undemanding

text 1 = contents, words, content, wording, body, subject matter 2 = words, wording 3 = transcript, script

texture = feel, consistency, structure, surface, tissue, grain

thank = say thank you to, show your appreciation to

thanks PLURAL NOUN = gratitude, appreciation, credit, recognition, acknowledgment, gratefulness
• PHRASES **thanks to** = because of, through, due to, as a result of, owing to

thaw = melt, dissolve, soften, defrost, warm, liquefy, unfreeze ≠ freeze

theatrical 1 = dramatic, stage, Thespian 2 = exaggerated, dramatic, melodramatic, histrionic, affected, mannered, showy, ostentatious ≠ natural

theft = stealing, robbery, thieving, fraud, embezzlement, pilfering, larceny, purloining

theme 1 = motif, leitmotif 2 = subject, idea, topic, essence, subject matter, keynote, gist

theological = religious,

ecclesiastical, doctrinal

theoretical 1 = abstract, speculative ≠ practical 2 = hypothetical, academic, notional, unproven, conjectural, postulatory

theory = belief, feeling, speculation, assumption, hunch, presumption, conjecture, surmise

therapeutic = beneficial, healing, restorative, good, corrective, remedial, salutary, curative ≠ harmful

therapist = psychologist, analyst, psychiatrist, shrink (informal), counsellor, healer, psychotherapist, psychoanalyst

therapy = remedy, treatment, cure, healing, method of healing

therefore = consequently, so, thus, as a result, hence, accordingly, thence, ergo

thesis 1 = proposition, theory, hypothesis, idea, view, opinion, proposal, contention 2 = dissertation, paper, treatise, essay, monograph

thick 1 = bulky, broad, big, large, fat, solid, substantial, hefty ≠ thin 2 = wide, across, deep, broad, in extent or diameter 3 = dense, close, heavy, compact, impenetrable, lush 4 = heavy, heavyweight, dense, chunky, bulky, woolly 5 = opaque, heavy, dense, impenetrable 6 = viscous, concentrated, stiff, condensed, gelatinous, semi-solid, viscid ≠ runny **7** = <u>crowded</u>, full, covered, bursting, bristling, brimming ≠ empty **8** (*Informal*) = <u>stupid</u>, slow, dense, dopey (*informal*), moronic, obtuse, brainless, dumb-ass (*informal*) ≠ clever **9** (*Informal*) = <u>friendly</u>, close, intimate, familiar, pally (*informal*), devoted, inseparable ≠ unfriendly

thicken = <u>set</u>, condense, congeal, clot, jell, coagulate ≠ thin

thief = <u>robber</u>, burglar, stealer, plunderer, shoplifter, embezzler, pickpocket, pilferer

thin 1 = <u>narrow</u>, fine, attenuated ≠ thick **2** = <u>slim</u>, spare, lean, slight, slender, skinny, skeletal, bony ≠ fat **3** = <u>meagre</u>, sparse, scanty, poor, scattered, inadequate, insufficient, deficient ≠ plentiful **4** = <u>fine</u>, delicate, flimsy, sheer, skimpy, gossamer, diaphanous, filmy ≠ thick **5** = <u>unconvincing</u>, inadequate, feeble, poor, weak, superficial, lame, flimsy ≠ convincing **6** = <u>wispy</u>, thinning, sparse, scarce, scanty

thing NOUN **1** = <u>substance</u>, stuff, being, body, material, fabric, entity **2** (*Informal*) = <u>phobia</u>, fear, complex, horror, terror, hang-up (*informal*), aversion, neurosis **3** (*Informal*) = <u>obsession</u>, liking, preoccupation, mania, fetish, fixation, soft spot, predilection
● PLURAL NOUN **1** = <u>possessions</u>, stuff, gear, belongings, effects, luggage, clobber (*Brit. slang*), chattels **2** = <u>equipment</u>, gear, tools, stuff, tackle, implements, kit, apparatus **3** = <u>circumstances</u>, the situation, the state of affairs, matters, life, affairs

think VERB **1** = <u>believe</u>, be of the opinion, be of the view **2** = <u>judge</u>, consider, estimate, reckon, deem, regard as **3** = <u>ponder</u>, reflect, contemplate, deliberate, meditate, ruminate, cogitate, be lost in thought
● PHRASES **think something up** = <u>devise</u>, create, come up with, invent, contrive, visualize, concoct, dream something up

thinker = <u>philosopher</u>, intellect (*informal*), wise man, sage, brain (*informal*), theorist, mastermind

thinking NOUN = <u>reasoning</u>, idea, view, position, theory, opinion, judgment, conjecture
● ADJECTIVE = <u>thoughtful</u>, intelligent, reasoning, rational, philosophical, reflective, contemplative, meditative

thirst 1 = <u>dryness</u>, thirstiness, drought **2** = <u>craving</u>, appetite, longing, desire, passion, yearning, hankering, keenness ≠ aversion

thorn = <u>prickle</u>, spike, spine, barb

thorough 1 = <u>comprehensive</u>, full, complete, sweeping, intensive, in-depth, exhaustive ≠ cursory **2** = <u>careful</u>, conscientious, painstaking, efficient, meticulous, exhaustive, assiduous ≠ careless **3** = <u>complete</u>, total, absolute, utter, perfect, outright, unqualified, out-and-out ≠ partial

thoroughly 1 = <u>carefully</u>, fully, efficiently, meticulously, painstakingly, scrupulously, assiduously, intensively ≠ carelessly **2** = <u>fully</u> **3** = <u>completely</u>, quite, totally, perfectly, absolutely, utterly, downright, to the hilt ≠ partly

though CONJUNCTION = <u>although</u>, while, even if, even though, notwithstanding

● ADVERB = <u>nevertheless</u>, still, however, yet, nonetheless, for all that, notwithstanding

thought 1 = <u>thinking</u>, consideration, reflection, deliberation, musing, meditation, rumination, cogitation **2** = <u>opinion</u>, view, idea, concept, notion, judgment **3** = <u>consideration</u>, study, attention, care, regard, scrutiny, heed **4** = <u>intention</u>, plan, idea, design, aim, purpose, object, notion **5** = <u>hope</u>, expectation, prospect, aspiration, anticipation

thoughtful 1 = <u>reflective</u>, pensive, contemplative, meditative, serious, studious, deliberative, ruminative ≠ shallow **2** = <u>considerate</u>, kind, caring, kindly, helpful, attentive, unselfish, solicitous ≠ inconsiderate

thrash VERB **1** = <u>defeat</u>, beat, crush, slaughter (*informal*), rout, trounce, run rings around (*informal*), wipe the floor with (*informal*) **2** = <u>beat</u>, wallop, whip, belt (*informal*), cane, flog, scourge, spank **3** = <u>thresh</u>, flail, jerk, writhe, toss and turn

● PHRASES **thrash something out** = <u>settle</u>, resolve, discuss, debate, solve, argue out, have something out, talk something over

thrashing 1 = <u>defeat</u>, beating, hammering (*informal*), hiding (*informal*), rout, trouncing, drubbing **2** = <u>beating</u>, hiding (*informal*), belting (*informal*), whipping, flogging

thread NOUN **1** = <u>strand</u>, fibre, yarn, filament, line, string, twine **2** = <u>theme</u>, train of thought, direction, plot, drift, story line

● VERB = <u>move</u>, pass, ease, thrust, squeeze through, pick your way

threat 1 = <u>danger</u>, risk, hazard, menace, peril **2** = <u>threatening remark</u>, menace **3** = <u>warning</u>, foreshadowing, foreboding

threaten 1 = <u>intimidate</u>, bully, menace, terrorize, lean on (slang), pressurize, browbeat ≠ defend 2 = <u>endanger</u>, jeopardize, put at risk, imperil, put in jeopardy, put on the line ≠ protect 3 = <u>be imminent</u>, impend

threshold 1 = <u>entrance</u>, doorway, door, doorstep 2 = <u>start</u>, beginning, opening, dawn, verge, brink, outset, inception ≠ end 3 = <u>limit</u>, margin, starting point, minimum

thrift = <u>economy</u>, prudence, frugality, saving, parsimony, carefulness, thriftiness ≠ extravagance

thrill NOUN = <u>pleasure</u>, kick (informal), buzz (slang), high, stimulation, tingle, titillation ≠ tedium

● VERB = <u>excite</u>, stimulate, arouse, move, stir, electrify, titillate, give someone a kick

thrilling = <u>exciting</u>, gripping, stimulating, stirring, sensational, rousing, riveting, electrifying ≠ boring

thrive = <u>prosper</u>, do well, flourish, increase, grow, develop, succeed, get on ≠ decline

thriving = <u>successful</u>, flourishing, healthy, booming, blooming, prosperous, burgeoning ≠ unsuccessful

throb VERB 1 = <u>pulsate</u>, pound, beat, pulse, thump, palpitate 2 = <u>vibrate</u>, pulsate, reverberate, shake, judder (informal)

● NOUN 1 = <u>pulse</u>, pounding, beat, thump, thumping, pulsating, palpitation 2 = <u>vibration</u>, throbbing, reverberation, judder (informal), pulsation

throng NOUN = <u>crowd</u>, mob, horde, host, pack, mass, crush, swarm

● VERB 1 = <u>crowd</u>, flock, congregate, converge, mill around, swarm around ≠ disperse 2 = <u>pack</u>, crowd

throttle = <u>strangle</u>, choke, garrotte, strangulate

through PREPOSITION 1 = <u>via</u>, by way of, by, between, past, from one side to the other of 2 = <u>because of</u>, by way of, by means of 3 = <u>using</u>, via, by way of, by means of, by virtue of, with the assistance of 4 = <u>during</u>, throughout, for the duration of, in

● ADJECTIVE = <u>completed</u>, done, finished, ended

● PHRASES **through and through** = <u>completely</u>, totally, fully, thoroughly, entirely, altogether, wholly, utterly

throughout PREPOSITION 1 = <u>right through</u>, everywhere in, during the whole of, through the whole of 2 = <u>all over</u>, everywhere in, through the whole of

● ADVERB 1 = <u>from start to finish</u>, right through 2 = <u>all through</u>, right through

throw VERB 1 = <u>hurl</u>, toss, fling, send, launch, cast, pitch, chuck (*informal*) 2 = <u>toss</u>, fling, chuck (*informal*), cast, hurl, sling 3 (*Informal*) = <u>confuse</u>, baffle, faze, astonish, confound, disconcert, dumbfound

● NOUN = <u>toss</u>, pitch, fling, sling, lob (*informal*), heave

thrust VERB = <u>push</u>, force, shove, drive, plunge, jam, ram, propel

● NOUN 1 = <u>stab</u>, pierce, lunge 2 = <u>push</u>, shove, poke, prod 3 = <u>momentum</u>, impetus, drive

thug NOUN = <u>ruffian</u>, hooligan, tough, heavy (*slang*), gangster, bully boy, bruiser (*informal*), tsotsi (*S. African*)

thump VERB = <u>strike</u>, hit, punch, pound, beat, knock, smack, clout (*informal*)

● NOUN 1 = <u>blow</u>, knock, punch, rap, smack, clout (*informal*), whack, swipe 2 = <u>thud</u>, crash, bang, clunk, thwack

thunder NOUN = <u>rumble</u>, crash, boom, explosion

● VERB 1 = <u>rumble</u>, crash, boom, roar, resound, reverberate, peal 2 = <u>shout</u>, roar, yell, bark, bellow

thus 1 = <u>therefore</u>, so, hence, consequently, accordingly, for

this reason, ergo, on that account 2 = <u>in this way</u>, so, like this, as follows

thwart = <u>frustrate</u>, foil, prevent, snooker, hinder, obstruct, outwit, stymie ≠ assist

tick NOUN 1 = <u>check mark</u>, mark, line, stroke, dash 2 = <u>click</u>, tapping, clicking, ticktock 3 (*Brit. informal*) = <u>moment</u>, second, minute, flash, instant, twinkling, split second, trice

● VERB 1 = <u>mark</u>, indicate, check off 2 = <u>click</u>, tap, ticktock

ticket 1 = <u>voucher</u>, pass, coupon, card, slip, certificate, token, chit 2 = <u>label</u>, tag, marker, sticker, card, slip, tab, docket

tide 1 = <u>current</u>, flow, stream, ebb, undertow, tideway 2 = <u>course</u>, direction, trend, movement, tendency, drift

tidy ADJECTIVE 1 = <u>neat</u>, orderly, clean, spruce, well-kept, well-ordered, shipshape ≠ untidy 2 = <u>organized</u>, neat, methodical 3 (*Informal*) = <u>considerable</u>, large, substantial, goodly, healthy, generous, handsome, ample ≠ small

● VERB = <u>neaten</u>, straighten, order, clean, groom, spruce up ≠ disorder

tie VERB 1 = <u>fasten</u>, bind, join, link, connect, attach, knot ≠ unfasten 2 = <u>tether</u>, secure 3 = <u>restrict</u>, limit, confine, bind, restrain, hamper, hinder ≠ free 4 = <u>draw</u>, be level, match, equal

• NOUN 1 = <u>fastening</u>, binding, link, bond, knot, cord, fetter, ligature 2 = <u>bond</u>, relationship, connection, commitment, liaison, allegiance, affiliation 3 = <u>draw</u>, dead heat, deadlock, stalemate

tier = <u>row</u>, bank, layer, line, level, rank, storey, stratum

tight 1 = <u>close-fitting</u>, narrow, cramped, snug, constricted, close ≠ loose 2 = <u>secure</u>, firm, fast, fixed 3 = <u>taut</u>, stretched, rigid ≠ slack 4 = <u>close</u>, even, well-matched, hard-fought, evenly-balanced ≠ uneven 5 (*Informal*) = <u>miserly</u>, mean, stingy, grasping, parsimonious, niggardly, tightfisted ≠ generous 6 (*Informal*) = <u>drunk</u>, intoxicated, plastered (*slang*), under the influence (*informal*), tipsy, paralytic (*informal*), inebriated, out to it (*Austral. & N.Z. slang*) ≠ sober

tighten = <u>close</u>, narrow, strengthen, squeeze, harden, constrict ≠ slacken

till[1] = <u>cultivate</u>, dig, plough, work

till[2] = <u>cash register</u>, cash box

tilt VERB = <u>slant</u>, tip, slope, list, lean, heel, incline

• NOUN 1 = <u>slope</u>, angle, inclination, list, pitch, incline,

slant, camber 2 (*Medieval history*) = <u>joust</u>, fight, tournament, lists, combat, duel

timber 1 = <u>beams</u>, boards, planks 2 = <u>wood</u>, logs

time NOUN 1 = <u>period</u>, term, space, stretch, spell, span 2 = <u>occasion</u>, point, moment, stage, instance, point in time, juncture 3 = <u>age</u>, duration 4 = <u>tempo</u>, beat, rhythm, measure

• VERB = <u>schedule</u>, set, plan, book, programme, set up, fix, arrange

timeless = <u>eternal</u>, lasting, permanent, enduring, immortal, everlasting, ageless, changeless ≠ temporary

timely = <u>opportune</u>, appropriate, well-timed, suitable, convenient, judicious, propitious, seasonable ≠ untimely

timetable 1 = <u>schedule</u>, programme, agenda, list, diary, calendar 2 = <u>syllabus</u>, course, curriculum, programme, teaching programme

tinge NOUN 1 = <u>tint</u>, colour, shade 2 = <u>trace</u>, bit, drop, touch, suggestion, dash, sprinkling, smattering

• VERB = <u>tint</u>, colour

tinker = <u>meddle</u>, play, potter, fiddle (*informal*), dabble, mess about

tint NOUN 1 = <u>shade</u>, colour, tone, hue 2 = <u>dye</u>, wash, rinse, tinge, tincture

● VERB = <u>dye</u>, colour

tiny = <u>small</u>, little, minute, slight, miniature, negligible, microscopic, diminutive ≠ huge

tip¹ NOUN 1 = <u>end</u>, point, head, extremity, sharp end, nib, prong 2 = <u>peak</u>, top, summit, pinnacle, zenith, spire, acme, vertex

● VERB = <u>cap</u>, top, crown, surmount, finish

tip² VERB 1 = <u>reward</u>, remunerate, give a tip to, sweeten (*informal*) 2 = <u>predict</u>, back, recommend, think of

● NOUN 1 = <u>gratuity</u>, gift, reward, present, sweetener (*informal*) 2 = <u>hint</u>, suggestion, piece of advice, pointer

tip³ VERB 1 = <u>pour</u>, drop, empty, dump, drain, discharge, unload, jettison 2 (*Brit.*) = <u>dump</u>, empty, unload, pour out

● NOUN (*Brit.*) = <u>dump</u>, midden, rubbish heap, refuse heap

tire 1 = <u>exhaust</u>, drain, fatigue, weary, wear out ≠ refresh 2 = <u>flag</u>, become tired, fail 3 = <u>bore</u>, weary, exasperate, irritate, irk

tired 1 = <u>exhausted</u>, fatigued, weary, flagging, drained, sleepy, worn out, drowsy, tuckered out (*Austral. & N.Z. informal*) ≠ energetic 2 = <u>bored</u>, fed up, weary, sick, hoha (*N.Z.*)

tiny → together

≠ enthusiastic about 3 = <u>hackneyed</u>, stale, well-worn, old, corny (*slang*), threadbare, trite, clichéd ≠ original

tiring = <u>exhausting</u>, demanding, wearing, tough, exacting, strenuous, arduous, laborious

title 1 = <u>name</u>, designation, term, handle (*slang*), moniker *or* monicker (*slang*) 2 (*Sport*) = <u>championship</u>, trophy, bays, crown, honour 3 (*Law*) = <u>ownership</u>, right, claim, privilege, entitlement, tenure, prerogative, freehold

toast¹ 1 = <u>brown</u>, grill, crisp, roast 2 = <u>warm (up)</u>, heat (up), thaw, bring back to life

toast² NOUN 1 = <u>tribute</u>, compliment, salute, health, pledge, salutation 2 = <u>favourite</u>, celebrity, darling, talk, pet, focus of attention, hero *or* heroine, blue-eyed boy *or* girl (*Brit. informal*)

● VERB = <u>drink to</u>, honour, salute, drink (to) the health of

together ADVERB 1 = <u>collectively</u>, jointly, as one, with each other, in conjunction, side by side, mutually, in partnership ≠ separately 2 = <u>at the same time</u>, simultaneously, concurrently, contemporaneously, at one fell swoop

● ADJECTIVE (*Informal*) = self-possessed, composed, well-balanced, well-adjusted

toil VERB 1 = labour, work, struggle, strive, sweat (*informal*), slave, graft (*informal*), slog 2 = struggle, trek, slog, trudge, fight your way, footslog

● NOUN = hard work, effort, application, sweat, graft (*informal*), slog, exertion, drudgery ≠ idleness

toilet 1 = lavatory, bathroom, loo (*Brit. informal*), privy, cloakroom (*Brit.*), urinal, latrine, washroom, dunny (*Austral. & N.Z. old-fashioned informal*), bogger (*Austral. slang*), brasco (*Austral. slang*) 2 = bathroom, gents or ladies (*Brit. informal*), privy, latrine, water closet, ladies' room, W.C.

token NOUN = symbol, mark, sign, note, expression, indication, representation, badge

● ADJECTIVE = nominal, symbolic, minimal, hollow, superficial, perfunctory

tolerance 1 = broad-mindedness, indulgence, forbearance, permissiveness, open-mindedness ≠ intolerance 2 = endurance, resistance, stamina, fortitude, resilience, toughness, staying power, hardiness 3 = resistance, immunity, resilience, non-

susceptibility

tolerant = broad-minded, understanding, open-minded, catholic, long-suffering, permissive, forbearing, unprejudiced ≠ intolerant

tolerate 1 = endure, stand, take, stomach, put up with (*informal*) 2 = allow, accept, permit, take, brook, put up with (*informal*), condone ≠ forbid

toll[1] VERB = ring, sound, strike, chime, knell, clang, peal

● NOUN = ringing, chime, knell, clang, peal

toll[2] 1 = charge, tax, fee, duty, payment, levy, tariff 2 = damage, cost, loss, roll, penalty, sum, number, roster 3 = adverse effects, price, cost, suffering, damage, penalty, harm

tomb = grave, vault, crypt, mausoleum, sarcophagus, catacomb, sepulchre

tone NOUN 1 = pitch, inflection, intonation, timbre, modulation 2 = volume, timbre 3 = character, style, feel, air, spirit, attitude, manner, mood 4 = colour, shade, tint, tinge, hue

● VERB = harmonize, match, blend, suit, go well with

● PHRASES **tone something down** = moderate, temper, soften, restrain, subdue, play down = reduce, moderate

tongue = language, speech, dialect, parlance

tonic = stimulant, boost, pick-me-up (informal), fillip, shot in the arm (informal), restorative

too 1 = also, as well, further, in addition, moreover, besides, likewise, to boot 2 = excessively, very, extremely, overly, unduly, unreasonably, inordinately, immoderately

tool 1 = implement, device, appliance, machine, instrument, gadget, utensil, contraption 2 = puppet, creature, pawn, stooge (slang), minion, lackey, flunkey, hireling

top NOUN 1 = peak, summit, head, crown, height, ridge, brow, crest ≠ bottom 2 = lid, cover, cap, plug, stopper, bung 3 = first place, head, peak, lead, high point
● ADJECTIVE 1 = highest, loftiest, furthest up, uppermost 2 = leading, best, first, highest, head, finest, elite, foremost ≠ lowest 3 = chief, most important, principal, most powerful, highest, head, leading, main 4 = prime, best, select, first-class, quality, choice, excellent, premier
● VERB 1 = lead, head, be at the top of, be first in 2 = cover, garnish, finish, crown, cap 3 = surpass, better, beat, improve

on, cap, exceed, eclipse, excel ≠ not be as good as

topic = subject, point, question, issue, matter, theme, subject matter

topical = current, popular, contemporary, up-to-date, up-to-the-minute, newsworthy

topple 1 = fall over, fall, collapse, tumble, overturn, totter, keel over, overbalance 2 = knock over 3 = overthrow, overturn, bring down, oust, unseat, bring low

torment NOUN = suffering, distress, misery, pain, hell, torture, agony, anguish ≠ bliss
● VERB 1 = torture, distress, rack, crucify ≠ comfort 2 = tease, annoy, bother, irritate, harass, hassle (informal), pester, vex

torn 1 = cut, split, rent, ripped, ragged, slit, lacerated 2 = undecided, uncertain, unsure, wavering, vacillating, in two minds (informal), irresolute

tornado = whirlwind, storm, hurricane, gale, cyclone, typhoon, tempest, squall

torture VERB 1 = torment, abuse, persecute, afflict, scourge, molest, crucify, mistreat ≠ comfort 2 = distress, torment, worry, trouble, rack, afflict, harrow, inflict anguish on
● NOUN 1 = ill-treatment, abuse, torment, persecution,

maltreatment, harsh treatment
2 = <u>agony</u>, suffering, anguish, distress, torment, heartbreak ≠ bliss

toss VERB **1** = <u>throw</u>, pitch, hurl, fling, launch, cast, flip, sling **2** = <u>shake</u> **3** = <u>thrash (about)</u>, twitch, wriggle, squirm, writhe
● NOUN = <u>throw</u>, pitch, lob (*informal*)

tot NOUN **1** = <u>infant</u>, child, baby, toddler, mite, littlie (*Austral. informal*), ankle-biter (*Austral. slang*), tacker (*Austral. slang*) **2** = <u>measure</u>, shot (*informal*), finger, nip, slug, dram, snifter (*informal*)
● PHRASES **tot something up** = <u>add up</u>, calculate, total, reckon, compute, tally, enumerate, count up

total NOUN = <u>sum</u>, entirety, grand total, whole, aggregate, totality, full amount, sum total ≠ part
● ADJECTIVE = <u>complete</u>, absolute, utter, whole, entire, undivided, overarching, thoroughgoing ≠ partial
● VERB **1** = <u>amount to</u>, make, come to, reach, equal, run to, number, add up to **2** = <u>add up</u>, work out, compute, reckon, tot up ≠ subtract

totally = <u>completely</u>, entirely, absolutely, fully, comprehensively, thoroughly, wholly, utterly ≠ partly

touch VERB **1** = <u>feel</u>, handle, finger, stroke, brush, make contact with, caress, fondle **2** = <u>come into contact</u>, meet, contact, border, graze, adjoin, be in contact, abut **3** = <u>tap</u> **4** = <u>affect</u>, influence, inspire, impress **5** = <u>consume</u>, take, drink, eat, partake of **6** = <u>move</u>, stir, disturb **7** = <u>match</u>, rival, equal, compare with, parallel, hold a candle to (*informal*)
● NOUN **1** = <u>contact</u>, push, stroke, brush, press, tap, poke, nudge **2** = <u>feeling</u>, handling, physical contact **3** = <u>bit</u>, spot, trace, drop, dash, small amount, jot, smattering **4** = <u>style</u>, method, technique, way, manner, trademark
● PHRASES **touch and go** = <u>risky</u>, close, near, critical, precarious, nerve-racking ◆ **touch on** or **upon something** = <u>refer to</u>, cover, raise, deal with, mention, bring in, speak of, hint at

touching = <u>moving</u>, affecting, sad, stirring, critical, poignant, emotive, pitiable

tough ADJECTIVE **1** = <u>strong</u> ≠ weak **2** = <u>hardy</u>, strong, seasoned, strapping, vigorous, sturdy, stout **3** = <u>violent</u>, rough, ruthless, pugnacious, hard-bitten **4** = <u>strict</u>, severe, stern, hard, firm, resolute, merciless, unbending ≠ lenient **5** = <u>hard</u>, difficult, troublesome, uphill, strenuous, arduous, laborious **6** = <u>resilient</u>, hard, resistant, durable, strong, solid, rugged, sturdy ≠ fragile

• NOUN = <u>ruffian</u>, bully, thug, hooligan, bruiser (*informal*), roughneck (*slang*), tsotsi (*S. African*)

tour NOUN = <u>journey</u>, expedition, excursion, trip, outing, jaunt, junket

• VERB **1** = <u>travel round</u>, travel through, journey round, trek round, go on a trip through **2** = <u>visit</u>, explore, go round, inspect, walk round, drive round, sightsee

tourist = <u>traveller</u>, voyager, tripper, globetrotter, holiday-maker, sightseer, excursionist

tournament = <u>competition</u>, meeting, event, series, contest

tow = <u>drag</u>, draw, pull, haul, tug, yank, lug

towards 1 = <u>in the direction of</u>, to, for, on the way to, en route for **2** = <u>regarding</u>, about, concerning, respecting, in relation to, with regard to, with respect to, apropos

tower = <u>column</u>, pillar, turret, belfry, steeple, obelisk

toxic = <u>poisonous</u>, deadly, lethal, harmful, pernicious, noxious, septic, pestilential ≠ harmless

toy NOUN = <u>plaything</u>, game, doll

• PHRASES **toy with something** = <u>play with</u>, consider, trifle with, dally with, entertain the possibility of, amuse yourself with, think idly of

trace VERB **1** = <u>search for</u>, track, unearth, hunt down **2** = <u>find</u>, track (down), discover, detect, unearth, hunt down, ferret out, locate **3** = <u>outline</u>, sketch, draw **4** = <u>copy</u>, map, draft, outline, sketch, reproduce, draw over

• NOUN **1** = <u>bit</u>, drop, touch, shadow, suggestion, hint, suspicion, tinge **2** = <u>remnant</u>, sign, record, mark, evidence, indication, vestige **3** = <u>track</u>, trail, footstep, path, footprint, spoor, footmark

track NOUN **1** = <u>path</u>, way, road, route, trail, pathway, footpath **2** = <u>course</u>, line, path, orbit, trajectory **3** = <u>line</u>, tramline

• VERB = <u>follow</u>, pursue, chase, trace, tail (*informal*), shadow, trail, stalk

• PHRASES **track something or someone down** = <u>find</u>, discover, trace, unearth, dig up, hunt down, sniff out, run to earth or ground

tract[1] = <u>area</u>, region, district, stretch, territory, extent, plot, expanse

tract[2] = <u>treatise</u>, essay, booklet, pamphlet, dissertation, monograph, homily

trade NOUN 1 = <u>commerce</u>, business, transactions, dealing, exchange, traffic, truck, barter 2 = <u>job</u>, employment, business, craft, profession, occupation, line of work, métier

● VERB 1 = <u>deal</u>, do business, traffic, truck, bargain, peddle, transact, cut a deal 2 = <u>exchange</u>, switch, swap, barter 3 = <u>operate</u>, run, deal, do business

trader = <u>dealer</u>, supplier, merchant, seller, purveyor

tradition 1 = <u>customs</u>, institution, ritual, folklore, lore, tikanga (*N.Z.*) 2 = <u>established practice</u>, custom, convention, habit, ritual

traditional 1 = <u>old-fashioned</u>, old, established, conventional, usual, accustomed, customary, time-honoured ≠ revolutionary 2 = <u>folk</u>, old

traffic NOUN 1 = <u>transport</u>, vehicles, transportation, freight 2 = <u>trade</u>, commerce, business, exchange, truck, dealings, peddling

● VERB = <u>trade</u>, deal, exchange, bargain, do business, peddle, cut a deal, have dealings

tragedy = <u>disaster</u>, catastrophe, misfortune, adversity, calamity ≠ fortune

tragic 1 = <u>distressing</u>, sad, appalling, deadly, unfortunate, disastrous, dreadful, dire ≠ fortunate 2 = <u>sad</u>, miserable, pathetic, mournful ≠ happy

trail NOUN 1 = <u>path</u>, track, route, way, course, road, pathway, footpath 2 = <u>tracks</u>, path, marks, wake, trace, scent, footprints, spoor 3 = <u>wake</u>, stream, tail

● VERB 1 = <u>follow</u>, track, chase, pursue, dog, hunt, shadow, trace 2 = <u>drag</u>, draw, pull, sweep, haul, tow, dangle, droop 3 = <u>lag</u>, follow, drift, wander, linger, trudge, plod, meander

train VERB 1 = <u>instruct</u>, school, prepare, coach, teach, guide, educate, drill 2 = <u>exercise</u>, prepare, work out, practise, do exercise, get into shape 3 = <u>aim</u>, point, level, position, direct, focus, sight, zero in

● NOUN = <u>sequence</u>, series, chain, string, set, cycle, trail, succession

trainer = <u>coach</u>, manager, guide, adviser, tutor, instructor, counsellor, guru

trait = <u>characteristic</u>, feature, quality, attribute, quirk, peculiarity, mannerism, idiosyncrasy

traitor = <u>betrayer</u>, deserter, turncoat, renegade, defector, Judas, quisling, apostate, fizgig (*Austral. slang*) ≠ loyalist

tramp VERB = <u>trudge</u>, stump, toil, plod, traipse (*informal*)

trample → transparent

2 = <u>hike</u>, walk, trek, roam, march, ramble, slog, rove
● NOUN 1 = <u>vagrant</u>, derelict, drifter, down-and-out, derro (*Austral. slang*) 2 = <u>tread</u>, stamp, footstep, footfall 3 = <u>hike</u>, march, trek, ramble, slog

trample *often with* **on** = <u>stamp</u>, crush, squash, tread, flatten, run over, walk over

trance = <u>daze</u>, dream, abstraction, rapture, reverie, stupor, unconsciousness

transaction = <u>deal</u>, negotiation, business, enterprise, bargain, undertaking

transcend = <u>surpass</u>, exceed, go beyond, rise above, eclipse, excel, outstrip, outdo

transcript = <u>copy</u>, record, manuscript, reproduction, duplicate, transcription

transfer VERB = <u>move</u>, transport, shift, relocate, transpose, change
● NOUN = <u>transference</u>, move, handover, change, shift, transmission, translation, relocation

transform 1 = <u>change</u>, convert, alter, transmute 2 = <u>make over</u>, remodel, revolutionize

transformation 1 = <u>change</u>, conversion, alteration, metamorphosis, transmutation 2 = <u>revolution</u>, sea change

transit = <u>movement</u>, transfer,

transport, passage, crossing, transportation, carriage, conveyance

transition = <u>change</u>, passing, development, shift, conversion, alteration, progression, metamorphosis

transitional 1 = <u>changing</u>, passing, fluid, intermediate, unsettled, developmental 2 = <u>temporary</u>, working, acting, short-term, interim, fill-in, caretaker, provisional

translate = <u>render</u>, put, change, convert, interpret, decode, construe, paraphrase

translation = <u>interpretation</u>, version, rendering, rendition, decoding, paraphrase

transmission 1 = <u>transfer</u>, spread, spreading, passing on, circulation, dispatch, relaying, mediation 2 = <u>broadcasting</u>, showing, putting out, relaying, sending 3 = <u>programme</u>, broadcast, show, production, telecast

transmit 1 = <u>broadcast</u>, televise, relay, air, radio, send out, disseminate, beam out 2 = <u>pass on</u>, carry, spread, send, bear, transfer, hand on, convey

transparent 1 = <u>clear</u>, sheer, see-through, lucid, translucent, crystalline, limpid, diaphanous ≠ opaque 2 = <u>obvious</u>, plain, patent, evident, explicit, manifest, recognizable, unambiguous ≠ uncertain

transplant 1 = <u>implant</u>, transfer, graft 2 = <u>transfer</u>, take, bring, carry, remove, transport, shift, convey

transport NOUN 1 = <u>vehicle</u>, transportation, conveyance 2 = <u>transference</u>, carrying, delivery, distribution, transportation, shipment, freight, haulage 3 *often plural* = <u>ecstasy</u>, delight, heaven, bliss, euphoria, rapture, enchantment, ravishment ≠ despondency
● VERB 1 = <u>convey</u>, take, move, bring, send, carry, bear, transfer 2 = <u>enrapture</u>, move, delight, entrance, enchant, captivate, ravish 3 (*History*) = <u>exile</u>, banish, deport

trap NOUN 1 = <u>snare</u>, net, gin, pitfall, noose 2 = <u>ambush</u>, set-up (*informal*) 3 = <u>trick</u>, set-up (*informal*), deception, ploy, ruse, trickery, subterfuge, stratagem
● VERB 1 = <u>catch</u>, snare, ensnare, entrap, take, corner, bag, lay hold of 2 = <u>trick</u>, fool, cheat, lure, seduce, deceive, dupe, beguile 3 = <u>capture</u>, catch, arrest, seize, take, secure, collar (*informal*), apprehend

trash 1 = <u>nonsense</u>, rubbish, rot, drivel, twaddle, tripe (*informal*), moonshine, hogwash, kak (*S.* *African taboo slang*), bizzo (*Austral. slang*), bull's wool (*Austral. & N.Z. slang*) ≠ sense 2 (*Chiefly U.S. & Canad.*) = <u>litter</u>, refuse, waste, rubbish, junk (*informal*), garbage, dross

trauma 1 = <u>shock</u>, suffering, pain, torture, ordeal, anguish 2 = <u>injury</u>, damage, hurt, wound, agony

traumatic = <u>shocking</u>, upsetting, alarming, awful, disturbing, devastating, painful, distressing ≠ calming

travel VERB = <u>go</u>, journey, move, tour, progress, wander, trek, voyage
● NOUN *usually plural* = <u>journey</u>, wandering, expedition, globetrotting, tour, trip, voyage, excursion

traveller or (*U.S.*) **traveler** = <u>voyager</u>, tourist, explorer, globetrotter, holiday-maker, wayfarer

tread VERB = <u>step</u>, walk, march, pace, stamp, stride, hike
● NOUN = <u>step</u>, walk, pace, stride, footstep, gait, footfall

treason = <u>disloyalty</u>, mutiny, treachery, duplicity, sedition, perfidy, lese-majesty, traitorousness ≠ loyalty

treasure 1 = <u>riches</u>, money, gold, fortune, wealth, valuables, jewels, cash

2 (*Informal*) = **angel**, darling, jewel, gem, paragon, nonpareil
● VERB = **prize**, value, esteem, adore, cherish, revere, hold dear, love

treasury = **storehouse**, bank, store, vault, hoard, cache, repository

treat VERB 1 = **behave towards**, deal with, handle, act towards, use, consider, serve, manage 2 = **take care of**, minister to, attend to, give medical treatment to, doctor (*informal*), nurse, care for, prescribe medicine for 3 = **provide**, stand (*informal*), entertain, lay on, regale
● NOUN 1 = **entertainment**, party, surprise, gift, celebration, feast, outing, excursion 2 = **pleasure**, delight, joy, thrill, satisfaction, enjoyment, source of pleasure, fun

treatment 1 = **care**, medical care, nursing, medicine, surgery, therapy, healing, medication 2 = **cure**, remedy, medication, medicine 3 *often with of* = **handling**, dealings with, behaviour towards, conduct towards, management, manipulation, action towards

treaty = **agreement**, pact, contract, alliance, convention, compact, covenant, entente

trek VERB 1 = **journey**, march,

hike, tramp, rove, go walkabout (*Austral.*) 2 = **trudge**, traipse (*informal*), footslog, slog
● NOUN 1 = **slog**, tramp 2 = **journey**, hike, expedition, safari, march, odyssey

tremble VERB 1 = **shake**, shiver, quake, shudder, quiver, totter 2 = **vibrate**, shake, quake, wobble
● NOUN = **shake**, shiver, quake, shudder, wobble, tremor, quiver, vibration

tremendous 1 = **huge**, great, enormous, terrific, formidable, immense, gigantic, colossal ≠ tiny 2 = **excellent**, great, wonderful, brilliant, amazing, extraordinary, fantastic (*informal*), marvellous, booshit (*Austral. slang*), exo (*Austral. slang*), sik (*Austral. slang*) ≠ terrible

trench = **ditch**, channel, drain, gutter, trough, furrow, excavation

trend 1 = **tendency**, swing, drift, inclination, current, direction, flow, leaning 2 = **fashion**, craze, fad (*informal*), mode, thing, style, rage, vogue

trendy (*Brit. informal*) = **fashionable**, with it (*informal*), stylish, in fashion, in vogue, modish, voguish

trial 1 (*Law*) = **hearing**, case, court case, inquiry, tribunal, lawsuit, appeal, litigation 2 = **test**, experiment, evaluation, audition, dry run (informal), assessment, probation, appraisal **3** = <u>hardship</u>, suffering, trouble, distress, ordeal, adversity, affliction, tribulation

tribe = <u>race</u>, people, family, clan, hapu (N.Z.), iwi (N.Z.)

tribunal = <u>hearing</u>, court, trial

tribute = <u>accolade</u>, testimonial, eulogy, recognition, compliment, commendation, panegyric ≠ criticism

trick NOUN **1** = <u>joke</u>, stunt, spoof (informal), prank, practical joke, antic, jape, leg-pull (Brit. informal) **2** = <u>deception</u>, trap, fraud, manoeuvre, ploy, hoax, swindle, ruse **3** = <u>sleight of hand</u>, stunt, legerdemain **4** = <u>secret</u>, skill, knack, hang (informal), technique, know-how (informal) **5** = <u>mannerism</u>, habit, characteristic, trait, quirk, peculiarity, foible, idiosyncrasy
● VERB = <u>deceive</u>, trap, take someone in (informal), fool, cheat, con (informal), kid (informal), mislead

trickle VERB = <u>dribble</u>, run, drop, stream, drip, ooze, seep, exude
● NOUN = <u>dribble</u>, drip, seepage, thin stream

tricky 1 = <u>difficult</u>, sensitive, complicated, delicate, risky, hairy (informal), problematic, thorny ≠ simple **2** = <u>crafty</u>, scheming, cunning, slippery, sly, devious,

wily, artful ≠ open

trifle = <u>knick-knack</u>, toy, plaything, bauble, bagatelle

trifling = <u>insignificant</u>, trivial, worthless, negligible, unimportant, paltry, measly ≠ significant

trigger = <u>bring about</u>, start, cause, produce, generate, prompt, provoke, set off ≠ prevent

trim ADJECTIVE **1** = <u>neat</u>, smart, tidy, spruce, dapper, natty (informal), well-groomed, shipshape ≠ untidy **2** = <u>slender</u>, fit, slim, sleek, streamlined, shapely, svelte, willowy
● VERB **1** = <u>cut</u>, crop, clip, shave, tidy, prune, pare, even up **2** = <u>decorate</u>, dress, array, adorn, ornament, embellish, deck out, beautify
● NOUN **1** = <u>decoration</u>, edging, border, piping, trimming, frill, embellishment, adornment **2** = <u>condition</u>, health, shape (informal), fitness, wellness, fettle **3** = <u>cut</u>, crop, clipping, shave, pruning, shearing, tidying up

trimming NOUN = <u>decoration</u>, edging, border, piping, frill, embellishment, adornment, ornamentation
● PLURAL NOUN = <u>extras</u>, accessories, ornaments, frills, trappings,

paraphernalia

trinity = <u>threesome</u>, trio, triad, triumvirate

trio = <u>threesome</u>, trinity, trilogy, triad, triumvirate

trip NOUN **1** = <u>journey</u>, outing, excursion, day out, run, drive, tour, spin (*informal*) **2** = <u>stumble</u>, fall, slip, misstep

● VERB **1** = <u>stumble</u>, fall, fall over, slip, tumble, topple, stagger, misstep **2** = <u>skip</u>, dance, hop, gambol

● PHRASES **trip someone up** = <u>catch out</u>, trap, wrongfoot

triple ADJECTIVE **1** = <u>treble</u>, three times **2** = <u>three-way</u>, threefold, tripartite

● VERB = <u>treble</u>, increase threefold

triumph NOUN **1** = <u>success</u>, victory, accomplishment, achievement, coup, feat, conquest, attainment ≠ failure **2** = <u>joy</u>, pride, happiness, rejoicing, elation, jubilation, exultation

● VERB **1** *often with* **over** = <u>succeed</u>, win, overcome, prevail, prosper, vanquish ≠ fail **2** = <u>rejoice</u>, celebrate, glory, revel, gloat, exult, crow

triumphant 1 = <u>victorious</u>, winning, successful, conquering ≠ defeated **2** = <u>celebratory</u>, jubilant, proud, elated, exultant, cock-a-hoop

trinity → trouble

trivial = <u>unimportant</u>, small, minor, petty, meaningless, worthless, trifling, insignificant ≠ important

troop NOUN = <u>group</u>, company, team, body, unit, band, crowd, squad

● PLURAL NOUN = <u>soldiers</u>, men, armed forces, servicemen, army, soldiery

● VERB = <u>flock</u>, march, stream, swarm, throng, traipse (*informal*)

trophy 1 = <u>prize</u>, cup, award, laurels **2** = <u>souvenir</u>, spoils, relic, memento, booty, keepsake

tropical = <u>hot</u>, stifling, steamy, torrid, sultry, sweltering ≠ cold

trot VERB = <u>run</u>, jog, scamper, lope, canter

● NOUN = <u>run</u>, jog, lope, canter

trouble NOUN **1** = <u>bother</u>, problems, concern, worry, stress, difficulty (*informal*), anxiety, distress **2** *usually plural* = <u>distress</u>, problem, worry, pain, anxiety, grief, torment, sorrow ≠ pleasure **3** = <u>ailment</u>, disease, failure, complaint, illness, disorder, defect, malfunction **4** = <u>disorder</u>, fighting, conflict, bother, unrest, disturbance, to-do (*informal*), furore, biffo (*Austral. slang*) ≠ peace **5** = <u>effort</u>, work, thought, care, labour, pains, hassle (*informal*), inconvenience ≠ convenience

● VERB 1 = <u>bother</u>, worry, upset, disturb, distress, plague, pain, sadden ≠ <u>please</u> 2 = <u>afflict</u>, hurt, bother, cause discomfort to, pain, grieve 3 = <u>inconvenience</u>, disturb, burden, put out, impose upon, incommode ≠ <u>relieve</u> 4 = <u>take pains</u>, take the time, make an effort, exert yourself ≠ avoid

troublesome 1 = <u>bothersome</u>, trying, taxing, demanding, difficult, worrying, annoying, tricky ≠ <u>simple</u> 2 = <u>disorderly</u>, violent, turbulent, rebellious, unruly, rowdy, undisciplined, uncooperative ≠ well-behaved

trough = <u>manger</u>, water trough

truce = <u>ceasefire</u>, peace, moratorium, respite, lull, cessation, let-up (informal), armistice

true 1 = <u>correct</u>, right, accurate, precise, factual, truthful, veracious ≠ <u>false</u> 2 = <u>actual</u>, real, genuine, proper, authentic, dinkum (Austral. & N.Z. informal) 3 = <u>faithful</u>, loyal, devoted, dedicated, steady, reliable, staunch, trustworthy ≠ unfaithful 4 = <u>exact</u>, perfect, accurate, precise, spot-on (Brit. informal), on target, unerring ≠ inaccurate

truly 1 = <u>genuinely</u>, correctly, truthfully, rightly, precisely, exactly, legitimately, authentically ≠ falsely 2 = <u>really</u>, very, greatly,

indeed, extremely 3 = <u>faithfully</u>, steadily, sincerely, staunchly, dutifully, loyally, devotedly

trumpet NOUN = <u>horn</u>, clarion, bugle

● VERB = <u>proclaim</u>, advertise, tout (informal), announce, broadcast, shout from the rooftops ≠ keep secret

trunk 1 = <u>stem</u>, stalk, bole 2 = <u>chest</u>, case, box, crate, coffer, casket 3 = <u>body</u>, torso 4 = <u>snout</u>, nose, proboscis

trust VERB 1 = <u>believe in</u>, have faith in, depend on, count on, bank on, rely upon ≠ distrust 2 = <u>entrust</u>, commit, assign, confide, consign, put into the hands of, allow to look after, hand over 3 = <u>expect</u>, hope, suppose, assume, presume, surmise

● NOUN = <u>confidence</u>, credit, belief, faith, expectation, conviction, assurance, certainty ≠ distrust

trusting or **trustful** = <u>unsuspecting</u>, naive, gullible, unwary, credulous, unsuspicious ≠ suspicious

truth 1 = <u>reality</u>, fact(s), real life 2 = <u>truthfulness</u>, fact, accuracy, precision, validity, legitimacy, veracity, genuineness ≠ inaccuracy

try VERB 1 = <u>attempt</u>, seek, aim, strive, struggle, endeavour, have a

go, make an effort
2 = <u>experiment with</u>, try out, put to the test, test, taste, examine, investigate, sample
● NOUN = <u>attempt</u>, go (*informal*), shot (*informal*), effort, crack (*informal*), stab (*informal*), bash (*informal*), whack (*informal*)

trying = <u>annoying</u>, hard, taxing, difficult, tough, stressful, exasperating, tiresome
≠ straightforward

tuck VERB = <u>push</u>, stick, stuff, slip, ease, insert, pop (*informal*)
● NOUN **1** (*Brit. informal*) = <u>food</u>, grub (*slang*), kai (*N.Z. informal*), nosh (*slang*) **2** = <u>fold</u>, gather, pleat, pinch

tug VERB **1** = <u>pull</u>, pluck, jerk, yank, wrench **2** = <u>drag</u>, pull, haul, tow, lug, heave, draw
● NOUN = <u>pull</u>, jerk, yank

tuition = <u>training</u>, schooling, education, teaching, lessons, instruction, tutoring, tutelage

tumble VERB = <u>fall</u>, drop, topple, plummet, stumble, flop
● NOUN = <u>fall</u>, drop, trip, plunge, spill, stumble

tumour = <u>growth</u>, cancer, swelling, lump, carcinoma (*Pathology*), sarcoma (*Medical*)

tune NOUN **1** = <u>melody</u>, air, song, theme, strain(s), jingle, ditty **2** = <u>harmony</u>, pitch, euphony
● VERB **1** = <u>tune up</u>, adjust

2 = <u>regulate</u>, adapt, modulate, harmonize, attune, pitch

tunnel NOUN = <u>passage</u>, underpass, passageway, subway, channel, hole, shaft
● VERB = <u>dig</u>, burrow, mine, bore, drill, excavate

turbulent = <u>stormy</u>, rough, raging, tempestuous, furious, foaming, agitated, tumultuous
≠ calm

turf NOUN **1** = <u>grass</u>, sward **2** = <u>sod</u>
● PHRASES **the turf** = <u>horse-racing</u>, the flat, racing

turmoil = <u>confusion</u>, disorder, chaos, upheaval, disarray, uproar, agitation, commotion ≠ peace

turn VERB **1** = <u>change course</u>, swing round, wheel round, veer, move, switch, shift, swerve **2** = <u>rotate</u>, spin, go round (and round), revolve, roll, circle, twist, spiral **3** = <u>change</u>, transform, shape, convert, alter, mould, remodel, mutate **4** = <u>shape</u>, form, fashion, cast, frame, mould, make **5** = <u>go bad</u>, go off (*Brit. informal*), curdle **6** = <u>make rancid</u>, spoil, sour, taint
● NOUN **1** = <u>rotation</u>, cycle, circle, revolution, spin, twist, whirl, swivel **2** = <u>change of direction</u>, shift, departure, deviation **3** = <u>direction</u>, course, tack, tendency, drift **4** = <u>opportunity</u>, go, time, try, chance, crack

(*informal*), stint **5** = <u>deed</u>, service, act, action, favour, gesture

• PHRASES **turn on someone** = <u>attack</u>, assault, fall on, round on, lash out at, assail, lay into (*informal*), let fly at ◆ **turn someone on** (*Informal*) = <u>arouse</u>, attract, excite, thrill, stimulate, please, titillate ◆ **turn something down 1** = <u>refuse</u>, decline, reject, spurn, rebuff, repudiate **2** = <u>lower</u>, soften, mute, lessen, muffle, quieten ◆ **turn something in** = <u>hand in</u>, return, deliver, give up, hand over, submit, surrender, tender ◆ **turn something off** = <u>switch off</u>, turn out, put out, stop, cut out, shut down, unplug, flick off ◆ **turn something on** = <u>switch on</u>, activate, start, start up, ignite, kick-start ◆ **turn something up 1** = <u>find</u>, reveal, discover, expose, disclose, unearth, dig up **2** = <u>increase</u>, raise, boost, enhance, intensify, amplify ◆ **turn up 1** = <u>arrive</u>, come, appear, show up (*informal*), attend, put in an appearance, show your face **2** = <u>come to light</u>, show up, pop up, materialize

turning = <u>turn-off</u>, turn, bend, curve, junction, crossroads, side road, exit

turning point = <u>crossroads</u>, change, crisis, crux, moment of truth

turnout = <u>attendance</u>, crowd, audience, gate, assembly, congregation, number, throng

turnover 1 = <u>output</u>, business, productivity **2** = <u>movement</u>, coming and going, change

turtle ▸ **reptiles**

tutor NOUN = <u>teacher</u>, coach, instructor, educator, guide, guardian, lecturer, guru
• VERB = <u>teach</u>, educate, school, train, coach, guide, drill, instruct

twig = <u>branch</u>, stick, sprig, shoot, spray

twilight 1 = <u>dusk</u>, evening, sunset, early evening, nightfall, sundown, gloaming (*Scot. poetic*), close of day, evo (*Austral. slang*) ≠ dawn **2** = <u>half-light</u>, gloom, dimness, semi-darkness

twin NOUN = <u>double</u>, counterpart, mate, match, fellow, clone, duplicate, lookalike
• VERB = <u>pair</u>, match, join, couple, link, yoke

twinkle VERB = <u>sparkle</u>, flash, shine, glitter, gleam, blink, flicker, shimmer
• NOUN = <u>sparkle</u>, flash, spark, gleam, flicker, shimmer, glimmer

twist VERB **1** = <u>coil</u>, curl, wind, wrap, screw, twirl **2** = <u>intertwine</u> **3** = <u>distort</u>, screw up, contort, mangle, mangulate (*Austral. slang*) ≠ straighten
• NOUN **1** = <u>surprise</u>, change, turn,

development, revelation
2 = <u>development</u>, emphasis, variation, slant **3** = <u>wind</u>, turn, spin, swivel, twirl **4** = <u>curve</u>, turn, bend, loop, arc, kink, zigzag, dog-leg

twitch VERB **1** = <u>jerk</u>, flutter, jump, squirm **2** = <u>pull (at)</u>, tug (at), pluck (at), yank (at)
● NOUN = <u>jerk</u>, tic, spasm, jump, flutter

tycoon = <u>magnate</u>, capitalist, baron, industrialist, financier, fat cat (*slang, chiefly U.S.*), mogul, plutocrat

type = <u>kind</u>, sort, class, variety, group, order, style, species

typical 1 = <u>archetypal</u>, standard, model, normal, stock, representative, usual, regular ≠ unusual **2** = <u>characteristic</u> **3** = <u>average</u>, normal, usual, routine, regular, orthodox, predictable, run-of-the-mill

tyranny = <u>oppression</u>, cruelty, dictatorship, authoritarianism, despotism, autocracy, absolutism, high-handedness ≠ liberality

U

ubiquitous = <u>ever-present</u>, pervasive, omnipresent, everywhere, universal

ugly 1 = <u>unattractive</u>, homely (*chiefly U.S.*), plain, unsightly, unlovely, unprepossessing, ill-favoured ≠ beautiful
2 = <u>unpleasant</u>, shocking, terrible, nasty, distasteful, horrid, objectionable, disagreeable ≠ pleasant **3** = <u>bad-tempered</u>, dangerous, menacing, sinister, baleful

ulcer = <u>sore</u>, abscess, peptic ulcer, gumboil

ultimate 1 = <u>final</u>, last, end **2** = <u>supreme</u>, highest, greatest, paramount, superlative **3** = <u>worst</u>, greatest, utmost, extreme **4** = <u>best</u>, greatest, supreme, optimum, quintessential

ultimately 1 = <u>finally</u>, eventually, in the end, after all, at last, sooner or later, in due time **2** = <u>fundamentally</u>, essentially, basically, primarily, at heart, deep down

umpire NOUN = <u>referee</u>, judge, arbiter, arbitrator
● VERB = <u>referee</u>, judge, adjudicate, arbitrate

unable = <u>incapable</u>, powerless, unfit, impotent, unqualified, ineffectual ≠ able

unanimous 1 = <u>agreed</u>, united, in agreement, harmonious, like-minded, of the same mind ≠ divided **2** = <u>united</u>, common, concerted, solid, consistent, harmonious, undivided, congruent ≠ split

unarmed = defenceless, helpless, unprotected ≠ armed

unaware = ignorant, unconscious, oblivious, uninformed, unknowing, not in the loop (*informal*) ≠ aware

unbearable = intolerable, insufferable, too much (*informal*), unacceptable ≠ tolerable

unborn = expected, awaited, embryonic

uncertain = unsure, undecided, vague, unclear, dubious, hazy, irresolute ≠ sure

uncertainty
1 = unpredictability, precariousness, ambiguity, unreliability, fickleness, chanciness, changeableness ≠ predictability 2 = doubt, confusion ≠ confidence
3 = hesitancy, indecision

uncomfortable 1 = uneasy, troubled, disturbed, embarrassed, awkward, discomfited ≠ comfortable 2 = painful, awkward, rough

uncommon 1 = rare, unusual, odd, novel, strange, peculiar, scarce, queer ≠ common
2 = extraordinary, remarkable, special, outstanding, distinctive, exceptional, notable ≠ ordinary

uncompromising = inflexible, strict, rigid, firm, tough, inexorable, intransigent, unbending

unconditional = absolute, full, complete, total, positive, entire, outright, unlimited ≠ qualified

unconscious 1 = senseless, knocked out, out cold (*informal*), out, stunned, dazed, in a coma, stupefied ≠ awake 2 = unaware, ignorant, oblivious, unknowing ≠ aware 3 = unintentional, unwitting, inadvertent, accidental ≠ intentional

uncover 1 = reveal, expose, disclose, divulge, make known ≠ conceal 2 = open, unveil, unwrap, show, strip, expose, bare, lay bare

under PREPOSITION 1 = below, beneath, underneath ≠ over
2 = subordinate to, subject to, governed by, secondary to
● ADVERB = below, down, beneath ≠ up

undercover = secret, covert, private, hidden, concealed ≠ open

underdog = weaker party, little fellow (*informal*), outsider

underestimate
1 = undervalue, understate, diminish, play down, minimize, downgrade, miscalculate, trivialize ≠ overestimate
2 = underrate, undervalue, belittle ≠ overrate

assume, fancy

understandable = reasonable, natural, justified, expected, inevitable, legitimate, predictable, accountable

understanding NOUN

1 = perception, knowledge, grasp, sense, know-how (*informal*), judgment, awareness, appreciation ≠ ignorance

2 = agreement, deal, promise, arrangement, accord, contract, bond, pledge ≠ disagreement

3 = belief, view, opinion, impression, interpretation, feeling, idea, notion

● ADJECTIVE = sympathetic, kind, compassionate, considerate, patient, sensitive, tolerant ≠ unsympathetic

undertake = agree, promise, contract, guarantee, engage, pledge

undertaking 1 = task, business, operation, project, attempt, effort, affair, venture 2 = promise, commitment, pledge, word, vow, assurance

underwear = underclothes, lingerie, undies (*informal*), undergarments, underthings, brookies (*S. African informal*), underdaks (*Austral. slang*)

underworld 1 = criminals, gangsters, organized crime, gangland (*informal*) 2 = nether

---

> *Word Power*
>
> **underestimate** –
> *Underestimate* is sometimes wrongly used where *overestimate* is meant: *the importance of his work cannot be overestimated* (not *cannot be underestimated*).

undergo = experience, go through, stand, suffer, bear, sustain, endure

underground ADJECTIVE

1 = subterranean, basement, lower-level, sunken, covered, buried, subterrestrial 2 = secret, covert, hidden, guerrilla, revolutionary, confidential, dissident, closet

● PHRASES **the underground**

1 = the tube (*Brit.*), the subway, the metro 2 = the Resistance, partisans, freedom fighters

underline 1 = emphasize, stress, highlight, accentuate ≠ minimize

2 = underscore, mark

underlying = fundamental, basic, prime, primary, elementary, intrinsic

undermine = weaken, sabotage, subvert, compromise, disable ≠ reinforce

understand 1 = comprehend, get, take in, perceive, grasp, see, follow, realize 2 = believe, gather, think, see, suppose, notice,

world, Hades, nether regions

underwrite = <u>finance</u>, back, fund, guarantee, sponsor, insure, ratify, subsidize

undesirable = <u>unwanted</u>, unwelcome, disagreeable, objectionable, unacceptable, unsuitable, unattractive, distasteful ≠ desirable

undo 1 = <u>open</u>, unfasten, loose, untie, unbutton, disentangle 2 = <u>reverse</u>, cancel, offset, neutralize, invalidate, annul 3 = <u>ruin</u>, defeat, destroy, wreck, shatter, upset, undermine, overturn

undone = <u>unfinished</u>, left, neglected, omitted, unfulfilled, unperformed ≠ finished

undoubtedly = <u>certainly</u>, definitely, surely, doubtless, without doubt, assuredly

unearth 1 = <u>discover</u>, find, reveal, expose, uncover 2 = <u>dig up</u>, excavate, exhume, dredge up

unearthly = <u>eerie</u>, strange, supernatural, ghostly, weird, phantom, uncanny, spooky (*informal*)

uneasy 1 = <u>anxious</u>, worried, troubled, nervous, disturbed, uncomfortable, edgy, perturbed ≠ relaxed 2 = <u>precarious</u>, strained, uncomfortable, tense, awkward, shaky, insecure

unemployed = <u>out of work</u>, redundant, laid off, jobless, idle ≠ working

unfair 1 = <u>biased</u>, prejudiced, unjust, one-sided, partial, partisan, bigoted 2 = <u>unscrupulous</u>, dishonest, unethical, wrongful, unsporting ≠ ethical

unfit 1 = <u>out of shape</u>, feeble, unhealthy, flabby, in poor condition ≠ healthy 2 = <u>incapable</u>, inadequate, incompetent, no good, useless, unqualified ≠ capable 3 = <u>unsuitable</u>, inadequate, useless, unsuited ≠ suitable

unfold 1 = <u>reveal</u>, tell, present, show, disclose, uncover, divulge, make known 2 = <u>open</u>, spread out, undo, expand, unfurl, unwrap, unroll

unfortunate 1 = <u>disastrous</u>, calamitous, adverse, ill-fated ≠ opportune 2 = <u>regrettable</u>, deplorable, lamentable, unsuitable, unbecoming ≠ becoming 3 = <u>unlucky</u>, unhappy, doomed, cursed, unsuccessful, hapless, wretched ≠ fortunate

unhappy 1 = <u>sad</u>, depressed, miserable, blue, melancholy, mournful, dejected, despondent ≠ happy 2 = <u>unlucky</u>, unfortunate, hapless, cursed, wretched, ill-fated ≠ fortunate

unhealthy 1 = <u>harmful</u>, detrimental, unwholesome, insanitary, insalubrious ≠ beneficial **2** = <u>sick</u>, sickly, unwell, delicate, crook (*Austral. & N.Z. informal*), ailing, frail, feeble, invalid ≠ well **3** = <u>weak</u>, ailing ≠ strong

unification = <u>union</u>, uniting, alliance, coalition, federation, confederation, amalgamation, coalescence

uniform NOUN **1** = <u>regalia</u>, suit, livery, colours, habit **2** = <u>outfit</u>, dress, costume, attire, gear (*informal*), get-up (*informal*), ensemble, garb
● ADJECTIVE **1** = <u>consistent</u>, unvarying, similar, even, same, matching, regular, constant ≠ varying **2** = <u>alike</u>, similar, like, same, equal

unify = <u>unite</u>, join, combine, merge, consolidate, confederate, amalgamate ≠ divide

union 1 = <u>joining</u>, uniting, unification, combination, coalition, merger, mixture, blend **2** = <u>alliance</u>, league, association, coalition, federation, confederacy

unique 1 = <u>distinct</u>, special, exclusive, peculiar, only, single, lone, solitary **2** = <u>unparalleled</u>, unmatched, unequalled, matchless, without equal

> ### Word Power
>
> **unique** – Unique with the meaning 'being the only one' or 'having no equal' describes an absolute state: *a case unique in British law*. In this use it cannot therefore be qualified; something is either *unique* or *not unique*. However, *unique* is also very commonly used in the sense of 'remarkable' or 'exceptional', particularly in the language of advertising, and in this meaning it can be used with qualifying words such as *rather*, *quite*, etc. Since many people object to this use, it is best avoided in formal and serious writing.

unit 1 = <u>entity</u>, whole, item, feature **2** = <u>section</u>, company, group, force, detail, division, cell, squad **3** = <u>measure</u>, quantity, measurement **4** = <u>part</u>, section, segment, class, element, component, constituent, tutorial

unite 1 = <u>join</u>, link, combine, couple, blend, merge, unify, fuse ≠ separate **2** = <u>cooperate</u>, ally, join forces, band, pool, collaborate ≠ split

unity 1 = <u>union</u>, unification, coalition, federation, integration, confederation, amalgamation **2** = <u>wholeness</u>, integrity, oneness, union, entity, singleness

≠ disunity 3 = <u>agreement</u>, accord, consensus, harmony, solidarity, unison, assent, concord ≠ disagreement

universal 1 = <u>widespread</u>, general, common, whole, total, unlimited, overarching 2 = <u>global</u>, worldwide, international, pandemic

universally = <u>without exception</u>, everywhere, always, invariably

universe = <u>cosmos</u>, space, creation, nature, heavens, macrocosm, all existence

unknown 1 = <u>strange</u>, new, undiscovered, uncharted, unexplored, virgin, remote, alien 2 = <u>unidentified</u>, mysterious, anonymous, unnamed, nameless, incognito 3 = <u>obscure</u>, humble, unfamiliar ≠ famous

unlike 1 = <u>different from</u>, dissimilar to, distinct from, unequal to ≠ similar to 2 = <u>contrasted with</u>, in contradiction to, in contrast with or to, as opposed to, differently from, opposite to

unlikely 1 = <u>improbable</u>, doubtful, remote, slight, faint ≠ probable 2 = <u>unbelievable</u>, incredible, implausible, questionable ≠ believable

unload 1 = <u>empty</u>, clear, unpack, dump, discharge 2 = <u>unburden</u>

unnatural 1 = <u>abnormal</u>, odd, strange, unusual, extraordinary, perverted, queer, irregular ≠ normal 2 = <u>false</u>, forced, artificial, affected, stiff, feigned, stilted, insincere ≠ genuine

unpleasant 1 = <u>nasty</u>, bad, horrid, distasteful, displeasing, objectionable, disagreeable ≠ nice 2 = <u>obnoxious</u>, rude ≠ likable or likeable

unravel 1 = <u>solve</u>, explain, work out, resolve, figure out (informal) 2 = <u>undo</u>, separate, disentangle, free, unwind, untangle

unrest = <u>discontent</u>, rebellion, protest, strife, agitation, discord, sedition, dissension ≠ peace

unsettled 1 = <u>unstable</u>, shaky, insecure, disorderly, unsteady 2 = <u>restless</u>, tense, shaken, confused, disturbed, anxious, agitated, flustered 3 = <u>inconstant</u>, changing, variable, uncertain

unstable 1 = <u>changeable</u>, volatile, unpredictable, variable, fluctuating, fitful, inconstant ≠ constant 2 = <u>insecure</u>, shaky, precarious, unsettled, wobbly, tottering, unsteady 3 = <u>unpredictable</u>, irrational, erratic, inconsistent, temperamental, capricious, changeable ≠ level-headed

unthinkable 1 = <u>impossible</u>, out of the question,

inconceivable, absurd, unreasonable 2 = **inconceivable**, incredible, unimaginable

untold 1 = **indescribable**, unthinkable, unimaginable, undreamed of, unutterable, inexpressible 2 = **countless**, incalculable, innumerable, myriad, numberless, uncountable

untrue 1 = **false**, lying, wrong, mistaken, incorrect, inaccurate, dishonest, deceptive ≠ true 2 = **unfaithful**, disloyal, deceitful, treacherous, faithless, false, untrustworthy, inconstant ≠ faithful

unusual 1 = **rare**, odd, strange, extraordinary, different, curious, queer, uncommon ≠ common 2 = **extraordinary**, unique, remarkable, exceptional, uncommon, singular, unconventional ≠ average

upbeat (*Informal*) = **cheerful**, positive, optimistic, encouraging, hopeful, cheery

upbringing = **education**, training, breeding, rearing, raising

update = **bring up to date**, improve, correct, renew, revise, upgrade, amend, overhaul

upgrade 1 = **improve**, better, update, reform, add to, enhance, refurbish, renovate 2 = **promote**, raise, advance, boost, move up, elevate, kick upstairs (*informal*),

give promotion to ≠ demote

upheaval = **disturbance**, revolution, disorder, turmoil, disruption

uphill 1 = **ascending**, rising, upward, mounting, climbing ≠ descending 2 = **arduous**, hard, taxing, difficult, tough, exhausting, gruelling, strenuous

uphold 1 = **support**, back, defend, aid, champion, maintain, promote, sustain 2 = **confirm**, endorse

uplift VERB = **improve**, better, raise, advance, inspire, refine, edify
• NOUN = **improvement**, enlightenment, advancement, refinement, enhancement, enrichment, edification

upper 1 = **topmost**, top ≠ bottom 2 = **higher**, high ≠ lower 3 = **superior**, senior, higher-level, greater, top, important, chief, most important ≠ inferior

upper class = **aristocratic**, upper-class, noble, high-class, patrician, blue-blooded, highborn

upright 1 = **vertical**, straight, standing up, erect, perpendicular, bolt upright ≠ horizontal 2 = **honest**, good, principled, just, ethical, honourable, righteous, conscientious ≠ dishonourable

uprising = **rebellion**, rising,

revolution, revolt, disturbance, mutiny, insurrection, insurgence

uproar 1 = <u>commotion</u>, noise, racket, riot, turmoil, mayhem, din, pandemonium **2** = <u>protest</u>, outrage, complaint, objection, fuss, stink (*informal*), outcry, furore

upset ADJECTIVE 1 = <u>distressed</u>, shaken, disturbed, worried, troubled, hurt, bothered, unhappy **2** = <u>sick</u>, queasy, bad, ill **3** = <u>overturned</u>, upside down, capsized, spilled

● **VERB 1** = <u>distress</u>, trouble, disturb, worry, alarm, bother, grieve, agitate **2** = <u>tip over</u>, overturn, capsize, knock over, spill **3** = <u>mess up</u>, spoil, disturb, change, confuse, disorder, unsettle, disorganize

● **NOUN 1** = <u>distress</u>, worry, trouble, shock, bother, disturbance, agitation **2** = <u>reversal</u>, shake-up (*informal*), defeat **3** = <u>illness</u>, complaint, disorder, bug (*informal*), sickness, malady

upside down or **upside-down ADVERB** = <u>wrong side up</u>

● **ADJECTIVE 1** = <u>inverted</u>, overturned, upturned **2** (*Informal*) = <u>confused</u>, disordered, chaotic, muddled, topsy-turvy, higgledy-piggledy (*informal*)

up-to-date 1 = <u>modern</u>,

fashionable, trendy (*Brit. informal*), current, stylish, in vogue, up-to-the-minute ≠ out of date

urban = <u>civic</u>, city, town, metropolitan, municipal, dorp (*S. African*)

urge VERB 1 = <u>beg</u>, exhort, plead, implore, beseech, entreat **2** = <u>advocate</u>, recommend, advise, support, counsel ≠ discourage

● **NOUN** = <u>impulse</u>, longing, wish, desire, drive, yearning, itch (*informal*), thirst ≠ reluctance

urgency = <u>importance</u>, need, necessity, gravity, pressure, hurry, seriousness, extremity

urgent = <u>crucial</u>, desperate, pressing, great, important, crying, critical, immediate ≠ unimportant

usage 1 = <u>use</u>, operation, employment, running, control, management, handling **2** = <u>practice</u>, method, procedure, habit, regime, custom, routine, convention

use VERB 1 = <u>employ</u>, utilize, work, apply, operate, exercise, practise, resort to **2** *sometimes with* **up** = <u>consume</u>, exhaust, spend, run through, expend **3** = <u>take advantage of</u>, exploit, manipulate

● **NOUN 1** = <u>usage</u>, employment, operation, application **2** = <u>purpose</u>, end, reason, object

3 = <u>good</u>, point, help, service, value, benefit, profit, advantage

used = <u>second-hand</u>, cast-off, nearly new, shopsoiled ≠ new

used to = <u>accustomed to</u>, familiar with

useful = <u>helpful</u>, effective, valuable, practical, profitable, worthwhile, beneficial, fruitful ≠ useless

useless 1 = <u>worthless</u>, valueless, impractical, fruitless, unproductive, ineffectual, unsuitable ≠ useful 2 = <u>pointless</u>, futile, vain ≠ worthwhile 3 (*Informal*) = <u>inept</u>, no good, hopeless, incompetent, ineffectual

usher VERB = <u>escort</u>, lead, direct, guide, conduct

● NOUN = <u>attendant</u>, guide, doorman, escort, doorkeeper

usual = <u>normal</u>, customary, regular, general, common, standard, ordinary, typical ≠ unusual

usually = <u>normally</u>, generally, mainly, commonly, mostly, on the whole, as a rule, habitually

utility = <u>usefulness</u>, benefit, convenience, practicality, efficacy, serviceableness

utilize = <u>use</u>, employ, deploy, take advantage of, make use of, put to use, bring into play, avail yourself of

utmost ADJECTIVE 1 = <u>greatest</u>, highest, maximum, supreme, paramount, pre-eminent 2 = <u>farthest</u>, extreme, last, final

● NOUN = <u>best</u>, greatest, maximum, highest, hardest

utter¹ = <u>say</u>, state, speak, voice, express, deliver, declare, mouth

utter² = <u>absolute</u>, complete, total, sheer, outright, thorough, downright, unmitigated

utterly = <u>totally</u>, completely, absolutely, perfectly, fully, entirely, extremely, thoroughly

V

vacancy 1 = <u>opening</u>, job, post, place, position, role, situation, opportunity 2 = <u>room</u>, space, available accommodation, unoccupied room

vacant 1 = <u>empty</u>, free, available, abandoned, deserted, for sale, on the market, void ≠ occupied 2 = <u>unfilled</u>, unoccupied ≠ taken 3 = <u>blank</u>, vague, dreamy, empty, abstracted, idle, vacuous, inane ≠ thoughtful

vacuum 1 = <u>gap</u>, lack, absence, space, deficiency, void 2 = <u>emptiness</u>, space, void, gap, nothingness, vacuity

vague 1 = <u>unclear</u>, indefinite, hazy, confused, loose, uncertain,

unsure, superficial ≠ clear
2 = <u>imprecise</u>, unspecified, generalized, rough, loose, ambiguous, hazy, equivocal 3 = <u>absent-minded</u>, distracted, vacant, preoccupied, oblivious, inattentive 4 = <u>indistinct</u>, unclear, faint, hazy, indeterminate, nebulous, ill-defined ≠ distinct

vain ADJECTIVE 1 = <u>futile</u>, useless, pointless, unsuccessful, idle, worthless, senseless, fruitless ≠ successful 2 = <u>conceited</u>, narcissistic, proud, arrogant, swaggering, egotistical, self-important ≠ modest
● PHRASES **in vain** 1 = <u>useless</u>, to no avail, unsuccessful, fruitless, vain 2 = <u>uselessly</u>, to no avail, unsuccessfully, fruitlessly, vainly, ineffectually

valid 1 = <u>sound</u>, good, reasonable, telling, convincing, rational, logical, viable ≠ unfounded 2 = <u>legal</u>, official, legitimate, genuine, authentic, lawful, bona fide ≠ invalid

validity 1 = <u>soundness</u>, force, power, weight, strength, cogency 2 = <u>legality</u>, authority, legitimacy, right, lawfulness

valley 1 = <u>hollow</u>, dale, glen, vale, depression, dell

valuable ADJECTIVE 1 = <u>useful</u>, important, profitable, worthwhile, beneficial, helpful ≠ useless

2 = <u>treasured</u>, prized, precious 3 = <u>precious</u>, expensive, costly, dear, high-priced, priceless, irreplaceable ≠ worthless
● PLURAL NOUN = <u>treasures</u>, prized possessions, precious items, heirlooms, personal effects, costly article

value NOUN 1 = <u>importance</u>, benefit, worth, merit, point, service, sense, profit ≠ worthlessness 2 = <u>cost</u>, price, worth, rate, market price, face value, asking price, selling price
● PLURAL NOUN = <u>principles</u>, morals, ethics, mores, standards of behaviour, (moral) standards
● VERB 1 = <u>appreciate</u>, rate, prize, regard highly, respect, admire, treasure, esteem ≠ undervalue 2 = <u>evaluate</u>, price, estimate, rate, cost, assess, set at, appraise

vanish 1 = <u>disappear</u>, dissolve, evaporate, fade away, melt away, evanesce ≠ appear 2 = <u>die out</u>, disappear, pass away, end, fade, dwindle, cease to exist, become extinct

vanity = <u>pride</u>, arrogance, conceit, narcissism, egotism, conceitedness ≠ modesty

variable = <u>changeable</u>, unstable, fluctuating, shifting, flexible, uneven, temperamental, unsteady ≠ constant

variant NOUN = <u>variation</u>, form,

version, development, alternative, adaptation, revision, modification
● **ADJECTIVE** = <u>different</u>, alternative, modified, divergent

variation 1 = <u>alternative</u>, variety, modification, departure, innovation, variant 2 = <u>variety</u>, change, deviation, difference, diversity, diversion, novelty ≠ uniformity

varied = <u>different</u>, mixed, various, diverse, assorted, miscellaneous, sundry, motley ≠ unvarying

variety 1 = <u>diversity</u>, change, variation, difference, diversification, heterogeneity, multifariousness ≠ uniformity 2 = <u>range</u>, selection, assortment, mix, collection, line-up, mixture, array 3 = <u>type</u>, sort, kind, class, brand, species, breed, strain

various 1 = <u>different</u>, assorted, miscellaneous, varied, distinct, diverse, disparate, sundry ≠ similar 2 = <u>many</u>, numerous, countless, several, abundant, innumerable, sundry, profuse

---

Word Power

various – The use of *different* after *various*, which seems to be most common in speech, is unnecessary and should be avoided in serious writing: *the disease exists in various forms* (not *in various different forms*).

---

varnish NOUN = <u>lacquer</u>, polish, glaze, gloss
● **VERB** = <u>lacquer</u>, polish, glaze, gloss

vary 1 = <u>differ</u>, be different, be dissimilar, disagree, diverge 2 = <u>change</u>, shift, swing, alter, fluctuate, oscillate, see-saw 3 = <u>alternate</u>

vast = <u>huge</u>, massive, enormous, great, wide, immense, gigantic, monumental ≠ tiny

vault[1] 1 = <u>strongroom</u>, repository, depository 2 = <u>crypt</u>, tomb, catacomb, cellar, mausoleum, charnel house, undercroft

vault[2] = <u>jump</u>, spring, leap, clear, bound, hurdle

veer = <u>change direction</u>, turn, swerve, shift, sheer, change course

vehicle 1 = <u>conveyance</u>, machine, motor vehicle 2 = <u>medium</u>, means, channel, mechanism, organ, apparatus

veil NOUN 1 = <u>mask</u>, cover, shroud, film, curtain, cloak 2 = <u>screen</u>, mask, disguise, blind 3 = <u>film</u>, cover, curtain, cloak, shroud
● **VERB** = <u>cover</u>, screen, hide, mask, shield, disguise, conceal, obscure ≠ reveal

veiled = <u>disguised</u>, implied, hinted at, covert, masked, concealed, suppressed

vein 1 = blood vessel 2 = mood, style, note, tone, mode, temper, tenor 3 = seam, layer, stratum, course, current, bed, deposit, streak

velocity = speed, pace, rapidity, quickness, swiftness

vengeance = revenge, retaliation, reprisal, retribution, requital ≠ forgiveness

vent NOUN = outlet, opening, aperture, duct, orifice
● VERB = express, release, voice, air, discharge, utter, emit, pour out ≠ hold back

venture NOUN = undertaking, project, enterprise, campaign, risk, operation, activity, scheme
● VERB 1 = go, travel, journey, set out, wander, stray, plunge into, rove 2 = dare, presume, have the courage to, be brave enough, hazard, go out on a limb (*informal*), take the liberty, go so far as 3 = put forward, volunteer

verbal = spoken, oral, word-of-mouth, unwritten

verdict = decision, finding, judgment, opinion, sentence, conclusion, conviction, adjudication

verge NOUN 1 = brink, point, edge, threshold 2 = border, edge, margin, limit, boundary, threshold, brim
● PHRASES **verge on something**

= come near to, approach, border on, resemble, incline to, be similar to, touch on, be more or less

verify 1 = check, make sure, examine, monitor, inspect 2 = confirm, prove, substantiate, support, validate, bear out, corroborate, authenticate ≠ disprove

versatile 1 = adaptable, flexible, all-round, resourceful, multifaceted ≠ unadaptable 2 = all-purpose, variable, adjustable ≠ limited

versed = knowledgeable, experienced, seasoned, familiar, practised, acquainted, well-informed, proficient ≠ ignorant

version 1 = form, variety, variant, sort, class, design, style, model 2 = adaptation, edition, interpretation, form, copy, rendering, reproduction, portrayal 3 = account, report, description, record, reading, story, view, understanding

vertical = upright, sheer, perpendicular, straight (up and down), erect, plumb, on end, precipitous, vertiginous ≠ horizontal

very ADVERB = extremely, highly, greatly, really, deeply, unusually, profoundly, decidedly
● ADJECTIVE = exact, precise, selfsame 2 = ideal

Word Power

very – In strict usage, adverbs of degree such as *very*, *too*, *quite*, *really*, and *extremely* are used only to qualify adjectives: *he is very happy*; *she is too sad*. By this rule, these words should not be used to qualify past participles that follow the verb *to be*, since they would then be technically qualifying verbs. With the exception of certain participles, such as *tired* or *disappointed*, that have come to be regarded as adjectives, all other past participles are qualified by adverbs such as *much*, *greatly*, *seriously*, or *excessively*: *he has been much* (not *very*) *inconvenienced*; *she has been excessively* (not *too*) *criticized*.

vessel 1 = <u>ship</u>, boat, craft **2** = <u>container</u>, receptacle, can, bowl, tank, pot, drum, barrel

vest VERB

● PHRASES **vest in something** or **someone** usually passive = <u>place</u>, invest, entrust, settle, confer, endow, bestow, consign

◆ **vest with something** usually passive = <u>endow with</u>, entrust with

vet = <u>check</u>, examine, investigate, review, appraise, scrutinize

veteran NOUN = <u>old hand</u>, past master, warhorse (*informal*), old

stager ≠ novice

● ADJECTIVE = <u>long-serving</u>, seasoned, experienced, old, established, qualified, mature, practised

veto VERB = <u>ban</u>, block, reject, rule out, turn down, forbid, boycott, prohibit ≠ pass

● NOUN = <u>ban</u>, dismissal, rejection, vetoing, boycott, embargo, prohibiting, prohibition ≠ ratification

viable = <u>workable</u>, practical, feasible, suitable, realistic, operational, applicable, usable ≠ unworkable

vibrant 1 = <u>energetic</u>, dynamic, sparkling, vivid, spirited, storming, alive, vigorous **2** = <u>vivid</u>, bright, brilliant, intense, clear, rich, glowing

vice 1 = <u>fault</u>, failing, weakness, limitation, defect, deficiency, flaw, shortcoming ≠ good point **2** = <u>wickedness</u>, evil, corruption, sin, depravity, immorality, iniquity, turpitude ≠ virtue

vice versa = <u>the other way round</u>, conversely, in reverse, contrariwise

vicious 1 = <u>savage</u>, brutal, violent, cruel, ferocious, barbarous ≠ gentle **2** = <u>malicious</u>, vindictive, spiteful, mean, cruel, venomous

victim 1 = <u>casualty</u>, sufferer,

victor → violate

fatality ≠ survivor 2 = **scapegoat**, sacrifice, martyr

victor = **winner**, champion, conqueror, vanquisher, prizewinner ≠ loser

victorious = **winning**, successful, triumphant, first, champion, conquering, vanquishing, prizewinning ≠ losing

victory = **win**, success, triumph, conquest, walkover (*informal*) ≠ defeat

vie = **compete**, struggle, contend, strive

view NOUN 1 *sometimes plural* = **opinion**, belief, feeling, attitude, impression, conviction, point of view, sentiment 2 = **scene**, picture, sight, prospect, perspective, landscape, outlook, spectacle 3 = **vision**, sight, visibility, range of vision, eyeshot
• VERB = **regard**, see, consider, perceive, treat, estimate, reckon, deem

viewer = **watcher**, observer, spectator, onlooker

vigorous 1 = **strenuous**, energetic, arduous, hard, taxing, active, rigorous 2 = **spirited**, lively, energetic, active, dynamic, animated, forceful, feisty (*informal*) ≠ lethargic 3 = **strong**, powerful, lively, lusty ≠ weak

vigorously 1 = **energetically**,

hard, forcefully, strongly, strenuously, lustily 2 = **forcefully**, strongly, vehemently, strenuously

vigour or (*U.S.*) **vigor** = **energy**, vitality, power, spirit, strength, animation, verve, gusto ≠ weakness

vile 1 = **wicked**, evil, corrupt, perverted, degenerate, depraved, nefarious ≠ honourable 2 = **disgusting**, foul, revolting, offensive, nasty, sickening, horrid, repulsive, yucko (*Austral. slang*) ≠ pleasant

villain 1 = **evildoer**, criminal, rogue, scoundrel, wretch, reprobate, miscreant, blackguard 2 = **baddy** (*informal*), antihero ≠ hero

vindicate 1 = **clear**, acquit, exonerate, absolve, let off the hook, exculpate ≠ condemn 2 = **support**, defend, excuse, justify

vintage NOUN (always used of wines) = **harvest**
• ADJECTIVE 1 (always used of wines) = **high-quality**, best, prime, quality, choice, select, superior 2 = **classic**, old, veteran, historic, heritage, enduring, antique, timeless

violate 1 = **break**, infringe, disobey, transgress, ignore, defy, disregard, flout ≠ obey 2 = **invade**, infringe on, disturb, upset, shatter, disrupt, impinge on, encroach on **3** = <u>desecrate</u>, profane, defile, abuse, pollute, deface, dishonour, vandalize ≠ honour **4** = <u>rape</u>, molest, sexually assault, ravish, abuse, assault, interfere with, sexually abuse

violation 1 = <u>breach</u>, abuse, infringement, contravention, abuse, trespass, transgression, infraction **2** = <u>invasion</u>, intrusion, trespass, breach, disturbance, disruption, interruption, encroachment **3** = <u>desecration</u>, sacrilege, defilement, profanation, spoliation **4** = <u>rape</u>, sexual assault, molesting, ravishing (old-fashioned), abuse, sexual abuse, indecent assault, molestation

violence 1 = <u>brutality</u>, bloodshed, savagery, fighting, terrorism **2** = <u>force</u>, power, strength, might, ferocity, forcefulness, powerfulness **3** = <u>intensity</u>, force, cruelty, severity, fervour, vehemence

violent 1 = <u>brutal</u>, aggressive, savage, wild, fierce, bullying, cruel, vicious ≠ gentle **2** = <u>sharp</u> **3** = <u>passionate</u>, uncontrollable, unrestrained **4** = <u>fiery</u>, fierce, passionate

VIP = <u>celebrity</u>, big name, star, somebody, luminary, big hitter (informal), heavy hitter (informal)

virgin NOUN = <u>maiden</u>, girl (archaic)
● ADJECTIVE = <u>pure</u>, chaste, immaculate, virginal, vestal, uncorrupted, undefiled ≠ corrupted

virtual = <u>practical</u>, essential, in all but name

virtually = <u>practically</u>, almost, nearly, in effect, in essence, as good as, in all but name

virtue 1 = <u>goodness</u>, integrity, worth, morality, righteousness, probity, rectitude, incorruptibility ≠ vice **2** = <u>merit</u>, strength, asset, plus (informal), attribute, good point, strong point ≠ failing **3** = <u>advantage</u>, benefit, merit, credit, usefulness, efficacy

visible = <u>perceptible</u>, observable, clear, apparent, evident, manifest, in view, discernible ≠ invisible

vision 1 = <u>image</u>, idea, dream, plans, hopes, prospect, ideal, concept **2** = <u>hallucination</u>, illusion, apparition, revelation, delusion, mirage, chimera **3** = <u>sight</u>, seeing, eyesight, view, perception **4** = <u>foresight</u>, imagination, perception, insight, awareness, inspiration, innovation, creativity

visionary NOUN **1** = <u>idealist</u>, romantic, dreamer, daydreamer ≠ realist **2** = <u>prophet</u>, diviner, mystic, seer, soothsayer, sibyl,

scryer, spaewife (*Scot.*)
● ADJECTIVE 1 = idealistic, romantic, unrealistic, utopian, speculative, impractical, unworkable, quixotic ≠ realistic
2 = prophetic, mystical, predictive, oracular, sibylline

visit VERB 1 = call on, drop in on (*informal*), stay at, stay with, stop by, spend time with, look someone up, go see (*U.S.*)
2 = stay in, stop by
● NOUN 1 = call, social call 2 = trip, stop, stay, break, tour, holiday, vacation (*informal*), stopover

visitor = guest, caller, company, manu(w)hiri (*N.Z.*)

vista = view, scene, prospect, landscape, panorama, perspective

visual 1 = optical, optic, ocular
2 = observable, visible, perceptible, discernible ≠ imperceptible

vital 1 = essential, important, necessary, key, basic, significant, critical, crucial ≠ unnecessary
2 = lively, vigorous, energetic, spirited, dynamic, animated, vibrant, vivacious ≠ lethargic

vitality = energy, vivacity, life, strength, animation, vigour, exuberance, liveliness ≠ lethargy

vivid 1 = clear, detailed, realistic, telling, moving, affecting, arresting, powerful ≠ vague
2 = bright, brilliant, intense, clear,

rich, glowing, colourful ≠ dull

vocabulary 1 = language, words, lexicon 2 = wordbook, dictionary, glossary, lexicon

vocal 1 = outspoken, frank, forthright, strident, vociferous, articulate, expressive, eloquent ≠ quiet 2 = spoken, voiced, uttered, oral, said

vocation = profession, calling, job, trade, career, mission, pursuit

vogue = fashion, trend, craze, style, mode, passing fancy, dernier cri (*French*)

voice NOUN 1 = tone, sound, articulation 2 = utterance
3 = opinion, will, feeling, wish, desire 4 = say, view, vote, comment, input
● VERB = express, declare, air, raise, reveal, mention, mouth, pronounce

(*Related Words*)
adjective: vocal

void NOUN 1 = gap, space, lack, hole, emptiness 2 = emptiness, space, vacuum, oblivion, blankness, nullity, vacuity
● ADJECTIVE = invalid, null and void, inoperative, useless, ineffective, worthless
● VERB = invalidate, nullify, cancel, withdraw, reverse, undo, repeal, quash

volatile 1 = changeable, shifting, variable, unsettled, unstable,

volley → waddle

explosive, unreliable, unsteady ≠ **stable 2** = temperamental, erratic, mercurial, up and down (*informal*), fickle, over-emotional ≠ calm

volley = barrage, blast, burst, shower, hail, bombardment, salvo, fusillade

volume 1 = amount, quantity, level, body, total, measure, degree, mass **2** = capacity, size, mass, extent, proportions, dimensions, bulk, measurements **3** = book, work, title, opus, publication, manual, tome, treatise **4** = loudness, sound, amplification

voluntarily = willingly, freely, by choice, off your own bat, of your own accord, of your own volition

voluntary 1 = intentional, deliberate, planned, calculated, wilful ≠ unintentional **2** = optional, discretionary, up to the individual, open, unforced, at your discretion, open to choice ≠ obligatory **3** = unpaid, free, willing, pro bono (*Law*)

volunteer = offer, step forward ≠ refuse

vomit 1 = be sick, throw up (*informal*), spew, chuck (*Austral. & N.Z. informal*), heave (*slang*), retch **2** *often with* **up** = bring up, throw up, regurgitate, emit (*informal*), disgorge, spew out *or* up

vote NOUN = poll, election, ballot, referendum, popular vote, plebiscite, straw poll, show of hands
● VERB = cast your vote

voucher = ticket, token, coupon, pass, slip, chit, chitty (*Brit. informal*), docket

vow VERB = promise, pledge, swear, commit, engage, affirm, avow, bind yourself
● NOUN = promise, commitment, pledge, oath, profession, avowal

voyage NOUN = journey, trip, passage, expedition, crossing, sail, cruise, excursion
● VERB = travel, journey, tour, cruise, steam, take a trip, go on an expedition

vulgar 1 = tasteless, common ≠ tasteful **2** = crude, rude, coarse, indecent, tasteless, risqué, ribald **3** = uncouth, unrefined, impolite, ill-bred ≠ refined

vulnerable 1 = susceptible, helpless, unprotected, defenceless, exposed, weak, sensitive, tender ≠ immune **2** = exposed, open, unprotected, defenceless, accessible, wide open, assailable ≠ well-protected

W

waddle = shuffle, totter, toddle, sway, wobble

wade 1 = <u>paddle</u>, splash, splash about, slop 2 = <u>walk through</u>, cross, ford, travel across

wag VERB 1 = <u>wave</u>, shake, waggle, stir, quiver, vibrate, wiggle 2 = <u>waggle</u>, wave, shake, flourish, brandish, wobble, wiggle 3 = <u>shake</u>, bob, nod
● NOUN 1 = <u>wave</u>, shake, quiver, vibration, wiggle, waggle. 2 = <u>nod</u>, bob, shake

wage NOUN often plural
= <u>payment</u>, pay, remuneration, fee, reward, income, allowance, recompense
● VERB = <u>engage in</u>, conduct, pursue, carry on, undertake, practise, prosecute, proceed with

wail VERB = <u>cry</u>, weep, grieve, lament, howl, bawl, yowl
● NOUN = <u>cry</u>, moan, howl, lament, yowl

wait VERB 1 = <u>stay</u>, remain, stop, pause, rest, linger, loiter, tarry ≠ go 2 = <u>stand by</u>, hold back, hang fire 3 = <u>be postponed</u>, be suspended, be delayed, be put off, be put back, be deferred, be put on hold (*informal*), be shelved
● NOUN = <u>delay</u>, gap, pause, interval, stay, rest, halt, hold-up

waiter or **waitress**
= <u>attendant</u>, server, flunkey, steward or stewardess, servant

waive 1 = <u>give up</u>, relinquish,

renounce, forsake, drop, abandon, set aside, dispense with ≠ claim 2 = <u>disregard</u>, ignore, discount, overlook, set aside, pass over, dispense with, brush aside

wake[1] VERB 1 = <u>awake</u>, stir, awaken, come to, arise, get up, rouse, get out of bed ≠ fall asleep 2 = <u>awaken</u>, arouse, rouse, waken 3 = <u>evoke</u>, recall, renew, stimulate, revive, induce, arouse, call up
● NOUN = <u>vigil</u>, watch, funeral, deathwatch, tangi (*N.Z.*)

Word Power

wake – Both *wake* and its synonym *waken* can be used either with or without an object: *I woke/wakened my sister*, and also *I woke/wakened (up) at noon*. *Wake, wake up*, and occasionally *waken*, can also be used in a figurative sense, for example *seeing him again woke painful memories*; and *it's time he woke up to his responsibilities*. The verbs *awake* and *awaken* are more commonly used in the figurative than the literal sense, for example *he awoke to the danger he was in*.

---

wake[2] NOUN = <u>slipstream</u>, wash, trail, backwash, train, track, waves, path
● PHRASES **in the wake of** = <u>in the aftermath of</u>, following, because of, as a result of, on

account of, as a consequence of

walk VERB 1 = stride, stroll, go, move, step, march, pace, hike 2 = travel on foot 3 = escort, take, see, show, partner, guide, conduct, accompany

● NOUN 1 = stroll, hike, ramble, march, trek, trudge, promenade, saunter 2 = gait, step, bearing, carriage, tread 3 = path, footpath, track, way, road, lane, trail, avenue, berm (N.Z.)

● PHRASES **walk of life** = area, calling, business, line, trade, class, field, career

walker = hiker, rambler, wayfarer, pedestrian

wall 1 = partition, screen, barrier, enclosure 2 = barrier, obstacle, barricade, obstruction, check, bar, fence, impediment

wallet = purse, pocketbook, pouch, case, holder, money-bag

wander VERB = roam, walk, drift, stroll, range, stray, ramble, prowl

● NOUN = excursion, walk, stroll, cruise, ramble, meander, promenade, mosey (informal)

wanderer = traveller, rover, nomad, drifter, gypsy, explorer, rambler, voyager

wane 1 = decline, weaken, diminish, fail, fade, decrease, dwindle, lessen ≠ grow 2 = diminish, decrease, dwindle ≠ wax

want VERB 1 = wish for, desire, long for, crave, covet, hope for, yearn for, thirst for 2 = need, demand, require, call for 3 = should, need, must, ought 4 = desire, long for, crave, wish for, yearn for, thirst for, hanker after, burn for 5 = lack, need, require, miss

● NOUN 1 = lack, need, absence, shortage, deficiency, famine, scarcity, dearth ≠ abundance 2 = poverty, hardship, privation, penury, destitution, neediness, pennilessness ≠ wealth 3 = wish, will, need, desire, requirement, longing, appetite, craving

wanting 1 = deficient, poor, inadequate, insufficient, faulty, defective, imperfect, unsound, bodger or bodgie (Austral. slang) ≠ adequate 2 = lacking, missing, absent, incomplete, short, shy ≠ complete

war NOUN 1 = conflict, drive, attack, fighting, fight, operation, battle, movement ≠ peace 2 = campaign, drive, attack, operation, movement, push, mission, offensive

● VERB = fight, battle, clash, wage war, campaign, combat, do battle, take up arms ≠ make peace

ward NOUN 1 = room, department, unit, quarter, division, section, apartment, cubicle 2 = district, constituency, area, division, zone, parish, precinct **3** = <u>dependant</u>, charge, pupil, minor, protégé

● PHRASES **ward someone off** = <u>drive off</u>, resist, fight off, hold off, repel, fend off ◆ **ward something off 1** = <u>avert</u>, fend off, stave off, avoid, frustrate, deflect, repel **2** = <u>parry</u>, avert, deflect, avoid, repel, turn aside

warden 1 = <u>steward</u>, guardian, administrator, superintendent, caretaker, curator, custodian **2** = <u>jailer</u>, prison officer, guard, screw (*slang*) **3** = <u>governor</u>, head, leader, director, manager, chief, executive, commander, baas (*S. African*) **4** = <u>ranger</u>, keeper, guardian, protector, custodian, official

wardrobe 1 = <u>clothes cupboard</u>, cupboard, closet (*U.S.*), cabinet **2** = <u>clothes</u>, apparel, attire

warehouse = <u>store</u>, depot, storehouse, repository, depository, stockroom

wares = <u>goods</u>, produce, stock, products, stuff, commodities, merchandise

warfare = <u>war</u>, fighting, battle, conflict, combat, hostilities, enmity ≠ peace

warm ADJECTIVE **1** = <u>balmy</u>, mild, temperate, pleasant, fine, bright, sunny, agreeable ≠ cool **2** = <u>cosy</u>, snug, toasty (*informal*),

comfortable, homely, comfy (*informal*) **3** = <u>moderately hot</u>, heated ≠ cool **4** = <u>thermal</u>, winter, thick, chunky, woolly ≠ cool **5** = <u>mellow</u>, relaxing, pleasant, agreeable, restful **6** = <u>affable</u>, kindly, friendly, affectionate, loving, tender, amicable, cordial ≠ unfriendly **7** = <u>near</u>, close, hot, near to the truth

● VERB = <u>warm up</u>, heat, thaw (out), heat up ≠ cool down

● PHRASES **warm something or someone up** = <u>heat</u>, thaw, heat up

warmth 1 = <u>heat</u>, snugness, warmness, comfort, homeliness, hotness ≠ coolness **2** = <u>affection</u>, feeling, love, goodwill, kindness, tenderness, cordiality, kindliness ≠ hostility

warn 1 = <u>notify</u>, tell, remind, inform, alert, tip off, give notice, make someone aware **2** = <u>advise</u>, urge, recommend, counsel, caution, commend, exhort, admonish

warning 1 = <u>caution</u>, information, advice, injunction, notification **2** = <u>notice</u>, notification, sign, alarm, announcement, alert, tip-off (*informal*) **3** = <u>omen</u>, sign, forecast, indication, prediction, prophecy, foreboding, portent, rahui (*N.Z.*) **4** = <u>reprimand</u>, admonition

warp VERB 1 = <u>distort</u>, bend, twist, buckle, deform, disfigure, contort, malform 2 = <u>become distorted</u>, bend, twist, contort, become deformed, become misshapen 3 = <u>pervert</u>, twist, corrupt, degrade, deprave, debase, debauch, lead astray

• NOUN = <u>twist</u>, bend, defect, flaw, distortion, imperfection, kink, contortion

warrant VERB 1 = <u>call for</u>, demand, require, merit, rate, earn, deserve, permit 2 = <u>guarantee</u>, declare, pledge, promise, ensure, affirm, certify, attest

• NOUN 1 = <u>authorization</u>, permit, licence, permission, authority, sanction 2 = <u>justification</u>, reason, grounds, basis, licence, rationale, vindication, authority

warranty = <u>guarantee</u>, promise, contract, bond, pledge, certificate, assurance, covenant

warrior = <u>soldier</u>, combatant, fighter, gladiator, trooper, man-at-arms

wary 1 = <u>suspicious</u>, sceptical, guarded, distrustful, chary 2 = <u>watchful</u>, careful, alert, cautious, vigilant, circumspect, heedful ≠ careless

wash VERB 1 = <u>clean</u>, scrub, sponge, rinse, scour, cleanse 2 = <u>launder</u>, clean, rinse, dry-clean 3 = <u>rinse</u>, clean, scrub, lather 4 = <u>bathe</u>, bath, clean yourself, soak, douse, scrub yourself down 5 = <u>move</u>, overcome, touch, upset, stir, disturb, perturb, surge through 6 (*Informal*) (always used in negative constructions) = <u>be plausible</u>, stand up, hold up, pass muster, hold water, stick, carry weight, be convincing

• NOUN 1 = <u>laundering</u>, cleaning, clean, cleansing 2 = <u>bathe</u>, dip, soak, scrub, rinse 3 = <u>backwash</u>, slipstream, path, trail, train, track, waves, aftermath 4 = <u>splash</u>, surge, swell, rise and fall, undulation 5 = <u>coat</u>, film, covering, layer, coating, overlay

• PHRASES **wash something** or **someone away** = <u>sweep away</u>, carry off, bear away ◆ **wash something away** = <u>erode</u>, wear something away

wasp ▸ ants, bees, and wasps

waste VERB 1 = <u>squander</u>, throw away, blow (*slang*), lavish, misuse, dissipate, fritter away ≠ save 2 = <u>wear out</u>, wither

• NOUN 1 = <u>squandering</u>, misuse, extravagance, frittering away, dissipation, wastefulness, prodigality ≠ saving 2 = <u>rubbish</u>, refuse, debris, scrap, litter, garbage, trash, leftovers

• PLURAL NOUN = <u>desert</u>, wilderness, wasteland

• ADJECTIVE 1 = <u>unwanted</u>, useless,

worthless, unused, leftover, superfluous, unusable, supernumerary ≠ necessary 2 = uncultivated, wild, bare, barren, empty, desolate, unproductive, uninhabited ≠ cultivated

● PHRASES **waste away** = decline, dwindle, wither, fade, crumble, decay, wane, wear out

> *Word Power*
>
> **waste** – *Waste* and *wastage* are to some extent interchangeable, but many people think that *wastage* should not be used to refer to loss resulting from human carelessness, inefficiency, etc.: *a waste (not a wastage) of time, money, effort,* etc.

watch VERB 1 = look at, observe, regard, eye, see, view, contemplate, eyeball (*slang*) 2 = spy on, follow, track, monitor, keep an eye on, stake out, keep tabs on (*informal*), keep watch on 3 = guard, keep, mind, protect, tend, look after, shelter, take care of

● NOUN 1 = wristwatch, timepiece, chronometer 2 = guard, surveillance, observation, vigil, lookout

watchdog 1 = guardian, monitor, protector, custodian, scrutineer 2 = guard dog

water NOUN = liquid, H₂O, wai (*N.Z.*)

● PLURAL NOUN = sea, main, waves, ocean, depths, briny

● VERB 1 = sprinkle, spray, soak, irrigate, hose, dampen, drench, douse 2 = get wet, cry, weep, become wet, exude water

● PHRASES **water something down** = dilute, weaken, water, doctor, thin

(*Related Words*)

adjective: aquatic

waterfall = cascade, fall, cataract

wave VERB 1 = signal, sign, gesture, gesticulate 2 = guide, point, direct, indicate, signal, motion, gesture, nod 3 = brandish, swing, flourish, wag, shake 4 = flutter, flap, stir, shake, swing, wag, oscillate

● NOUN 1 = gesture, sign, signal, indication, gesticulation 2 = ripple, breaker, swell, ridge, roller, billow 3 = outbreak, rash, upsurge, flood, surge, ground swell 4 = stream, flood, surge, spate, current, flow, rush, tide

waver 1 = hesitate, dither (*chiefly Brit.*), vacillate, falter, fluctuate, seesaw, hum and haw ≠ be decisive 2 = flicker, shake, tremble, wobble, quiver, totter

wax 1 = increase, grow, develop, expand, swell, enlarge, magnify

≠ wane 2 = <u>become fuller</u>, enlarge

way 1 = <u>method</u>, means, system, process, technique, manner, procedure, mode 2 = <u>manner</u>, style, fashion, mode 3 *often plural* = <u>custom</u>, manner, habit, style, practice, nature, personality, wont, tikanga (*N.Z.*) 4 = <u>route</u>, direction, course, road, path 5 = <u>access</u>, road, track, channel, route, path, trail, pathway 6 = <u>journey</u>, approach, passage 7 = <u>distance</u>, length, stretch

wayward = <u>erratic</u>, unruly, unmanageable, unpredictable, capricious, ungovernable, inconstant ≠ obedient

weak 1 = <u>feeble</u>, frail, debilitated, fragile, sickly, puny, unsteady, infirm ≠ strong 2 = <u>slight</u>, faint, feeble, pathetic, hollow 3 = <u>fragile</u>, brittle, flimsy, fine, delicate, frail, dainty, breakable 4 = <u>unsafe</u>, exposed, vulnerable, helpless, unprotected, defenceless, unguarded ≠ secure 5 = <u>unconvincing</u>, unsatisfactory, lame, flimsy, pathetic ≠ convincing 6 = <u>tasteless</u>, thin, diluted, watery, runny, insipid ≠ strong

weaken 1 = <u>reduce</u>, undermine, moderate, diminish, lessen, sap ≠ boost 2 = <u>wane</u>, diminish, dwindle, lower, flag, fade, lessen ≠ grow 3 = <u>sap the strength of</u>

≠ strengthen

weakness 1 = <u>frailty</u>, fatigue, exhaustion, fragility, infirmity, feebleness, decrepitude ≠ strength 2 = <u>liking</u>, appetite, penchant, soft spot, passion, inclination, fondness, partiality ≠ aversion 3 = <u>powerlessness</u>, vulnerability, meekness, spinelessness, timorousness, cravenness, cowardliness 4 = <u>inadequacy</u>, deficiency, transparency, lameness, hollowness, implausibility, flimsiness, unsoundness 5 = <u>failing</u>, fault, defect, deficiency, flaw, shortcoming, blemish, imperfection ≠ strong point

wealth 1 = <u>riches</u>, fortune, prosperity, affluence, money, opulence ≠ poverty 2 = <u>property</u>, capital, fortune 3 = <u>abundance</u>, plenty, richness, profusion, fullness, cornucopia, copiousness ≠ lack

wealthy = <u>rich</u>, prosperous, affluent, well-off, flush (*informal*), opulent, well-heeled (*informal*), well-to-do ≠ poor

wear VERB 1 = <u>be dressed in</u>, have on, sport (*informal*), put on 2 = <u>show</u>, present, bear, display, assume, put on, exhibit 3 = <u>deteriorate</u>, fray, wear thin ● NOUN 1 = <u>clothes</u>, things, dress, gear (*informal*), attire, costume, garments, apparel **2** = <u>damage</u>, wear and tear, erosion, deterioration, attrition, corrosion, abrasion ≠ repair

● **PHRASES wear off** = <u>subside</u>, disappear, fade, diminish, decrease, dwindle, wane, peter out

wearing = <u>tiresome</u>, trying, fatiguing, oppressive, exasperating, irksome, wearisome ≠ refreshing

weary ADJECTIVE **1** = <u>tired</u>, exhausted, drained, worn out, done in (*informal*), flagging, fatigued, sleepy, clapped out (*Austral. & N.Z. informal*) ≠ energetic **2** = <u>tiring</u>, arduous, tiresome, laborious, wearisome ≠ refreshing

● **VERB** = <u>grow tired</u>, tire, become bored ≠ invigorate

weather NOUN = <u>climate</u>, conditions, temperature, forecast, outlook, meteorological conditions, elements

● **VERB** = <u>withstand</u>, stand, survive, overcome, resist, brave, endure, come through ≠ surrender to

weave 1 = <u>knit</u>, intertwine, plait, braid, entwine, interlace **2** = <u>zigzag</u>, wind, crisscross **3** = <u>create</u>, tell, recount, narrate, build, relate, make up, spin

web 1 = <u>cobweb</u>, spider's web **2** = <u>mesh</u>, lattice **3** = <u>tangle</u>, network

wed 1 = <u>get married to</u>, be united to ≠ divorce **2** = <u>get married</u>, marry, be united, tie the knot (*informal*), take the plunge (*informal*) ≠ divorce **3** = <u>unite</u>, combine, join, link, ally, blend, merge, interweave ≠ divide

wedding = <u>marriage</u>, nuptials, wedding ceremony, marriage service, wedding service

wedge VERB = <u>squeeze</u>, force, lodge, jam, crowd, stuff, pack, thrust

● **NOUN** = <u>block</u>, lump, chunk

weep = <u>cry</u>, shed tears, sob, whimper, mourn, lament, blubber, snivel ≠ rejoice

weigh 1 = <u>have a weight of</u>, tip the scales at (*informal*) **2** often with **up** = <u>consider</u>, examine, contemplate, evaluate, ponder, think over, reflect upon, meditate upon **3** = <u>compare</u>, balance, contrast, juxtapose, place side by side **4** = <u>matter</u>, carry weight, count

weight NOUN **1** = <u>heaviness</u>, mass, poundage, load, tonnage **2** = <u>importance</u>, force, power, value, authority, influence, impact, import, mana (*N.Z.*)

● **VERB 1** often with **down** = <u>load</u> **2** = <u>bias</u>, load, slant, unbalance

weird 1 = <u>strange</u>, odd, unusual, bizarre, mysterious, queer, eerie, unnatural ≠ normal **2** = bizarre, odd, strange, unusual, queer, unnatural, creepy (*informal*), freakish ≠ ordinary

welcome VERB **1** = greet, meet, receive, embrace, hail, karanga (*N.Z.*), mihi (*N.Z.*) ≠ reject **2** = accept gladly, appreciate, embrace, approve of, be pleased by, give the thumbs up to (*informal*), be glad about, express pleasure *or* satisfaction at
● NOUN = greeting, welcoming, reception, acceptance, hail, hospitality, salutation ≠ rejection
● ADJECTIVE **1** = pleasing, appreciated, acceptable, pleasant, desirable, refreshing, delightful, gratifying ≠ unpleasant **2** = wanted ≠ unwanted **3** = free

weld 1 = join, link, bond, bind, connect, fuse, solder **2** = unite, combine, blend, unify, fuse

welfare 1 = wellbeing, good, interest, health, security, benefit, safety, protection **2** = state benefit, support, benefits, pensions, dole (*slang*), social security, unemployment benefit, state benefits

well¹ ADVERB **1** = skilfully, expertly, adeptly, professionally, correctly, properly, efficiently, adequately ≠ badly **2** = satisfactorily, nicely, smoothly, successfully, pleasantly, splendidly, agreeably ≠ badly **3** = thoroughly, completely, fully,

carefully, effectively, efficiently, rigorously **4** = intimately, deeply, fully, profoundly ≠ slightly **5** = favourably, highly, kindly, warmly, enthusiastically, approvingly, admiringly, with admiration ≠ unfavourably **6** = considerably, easily, very much, significantly, substantially, markedly **7** = fully, highly, greatly, amply, very much, thoroughly, considerably, substantially **8** = possibly, probably, certainly, reasonably, conceivably, justifiably **9** = decently, right, kindly, fittingly, fairly, properly, politely, suitably ≠ unfairly **10** = prosperously, comfortably, splendidly, in comfort, in (the lap of) luxury, without hardship
● ADJECTIVE **1** = healthy, sound, fit, blooming, in fine fettle, in good condition ≠ ill **2** = satisfactory, right, fine, pleasing, proper, thriving ≠ unsatisfactory **3** = advisable, proper, agreeable ≠ inadvisable

well² NOUN = hole, bore, pit, shaft
● VERB **1** = flow, spring, pour, jet, surge, gush, spurt, spout **2** = rise, increase, grow, mount, surge, intensify

wet ADJECTIVE **1** = damp, soaking, saturated, moist, watery, soggy, sodden, waterlogged ≠ dry **2** = rainy, damp, drizzly, showery, raining, pouring, drizzling,

teeming ≠ sunny **3** (*Informal*)
= <u>feeble</u>, soft, weak, ineffectual,
weedy (*informal*), spineless,
effete, timorous

● VERB = <u>moisten</u>, spray, dampen,
water, soak, saturate, douse,
irrigate ≠ dry

● NOUN **1** = <u>rain</u>, drizzle ≠ fine
weather **2** = <u>moisture</u>, water,
liquid, damp, humidity,
condensation, dampness,
wetness ≠ dryness

whack (*Informal*) VERB = <u>strike</u>,
hit, belt (*informal*), bang, smack,
thrash, thump, swipe

● NOUN **1** = <u>blow</u>, hit, stroke, belt
(*informal*), bang, smack, thump,
swipe **2** (*Informal*) = <u>share</u>, part,
cut (*informal*), bit, portion, quota
3 (*Informal*) = <u>attempt</u>, go
(*informal*), try, turn, shot
(*informal*), crack (*informal*), stab
(*informal*), bash (*informal*)

**whale ► whales and
dolphins**

wharf = <u>dock</u>, pier, berth, quay,
jetty, landing stage

wheel NOUN = <u>disc</u>, ring, hoop

● VERB **1** = <u>push</u>, trundle, roll
2 = <u>turn</u>, swing, spin, revolve,
rotate, whirl, swivel **3** = <u>circle</u>, go
round, twirl, gyrate

whereabouts = <u>position</u>,
situation, site, location

whiff = <u>smell</u>, hint, scent, sniff,
aroma, odour

whim = <u>impulse</u>, caprice, fancy,
urge, notion

whine VERB **1** = <u>cry</u>, sob, wail,
whimper, sniffle, snivel, moan
2 = <u>complain</u>, grumble, gripe
(*informal*), whinge (*informal*),
moan, grouse, grizzle (*informal*,
chiefly Brit.*), grouch (*informal*)

● NOUN **1** = <u>cry</u>, moan, sob, wail,
whimper **2** = <u>drone</u>, note, hum
3 = <u>complaint</u>, moan, grumble,
grouse, gripe (*informal*), whinge
(*informal*), grouch (*informal*)

whip NOUN = <u>lash</u>, cane, birch,
crop, scourge, cat-o'-nine-tails

● VERB **1** = <u>lash</u>, cane, flog, beat,
strap, thrash, birch, scourge
2 (*Informal*) = <u>dash</u>, shoot, fly,
tear, rush, dive, dart, whisk
3 = <u>whisk</u>, beat, mix vigorously,
stir vigorously **4** = <u>incite</u>, drive,
stir, spur, work up, get going,
agitate, inflame

whirl VERB **1** = <u>spin</u>, turn, twist,
rotate, twirl **2** = <u>rotate</u>, roll, twist,
revolve, swirl, twirl, pirouette
3 = <u>feel dizzy</u>, swim, spin, reel, go
round

● NOUN **1** = <u>revolution</u>, turn, roll,
spin, twist, swirl, rotation, twirl
2 = <u>bustle</u>, round, series,
succession, flurry, merry-go-
round **3** = <u>confusion</u>, daze, dither
(*chiefly Brit.*), giddiness
4 = <u>tumult</u>, spin

whisk VERB **1** = <u>flick</u>, whip, sweep,

Whales and dolphins

beluga	porpoise
baleen whale	right whale or (Austral.) bay
blue whale or sulphur-bottom	whale
bottlenose dolphin	rorqual
bowhead	sperm whale or cachalot
humpback whale	toothed whale
killer whale, grampus, or orca	whalebone whale
narwhal	white whale

brush 2 = <u>beat</u>, mix vigorously, stir vigorously, whip, fluff up
● NOUN **1** = <u>flick</u>, sweep, brush, whip **2** = <u>beater</u>, mixer, blender

whisper VERB **1** = <u>murmur</u>, breathe ≠ shout **2** = <u>rustle</u>, sigh, hiss, swish
● NOUN **1** = <u>murmur</u>, mutter, mumble, undertone **2** (Informal) = <u>rumour</u>, report, gossip, innuendo, insinuation **3** = <u>rustle</u>, sigh, hiss, swish

white = <u>pale</u>, wan, pasty, pallid, ashen
➤ **shades from black to white**

white-collar = <u>clerical</u>, professional, salaried, nonmanual

whittle VERB = <u>carve</u>, cut, hew, shape, trim, shave, pare
● PHRASES **whittle something** or **someone down** = <u>reduce</u>, cut down, cut, decrease, prune, scale down ◆ **whittle something away** = <u>undermine</u>, reduce, consume, erode, eat away, wear away

whole NOUN = <u>unit</u>, ensemble, entirety, totality ≠ part
● ADJECTIVE **1** = <u>complete</u>, full, total, entire, uncut, undivided, unabridged ≠ partial
2 = <u>undamaged</u>, intact, unscathed, unbroken, untouched, unharmed, in one piece ≠ damaged
● PHRASES **on the whole 1** = <u>all in all</u>, altogether, all things considered, by and large
2 = <u>generally</u>, in general, as a rule, chiefly, mainly, mostly, principally, on average

wholesale ADJECTIVE = <u>extensive</u>, total, mass, sweeping, broad, comprehensive, wide-ranging, blanket ≠ limited
● ADVERB = <u>extensively</u>, comprehensively, across the board, indiscriminately

wholly = <u>completely</u>, totally, perfectly, fully, entirely, altogether, thoroughly, utterly

≠ partly

whore = <u>prostitute</u>, tart
(*informal*), streetwalker, call girl

wide ADJECTIVE 1 = <u>spacious</u>,
broad, extensive, roomy,
commodious ≠ confined
2 = <u>baggy</u>, full, loose, ample,
billowing, roomy, voluminous,
capacious 3 = <u>expanded</u>, dilated,
distended ≠ shut 4 = <u>broad</u>,
extensive, wide-ranging, large,
sweeping, vast, immense,
expansive ≠ restricted
5 = <u>extensive</u>, general, far-
reaching, overarching 6 = <u>large</u>,
broad, vast, immense 7 = <u>distant</u>,
remote, off course, off target
● ADVERB 1 = <u>fully</u>, completely
≠ partly 2 = <u>off target</u>, astray, off
course, off the mark

widen 1 = <u>broaden</u>, expand,
enlarge, dilate, spread, extend,
stretch ≠ narrow 2 = <u>get wider</u>,
spread, extend, expand, broaden
≠ narrow

widespread = <u>common</u>,
general, popular, broad,
extensive, universal, far-reaching,
pervasive ≠ limited

width = <u>breadth</u>, extent, span,
scope, diameter, compass,
thickness, girth

wield 1 = <u>brandish</u>, flourish,
manipulate, swing, use, manage,
handle, employ 2 = <u>exert</u>,
maintain, exercise, have, possess

wife = <u>spouse</u>, partner, mate,
bride, better half (*humorous*),
vrou (*S. African*), wahine (*N.Z.*)

wild ADJECTIVE 1 = <u>untamed</u>,
fierce, savage, ferocious,
unbroken, feral, undomesticated,
free, warrigal (*Austral. literary*)
≠ tame 2 = <u>uncultivated</u>, natural
≠ cultivated 3 = <u>stormy</u>, violent,
rough, raging, choppy,
tempestuous, blustery
4 = <u>excited</u>, crazy (*informal*),
enthusiastic, raving, hysterical
≠ unenthusiastic
5 = <u>uncontrolled</u>, disorderly,
turbulent, wayward, unruly,
rowdy, unfettered, riotous ≠ calm
6 = <u>mad</u> (*informal*), furious,
fuming, infuriated, incensed,
enraged, very angry, irate, tooshie
(*Austral. slang*), off the air (*Austral.
slang*) 7 = <u>uncivilized</u>, fierce,
savage, primitive, ferocious,
barbaric, brutish, barbarous
≠ civilized
● PLURAL NOUN = <u>wilderness</u>,
desert, wasteland, middle of
nowhere (*informal*), backwoods,
back of beyond (*informal*)

wilderness = <u>wilds</u>, desert,
wasteland, uncultivated region

will NOUN 1 = <u>determination</u>,
drive, purpose, commitment,
resolution, resolve, spine,
backbone 2 = <u>wish</u>, mind, desire,
intention, fancy, preference,
inclination 3 = <u>choice</u>,

prerogative, volition 4 = <u>decree</u>, wish, desire, command, dictate, ordinance 5 = <u>testament</u>, bequest(s), last wishes, last will and testament

● VERB 1 = <u>wish</u>, want, prefer, desire, see fit 2 = <u>bequeath</u>, give, leave, transfer, gift, hand on, pass on, confer

willing 1 = <u>inclined</u>, prepared, consenting, agreeable, compliant, amenable ≠ unwilling 2 = <u>ready</u>, game (*informal*) ≠ reluctant

willingly = <u>readily</u>, freely, gladly, happily, eagerly, voluntarily, cheerfully, by choice ≠ unwillingly

willingness = <u>inclination</u>, will, agreement, wish, consent, volition ≠ reluctance

wilt 1 = <u>droop</u>, wither, sag, shrivel 2 = <u>weaken</u>, languish, droop 3 = <u>wane</u>, flag, fade

win VERB 1 = <u>be victorious in</u>, succeed in, prevail in, come first in, be the victor in ≠ lose 2 = <u>be victorious</u>, succeed, triumph, overcome, prevail, conquer, come first, sweep the board ≠ lose 3 = <u>gain</u>, get, land, achieve, earn, secure, obtain, acquire ≠ forfeit

● NOUN = <u>victory</u>, success, triumph, conquest ≠ defeat

● PHRASES **win someone over** or **round** = <u>convince</u>, influence, persuade, convert, sway, prevail

upon, bring *or* talk round

wince VERB = <u>flinch</u>, start, shrink, cringe, quail, recoil, cower, draw back

● NOUN = <u>flinch</u>, start, cringe

wind[1] NOUN 1 = <u>air</u>, blast, hurricane, breeze, draught, gust, zephyr 2 = <u>flatulence</u>, gas 3 = <u>breath</u>, puff, respiration 4 = <u>nonsense</u>, talk, boasting, hot air, babble, bluster, humbug, twaddle (*informal*), bizzo (*Austral. slang*), bull's wool (*Austral. & N.Z. slang*)

● PHRASES **get wind of something** = <u>hear about</u>, learn of, find out about, become aware of, be told about, be informed of, be made aware of, hear tell of

wind[2] VERB 1 = <u>meander</u>, turn, bend, twist, curve, snake, ramble, twist and turn 2 = <u>wrap</u>, twist, reel, curl, loop, coil 3 = <u>coil</u>, curl, spiral, encircle

● PHRASES **wind someone up** (*Informal*) 1 = <u>irritate</u>, excite, anger, annoy, exasperate, nettle, work someone up, pique 2 = <u>tease</u>, kid (*informal*), have someone on (*informal*), annoy, rag (*informal*), rib (*informal*), josh (*informal*), vex ◆ **wind something up** 1 = <u>end</u>, finish, settle, conclude, tie up, wrap up, finalize 2 = <u>close down</u>, close, dissolve, terminate, put something into liquidation

♦ **wind up** = end up, be left, finish up, fetch up (*informal*), land up

windfall = godsend, find, jackpot, bonanza, manna from heaven ≠ misfortune

windy = breezy, wild, stormy, windswept, blustery, gusty, squally, blowy ≠ calm

wing NOUN 1 = faction, group, arm, section, branch
● VERB 1 = fly, soar, glide, take wing 2 = wound, hit, clip

wink VERB 1 = blink, bat, flutter 2 = twinkle, flash, shine, sparkle, gleam, shimmer, glimmer
● NOUN = blink, flutter

winner = victor, champion, master, champ (*informal*), conqueror, prizewinner ≠ loser

winning ADJECTIVE 1 = victorious, first, top, successful, unbeaten, conquering, triumphant, undefeated 2 = charming, pleasing, attractive, engaging, cute, disarming, enchanting, endearing ≠ unpleasant
● PLURAL NOUN = spoils, profits, gains, prize, proceeds, takings

wipe VERB 1 = clean, polish, brush, rub, sponge, mop, swab 2 = erase, remove
● NOUN = rub, brush
● PHRASES **wipe something** or **someone out** = destroy, massacre, erase, eradicate, obliterate, annihilate, exterminate, expunge

wisdom = understanding, learning, knowledge, intelligence, judgment, insight, enlightenment, erudition ≠ foolishness

wise 1 = sage, clever, intelligent, sensible, enlightened, discerning, perceptive, erudite ≠ foolish 2 = sensible, clever, intelligent, prudent, judicious ≠ unwise

wish NOUN 1 = desire, want, hope, urge, intention, fancy (*informal*), ambition, yen (*informal*) ≠ aversion
● VERB = want, feel, choose, please, desire, think fit
● PHRASES **wish for something** = desire, want, hope for, long for, crave, aspire to, yearn for, hanker for

wit 1 = humour, quips, banter, puns, repartee, wordplay, witticisms, badinage ≠ seriousness 2 = humorist, card (*informal*), comedian, wag, joker, dag (*N.Z. informal*) 3 *often plural* = cleverness, sense, brains, wisdom, common sense, intellect, ingenuity, acumen ≠ stupidity

witch = enchantress, magician, hag, crone, sorceress, Wiccan

witchcraft = magic, voodoo, wizardry, black magic, enchantment, occultism, sorcery,

Wicca, makutu (*N.Z.*)

withdraw 1 = <u>remove</u>, take off, pull out, extract, take away, pull back, draw out, draw back 2 = <u>take out</u>, extract, draw out

withdrawal = <u>removal</u>, ending, stopping, taking away, abolition, elimination, cancellation, termination

withdrawn = <u>uncommunicative</u>, reserved, retiring, distant, shy, taciturn, introverted, unforthcoming ≠ outgoing

wither 1 = <u>wilt</u>, decline, decay, disintegrate, perish, shrivel ≠ flourish 2 = <u>waste</u>, decline, shrivel 3 = <u>fade</u>, decline, perish ≠ increase

withering = <u>scornful</u>, devastating, humiliating, snubbing, hurtful, mortifying

withhold 1 = <u>keep secret</u>, refuse, hide, reserve, retain, conceal, suppress, hold back ≠ reveal 2 = <u>hold back</u>, suppress, keep back ≠ release

withstand = <u>resist</u>, suffer, bear, oppose, cope with, endure, tolerate, stand up to ≠ give in to

witness NOUN 1 = <u>observer</u>, viewer, spectator, looker-on, watcher, onlooker, eyewitness, bystander 2 = <u>testifier</u>
● VERB 1 = <u>see</u>, view, watch, note, notice, observe, perceive

2 = <u>countersign</u>, sign, endorse, validate

witty = <u>humorous</u>, funny, clever, amusing, sparkling, whimsical, droll, piquant ≠ dull

wizard = <u>magician</u>, witch, shaman, sorcerer, occultist, magus, conjuror, warlock, tohunga (*N.Z.*)

wobble VERB 1 = <u>shake</u>, rock, sway, tremble, teeter, totter 2 = <u>tremble</u>, shake
● NOUN 1 = <u>unsteadiness</u>, shake, tremble 2 = <u>unsteadiness</u>, shake, tremor

woe 1 = <u>misery</u>, distress, grief, agony, gloom, sadness, sorrow, anguish ≠ happiness 2 = <u>problem</u>, grief, misery, sorrow

woman 1 = <u>lady</u>, girl, female, sheila (*Austral. & N.Z. informal*), vrou (*S. African*), adult female, charlie (*Austral. slang*), chook (*Austral. slang*), wahine (*N.Z.*) ≠ man

womanly 1 = <u>feminine</u>, motherly, female, warm, tender, matronly, ladylike 2 = <u>curvaceous</u>, ample, voluptuous, shapely, curvy (*informal*), busty (*informal*), buxom, full-figured

wonder VERB 1 = <u>think</u>, question, puzzle, speculate, query, ponder, meditate, conjecture 2 = <u>be amazed</u>, stare, marvel, be astonished, gape
● NOUN 1 = <u>amazement</u>, surprise,

admiration, awe, fascination, astonishment, bewilderment, wonderment 2 = <u>phenomenon</u>, sight, miracle, spectacle, curiosity, marvel, prodigy, rarity

wonderful 1 = <u>excellent</u>, great (*informal*), brilliant, outstanding, superb, fantastic (*informal*), tremendous, magnificent, booshit (*Austral. slang*), exo (*Austral. slang*), sik (*Austral. slang*) ≠ terrible 2 = <u>remarkable</u>, amazing, extraordinary, incredible, astonishing, staggering, startling, phenomenal ≠ ordinary

woo 1 = <u>seek</u>, cultivate 2 = <u>court</u>, pursue

wood 1 = <u>timber</u>, planks, planking, lumber (*U.S.*) 2 *or* **woods** = <u>woodland</u>, forest, grove, thicket, copse, coppice 3 = <u>firewood</u>, fuel, logs, kindling

wooded = <u>tree-covered</u>, forested, timbered, sylvan (*poetic*), tree-clad

wooden 1 = <u>made of wood</u>, timber, woody, ligneous 2 = <u>expressionless</u>, lifeless, deadpan, unresponsive

wool 1 = <u>fleece</u>, hair, coat 2 = <u>yarn</u>

word NOUN 1 = <u>term</u>, name, expression 2 = <u>chat</u>, tête-à-tête, talk, discussion, consultation, confab (*informal*), heart-to-heart,

powwow (*informal*) 3 = <u>comment</u>, remark, utterance 4 = <u>message</u>, news, report, information, notice, intelligence, dispatch, communiqué 5 = <u>promise</u>, guarantee, pledge, vow, assurance, oath 6 = <u>command</u>, order, decree, bidding, mandate ● VERB = <u>express</u>, say, state, put, phrase, utter, couch, formulate

Related Words
adjectives: lexical, verbal

wording = <u>phraseology</u>, words, language, phrasing, terminology

work VERB 1 = <u>be employed</u>, be in work 2 = <u>labour</u>, sweat, slave, toil, slog (away), drudge, peg away, exert yourself ≠ relax 3 = <u>function</u>, go, run, operate, be in working order ≠ be out of order 4 = <u>succeed</u>, work out, pay off (*informal*), be successful, be effective, do the trick (*informal*), do the business (*informal*), get results 5 = <u>cultivate</u>, farm, dig, till, plough 6 = <u>operate</u>, use, move, control, drive, manage, handle, manipulate 7 = <u>manipulate</u>, form, fashion, shape, mould, knead ● NOUN 1 = <u>employment</u>, business, job, trade, duty, profession, occupation, livelihood ≠ play 2 = <u>effort</u>, industry, labour, sweat, toil, exertion, drudgery, elbow grease (*facetious*) ≠ leisure 3 = <u>task</u>, jobs, projects, commissions, duties, assignments, chores, yakka (*Austral. & N.Z. informal*) 4 = <u>handiwork</u>, doing, act, feat, deed 5 = <u>creation</u>, piece, production, opus, achievement, composition, handiwork

• **PLURAL NOUN 1** = <u>factory</u>, plant, mill, workshop **2** = <u>writings</u>, output, canon, oeuvre (*French*) **3** = <u>mechanism</u>, workings, parts, action, movement, machinery

• **PHRASES work something out** = <u>solve</u>, find out, calculate, figure out

worker = <u>employee</u>, hand, labourer, workman, craftsman, artisan, tradesman

workman = <u>labourer</u>, hand, worker, employee, mechanic, operative, craftsman, artisan

workshop 1 = <u>factory</u>, plant, mill **2** = <u>workroom</u>, studio

world 1 = <u>earth</u>, planet, globe **2** = <u>mankind</u>, man, everyone, the public, everybody, humanity, humankind **3** = <u>sphere</u>, area, field, environment, realm, domain **4** (usually used in phrase *a world of difference*) = <u>huge amount</u>, mountain, wealth, great deal, good deal, abundance, enormous amount, vast amount

worldly 1 = <u>earthly</u>, physical, secular, terrestrial, temporal, profane ≠ spiritual

2 = <u>materialistic</u>, grasping, selfish, greedy ≠ nonmaterialistic **3** = <u>worldly-wise</u>, knowing, experienced, sophisticated, cosmopolitan, urbane, blasé ≠ naive

worn = <u>ragged</u>, frayed, shabby, tattered, tatty, threadbare, the worse for wear

worried = <u>anxious</u>, concerned, troubled, afraid, frightened, nervous, tense, uneasy ≠ unworried

worry VERB 1 = <u>be anxious</u>, be concerned, be worried, brood, fret, agonize, get in a lather (*informal*) ≠ be unconcerned **2** = <u>trouble</u>, upset, bother, disturb, annoy, unsettle, pester, vex ≠ soothe

• **NOUN 1** = <u>anxiety</u>, concern, fear, trouble, unease, apprehension, misgiving, trepidation ≠ peace of mind **2** = <u>problem</u>, care, trouble, bother, hassle (*informal*)

worsen 1 = <u>deteriorate</u>, decline, sink, decay, get worse, degenerate, go downhill (*informal*) ≠ improve

2 = <u>aggravate</u>, damage, exacerbate, make worse ≠ improve

worship VERB 1 = <u>revere</u>, praise, honour, adore, glorify, exalt, pray to, venerate ≠ dishonour **2** = <u>love</u>, adore, idolize, put on a pedestal

≠ despise

● NOUN = <u>reverence</u>, praise, regard, respect, honour, glory, devotion, adulation

worth 1 = <u>value</u>, price, rate, cost, estimate, valuation
≠ worthlessness 2 = <u>merit</u>, value, quality, importance, excellence, goodness, worthiness
≠ unworthiness 3 = <u>usefulness</u>, value, quality, importance, excellence, goodness
≠ uselessness

worthless 1 = <u>valueless</u>, rubbishy, negligible ≠ valuable 2 = <u>useless</u>, unimportant, ineffectual, negligible ≠ useful 3 = <u>good-for-nothing</u>, vile, despicable, contemptible
≠ honourable

worthwhile = <u>useful</u>, valuable, helpful, profitable, productive, beneficial, meaningful, constructive ≠ useless

worthy = <u>praiseworthy</u>, deserving, valuable, worthwhile, admirable, virtuous, creditable, laudable ≠ disreputable

would-be = <u>budding</u>, self-styled, wannabe (*informal*), unfulfilled, self-appointed

wound NOUN 1 = <u>injury</u>, cut, hurt, trauma (*Pathology*), gash, lesion, laceration 2 *often plural* = <u>trauma</u>, offence, slight, insult

● VERB 1 = <u>injure</u>, cut, wing, hurt,

pierce, gash, lacerate 2 = <u>offend</u>, hurt, annoy, sting, mortify, cut to the quick

wrangle VERB = <u>argue</u>, fight, row, dispute, disagree, contend, quarrel, squabble

● NOUN = <u>argument</u>, row, dispute, quarrel, squabble, bickering, tiff, altercation

wrap VERB 1 = <u>cover</u>, enclose, shroud, swathe, encase, enfold, bundle up 2 = <u>pack</u>, package, parcel (up), tie up, gift-wrap
≠ unpack 3 = <u>bind</u>, swathe
≠ unwind

● NOUN = <u>cloak</u>, cape, stole, mantle, shawl

● PHRASES **wrap something up** 1 = <u>giftwrap</u>, pack, package, bundle up 2 (*Informal*) = <u>end</u>, conclude, wind up, terminate, finish off, round off, polish off

wrath = <u>anger</u>, rage, temper, fury, resentment, indignation, ire, displeasure ≠ satisfaction

wreck VERB 1 = <u>destroy</u>, break, smash, ruin, devastate, shatter, spoil, demolish ≠ build 2 = <u>spoil</u>, ruin, devastate, shatter, crool *or* cruel (*Austral. slang*) ≠ save

● NOUN = <u>shipwreck</u>, hulk

wreckage = <u>remains</u>, pieces, ruin, fragments, debris, rubble

wrench VERB 1 = <u>twist</u>, force, pull, tear, rip, tug, jerk, yank 2 = <u>sprain</u>, strain, rick

● **NOUN 1** = <u>twist</u>, pull, rip, tug, jerk, yank **2** = <u>sprain</u>, strain, twist **3** = <u>blow</u>, shock, upheaval, pang **4** = <u>spanner</u>, adjustable spanner

wrestle = <u>fight</u>, battle, struggle, combat, grapple, tussle, scuffle

wrinkle NOUN **1** = <u>line</u>, fold, crease, furrow, crow's-foot, corrugation **2** = <u>crease</u>, fold, crumple, furrow, crinkle, corrugation

● **VERB 1** = <u>crease</u>, gather, fold, crumple, rumple, pucker, corrugate ≠ smooth

writ = <u>summons</u>, document, decree, indictment, court order, subpoena, arraignment

write 1 = <u>record</u>, scribble, inscribe, set down, jot down **2** = <u>compose</u>, draft, pen, draw up **3** = <u>correspond</u>, get in touch, keep in touch, write a letter, drop a line, drop a note

writer = <u>author</u>, novelist, hack, scribbler, scribe, wordsmith, penpusher

writing = <u>script</u>, hand, printing, fist (informal), scribble, handwriting, scrawl, calligraphy

wrong ADJECTIVE **1** = <u>amiss</u>, faulty, unsatisfactory, not right, defective, awry **2** = <u>incorrect</u>, mistaken, false, inaccurate, untrue, erroneous, wide of the mark, fallacious **3** = <u>inappropriate</u>, incorrect, unsuitable, unacceptable, undesirable, incongruous, unseemly, unbecoming ≠ correct **4** = <u>bad</u>, criminal, illegal, evil, unlawful, immoral, unjust, dishonest ≠ moral **5** = <u>defective</u>, faulty, awry, askew

● ADVERB **1** = <u>incorrectly</u>, badly, wrongly, mistakenly, erroneously, inaccurately ≠ correctly **2** = <u>amiss</u>, astray, awry, askew

● NOUN = <u>offence</u>, injury, crime, error, sin, injustice, misdeed, transgression ≠ good deed

● VERB = <u>mistreat</u>, abuse, hurt, harm, cheat, take advantage of, oppress, malign ≠ treat well

X

X-ray = <u>radiograph</u>, x-ray image

Y

yank VERB = <u>pull</u>, tug, jerk, seize, snatch, pluck, hitch, wrench

● NOUN = <u>pull</u>, tug, jerk, snatch, hitch, wrench, tweak

yarn 1 = <u>thread</u>, fibre, cotton, wool **2** (Informal) = <u>story</u>, tale, anecdote, account, narrative, fable, reminiscence, urban myth

yawning = <u>gaping</u>, wide, huge, vast, cavernous

Shades of yellow

amber	daffodil	oatmeal	straw
buff	gold *or* golden	ochre	tea rose
canary yellow	lemon	old gold	topaz
champagne	maize	primrose	tortoiseshell
cinnamon	mustard	saffron	

yearly ADJECTIVE = <u>annual</u>, each year, every year, once a year
● ADVERB = <u>annually</u>, every year, by the year, once a year, per annum

yearn often with **for** = <u>long</u>, desire, hunger, ache, crave, covet, itch, hanker after

yell VERB = <u>scream</u>, shout, cry out, howl, call out, wail, shriek, screech ≠ whisper
● NOUN = <u>scream</u>, cry, shout, roar, howl, shriek, whoop, screech ≠ whisper

yellow ► shades of yellow

yen = <u>longing</u>, desire, craving, yearning, passion, hunger, ache, itch

yet ADVERB 1 = <u>so far</u>, until now, up to now, still, as yet, even now, thus far, up till now 2 = <u>now</u>, right now, just now, so soon 3 = <u>still</u>, in addition, besides, to boot, into the bargain
● CONJUNCTION = <u>nevertheless</u>, still, however, for all that, notwithstanding, just the same, be that as it may

yield VERB 1 = <u>bow</u>, submit, give in, surrender, succumb, cave in (*informal*), capitulate 2 = <u>relinquish</u>, resign, hand over, surrender, turn over, make over, give over, bequeath ≠ retain ≠ resist 3 = <u>produce</u>, give, provide, return, supply, bear, net, earn ≠ use up
● NOUN 1 = <u>produce</u>, crop, harvest, output 2 = <u>profit</u>, return, income, revenue, earnings, takings ≠ loss

yielding 1 = <u>soft</u>, pliable, springy, elastic, supple, spongy, unresisting 2 = <u>submissive</u>, obedient, compliant, docile, flexible, accommodating, pliant, acquiescent ≠ obstinate

yob *or* **yobbo** = <u>thug</u>, hooligan, lout, hoon (*Austral. & N.Z. slang*), ruffian, roughneck (*slang*), tsotsi (*S. African*), cougan (*Austral. slang*), scozza (*Austral. slang*), bogan (*Austral. slang*)

young ADJECTIVE 1 = <u>immature</u>, juvenile, youthful, little, green, junior, infant, adolescent ≠ old 2 = <u>early</u>, new, undeveloped, fledgling ≠ advanced
● PLURAL NOUN = <u>offspring</u>, babies,

litter, family, issue, brood, progeny ≠ parents

youngster = youth, girl, boy, kid (*informal*), lad, teenager, juvenile, lass

youth 1 = immaturity, adolescence, boyhood *or* girlhood, salad days ≠ old age

2 = boy, lad, youngster, kid (*informal*), teenager, young man, adolescent, teen (*informal*) ≠ adult

youthful = young, juvenile, childish, immature, boyish, girlish ≠ elderly

Z

zeal = enthusiasm, passion, zest, spirit, verve, fervour, eagerness,

gusto ≠ apathy

zero 1 = nought, nothing, nil

2 = rock bottom, the bottom, an all-time low, a nadir, as low as you can get

zip VERB = speed, shoot, fly, flash, zoom, whizz (*informal*)

● NOUN (*Informal*) = energy, drive, vigour, verve, zest, gusto, liveliness ≠ lethargy

zone = area, region, section, sector, district, territory, belt, sphere

zoom = speed, shoot, fly, rush, flash, dash, whizz (*informal*), hurtle

WORD
POWER

Supplement

CONTENTS

WORD POWER

CONTENTS

WORD POWER

ACTORS

Male

Woody Allen (*U.S.*)
Fred Astaire (*U.S.*)
Richard Attenborough (*English*)
Jean-Louis Barrault (*French*)
John Barrymore (*U.S.*)
Alan Bates (*English*)
Warren Beatty (*U.S.*)
Jean-Paul Belmondo (*French*)
Alan Bennett (*English*)
Dirk Bogarde (*English*)
Humphrey Bogart (*U.S.*)
Charles Boyer (*French*)
Kenneth Branagh (*English*)
Marlon Brando (*U.S.*)
Adrien Brody (*U.S.*)
Mel Brooks (*U.S.*)
Richard Burbage (*English*)
Richard Burton (*Welsh*)
Glen Byam Shaw (*English*)
James Cagney (*U.S.*)
Michael Caine (*English*)
Simon Callow (*English*)
Robert Carlyle (*Scottish*)
Jim Carrey (*U.S.*)
Charlie Chaplin (*English*)
Maurice Chevalier (*French*)
John Cleese (*English*)
George Clooney (*U.S.*)
Sean Connery (*Scottish*)
Peter Cook (*English*)

Chris Cooper (*U.S.*)
Gary Cooper (*U.S.*)
Kevin Costner (*U.S.*)
Noel Coward (*English*)
Michael Crawford (*English*)
Tom Cruise (*U.S.*)
James Dean (*U.S.*)
Robert De Niro (*U.S.*)
Gerard Depardieu (*French*)
Vittorio de Sica (*Italian*)
John Dexter (*English*)
Leonardo DiCaprio (*U.S.*)
Kirk Douglas (*U.S.*)
Michael Douglas (*U.S.*)
Clint Eastwood (*U.S.*)
Douglas Fairbanks Jr. (*U.S.*)
Douglas Fairbanks Snr. (*U.S.*)
WC Fields (*U.S.*)
Albert Finney (*English*)
Errol Flynn (*Australian*)
Henry Fonda (*U.S.*)
Harrison Ford (*U.S.*)
Jean Gabin (*France*)
Clark Gable (*U.S.*)
David Garrick (*English*)
Mel Gibson (*Australian*)
John Gielgud (*English*)
Cary Grant (*English-U.S.*)
Alec Guinness (*English*)
Gene Hackman (*U.S.*)
Tom Hanks (*U.S.*)

4

Male (continued)

Oliver Hardy (*U.S.*)
Rex Harrison (*English*)
Dustin Hoffman (*U.S.*)
Bob Hope (*U.S.*)
Anthony Hopkins (*Welsh*)
Michael Hordern (*English*)
Leslie Howard (*English*)
Trevor Howard (*English*)
Rock Hudson (*U.S.*)
Barry Humphries (*Australian*)
John Hurt (*English*)
Jeremy Irons (*English*)
Henry Irving (*English*)
Derek Jacobi (*English*)
Al Jolson (*U.S.*)
Boris Karloff (*English*)
Edmund Kean (*English*)
Buster Keaton (*U.S.*)
Harvey Keitel (*U.S.*)
Gene Kelly (*U.S.*)
John Kemble (*English*)
Burt Lancaster (*U.S.*)
Charles Laughton (*English-U.S.*)
Stan Laurel (*English-U.S.*)
Bruce Lee (*U.S.*)
Christopher Lee (*English*)
Harold Lloyd (*U.S.*)
Bela Lugosi (*Hungarian*)
Ewan McGregor (*Scottish*)

Ian McKellen (*English*)
Steve McQueen (*U.S.*)
William Macready (*English*)
James Mason (*English*)
Raymond Massey (*Canadian*)
Marcello Mastroianni (*Italian*)
Bernard Miles (*English*)
John Mills (*English*)
Robert Mitchum (*U.S.*)
Dudley Moore (*English*)
Robert Morley (*English*)
Sam Neill (*N.Z.*)
Paul Newman (*U.S.*)
Jack Nicholson (*U.S.*)
Liam Neeson (*Irish*)
David Niven (*English*)
Gary Oldman (*English*)
Laurence Olivier (*English*)
Peter O'Toole (*Irish-British*)
Al Pacino (*U.S.*)
Gregory Peck (*U.S.*)
Donald Pleasence (*English*)
Anthony Quayle (*English*)
Anthony Quinn (*U.S.*)
Daniel Radcliffe (*English*)
Ronald Reagan (*U.S.*)
Robert Redford (*U.S.*)
Michael Redgrave (*English*)
Fernando Rey (*Spanish*)
Ralph Richardson (*English*)
Paul Robeson (*U.S.*)

WORD POWER

WORD POWER

Male (continued)

Edward G Robinson (*U.S.*)
Tim Roth (*English*)
Arnold Schwarzenegger (*Austrian-U.S.*)
Paul Scofield (*English*)
Peter Sellers (*English*)
Sam Shepard (*U.S.*)
Sylvester Stallone (*U.S.*)
Konstantin Stanislavsky (*Russian*)
James Stewart (*U.S.*)
Donald Sutherland (*Canadian*)

Jacques Tati (*French*)
Spencer Tracy (*U.S.*)
John Travolta (*U.S.*)
Peter Ustinov (*English*)
Rudolph Valentino (*Italian-U.S.*)
Max Von Sydow (*Swedish*)
John Wayne (*U.S.*)
Johnny Weissmuller (*U.S.*)
Orson Welles (*U.S.*)
Elijah Wood (*U.S.*)

Female

Yvonne Arnaud (*French*)
Peggy Ashcroft (*English*)
Tallulah Bankhead (*U.S.*)
Brigitte Bardot (*French*)
Ingrid Bergman (*Swedish-U.S.*)
Sarah Bernhardt (*French*)
Clara Bow (*U.S.*)
Fanny Brice (*U.S.*)
Glenn Close (*U.S.*)
Claudette Colbert (*French-U.S.*)
Joan Crawford (*U.S.*)
Bette Davis (*U.S.*)
Geena Davis (*U.S.*)
Judy Davis (*Australian*)

Judi Dench (*English*)
Catherine Deneuve (*French*)
Marlene Dietrich (*German*)
Faye Dunaway (*U.S.*)
Edith Evans (*English*)
Jane Fonda (*U.S.*)
Jodie Foster (*U.S.*)
Greta Garbo (*Swedish*)
Ava Gardner (*U.S.*)
Judy Garland (*U.S.*)
Lillian Gish (*U.S.*)
Joyce Grenfell (*English*)
Jean Harlow (*U.S.*)
Audrey Hepburn (*Belgian-U.S.*)
Katharine Hepburn (*U.S.*)

Female (continued)

Wendy Hiller (*English*)
Holly Hunter (*U.S.*)
Isabelle Huppert (*French*)
Glenda Jackson (*English*)
Diane Keaton (*U.S.*)
Grace Kelly (*U.S.*)
Fanny Kemble (*English-U.S.*)
Nicole Kidman (*Australian*)
Jessica Lange (*U.S.*)
Gertrude Lawrence (*English*)
Vivien Leigh (*English*)
Lotte Lenya (*Austrian*)
Margaret Lockwood (*English*)
Jennifer Lopez (*Puerto Rican*)
Sophia Loren (*Italian*)
Siobhan McKenna (*Irish*)
Shirley MacLaine (*U.S.*)
Melina Mercouri (*Greek*)
Liza Minnelli (*U.S.*)
Helen Mirren (*English*)
Marilyn Monroe (*U.S.*)
Jeanne Moreau (*French*)
Michelle Pfeiffer (*U.S.*)
Mary Pickford (*U.S.*)
Joan Plowright (*English*)
Jian Qing (*Chinese*)

Vanessa Redgrave (*English*)
Julia Roberts (*U.S.*)
Flora Robson (*English*)
Ginger Rogers (*U.S.*)
Margaret Rutherford (*English*)
Susan Sarandon (*U.S.*)
Delphine Seyrig (*French*)
Sarah Siddons (*English*)
Simone Signoret (*French*)
Maggie Smith (*English*)
Meryl Streep (*U.S.*)
Barbra Streisand (*U.S.*)
Janet Suzman (*South African*)
Elizabeth Taylor (*English-U.S.*)
Shirley Temple (*U.S.*)
Ellen Terry (*English*)
Emma Thompson (*English*)
Sybil Thorndike (*English*)
Sigourney Weaver (*U.S.*)
Raquel Welch (*U.S.*)
Mae West (*U.S.*)
Billie Whitelaw (*English*)
Kate Winslet (*English*)
Peg Woffington (*Irish*)
Catherine Zeta-Jones (*Welsh*)

WORD POWER

ADMINISTRATIVE REGIONS

French regions

Alsace	Île-de-France
Aquitaine	Languedoc-Roussillon
Auvergne	Limousin
Basse-Normandie	Lorraine
Brittany	Midi-Pyrénées
Burgundy	Nord-Pas-de-Calais
Centre	Pays de Loire
Champagne-Ardenne	Picardie
Corsica	Poitou-Charentes
Franche-Comté	Provence-Alpes-Côte d'Azur
Haute-Normandie	Rhône-Alpes

French départements

Ain	Corse	Haute Marne
Aisne	Cote d'Or	Haute Savoie
Allier	Côtes du Nord	Haute Vienne
Alpes de Haute Provence	Creuse	Hautes Alpes
Alpes Maritimes	Deux Sèvres	Hautes Pyrénées
Ardèche	Dordogne	Hauts de Seine
Ardennes	Doubs	Hérault
Ariège	Drôme	Ille et Vilaine
Aube	Essone	Indre
Aude	Eure	Indre et Loire
Aveyron	Eure et Loir	Isère
Bas Rhin	Finistère	Jura
Bouches du Rhône	Gard	Landes
Calvados	Gayane	Loir et Cher
Cantal	Gers	Loire
Charente	Gironde	Loire Atlantique
Charente Maritime	Guadeloupe	Loiret
Cher	Haut Rhin	Lot
Corrèze	Haute Garonne	Lot et Garonne
	Haute Loire	Lozère

8

French départements (continued)

Maine et Loire	Pas de Calais	Tarn
Manche	Puy de Dôme	Tarn et Garonne
Marne	Pyrénées Atlantiques	Territoire de
Martinique	Pyrénées Orientales	Belfort
Mayenne	Réunion	Val d'Oise
Meurthe et Moselle	Rhône	Val de Marne
Meuse	Saône	Var
Morbihan	Saône et Loire	Vaucluse
Moselle	Sarthe	Vendée
Niveres	Savoie	Vienne
Nord	Seine et Marne	Vosges
Oise	Seine Maritime	Yonne
Orne	Seine Saint Denis	Yvelines
Paris	Somme	

German states

Baden-Württemberg	Mecklenburg-West Pomerania
Bavaria	North Rhine-Westphalia
Berlin	Rhineland-Palatinate
Brandenburg	Saarland
Bremen	Saxony
Hamburg	Saxony-Anhalt
Hessen	Schleswig-Holstein
Lower Saxony	Thuringia

Italian regions

Abruzzo	Lazio	Sardinia
Basilicata	Liguria	Sicily
Calabria	Lombardy	Trentino-Alto Adige
Campania	Marche	Tuscany
Emilia-Romagna	Molise	Umbria
Friuli-Venezia	Piedmont	Valle d'Aosta
Giulia	Puglia	Veneto

Italian provinces

Agrigento	Forlì	Pescara
Alessandria	Frosinone	Piacenza
Ancona	Genova	Pisa
Aosta	Gorizia	Pistoia
Arezzo	Grosseto	Pordenone
Ascoli Piceno	Imperia	Potenza
Asti	Isernia	Prato
Avellino	L'Aquila	Ragusa
Bari	La Spezia	Ravenna
Belluno	Latina	Reggio di Calabria
Benevento	Lecce	Reggio Emilia
Bergamo	Lecco	Rieti
Bologna	Livorno	Rimini
Bolzano	Lodi	Roma
Brescia	Lucca	Rovigo
Brindisi	Macerata	Salerno
Cagliari	Mantova	Sassari
Caltanissetta	Massa Carrara	Savona
Campobasso	Matera	Siena
Caserta	Messina	Siracusa
Catania	Milano	Sondrio
Catanzaro	Modena	Taranto
Chieti	Napoli	Teramo
Como	Novara	Terni
Cosenza	Nuoro	Torino
Cremona	Oristano	Trapani
Crotone	Padova	Trento
Cuneo	Palermo	Treviso
Enna	Parma	Trieste
Ferrara	Pavia	Udine
Firenze	Perugia	Varese
Foggia	Pesaro	Venezia

WORD POWER

ADMINISTRATIVE REGIONS

Italian provinces (continued)

Verbania	Vibo Valentia	Repubblica di San
Vercelli	Vicenza	Marino
Verona	Viterbo	

Spanish regions

Andalucía	Castilla-La Mancha	Murcia
Aragón	Castilla-León	Navarra
Asturias	Catalonia	Valencian
Balearic Islands	Extremadura	Community
Basque Country	Galicia	Ceuta
Canary Islands	La Rioja	Melilla
Cantabria	Madrid	

Spanish provinces

Álava	Ciudad Real	Orense
Albacete	Girona	Palencia
Alhucemas	Granada	Pontevedra
Alicante	Gualalajara	Salamanca
Almeria	Guipúzcoa	Santa Cruz de
Asturias	Huelva	Tenerife
Ávila	Huesca	Segovia
Badajoz	Jaén	Sevilla
Balearics	La Coruna	Soria
Barcelona	La Rioja	Tarragona
Burgos	Las Palmas	Teruel
Cácares	León	Toledo
Cádiz	Lleida	Valencia
Cantabria	Lugo	Valladolid
Castellón	Madrid	Vélez de la Gomera
Chafarinas	Málaga	Vizcaya
Cordoba	Melilla	Zamora
Cuenca	Murcia	Zaragoza
Ceuta	Navarra	

WORD POWER

Agostino di Duccio (*Italian*)
Josef Albers (*German-U.S.*)
Leon Battista Alberti (*Italian*)
Washington Allston (*U.S.*)
Lawrence Alma-Tadema
  (*Dutch-English*)
Albrecht Altdorfer (*German*)
Fra Angelico (*Italian*)
Pietro Annigoni (*Italian*)
Antonello da Messina (*Italian*)
Apelles (*Greek*)
Karel Appel (*Dutch*)
Aleksandr Porfiryevich
  Archipenko (*Russian*)
Giuseppe Arcimboldo
  (*Italian*)
Jean or Hans Arp (*French*)
John James Audubon (*U.S.*)
Frank Auerbach (*English-
  German*)
Francis Bacon (*Irish*)
Leon Nikolayevich Bakst
  (*Russian*)
Balthus (*Polish-French*)
Frédéric August Bartholdi
  (*French*)
Fra Bartolommeo (*Italian*)
Max Beckmann (*German*)
Vanessa Bell (*English*)
Giovanni Bellini (*Italian*)
Thomas Hart Benton
  (*U.S.*)

Gian Lorenzo Bernini (*Italian*)
Joseph Beuys (*German*)
Peter Blake (*English*)
William Blake (*English*)
Umberto Boccioni (*Italian*)
David Bomberg (*English*)
Rosa Bonheur (*French*)
Pierre Bonnard (*French*)
Richard Parkes Bonnington
  (*English*)
Gutzon Borglum (*U.S.*)
Hieronymus Bosch (*Dutch*)
Sandro Botticelli (*Italian*)
Francois Boucher (*French*)
Eugène Boudin (*French*)
Arthur Boyd (*Australian*)
Donato Bramante (*Italian*)
Constantin Brancusi
  (*Romanian*)
Georges Braque (*French*)
Brassaï (*French*)
Agnolo Bronzino (*Italian*)
Ford Madox Brown (*English*)
Jan Brueghel (*Flemish*)
Pieter Brueghel the Elder
  (*Flemish*)
Pieter Brueghel the Younger
  (*Flemish*)
Bernard Buffet (*French*)
Edward Burne-Jones (*English*)
Edward Burra (*English*)
Reg Butler (*English*)

Alexander Calder (*U.S.*)
Callimachus (*Greek*)
Robert Campin (*Flemish*)
Antonio Canova (*Italian*)
Michelangelo Merisi da
  Caravaggio (*Italian*)
Anthony Caro (*English*)
Vittore Carpaccio (*Italian*)
Agostino Carracci (*Italian*)
Annibale Carracci (*Italian*)
Ludovico Carracci (*Italian*)
Mary Cassatt (*U.S.*)
Pietro Cavallini (*Italian*)
Benvenuto Cellini (*Italian*)
Lynn Chadwick (*English*)
Marc Chagall (*Russian-
  French*)
Philippe de Champaigne
  (*French*)
Jean-Baptiste Siméon Chardin
  (*French*)
Giorgio de Chirico (*Italian*)
Giovanni Cimabue (*Italian*)
Claude Lorrain (*French*)
François Clouet (*French*)
Jean Clouet (*French*)
John Constable (*English*)
John Copley (*U.S.*)
Jean Baptiste Camille Corot
  (*French*)
Antonio Allegri da Corregio
  (*Italian*)

Gustave Courbet (*French*)
David Cox (*English*)
Antoine Coypel (*French*)
Lucas Cranach (*German*)
Walter Crane (*English*)
John Crome (*English*)
Aelbert Cuyp or Kuyp (*Dutch*)
Paul Cézanne (*French*)
Richard Dadd (*English*)
Salvador Dalí (*Spanish*)
Francis Danby (*Irish*)
Charles François Daubigny
  (*French*)
Honoré Daumier (*French*)
Jacques Louis David (*French*)
Peter de Wint (*English*)
Hilaire Germain Edgar Degas
  (*French*)
Eugène Delacroix (*French*)
Paul Delaroche (*French*)
Robert Delaunay (*French*)
Paul Delvaux (*Belgian*)
Maurice Denis (*French*)
André Derain (*French*)
William Dobell (*Australian*)
Domenichino (*Italian*)
Domenico del Barbiere
  (*Italian*)
Donatello (*Italian*)
Gerrit Dou (*Dutch*)
George Russell Drysdale
  (*Australian*)

WORD POWER

13

WORD POWER

Jean Dubuffet (*French*)

Duccio di Buoninsegna (*Italian*)

Marcel Duchamp (*French-U.S.*)

Raoul Dufy (*French*)

Albrecht Dürer (*German*)

Thomas Eakins (*U.S.*)

El Greco (*Greek-Spanish*)

James Ensor (*Belgian*)

Jacob Epstein (*British*)

Max Ernst (*German*)

Henri Fantin-Latour (*French*)

Lyonel Feininger (*U.S.*)

John Flaxman (*English*)

Jean Fouquet (*French*)

Jean Honoré Fragonard (*French*)

Lucian Freud (*English*)

Caspar David Friedrich (*German*)

Roger Fry (*English*)

Henry Fuseli (*Swiss*)

Naum Gabo (*Russian-U.S.*)

Thomas Gainsborough (*English*)

Henri Gaudier-Brzeska (*French*)

Paul Gauguin (*French*)

Gentile da Fabriano (*Italian*)

Lorenzo Ghiberti (*Italian*)

Domenico Ghirlandaio (*Italian*)

Alberto Giacometti (*Swiss*)

Giambologna (*Italian*)

Grinling Gibbons (*Dutch*)

Gilbert (Proesch) and George (Passmore) (*English*)

Eric Gill (*English*)

Giorgione da Castelfranco (*Italian*)

Giotto di Bondone (*Italian*)

Giulio Romano (*Italian*)

Hugo van der Goes (*Flemish*)

Julio González (*Spanish*)

Arshile Gorky (*U.S.*)

Francisco de Goya (*Spanish*)

Jan van Goyen (*Dutch*)

Duncan Grant (*Scottish*)

Jean Baptiste Greuze (*French*)

Juan Gris (*Spanish*)

Antoine Jean Gros (*French*)

George Grosz (*German-U.S.*)

Grünewald (*German*)

Francesco Guardi (*Italian*)

François Gérard (*French*)

Théodore Géricault (*French*)

Frans Hals (*Dutch*)

Richard Hamilton (*English*)

Ando Hiroshige (*Japanese*)

Damien Hirst (*English*)

Meindert Hobbema (*Dutch*)

David Hockney (*English*)

Hans Hofmann (*German-U.S.*)

William Hogarth (*English*)

Katsushika Hokusai (*Japanese*)

Hans Holbein (*German*)

Winslow Homer (*U.S.*)

Pieter de Hooch or Hoogh (*Dutch*)

Edward Hopper (*U.S.*)

Jean Antoine Houdon (*French*)

William Holman Hunt (*English*)

Jean Auguste Dominique Ingres (*French*)

Augustus John (*Welsh*)

Gwen John (*Welsh*)

Jasper Johns (*U.S.*)

Johan Barthold Jongkind (*Dutch*)

Jacob Jordaens (*Flemish*)

Wassily Kandinsky (*Russian*)

Angelica Kauffmann (*Swiss*)

Ernst Ludwig Kirchner (*German*)

Ron B. Kitaj (*U.S.*)

Paul Klee (*Swiss*)

Gustav Klimt (*Austrian*)

Franz Kline (*U.S.*)

Godfrey Kneller (*German-English*)

Laura Knight (*English*)

Oscar Kokoschka (*Austrian*)

Willem de Kooning (*Dutch-U.S.*)

Leon Kossoff (*English*)

Georges de La Tour (*French*)

Edwin Landseer (*English*)

Thomas Lawrence (*English*)

Charles Lebrun (*French*)

Fernand Léger (*French*)

Wilhelm Lehmbruck (*German*)

Frederic Leighton (*English*)

Peter Lely (*Dutch-English*)

Leonardo da Vinci (*Italian*)

Wyndham Lewis (*British*)

Roy Lichtenstein (*U.S.*)

Norman Alfred William Lindsay (*Australian*)

Jacques Lipchitz (*Lithuanian-U.S.*)

Filippino Lippi (*Italian*)

L(awrence) S(tephen) Lowry (*English*)

Lysippus (*Greek*)

Jan Mabuse (*Flemish*)

Charles Rennie Mackintosh (*Scottish*)

René Magritte (*Belgian*)

Aristide Maillol (*French*)

Kasimir Severinovich Malevich (*Russian*)

WORD POWER

Edouard Manet (*French*)
Andrea Mantegna (*Italian*)
Franz Marc (*German*)
John Martin (*English*)
Simone Martini (*Italian*)
Masaccio (*Italian*)
Quentin Massys (*Flemish*)
Henri Matisse (*French*)
Hans Memling or Memlinc
  (*Flemish*)
Franz Xavier Messerschmidt
  (*Austrian*)
Ivan Mestrovic (*Yugoslav-U.S.*)
Michelangelo Buonarroti
  (*Italian*)
Michelozzi Michelozzo
  (*Italian*)
John Everett Millais (*English*)
Jean François Millet (*French*)
Joan Miró (*Spanish*)
Amedeo Modigliani (*Italian*)
László Moholy-Nagy
  (*Hungarian*)
Piet Mondrian (*Dutch*)
Claude Oscar Monet (*French*)
Henry Moore (*British*)
Gustave Moreau (*French*)
Berthe Morisot (*French*)
William Morris (*English*)
Samuel Finley Breese Morse
  (*U.S.*)
Grandma Moses (*U.S.*)

Edvard Munch (*Norwegian*)
Alfred Munnings (*English*)
Bartolomé Esteban Murillo
  (*Spanish*)
Myron (*Greek*)
Paul Nash (*English*)
Ernst Wilhelm Nay (*German*)
Barnett Newman (*U.S.*)
Ben Nicholson (*English*)
Sidney Nolan (*Australian*)
Emil Nolde (*German*)
Joseph Nollekens (*Dutch-
  English*)
Georgia O'Keefe (*U.S.*)
Claes Oldenburg (*Swedish-
  U.S.*)
Orcagna (*Italian*)
José Clemente Orozco
  (*Mexican*)
Jean Baptiste Oudry (*French*)
Palma Vecchio (*Italian*)
Samuel Palmer (*English*)
Eduardo Paolozzi (*Scottish*)
Parmigianino (*Italian*)
Victor Pasmore (*English*)
Joachim Patinir or Patenier
  (*Flemish*)
Perugino (*Italian*)
Baldassare Peruzzi (*Italian*)
Antoine Pevsner (*Russian-
  French*)
Phidias (*Greek*)

16

Francis Picabia (*French*)
Pablo Picasso (*Spanish*)
Piero della Francesca (*Italian*)
Piero di Cosimo (*Italian*)
Pietro da Cortona (*Italian*)
Jean Baptiste Pigalle (*French*)
Germain Pilon (*French*)
Pinturicchio (*Italian*)
John Piper (*English*)
Pisanello (*Italian*)
Andrea Pisano (*Italian*)
Giovanni Pisano (*Italian*)
Nicola Pisano (*Italian*)
Camille Pissarro (*French*)
Antonio del Pollaiuolo
(*Italian*)
Piero del Pollaiuolo (*Italian*)
Jackson Pollock (*U.S.*)
Polyclitus (*Greek*)
Polygnotus (*Greek*)
Pontormo (*Italian*)
Paulus Potter (*Dutch*)
Nicolas Poussin (*French*)
Praxiteles (*Greek*)
Pierre Paul Prud'hon (*French*)
Pierre Puget (*French*)
Pierre Puvis de Chavannes
(*French*)
Jacopa della Quercia (*Italian*)
Arthur Rackham (*English*)
Henry Raeburn (*Scottish*)
Allan Ramsay (*Scottish*)

Raphael (*Italian*)
Robert Rauschenberg (*U.S.*)
Man Ray (*U.S.*)
Odilon Redon (*French*)
Rembrandt Harmensz van
Rijn (*Dutch*)
Guido Reni (*Italian*)
Pierre Auguste Renoir
(*French*)
Joshua Reynolds (*English*)
José de Ribera (*Spanish*)
Bridget Riley (*English*)
Diego Rivera (*Mexican*)
Andrea della Robbia (*Italian*)
Luca della Robbia (*Italian*)
Alexander Mikhailovich
Rodchenko (*Russian*)
Auguste Rodin (*French*)
George Romney (*English*)
Salvator Rosa (*Italian*)
Dante Gabriel Rossetti
(*English*)
Mark Rothko (*U.S.*)
Geroges Rouault (*French*)
Louis-François Roubiliac *or*
Roubillac (*French*)
Henri Julien Rousseau
(*French*)
Théodore Rousseau (*French*)
Peter Paul Rubens (*Flemish*)
Rublyov *or* Rublev Andrei
(*Russian*)

17

——— ARTISTS ———

WORD POWER

Jacob van Ruisdael (*Dutch*)

Philipp Otto Runge (*German*)

Salomen van Ruysdael (*Dutch*)

John Singer Sargent (*U.S.*)

Egon Schiele (*Austrian*)

Martin Schongauer (*German*)

Kurt Schwitters (*German*)

Scopas (*Greek*)

Maurice Sendak (*U.S.*)

Sesshu (*Japanese*)

Georges Seurat (*French*)

Ben Shahn (*U.S.*)

Walter Richard Sickert (*British*)

Paul Signac (*French*)

Luca Signorelli (*Italian*)

David Alfaro Siqueiros (*Mexican*)

Alfred Sisley (*French*)

John Sloan (*U.S.*)

Claus Sluter (*Dutch*)

David Smith (*U.S.*)

Chaim Soutine (*Lithuanian-French*)

Stanley Spencer (*English*)

Jan Steen (*Dutch*)

Veit Stoss (*German*)

George Stubbs (*English*)

Graham Sutherland (*English*)

Yves Tanguy (*French*)

Vladimir Tatlin (*Russian*)

David Teniers the Elder (*Flemish*)

David Teniers the Younger (*Flemish*)

Gerard Ter Borch *or* Terborch (*Dutch*)

Hendrik Terbrugghen (*Dutch*)

James Thornhill (*English*)

Bertel Thorvaldsen (*Danish*)

Giambattista Tiepolo (*Italian*)

Jacopo Tintoretto (*Italian*)

James Jacques Joseph Tissot (*French*)

Titian (*Italian*)

Henri Marie Raymond de Toulouse-Lautrec (*French*)

J(oseph) M(allord) W(illiam) Turner (*English*)

Paolo Uccello (*Italian*)

Utagawa Kuniyoshi (*Japanese*)

Maurice Utrillo (*French*)

Adriaen van de Velde (*Dutch*)

Willem van de Velde the Elder (*Dutch*)

Willem van de Velde the Younger (*Dutch*)

Rogier van der Weyden (*Flemish*)

Anthony Van Dyck (*Flemish*)

Jan van Eyck (*Flemish*)

Vincent van Gogh (*Dutch*)

Victor Vasarely (*Hungarian-French*)

Giorgio Vasari (*Italian*)

Diego Rodríguez de Silva y Velázquez (*Spanish*)

Jan Vermeer (*Dutch*)

Paolo Veronese (*Italian*)

Andrea del Verrocchio (*Italian*)

Élisabeth Vigée-Lebrun (*French*)

Jacques Villon (*French*)

Maurice de Vlaminck (*French*)

Andy Warhol (*U.S.*)

Jean Antoine Watteau (*French*)

George Frederick Watts (*English*)

Benjamin West (*U.S.*)

James Abbott McNeill Whistler (*U.S.*)

Richard Wilson (*Welsh*)

Joseph Wright (*English*)

Xia Gui *or* Hsia Kuei (*Chinese*)

Zeuxis (*Greek*)

Johann Zoffany (*German*)

Anders Zorn (*Swedish*)

Gaetano Giulio Zumbo (*Italian*)

Francisco Zurbarán (*Spanish*)

WORD POWER

AUSTRALIAN STATES AND TERRITORIES

Australian Capital Territory
New South Wales
Northern Territory
Queensland

South Australia
Tasmania
Victoria
Western Australia

CANADIAN PROVINCES

Province	Abbreviation	Province	Abbreviation
Alberta	AB	Nunavut	NU
British Columbia	BC	Ontario	ON
Manitoba	MB	Prince Edward Island	PE
New Brunswick	NB	Quebec	PQ
Newfoundland	NF	Saskatchewan	SK
Northwest Territories	NWT	Yukon Territory	YT
Nova Scotia	NS		

WORD POWER

City	*Country*
Abu Dhabi	United Arab Emirates
Abuja	Nigeria
Accra	Ghana
Addis Ababa	Ethiopia
Astana	Kazakhstan
Algiers	Algeria
Amman	Jordan
Amsterdam	Netherlands
Andorra la Vella	Andorra
Ankara	Turkey
Antananarivo	Madagascar
Apia	Samoa
Ashkhabad	Turkmenistan
Asmara	Eritrea
Asunción	Paraguay
Athens	Greece
Baghdad	Iraq
Baku	Azerbaijan
Bamako	Mali
Bandar Seri Begawan	Brunei
Bangkok	Thailand
Bangui	Central African Republic
Banjul	Gambia
Basseterre	St. Kitts and Nevis
Beijing	People's Republic of China
Beirut *or* Beyrouth	Lebanon
Belfast	Northern Ireland
Belgrade	Yugoslavia (Serbia and Montenegro)
Belmopan	Belize
Berlin	Germany

WORD POWER

21

City	Country
Berne	Switzerland
Bishkek	Kyrgyzstan
Bissau	Guinea-Bissau
Bloemfontein	judicial capital of South Africa
Bogotá	Colombia
Brasília	Brazil
Bratislava	Slovakia
Brazzaville	Congo (Republic of)
Bridgetown	Barbados
Brussels	Belgium
Bucharest	Romania
Budapest	Hungary
Buenos Aires	Argentina
Bujumbura	Burundi
Cairo	Egypt
Canberra	Australia
Cape Town	legislative capital of South Africa
Caracas	Venezuela
Cardiff	Wales
Castries	St. Lucia
Cayenne	French Guiana
Colombo	Sri Lanka
Conakry *or* Konakry	Guinea
Copenhagen	Denmark
Dakar	Senegal
Damascus	Syria
Delhi	India
Dhaka *or* Dacca	Bangladesh
Dili	East Timor
Djibouti *or* Jibouti	Djibouti *or* Jibouti
Dodoma	Tanzania

WORD POWER

22

City	Country
Doha	Qatar
Douglas	Isle of Man
Dublin	Republic of Ireland
Dushanbe	Tajikistan
Edinburgh	Scotland
Fort-de-France	Martinique
Freetown	Sierra Leone
Funafuti	Tuvalu
Gaborone	Botswana
Georgetown	Guyana
Guatemala	Guatemala City
Hanoi	Vietnam
Harare	Zimbabwe
Havana	Cuba
Helsinki	Finland
Honiara	Solomon Islands
Islamabad	Pakistan
Jakarta *or* Djakarta	Indonesia
Jerusalem	Israel
Kabul	Afghanistan
Kampala	Uganda
Katmandu *or* Kathmandu	Nepal
Khartoum *or* Khartum	Sudan
Kiev	Ukraine
Kigali	Rwanda
Kingston	Jamaica
Kingstown	St. Vincent and the Grenadines
Kinshasa	Congo (Democratic Republic of)
Kishinev	Moldova
Palikir	Micronesia
Koror	Palau

WORD POWER

WORD POWER

City	Country
Kuala Lumpur	Malaysia
Kuwait	Kuwait
La Paz	administrative capital of Bolivia
Libreville	Gabon
Lilongwe	Malawi
Lima	Peru
Lisbon	Portugal
Ljubljana	Slovenia
Lomé	Togo
London	United Kingdom
Luanda	Angola
Lusaka	Zambia
Luxembourg	Luxembourg
Madrid	Spain
Majuro	Marshall Islands
Malabo	Equatorial Guinea
Malé	Maldives
Managua	Nicaragua
Manama	Bahrain
Manila	Philippines
Maputo	Mozambique
Maseru	Lesotho
Mbabane	Swaziland
Mexico City	Mexico
Minsk	Belarus
Mogadishu	Somalia
Monaco-Ville	Monaco
Monrovia	Liberia
Montevideo	Uruguay
Moroni	Comoros
Moscow	Russia

City	Country
Muscat	Oman
Nairobi	Kenya
Nassau	Bahamas
Ndjamena	Chad
Niamey	Niger
Nicosia	Cyprus
Nouakchott	Mauritania
Nuku'alofa	Tonga
Nuuk	Greenland
Oslo	Norway
Ottawa	Canada
Ouagadougou	Burkina-Faso
Panama City	Panama
Paramaribo	Suriname
Paris	France
Phnom Penh	Cambodia
Pishpek	Kirghizia
Port-au-Prince	Haiti
Port Louis	Mauritius
Port Moresby	Papua New Guinea
Port of Spain	Trinidad and Tobago
Porto Novo	Benin
Prague	Czech Republic
Praia	Cape Verde
Pretoria	administrative capital of South Africa
Pristina	Kosovo (Federal Republic of Yugoslavia)
Pyongyang	North Korea
Quito	Ecuador
Rabat	Morocco

WORD POWER

City	Country
Reykjavik	Iceland
Riga	Latvia
Riyadh	Saudi Arabia
Rome	Italy
Roseau	Dominica
Sana'a	Yemen
San José	Costa Rica
San Juan	Puerto Rico
San Marino	San Marino
San Salvador	El Salvador
Santiago	Chile
Santo Domingo	Dominican Republic
São Tomé	São Tomé and Principe
Sarajevo	Bosnia and Herzegovina
Seoul	South Korea
Singapore	Singapore
Skopje	Macedonia
Sofia	Bulgaria
St. George's	Grenada
St. John's	Antigua and Barbuda
Stockholm	Sweden
Sucre	legislative and judicial capital of Bolivia
Suva	Fiji
Taipei	Taiwan
Tallinn	Estonia
Tarawa	Kiribati
Tashkent	Uzbekistan
Tbilisi	Georgia
Tegucigalpa	Honduras
Tehran	Iran

City	Country
Tel Aviv	Israel
Thimphu	Bhutan
Tirana	Albania
Tokyo	Japan
Tripoli	Libya
Tunis	Tunisia
Ulan Bator	Mongolia
Vaduz	Liechtenstein
Valletta	Malta
Vatican City	Vatican City
Victoria	Seychelles
Vienna	Austria
Vientiane	Laos
Port Vila	Vanuatu
Vilnius	Lithuania
Warsaw	Poland
Washington DC	United States of America
Wellington	New Zealand
Windhoek	Namibia
Yamoussoukro	Côte d'Ivoire
Yangon (Rangoon)	Myanmar (Burma)
Yaoundé *or* Yaunde	Cameroon
Yaren	Nauru
Yerevan	Armenia
Zagreb	Croatia

WORD POWER

—— COUNTIES ——

English counties

Bedfordshire
Berkshire
Bristol
Buckinghamshire
Cambridgeshire
Cheshire
Cornwall
Cumbria
Derbyshire
Devon
Dorset
Durham
East Riding of Yorkshire
East Sussex
Essex
Gloucestershire
Greater London
Greater Manchester
Hampshire
Herefordshire
Hertfordshire
Isle of Wight
Kent
Lancashire

Leicestershire
Lincolnshire
Merseyside
Norfolk
Northamptonshire
Northumberland
North Yorkshire
Nottinghamshire
Oxfordshire
Rutland
Shropshire
Somerset
South Yorkshire
Staffordshire
Suffolk
Surrey
Tyne and Wear
Warwickshire
West Midlands
West Sussex
West Yorkshire
Wiltshire
Worcestershire

Scottish counties

Aberdeen City
Aberdeenshire
Angus
Argyll and Bute
City of Edinburgh
Clackmannanshire

Dumfries and Galloway
Dundee City
East Ayrshire
East Dunbartonshire
East Lothian
East Renfrewshire

Scottish counties (continued)

Falkirk
Fife
Glasgow City
Highland
Inverclyde
Midlothian
Moray
North Ayrshire
North Lanarkshire
Orkney

Perth and Kinross
Renfrewshire
Scottish Borders
Shetland
South Ayrshire
South Lanarkshire
Stirling
West Dunbartonshire
Western Isles (Eilean Siar)
West Lothian

Welsh counties

Clwyd
Dyfed
Gwent

Gwynedd
Mid Glamorgan
Powys

South Glamorgan
West Glamorgan

Northern Irish counties

Antrim
Armagh
Belfast City

Down
Fermanagh
Londonderry

Londonderry City
Tyrone

Republic of Ireland counties

Carlow
Cavan
Clare
Cork
Donegal
Dublin
Galway
Kerry
Kildare

Kilkenny
Laois
Leitrim
Limerick
Longford
Louth
Mayo
Meath
Monaghan

Offaly
Roscommon
Sligo
Tipperary
Waterford
Westmeath
Wexford
Wicklow

WORD POWER

WORD POWER

Afghanistan
Albania
Algeria
American Samoa
Andorra
Angola
Antigua and Barbuda
Argentina
Armenia
Australia
Austria
Azerbaijan
Bahamas
Bahrain
Bangladesh
Barbados
Belarus
Belau
Belgium
Belize
Benin
Bhutan
Bolivia
Bosnia and Herzegovina
Botswana
Brazil
Brunei
Bulgaria
Burkina-Faso
Burundi
Cambodia
Cameroon
Canada
Cape Verde
Central African Republic

Chad
Chile
Colombia
Comoros
Congo (Republic of)
Congo (Democratic Republic of)
Costa Rica
Côte d'Ivoire
Croatia
Cuba
Cyprus
Czech Republic
Denmark
Djibouti
Dominica
Dominican Republic
East Timor
Ecuador
Egypt
El Salvador
England
Equatorial Guinea
Eritrea
Estonia
Ethiopia
Fiji
Finland
France
Gabon
Gambia
Georgia
Germany
Ghana
Greece

Greenland
Grenada
Guatemala
Guinea
Guinea-Bissau
Guyana
Haiti
Honduras
Hungary
Iceland
India
Indonesia
Iran
Iraq
Israel
Italy
Jamaica
Japan
Jordan
Kazakhstan
Kenya
Kirghizia
Kiribati
Kuwait
Laos
Latvia
Lebanon
Lesotho
Liberia
Libya
Liechtenstein
Lithuania
Luxembourg
Macedonia
Madagascar

Malawi
Malaysia
Mali
Malta
Marshall Islands
Mauritania
Mauritius
Mexico
Micronesia
Moldova
Monaco
Mongolia
Morocco
Mozambique
Myanmar
Namibia
Nauru
Nepal
Netherlands
New Zealand
Nicaragua
Niger
Nigeria
Northern Ireland
North Korea
Norway
Oman
Pakistan
Panama
Papua New Guinea
Paraguay
People's Republic of China
Peru
Philippines
Poland

WORD POWER

31

WORD POWER

Portugal
Puerto Rico
Qatar
Republic of Ireland
Republic of Maldives
Romania
Russia
Rwanda
St Kitts and Nevis
St Lucia
St Vincent and the Grenadines
Samoa
San Marino
São Tomé and Principe
Saudi Arabia
Scotland
Senegal
Seychelles
Sierra Leone
Singapore
Slovakia
Slovenia
Solomon Islands
Somalia
South Africa
South Korea
Spain
Sri Lanka
Sudan
Surinam
Swaziland

Sweden
Switzerland
Syria
Taiwan
Tajikistan
Tanzania
Thailand
Togo
Tonga
Trinidad and Tobago
Tunisia
Turkey
Turkmenistan
Tuvalu
Uganda
Ukraine
United Arab Emirates
United Kingdom
United States of America
Uruguay
Uzbekistan
Vanuatu
Vatican City
Venezuela
Vietnam
Wales
Yemen
Yugoslavia (Serbia and
   Montenegro)
Zambia
Zimbabwe

Country	*Currency*
Afghanistan	afghani
Albania	lek
Algeria	Algerian dinar
Andorra	euro
Angola	kwanza
Antigua and Barbuda	East Caribbean dollar
Argentina	peso
Armenia	dram
Australia	Australian dollar
Austria	euro
Azerbaijan	manat
Bahamas	Bahamian dollar
Bahrain	dinar
Bangladesh	taka
Barbados	Barbados dollar
Belarus	rouble
Belgium	euro
Belize	Belize dollar
Benin	CFA franc
Bhutan	ngultrum
Bolivia	boliviano
Bosnia-Herzegovina	convertible marka
Botswana	pula
Brazil	real
Brunei	Brunei dollar
Bulgaria	lev
Burkina-Faso	CFA franc
Burundi	Burundi franc
Cambodia	riel
Cameroon	CFA franc
Canada	Canadian dollar
Cape Verde	escudo
Central African Republic	CFA franc

WORD POWER

Country	Currency
Chad	CFA franc
Chile	peso
China	yuan
Colombia	peso
Comoros	Comorian franc
Congo (Republic of)	CFA franc
Congo (Democratic Republic of)	Congolese franc
Costa Rica	cólon
Côte d'Ivoire	CFA franc
Croatia	kuna
Cuba	peso
Cyprus	pound
Czech Republic	koruna
Denmark	krone
Djibouti	Djibouti franc
Dominica	East Caribbean dollar
Dominican Republic	peso
East Timor	US dollar
Ecuador	US dollar
Egypt	pound
El Salvador	cólon
Equatorial Guinea	CFA franc
Eritrea	nakfa
Estonia	kroon
Ethiopia	birr
Fiji	Fiji dollar
Finland	euro
France	euro
French Guiana	French franc
Gabon	CFA franc
Gambia	dalasi
Germany	euro
Ghana	cedi

Country	Currency
Greece	euro
Greenland	Danish krone
Grenada	East Caribbean dollar
Guatemala	quetzal
Guinea	Guinea franc
Guinea-Bissau	CFA franc
Guyana	Guyana dollar
Haiti	gourde
Honduras	lempira
Hungary	forint
Iceland	krona
India	rupee
Indonesia	rupiah
Iran	rial
Iraq	dinar
Ireland (Republic of)	euro
Israel	shekel
Italy	euro
Jamaica	Jamaican dollar
Japan	yen
Jordan	dinar
Kazakhstan	tenge
Kenya	shilling
Kirghizia	som
Kiribati	Australian dollar
Kosovo	dinar; euro
Kuwait	dinar
Kyrgyzstan	som
Laos	kip
Latvia	lat
Lebanon	pound
Lesotho	loti
Liberia	Liberian dollar

WORD POWER

35

—— CURRENCIES ——

Country	Currency
Libya	dinar
Liechtenstein	Swiss franc
Lithuania	litas
Luxembourg	euro
Macedonia	denar
Madagascar	Malagasy franc
Malawi	kwacha
Malaysia	ringgit
Maldives (Republic of)	rufiyaa
Mali	CFA franc
Malta	lira
Marshall Islands	U.S. dollar
Mauritania	ouguiya
Mauritius	rupee
Mexico	peso
Micronesia	U.S. dollar
Moldova	leu
Monaco	French franc
Mongolia	tugrik
Montenegro	euro
Montserrat	East Caribbean dollar
Morocco	dirham
Mozambique	metical
Myanmar	kyat
Namibia	Namibian dollar
Nauru	Australian dollar
Nepal	rupee
Netherlands	euro
New Zealand	New Zealand dollar
Nicaragua	córdoba
Niger	CFA franc
Nigeria	naira
North Korea	won

Country	*Currency*
Norway	krone
Oman	rial
Pakistan	rupee
Palau	U.S. dollar
Panama	balboa
Papua New Guinea	kina
Paraguay	guarani
Peru	new sol
Philippines	Philippine peso
Poland	zloty
Portugal	euro
Qatar	riyal
Romania	leu
Russia	rouble
Rwanda	Rwanda franc
St. Kitts and Nevis	East Caribbean dollar
St. Lucia	East Caribbean dollar
St. Vincent and the Grenadines	East Caribbean dollar
Samoa	tala
San Marino	euro
São Tomé and Principe	dobra
Saudi Arabia	riyal
Senegal	CFA franc
Seychelles	rupee
Sierra Leone	leone
Singapore	Singapore dollar
Slovakia	koruna
Slovenia	tolar
Solomon Islands	Solomon Islands dollar
Somalia	shilling
South Africa	rand
South Korea	won
Spain	euro

WORD POWER

WORD POWER

Country	Currency
Sri Lanka	rupee
Sudan	dinar
Surinam	guilder
Swaziland	lilangeni
Sweden	krona
Switzerland	Swiss franc
Syria	pound
Taiwan	Taiwan dollar
Tajikistan	somoni
Tanzania	shilling
Thailand	baht
Togo	CFA franc
Tonga	pa'anga
Trinidad and Tobago	Trinidad and Tobago dollar
Tunisia	dinar
Turkey	Turkish lira
Turkmenistan	manat
Tuvalu	Australian dollar
Uganda	shilling
Ukraine	hryvna
United Arab Emirates	dirham
United Kingdom	pound sterling
United States of America	U.S. dollar
Uruguay	peso
Uzbekistan	sum
Vanuatu	vatu
Vatican City	euro
Venezuela	bolívar
Vietnam	dong
Yemen	riyal
Yugoslavia (Serbia)	dinar
Zambia	kwacha
Zimbabwe	Zimbabwe dollar

Aeschylus (*Greek*)

Edward Albee (*U.S.*)

Robert Amos (*Australian*)

Jean Anouilh (*French*)

Aristophanes (*Greek*)

Alan Ayckbourn (*English*)

Pierre Augustin Caron de Beaumarchais (*French*)

Francis Beaumont (*English*)

Samuel Beckett (*Irish*)

Brendan Behan (*Irish*)

Richard Beynon (*Australian*)

Alan Bleasdale (*English*)

Edward Bond (*English*)

Bertolt Brecht (*German*)

Eugene Brieux (*French*)

Pedro Calderón de la Barca (*Spanish*)

George Chapman (*English*)

Anton Pavlovich Chekhov (*Russian*)

William Congreve (*English*)

Pierre Corneille (*French*)

Noël (Pierce) Coward (*English*)

Thomas Dekker (*English*)

John Dryden (*English*)

T(homas) S(tearns) Eliot (*U.S.-British*)

Louis Esson (*Australian*)

Euripides (*Greek*)

John Fletcher (*English*)

Dario Fo (*Italian*)

John Ford (*English*)

Brian Friel (*Irish*)

John Galsworthy (*English*)

Jean Genet (*French*)

W(illiam) S(chwenk) Gilbert (*English*)

(Hippolyte) Jean Giraudoux (*French*)

Johann Wolfgang von Goethe (*German*)

Nikolai Gogol (*Russian*)

Oliver Goldsmith (*Irish*)

Oriel Gray (*Australian*)

Robert Greene (*English*)

David Hare (*English*)

Gerhart Johann Robert Hauptmann (*German*)

Václav Havel (*Czech*)

Alfred Hayes (*U.S.*)

(Christian) Friedrich Hebbel (*German*)

Dorthy Hewett (*Australian*)

Thomas Heywood (*English*)

Jack Hibberd (*Australian*)

Sidney Howard (*U.S.*)

Henrik Ibsen (*Norwegian*)

William Motter Inge (*U.S.*)

Eugène Ionesco (*Romanian-French*)

Ben Jonson (*English*)

George Kaiser (*German*)

WORD POWER

WORD POWER

Tony Kushner (*U.S.*)
Thomas Kyd (*English*)
Ray Lawler (*Australian*)
Liz Lochhead (*Scottish*)
Lope de Vega (*Spanish*)
Federico Garcia Lorca
(*Spanish*)
Maurice Maeterlinck (*Belgian*)
David Mamet (*U.S.*)
Christopher Marlowe
(*English*)
John Marston (*English*)
Menander (*Greek*)
Arthur Miller (*U.S.*)
Molière (*French*)
Barry Oakley (*Australian*)
Sean O'Casey (*Irish*)
Eugene (Gladstone) O'Neill
(*U.S.*)
Joe Orton (*English*)
John Osborne (*English*)
Thomas Otway (*English*)
John Patrick (*U.S.*)
Arthur Wing Pinero (*English*)
Harold Pinter (*English*)
Luigi Pirandello (*Italian*)
Titus Maccius Plautus
(*Roman*)
Hal Porter (*Australian*)
Aleksander Sergeyevich
Pushkin (*Russian*)
Jean Baptiste Racine (*French*)

Terence Mervyn Rattigan
(*English*)
John Romeril (*Australian*)
Willy Russell (*English*)
Thomas Sackville (*English*)
Jean-Paul Sartre (*French*)
Johann Christoph Friedrich
von Schiller (*German*)
Lucius Annaeus Seneca
(*Roman*)
Alan Seymour (*Australian*)
Peter Shaffer (*English*)
William Shakespeare (*English*)
George Bernard Shaw (*Irish*)
Sam Shepard (*U.S.*)
Richard Brinsley Sheridan
(*Irish*)
Robert Sherwood (*U.S.*)
Sophocles (*Greek*)
Wole Soyinka (*Nigerian*)
Tom Stoppard (*Czech-English*)
August Strindberg (*Swedish*)
John Millington Synge (*Irish*)
John Webster (*English*)
Oscar Wilde (*Irish*)
Thornton Wilder (*U.S.*)
Tennessee Williams (*U.S.*)
David Keith Williamson
(*Australian*)
William Wycherly (*English*)

EUROPEAN UNION

EU member states

1958 Belgium	1973 United Kingdom
1958 France	1981 Greece
1958 Germany	1986 Portugal
1958 Italy	1986 Spain
1958 Luxembourg	1995 Finland
1958 The Netherlands	1995 Sweden
1973 Denmark	1995 Austria
1973 Republic of Ireland	

EU applications under consideration

Cyprus	Poland
Estonia	Switzerland
Hungary	Czech Republic

NEW ZEALAND TERRITORIES

Cook Islands	the Ross Dependency
Niue	Tokelau *or* Union Islands

—— NOVELISTS ——

Peter Abrahams (*South African*)
Chinua Achebe (*Nigerian*)
Peter Ackroyd (*English*)
Douglas Adams (*English*)
Richard Adams (*English*)
Alain-Fournier (*French*)
Brian Aldiss (*English*)
James Aldridge (*Australian*)
Al Alvarez (*English*)
Eric Ambler (*English*)
Kingsley Amis (*English*)
Martin Amis (*English*)
Mulk Raj Anand (*Indian*)
Maya Angelou (*U.S.*)
Lucius Apuleius (*Roman*)
Jeffrey Archer (*English*)
Isaac Asimov (*U.S.*)
Margaret Atwood (*Canadian*)
Louis Auchincloss (*U.S.*)
Jane Austen (*English*)
Beryl Bainbridge (*English*)
R M Ballantyne (*Scottish*)
J G Ballard (*English*)
Honoré de Balzac (*French*)
Iain Banks (*Scottish*)
Lynne Reid Banks (*English*)
Elspeth Barker (*Scottish*)
Pat Barker (*English*)
Julian Barnes (*English*)
Stanley Barstow (*English*)
John Barth (*U.S.*)
H E Bates (*English*)

Nina Bawden (*English*)
Simone de Beauvoir (*French*)
Sybille Bedford (*British*)
Max Beerbohm (*English*)
Aphra Behn (*English*)
Saul Bellow (*Canadian*)
Andrei Bely (*Russian*)
David Benedictus (*English*)
(Enoch) Arnold Bennett (*English*)
John Berger (*English*)
Thomas Berger (*U.S.*)
Maeve Binchy (*Irish*)
R(ichard) D(oddridge) Blackmore (*English*)
Alan Bleasdale (*English*)
Heinrich Böll (*German*)
Elizabeth Bowen (*Irish*)
Paul Bowles (*U.S.*)
William Boyd (*Scottish*)
Malcolm Bradbury (*English*)
Barbara Taylor Bradford (*English*)
Melvin Bragg (*English*)
John Braine (*English*)
André Brink (*South African*)
Vera Brittain (*English*)
Louis Bromfield (*U.S.*)
Anne Brontë (*English*)
Charlotte Brontë (*English*)
Emily (Jane) Brontë (*English*)
Christina Brooke-Rose (*English*)

Anita Brookner (*English*)

Brigid Brophy (*English*)

George Douglas Brown (*Scottish*)

George Mackay Brown (*Scottish*)

John Buchan (*Scottish*)

Pearl Buck (*U.S.*)

Mikhail Afanaseyev Bulgakov (*Russian*)

John Bunyan (*English*)

Anthony Burgess (*British*)

Fanny Burney (*English*)

Edgar Rice Burrows (*U.S.*)

William Burroughs (*U.S.*)

Samuel Butler (*English*)

A S Byatt (*English*)

Italo Calvino (*Italian*)

Albert Camus (*French*)

Elias Canetti (*Bulgarian*)

Truman Capote (*U.S.*)

Peter Carey (*Australian*)

Angela Carter (*English*)

Barbara Cartland (*English*)

Willa Cather (*U.S.*)

Camilo José Cela (*Spanish*)

Miguel de Cervantes (*Spanish*)

Raymond Chandler (*U.S.*)

G K Chesterton (*English*)

Agatha (Mary Clarissa) Christie (*English*)

Arthur C Clarke (*English*)

James Clavell (*U.S.*)

Jon Cleary (*Australian*)

J M Coetzee (*South African*)

Colette (*French*)

(William) Wilkie Collins (*English*)

Ivy Compton-Burnett (*English*)

Richard Condon (*U.S.*)

Evan Connell (*U.S.*)

Joseph Conrad (*Polish-British*)

Catherine Cookson (*English*)

James Fenimore Cooper (*U.S.*)

Jilly Cooper (*English*)

William Cooper (*English*)

Maria Corelli (*English*)

Stephen Crane (*U.S.*)

Lionel Davidson (*English*)

(William) Robertson Davies (*Canadian*)

Daniel Defoe (*English*)

Len Deighton (*English*)

E M Delafield (*English*)

Don DeLillo (*U.S.*)

Thomas de Quincy (*English*)

Anita Desai (*Indian*)

Peter De Vries (*U.S.*)

Charles (John Huffam) Dickens (*English*)

Monica Dickens (*English*)

Joan Didion (*U.S.*)

Isak Dinesen (*Danish*)

Benjamin Disraeli (*English*)

J P Donleavy (*Irish*)

John Roderigo Dos Passos (*U.S.*)
Fyodor Mikhailovich Dostoevsky (*Russian*)
Arthur Conan Doyle (*Scottish*)
Roddy Doyle (*Irish*)
Margaret Drabble (*English*)
Maureen Duffy (*English*)
Alexandre Dumas (*French*)
Daphne Du Maurier (*English*)
Nell Dunn (*English*)
Gerald Durrell (*English*)
Laurence Durrell (*English*)
Umberto Eco (*Italian*)
Maria Edgeworth (*English*)
George Eliot (*English*)
Stanley Elkin (*U.S.*)
Alice Thomas Ellis (*English*)
Ben Elton (*English*)
Zöe Fairbairns (*English*)
Philip José Farmer (*U.S.*)
Howard Fast (*U.S.*)
William Faulkner (*U.S.*)
Elaine Feinstein (*English*)
Helen Fielding (*English*)
Henry Fielding (*English*)
Eva Figes (*British*)
F(rancis) Scott (Key) Fitzgerald (*U.S.*)
Penelope Fitzgerald (*English*)
Gustave Flaubert (*French*)
Ian Fleming (*English*)

Ford Madox Ford (*English*)
Richard Ford (*U.S.*)
C S Forester (*English*)
E M Forster (*English*)
Frederick Forsyth (*English*)
John Fowles (*English*)
Janet Paterson Frame (*New Zealand*)
Dick Francis (*English*)
Antonia Fraser (*English*)
Michael Frayn (*English*)
Nicholas Freeling (*English*)
Marilyn French (*U.S.*)
Roy Fuller (*English*)
William Gaddis (*U.S.*)
Janice Galloway (*Scottish*)
John Galsworthy (*English*)
Gabriel García Márquez (*Colombian*)
Helen Garner (*Australian*)
Elizabeth Gaskell (*English*)
William Alexander Gerhardie (*English*)
Lewis Grassic Gibbon (*Scottish*)
Stella Gibbons (*English*)
André Gide (*French*)
Penelope Gilliat (*English*)
George Gissing (*English*)
Ellen Glasgow (*U.S.*)
(Margaret) Rumer Godden (*English*)
William Godwin (*English*)

Johann Wolfgang von Goethe (*German*)

Nikolai Vasilievich Gogol (*Russian*)

Herbert Gold (*U.S.*)

William (Gerald) Golding (*English*)

William Goldman (*U.S.*)

Oliver Goldsmith (*Anglo-Irish*)

Ivan Aleksandrovich Goncharov (*Russian*)

Nadine Gordimer (*South African*)

Maxim Gorky (*Russian*)

Edmund Gosse (*English*)

Winston Graham (*English*)

Günter (Wilhelm) Grass (*German*)

Robert Graves (*English*)

Alasdair Gray (*Scottish*)

Graham Greene (*English*)

John Grisham (*U.S.*)

George Grossmith (*English*)

Weedon Grossmith (*English*)

David Guterson (*U.S.*)

Rider Haggard (*English*)

Arthur Hailey (*Anglo-Canadian*)

Thomas Hardy (*English*)

L(eslie) P(oles) Hartley (*English*)

Nathaniel Hawthorne (*U.S.*)

Shirley Hazzard (*U.S.*)

Robert A Heinlein (*U.S.*)

Joseph Heller (*U.S.*)

Ernest Hemingway (*U.S.*)

Hermann Hesse (*German*)

Georgette Heyer (*English*)

Patricia Highsmith (*U.S.*)

Susan Hill (*English*)

James Hilton (*English*)

Barry Hines (*English*)

Russell Hoban (*U.S.*)

James Hogg (*Scottish*)

Winifred Holtby (*English*)

Anthony Hope (*English*)

Paul Horgan (*U.S.*)

Elizabeth Jane Howard (*English*)

Thomas Hughes (*English*)

Victor (Marie) Hugo (*French*)

Keri Hulme (*New Zealand*)

Evan Hunter (*U.S.*)

Zora Neale Hurston (*U.S.*)

Aldous Huxley (*English*)

Hammond Innes (*English*)

John Irving (*U.S.*)

Christopher Isherwood (*English-U.S.*)

Kazuo Ishiguro (*British*)

Henry James (*U.S.-British*)

P D James (*English*)

Ruth Prawer Jhabvala (*Anglo-Polish*)

Erica Jong (*U.S.*)

WORD POWER

James Joyce (*Irish*)

Franz Kafka (*Czech*)

Johanna Kaplan (*U.S.*)

Nikos Kazantazakis (*Greek*)

Molly Keane (*Anglo-Irish*)

James Kelman (*Scottish*)

Thomas Keneally (*Australian*)

Margaret Kennedy (*English*)

Jack Kerouac (*U.S.*)

Ken Kesey (*U.S.*)

Francis King (*English*)

Stephen King (*U.S.*)

Charles Kingsley (*English*)

Rudyard Kipling (*English*)

Milan Kundera (*French-Czech*)

Pierre Choderlos de Laclos (*French*)

George Lamming (*Barbadian*)

Guiseppe Tomasi di Lampedusa (*Italian*)

D H Lawrence (*English*)

John Le Carré (*English*)

Harper Lee (*U.S.*)

Laurie Lee (*English*)

Sheridan Le Fanu (*Irish*)

Ursula Le Guin (*U.S.*)

Rosamond Lehmann (*English*)

Mikhail Yurievich Lermontov (*Russian*)

Doris Lessing (*Rhodesian*)

Primo Levi (*Italian*)

(Harry) Sinclair Lewis (*U.S.*)

Penelope Lively (*English*)

David Lodge (*English*)

Jack London (*U.S.*)

(Clarence) Malcolm Lowry (*English*)

Alison Lurie (*U.S.*)

Rose Macauley (*English*)

Carson McCullers (*U.S.*)

George MacDonald (*Scottish*)

Ian McEwan (*English*)

William McIlvanney (*Scottish*)

Colin MacInnes (*English*)

Compton MacKenzie (*English*)

Henry MacKenzie (*Scottish*)

Bernard McLaverty (*Irish*)

Alistair MacLean (*Scottish*)

Naguib Mahfouz (*Egyptian*)

Norman Mailer (*U.S.*)

Bernard Malamud (*U.S.*)

David Malouf (*Australian*)

(Cyril) Wolf Mankowitz (*English*)

Thomas Mann (*German*)

Olivia Manning (*English*)

Kamala Markandaya (*Indian*)

Frederick Marryat (*English*)

Ngaio Marsh (*New Zealand*)

Allan Massie (*Scottish*)

Somerset Maugham (*English*)

Guy de Maupassant (*French*)

Francois Mauriac (*French*)

Herman Melville (*U.S.*)

George Meredith (*English*)

James A Michener (*U.S.*)

NOVELISTS

Henry Miller (*U.S.*)
Yukio Mishima (*Japanese*)
Julian Mitchell (*English*)
Margaret Mitchell (*U.S.*)
Naomi Mitchison (*Scottish*)
Nancy Mitford (*English*)
Timothy Mo (*British*)
Nicholas Monsarrat (*English*)
Michael Moorcock (*English*)
Brian Moore (*Irish-Canadian*)
Toni Morrison (*U.S.*)
John Mortimer (*English*)
Penelope Mortimer (*Welsh*)
Nicholas Mosley (*English*)
Iris Murdoch (*Irish*)
Vladimir Vladimirovich
    Nabokov (*Russian-U.S.*)
V S Naipaul (*Trinidadian*)
P H Newby (*English*)
Ngugi wa Thiong'o (*Kenyan*)
Robert Nye (*English*)
Joyce Carol Oates (*U.S.*)
Edna O'Brien (*Irish*)
Kenzaburo Oë (*Japanese*)
Liam O'Flaherty (*Irish*)
John O'Hara (*U.S.*)
Ben Okri (*Nigerian*)
Margaret Oliphant (*Scottish*)
Michael Ondaatje (*Canadian*)
Baroness Emmuska Orczy
    (*Hungarian-British*)
George Orwell (*English*)
Ouida (*English*)

Cynthia Ozick (*U.S.*)
Boris Leonidovich Pasternak
    (*Russian*)
Allan Paton (*South African*)
Thomas Love Peacock
    (*English*)
Mervyn Peake (*English*)
Harold Porter (*Australian*)
Katherine Anne Porter (*U.S.*)
Anthony Powell (*English*)
John Cowper Powys (*English*)
Terry Pratchett (*English*)
J B Priestley (*English*)
V S Pritchett (*English*)
E Annie Proulx (*U.S.*)
Marcel Proust (*French*)
Mario Puzo (*U.S.*)
Thomas Pynchon (*U.S.*)
Ellery Queen (*U.S.*)
Ann Radcliffe (*English*)
Raja Rao (*Indian*)
Frederic Raphael (*U.S.*)
Piers Paul Read (*English*)
Erich Maria Remarque
    (*German*)
Mary Renault (*English*)
Ruth Rendell (*English*)
Jean Rhys (*British*)
Dorothy Richardson (*English*)
Samuel Richardson (*English*)
Mordecai Richler
    (*Canadian*)
Harold Robbins (*U.S.*)

WORD POWER

WORD POWER

Frederick William Rolfe (*English*)
Henry Roth (*U.S.*)
(Ahmed) Salman Rushdie (*Indian-British*)
Vita Sackville-West (*English*)
Marquis de Sade (*French*)
Antoine de Saint-Exupéry (*French*)
Saki (*British*)
J D Salinger (*U.S.*)
George Sand (*French*)
William Saroyan (*U.S.*)
Jean-Paul Sartre (*French*)
Dorothy L Sayers (*English*)
Olive Schreiner (*South African*)
Walter Scott (*Scottish*)
Hubert Selby Jr (*U.S.*)
Tom Sharpe (*English*)
Mary Shelley (*English*)
Carol Shields (*Canadian-American*)
Mikhail Alexandrovich Sholokhov (*Russian*)
Nevil Shute (*Anglo-Austrian*)
Alan Sillitoe (*English*)
Georges Simenon (*Belgian*)
Claude Simon (*French*)
Isaac Bashevis Singer (*U.S.*)
Iain Crichton Smith (*Scottish*)
Zadie Smith (*British*)

Tobias George Smollett (*Scottish*)
C P Snow (*English*)
Alexander Isayevich Solzhenitsyn (*Russian*)
Muriel Spark (*Scottish*)
Howard Spring (*Welsh*)
C K Stead (*New Zealand*)
Gertrude Stein (*U.S.*)
John Steinbeck (*U.S.*)
Stendhal (*French*)
Laurence Sterne (*Irish-British*)
Robert Louis Stevenson (*Scottish*)
J I M Stewart (*Scottish*)
Mary Stewart (*English*)
Bram Stoker (*Irish*)
Robert Stone (*U.S.*)
David Storey (*English*)
Harriet Elizabeth Beecher Stowe (*U.S.*)
William Styron (*U.S.*)
Patrick Süskind (*German*)
Graham Swift (*English*)
Jonathan Swift (*Irish*)
Julian Symons (*English*)
Emma Tennant (*English*)
William Makepeace Thackeray (*English*)
Paul Theroux (*U.S.*)
J(ohn) R(onald) R(euel) Tolkien (*English*)
Leo Tolstoy (*Russian*)

John Kennedy Toole (*U.S.*)
Nigel Tranter (*Scottish*)
Rose Tremain (*English*)
William Trevor (*Irish*)
Anthony Trollope (*English*)
Joanna Trollope (*English*)
Frank Tuohy (*English*)
Ivan Sergeyevich Turgenev (*Russian*)
Amos Tutuola (*Nigerian*)
Mark Twain (*U.S.*)
Anne Tyler (*U.S.*)
John Updike (*U.S.*)
Edward (Falaise) Upward (*English*)
Leon Uris (*U.S.*)
Laurens Van der Post (*South African*)
Peter Vansittart (*English*)
Mario Vargas Llosa (*Peruvian*)
Jules Verne (*French*)
Gore Vidal (*U.S.*)
Voltaire (*French*)
Kurt Vonnegut (*U.S.*)
John Wain (*English*)
Alice Walker (*U.S.*)
Horace Walpole (*English*)
Marina Warner (*English*)
Robert Penn Warren (*U.S.*)
Keith Waterhouse (*English*)
Evelyn Waugh (*English*)
Fay Weldon (*English*)

H G Wells (*English*)
Irvine Welsh (*Scottish*)
Eudora Welty (*U.S.*)
Mary Wesley (*English*)
Morris West (*Australian*)
Rebecca West (*Irish*)
Edith Wharton (*U.S.*)
Antonia White (*English*)
Patrick White (*Australian*)
T H White (*English*)
Oscar Wilde (*Irish*)
Thornton Wilder (*U.S.*)
Michael Wilding (*Australian*)
A(ndrew) N(orman) Wilson (*English*)
Jeanette Winterson (*English*)
P(elham) G(renville) Wodehouse (*English-U.S.*)
Thomas Clayton Wolfe (*U.S.*)
Tom Wolfe (*U.S.*)
Tobias Wolff (*U.S.*)
Virginia Woolf (*English*)
Herman Wouk (*U.S.*)
Richard Nathaniel Wright (*U.S.*)
Frank Yerby (*U.S.*)
Marguerite Yourcenar (*French*)
Evgeny Ivanovich Zamyatin (*Russian*)
Emile Zola (*French*)

WORD POWER

WORD POWER

Dannie Abse (*Welsh*)

(Karen) Fleur Adcock (*New Zealander*)

Conrad (Potter) Aiken (*U.S.*)

Anna Akhamatova (*Russian*)

Maya Angelou (*U.S.*)

Guillaume Apollinaire (*French*)

Ludovico Ariosto (*Italian*)

Matthew Arnold (*English*)

W(ystan) H(ugh) Auden (*English-U.S.*)

Charles Pierre Baudelaire (*French*)

Patricia Beer (*English*)

Hilaire Belloc (*British*)

John Berryman (*U.S.*)

John Betjeman (*English*)

Elizabeth Bishop (*U.S.*)

William Blake (*English*)

Edmund Blunden (*English*)

Joseph Brodsky (*Russian-American*)

Rupert (Chawner) Brooke (*English*)

Gwendolyn Brooks (*U.S.*)

Elizabeth Barrett Browning (*English*)

Robert Browning (*English*)

Robert Burns (*Scottish*)

(George Gordon) Byron (*British*)

Callimachus (*Greek*)

Luis Vaz de Camoëns (*Portuguese*)

Thomas Campion (*English*)

Raymond Carver (*U.S.*)

Gaius Valerius Catullus (*Roman*)

Charles Causley (*English*)

Geoffrey Chaucer (*English*)

Amy Clampitt (*U.S.*)

John Clare (*English*)

Samuel Taylor Coleridge (*English*)

William Cowper (*English*)

George Crabbe (*English*)

e(dward) e(stlin) cummings (*U.S.*)

Dante (Alighieri) (*Italian*)

Cecil Day Lewis (*Irish*)

Walter de la Mare (*English*)

Emily Dickinson (*U.S.*)

John Donne (*English*)

H D (Hilda Doolittle) (*U.S.*)

John Dryden (*English*)

Carol Ann Duffy (*Scottish*)

William Dunbar (*Scottish*)

Douglas Dunn (*Scottish*)

Geoffrey Dutton (*Australian*)

T(homas) S(tearns) Eliot (*U.S.-British*)

Ebenezer Elliot (the Corn Law Rhymer) (*English*)

Paul Éluard (*French*)

Ralph Waldo Emerson (*U.S.*)

William Empson (*English*)

Edward Fitzgerald (*English*)

Robert Fitzgerald (*Australian*)

Robert (Lee) Frost (*U.S.*)

Allen Ginsberg (*U.S.*)

Johann Wolfgang von Goethe (*German*)

Robert Graves (*English*)

Thomas Gray (*English*)

Thom Gunn (*English*)

Seamus Heaney (*Irish*)

Adrian Henri (*English*)

Robert Henryson (*Scottish*)

George Herbert (*English*)

Robert Herrick (*English*)

Hesiod (*Greek*)

Geoffrey Hill (*English*)

Ralph Hodgson (*English*)

Homer (*Greek*)

Thomas Hood (*English*)

Gerard Manley Hopkins (*English*)

Horace (*Roman*)

A(lfred) E(dward) Housman (*English*)

Ted Hughes (*English*)

Elizabeth Jennings (*English*)

Samuel Johnson (*English*)

Ben Jonson (*English*)

Juvenal (*Roman*)

Patrick Kavanagh (*Irish*)

John Keats (*English*)

Sidney Keyes (*English*)

(Joseph) Rudyard Kipling (*English*)

Jean de La Fontaine (*French*)

Alphonse Marie Louis de Prat de Lamartine (*French*)

Walter Savage Landor (*English*)

William Langland (*English*)

Philip Larkin (*English*)

Tom Leonard (*Scottish*)

Henry Wadsworth Longfellow (*U.S.*)

Amy Lowell (*U.S.*)

Robert Lowell (*U.S.*)

Richard Lovelace (*English*)

Lucretius (*Roman*)

Thomas Macauley (*English*)

Norman MacCaig (*Scottish*)

Hugh MacDiarmid (*Scottish*)

Roger McGough (*English*)

Sorley MacLean (*Scottish*)

Louis MacNeice (*Irish*)

Stéphane Mallarmé (*French*)

Martial (*Roman*)

Andrew Marvell (*English*)

John Masefield (*English*)

Edna St Vincent Millay (*U.S.*)

John Milton (*English*)

Marianne Moore (*U.S.*)

—— POETS ——

Edwin Morgan (*Scottish*)
Andrew Motion (*English*)
Edwin Muir (*Scottish*)
Ogden Nash (*U.S.*)
Pablo Neruda (*Chilean*)
Frank O'Hara (*U.S.*)
Omar Khayyam (*Persian*)
Ovid (*Roman*)
Wilfred Owen (*British*)
Brian Patten (*English*)
Octavio Paz (*Mexican*)
Petrarch (*Italian*)
Pindar (*Greek*)
Sylvia Plath (*U.S.*)
Alexander Pope (*English*)
Peter Porter (*Australian*)
Ezra (Loomis) Pound (*U.S.*)
Sextus Propertius (*Roman*)
Aleksander Sergeyevich Pushkin (*Russian*)
Kathleen Raine (*English*)
Adrienne Rich (*U.S.*)
Laura Riding (*U.S.*)
Rainer Maria Rilke (*Austro-German*)
Arthur Rimbaud (*French*)
(John Wilmot) Rochester (*English*)
Theodore Huebner Roethke (*U.S.*)
Isaac Rosenberg (*English*)

Christina Georgina Rossetti (*English*)
Dante Gabriel Rossetti (*English*)
Saint-John Perse (*French*)
Sappho (*Greek*)
Siegfried Sassoon (*English*)
Johann Christoph Friedrich von Schiller (*German*)
Delmore Schwarz (*U.S.*)
Sir Walter Scott (*Scottish*)
Jaroslav Seifert (*Czech*)
William Shakespeare (*English*)
Percy Bysshe Shelley (*English*)
Sir Philip Sidney (*English*)
Edith Sitwell (*English*)
John Skelton (*English*)
Christopher Smart (*English*)
Stevie Smith (*English*)
Robert Southey (*English*)
Stephen Spender (*English*)
Edmund Spenser (*English*)
Wallace Stevens (*U.S.*)
Algernon Charles Swinburne (*English*)
Wislawa Szymborska (*Polish*)
Torquato Tasso (*Italian*)
Alfred, Lord Tennyson (*English*)
Dylan (Marlais) Thomas (*Welsh*)
Edward Thomas (*English*)

POETS

R(onald) S(tuart) Thomas (*Welsh*)
James Thomson (*Scottish*)
Paul Verlaine (*French*)
Alfred Victor de Vigny (*French*)
François Villon (*French*)
Virgil (*Roman*)
Derek Walcott (*West Indian*)
Francis Charles Webb (*Australian*)
Walt Whitman (*U.S.*)
William Wordsworth (*English*)
Judith Wright (*Australian*)
Thomas Wyatt (*English*)
W(illiam) B(utler) Yeats (*Irish*)

WORD POWER

British Prime Ministers

Prime Minister	Party	Term of office
Robert Walpole	Whig	1721–42
Earl of Wilmington	Whig	1742–43
Henry Pelham	Whig	1743–54
Duke of Newcastle	Whig	1754–56
Duke of Devonshire	Whig	1756–57
Duke of Newcastle	Whig	1757–62
Earl of Bute	Tory	1762–63
George Grenville	Whig	1763–65
Marquess of Rockingham	Whig	1765–66
Duke of Grafton	Whig	1766–70
Lord North	Tory	1770–82
Marquess of Rockingham	Whig	1782
Earl of Shelburne	Whig	1782–83
Duke of Portland	Coalition	1783
William Pitt	Tory	1783–1801
Henry Addington	Tory	1801–04
William Pitt	Tory	1804–06
Lord Grenville	Whig	1806–07
Duke of Portland	Tory	1807–09
Spencer Perceval	Tory	1809–12
Earl of Liverpool	Tory	1812–27
George Canning	Tory	1827
Viscount Goderich	Tory	1827–28
Duke of Wellington	Tory	1828–30
Earl Grey	Whig	1830–34
Viscount Melbourne	Whig	1834
Robert Peel	Conservative	1834–35
Viscount Melbourne	Whig	1835–41
Robert Peel	Conservative	1841–46

British Prime Ministers (continued)

Prime Minister	Party	Term of office
Lord John Russell	Liberal	1846–52
Earl of Derby	Conservative	1852
Lord Aberdeen	Peelite	1852–55
Viscount Palmerston	Liberal	1855–58
Earl of Derby	Conservative	1858–59
Viscount Palmerston	Liberal	1859–65
Lord John Russell	Liberal	1865–66
Earl of Derby	Conservative	1866–68
Benjamin Disraeli	Conservative	1868
William Gladstone	Liberal	1868–74
Benjamin Disraeli	Conservative	1874–80
William Gladstone	Liberal	1880–85
Marquess of Salisbury	Conservative	1885–86
William Gladstone	Liberal	1886
Marquess of Salisbury	Conservative	1886–92
William Gladstone	Liberal	1892–94
Earl of Rosebery	Liberal	1894–95
Marquess of Salisbury	Conservative	1895–1902
Arthur James Balfour	Conservative	1902–05
Henry Campbell-Bannerman	Liberal	1905–08
Herbert Henry Asquith	Liberal	1908–15
Herbert Henry Asquith	Coalition	1915–16
David Lloyd George	Coalition	1916–22
Andrew Bonar Law	Conservative	1922–23
Stanley Baldwin	Conservative	1923–24
James Ramsay MacDonald	Labour	1924
Stanley Baldwin	Conservative	1924–29
James Ramsay MacDonald	Labour	1929–31
James Ramsay MacDonald	Nationalist	1931–35

British Prime Ministers (continued)

Prime Minister	Party	Term of office
Stanley Baldwin	Nationalist	1935–37
Arthur Neville Chamberlain	Nationalist	1937–40
Winston Churchill	Coalition	1940–45
Clement Attlee	Labour	1945–51
Winston Churchill	Conservative	1951–55
Anthony Eden	Conservative	1955–57
Harold Macmillan	Conservative	1957–63
Alec Douglas-Home	Conservative	1963–64
Harold Wilson	Labour	1964–70
Edward Heath	Conservative	1970–74
Harold Wilson	Labour	1974–76
James Callaghan	Labour	1976–79
Margaret Thatcher	Conservative	1979–90
John Major	Conservative	1990–97
Tony Blair	Labour	1997–

WORD POWER

Australian Prime Ministers

Prime Minister	Party	Term of office
Edmund Barton	Protectionist	1901–03
Alfred Deakin	Protectionist	1903–04
John Christian Watson	Labor	1904
George Houston Reid	Free Trade	1904–05
Alfred Deakin	Protectionist	1905–08
Andrew Fisher	Labor	1908–09
Alfred Deakin	Fusion	1909–10
Andrew Fisher	Labor	1910–13
Joseph Cook	Liberal	1913–14
Andrew Fisher	Labor	1914–15
William Morris Hughes	National Labor	1915–17
William Morris Hughes	Nationalist	1917–23
Stanley Melbourne Bruce	Nationalist	1923–29
James Henry Scullin	Labor	1929–31
Joseph Aloysius Lyons	United	1931–39
Earle Christmas Page	Country	1939
Robert Gordon Menzies	United	1939–41
Arthur William Fadden	Country	1941
John Joseph Curtin	Labor	1941–45
Joseph Benedict Chifley	Labor	1945–49
Robert Gordon Menzies	Liberal	1949–66
Harold Edward Holt	Liberal	1966–67
John McEwen	Country	1967–68
John Grey Gorton	Liberal	1968–71
William McMahon	Liberal	1971–72
Edward Gough Whitlam	Labor	1972–75
John Malcolm Fraser	Liberal	1975–83
Robert James Lee Hawke	Labor	1983–91
Paul Keating	Labor	1991–96
John Howard	Liberal	1996–

WORD POWER

PRIME MINISTERS

Canadian Prime Ministers

Prime Minister	Party	Term of office
John A. MacDonald	Conservative	1867–73
Alexander Mackenzie	Liberal	1873–78
John A. MacDonald	Conservative	1878–91
John J.C. Abbot	Conservative	1891–92
John S.D. Thompson	Conservative	1892–94
Mackenzie Bowell	Conservative	1894–96
Charles Tupper	Conservative	1896
Wilfrid Laurier	Liberal	1896–1911
Robert Borden	Conservative	1911–20
Arthur Meighen	Conservative	1920–21
William Lyon Mackenzie King	Liberal	1921–1926
Arthur Meighen	Conservative	1926
William Lyon Mackenzie King	Liberal	1926–30
Richard Bedford Bennet	Conservative	1930–35
William Lyon Mackenzie King	Liberal	1935–48
Louis St. Laurent	Liberal	1948–57
John George Diefenbaker	Conservative	1957–63
Lester Bowles Pearson	Liberal	1963–68
Pierre Elliott Trudeau	Liberal	1968–79
Joseph Clark	Conservative	1979–80
Pierre Elliott Trudeau	Liberal	1980–84
John Turner	Liberal	1984
Brian Mulroney	Conservative	1984–93
Kim Campbell	Conservative	1993
Joseph Jacques Jean Chrétien	Liberal	1993–

New Zealand Prime Ministers

Prime Minister	Party	Term of office
Henry Sewell	–	1856
William Fox	–	1856
Edward William Stafford	–	1856–61
William Fox	–	1861–62
Alfred Domett	–	1862–63
Frederick Whitaker	–	1863–64
Frederick Aloysius Weld	–	1864–65
Edward William Stafford	–	1865–69
William Fox	–	1869–72
Edward William Stafford	–	1872
William Fox	–	1873
Julius Vogel	–	1873–75
Daniel Pollen	–	1875–76
Julius Vogel	–	1876
Harry Albert Atkinson	–	1876–77
George Grey	–	1877–79
John Hall	–	1879–82
Frederic Whitaker	–	1882–83
Harry Albert Atkinson	–	1883–84
Robert Stout	–	1884
Harry Albert Atkinson	–	1884
Robert Stout	–	1884–87
Harry Albert Atkinson	–	1887–91
John Ballance	–	1891–93
Richard John Seddon	Liberal	1893–1906
William Hall-Jones	Liberal	1906
Joseph George Ward	Liberal/National	1906–12
Thomas Mackenzie	National	1912
William Ferguson Massey	Reform	1912–25

New Zealand Prime Ministers (continued)

Prime Minister	Party	Term of office
Francis Henry Dillon Bell	Reform	1925
Joseph Gordon Coates	Reform	1925–28
Joseph George Ward	Liberal/National	1928–30
George William Forbes	United	1930–35
Michael Joseph Savage	Labour	1935–40
Peter Fraser	Labour	1940–49
Sidney George Holland	National	1949–57
Keith Jacka Holyoake	National	1957
Walter Nash	Labour	1957–60
Keith Jacka Holyoake	National	1960–72
John Ross Marshall	National	1972
Norman Eric Kirk	Labour	1972–74
Wallace Edward Rowling	Labour	1974–75
Robert David Muldoon	National	1975–84
David Russell Lange	Labour	1984–89
Geoffrey Palmer	Labour	1989–90
Mike Moore	Labour	1990
Jim Bolger	National	1990–97
Jenny Shipley	National	1997–99
Helen Clark	Labour	1999–

SOUTH AFRICAN PROVINCES

Province	*Capital*
Eastern Cape	Bisho
Free State	Bloemfontein
Gauteng	Johannesburg
KwaZulu-Natal	Pietermaritzburg
Limpopo	Pietersburg
Mpumalanga	Nelspruit
North-West	Mafikeng
Northern Cape	Kimberley
Western Cape	Cape Town

WORD POWER

——— U.S. PRESIDENTS ———

President	Party	Term of office
1. George Washington	Federalist	1789–97
2. John Adams	Federalist	1797–1801
3. Thomas Jefferson	Democratic Republican	1801–1809
4. James Madison	Democratic Republican	1809–1817
5. James Monroe	Democratic Republican	1817–25
6. John Quincy Adams	Democratic Republican	1825–29
7. Andrew Jackson	Democrat	1829–37
8. Martin Van Buren	Democrat	1837–41
9. William Henry Harrison	Whig	1841
10. John Tyler	Whig	1841–45
11. James K. Polk	Democrat	1845–49
12. Zachary Taylor	Whig	1849–50
13. Millard Fillmore	Whig	1850–53
14. Franklin Pierce	Democrat	1853–57
15. James Buchanan	Democrat	1857–61
16. Abraham Lincoln	Republican	1861–65
17. Andrew Johnson	Republican	1865–69
18. Ulysses S. Grant	Republican	1869–77
19. Rutherford B. Hayes	Republican	1877–81
20. James A. Garfield	Republican	1881
21. Chester A. Arthur	Republican	1881–85
22. Grover Cleveland	Democrat	1885–89
23. Benjamin Harrison	Republican	1889–93
24. Grover Cleveland	Democrat	1893–97
25. William McKinley	Republican	1897–1901
26. Theodore Roosevelt	Republican	1901–1909
27. William Howard Taft	Republican	1909–13
28. Woodrow Wilson	Democrat	1913–21
29. Warren G. Harding	Republican	1921–23
30. Calvin Coolidge	Republican	1923–29

U.S. PRESIDENTS

President	Party	Term of office
31. Herbert C. Hoover	Republican	1929–33
32. Franklin D. Roosevelt	Democrat	1933–45
33. Harry S. Truman	Democrat	1945–53
34. Dwight D. Eisenhower	Republican	1953–61
35. John F. Kennedy	Democrat	1961–63
36. Lyndon B. Johnson	Democrat	1963–69
37. Richard M. Nixon	Republican	1969–74
38. Gerald R. Ford	Republican	1974–77
39. James E. Carter, Jr	Democrat	1977–81
40. Ronald W. Reagan	Republican	1981–89
41. George H. W. Bush	Republican	1989–93
42. William J. Clinton	Democrat	1993–2001
43. George W. Bush	Republican	2001–

U.S. STATES

State	Abbreviation	Zip Code
Alabama	Ala.	AL
Alaska	Alas.	AK
Arizona	Ariz.	AZ
Arkansas	Ark.	AR
California	Cal.	CA
Colorado	Colo.	CO
Connecticut	Conn.	CT
Delaware	Del.	DE
District of Columbia	D.C.	DC
Florida	Fla.	FL
Georgia	Ga.	GA
Hawaii	Haw.	HI
Idaho	Id. or Ida.	ID
Illinois	Ill.	IL
Indiana	Ind.	IN
Iowa	Ia. or Io.	IA

WORD POWER

State	Abbreviation	Zip Code
Kansas	Kan. *or* Kans.	KS
Kentucky	Ken.	KY
Louisiana	La.	LA
Maine	Me.	ME
Maryland	Md.	MD
Massachusetts	Mass.	MA
Michigan	Mich.	MI
Minnesota	Minn.	MN
Mississippi	Miss.	MS
Missouri	Mo.	MO
Montana	Mont.	MT
Nebraska	Neb.	NE
Nevada	Nev.	NV
New Hampshire	N.H.	NH
New Jersey	N.J.	NJ
New Mexico	N.M. *or* N.Mex.	NM
New York	N.Y.	NY
North Carolina	N.C.	NC
North Dakota	N.D. *or* N.Dak.	ND
Ohio	O.	OH
Oklahoma	Okla.	OK
Oregon	Oreg.	OR
Pennsylvania	Pa., Penn., *or* Penna.	PA
Rhode Island	R.I.	RI
South Carolina	S.C.	SC
South Dakota	S.Dak.	SD
Tennessee	Tenn.	TN
Texas	Tex.	TX
Utah	Ut.	UT
Vermont	Vt.	VT
Virginia	Va.	VA
Washington	Wash.	WA
West Virginia	W.Va.	WV
Wisconsin	Wis.	WI
Wyoming	Wyo.	WY

WORD POWER